MOHAMMED AYUB KHUHRO
A LIFE OF COURAGE IN POLITICS

MOHAMMED AYUB KHUHRO
A LIFE OF COURAGE IN POLITICS

*To Mr Jason Flewelling
with all best wishes
Hamida Khuhro
27 October 2009
Karachi*

HAMIDA KHUHRO

FEROZSONS (PVT.) LTD.
LAHORE-RAWALPINDI-KARACHI

ISBN 969 0 01424 2

First Published 1998 by
Ferozsons (Pvt) Ltd.
60, Shahrah-e-Quaid-e-Azam, Lahore-Pakistan
277, Peshawar Road, Rawalpindi
Mehran Heights, Main Clifton Road, Karachi

Khuhro, Hamida

Mohammed Ayub Khuhro–A Life of Courage in Politics

Copyright © Ferozsons (Pvt) Ltd., 1998 and Khuhro, Hamida

All Rights Reserved.
No part of this publication may be
reproduced, stored in a retrieval system, or
transmitted, in any form or by any means
(electronic or otherwise), without
the prior written permission
of the Publisher.

Typeset in 10 on 12 point Palatino
Designed, Printed and Bound in Pakistan by
Ferozsons (Pvt) Ltd., Lahore.

For my mother

all her grandchildren

and their generation

PREFACE

My father, Mohammed Ayub Khuhro, wanted me write his biography in his lifetime but unfortunately that was not to be. It was only sometime after his death in October 1980 that I began seriously to write the story of his long, sometimes controversial and always courageous, political life. It has not been an easy task since I am not only his daughter but also a historian by training added to which I am describing events which took place relatively recently so that analysis and even narration has been fraught with complexities. However, as the work progressed, I found it an increasingly rewarding and exciting encounter with the facts leading up to independence in the sub-continent and the early years of Pakistan. Now fifty years after the fateful inception of our country, people are looking back at what really happened. This book will answer many questions because my father's political life spanned the most decisive period in the history of the sub-continent. He was intimately linked with the emergence of the province of Sind from being a 'backwater of Indian history' and one of the smallest provinces of the British Empire of India to its becoming the cornerstone of the struggle for Pakistan and the key to the demand for a separate Muslim state in the sub-continent.

He was fully involved in the great events of the freedom movement and worked in a key capacity during the struggle for the achievement of independence, the creation of Pakistan. As the two countries were created from the womb of undivided India, my father was just 46 years of age on Pakistan's independence day 14 August 1947. It was also his birthday.

He was at peak political strength, having a great deal to his credit already and looking forward to the achievement of his lifetime hopes in a free Pakistan. The next thirty-three years his life were inextricably linked up with the ups and downs in Pakistan's own career. He bore the brunt of the anti-democratic and centralising actions of the power brokers of the country as he championed the rights of the provinces against an overmighty Centre. He suffered spectacularly for his political beliefs right from the first year of Pakistan's inception to the imposition of the Martial Law twenty years later. He fought to retain the city of Karachi in Sind in 1948 and lost but then saw its re-unification with the province in 1969 and laid the framework for its destiny as one of the world's megacities. He played his role at a particularly turbulent time in the history of the sub-continent. His unwavering (and fearless) stand on the many issues of politics and his fortitude in the face of adversity earned him the popular sobriquet 'The iron man of Sind'.

The primary focus for his life had always been the land of his birth, Sind.

This was a region that came late within the Imperial rule of the British. In my father's youth there were still people who could remember the Talpur regime and certainly the arrival and establishment of British rule in the 'forties of the 19th century. He grew up in Larkana, the garden of Sind in those days, where his family was a landowning *zamindar* family. Firmly rooted in the tradition of Sind my father nevertheless imbibed fully the lessons of modern education and democracy which were so tentatively planted in the sub-continent by the British. He admired the achievements of the West and believed that democracy was the route which India could take to transform itself from a deeply traditional society into a progressive well administered state. For Sind and for the Muslims of the sub-continent this was the path he wanted. He believed that things went wrong in Pakistan only when the rulers deviated from these principles.

Sind, nurtured by the mighty river Indus had spawned from time immemorial a series of sophisticated civilisations where people of necessity lived in harmony and tranquillity. The river's water brought untold richness of crops and prosperity to the people but it was fickle and upredictable. People could never accumulate too much before disaster might strike; they lived with this and developed degrees of toleration towards each other because they never knew when they would need another's help. They also had a keen respect for nature and had a religion to cope. No empire bothered too much with them – it was too difficult to regimentalise the seething passion of the mighty Indus when it decided every few years or so to unleash its more deadly side.

My father understood, as every Sindhi does, the unique vagaries of life on the edge of the Indus and was able to express the needs of his countrymen and women and act as essential conduit to the British rulers. He learnt the value of the politics of association and organised the people of Sind to participate in the freedom movement. He interpreted the needs of his people and articulated them at national and all India forums. Through his political activities, his participation in the Councils and Legislatures provided by the Imperial power, he sought to make a significant difference in the life of his people and when he felt that the response from the Imperial power was inadequate he threw in his lot with the national parties which were striving for freedom from Imperial control. He provided the solid support for the struggle for emancipation and freedom of the country. In this struggle the crucial factor was the people's support gathered and consolidated by grassroots politicians like my father, on whose work and strength depended the success or failure of the national leaders in the negotiations at Delhi and Simla.

Essentially his was an eternal struggle to make people outside Sind to understand what real community meant, a cohesive whole, a real togetherness which he experienced from his everyday life and knew his ancestors had. Perhaps he never properly understood that others could act from individual motives and not from a community point of view.

It was this lack of concern for himself and his role in the momentous history of the sub-continent he shaped and wrestled with that prompted him to write in a letter to his old friend and colleague and often political foe, G. M. Syed, "I am starting to write my biography and I shall also record my version of all these past events, and you will please make the necessary corrections in your book in some form if possible. God alone knows how long you and I will live, both being old now and I do not want the past history of Sind wrongly recorded even in its smallest details."

I have tried my best to follow those guidelines.

HAMIDA KHUHRO
Karachi.
12 January 1997

ACKNOWLEDGEMENTS

My father left an almost complete archive of his political life dating from the twenties to the end of his life in 1980. There are some gaps ofcourse particularly as important papers were lost at the time of the imposition of the first Martial Law regime in 1958 when not only were his personal papers taken but the offices of Muslim League were sealed and the papers seized. Some papers were finally retrieved through the efforts of dedicated historians such as Dr. Zaidi, but there was necessarily some lacuna.

I have researched extensively for the last fifteen years and more and as far as possible seen every collection of documents relating to his life and to the area and the period. Apart from my father's papers the most useful and extensive material was in India Office Library. Here I have spent many years starting from when it was located in the splendid India Office building in Whitehall where as a Ph.D. student I was working on British Imperial rule in Sind to my work in relation to my father's life and times at the less elegant surroundings of Blackfriars Bridge Road. In this research I was given most invaluable help by many good friends but most particularly Martin Moir and Richard Bingle who between them had an unparalleled knowledge of the official record and manuscripts in the IOL. My most heartfelt thanks to them both.

I would also like to thank Dr. Atique Zafar Shaikh and the staff of Pakistan National Archives in Islamabad who were extremely courteous and helpful in my researches over the years. I am extremely grateful to Herald Publication and in particular Mr. Hameed Haroon for allowing me to use the Dawn library over several years, for the use of painting of the Quaid-e-Azam reading DAWN and also for the use of a 1938 photograph. My thanks also to Ghulam Mustafa Khuhro for locating *Twarikh Ganjina Jahan Numa*, and through him the Makhdum family of Khuhra Sharif for their love of learning and libraries.

I am extremely indebted to my late respected honorary uncle and friend G. M. Syed, who was extremely helpful in giving me his personal recollections in addition to allowing me to use his rich collection of papers. I remember with gratitude the extensive interviews given to me by the late Pir Ali Mohammed Rashdi, whose unique knowledge of politics of Sind and of the world and his frankness in discussing many incidents and characters gave me a valuable insight into the politics of India as well as this province.

I remember with gratitude and affection long talks with the late Mian Mumtaz Daultana who gave me the benefit of his analysis of events leading up to and after the independence of the sub-continent.

Over the years I talked to many people leaders as well workers, involved in the drama of the freedom movement and of politics in this region. I talked to British officials who had served in Sind including that great historian of Sind H. T. Lambrick, Sir Hugh Dow an unrelenting foe of my father but benign in his old age, Sir Francis Mudie the last Imperial Governor of Sind and a friend of my father, and many other Old Sind Hands including Sir Patrick Cadell, Sir Sidney Ridley, Sir Charles Clee, Sir Godfrey Davis the ex-Chief Judge of Sind and many others. I had long and useful discussions with the late Sir Penderell Moon, the maverick I.C.S. officer and a brilliant historian and was always inspired by the late Professor Jack Gallagher who thought I could write history if I tried.

I am extremely grateful to my editor Elisabeth Davies for her careful reading of the manuscript, her valuable suggestions for clarifying a highly complex narrative and her meticulous corrections of the text. I would like to thank Daniel Lawton of the U.S. Foreign Service for his reading my earlier chapters and giving me his useful suggestions and for assuring me that the book was readable. I would like to thank my mother for her encouragement and support and her help in finding papers and photographs; my brothers and sisters and friends for reading the chapters as they were written and encouraging me to go on. I would like above all to thank my husband for daily encouragement and help and for putting up with a mess of papers about the house for so many years.

In the end I would like to record my deep appreciation of the personal interest taken by Mr. Zaheer Salam Ferozsons in the publication of the book. He has been extremely co-operative and understanding at all stages of its production and has gone out of his way to expedite the publication. My warmest gratitude to Ms. Gul Afshan of Ferozsons for her expertise, her patience and her helpfulness in getting this book published.

Note on spellings

The spelling used for the name of the province throughout the book is **Sind**, the official spelling throughout the British period and for over forty years afterwards, until it was changed to **Sindh** after 1988.

Otherwise the spelling of names of persons and places varies considerably as I have tried to retain the original spellings in quotations.

CONTENTS

Preface ... 7

Acknowledgements ... 11

BOOK I (1901–1935)

1 The Ancient Land of Sind ... 17
2 Sindhi Zamindar ... 27
3 Entry into Politics ... 37
4 Bombay Legislator ... 51
5 Confrontations ... 73
6 Achieving Autonomy for Sind ... 87
7 Setting the Framework ... 111

BOOK II (1936–1946)

8 Making Autonomy Work ... 131
9 Establishing Muslim League in Sind ... 151
10 Masjid Manzilgah ... 169
11 The Coalition Government ... 193
12 Political Seesaw ... 203
13 The Hur Uprising ... 223
14 In the Sessions Court at Sukkur ... 249
15 Working for Freedom ... 269

BOOK III (1947–1980)

16	Premier of Sind	… 315
17	Under Siege	… 349
18	Disillusion	… 371
19	Dealing with an Over Mighty Centre	… 387
20	Authoritarianism Triumphant	… 411
21	Targeted under Dictatorships	… 447
22	Intimations of Disaster	… 459
23	A Revealing Exchange of Letters	… 481
24	A Test of Endurance	… 501
25	A Quiet Exit	… 513
	Endnotes	… 531
	Bibliography	… 553
	Abbreviations	… 558
	Glossary	… 559
	Index	… 563

BOOK I
(1901–1935)

1

THE ANCIENT LAND OF SIND

The Sind that Mohammed Ayub Khuhro was born in was a sparsely populated, unspoilt corner of the Indian sub-continent; a gift of the mighty river Indus, just as Egypt was the gift of the river Nile; difficult of access because of the great Thar desert which cut it off from the rest of the sub-continent on the east and guarded on the west by the mountains and the fierce tribes of Baluchistan.

Sometimes called a 'backwater of Indian history', Sind was, if not a backwater of the Bombay Presidency, at least and literally, the hunting ground of the powerful bureaucrats, the top officials of the Bombay Presidency who took their annual winter tours in Sind, shooting wildfowl on the lakes and making leisurely journeys up the Indus, holding *durbars* and *kutcheries*, crowded with local notables, handing out honours or rebukes, conferring 'chairs' or issuing warnings and generally spreading awe in the countryside at the might of the British Empire. The pomp and splendour of *Lat Sahib*[1] and to a lesser extent that of the Commissioner-in-Sind and lesser officials, was for the *raiyat* of Sind, a wonder to behold. For the Bombay 'civilians', Sind was a very desirable perquisite. Added to the Bombay Presidency in 1847, the oldest possession of the British in India,[2] it was unspoilt by the rising middle and Babu classes spawned by British imperial necessity which infested the older parts of the presidency. Sind, 'Young Egypt', was a paradise for the bureaucrats tired of the complaints and importunities of 'westernized' Bombayites. This country of lakes and wildfowl, placid *raiyat*, pliant *zamindars*, and picturesque *sirdars* was just the place to revive the jaded spirits of the guardians of the empire.

The addition of Sind to British possessions came late in the history of the conquest of India and was an interesting footnote to the history of British empire building. By the end of the first quarter of the nineteenth century the British East India Company had become the 'paramount' power in India having acquired large areas in northern and southern India. Most of the states which had become independent during the decline of the Mughal power were now under their 'protection' and the Mughal emperor was himself a pensioner of the British. The 'Angrez sarkar' was the acknowledged master of all it surveyed. The only major states still independent of direct or indirect British authority were Punjab and Sind in the north-west of the sub-continent guarding the passes of Khyber and Bolan respectively. With the rise of Napoleon in France and his obvious interest in the east, particularly after his conquest of Egypt, the British, nervous of his intentions and anxious to safeguard their Indian interests, became more active in the affairs of Persia and Afghanistan. They warily watched the French and after 1815, the Russian 'menace' in these areas. The 'Great Game' had begun and with it the interest and interference in Sind and the Punjab.

Conquered and added to the British Indian empire in 1843 in the aftermath of the disastrous Kabul campaign of 1842, Sind had been annexed in a manner which scandalized even the hardened consciences of the British ruling class in the heyday of imperial expansion.* In the acquisition of this new territory Lord Ellenborough, the Governor General, was salvaging some of the British pride which had been so thoroughly humbled in the retreat from Afghanistan. Sind with its antiquated arms and prediluvian army, was no match for the experienced troops and modern weapons of the British Sepoy army and was easily taken.

The new addition to the empire was unique in many ways and different from the rest of the Company's acquisitions. Annexed by expanding empires from time to time both from the east (Pandava, Maurya, Dehli Sultanate and the Mughals) and from the west (Aryan, Achaemenian, Sassanid, Greek, Arab) – Sind, the westernmost province of historic India, bordering on the Arabian sea, had enjoyed long periods of independence and developed a distinctive culture of its own. Geographically it was prone to isolation. On the west it was guarded by the Sulaiman range of the Himalayas and fierce Baluch tribes and on the east by the Great Thar Desert. The river Indus, the Sindhu of the Aryans, was the lifeline, the *raison d'etre* of Sind. It was the Sindhu which gave its name not only to Sind, but to Hindu, Hindustan, India – all variants of the name Sindhu.

The Talpur Chiefs of Sind from whom the British took over had ruled the country for about sixty years and had themselves become rulers by defeating the Kalhoras, a Sindhi tribe who in their turn, had wrested the independence of Sind from the declining power of the imperial Mughuls. Talpurs were a minor Baluch tribe, religious disciples of the Kalhoras, who had been summoned to Sind to join the Kalhora armies. They had come with their camel caravans, wild hill men in their baggy trousers, long shirts, long matted hair and huge turbans, carrying their sheep across the hill streams, their women on camels, and bards singing of the great deeds of Baluch heroes. The Talpurs ruled Sind from 1783 to 1843 and in that year on 17 February at the battle of Miani and subsequently at the battle of Dubbo on 22 March, the Talpur armies were defeated decisively and Sind became part of the British empire.

At the time of the British conquest the area of Sind was approximately 52,994 square miles and its population was approximately 2,200,000, most of which was Muslim. Traditionally Sind was conveniently divided into three geographical regions corresponding with the incline of the river: *Siro* (the head) or upper Sind, *Wicholo* (middle) from Dadu town to Hyderabad, and *Lar* (incline) or lower Sind from Hyderabad to the sea. When Sir Charles Napier the conquering general became Governor of Sind he divided it into three "collectorates" – Karachi, Hyderabad and Shikarpur for administrative purposes. His trusted army officers were ap-

---

* The satirical English journal *Punch* pinpointed the ethical problem involved in the conquest by making up a Latin pun on the word Sind. According to this joke Charles Napier, the conqueror of Sind sent a telegram home "*Peccavi* -I have Scinde." *Punch*, vol. 6, 1844, p. 209.

pointed as heads of the divisions and were known as Collectors. Their main function, as the name implies, was to collect revenue, to maintain law and order, and to collect information regarding their charges which could lead not only to the accumulation of knowledge but more specially to better administration and enhancement of revenue. A great deal of basic information was collected in these early years which is still the basis of our knowledge about Sind at the time of the British takeover. This includes geographical and historical facts about the province as well as its people, tribes and customs, which would otherwise have been lost. The Deputy Collector for the Shikarpur Collectorate which included Larkana at this time, was Lieutenant Hugh James of 44th Regiment, Bengal Native Infantry who wrote an invaluable report on the "Pergunnah of Chandookah", as Larkana was known at the time. In this he made a detailed survey of the history, geography, irrigation and the agriculture of Larkana and summed up: "With great facilities for irrigation, Chandookah has not unjustly been styled the Garden of Upper Sind and... proved a source of wealth to the Ameers."

In the days before the construction of the Sukkur Barrage* most cultivation in Sind was on the banks of the river and depended on the annual inundation. There was a network of canals mostly of the inundation variety, only a few being perennial. Cultivation therefore did not extend to any great depth beyond the river. Sind resembled Egypt in that there was intensive cultivation a few miles on either side of the river, then fading away on both sides into arid zones. On the right of the river the cultivable area giving way to the mountains bordering Baluchistan and on the left bank tapering away to the great Thar desert. The annual floods with the overlay of silt which covered the banks made Sind a very fertile region where cultivation was trouble free, requiring only minimum effort of seeds scattered on the soil which in due course yielded magnificent crops. The small population lived a prosperous life in towns and villages in easy reach of the river.

Sind also had some of the most wonderful forests and lakes in the Indian subcontinent where migrating birds of great variety would make their annual journey to escape the cold regions of the north. Sind to which the British came was an idyllic country where nature and people's beliefs and lifestyle harmonized to a remarkable extent. Sufiism – the most relaxed form of Islam – was the favoured religion and the shrines of sufi saints, crowded with both Hindus and Muslims, bore witness to this fact. Although the great majority of the population (approximately 75%) was Muslim the two communities lived in harmony.

Most of the Muslims of Sind were engaged in agriculture. The landowners were known as zamindars and were heir to an ancient land tenure system which had taken shape over the centuries, occasionally rationalized by some great administrator such as Akbar the Great, or a wise viceroy such as Nawab Wali Mohammed

---

* The Lloyd Barrage at Sukkur or the Sukkur Barrage as it came to be known was completed in 1932 and was one of the major irrigation projects of the British Empire. It was the biggest irrigation work of its kind in the world at the time. It was not only a marvel of engineering but also aesthetically one of the finest public works anywhere. The Barrage made the water-supply of upper Sind perennial and greatly increased the acreage under cultivation. There have been long term disastrous efforts on the ecology such as the salination and water-logging of large areas of land but these effects became apparent only a long time later. One of the recommendations of the planners of the barrage had been to line the canals which however was never carried out because of the expenditure involved and perhaps if it had been the effects would not have been so dire.

Laghari the *Wazir* of the Talpur rulers of Sind. Originally the land had been settled by tribes which had moved into the lower Indus valley and started cultivating it. These tribes built their own villages which were temporary settlements on the banks of the river, liable to be moved during the season of floods, taken to a high ground and then rebuilt when the river had receded. The more established villages which were built by the heads of the tribes were usually the largest and these were where the zamindar lived. These villages had a *kot* or high wall enclosing the brick built house of the *wadero* (the *sirdar* or the zamindar) and his relatives. The other inhabitants of the village lived in houses of unbaked clay with thatched roofs of straw and wattle. The population of the village was made up of *haris* (cultivators) and village artisans such as the carpenter, the cloth weaver, the potter and the *razo* or the builder. There was also the *bania* (the money lender and shopkeeper), *kamdars* (land stewards), *munshis* (book keeping clerks), the *mulla* (the village priest) and other persons connected with the tending of the land and village life. Most villages had their resident *fakir* or holy mendicant who was usually an eccentric and was credited with spiritual power and a special relationship with the Almighty. A village without its *fakir* was a village not considered blessed.

Rural Sind revolved round the zamindar. He was the owner of land which was the source of the livelihood of the great majority of the people. He was the head of the village and the guardian of its security, the dispenser of justice and the channel of communication to the greater powers and authorities beyond the village world. Life in the village was happy or miserable depending on the kind of zamindar it had. If he was fair though strict, hard rather than soft, but not cruel, then he was the best kind of zamindar. A weak man was as bad as a tyrant. Fairness and a good understanding of the people were the most prized qualities in the head of the village. It was his business to know the character of the people in his villages so that he was never taken by surprise by events. He held his daily *kutcheries* or gatherings in his *autaq* where the news of the village, of the neighbourhood and of the world were brought by his *kamdars*, by the traveller and the occasional visitor from the outside world. He kept track of the small and big crimes in the area, the state of the river, of the latest development in the world outside–whether it was the annual visit of the *Lat Sahib* to Sind or the idiosyncrasies of the Commissioner-in-Sind or of the incoming Collector of the District. Here the *wadero* in his *kutcheri* or perhaps on his occasional visit to the nearest town came to know whether the Queen Empress Victoria was likely to declare war on the Kaiser or if the *Khalifa* in Istanbul was going to side with Germany or the *Angrez Sarkar* and he would hear with a good deal of satisfaction of the latest exploits of Kemal Pasha against the European allies.

The *wadero* needed to be shrewd in his assessment of political trends as they would affect the interests of his community, as indeed he was aware of the prospect of floods or drought. Inhabiting a region dependent on irrigation and therefore on the goodwill of the government which was responsible for the administration of water, it was essential for the zamindar to be on the right side of the government or at least to handle his relations with the administration with the utmost tact. The displeasure of the government could easily result in the stoppage of water or the diversion of the *karez* (water channels) which fed his lands. This affected not only the welfare of the zamindar himself but of hundreds of *hari* families cultivating his lands. It meant the ruination of the villages under his control. The zamindar was thus in a very delicate position *vis-a-vis* the administration. On the one hand he had to have his position recognized by the rulers but on the other he had to be careful not to appear to his people and his peers as too sycophantic. The life of a zamindar particularly in a colonial setting was largely that of a skilful tightrope walk.

Although in theory land belonged to the government of the day, because the ancient tribes had brought the land into cultivation and had settled on those lands, in effect it belonged to the zamindars, literary the 'land owners'. The prevailing system of land tenure or the system of cultivation was 'crop sharing'. The land was allotted to the cultivator or *hari* by the zamindar. There was a substantial number of *maurusi* or hereditary haris who traditionally cultivated land allocated by the zamindar but could not be moved by him. There was also itinerant labour which came for cotton picking or for canal clearance and digging of watercourses. This seasonal migrant labour was provided in northern Sind by the nomadic Brahui and Baluch tribes who came south with their sheep and goats to set up small settlements wherever work was available. Similarly in Middle and Lower Sind nomadic Kolhis and Bhils provided labour when necessary. Migrant Pathans, as well as Kolhi and Gaad tribesmen provided the labour for road building and canal clearance.

While this seasonal migrant labour was at the bottom of the social scale, at the very top of Sindhi society, during the rule of the Talpurs just before the British conquest of Sind, were the *jagirdars* – the military commanders of the regime and the 'feudal' lords of Sind. The most influential *jagirdars* were those related to the Talpur rulers or other important Baluch tribes such as the Lagharis, the tribe of Nawab Wali Mohammed, the trusted elder statesman of the Talpurs. The Baluch *sirdars* had their holdings of land round about the capital Hyderabad and the lesser capitals of Khairpur and Mirpurkhas, and were therefore conveniently placed to get their levies ready for the defence of the state. *Jagirdars* were not themselves responsible for the cultivation or administration of the lands in their *jagir* which was done by the hereditary landowners, the zamindars. The *jagirdars* merely collected the revenue of the lands assigned to them by the government and were therefore in *locus standi* for the government.[3] The rural society of Sind thus formed a pyramid with the small number of *jagirdars* at the apex with the larger layer of *zamindars* below followed by the village heirarchy of the *mulla*, who looked after the mosque and was the village teacher as well. Then there were the different types of artisans and skilled workers, the cultivators hereditary and non hereditary, and at the base the seasonal labour, the Brahuis, the gypsies-Oads, Bhils and Kolhis.

After the British completed the conquest of the country in 1843 they cut down the *jagir* holdings drastically, limiting them to the immediate members of the late ruling family and some of their close circle of Baluch *sirdars* or giving them as a political bribe to the border tribes such as the Chandia and the Magsi tribes on the Sind–Baluchistan border, who were too troublesome to control through regular district administration. By the end of the 19th century there were only such land grants or *jagirs* as were considered politically essential. The grants that the previous governments had made to the educational establishments and religious shrines were also cut or stopped altogether.

Pre-British rural (and urban) Sind owed allegiance to the rulers at Hyderabad where the Talpurs had their court and their Establishment which included the greater and lesser jagirdars, the chief *wazir*, other advisers and the secretariat of the *diwan* and his *Amil* assistants. The city of Hyderabad, the custom built capital of the great Kalhora ruler Ghulam Shah was planned around the main citadel – the Pucca Qila – the huge brick built fort standing on the edge of the hill with the Shahi Bazaar leading from its main gate and extending for about two miles along the spine of the hill. The Pucca Qila included the buildings which were the residences of the ruling family, the treasury, the armoury and other official buildings as well as the court itself. The great nobles, Nawab Wali Mohammed, Mirza Ismail and others had their own 'camps' or permanent settlements on the outskirts of the town – Tando Wali Mohammed, Tando Agha, Tando Mir Mahmood, Tando Thorho and so on. Through the centre of the town, leading off from the main gate of the fort was the Shahi Bazaar the main business and trading centre of the capital. On either side of the Bazaar were the lanes, *ghitties*, leading down the hill, each devoted to a different caste or craft. Nearer the fort were the *ghitties* where the Amil families lived within easy distance of the Mirs' courts and offices. Further down were the ghitties of swordmakers, silk-weavers, wood workers, gold and silver jewellers and all the other skills and trades needed to keep the Talpur court and the citizens supplied. Hyderabad was thus a bustling capital with its Court, its courtiers and feudal nobility – the *jagirdars*, the officials, the artisans and craftsmen, the shopkeepers and traders – all the paraphernalia to supply the capital, each in their appointed place.

Temperamentally Sindhis are a tolerant people and there was hardly if ever a case of religious persecution. Some instances of persecution of Hindus were publicised after the British conquest but these were very obviously highly exaggerated and motivated by the needs of the conquering power to justify the conquest on moral grounds and show the displaced rulers as cruel and unjust which patently they were not.

The majority of the population of Sind was Muslim and the largest minority was Hindu. With well demarcated areas of occupation and with a shared spiritual heritage of saints and folklore, the two great communities lived in harmony. Hindus of Sind were not 'caste' Hindus as in the rest of India. In Sind Hindus had migrated originally from the Punjab and were followers of Guru Nanak. They were known as Nanak Panthis or Nanak Shahis. Basically they were divided vertically in two sections. Amils were the administrators of the Kalhora and Talpur rulers and their most trusted officers and advisers. It was Diwan Gidumal the adviser of Mian Ghulam Shah Kalhoro who was entrusted with the task of selecting the site of the new capital which eventually became the city of Hyderabad. Amils provided the bureaucracy of the Kalhoras, and after them, of the Talpurs. They were the all-purpose officers – advisers, clerks, gofers and even envoys and ambassadors, known by the generic title of *Munshi*, a title which covered a multitude of functions from those of mere clerks to the most trusted advisers and senior officers of the kingdom. The office of treasurer or *Diwan* (finance minister) was the monopoly of Amils and to this day the families which performed this function traditionally are called Diwan.

The other Hindu caste in Sind was that of Bhaiband, the business community – the bankers and traders of Sind who had carried their trade not only throughout Sind (there was a *bania* in every village) but were spread over the world and whose 'hundies' were recognized and honoured as far north as Moscow and south to south east Asia and beyond. The Bhaiband caste was spread throughout Sind but the most famous of them came from the village of Khudabad[4] in Dadu district. In the 17th and 18th centuries Shikarpur in upper Sind became the most important banking and trading centre, not only of Sind but of west Asia and northern India. Caravans laden with goods came from the north, west and from the south east to Shikarpur from where their goods were sent off in different directions. Shikarpuris were merchants and financiers and had achieved their ascendancy in the world of business and finance through sheer talent and hard work. Known as *Sind varkies*, they lived in far flung places of the world, leaving their wives and families home in Sind and visiting them rarely or as frequently as distance and work would allow. *Sind varkies* became a byword for devotion to business and it was this single mindedness which brought prosperity and fame to Sind above and beyond its importance as an independent Muslim kingdom in a corner of the Indian sub-continent of the eighteenth century. The financiers of Shikarpur were closely involved with the ruling élite of the Kalhora and Talpur periods and acted as their bankers and creditors.

As the nineteenth century advanced however the importance of Shikarpur began to decline. The trade routes to the north were affected by the politics of the Great Game and the trade with central Asia and Russia was affected by consequent tension on the north western borders of India. At the same time the spread of British power and influence in India meant that trade by sea was steadily replacing the ancient caravan trade of Asia. The local trade with west Asia, south Asia, central Asia and China declined steadily and was replaced to a large extent by trade with Europe or trade through European particularly British traders who carried their goods in ships to the east and the west. The completion of the British conquest of India therefore brought about a change in the traditional patterns of trade in Asia and with this change affected the importance of Shikarpur as a trading and financial centre.

The decline of Shikarpur did not however affect the resilient Bhaiband community of Sind which changed with the times and became the leading business community of Karachi when it became a modern port after the British conquest. Amils tended to stay on in Hyderabad which they helped to turn into one of the most beautiful towns in Asia, a centre of modern education teeming with beautiful gardens, schools, colleges and public buildings. In the British period Hyderabad was a centre of intellectul life, pulsating with ideas and movements – a centre of Hindu as well as Muslim culture. The important urban centres or towns of pre-colonial Sind were the capital Hyderabad, the important trading centre Shikarpur, the twin cities of Sukkur and Rohri on the river Indus with the historic island of Bukkur between them and Larkana, the centre of grain trade of upper Sind.

In middle Sind apart from Hyderabad there were the important cloth weaving centres of Gambat and Naseerabad. About a hundred miles north west of Hyderabad was the ancient pilgrimage centre of Sehwan, the Buddhist city of Siwistan, mentioned in the *Chachnama*[5] and conquered in the 8th century by Mohammed bin Qasim, which had retained its holy status throughout Hindu, Buddhist and Muslim periods of history. This was also the place where according to legend Alexander the Great had once camped and it boasted a fort built by him. Lower down the river from Hyderabad was Thatta the capital of the medieval Samma dynasty – once a dazzling city of 400 colleges – which was pillaged and destroyed by the Portugese in the fifteenth century and was never able to regain its importance. At the western end of the Indus delta, situated on the Arabian sea, was the port of Karachi, replacing the river ports of Shah Bandar and Lahri Bandar and just rising in importance at the time of the British advent into Sind.

Napier as well as Lord Ellenborough, the Governor General at the time of the conquest, had very high hopes of Sind. They were anxious to have an exemplary administration. Writing to Napier, Ellenborough eloquently expressed these hopes: "...in Sind we must do all for futurity, we have to create an Egypt, and we must not allow little views of present advantage to interfere with the realization of the greatest future objects. We must redeem the character we have lost in India, on this new field for the exercise of European mind in the administration of an Asiatic Province. We must do as much by the people as we can, not only by and for ourselves. We must look to our reward hereafter, in the certain improvement of the country under a really enlightened government."[6]

Napier dreamt of the day when the river Indus would become the highway of north western India, busy with ships and boats carrying trade from the inaccessible regions of the north west – Afghanistan, Central Asia, the borders of the Russian empire, down the Indus to the sea and thence to Europe. Ellenborough and Napier had grandiose schemes which involved building a modern infrastructure in Sind – a modern port at Karachi, railways up to the Punjab and beyond, roads, navigable canals, removal of tolls and trade duties – all major undertakings requiring major expenditure which the East India Company would not be willing to undertake. Whatever money Napier could get hold of was spent on canal surveys, on the preliminary work for a harbour at Karachi and on setting up a new administration. Major Scott, a nephew of the Scottish novelist Sir Walter Scott, was Napier's man in charge of the Canal Department with Richard Burton who was to become famous as an explorer and an orientalist, as his deputy. Scott drew up comprehensive plans for a network of canals which included a barrage. This plan worked out before 1849 was eventually realised in 1932 with the building of the Sukkur Barrage. But long before Napier could realize even a part of his dreams for Sind he had gone and Sind was attached to the giant Bombay Presidency where its affairs were no longer of primary or urgent concern either to the presidency government or to the Central government at Calcutta. Sind retired to being a 'backwater' once more.

Some ripples were caused in the backwater by the appointment in 1849 of an outstanding administrator, H. B. E. (Bartle) Frere, who tried under difficult circumstances to build a modern system of communications and to make some much needed corrections and improvements in the administration. Frere with the strong support and co-operation of General John Jacob (of Jacobabad)[7] managed to build a railway from Karachi to Kotri, connecting Karachi to the river and the steamboat service up to Multan where the railway again took over to the Punjab and east to Delhi. Frere also went forward with the building of the port and with the improvement of administration. He also tried to liberalize the oppressive, almost punitive, system of revenue assessment set up by Napier and Pringle, although it would not be until the late nineteenth and early twentieth century that a reasonable system of revenue assessment would be worked out.

Frere's greatest and most valuable contribution was the system of education that he set up in Sind. He recognised the status of the Sindhi language and confirmed it as the language of the courts, education and administration in addition to English. He also got a report on the state of indigenous education in Sind which, deprived of funds and grants after the British conquest, had deteriorated greatly but the ruins of the structure remained to give some idea of its extent and quality.[8] He set up a system of state aided schools which imparted a 'secular' education as distinct from the traditional religious education, and which included some basic science subjects as well as the traditional humanities. But whatever schemes Frere had for Sind had to be drastically cut after the Revolt of 1857 which left the British in India disillusioned and paranoid – and made their first priority for expenditure the armed forces – a priority which left very little to spare for education and other 'enlightened' projects. As a result severe cuts had to be made in the sanctioned allocations. In the face of these realities Frere's system continued to limp along but the bright vision of the first colonial pioneers was never to be realised.

On the frontier of upper Sind Jacob was busy 'pacifying' and settling the Baluch tribes and building up a system of indirect rule which was based on the recognition of a hierarchy of tribes under the chief sirdar – the Khan of Kalat, the Beglar Begi. The tribes on the undefined borders of Sind – the Mazaris, the Bugtis and the Marris and other powerful and less powerful tribes – were handled with great tact and a system established which continues to the present day. The autonomy of major tribes was recognized with the proviso that in some areas the paramountcy of the Khan of Kalat was acknowledged. But the autonomy was exercised within limits set by the British imperial government. Annual *jirgas* were organised where the Commissioner-in-Sind or the Governor of Bombay came to preside over 'horse and cattle shows' with gatherings of notables of Sind and Baluchistan. Here the *sirdars* of the eastern Baluch tribes as well as those of Sind held their *jirgas* under the watchful eye of the senior British officials and were made to feel important and indispensable. These annual winter gatherings at Jacobabad and Sibi were the masterstroke of administration of the British in India – the very epitome of indirect rule which proved such a successful instrument in ruling the sub-continent. It was this ostentatious honouring of tribal chiefs and the recognition of their authority, the structuring of the hierarchy and the institutionalising of the system of arbitration that made the Sind frontier so peaceful and trouble free compared to the frontier of the Punjab, which was the tribal belt of the north west frontier.

In the rest of Sind the British, while they ruled in as arbitrary a manner as suited them, were careful to disguise their despotism in the very convincing garb of the 'rule of law'. They codified both the civil and criminal law, and worked out rules and regulations according to which the lives of their Indian subjects would be governed. To begin with the laws they framed in Sind were quite unrelated to local conditions since these were derived from the experience of the British administration in the Bombay Presidency where conditions were qiute different from those of Sind. As a result many people were confused and suffered a great deal of hardship. Families were ruined because of inappropriate laws and their inability to deal with them. A new class arose which could manipulate and use the new system to its advantage.

Far reaching changes were forced through not only in civil and criminal areas but also in economic relations which greatly affected the social structure. These changes were due in large part to the introduction of the new concept of secular education in the country which replaced a mainly religious one. This produced the lower cadre officers of the empire but would in time familiarize Indians with European thought.

In the immediate future the new education produced clerks for the Collector's and Commissioner's offices, the *tapedars*, and the *mukhtiarkars*, the 'native' officers on whose expertise and know-how the British Collector and Superintendent of Police relied for their information of local customs and indeed for the day to day events and the state of the people and the district. These clerks and *mukhtiarkars*, therefore exerted an influence on the administration and on the people – on the rulers and the ruled – which was quite out of proportion to their actual position. They were necessary go-betweens, speaking a sort of English, and were essential to the British officials. These native officials were the ones who arranged the tours, got in touch with the local zamindars, got tents organized, goats and chickens for the sahib's meals and arranged interviews for the humble petitioner as well as the great nawab.

Above all, the next hundred years saw the laying of the infrastructure of the 'modern' state. Thus Sind, as indeed the rest of India, was dragged 'kicking and screaming' into the modern world. The people soon became familiar with railways, the telegraph, printing presses, political and social organisation which heralded the beginnings of a representative democratic system – the *sine qua non* of a modern state. Naturally the lives of the people of India and in this case of Sind were affected in a profound way by these fundamental changes and a veritable revolution took place over the next few decades which affected not only the civil and criminal aspects of the legal system but also the social structure, in the rise of a new privileged class and the destruction of the old. As the twentieth century dawned in the sub-continent and in Sind it was giving birth to a new age in the history of this ancient land. Mohammed Ayub Khuhro was born simultaneously with the birth of this new century and was to be intimately concerned with its turbulent progress for over half a century.

2

SINDHI ZAMINDAR

Mohammed Ayub Khuhro was born on 14 August 1901, the eldest son of *Wadero* Shah Mohammed Khuhro, the *pagdar* of the Khuhro clan and zamindar of Larkana and Khairpur State in upper Sind. Mohammed Ayub's family belonged to the Sammat ethnic group or *zat* which originated from the Sammas, a branch of the Yadav tribe of the Induvarsi Rajputs. According to legend Sammas claim descent from Lord Krishna alias Shama and a woman called Sami. Khuhros belong to the Abro clan of the Sammas. According to tradition Khuhro settled in the fertile tract near the river Indus around modern Gambat in Khairpur district of upper Sind where the ancient madressah town of Khuhra bears testimony to their arrival and settlement.[1]

The Makhdums of Khuhra have in their possession an early 18th century manuscript based on earlier histories and manuscript sources which gives an Arab ancestry of the Khuhros. Modestly, Khuhros only claimed descent from Amr, known as Abu l-Hakam, a kinsman of the Holy Prophet who was called Abu Jahal (the father of ignorance), by the Muslims. Khuhros were descended from Samon a grandson of Abu Jahal who converted to Islam during the days of Khalifa Hazrat Ali. After the martyrdom of Imam Husain, Samon left Madina Mukarammah and went to Syria in the service of Marwan, the Ommayed ruler. "Because Marwan was wise and intelligent man and Samon was a clever man he became a favourite of Marwan. In the reign of Walid bin Abul Malik he accompanied the victor of Sind Mohammad bin Qasim to Sind *vilayet* and was martyred there."[2]

Samon had four sons Unar, Panhwar, Larik and Khuhro, the last being the progenitor of the Khuhro clan. The Khuhro clan founded and settled in the town of Khuhra in the Gambat region of Khairpur on the left bank of the Indus. Khuhra was "a town of good status" when in the earlier part of the seventeenth century, (between A.H. 1041–1062), the Makhdum family which had originally come to Sind from Baghdad in the time of Khalifa Muta'sim Billah came and settled in Khuhra.

Makhdum Mohammad Aqil (circa early 18th century) gives an account of the flood which occurred in the 1720s and which forced some people to move across the river to the Right bank. The family of Mohammad Ayub Khuhro settled on the Right bank in the Larkana area founding a village which they named after their patron saint, Makhdum Mohammad Aqil. Traditionally Khuhros were prudent land managers, religiously devout without being zealots, and highly educated according to the traditions of the day. Every Khuhro village was intensely proud of its *maktab* or Madressah.

Mohammed Ayub's father was the *pagdar*, the 'wearer of the turban' or head of the Khuhro tribe. The family had built its main village, Aqil, between the great natural canals of Nara and Ghar a few miles from Larkana. The inundations would force the village to move several times. Aqilai Khuhros were hard working and prosperous *zamindars*, with good sized holdings in Larkana. They were regarded as decent and fair minded and eschewed strong arm tactics which were not uncharacteristic of the tribes living in northern Sind. They cultivated large areas of *katcha* (lands on the banks of the river which became extremely fertile after the annual inundation) as well as regular *pucca* (canal irrigated land) land.

In the time of the Kalhoras and then of the Talpurs, the Khuhro *pagdars* were of sufficient status to be summoned periodically to pay their respects to the court at Hyderabad. Thus *Wadero* Jan Mohammed (Kalhora period) and *Wadero* Dost Mohammed (Talpur period) would make their preparations for the long journey, say their farewells and set off for Hyderabad in their river house boats or *jumptees*. These journeys would be undertaken in the winter when the floods had subsided and the crops had been gathered so there were enough funds to be able to take suitable presents for the Amirs. The journey itself would take a few weeks and it was hoped that the *Wadero* would be back before the next inundation of the river. The *Wadero* would remain at the Court for sometime, give the *hal ahwal* or the account of conditions and any events of interest, as etiquette required, to the Amirs and receive his *inam-lungi* or dress of honour and sometimes a sword as well and return as soon as he could to his native village.

During the Talpur period the *pargana* of Chandukah as Larkana was called, was under the governorship of Nawab Wali Mohammed Laghari one of the most remarkable administrators produced by Sind. Larkana prospered exceedingly during his tenure. It was, in these pre- Barrage times, the most fertile and rich agricultural areas in the whole of Sind. Hugh James, the first British officer incharge of the area, in his *Report on the Pergunnah of Chandukah* wrote of it: "With great facilities for irrigation, Chandookah has not unjustly been styled the Garden of Upper Sind", and also that it was a great source of wealth to the Amirs. The *paragana* or the district covered as James says "a large portion of Upper Sind." Its importance to the Amirs can be guaged from the fact that they appointed their most able administrator Nawab Wali Mohammed to put it in order.*

At the time the British conquered Sind *Wadero* Dost Mohammed was still alive though an old man and had just one son Mohammed Ayub. The situation was uncertain and the new administration was bringing in many changes imperfectly understood by the populace. The ruling families of Hyderabad and Khairpur had been defeated. The conquerors were taking hostages not only from the ruling families but also from many prominent tribes particularly of central Sind.[3] The familiar world was in shreds and a new unknown race with its unknown ways ruled the country. There were a number of cases to miscarriage of justice as for instance

---

* Larkana or Chanduka was Nawab Wali Mohammed's last charge. He died in Larkana and was initially buried in a garden on the outskirts of the town, the Tajar *bagh* or the 'garden of the tomb. The garden now renamed Jinnah bagh is in the middle of the present day town of Larkana.

when a Chandia Chief of lower Sind was hanged in Karachi while Charles Napier was still Governor.[4]

The Khuhro family was involved in another episode which had tragic results. Under the traditional system of administration prevailing in Sind at the time of the conquest the responsibility for law and order lay in the hands of the village or tribal heads. The zamindars knew their villages and the social situation within their jurisdiction, intimately. Every village and every community had the services of the *paggi* or *peri*, an expert tracker who could identify and follow the track of man or beast in his area without any possibility of error. As a result there was seldom a crime which went untraced and unpunished. The punishment was usually a fine or at the very most banishment from the village. In rare cases when murder could not be compensated by blood money and the victim's relations insisted on the "life for life" principle, the matter went up to the court of the Amirs at Hyderabad where more often than not the aggrieved party was induced to accept compensation and only in rare cases was the death penalty inflicted. Justice was cheap, swift and on the whole, sure. The advent of the British threw the system into some confusion particularly because of the threatening and contradictory nature of Napier's proclamations. One particular order which caused most confusion and threw the traditional system into disarray was the one which insisted that all criminals should be given over to the police and not punished locally as was the case hitherto. And just such a case occurred in Aqil, the Khuhro village.

Soon after the establishment of British rule, a case of theft occurred in Aqil. The thief was duly caught and according to the newly proclaimed laws was sent by the head of the village to be handed over to police custody in Larkana which was the nearest town. The villagers in charge of taking the man into town were rather high handed in their treatment of the thief and dealt him some blows in the course of the journey as a result of which the thief died in their custody. For this mishap the authorities held the village (and tribal) head *Wadero* Mohammed Ayub Khuhro responsible. *Wadero* Mohammed Ayub was arrested and put into the district jail which was at the district headquarters of Shikarpur. Here he was held for several months awaiting trial but because of the shock of the disgrace he felt himself to have suffered and partly because of the conditions in the jail, Khuhro fell ill and died before the trial could take place. During his illness his eldest son Shah Mohammed a boy in his teens, came and stayed in Shikarpur to be near his father. A good deal of expense was incurred in maintaining an establishment in Shikarpur and in bribing police and jail officials to get some facilities for the prisoner. As Mohammed Ayub was an only child there were no responsible person to look after the property in his absence and the family was forced to take loans from moneylenders. The death of Mohammed Ayub left his young wife and sons to fend for themselves, heavily in debt, in very difficult circumstances and without the support of dependable relations.

Mohammed Ayub's wife, Emnah, was a woman of great courage and intelligence. Thrown back on her own resources and conscious that the future of the family, its social status and its very survival depended on her, she determinedly met the situation. Fortunately Emnah had the character to be able to do so. Acting in a most uncharacteristic manner for women of her time and social circumstance,

Emnah took a realistic look at her situation and decided to rescue her family from the dire circumstances and ruin facing it. She summoned the local moneylenders and sitting behind a screen talked business with them. She had already mortgaged her jewellery, now she took loans to finance herself while she picked up the pieces of the *zamindari*. She encouraged her sons to work while she kept a personal check on the *kamdars* who brought their accounts to her and took orders from her. She handed out the money for seed, for the *haris* and kept ready the required sums needed to pay the government tax at a time when many of her contemporary zamindar families were being ruined because of the severity of the new land revenue laws. She not only managed to save her lands and to pay off her debts but also expanded the property by encouraging her young sons to take land on lease from the government, to farm it and later to buy it.

She handled her finances expertly and instilled the habits of frugality and hard work in her children which were to become legendary in the annals of Larkana. Although in strict *purdah*, she kept iron control on her lands and on the *raj*. She herself did the *faislas* (settlement of disputes, arbitration and control of the law and order in the community) and till the end of her life she continued to do so. Once a year she would get into her travelling ox cart or *chhakro* duly arranged with purdah, carpets and cushions, with sacks (guni bags) of wheat and sugar, and visited all the families who had been bereaved or where there had been marriages and circumcisions during the course of the year, distributing the customary amount of wheat and sugar, making her visits of condolence and congratulation.

By the time she died late in the century, her sons Shah Mohammed and Jan Mohammed were among the leading *zamindars* of the district and while Shah Mohammed concentrated all his energies on the improvement and expansion of the *zamindari*, Jan Mohammed enjoyed the social and political life of the district. He was elected member of the District Local Board, which came into being as a result of Lord Ripon's reforms introducing local self government in India between 1883 and 1885, and which offered the only representative or quasi political position available to Indians at this time. *Wadero* Jan Mohammed retained his membership till late in life and eventually relinquished it in favour of his nephew Mohammed Ayub Khuhro.

Mohammed Ayub, the eldest son of *Wadero* Shah Mohammed was born in 1901, when the latter was in his late 'fifties, which was considered an advanced age at the time. Although he had three more sons and several daughters his first born son was his undoubted favourite. Father of several daughters no son had been born to him for nearly forty years of married life. Unusually for a Muslim *zamindar* of the time, he had just one wife and he did not marry again during her lifetime. He did however beseech saints and *murshids* and spent nights praying in the company of *fakirs* entreating the Almighty for a son. The *Fakirs* promised that a son would be given to him who, moreover, would raise the honour of his clan and spend his life helping his people. Eventually this promise was fulfilled and a son was born in the summer of 1901. As long as he was alive Shah Mohammed revered saints and *fakirs* and took his son to visit them regularly. He was careful not to displease the holy men and always to keep them propitiated. He was very particular that at least one holy mendicant should always be living in his village as a kind of permanent blessing.

When Mohammed Ayub was about twelve years old the holy man 'in residence' in Aqil was Fakir Shahabuddin who lived just outside the village in a hut, sitting most of the time on a *manah* which was a sort of platform on stilts made up of sticks and thatch. People would take him food which they would put in a pot kept just outside his hut. Every offering would go into this pot whether it was rice or lentils or spinach or meat or fish. No one actually saw him eat this food but presumably he did. He would spend his nights praying and Mohammed Ayub would quite often go with his father to pay his respects–the *Fakir* would sometimes come down from his platform and sit with them. Once Fakir Shahabuddin was annoyed with Shah Mohammed and put a curse on the village shouting "fire, fire" and sure enough there was a fire and village suffered substantial damage. Another holy man, Karam Fakir, a wandering mendicant from Khairpur was a great friend of *Wadero* Jan Mohammed and would quite often visit him in Aqil. Mohammed Ayub who remembered him quite well even in later life, recollected: "One day I was with my uncle in a tonga and we were going across the level crossing near Larkana station when we saw Karam Fakir walking along. My uncle immediately asked the tonga-wallah to stop and both of us got down from the tonga. My uncle bent down to *salaam* him and touch his feet and asked me to do the same. He then asked Karam Fakir where he was going. The Fakir answered that he was going to Sehwan to visit the shrine of Qalandar Lal Shahbaz. My uncle asked him to say a few words of blessing for me and the Fakir replied, 'This boy will do well. Mirs and Pirs and even their women will salute him.' That was the last time I saw him as he died soon afterwards."[5] This tradition of reverence for holy men lingered in the family and it was firmly believed that absence of fakirs meant deprivation of the blessing of Almighty Allah. For most of his life and in all his houses Mohammed Ayub had at least one *majzoub* (handicapped) *fakir* in residence and there were strict instructions that these *Allah lok* (God's people) were not to be disturbed.

Mohammed Ayub had his early schooling in his village. After four years of Sindhi a tutor was engaged from the nearby village of Dodo to teach him English and Persian. At the age of twelve his uncle felt that he was old enough to go to a school in Larkana. The Larkana Madressah had been established in 1901-2, at the initiative of the Collector Abbot who was determined that the children of zamindars should acquire modern education. He took donations from the district zamindars and established what became one of the best schools in Sind. Abbot and the Collectors after him worked out a technique to overcome the reluctance of the zamindars to send their sons to school. When a zamindar came to call on the Collector, as most of them would do about once every two months or so, the Collector would ask the zamindar how many children he had and of what age. Then he would bring up the matter of their education and tell the zamindar that he must send his sons to the madressah. If there was any reluctance the Collector would issue orders that the offending zamindar was to be denied an interview and his privilege of a 'chair' in the 'durbar' was to be taken away. Naturally the zamindar would be very alarmed at this and would hasten to send his sons to the Madressah.

When Mohammed Ayub was at school many of these forced admissions took place and zamindars from as far as Khairpur sent their sons to the Larkana Madressah. There was a regular school board to look after the affairs of the Madressah which consisted of leading zamindars as well as officials. The Chairman of the Board was W. Hudson, the Collector of Larkana at the time and among the members of the School Board was Sir Shahnawaz Bhutto, not the chief but certainly the most well-known and influential zamindar of the large Bhutto clan. Another local notable who was a member of the Madressah Board was Sarai Shah Mohammed Lahori, a substantial zamindar of the district. The Madressah was served by a staff of well qualified and devoted teachers. The headmaster was Kazi Jan Mohammed of Shikarpur who retired shortly after Mohammed Ayub's admission and his place was taken by Chaudhri Abdul Ghani from Lahore, an excellent teacher and one of the best headmasters the school ever had. The rest of the teachers- Naik Mohammed who taught English, Subhan Ali Shah of Sukkur, the maths teacher, Ghulam Sarwar Qadri, the Sindhi teacher, Nawaz Ali Jaffri in charge of history and geography–were all good and dedicated teachers.

Mohammed Ayub joined the Madressah in the third standard and was the youngest student in his class. Among his contemporaries in school were (later Khan Sahib) Kehar from a neighbouring village and Sardar Wahid Baksh Bhutto, both a class senior to Mohammed Ayub and Omar bin Mohammed Daudpoto who later became a renowned scholar of Arabic and Persian and a well-known educationist. The latter came to the Madressah straight from his village where his brilliance had been recognized by the local teachers and officials who arranged for him to get a 'free boardship' in the Madressah. Daudpoto came from a poor family and it was to the credit of the system that his talent was recognized and he was given a chance to cultivate it. Daudpoto was the first son of a village artisan who attended the Larkana Madressah which was at this time the exclusive domain of the zamindari children. Daudpoto, in his autobiography, describes his arrival at the Madressah–

"I was wearing a coarse *bafta* cloth shirt, blue indigo dyed shalwar with embroidered edges and a white turban, a pair of village made slippers and a home-made pathan type jacket",[6]

all this long before handcrafted materials came into fashion. Carrying an old tin trunk on his head Daudpoto arrived at the school and immediately became an object of ridicule among the well dressed and snobbish sons of zamindars. This ridicule lasted a very short time however as the village hick proved himself by far the cleverest boy in the school. Daudpoto was in fact helped by a number of people and among the list of his benefactors he gives the name of Shah Mohammed Khuhro.[7] Young Mohammed Ayub took advantage of the brilliant Daudpoto's presence and was tutored by him in Persian and Arabic. The friendship which was begun at the Madressah continued all their lives and Daudpoto mentions it in very warm terms in his autobiography. Daudpoto became a notable scholar of Arabic and went on to receive his doctorate at Cambridge University. Apart from Daudpoto there were a number of men of talent and scholarship in Sind in his generation who came from humble backgrounds and who were able to use even the admittedly limited opportunities of the time, to achieve distinction.

Mohammed Ayub's transfer to Larkana to a school where English was taught was not to the liking of his father who was a very conservative man and felt that knowledge of the Sindhi language, basic arithmetic and perhaps a bit of Persian, was quite enough education for a zamindar's son, who was not after all in the business of finding a job in a government department. It was therefore much against his father's wishes and at the insistence of his uncle Jan Mohammed that Mohammed Ayub was sent to school. Jan Mohammed realised that the old world with its unchanging ways was over and that survival with honour in this new order was dependent on education and above all in being conversant with the English language, the channel of communication with the *Angrez Sarkar*. Initially Khuhro moved into a hostel of the school and describes the routine of student life:

"The routine at the madressah was fairly strict and discipline was carefully observed. We were woken up for Fajr prayers and there was no breakfast unless we said our prayers. After studies around one o'clock we said our mid-day prayers and then had lunch. In the afternoon we had carefully allotted time for games and study. Games like football etc. were played under supervision and for older boys there was tennis."[8]

Wadero Shah Mohammed who had been reluctant to send his son to a school at all, could not bring himself to trust hostels and insisted that his son should stay in his own establishment in Larkana. Khuhro walked the short distance to school every morning passing by the city court house on his way. Here he would hear the court bailiffs shouting out every day– "The lands of so and so forfeited for debt ex parte." At the same time there were numbers of illiterate *haris* and *khatedars* or small holders, crowded round the entrance of the courts, quite helpless to prevent the forfeiture of their property and the destruction of their life and future. In most cases the dispossessed land-owner only came to know of his misfortune when the court notice was served on him and he had to hand his property over to the *bania*. Mohammed Ayub was deeply affected by these proceedings and was fully aware of the social injustice caused by them. Many of the people affected were friends and neighbours, all of them were Muslims.

In fact by the early 'forties it was being generally said that over 30% of the agricultural property of Muslim agriculturists was in the hands of urban capitalists and moneylenders who were as it happened, all Hindus. It is certainly true that the biggest and best orchards and some of the choicest lands had transferred to the hands of the Hindu capitalists by this time. When Mohammed Ayub was going to school in Larkana the process of this transfer was in full swing and Larkana though perhaps not the worst affected in this way (the richest lands transferred were in Hyderabad and neighbouring districts of the *wicholo* or middle Sind), there was enough land transfer to cause noticeable hardship. The bare faced injustice of the proceedings to forfeit the lands of the indebted *haris* left a deep impression on Mohammed Ayub and one of the major causes of his political life was to be the fight to right this wrong through the necessary legislation-the Land Alienation Bill and the Debt Reconciliation Bill–a fight that was to prove long and arduous.

The time Mohammed Ayub spent at the Larkana Madressah was a very happy one. Here he made life long friendships with Kehar, with the Phull family, with other contemporaries at school who would be associated with him throughout his long career as zamindar, politician and statesman. It was here while he was a student of Class IV that he first met Shahnawaz Bhutto who was to become a good friend albeit with occasional differences regarding politics. Bhutto was a member of a cadet branch of the well-known zamindar family, and although a comparatively small land holder in relation to other members of his family, he had a working knowledge of English and had achieved a good deal of importance in the district and later in the Presidency, through his tact and judicious courtship of the British officials. Bhutto was a member of the Board of Governors of the school and it was customary that sometimes a member of the Board would come and inspect the school and take *viva voce* examination of some classes. Bhutto was very kind to young Khuhro asking him about his family, sending regards to his father and uncle and then passing him with the best marks in class. In future life Khuhro always recollected that no matter how difficult the circumstances, Shahnawaz Bhutto never allowed annoyance to show and was always charming and avuncular in his attitude to Khuhro, often giving him the benefit of his worldly advice.

At this time the Madressah was not yet entitled to hold the matriculation examination and for the last two years of his schooling Mohammed Ayub had to go to Sind Madressah at Karachi. The Sind Madressah was established in 1885[9] by the efforts of Khan Bahadur Hassanally Bey Effendi to enable and encourage Muslim families to send their children for modern education and to learn the English language. The school, with its residential 'houses' was a collection of graceful edifices built on the traditional quadrangle principle which echoed the planning of ancient Muslim universities as well as Oxford and Cambridge. The Sind Madressah had done remarkable pioneering work in the field of education and it was the foremost school for Muslims in the province. Here Mohammed Ali Jinnah had taken admission in 1887 and the list of the school alumni contained most of the distinguished names in the modern history of Sind.

Having passed his matriculation examination with honours, in 1920 Khuhro took admission in Dayaram Jethmal Sind College (D. J. Sind College), the premier educational institution in Sind, again much against the wishes of his father. *Wadero* Shah Mohammed, who was nearing the end of his life and felt that all this study of English and secular subjects was highly improper for a Muslim and would lead to the loosening of moral standards; but most importantly would distract a zamindar from his proper work which was to look after his zamindari. But once again his younger brother Jan Mohammed prevailed, insisting that Mohammed Ayub continue his studies and the zamindari would be looked after in good time. The Principal of D. J. College at this time was S. C. Shahani, one of the most dynamic heads the college has ever had. He was himself a zamindar and later became a politician when he was elected to the Viceroy's Council. It was he who conceived the idea of an engineering college with a view particularly to provide engineers for the Sukkur Barrage then being built and it was through his efforts that N. E. D. Engineering College was established in 1922. He was also responsible for the first Law College in Sind which was set up in 1926 and named after him, the S. C. Shahani Law College. Shahani took a special interest in Khuhro regarding him as a fairly rare phenomenon – a Muslim zamindar's son who had come as far as college and was a outstanding student. In Khuhro's class there were only seven Muslim students in a class of eighty. Khuhro was given the best rooms in Metharam hostel which was just opposite the College itself and had his own servants including a cook. He was frequently a guest at Shahani's house which was in the grounds of Metharam hostel.

It was at 'D. J.' that Khuhro got to know Dr. Hotchand Gurbaxani, the great Sindhi and Persian scholar who edited one of the best known and authoritative versions of *Shah jo Risalo*. Dr. Gurbaxani was at this time Professor of Persian at the college. He became a friend of Khuhro and throughout his life retained the warm friendship. After retirement when he was living on the other side of Patel Park* from Khuhro's house in Karachi, he met Khuhro almost every day when the latter was in Karachi, walking across the park in the evening to spend a few hours discussing the state of politics and Sindhi and Persian poetry. Unfortunately Khuhro's hopes of a higher education remained unfulfilled as barely a year after his joining D. J. Sind College, in March 1921 his father died after a short illness and he had to return home to look after his affairs.

Wadero Jan Mohammed was still alive but an old man and in the circumstances there was no alternative to Khuhro's returning to zamindari concerns. With the help of his uncle these affairs were soon settled. Khuhro had an affinity with figures and was well able to understand the somewhat complicated accounts brought to him by the *kamdars*. Throughout his life he would remain meticulous in checking these accounts and being able to notice any discrepancies however slight. Land stewards found it difficult to fool him even when he was busy with politics. He was also familiar with the land and the *haris* who cultivated it. He would ride across the fields early in the morning to the Aqil *bund*, (earth barrier) to check the inundation and then once or twice a week take the ferry across to the *kutcha* where the inundation crop was growing luxuriantly.

He had been in the habit of accompanying his father and uncle since his early years and later accompanying any official who came to inspect the crops. Of these officials Khuhro noted,

"The British district officers were extremely conscientious in their duties. In my school days I remember the Assistant Collector used to come to survey the lands riding on his horse. I used to be sent off by my father with him and I would see the thorough checking he did of the fields, channels etc."[10]

Now responsible for the zamindari he was quite happy to ride across the fields in the morning and enquire about the welfare of the villagers and keep an eye on the condition of the crops. He maintained the friendships of his father and uncle with the neighbouring zamindars and the officials of the district. He participated in the annual *jirgas* to decide disputes and cattle thefts with the neighbouring zamindars.

As head of the tribe and an active working zamindar he participated in local affairs and was fully immersed with the problems that beset the zamindar class as well as the agricultural sector in general. He realised that zamindars and agricultural interests needed a voice which could be heard in the highest reaches of officialdom. Since the locally recruited officials were on the whole of an urban background and too busy pursuing their promotions, the case for the rural areas where the majority of the people lived was going by default. The representatives for Larkana, for instance, were seriously handicapped because of their lack of English, the language in which the official and legislative business was carried on or were too dependent on official goodwill or too sycophantic to bring up any problems that could cause a frown on the brow of the officialdom. So if the case was to be put up it had to be done by the new generation of enthusiastic and English

---

* Patel Park was renamed Nishtar Park after Partition.

knowing young men.

Khuhro was by no means reluctant to give time to public affairs. He was already familiar with the issues that were exercising the politicians and had seen and met some of the great men of the day during the *khilafat* agitation. He was drawn to the world of politics. He wanted to participate in the exciting and stimulating events that were taking place in the country following the end of the Great War. He felt that the solution of the problems of rural Sind, of the heavily disadvantaged Muslims, lay not in the villages themselves but in the urban world where laws were made and policies laid down which had such far reaching implications for the helpless cultivator of the soil. Not only was Khuhro strongly drawn to the world of policy makers but his training and indeed the hopes of his uncle had been that he would join that world. Fortunately Mohammed Ayub's younger brother Mohammed Nawaz was showing every sign of becoming a good traditional zamindar and so the conduct of the zamindari could be safely left in his charge with the periodic supervision of the elder brother.

It was said in Aqil that *Wadero* Jan Mohammed, whose duty it was to provide *rasai* for the visiting Officer Sahibs in Larkana for the shooting season, was completely fed up with providing goats, chickens and village labour and had encouraged his nephew to acquire an English education so that he could talk to the Sahibs on (more or less) equal terms and rid the zamindars of this tedious and annoying duty. This objective, among more momentous ones, was certainly achieved by the political life of Mohammed Ayub Khuhro.

3

ENTRY INTO POLITICS

By the time Khuhro joined college in Karachi the Khilafat agitation and the civil disobedience movement had been launched by Gandhi in co-operation with the Muslim Khilafat leadership. At the outbreak of World War I the Indian political leadership had offered assistance to the colonial government in the war effort and they had hoped that India would be substantially advanced on the road to self-government after the war.

Constitutional reforms had been promised in various authoritative pronouncements by representatives of the British government. On 20 August 1917, Edwin Montagu, the Secretary of State for India made a statement in the House of Commons declaring that the policy of His Majesty's Government

> is that of the increasing association of Indians in every branch of the administration and the gradual development of self-governing institutions with a view to the progressive realisation of responsible government in India, as an integral part of the British Empire.[1]

In October, the same year, Montagu came to India staying in the sub-continent till April of the following year. He travelled extensively, met people and made an exhaustive survey of the problems and aspirations of the Indian peoples. It was hoped by the political leadership that India would be given Dominion Status like the other parts of the Empire. But what emerged after the war was not Dominion Status but what were regarded by Indians as very half hearted concessions, making obvious a clear distrust of Indians by the British rulers in stark contrast of their policy towards the White Dominions. The constitutional reforms which came to be known as the Montagu-Chelmsford Reforms after the names of the Secretary of State and the Viceroy, thus proved a great disappointment. The ensuing protests and the mass movement launched by Gandhi destroyed the moderate leadership of India. There was widespread belief that the moderate constitutional methods so far advocated by the fathers of Indian nationalism– Gokhale, Pheroze Shaw Mehta and others had proved ineffective and that a tougher breed of politicians would be able to bargain more effectively with the British rulers.

From 1919 onwards for a number of years India experienced the politics of mass mobilization- large scale public meetings, *hartals* (strikes and shutdowns), *Satyagraha* (demonstrations and 'sit ins'), processions and protests. Emotions ran high among both among Hindus and Muslims particularly after the notorious

Jallianwalla Bagh incident in which hundreds of innocent people gathered in an enclosed space and were shot down under the orders of a British officer, General Dyer. The *ulema* pronounced *fatwas* that the territories ruled by the British were *Darul Harb* (the zone of war ie. against the Muslims) and it was the duty of Muslims to emigrate to *Darul Islam* (the zone of Islam or peace). As a result of this dictum thousands of Muslim families sold off their properties particularly in Sind and Punjab and set off for 'zones of peace', in this case, Afghanistan, to live in a Muslim society.

Khuhro had his close encounter with the Khilafat movement when Larkana became the venue for the Khilafat conference of 1920. Jan Mohammed Junejo, a neighbouring *zamindar* and family friend was very active in Khilafat politics. He was "England returned", Bar at Law and an idealist. He was a leading light in the Civil Disobedience and Khilafat movements. In June 1920 he organized a successful three day Khilafat conference in Larkana and played host to the luminaries of Indian politics, the Ali brothers, Maulana Abul Kalam Azad and many others. The conference was held in a large hall on Empire road near the Khuhro house. Khuhro attended the conference and a dinner given by Jan Mohammed Junejo for the delegates. The British officials were concerned about the Khilafat activity and did their best to show that it did not have public support. They organized a sabotage operation and put in charge, the Native Assistant Commissioner Khan Bahadur Nabi Baksh, who appointed his brother Abdul Qadir Mohammed Hussain (Daftardar) to mobilize action against the Khilafat agitation. Abdul Qadir managed to persuade three important Larkana personalities, Shahnawaz Bhutto, Nawab Amir Ali Lahori and Ghulam Mohammed Isran to co-operate with him.[2]

The Junejo residence adjoined the Larkana Madressah wall and just opposite was a mosque with large grounds which was used as Eidgah *maidan* (grounds for Eid prayers). Meetings were held there to counter the Khilafat conference but in spite of official pressure there was little public response with at most two to three hundred people attending. Pro Khilafat maulvis started preaching outside the mosque grounds to great effect. Recognising the futility and the unpopularity of these meetings, Nawab Lahori pretended to be ill with heart trouble and lay on his *charpoy* (string bed) outside the mosque. Shahnawaz Bhutto left town. The counter movement ended in failure.

On 9 July amidst great emotional scenes the first *hijrat* train from India set off from Larkana under the leadership of Barrister Junejo titled *Rais al Muhajireen*. He had already resigned all his official posts and sold off his property to migrate to the *Darul Islam*, Afghanistan. Once in Afghanistan the *muhajireen* (emigrants) found themselves helpless and in a very difficult situation. No arrangements had been made to receive them or to house and feed them consequently they suffered a great deal - many of them returned home having lost their property and belongings.[3] Jan Mohammed Junejo returned to India in order to raise funds to enable the immigrants to return home but he fell ill and died at Ajmer where he had gone for a Khilafat conference in 1923.

For Khuhro, Junejo's struggle and death confirmed his own distaste for emotionalism and what he considered misdirected idealism. Here was food for thought. Junejo was educated, politically aware and patriotic. He had worked for and achieved an all India position early in life. Junejo's death was a dramatic example of what seemed to illustrate the futility of emotionalism. Junejo had invited Khuhro as the bright, up and coming educated young zamindar of the district who might be recruited to the cause. But even at that young age Khuhro was realistic enough to see that the Khilafat movement was a romantic movement and with its *fatwas* of *Darul Harb* was not going to serve the purpose of banishing the British or improving the lot of Muslims in India. Khuhro saw that the *Hijrat* movement was quite obviously a disaster for those who were participating in it. To sell off the family property and to set off into the unknown was not going to help restore the Khalifa to his position. Although affected by the passion of the student community where he was studying in D. J. Sind College, he was never convinced that 'Non Co-operation' was the answer to the problems of India. So when his father wrote to him to say that he should not take any rash step such as leaving college he could reassure him without hesitation.[4]

Khuhro came to the conclusion early on that if the Muslims were to advance they could not afford to indulge in the romantic dream of the Khilafatists. He realized only too well that the Khalifa in Istanbul would not provide an answer to problems of Sindhis particularly when the British had just won a world war. To Khuhro the best option, in fact the only option reinforced by the experience of friends such as Junejo, was to work within the system to better the conditions of the people. He was deeply impressed with the achievements of western science and with the power of a modern imperial government such as that of Britain. He could not see what Gandhi had to offer apart from emotionalism and chaos. The slogan of *Swaraj* or *Ram Rajya*, Gandhi's terms for self rule and ideal government, but couched in Hindu religious language, did not echo in the heart of the Mussalmans of Sind. The Non Co-operators did not inspire confidence as an alternative to the existing government of India. The denouement of the Non Co-operation movement with the Khilafat movement was rioting and bloodshed. Thousands were put in jail, students left educational institutions putting their futures in jeopardy. The waste reinforced his conviction of the futility of this kind of action. The efforts to preserve the Khalifa in Istanbul proved equally futile when Kemal Ataturk, the hero of the Muslim world, abolished the Khilafat itself.

The Montagu Chelmsford Reforms of 1919 established for India the principle of provincial autonomy. The Reforms were miserly in the amount of power or responsibility devolved to the Indians but they served to point the way to the constitutional future of India, that of provincial autonomy and federalism. The system of government established under the 'Montford Reforms' came to be popularly known as Dyarchy because the central idea of the reforms was the division of powers between the British officials who were 'nominated' members of the provincial governments and the 'natives' who were the elected members of the governments. The former were given the 'power' subjects such as law and order and finance and the latter the 'nation building' subjects such as education, public works and suchlike.

To the Indian politicians who were expecting reforms on the scale of those given to Australia and Canada, these driblets were a deep disappointment and were to provide the death knell of 'moderate' politics in India. It was obvious that reasoned arguments were not proving effective in gaining concessions from the colonial government. That there was a double standard in operation, one for the 'white' colonies and one for the non whites in the empire. Gandhi newly arrived from leading a struggle for civil rights for non whites in South Africa had offered co-operation in war time with the promise of Dominion Status and Home Rule after the war. Congress and Muslim League had formed a pact (The Lucknow Pact, 1916) which was to smooth the way for the forthcoming reforms. A spirit of compromise was evident but the reforms when they came were not only a grave disappointment but also shattered for ever the consensus which had worked during and after the war.

The Congress party was split between those who rejected the reforms outright and those who wanted to work with the reforms and 'wreck them from within'. Gandhi was convinced that only by taking the issue to the public and activating them–by mass contact–would the colonial government be forced to abdicate or devolve power. In this he tried to gain the co-operation of the Muslims by including the popular Khilafat cause. These tactics gained wide popularity for Gandhi and although for a time created a remarkable joint political action by the two communities, they failed to achieve positive results. The pressure on the Imperial government was not enough to force it to concede although it did promise to re-examine the working of the reforms after ten years. The negative result of Gandhi's mass contact movement were however very serious for the future of the country. The introduction of religious politics necessarily led to the oversimplification of the issues. Moreover the language and terminology of both Gandhi and the Khilafatists was religious which introduced a new and potentially divisive element into Indian politics which would ultimately defeat the feeble plant of secularism. *Ram Raj, Swaraj,* patriotic hymns like *Bande Mataram* as well as the concept of *Darul Harb* and *Darul Islam* were highly emotive terms which once brought to the fore in the consciousness of the people would not go away and were to lead to consequences not dreamt of by the leaders of Non Co-operation and Khilafat movements. The collapse of these movements led to religious revivalism and the rise of communal violence which appeared on the political and public scene on a wide scale for the first time in the 1920s.

Personal affairs as well as distrust of emotional politics kept Khuhro away from the Non Co-operation and Khilafat activities in the immediate post war period. But some involvement in public life was almost essential for a young man in his position. In 1922 Khuhro was elected to the District Local Board in place of his uncle Jan Mohammed who resigned to make way for him, and he began to take an active part in the local politics. From the very first he proved a keen member of District Local Board, getting to understand the problems of the area, determined to correct injustices and cut through the layers of patronage and veiled political dealings.

At this time the President of the District Local Board of Larkana was Khan Bahadur Shahnawaz Bhutto who had close links with the British officials and therefore a good deal of influence in official circles. Bhutto was a very shrewd man who understood the art of manipulation and managed local affairs with tact and finesse. For many years he had so organized the conduct of the Local Board meetings that all decisions were made at the behest of the President without any discussion. An official of the Board would stand up at the meeting and say, "Hoping to get the sanction of the Board, the President has taken such and such action.", and the decision would get the sanction. Finally at one meeting, sometime after he was elected, Khuhro protested that if this was the way the affairs of the Board were carried on there was no point in having the meetings at all and wasting the time of the members. Bhutto was very alarmed at this sign of rebellion and realized that if allowed to go further this could mean more trouble from the members and an end to his dominance. He asked Khuhro to come and see him and explained in a fatherly way that it was dangerous to air his views or protest publicly in this hot headed youthful way and that he should understand that if there was open debate, he would not be able to keep control over the Board and all kinds of elements would be able to raise their voices. So if Khuhro wanted anything in the way of scholarships or employment for his proteges or any other benefits Khuhro should come to see him and all would be settled in a gentlemanly manner and without fuss. Khuhro agreed and after that Bhutto took care to consult him whenever there were any scholarships, jobs or other patronage to be distributed.

Soon after his election to the Local Board Khuhro was also elected to Larkana Municipal Committee with the support of Nawab Lahori, a local notable. Khuhro worked seriously and hard at his new duties. The depth of understanding of local problems that he had already acquired by this time is reflected in his reply to a questionnaire the government circulated a couple of years later regarding the law and order problem, particularly cattle stealing which was a widespread crime in Sind. Khuhro's reply is worth quoting in detail to show not only his understanding of the peculiar problems of rural Sind and the chronic shortcomings of the administration but also his in-depth and analytical approach in dealing with issues. He explained that the geography of Sind encouraged a certain kind of crime:

"Cattle form a part of the wealth of almost every inhabitant of the rural area in the province and they are a good source of their income and livelihood. However the geographical position of the province and its topography both of them expose the province to dangers of cattle stealing. The province is bound on the north west by the hilly country of Baluchistan and the tribes of this area carry away the cattle of the villagers with impunity. Secondly the river Indus runs from the north to the south and divides the province into two. The hill tribes find it very easy to lift cattle to Baluchistan or from one half of the province to the other across the Indus. Cattle thieves also find easy refuge in the state of Khairpur which is outside the jurisdiction of the British administration. Thus cattle thieves find convenient shelter in the hills or in the riverine tracts or in the desert. These are the Rohillas of today. There is regular trade going on in cattle lifting and cattle is regularly sent across the river into different districts or into the hills. The ease with which this can be done is the reason why cattle stealing is so common in Sind."[5]

Khuhro explained that the current remedy was not adequate and it was necessary to separate the powers of the executive and judiciary. He further suggested:

"The application of Chapter VIII (C.P.O.) has done very little or no good. It could do more good if it were properly applied but it is usually used as a means of wreaking private vengeance. The basic problem for the misuse of this section is the corruption of the police. A great deal of mischief arises from the combination of judicial and executive authority in the same individual. A *badmash* should not be put up unless evidence collected against him by the police is authenticated by an independent judicial officer who is far above executive considerations and whose executive zeal can under no circumstances outrun his judicial discretion. But this is an ideal state of affairs and till it is attained, I am of the opinion that a *jirga* system be introduced i.e. Boards of respectable *zamindars*, in whom people may have confidence, be appointed in each *taluka*. The sub-divisional magistrate should be Chairman of *jirga* committee. The committee should meet once a month and discuss these offenses committed during those intervals and the *zamindar* who may be member of *jirga* or in whose *zamindari* or vicinity any theft has been committed, should bring the matter before the committee. The *zamindar* in whose area the theft has been committed should either produce the thief or give adequate information so that authorities can trace him. Police in such cases should be held dutybound to assist the Board to capture those abscondees. When the person is found guilty by a *jirga* he should be liable for up to three years imprisonment. Security should not be taken except in rare cases where the committee is fully satisfied of the penitence of the accused. Section 110 should therefore be so amended as to be in harmony with this system."[6]

Khuhro fully realised the importance of involving the community in the maintenance of law and order and advised that:

"the opinion of the villagers be necessarily invited when selecting the *jirga* committee members".

The village community would therefore have a veto on the membership and would be able to ensure that only public spirited, honest and responsible *zamindars* would be on the committee responsible for the maintenance of law and order. He further suggested:

"Each member should be given a certain number of villages in his charge according to the wishes of the respectable inhabitants of those villages. The police should have absolutely no power to run in *badmashes* nor should they have any hand in the matter. Their duty should only be to assist in capturing *badmashes* when directed by the committee."

Khuhro was thus very aware of the tendency of the irresponsible executive to high handedness and corruption and wanted to get public involvement to act as a check on the executive. He pointed out the defects of the present system and set out the logic behind his suggestions–

"It might be said that there is an inconsistency of opinion as I have expressed at one place that the executive and judicial should be separated for the purposes of Chapter VIII, while in the latter para I have shown the necessity of *jirga* committee to be appointed with powers vested in them to try these theft cases and punish the culprits. My object in showing two different factors is plain and simple. I am opposed to both the executive and judicial powers centred in one individual, because past experience shows that their judicial discretion has often been surmounted by executive consideration. Whereas if the boards which will be formed by the assembly of the pick of the 'taluka zamindars' they will thoroughly investigate, discuss and weigh everything properly and deliberately before arriving at any conclusion. In that case there is no danger of the diminution of the judicial discretion. The sub-divisional magistrate in this case will be the Chairman of the Committee and will therefore naturally understand both sides properly and will get no chance to draw his own hasty conclusion by being either too optimistic or too pessimistic."[7]

Khuhro was sceptical of the usefulness of appointing extra police officials or keeping a top heavy police administration at the sub-divisional level which would not be able establish contact with the people at the lower level and would be manipulated by lower grade police officials. As for the *patharidars* (local protectors and patrons of lawless elements) he gave the opinion that

"it is not in any way difficult to bring the patharidars within the clutches of the law. Almost all the patharidars are known to the local police but the police wilfully connives at their misdeeds, because they are the general suppliers and pay liberal gratuities in many forms to the local police."[8]

Khuhro put forward a solution to the law and order problem which was well suited to local conditions:

"There are in my opinion two ways to remedy these evils under the present circumstances: (i) The Criminal Tribes Settlement Act be brought in force in Sind without any loss of time. By so doing most of the *patharidars* will fall within the purview of that Act. (ii). The remaining *patharidars* will face their doom by the enforcement of the *jirga* system. It will hunt them out in all directions wherever they go to seek refuge. This system will make them liable to three years imprisonment each time and will automatically compel them to relinquish criminal habits.

I am strongly in favour of the compulsory registration of cattle and their being numbered provided this duty is entrusted to Local Boards and they are authorised to charge certain fixed fees for registration. If it is entrusted to the police it will make things much worse than before. Local Boards are public bodies and they are directly responsible to the people and they take public opinion into consideration. The elected President and Vice-President will watch all the movements of the staff deputed to this work, whereas police belong to another sphere and will not attach so much weight to ordinary complaints and there will be sufficient scope for ill doings and corruption.

I am opposed to the appointment of village headmen because the police will get such people appointed as will play into their hands. They will intensify the gravity of injustice and corruption through the instrument the village headmen.

I would recommend (i) immediate enforcement of the Criminal Tribes Act in Sind. (ii) Compulsory registration of cattle and (iii) the *jirga* system. These are the best solutions for the eradication of this evil in province of Sind. The Criminal Tribes Settlement Act should be thoroughly discussed in Council, public opinion and criticism be invited on it in full detail before it is applied to Sind. There are I think certain clauses which will undoubtedly invite considerable opposition. These should therefore be amended, improved or abrogated before bringing the Act into force."[9]

As is obvious from this analysis that Khuhro had a genuine understanding of the social structure and the administration even at his young age. Khuhro took pains to understand problems and had a great capacity for mastering detail. This was combined with exceptional clarity of thought. All these qualities were to stand him in good stead and would in time earn him the reputation of one the best administrators and Premiers of any province in the Indian sub-continent.

While Khuhro was gaining experience in Local Government elections for the Bombay Council were due at the end of 1923. Khuhro's friends were very keen that he should contest them. They felt that the representation of Sind was in the hands of an older and tired leadership which had been nurtured by the colonial officials to suit their needs rather than that of the electorate. Until the introduction of the reforms of 1919, the "natives" on the Viceroy's and Governors' Councils were nominated and dependent for their membership on the goodwill of British officials. This system was hardly conducive to independence of thought or action and had tended to encourage sycophants. Naturally local problems did not get much attention from nominated members who were more interested in accumulating favours and honours for themselves. With the introduction of elected assemblies the time was ripe and even overdue for an element of independence to be introduced even in so tractable a group as the members from Sind. Khuhro's leading 'backer' as candidate for the 1923 elections was Shaikh Mohammad Kadir, the *wazir* of Khairpur state.

Shaikh Mohammad Kadir was a remarkable personality and played an important part at this period in raising political consciousness among the Muslims of Sind. Originally from Surat in Gujerat, he started his career as a clerk in the Revenue department, and rose to the rank of Deputy Collector which at that time, except for the rare Collectorship of a district, was the highest rank available to a 'native' officer. In the early 'twenties he became *wazir* or the principal civil servant and 'adviser' appointed by the Viceroy's government in the state of Khairpur in Sind. This was a position of great influence particularly in upper Sind where, as the only 'native' officer of this rank not only was he the doyen of the Muslim officers but as the principal officer in a 'native state' he was in a considerable position of power and was in a position to wield considerable influence among the landowners and the politics of area. Shaikh Mohammad Kadir was passionately interested in the uplift of the Muslims of Sind. He was keen to see that the sons of zamindars were educated and that the Muslim community acquire political consciousness and be able to stand up to the might of the Hindu and British bureaucracy. He was a man of tact and diplomacy and through the judicious exercise of these talents as well as his position, he became a powerful figure in the society and politics of Sind in the early 'twenties.

In order to provide the Muslims of Sind with a voice he collected funds and started a Sindhi language newspaper from Sukkur, the *Sind_Zamindar* of which Khuhro, a major contributor to the funds for the newspaper and as a dynamic young man, became the Managing Director. *Sind Zamindar* championed the Muslim cause effectively for the next quarter of a century and helped to raise awareness of the situation in which the Muslim community found itself at this time. Unlike most of the press of the time it took a bold anti establishment line not hesitating to criticize the British officers and their policies. Kadir also collected funds for a public school for the sons of Muslim zamindars, to be built near Sukkur but this scheme could not be implemented as he was transferred from Khairpur by 1925 and the Muslim officers after him were not sufficiently interested to back such a scheme. Khuhro and other friends then used the funds to build a hostel in Karachi for Muslim boys from rural Sind which was used by several generations of boys until after Partition. The Leslie Wilson hostel, named after the then Governor Bombay Presidency and which after Partition became known as Jinnah Courts, was situated facing the new Governor's House and was a famous landmark of Karachi.

Khuhro's acquaintance with Shaikh Mohammed Kadir began almost as soon as he began his public career in 1921. The Khuhro family had considerable land holdings in Khairpur state which was situated on the opposite banks of the river Indus from Larkana District, and this fact made Khuhro a zamindar of Khairpur State and therefore a subject of the Mir of Khairpur. At this time the ruler of Khairpur was Mir Ali Nawaz Talpur, an eccentric and colourful personality whose extravagant lifestyle is legendary in the annals of Khairpur. His favourite passtimes, not unusual for the ruler of a 'native state', were hunting, music and dancing girls. His love affair with a famous courtesan of Lahore's Hira Mandi, Bali, was one of the more colourful episodes of Khairpur's history. For the satisfactory pursuit of these pleasures Mir Ali Nawaz needed rather more revenues than were normally produced by the small state of Khairpur with the result that from time to time demands were made on the landowners of Khairpur to pay revenues in advance or to pay more than the sums legitimately due from them.

Mohammed Ayub Khuhro was not a man to put up with these demands. He refused to pay in advance or to pay more than was due from him. The result of his curt refusal was that he earned the ire of the Mir and there was an open breach between the two. Shaikh Mohammad Kadir felt that apart from upsetting the Mir this quarrel could go against the interests of Khuhro who was on the threshold of what promised to be a bright political career. He therefore intervened to effect a reconciliation. He asked Khuhro to invite the Mir to a grand dinner and music party and undertook to make the Mir agree that no undue demands would be made on the zamindars of Khairpur. Khuhro held a banquet in the honour of the Mir where the best available musicians and singers were brought to perform, poets came to recite poems in honour of the guest and the host, trays of silver rupees were placed in front of the Mir from which he could shower his appreciation on the performers. No effort was spared to entertain the Mir in the style to which he was accustomed. After this reconciliation, relations between the Mir and Khuhro remained cordial, if not very close, throughout Mir Ali Nawaz's rule in Khairpur and the departure of Shaikh Mohammad Kadir did not affect those relations. Khuhro was always invited to the numerous functions held by the Mir whether they were purely music and dance for the entertainment of the Mir and his friends or official functions in honour of the visiting Commissioner or Governor.[10]

The backing by Shaikh Mohammed Kadir was to prove invaluable in the early phase of Khuhro's political career. He encouraged Khuhro to participate in political and social organizations at the Sind as well as all India level. In 1922-23 a session of Muslim Educational Conference was held in Hyderabad, Sind. This organization had been sponsored by the leading Muslims of the Bombay Presidency for the advancement of education in the community. The Hyderabad session was to be attended by the Governor of Bombay, Sir Leslie Wilson, as the guest of honour and such well known personalities as Sir Ross Masood, the grandson of Sir Sayed Ahmed Khan. Sir Currimbhoy, the businessman and philanthropist and Sir Ibrahim Rahimtoola of Bombay were present at the conference. Khuhro accompanied Kadir to this conference and met the men with whom he would be closely associated as a member of Bombay Legislative Council from the following year. In Sir Leslie Wilson he would find a rare phenomenon, a high British official who was genuinely sympathetic and ready to listen to the problems of the disadvantaged Muslims of Sind.

It was on this visit to Hyderabad that Khuhro met for the first and only time the leading Muslim nationalist politician of the time, Rais Ghulam Mohammed Bhurgri.

Bhurgri was at this time at the height of his career as the leading all India politician of Sind and an important figure both in Muslim League and the Congress parties. He was a member of the Bombay Council and a leading opponent of the worst aspects of colonialism. He was very conscious of the irresponsibility and the high-handedness of the official class and was leading an effective campaign to reduce their powers and give relief to the public from their unjustified demands. He was to preside over the annual session of Muslim League but unfortunately died at a comparatively early age in 1924. Bhurgri's circle of friends was very wide and he kept in touch with the political base through an extensive correspondence with friends and peers throughout the province. After every Council session he would write letters to influential zamindars, telling them of matters relating to Sind or to agriculture, any legislation or government decisions that were likely to affect them and of the political and general conditions obtaining in the country as a whole. Among his friends and correspondents was Mohammed Ayub Khuhro's uncle Jan Mohammed. Bhurgri was therefore aware of the hopes and ambitions of Jan Mohammed regarding his nephew and had followed his career at a distance.

One evening during this visit to Hyderabad Khuhro was walking up the *Tilak Charhi*, a fashionable promenade of Hyderabad when Rais Ghulam Mohammed passed by in his Victoria carriage. He saw Khuhro and stopped the carriage. He called Khuhro over and asked him if he was Mohammed Ayub, son of Shah Mohammed Khuhro. When Khuhro answered in the affirmative he asked him to get into the carriage and took him to his house where he chatted with the young man for a while, asking him about his education and future plans and approved his plans for a political future. This was the only time Khuhro met Rais Bhurgri who in spite of his early death left a great name in the political history of Sind.

The second election to the Bombay Legislative Council under the Montagu Chelmsford Reforms became due at the end of 1923. The Dyarchical system introduced by these Reforms meant a measure of responsible government for India and the recognition of the principle of provincial autonomy. At the provincial level a largely elected legislature with about 20% nominated members had been provided for. The Governor who was the executive head of the presidency was assisted by a cabinet which consisted of Executive Councillors who were nominated and Ministers who were chosen from among the elected legislators. The former were in charge of 'Reserved' subjects or those that the colonial government felt could only be entrusted to British officials such as Law and Order, Finance, etc. The elected Ministers were given 'transferred' subjects such as Health, Education, Public Works, etc. which could safely be entrusted to Indians. These were known as 'nation building' subjects. At this time Sind which was part of the Bombay Presidency, sent nineteen members to the Bombay Legislature of which fifteen were Muslims, three Hindus and one European. Larkana was the largest district in Sind with eleven *talukas* (sub divisions) and sent three members to Bombay, Sukkur, Hyderabad and Mirpurkhas districts sent two members each and Dadu, Thatta, Jacobabad and Nawabshah sent one member each. Karachi sent two Muslims, one member from the Indian Chamber of Commerce and one from the European Chamber of Commerce. Two Hindus were elected – one from Upper and one from Lower Sind. Those eligible for voting had to be tax payers in order to qualify as voters.

By the end of 1923 Khuhro had an impressive list of achievements to his credit.

He had only been in public life for two years but not only was he an active member of the District Local Board and Larkana Municipal Committee, he was Managing Director of *Sind Zamindar*, the leading Muslim newspaper in upper Sind. Following up his schoolboy concern for the indebted agriculturists whom he had daily seen being deprived of their lands in repayment of debts to moneylenders, he became very active in the Co-operative movement for agriculturists and had taken the initiative to organize both big and small zamindars and *khatedars* in order to try to save them from indebtedness and ruin. He was Chairman of the Agriculture Development Association and became Managing Director of the District Co-operative Credit Bank. He was also General Secretary of the Larkana District Mohammedan Association.

Khuhro was advised by his friends including Shaikh Mohammed Kadir to contest as he stood a good chance of winning and also because they felt that there was need for a public spirited young man in the jaded sycophantic politics of Sind. The other candidates who were contesting from Larkana District were Nawab Amir Ali Lahori, Pir Hamid Shah, Khan Bahadur Shah Nawaz Bhutto, Khan Bahadur Ghulam Mohammed Isran and Khan Sahib Karim Baksh Jatoi, all of them much older men than Khuhro. Some of them had been elected to the Assembly in the 1920 elections including Shahnawaz Bhutto and Isran as well as Khan Bahadur Dhani Baksh Jatoi the elder brother of K. B. Karim Baksh.

The elections were scheduled to take place in November 1923 and when Khuhro announced his candidature there was consternation among the established members, Khuhro describes the scene:

"originally I had no idea of contesting the elections. I was still not old enough to be member at twenty two years of age. About June or July 1923 preparations were afoot for the selection of candidates for Bombay Legislative Council elections scheduled to be held on 18th November 1923. Larkana consisted of eleven *talukas* (sub-divisions) from Ratodero to Sehwan and included the whole of Dadu district except Kotri *taluka* and had three `plural' seats i.e. seats with combined voting, each voter had three votes which he gave to one, two or three candidates. Elections were held every three years. The first elections under the Montagu–Chelmsford Reforms had been held in November 1920. Larkana had sent up S. N. Bhutto, K. B. Dhani Baksh Jatoi from the Mehar Dadu area and K. B. Ghulam Mohammed Isran from Kambar *taluka*. The most powerful and influential zamindars or their nominees got elected.

The sitting members Bhutto, Jatoi and Isran with the help of some other big zamindars and nawabs called a meeting of the district élite in Larkana Madressah – my old school. Of the sitting members Bhutto had some English and the other two members were not formally educated though they could read and write Sindhi. In that meeting a large number of zamindars, both great and small were present. The obvious intention of the organizers was that consensus be secured in favour of the sitting members. One could sense the object of the meeting. I had been persuaded to stand by some influential zamindars of the district and some friendly officials like the Chief Wazir of Khairpur State, Shaikh Mohammed Kadir and the late Shaikh Ghulam Mohammed, a good friend of my late father who had just retired from service as Deputy Collector, Larkana. Their main reason in their advising and encouraging me to stand for elections was that they wanted a young energetic and reasonably educated in English candidate to be member of the legislature from Larkana in order to fight for their rights–(i.e. for a better deal for the agriculture sector and for Muslim officials who were sparsely represented in Government service)–The zamindars particularly were unhappy with Bhutto, who according to them was too proud and arrogant to meet or mix with them or listen and get their grievances redressed by the government machinery. K. B. Bhutto was very influential in the district because of Government support. He was the nominated President of the Local Board, the European Collector yielding this place to him, and was also Honorary Ist Class Magistrate. He was leader of the Muslim group of members in the Bombay Legislature mainly because he was the only person barring Rais Bhurgri, who had some English education. Bhurgri was a nationalist and anti British member of the Congress and the zamindars did not follow his line which they felt was too hazardous. When the meeting took place in the Madressah, some of my friends attended. These included the late *Wadero* Sahib Khan Junejo, Sayed Noor Mohammed Shah, zamindar of Bakapur, *Wadero* Ghulam Qadir Dayo of Ratodero. Some zamindars, among them K. B. Amir Ali Lahori and Nawab Ghaibi Khan Chandio expressed the view that the same members should continue. Later however Lahori himself contested. My name was put forward by my friends saying that one seat should be given to this promising young man. The proposal was not palatable to those who had come to support unopposed election of sitting members. When it became known that I was a serious candidate a thorough search was made to find anything which would make me ineligible. It was objected that I was too young..."[11]

Without coming out directly against him Bhutto tried through his friends to get Khuhro's papers disqualified. He knew Khuhro's record as member of Larkana Local Board and Municipality and felt that he would disturb the even tenor of the docile and pro-Government group that was formed by the members from Sind. He was also shrewd enough to know that in the future an educated young man like Khuhro could prove a serious political contender not only on the Larkana level but at the provincial level and it would be better to nip this possible future threat, in the bud, as it were. He encouraged his friends therefore to put in objections to Khuhro's candidature on grounds of age. It was necessary to be twenty three years of age to qualify as candidate for Legislative Council membership and Khuhro was a year short. Khuhro was however able to get support from the British Civil Surgeon at Sukkur that he appeared to be of the required age and was accepted by the Collector of Larkana, J. B. Irwin, in whose impartiality could be no doubt and so the objections against Khuhro were dismissed and he was free to contest elections.

Elections to the Council in 1923 were a gentlemanly affair. Franchise was limited to those with a 'vested interest' in society – the tax payers – and all 'vagrant and irresponsible' elements were excluded. Most of the voters were under the patronage of landowners and there was a network of friendships, connections and influence which controlled the voting pattern. The candidate or his friends would call on the landowners or the tribal elders and ask for their vote. Once word was given there was no going back on it and the candidate could rely almost absolutely on those whose promises he had received. The voters would be brought to the polling stations by the landowner responsible for them and the expense of transport and food would be borne by him. It would be a matter of honour and etiquette that the candidate not be troubled by these matters of bringing the voters or paying for their transport and food. Once he had the assurance that the votes would be his, he could rest easy that they would get into the ballot box.

Khuhro found that his candidature was popular in the district. He was promised support from almost everyone he approached. Apart from friendship with the family the majority of zamindars of the district were tired of being taken for granted by the sitting candidates from the district. Most of the members who had gone to the 1920 Assembly were barely literate in Sindhi and quite inadequate when it came to the question of taking up issues in the Assembly. Also their main concern was to be on good terms with the officials and be able to entertain them to shoots and feasts to the wonder and envy of their friends and neighbours. Of all the members from Larkana, Shahnawaz Bhutto was the most senior but it was generally felt that he relied too much on official favour and was arrogant and inaccessible in his attitude to his fellow landowners and also to the general public. As one contemporary puts it "Sir Sahib's doors were closed in the evening and only officials were to be found giving Sir Sahib convivial company." Sir Shahnawaz was, with Sir Ghulam Hussain Hidayetullah, one of the two most trusted men of the British officialdom in Sind. But the Larkana voter was not satisfied with the honours and favours that were being enjoyed by Sir Sahib and wanted that the elected member be more active on their behalf. Hence Sir Shahnawaz found himself in difficulties and uncertain of winning had to resort to getting another candidate Ghulam Mohammed Isran, a close friend to withdraw in his favour. The elections duly took place and the successful candidates from Larkana were Sir Shahnawaz Bhutto, Khan Sahib Karim Baksh Jatoi and Mohammed Ayub Khuhro.

Sir Shahnawaz was aware that although he had won the election he had been under threat and that this was because of Khuhro's attracting the votes which would otherwise have gone to him, and that he had been able to manage his majority because of the withdrawal of Isran but although the critical situation had been resolved successfully the shock affected him deeply. He was however too subtle and too tactful a man to allow that to be seen. In fact he felt that the best tactics under the circumstances would be to disarm the man whom he saw as a potential rival. His attempt to get Khuhro disqualified had failed and now Khuhro, young, educated and energetic was a member of the Legislature. Bhutto bowed gracefully to the inevitable and decided to effect a reconciliation. He went to see Khuhro one morning and said: "Come, my boy! Isran intends to put an election petition against you. We will go and persuade him to withdraw." Khuhro knew very well that Isran would not have put in such a petition unless prompted by Bhutto but realised that the older man wanted to do him a favour and went along with him, accepting his tactics as the best way out of a situation of needless rivalry. The petition was withdrawn and cordial relations were re-established.

After the elections Sir Shahnawaz fell seriously ill and spent several months in Karachi in the cold season of 1923-24 recovering from his illness. As a result he was unable to attend the Spring session of the newly elected Council in February and March of 1924. During the period of his convalescence Bhutto was living in a house owned by the Dossuls, a Karachi business family, which was situated on the sea front at Karachi on the Jehangir Kothari Parade. Sea air was thought to ensure speedy recovery and Sir Shahnawaz spent sometime at Clifton. It was here that he became acquainted with his future wife, Lakhi Bai, the second Lady Bhutto and the mother of his youngest son Zulfiqar Ali who was to become Prime Minister of Pakistan nearly half a century later.

Lakhi Bai and Ruki Bai were two sisters whose family had originally come from Marwar in Rajasthan which for some curious reason was the place from where the most popular courtesans of Sind originated. Their mother was a famed courtesan of Hyderabad who counted many rich and well-known men among her clients. Her two daughters were also famed for their beauty and their singing talent in the entertainment world of Hyderabad and Karachi and were much sought after. Sir Shahnawaz, forced to spend months idling at the Karachi sea side, was anxious to have suitably entertaining company and this was provided by the young and beautiful Lakhi Bai, with whom Sir Shahnawaz fell passionately in love and who he determined to marry.

By April 1924 Khuhro was back from the Council session in Bombay and called on Sir Shahnawaz to ask after his health. In an interview with a writer Khuhro related an episode illustrating the extent of his close and cordial relations with Sir Shahnawaz at this time:

"I returned to Karachi after attending the Spring Session of the Legislative Assembly at Bombay in April 1924 and saw K. B. Shahnawaz several times at the Clifton house. I was living in the Carlton Hotel near Cantonment Station, at this time one of the best hotels in town, managed by an English woman, a Mrs. Caroe who also served the best food in town. As soon as K. B. Shahnawaz recovered sufficiently he took a room in the Carlton next to mine. A few days later he asked me to book a coupé in the Quetta Mail for his use but in my name for the next day, which I did. That evening he came to my room and asked me to accompany him on some important errand. I went outside with him and found a Victoria carriage waiting. We got in and drove towards the town near the area then known as Napier Road. Here K. B. Shahnawaz asked the carriage to stop, asked me to wait, got down and disappeared down the street. After a while he appeared with a lady in *burqa*, carrying a baby girl and we drove quickly back to the Cantonment Station where he and the lady boarded the train for Quetta."[12]

In Quetta where Bhutto was the guest of the brother of the Khan of Kelat, he married Lakhi Bai who was converted to Islam and took the name of Khurshid Begum. She was a woman of great charm and warmth of personality and Sir Shahnawaz was to remain devoted to her for the rest of his life. She always remained friendly with the Khuhros and even during periods of political antagonism between the families, maintained her cordial relationship with them. After the death of Sir Shahnawaz in the 'fifties she found friendship and consolation in the company of Khuhro's wife and family. After spending sometime in Baluchistan after their marriage the Bhuttos returned to Larkana where they stayed in Khuhro's house on Empire Road until Sir Shahnawaz made his own arrangements.

For Khuhro the first session of the Legislative Council he had attended at Bombay had been an enormously satisfying and enriching experience. It had opened worlds beyond the provincial boundaries which had been his horizons so far. With his natural self confidence he looked forward to valuable years for the advancement of his political objectives as legislator in Bombay.

4

BOMBAY LEGISLATOR

The spring session of the Bombay Legislative Council was due to start on 1 March 1924. Khuhro made his preparations to reach Bombay in time for it. To get to Bombay it was possible to go by sea, a four day journey in a small ship or to go by train on an almost two day long journey through Rajputana* and then south to Bombay. Khuhro along with some other members, some of them much older, who had never travelled outside Sind and were quite unfamiliar with either English or Hindustani, had asked Khuhro to make their travel arrangements along with his own. Khuhro willingly obliged thus leading a group of members to Bombay. He had decided to go by train, a more interesting journey than the one by sea. He boarded the train, then known as Raja's train because it travelled through the land of Rajas, at Hyderabad and travelled through the picturesque state of Rajputana, with peacocks strutting through the grass and deer and other animals coming up to the train quite unafraid. There was an atmosphere of charm and colourful bustle along the wayside stations. Khuhro and his companions travelled through to Jodhpur and then south to Ahmedabad on the B.B.C.I. and on to Bombay, arriving there two days after leaving Hyderabad.

Bombay, *urbs Prima in Indis*, was, in the nineteen twenties at the height of its glory. Capital of the biggest Presidency in India and the first city where the traveller from Europe landed, it was one of the finest example of a British colonial city. Sir Bartle Frere, the pioneering Commissioner-in-Sind had been Governor of Bombay from 1862 to 1869 had laid out plans and with the help of local philanthropists had built a splendid Victorian colonial city. "Without exception the finest modern city in Asia, and the noblest monument of British enterprise in the world" commented one visitor in 1891. Since then ofcourse Lutyens' New Delhi had been built and Curzon had added to the splendours of Calcutta, but there is no doubt that since the construction of Suez Canal Bombay had become a great centre of Indo–European trade and was a less hierarchical and hide-bound city than either Delhi and Calcutta, where Europeans and Indians mixed more easily and the atmosphere was therefore more liberal than in the other great cities of India.

One of the most famous landmarks of Bombay was the splendid Taj Mahal hotel, built at the initiative of the Parsi business magnate Tata. It was said that excluded from the nearby Watson's Hotel which was exclusively for Europeans,

---

* Rajasthan was known as Rajputana before Partition.

Tata resolved to build a grander hotel which Indians could use and the result was the Taj Hotel. The Taj was one of the great hotels of the Empire along with Raffles of Singapore and Shepheards of Cairo, and it was here that the out of town legislators, politicians and the top government officials as well as the Bombay's leading citizens, met and discussed politics and problems.

Khuhro was lucky to get a room at this hotel, this, the first time he was in Bombay. There was only a short time before the start of the session for Khuhro to call on senior colleagues and meet friends over tea, to familiarise himself with the geography of official Bombay, to go around in a Victoria carriage to look at the splendid buildings and parks of Bombay.

The Bombay Legislative Council met on the first of March at the Town Hall, a magnificent Palladian building situated at the top of Elphinstone Circle which included some of the most important architectural splendours of Bombay. The Council was presided over by Sir Ibrahim Rahimtoola whom Khuhro had already met the previous year at Hyderabad. There were approximately a hundred members both official and non official. The official Opposition party was the Swaraj Party under the leadership of M. R. Jayakar and ofcourse there were many distinguished politicians and officials in the Council. From among the members as well as outside the Council, Khuhro was to make many good friends in the following years. Among these were the Parsi philanthropist Sir Cowasji Jehangir, Chunilal Mehta, Sir Ali Mohammed Dehlavi, Rahimtoola, Maulvi Rafiuddin Ahmed of Poona, Navrojee Jehangir Wadia, K. F. Nariman, the distinguished scholar Abasaheb G. N. Mujumdar and other distinguished Parsis, Hindus, Muslims as well as the European members of the Council and the Government. Sir Henry Lawrence the distinguished ex-Commissioner-in-Sind, Sir Maurice Hayward, Sir Charlton Harrison the Chief Engineer of Lloyd Barrage at Sukkur were official nominated members as were other civil servants from the Presidency. From Sind Khuhro's colleagues included Seth Abdullah Haroon, Shahnawaz Bhutto, Ghulam Hussain Hidayetullah, Khan Saheb Serai Imambaksh Khan Jatoi of Nawabshah and Khan Saheb Karimbaksh Khan Jatoi of Mehar in Dadu District, Khan Saheb Sher Mohammed Khan Bijarani of Upper Sind Frontier District (later Jacobabad), Jan Mohammed Khan Bhurgri the brother of Rais Ghulam Mohammed Bhurgri, Saiyid Ghulam Nabi Shah of Thar Parkar, Mukhi Jethanand, Haji Gul Mohammed Khamiso, Haji Fazal Mohammed Laghari, Saiyid Mohammed Kamil Shah, Nur Mohammed Vakil, K. B. Jan Mohammed Pathan, Pir Rasulbaksh Shah of Ghotki, Durgadas Advani, Bhojsing Pahlajani and others.

Most of the Muslim and non Hindu members were generally regarded as pro-Government and only a number of Hindus belonged to the Swaraj party. Swarajists, a faction of the Congress, who, while they considered the Reforms of 1919 as falling far short of the promises made to India, felt that no purpose would be achieved by a boycott of the Councils and that the Reforms could be proved insufficient or 'wrecked' from within. Hence the Swaraj party provided a strong and skilful Opposition and the Government had to be alert to defend itself against it. The Muslim members from Sind were regarded as a solid pro Government block but were able quite often to use their votes to get concessions from the Government for their province which the Presidency bureaucracy would otherwise have been very reluctant to concede.

Khuhro's first opportunity to speak occurred just a fortnight after the start of the Session, in support of a Motion by R. G. Pradhan of Nasik District. This recommended that the process of revising the land revenue assessment be brought under closer regulation by statute as recommended by the Joint Committee appointed to consider the Government of India Bill, 1919. The motion also asked for a report on the nature and the form of legislation that should be undertaken. In supporting the Motion Khuhro put forward the case of the agriculturists of Sind. He suggested that a Committee to investigate the question of a revision settlement be appointed as early as possible, that it should have a clear non official majority and should include a fair representation of the interests of Sind with due reference to their importance. He spoke against the Government habit of increasing the rates of assessment even when prices were going down, and of basing the assessment on the produce of the best agricultural lands.

Khuhro offered a remedy to rescue the agriculturists from the clutches of the moneylender. He felt that the agricultural co-operative movement which had begun a short time earlier in Sind would go a long way to solve the problem and should be encouraged by the government, its success had been "nothing short of a miracle". Khuhro went on:

"I would [like to] explain to the Honourable House the condition of the agriculturists just before this movement started. Government used to advance a loan to the agriculturist in shape of a *taccavi*, but very few could take advantage out of that loan because the system was that when an agriculturist required it, he sent a petition to the Deputy Collector of the Division and then the petition was sent to the *mukhtiarkar* to investigate whether the man really deserved to have the loan and how much property he owned and whether he would utilize that amount for agricultural purposes. Sir, this investigation often took too long and often it was seen that the loan was refused and in some cases when the loan was granted, it was granted very late when it could not serve the purpose of the applicant."[1]

Khuhro explained the dilemma of the cultivator who quite often had no alternative but to go to the moneylender from whose clutches it would be impossible to extricate himself:

"Often when unnecessary delay was caused, the agriculturist used to run to the moneylenders, who charged at least 24% or even 36% interest, and I have seen cases where if anyone required Rs. 100/- they would [have to give] a receipt for Rs. 200/- and out of that 24% was allowed as interest on each Rs. 100/-. This was the condition of the agriculturists. If any amount was lent to the agriculturist by the moneylender, the property of the agriculturist would be mortgaged and very often a high rate of interest would be charged on that property. If they resisted paying that high rate of interest, they would be taken to court and the moneylenders would get decrees passed against them and they would be called upon to pay all the expenses."

Khuhro was very hopeful about the Co-operative Movement and explained its usefulness for the agriculturist arguing for greater capital and larger loans to give genuine help to the cultivator:

"At present the working capital utilised in this Co-operative Movement in Sind amounts to Rs. 51,00,000/-. This is quite a good sum but this sum is utilised only in a short period of six years. I think it will be increasing more and more every year, according to the demand. But the one thing that I want to point out is that at present a loan only to the extent of Rs. 500/- can be given to each shareholder of the co-operative society. This is a very small sum and may attract agriculturists who have got small holdings; but my suggestion is that there should be district banks to advance loans to those agriculturists who require much more money."[2]

Khuhro detailed the benefits for farmers in the movement:

"The other advantage that the agriculturists have derived out of this movement is that they have learnt the method of working together and co-operating with one another. At present the number of co-operative societies in Sind has reached nearly 600, though only six years have passed since their introduction. But I daresay that the movement has taken a very firm root and is very much appreciated by the agriculturists. I would request the Honourable Minister incharge to take more interest in this movement and to see that it develops more and more, and I hope my suggestion will be taken into consideration."[3]

The condition of the agriculturist was, however, beyond simple remedies like easy loans. As Khuhro put it, "A vast number of the smaller *khatedars* was heavily indebted to the *bania*. These unfortunate people were being dispossessed by the *banias* thus rapidly impoverishing the Muslim population. The Encumbered Estates Act which had been introduced into Sind had saved a number of the larger landowners but the plight of the poorer agriculturists was as bad as ever." Khuhro also made the point that:

"The condition of the *zamindars* of Sind is very bad and deserves pity. So many have already sold their properties and many are under heavy debts ... Thanks to the Government, Encumbered Estates Act was applied and it proved a very good weapon to save them from forced insolvency...the record of the Manager Encumbered Estates [will show] that from seventy to hundred *zamindars* every year go to seek his protection."[4]

Khuhro was in fact seeking the protection of Land Alienation Act and Debt Reconciliation Bills which had been introduced into some other provinces of British India including the Punjab, but that would prove to be a long haul in Sind and many years would pass before this legislation would become a possibility. Thus in his very first session in the Council, Khuhro started work on the political programme he had set for himself. Not only did he take every opportunity to speak on the difficulties faced by the agriculturists but also took up the cause of the Muslims in Sind.

"When I was elected to the Bombay Legislature I was determined that I would do my best to fully represent the cause of Sind, particularly the Muslims who were by and large very backward and disadvantaged in a province where they were in an overwhelming majority. They suffered in any case because of certain unavoidable disadvantages as they were largely a rural community. This meant that they had no ready access to schools and education. Secondly they were seriously under-represented in services and unfortunately as they were not in a position to get good education they could never stand against Hindus in competition for services. The Hindu official class was moreover determined to keep its monopoly and would avoid taking in Muslims into any vacant posts... Having achieved complete dominance they were unwilling to give up even a small part of their monopoly with the result that Muslims were becoming more and more resentful. Apart from a few sympathetic officers such as Sir Henry Lawrence, Commissioner in Sind before and during World War I period, the majority were indifferent."[5]

Sir Henry Lawrence who was related to the great Lawrences of the Punjab, John and Henry, was one of the more able and sensitive of the Commissioners that Sind was ever to have. He tried his utmost to recruit the Muslims and succeeded in appointing some Mukhtiarkars and Deputy Collectors. Khuhro, too young to know him in his days in Sind which covered the World War, became good friends with him in Bombay and always found him sympathetic to Sind problems. After Lawrence retired and went to live in Oxford, Khuhro on his first visit to England in 1933 when he went there for the Third Round Table Conference, spent a very pleasant weekend with the Lawrences at their Boar's Hill house at Oxford.

In the Autumn Session of 1924, Khuhro put the questions regarding the recruitment and ratio of Muslim officers in the revenue department to pinpoint the grievance of educated Sindhis:

"(a) Will Government be pleased to state whether it is a fact that in order to increase the number of Mohammedan *Mukhtiarkars* in Sind, the policy of direct recruitment of four *Mukhtiarkars* every year as probationers was initiated in 1918.

(b) If so, how many *Mukhtiarkars* were recruited in pursuance of that policy and how many of them are still in Government service?

(c) Is it a fact that Government intended to continue this policy for full ten years?

(d) If so will Government be pleased to furnish the total number of *Mukhtiarkars* in Sind, stating how many of them are Mohammedan, how many Hindus and how many belong to other communities?"[6]

Chunilal Mehta, the Minister in charge replied that in 1921 there were numerous reversions among acting *Mukhtiarkars* and owing to this cause and the reduction of appointments which were then imminent, there was little likelihood that vacancies would be available in which numerous probationary *Mukhtiarkars* could be placed. The scheme was temporarily suspended for this reason by the Commissioner-in-Sind. The Minister added that the Commissioner had subsequently been directed to revert to the policy of 1918. He also gave the figures which showed that out of total of eighty-two posts of Mukhtiarkars, fifty-six were Hindus, nineteen Muslims and five of other communities. In addition to putting questions in the Council, Khuhro also prepared a detailed note on the position of probationary *Mukhtiarkars* in Sind to aid the Government in the formulation of its policy:

"The policy outlined by Mr. Lawrence and accepted by the Government was, that every year there shall be recruitment of Mussalmans to the Revenue service upto the maximum limit of four *Mukhtiarkars*. There were very few Mussalman *Mukhtiarkars* in service then. In the interests of administration and justice as well as of our community it was thought necessary to recruit 4 Mussalmans every year for ten years. The policy continued with interruption for sometime and it is now considered necessary in some quarters to effect a change in it by recruiting 7 head *munshis* every year, one in each district. My

views on the subject are:—The question should be divided into three parts:
(a) Recruitment to the service.
(b) Material for recruitment.
(c) Method of recruitment.

With regard to (a), I am positively of opinion that the policy outlined by Mr.Lawrence and accepted by Government must continue—not only for ten years but for at least 15 years, for the reasons that it has had some interruptions, that recruitment every year has not reached the maximum of four, and that the number of *mukhtiarkars* in the province has largely increased and will increase on account of the Barrage operations. This question of recruitment should not be mixed up with how the recruitment has to be made. We want four Mussalmans directly recruited as Mukhtiarkars every year. How they are to be recruited I consider below.

With regard to (b) I am strongly of the opinion that material for recruitment should be the Sind Mussalman graduates. Whether the recruitment is made from Mussalman graduates direct or from them after training them for one year or so as *Head Munshis*, I have no objection. What I am anxious about is that the door for recruitment from Mussalman graduates direct should not be closed. It should remain open and if there are any worthy Muslim graduates outside the service available and willing for recruitment as probationers they should not be excluded. In other words recruitment may be made from (1) Worthy Muslim graduates outside service, and (2) Muslim graduates employed and trained as *Head Munshis*.

With regard to (c), I am aware of the complaint that some of the Muslim graduates taken up as probationary *Mukhtiarkars* have not proved successful. I am not quite sure if they are worse than many of the Hindu *mukhtiarkars* in the service. Ofcourse that is not the criterion by which I should judge these Muslim recruits in the service. They are ofcourse expected to turn out as efficient and capable administrators and be the pride of the community. I have so far, had no occasion to examine the *bona fides* of the complaint, but I must say that if the complaint is real, it has something to do with the more or less unsatisfactory method of recruitment. At present the recruitment is made by the Commissioner, who, I must admit, does his duty in this connection on the best of principles as far as possible but as he is not expected to know every candidate personally nor his antecedents precisely the recruitment is bound, in a measure, to be defective. I, therefore, suggest that he should be assisted in the task by a small committee or respectable Mussalmans in and out of service knowing the Sind conditions very well. This system is not unknown to the province. It has been approved of and followed by Government in the matter of recruitment of some other service, for instance, the sub-judges."[7]

In a province in which the population of Muslims was 75% and the vast majority of revenue payers were Muslims, it was a clear case of injustice that in the ranks of these important revenue officers there should be only 25% Muslims. In higher posts the ratio of Muslim officers was even lower. Khuhro had thus taken up a matter which was crucial to the welfare of the bulk of the population. As Khuhro said in his own words:

"I took up the cause of Muslim recruitment in services as a personal crusade.

Before I had left to attend the Council session in Bombay, the Muslim officers had made a representation to me in Hyderabad. Nabi Baksh Mohammed Hussain and some other senior officers had invited me to dinner and had given me some facts and figures. I decided that in addition to efforts that I might make in the Council and which might bring results in time I would try the direct approach in order to try and get immediate results. I walked into the office of Sir Maurice Hayward, the Home Member of the Executive Council and put the matter before him. I explained the position in Sind to him carefully and asked him bluntly if he thought it was fair that 75% of the population should have a representation so negligible in the services whether it was the administrative side, P.W.D., Judicial or other. I said that there was not a single Muslim District Judge or Assistant Judge in the whole of Sind. Sir Maurice heard me out patiently and then pulled out the Civil List from the drawer of his desk and looked through it. "What do you think of Abdullah Akhund ? If you agree I could promote him. He has worked under me when I was District Judge and he was Sub-Judge." At that time I had not met Abdullah Akhund who was a fine officer and was later to become a good friend of mine. I immediately agreed however that Akhund should be appointed and Sir Maurice there and then made a note of it and before I returned to Sind, orders of his promotion had reached already."[8]

Khuhro was encouraged by the positive response of Sir Maurice Hayward and decided to use this as one of the methods of approach to redress the balance of services in Sind. He made it a habit to meet high officers, Ministers and Executive Councillors and impress upon them the need to increase Muslim representation in the services as justice required that this should be done, since the prevailing under representation of Muslims in the officer cadres was nothing short of scandalous. Regarding the attitude of the British officers, particularly at the higher level in the Presidency Khuhro was on the whole satisfied:

"On the whole I found throughout my career that senior British Officials were fairminded and open to persuasion. Ofcourse they had their favourites and were susceptible to flattery, a tactic which I was temperamentally unable to use but which was used by some well-known colleagues of mine and which secured them high places in Government. In general I found British officers I encountered in Sind and Bombay to be men of high calibre and character. There were, however, some exceptions. Unfortunately of the three British Governors of Sind after 1936, two were certainly not the best examples of British officials in India."[9]

Khuhro was quite correct in his judgement about the governors who would be posted in Sind after the separation of the province from Bombay Presidency in 1936. The first Governor Sir Lancelot Graham was to prove a mediocre officer whose competence even the superior officers such as the Viceroy and the Secretary of State questioned.[10] The second Governor, Sir Hugh Dow was a man probably capable of being an efficient clerical or subordinate officer but lacked the imagination or generosity which was essential for the high post he was occupying. While in the Bombay Legislative Council, however, Khuhro was to develop a particularly good rapport with the two Governors of Bombay he encountered, Sir Leslie Wilson and his successor Sir Frederick Sykes. Wilson listened sympathetically to the problems of the Muslims and Khuhro had an extensive correspondence as well as frequent meetings with him on the subject of Muslim grievances.

Back in Larkana Khuhro pursued the start he had made with the Home Minister Sir Maurice Hayward. He wrote asking for Muslim sub-judges to be appointed in vacant posts and received an acknowledgement for his recommendations. The Secretary of the Home Department, Bombay wrote to him, dated 1 July 1924:

"I am desired by the Honourable Sir Maurice Hayward, Kt., I.C.S., to acknowledge receipt of your letter of 21st instant suggesting that a Mohammedan should be selected for the vacancy in the cadre of Subordinate Judges in Sind which is to be shortly filled up and to say that it will receive attention."[11]

At the same time Khuhro was fighting the case for Muslims with the Government of Sind. In June he was approached by the citizens of Miro Khan in Larkana District to stop the transfer of the Muslim *mukhtiarkar*. He immediately wrote to the Commissioner-in-Sind, Jean Louis Rieu, to stop the transfer. The Commissioner wrote back:

"I am unable to cancel Mr. Yar Mohammed's transfer... I am, however, sending a Mussalman *mukhtiarkar* to Miro Khan, and I hope that the Mussalmans of the *taluka* will be pleased." On 25 July Khuhro again wrote to Rieu, regarding the appointment of a Muslim sub-judge. Promptly on 28 July he received a reply: "Your letter of the 25th, regarding the appointment of a Muslim sub-judge. I quite recognize the importance of increasing the proportion of Mussalmans among the subordinate judiciary, and, as a matter of fact, before even your letter reached me I had written to Mr. Kennedy asking him to let me have the name of the best Mussalman candidates qualified for appointment. I am still waiting to hear from him on the subject."[12]

Some of the most distinguished names in the history of Sind were recognized and promoted by Khuhro in his struggle to get justice for the Muslims of Sind. In November 1924 he heard from the Secretary of the Home Department of the Presidency government:

"I am directed by the Governor in Council to acknowledge the receipt of your letter, dated the 12th November 1924, recommending the appointment of Mr. I. I. Kazi as an Assistant Judge in Sind."[13]

Acting on his belief that it was the attitude of the British officers at the top which had to be influenced in order to effect a quick remedy for the backwardness of Sindhi Muslims, Khuhro mounted his attack at the very top of the pile in Bombay. He had first met Sir Leslie Wilson, the Governor of Bombay on the occasion of his visit to Hyderabad to preside over the Educational Conference in 1923. Now he took the opportunity to renew the acquaintance and to put the case to the Governor. During the years of Sir Leslie Wilson's tenure as Governor, Khuhro kept him regularly informed about the condition, the grievances and the demands of the Muslims of Sind and about the province in general. This correspondence gives a unique insight into the conditions of Sind in the 'twenties. On 23 August 1924, a few weeks after Khuhro had returned from Bombay after his first Legislative Council session, Wilson wrote to him:

"I am sorry that I have not written to you before in connection with the talk which we had in my office in the Council Hall during the last sitting of the Council, but I had not forgotten about it and have been making enquiries and the departments are endeavouring to meet your wishes as far as possible:

I can assure you that it is my intention to see that the orders of Government with regard to the employment of Mussalmans in Sind are carried out, and, should you at any time hear of any case in which you think that this was not so, I should be grateful if you would let the Member or Minister in charge of the department know, or communicate with me.

With regard to the scholarships about which you spoke to me, I find that all the scholarships to go to England came to an end when the Reforms came into being, and I am informed that there are now no scholarships given by the Presidency for this purpose. As I daresay you are aware, however, Sir Fazulbhoy Currimbhoy has handed to me 10 lakhs, which I am handing to the University for Scholarships for Mohammedans so that they can proceed to England for education, and I am hoping to hear from the University soon with regard to the conditions under which they accept this very handsome gift.

I have been very distressed to hear about the floods in Sind and am keeping in close touch with all that is being done, and I can assure you that no effort will be spared to relieve as far as possible the distress which may be caused.

yours sincerely,

Leslie Wilson "[14]

Khuhro had been making enquiries about scholarships for Muslims to study in England because that was obviously the quickest way to get highly educated and competent Muslim officers into higher posts and it would also encourage education among Muslims in Sind. He was also very anxious that his old friend and fellow student, Daudpoto, who had proved himself a brilliant scholar should get a chance to pursue his studies at one of the great universities in England. He wrote to the Governor about the possibility of a scholarship and pursued the matter with the Government. He heard from Secretary, General Department, Government of Bombay on 9 September:

"I have inquired about Mr. Daudpoto. Govt. have decided to give him a scholarship of £300 per annum plus a bonus not exceeding £45 p.a. for two years (at least). He will also get a second class passage both ways. The delay in issue of orders is due to the fact that we await instructions from the High Commissioner whether there is room for him at Emmanual College, Cambridge. The H. C. has been expedited by cable."[15]

Daudpoto went to Cambridge the same year and completed his Doctorate in three years returning home in 1927 to a brilliant career of scholarship and government service.[16]

In continuation of his efforts to further the cause of Sindhi Muslims, Khuhro's next communication to the Governor is dated the next month, 17 September 1924 and covers matters of fundamental interest for Muslims of Sind ranging from zamindari problems to those of recruitment in services and education:

"Your Excellency,

I am highly grateful to Your Excellency for the kind sympathy shown and expressed in the letter, dated 23rd August '24. I am extremely sorry for not having communicated with Your Excellency for so long, for such important matters which are mentioned in your kind note and which are really the greatest grievances of the Sind Mussalmans. Before going into details I feel it my utmost duty to thank Your Excellency most heartily for the great favours shown by Your Excellency's Government towards the agriculturists of Sind. It was expressly put before Your Excellency by me on the occasion of the last interview, that great injustice has been done to Sind zamindars so far, in the matters of Land Settlement and the Fallow rules. A great step forward has been taken by Your Excellency's Government, to do justice to them which cannot go unthanked on the part of the Sind members on the Legislative Council. There is still much more to be done on the Fallow rules matter, for which I am communicating with the Rt. Hon. M. C. V. Mehta, the Member in charge Revenue Department. As regards the employment of Mohammedans, in the various departments of the Government in the province of Sind, we have indeed a very great grievance, which needs your Excellency's full sympathy. The greatest injustice is done to the Mussalmans in the services of the new Barrage scheme. I am sending questions to the Bombay Council, asking the member, of employed Hindus and Mohammedans separately. I shall lay the facts before Your Excellency as soon as I get the facts from the Hon: member in charge.

Secondly, in the year 1918, Government were appointing four probationary Mukhtiarkars in Sind, because the number of Mohammedan Mukhtiarkars in Sind was considerably low. This policy was pursued for only three years even though Government had decided to continue for ten years. The Mussalmans will be highly grateful to Your Excellency if this matter is revived in your time. I think the number of Mohammedan Mukhtiarkars is still very low and it is badly needed that Mussalmans should be appointed direct as Mukhtiarkars to reach the number of equality.

Thirdly, I am much grieved to inform Your Excellency that absolutely nothing has been done for the education of Mussalmans in Sind. This year, I have been told that even the scholarships, which were being given every year for higher education, have been on the contrary reduced. Scholarships is the help which can uplift the backward community of Mussalmans. I shall be highly indebted to Your Excellency if the full sympathy is shown in above matters, as very kindly expressed by Your Excellency in person as well as in communication.

It is a great pleasure to us that Your Excellency is going to visit Sind this year, and the Larkana district as well. We shall have an opportunity to meet Your Excellency and place these grievances before Your Excellency. It will be a very good opportunity to request Your Excellency to prevail upon the Commissioner-in-Sind, to remove those grievances..."[17]

The Governor was prompt in his reply:

"I received your letter of the 17th yesterday, and am glad that the agriculturists of Sind appreciate the recent action of Government. I will not say anything about the Fallow Rules matter, as you are in communication with the Hon. Member.

I am making the fullest enquiries with regard to the employment of Mohammedans in the various departments of the Government in the province of Sind, and you may rest assured that anything that can be done to meet the just claims of Mohammedans will be done.

My preliminary enquiries show me that since May 1919 out of 29 appointments of Mukhtiarkars and Resident Magistrates 9 such appointments were given to

Hindus, 3 to others and 17 to Mohammedans. The cause of the stagnation of promotion, which has prevented further appointments of Mohammedans, arises partly from reversion to normal conditions after the War, and partly from retrenchment measures, with the consequence that the scheme for making annually a certain number of direct appointments of Mohammedans as Mukhtiarkars had to be suspended for sometime. I am informed that this scheme was initiated at a time when promotion was rapid and a large number of temporary vacancies available, but since then, the substantive vacancies that have occurred have, up to the present, only just sufficed to admit of the gradual absorption of the surplus men who had been put into temporary vacancies. I am told that now only two men remain to be thus absorbed and after that the scheme will again come into operation.

With regard to your paragraph on the education of Mussalmans in Sind, I will not deal with that at the moment, for the whole question, which I agree is very urgent, is being looked into by the Minister.

I am very much looking forward to visiting Sind this year and, while I feel sure that unfortunately I shall not be able to meet all your grievances, I can promise you that it is the intention of Government within the limits of its financial capacity to do all that is possible."[18]

Pursuing the matter of the appointment of Mukhtiarkars, Khuhro was also in direct contact with the Sind administration. He heard from the Commissioner-in-Sind on 21 September:

"...your letter of the 11th instant regarding the maintenance of a due proportion of Mohammedan Mukhtiarkars on the acting list and to say that the question of communal representation in the services is being considered."[19]

On the same subject he heard from the Governor again on 22nd October:

"You will remember seeing me in the Council Hall and discussing the question, on which we have already corresponded, of directly recruited Mukhtiarkars.

I have been in correspondence with the Commissioner-in-Sind on this matter, and he informs me that it has not been possible, as I think I told you before, to resort to any such recruitment this year, up to the present, as there were a number of directly recruited Mukhtiarkars and Resident Magistrates (these two classes of appointments being graded together) who were in excess of the permanent cadre, and had first to be absorbed into vacancies as they occurred. Ten such officers have now been provided with permanent posts, but I am informed that the time has now arrived when there will soon be vacancies, and recruitment on the 50% basis will accordingly be reopened very shortly."[20]

Already thus by the end of his first year as Member, Bombay Legislative Council, Khuhro had identified his "causes" and was fully launched on the struggle to advance them. Instead of relying on rhetoric and emotion in the Bombay Council as most newly elected politicians and even old elected politicians were wont to do, Khuhro not only spoke in the Council detailing those grievances but also took them to the authorities where there was possibility of redress. Evidence shows that this approach bore fruit.

But merely to draw the attention of and activate the government in the matter of recruitment of Mukhtiarkars and Sub-Judges was not enough. Khuhro soon discovered that he had to find suitably qualified Muslims to be recruited to the jobs. Akhunds, Kazis and Daudpotos were thin on the ground. When the jobs were on offer the candidates to fill them had to be readily available. The appointing officers, forced out of their routine system of recruitment to look for Muslims, were not particularly sympathetic and only too ready to present the excuse that qualified Muslims were not available. Khuhro worked out a way around this obstacle. He suggested that the government should refer to Muslim organisations for suitable candidates. On 11 October, 1925, he wrote to Wilson:

"I do not think I need tell you that under your benign rule the Moslem element in public service of Sind which should be at least fifty percent, is not rigidly adhered to. The reason is not far to seek. The one wherewith we are invariably confronted is that there is a dearth of suitable Moslem candidature, for want of which the authorities are constrained to resort to its non-Moslem substitute. This when scrutinised in the light of our daily experience is entirely unfounded. For the cry of Sindhi qualified Moslems for Govt: service is daily gaining strength, and this is hardly consistent with the explanation given by local authorities for their not enforcing your benign edict. I do not mean to find fault with their failing, rather I have reasons to excuse it. The one great reason, according to me is, that the authorities are not in the proper know of things as private Mohammedan individuals or public Mohammedan bodies are.

I would therefore like that there should be some safeguard for the practical enforcement of your wholesome rule. I therefore request that it should be made encumbent upon the local authorities to call for names of suitable Mahommedan candidates from some recognized Moslem bodies in Sind, previous to making appointments. If this were done I am sure we will soon have your benign policy carried out."[21]

The Governor's reply to this letter reflected the difficulties that the policy of giving Muslims their due share in government service was already encountering from the reaction of the vested interest of the mainly Hindu bureaucracy which had had its own way for so long. Writing on 16 October he says:

"I have received your letter of the 11th October, but as I am doubtful if you will receive this before you leave Sind for the Council, I am sending it to the Council Hall, Poona.

I am sorry that the desire expressed not only by myself, but by Government, that the Muslim element in the public service in Sind should be at least 50% is not being strictly carried out. If I were to judge from the very strong complaints which I have been receiving from Hindu Members of Council from Sind, I should have thought that it was being carried out to the letter, even if not more strictly than that!

I can assure you that I am extremely anxious to see that this is done, and I fully accept your word that it is not. I am sure that the cause, provided there are a sufficient number of qualified Muslims, must be due to a faulty method of ascertaining the names of such Muslims when vacancies in Government appointments occur. I welcome your suggestion, which is similar to one I have already willingly acceded to in the Presidency, of some recognised Muslim bodies (I would prefer one only) being responsible for preparing lists of suitable Muslim candidates, and forwarding the names of such candidates to Government. It would also be possible for such a body to watch for advertisements for any vacancies, and assist a suitable Muslim candidate to make proper application for such a vacancy.

I shall hope to see you myself when you are in Poona, but at any rate, I hope you will discuss this matter with the Chief Secretary, whom I have informed of your letter."²²

Khuhro duly met the Governor at Poona and discussed the problems of Sind Muslims. The Governor agreed that it was a matter of priority that Muslims get their due share in Government service and wrote to Khuhro in confirmation of his view soon after the autumn session of the Bombay Council was over. In a letter, dated 30 November 1925 he wrote:

"When I saw you the other day, you spoke to me on the subject, among others, of the question of appointments being made known to members of the Mohammedan community. I told you, then, that definite instructions had been issued, and I felt sure that these instructions were being carried out. I enclose, for your information, a copy of the Government circular issued on the 23rd of July of this year, which deals with this question, and which gives very definite instructions for wide publicity to be given to any vacancies. I feel sure you will agree that Government could not do more.

With reference to the proposal which you mentioned to me of Mohammedan organisations being in a position to inform the authorities concerned of suitable Mohammedans available to fill vacancies in Government appointments, I welcome, as I told you, any such arrangement. It would, ofcourse, be far better if there one central body for the whole of Sind, which could be responsible for looking out for vacancies advertised or announced, and sending the names of any suitable applicants to the official making the announcement, with recommendations backed by such a body. I understand, however, that there is difficulty in Sind in such amalgamation, and, if it is found impossible for all the various districts to join together, then I suggest that this proposal should be carried out with Bodies as representative and as large as possible. It is difficult to anticipate the actual working of any such scheme, and practical experience only can say how it will work. I feel certain, however, that if the local representatives of Mahomedan bodies were to get in touch with the Collectors of the various Districts, there would be no practical difficulty in carrying out the proposal, although, ofcourse, I think it would be far easier, as I have said before, if these recommendations for appointments could be made from one central body representative of the Mahommedan interests in Sind."²³

Khuhro was only too aware of the justice of the Governor's comment that there should be a representative single body which would take on the responsibility of keeping lists of suitable candidates, matching them up against available jobs, keeping track of vacancies and bringing them to the attention of the candidates. All this implied an organized body with province wide support. With typical tenacity Khuhro set about getting such an organization into existence.

Sind Mohammedan Association had been set up in 1884 by Hassanally Effendi as the Sind branch of the Central National Mohammedan Association founded in 1877 by Syed Amir Ali, the renowned scholar, jurist and political worker from Calcutta. Syed Amir Ali was a pioneer of Muslim political organisation in India and had toured the country to encourage Muslims to organise themselves so as to properly represent their interests. By 1885 there were thirteen branches of National Mohammedan Association in India including Sind, and these increased to fifty-three by the end of the 'eighties. The Sind Mohammedan Association, which was one of the most enduring and successful of the branches functioned autonomously and had performed a very useful role in representing the Muslim cause. Although it was not "revolutionary" or "nationalistic" in the sense which came to be accepted after World War I, it nevertheless served the community well. Its approach was basically that of "gradualism" and of working in co-operation with the government in order to achieve the just rights of Muslims as loyal citizens of the British Empire.

Khuhro realised that the organisation was an ideal vehicle for his plans. He revived the activities of the Association, renewing its province wide membership and increasing it significantly. He regularized the receipts – the six rupee annual fee was regularly taken and a register of membership and accounts maintained.[24] In a short time the receipts were doubled and by 1928 quadrupled.

The revamped Sind Mohammedan Association thus became the primary means for the advancement for Sindhi Muslims from the mid-twenties to the time Sind was separated from the Bombay Presidency in the mid-thirties. Khuhro was variously General Secretary and Vice-President of the Association, while Sir Shahnawaz Bhutto, the senior politician from Sind, was to remain President for most of the period. The annual Address to the Governor (and occasionally to the Viceroy) was used by the Association to put the problems of the Muslims to the government and with its assurance of loyalty it was a practical way of keeping the issues before the government. Khuhro found it a very convenient adjunct to his personal struggle to get rights for the Sindhi people and it taught him a useful lesson in the virtues and usefulness of modern organisation. He was to use it most effectively in putting together the case for the separation of Sind, and it was under the banner of Sind Mohammedan Association that he presented the Muslim case to the Simon Commission in 1929.

As a measure to solve the problem of finding suitable candidates for Mukhtiarkars and other services, S. M. A. started to maintain registers for candidates in which matriculates were listed, and when there were not enough matriculates, lists of matric failed were compiled to help find Muslim candidates for jobs.[25] But the objective that Khuhro had set himself and the promise that the Governor had made that 50% at least of the appointments in Sind would go to Sindhi Muslims was more difficult to achieve. As time went on Khuhro realized that there were deeply entrenched vested interests already in place. There was no hope of redressing the balance unless extraordinary steps were taken and it was extremely difficult to get the colonial bureaucracy, steeped in routine and rigid in its attitudes, to adopt the flexible and far sighted attitude that was required. The successive Governors of the Bombay Presidency were usually men from the aristocracy, the ruling class of Britain itself, who on the whole had a broader view. But it was not enough for the Governor to be sympathetic and to issue a directive or circular. As Khuhro was to find throughout his career, the bureaucracy was adept at evasive tactics and in this case produced excuse after excuse for their failure to carry out the policy set down by the Governor.

After more than three years of effort to get equitable numbers of Muslims into services in Sind, Khuhro penned a 'statement' on the problem and sent it to the Governor with a letter, dated 30 July 1928:

"In the accompanying statement I have simply made an attempt to describe the number of appointments allotted to different communities in the cadre of Deputy Collectors and Mukhtiarkars.

I most respectfully submit to Your Excellency that the recent change in the policy by confirming Hindu Deputy Collectors in supersession of Mussalmans who are placed higher in the list of Ag.incumbents, by the previous Commissioners, has caused serious anxiety in the minds of Mussalmans of Sind. All the Mussalman Members of the Legislative Council representing Sind, feel very keenly about this sudden change in the policy which has placed our community at a very great disadvantage. The policy enunciated by Sir H. Lawrence when he was Commissioner-in-Sind and followed by Mr. Cadell and the Hon. Mr. Rieu (as Commissioner-in-Sind) was the just and reasonable policy. Even as late as two years ago, Mussalmans held 55% appointments in the cadre of Dy: Cs. [Deputy Commissioners] and within the last two years this radical change in policy has brought that change in proportion of 55% to 33%. I would therefore submit that there is every justification for the Mussalmans in feeling anxious over this matter. Besides even in the matter of acting appointments this policy is going to be repeated, whereby there is every apprehension that this policy will be perpetuated. I therefore submit that Your Excellency may kindly be pleased to order the abrogation of the recent order confirming all the 3 Hindu Ag. Dy: Cs. in supersession of Messrs. Channa and Isani two Muslim Ag. Dy: Cs. The revision I may respectfully submit is necessary in the interests of justice and equity."[26]

In his statement Khuhro detailed the appointments made in contravention of the directive of the Governor. He pointed out that appointments were being so manipulated that the Governor's orders were being flouted in spirit and excuses of a technical nature were being offered to cover up the non observance of the orders. That both in the case of Deputy Collectors and Mukhtiarkars there was demonstrable and clear violation of the directive. Khuhro cited chapter and verse to back his complaint and the Governor wrote back immediately:

"I received your letter of the 30th July yesterday afternoon, and am glad that you wrote to me on the question which you raise in that letter.

I am not, ofcourse, at the moment, acquainted with all the details of the various appointments of which you make mention in the statement which you attach to the letter, but I can assure you that there is no intention whatever, on the part of Government or myself, to change the policy which was brought into being during the times of Sir Henry Lawrence, Mr. Cadell, and Mr. Rieu, with regard to doing everything possible, as I think you know yourself, to encourage the appointments and promotion of Muslims wherever men suitable are available, and this policy, I can assure you, it is intended to continue.

I can only say that I will have enquiries made into what you say in your letter and statement, and will write to you again."[27]

True to his word Sir Leslie wrote again on 20 August giving what amounted to a detailed apologia of the bureaucracy and its justification for its lack of action:

"In continuation of my letter of the 1st August, I write to say that I have made very careful enquiries into the statements made in your letter of the 30th July, and in the statement accompanying it, and I am glad to find that the facts show that not only has there been no change in the policy of my Government to secure a sufficiently influential representation of Mohammedans in the Upper and Lower Branches of the Provincial Civil Service in Sind, but also that nothing has been done in the matter of appointments and promotions in that Service that is not in consonance with this policy.

2. I would in the first place venture to disabuse your mind of the idea that there are any orders in force directing that 50% of officiating and substantive vacancies in the cadres of Deputy Collectors and Mukhtiarkars should be assigned to Mohammedans.

You have probably in mind either the orders directing that 50 percent of the vacancies in the clerical line in Sind should be filled by Mohammedans, or the instruction issued in 1918, but no longer in effect, that half the number of annual vacancies in the Second Grade of Mukhtiarkars, subject to a maximum of four, should be assigned to Mohammedans.

3. The scheme for according due representation to your community was inaugurated ten years ago, and its outstanding feature has been the admission into the Second Grade of Mukhtiarkars, after a brief period of probation, of a fairly large number of Mohammedans, who by working their way through Lower and Upper branches of the Provincial Civil Service, will eventually redress the balance between the Mohammedan and other communities. How successfully the scheme has so far worked will be seen from the present state of the cadre of Second Grade Mukhtiarkars, in which 30 out of 55 men are Mohammedans. In the First Grade things can scarcely, from your point of view, be expected to be so satisfactory, looking to the reluctance of your community in the past to enter the public service in any appreciable numbers, and also to the new element not having had time to enter that grade. Nevertheless, thanks to the scheme for special training of Mohammedans as head munshis, their number will steadily increase. As regards the Deputy Collector's grade, I have only to remind you that your co-religionists have been assisted by Government in two ways; firstly by direct recruitment, and secondly by accelerating the promotion of First Grade Mohammedan Mukhtiarkars. In regard to the former, there are at present in Sind six Deputy Collectors who were directly recruited in that province, and they are all Mohammedans (including Mr. Sidiki who was recruited as a Mohammedan). A seventh, Mr. G. M. Isani, was transferred to the Presidency proper. Accelerated promotion can be resorted to only when the Mohammedan Mukhtiarkars are fairly senior, and when such promotion does not involve the supersession of officers of advanced age belonging to other communities with a long record of good work to their credit; and this my Government has been doing from time to time.

4. So much for the general policy. Coming now to details, I find that the confirmation of Messrs. Wadhwani, Punjabi and Gajria did not involve the supersession of any Mohammedan officer. As was pointed out to you recently, the serial order in which the names of the officiating Deputy Collectors appear in the Civil List does not necessarily indicate their relative precedence for substantive appointment to officiate. The list also does not contain the names of officers on foreign service whose claims to promotion cannot be disregarded. Two out of the three Hindu officers had over four years aggregate officiating service to their credit, the third, Mr. Wadhwani had virtually nine, while none

of the Mohammedan officers mentioned in your letter had officiated for more than $2\frac{1}{2}$ years; this will be evident from the rates of pay which they were drawing as officiating Deputy Collectors at the time when the promotions were sanctioned. The confirmation of the Hindu Deputy Collectors was a step which had long been overdue, and it was out of question at their age to keep them indefinitely out of the promotion which they had fully earned. They were all over fifty years of age, while the ages of the Muhammadans whose claims you have advanced ranged from 34 to 41. This bloc of Hindu officers is a legacy of the past which is now being worked off, and there is every reason to believe that, for the future, substantive appointments to the Deputy Collector's grade will be more equally shared by the two communities.

5. As I have already observed, the effects of the existing policy throughout the several grades of the Upper and Lower Branches of the Provincial Civil Service can only be felt in the course of time. Nevertheless, despite the reluctance of the members of your community generally to enter the Subordinate Revenue Service in the past, I do not see that they are at present so poorly represented in the Deputy Collector's grade as they might ordinarily have been expected to be. Out of the seven Deputy Collectors on the substantive list engaged on other duties, 3 are Mohammedans, 3 Hindus, and 1 Parsi; and out of the remaining 27, 11 are Mohammedans, 12 Hindus, and 4 Christians, leaving out of account 2 Mohammedans, Messrs. G. M. Isani and Abdul Kadir, now serving in the Presidency proper, who were confirmed as Deputy Collectors in Sind.

6. As regards appointments of officiating Deputy Collectors, the balance in the regular line is fairly even. But I am afraid I cannot agree that Muhammadans, irrespective of their efficiency, can be deputed to work under the Revenue Officer, Lloyd Barrage and Canals Construction. The Hindu officers working on the Barrage are all experts in their several lines, and whatever policy Government may formulate to advance the interests of the Mohammedans in the Provincial Civil Service, it cannot be blindly applied to special appointments borne outside its cadres.

7. In conclusion I would state that it is impossible to fix a proportion of recruitment on a communal basis in regard to higher appointments. Selection for them must be primarily on considerations of personal efficiency and merit. The best that Government can do is to ensure that the field of recruitment to the grade of Mukhtiarkars contains a due proportion of representatives of the Mohammedan and Hindu communities, and this is precisely what my Government has been doing for the last ten years.

8. I now trust that you, and the gentlemen who have associated themselves with you in the remarks which you have made in your letter and statement, will be relieved of the anxiety which the recent promotions appear to have caused, and will realise that, far from resiling from its attitude towards the Mohammedan community, my Government, is, in consultation with successive Commissioners, consistently seeking to advance in every practical way the interests of the Mohammedans in the public service in Sind."[28]

The Governor's letter was the Bombay bureaucracy's response to Muslim complaints and determination that their dominance would not be dented in any significant way. The allegation of the Governor that "the reluctance of the members of your community generally to enter the Subordinate Revenue Service in the past" was a familiar excuse used by those reluctant to appoint unfamiliar communities. Similarly the other reasons given – seniority, competence, due process and so on – were in reality a bid to postpone as far as possible the day when the Muslim majority would have to be accommodated in the services. Khuhro sent a tactful reply to the Governor, pointing out that despite the Governor's explanations in fact Muslims had legitimate grievances as regards their share in the services. Writing from Larkana on 12 September 1928 he said:

"Very many thanks for Your Excellency's kind letter, dated the 20th August last in response to my representation submitted to Your Excellency on 30th July last in connection with the recent appointments and confirmations of Deputy Collectors in Sind. I am highly grateful to Your Excellency for taking the trouble of examining the whole question so minutely and in such details. I must frankly submit to Your Excellency that the recent confirmation of all the three Hindu Deputy Collectors at one time, did come as a surprise to the Mussalmans of this province. But however it is a matter of gratification to note, which is so kindly mentioned by Your Excellency, that the substantive appointments to the posts of Deputy Collectors will be more equally shared by the two communities in the future. In this connection I deem it necessary to bring to Your Excellency's kind notice that the population of Mussalmans in this province being roughly 75 percent, they are legitimately entitled to more share in the public service than mere 50% of the vacancies in the departments precisely when Mussalmans possess minimum qualifications laid down for the various appointments or having considerable acting service behind them are available. Moreover this fact has also to be taken into consideration that Mussalmans are sparsely represented in the public service, all round in this province. Their number is unfortunately small in departments like P.W.D., Forest, etc. where technical and scientific qualifications are essentially needed and where Mussalmans are not available with these qualifications in fair numbers. I am led to think that this was one of the fundamental reasons why the Mussalmans have been encouraged to enter only those departments for which they had qualified themselves viz. Revenue, Judicial, Police, etc.

I venture to submit to Your Excellency that we Mussalmans of Sind fully rely on Your Excellency for giving us justice and fair treatment, which is often tempered with consideration and sympathy.

I once again thank Your Excellecy most heartily for giving the assurance that we will not be deprived of our legitimate share, on any occasion in the future, in the recruitment to public service in Your Excellency's regime."[29]

The fact was that even the Governor, no matter how good his intentions, had ultimately to rely on his subordinates to give him facts and brief him on the situation – and the structure of the British rule was such that the administration at the top had to rely on the word and assessment of the officers below and were almost incapable of independent investigation and assessment. Naturally therefore when the Governor asked for an opinion on the matter in hand he got the one which justified the actions of the administration. This excessive reliance on bureaucratic sources was a weakness in the British system which would prove fatal in the absence of any counterbalance from public representatives. Increasingly too, high calibre British recruits became less available for official service in India and provinces would be headed by mediocre men even more reliant on the bureaucracy.

Another problem facing the Muslims of Sind was the crucial and basic one of education. Soon after Khuhro's election, a Committee was formed to report on primary education with particular reference to the position of Mulla Schools, Khuhro, along with some other members of the Bombay Council made representation that Sind Muslim members should be appointed on the Committee. The Bombay Government agreed to give representation to Sind members and four members including Khuhro were appointed to the Committee. Khuhro, who had maintained a close interest in the education of Muslims of Sind, pursued the matter with his usual vigour. Writing to the Minister of Education, Government of Bombay, on 7 March 1926 he gave a succint review of the educational problems of Sind Muslims and pinpointed their special needs:

"You will, I trust, pardon me intruding upon your time; but the matter is so very pressing that I am compelled to encroach upon it.

1. I am sure His Excellency is fully aware of the backwardness of Muslim Education in Sind; and all along it has been our only aim in the lifetime of the present Council to do something to win the sympathy of His Excellency in that direction, so as to be able to make the Government do something to encourage it. While we all are conscious of the sympathy we have of His Excellency in this matter, we regret to see that the Department and the Education Ministry have done nothing to give impetus to Muslim education.

2. In 1924 we pressed upon the attention of the Hon'ble the Education Minister the urgency of reserving seats for Mussalman boys in the Government High Schools. His Excellency would perhaps be interested to know that in Bengal Mussalmans have better claim even on the aided institutions than we in Sind have even over Government High Schools. The reply formerly used to be that there are no Muslim boys to be admitted in the Government High Schools, and now when there are boys, we are refused admissions all the same. This and other things we duly brought to the notice of the representatives of the Government on our arrival in Bombay and we were given all sorts of hopes; but after a lapse of only a few days, we find that we are actually to be where we were and that there is no hope of any of those held out to us being realized. It is therefore that I have ventured to address you, owing to the urgency and importance of the subject.

3. His Excellency is fully aware of the fact that the Muslim population is mostly outside the District towns; and therefore the efforts of K. B. Mir Ghulam Mahommed in starting the Lawrence Madressah which teaches upto 5th standard deserved all possible support. We had approached His Excellency with the request to raise this school to the standard of a High School and to take it under Government control. Our appeal met with a sorry fate, even when His Excellency, the Finance member and other members were very sympathetic, the Department had its way. We were told that Government would take it under its control and teach upto Standard 3rd, when it is teaching even now upto the 5th Standard. So we requested this year that this School may kindly be taken up by Government upto 5th Standard. A bright prospect of our request being granted was held out to us at the beginning of the Council; and now we are given to understand that Government is thinking of giving some aid only to this School.

I need not mention here how the public of Sind has ever since 1910 been pressing for Middle Schools being started in the Mofussil in Sind, owing to the special features of that country. Even now when a philanthropic gentleman has done so much, the Government has so far done nothing to show its practical sympathy with Muslim education. I am hopeful that His Excellency will kindly be pleased to take up this School under Government control, at least upto 5th Standard.

4. We also drew the attention of the Hon'ble Education Minister to the urgent needs of the Sind Madressah and requested that an additional grant of Rs. 20,000/- be kindly made to that institution. We were given solid hopes about it. In personal conversation, the Hon'ble the Education Minister says that he has received a letter from His Excellency that a grant of Rs. 7,000/- to Rs. 10,000/- be made to the Madressah, he did not remember the actual figure. I am sure His Excellency, if he has written such a letter, could not have been aware of our request and the hope held out to us. I therefore request that His Excellency would be pleased to give us the figure we have prayed for.

5. We also requested that Rs. 30,000/- additional be given in scholarships; and we were encouraged to feel that our request would at once be granted; and His Excellency would be surprised to hear that we do not now hear a word about it, as if such a thing had not even been mentioned. I am sure His Excellency will realize how we are being kept on hopes, that are not to be fulfilled, at least the prospect of the fulfilment of which we do not see.

6. At the beginning of this letter I stated that we drew the attention of the Education Ministry to the fact that our boys were not being admitted in the Government High Schools. The Government saw the necessity of it and the most reasonableness of our request; but contrary to our expectations, the Government have fixed the proportion of Mussalman boys in the Karachi High School to be only 10 per cent, in Hyderabad 50 per cent, in Shikarpur 50 per cent, etc. To a question put to the Honourable Minister in the present sessions, the Minister was pleased to say that he had given Mussalmans 10 per cent in the Karachi High School because Mussalmans have a school of their own at Karachi. His Excellency if fully aware of the fact that the Karachi Madressah is not a school for the town but that it serves the whole of the province of Sind; and therefore to give only 10 per cent seats to Mussalmans at Karachi is hardly fair or just to the Mussalmans of Sind. But what is more astonishing is that at Hyderabad where the Amils have two of their best High Schools, and numerous branches of these scattered up over all the quarters of the town, Mussalmans have only 50 percent, though these Hindu schools have been in receipt of Government grants both building and recurring ever since they were founded and the benefits of which they have been reaping. At Karachi the existence of a Muslim High School gives us only 10 per cent seats and at Hyderabad the existence of two Hindu High Schools and their branches gives the Hindus 50 per cent seats. At Shikarpur where the Hindus have High School they have 50 per cent. So the net result is that Hindus have their own schools and also retain monopoly of Government High Schools.

What is specially troubling is that the Government have ordered that in future this share of seats – unfair as it is – should be given to Muslims in the 'lowest class'. If allowed to stand as they are, these orders will simply perpetuate the monopoly of Hindus over Government High Schools, in theory for seven years; but in actual practice for ever. We have discussed this matter with the General Secretary and I think he understands the reasonableness of our request. The Department has put forward the plea that they can never think of sending away any boys already in the School. You must be aware of the fact that in schools and colleges, even in England, no boys retain any lien on it. When there is decrease of classes or increase in the number of boys, the students are sent away. That happens in India everywhere and that would happen in any country. If you are so kind as to bear in mind the fact that in Hyderabad the orders were that boys of the Vernacular Practising School should only be taken up in the 1st Standard English of the Hyderabad High School. That school being located in the midst of the Amil quarters never had Muslim boys, with the result that Muslim boys were always in the past refused admission in the High School at Hyderabad. Nearly similar are also reasons for the non admission of Muslim boys in other High Schools of the Government. Thus you will, I trust, be good enough to see that we are being treated unfairly in the matter of admissions. I request therefore that His Excellency will be so pleased as to revise the percentage and to make the revised percentage provisional, so as to make revisions in future possible, when there is demand for greater admissions from Muslims and to give us for the present fullest share 'in all the classes'."[30]

From the moment of his installation as member of the Bombay Legislative Council therefore Khuhro was totally absorbed in the work which he felt had to be done to improve the conditions of Sindhi Muslims in the fields of agricultural indebtedness, facilities for education and encouragement in getting higher education, a just share of jobs and representation of the Muslim community at the decision making levels which he felt was necessary for any genuine improvement in their condition.

During this period though he could not help but be aware of the political events which were shaping the destiny of the sub-continent. Khuhro had stood aside from active participation in party politics. He felt that his constituents – the Muslims of Sind – would benefit less from the noisy activity of party politics than from the positive constructive work that he was engaged in. The process of steady work was not to last and Khuhro was caught up unwillingly in the shock waves caused by the communal frenzy which rocked India from the mid 'twenties onwards.

The communal outburst of the 'twenties came in the wake of what had been the biggest demonstration of intercommunal, particularly Hindu Muslim, political co-operation in the Khilafat and Non-Co-operation movements. By 1924 this 'Civil Dis-obedience Movement' had been called off by Gandhi as he felt that its non-violent nature had been violated. The passions that had been aroused by the mobilization of the masses of India then turned into a religious frenzy which resulted in communal riots all over India. These riots were the biggest and the most widespread manifestations of the religious animosity that India had ever seen but the elements that constituted this antipathy were latent in the Indian scene and Indian history.

The Mughal empire had during its two hundred years of ascendancy achieved a consensus society with the close association and co-operation with the Rajputs, the administrative and other Hindu elites of India. Thus while Akbar the Great relied on his Rajput generals as well as the generals who had come with Babur and Humayun from Central Asia, he also had Todar Mal to organise the revenue administration of his empire. Even Aurangzeb with the reputation of a religious bigot, was served faithfully and loyally by his Hindu as well as Muslim generals and civil administrators. It could be said therefore that although the people of the sub-continent were as religiously devout and fervent as they have always been historically, there had developed a mutual tolerance, mutual influence which was reflected not only in the style of the Mughal government but also in the commonality of many customs and modes of everyday life. On the religious level itself the mutual influence had developed a mystic *sufi* tradition which was reflected in the Bhakti tradition of Hinduism, in the teachings of the great Muslim saints of the sub-continent and in the rise of new religions such as Sikhism which its founder Guru Nanak had developed as a synthesis of Islamic and Hindu philosophy. This tradition of mutual tolerance might have grown and matured if local rulers had replaced the Mughals. In fact wherever local rulers established their independent states, the relations between the two communities were without rancour and generally mutually accommodating.

But with the establishment of British rule in India the situation changed basically. Now it was no longer a question of mutual accommodation – both the communities had to look to the British who were holding the ring and making the rules of the game. The British dealt expertly with the situation, dealing favoured son treatment to one and then the other community and practicing *par excellence* the ancient imperialist game of divide and rule. This became a matter of clear cut policy after the shock of the Revolt of 1857 which convinced the British that the unity and common purpose shown by the communities in that struggle had to be countered effectively if British control was to be maintained.

At the same time the curiosity of Western scholars, their researches into the ancient religions of India served to increase the consciousness of the newly Westernised Hindu middle classes of Calcutta and saw the rise of movements such as Brahmo Samaj. Then in turn the westernising influences of these early reformists gave way to the fundamentalist revivalists of Shuddhi movement. The Muslims had answered the Shuddhi movement by a revivalist movement of their own.

Inevitably there was a clash in the heightened passions of the 'twenties and this was to prove decisive for the future of India – the polarisation which occurred then was to prove impossible to bridge later – the leadership of India proved too short sighted and too cowardly to meet the challenge of both freeing India and keeping it together. In this crisis the most terrible failure was that of Gandhi who opened Pandora's box but did not have the wherewithal to gather in the troubles he released. Jinnah on the other hand, wisely in hindsight although much criticized at the time for his elitism, was opposed to taking serious political issues to the streets and subjecting them to the vagaries of mass movements and mass hysteria.

The fallout of communal tension in the rest of India necessarily affected even the peaceful and tolerant atmosphere of Sind and the years 1927-28 saw Hindu–Muslim clashes. In the aftermath of these troubles Khuhro found himself playing an important part.

5

CONFRONTATIONS

In the March of 1928 Khuhro had gone to visit his *katcha* lands in Phulloo, crossing over to the other side of the Indus and spending a few days there. He returned to Larkana on the mid morning of the 29th having made the journey of a few hours on boat and camel. Khuhro was expecting a good friend, Khan Bahadur Ali Hassan Hakro for lunch and while they were sitting at the table about 2.30 in the afternoon some notable businessmen of Larkana, Seth Khudadad Surahio, Seth Mohammed Din Khwaja and Khuhro's manager for his newspaper *Sind Zamindar*, Agha Nazar Ali Pathan, came running into the house and announced that there was a riot in the town and Muslims were being arrested indiscriminately by the police. The police was accompanied by a Hindu magistrate, Rupchand, and some of the Mahasabha activists of the town who were pointing out the people they wanted arrested.

The riot had been caused by the activities of the Hindu fundamentalists of the Shuddhi, Arya Samaj and Hindu Mahasabha movements who were busy scouring the countryside at the time trying to find and "reconvert" or *shuddhi* (purify) any person they suspected had been converted from Hinduism. A Hindu convert woman who had been married to a small landowner in a village near Dokri in Larkana District for more than fifteen years and was mother of several children had been reported as a kidnappee by Arya Samajist workers and they had got the Collector to issue a warrant. The police had brought her to Larkana but the Collector was very indecisive and kept her as *amanat* (i.e. in trust) in the house of a local notable, Nawab Lahori. The Collector of Larkana, Hamid Ali, was a somewhat vacillating character and was regarded rather warily by the Muslim circles as he had family connections with Congress. His wife was the daughter of Abbas Tayyabji of the well-known Tayyabjis of Bombay and a keen follower of Gandhi. The Collecter was thus suspected of Congress sympathies. He delayed taking action to diffuse the situation so it soon escalated into a confrontation. The husband and the children of the woman came to complain and ask that the woman be returned to her family but the Larkana administration took no notice.

The incident caused a great deal of resentment in the villages around Larkana as the action of the police was considered an attack on the home and family of a respectable man. A number of villagers entered the town and caused a disturbance. They stole soda water bottles from the shops and broke them, looted some shops and precipitated a minor riot. The Hindu population of the town panicked and insisted that there should be mass arrests. The extremist elements particularly the workers of Hindu Mahasabha, went around attacking any Muslim they found alone. In the melee about sixty nine people were injured, eleven of whom were Muslims and the rest Hindus but one Hindu died as a result of his injuries. The Hindus who were well organized and who formed the bulk of the administration determined to make an example of the rioters.

In fact the police made a large number of indiscriminate arrests at the say so of the Hindu political workers. The Muslim citizens felt helpless and unprotected as there was no voice of protest from the Muslim side. The most important Muslim leaders of the town, Sir Shahnawaz Bhutto and Nawab Lahori had refused to come out of their houses or show any interest or sympathy. The leading Muslim traders and community leaders then turned to Khuhro who responded immediately, driving around the town to assess the situation for himself:

"I immediately got into my car, and together with the leading citizens went round the town. I saw with my own eyes that what they said was all true. By this time fifty or sixty Mussalmans were arrested. I protested to the magistrate that his actions were extremely arbitrary and that he was arresting Muslims without proof and merely at the behest of their opponents and enemies. Mr. Hamid Ali had left the scene and gone for lunch saying that he had a Director of Agriculture coming to lunch and had put the Hindu magistrate Mr. Rupchand in charge of the whole matter in his absence. I also went and saw Hamid Ali and apprised him of what had happened. The Collector appeared to be quite complacent and did not show any emotion at what I felt was a serious injustice done to the people of the town. He did not react at all to my complaint. By the evening about a hundred Muslims were already in jail including the leaders of the business community who had come to see me. On realising that no redress was to be had from the officials I went home and immediately set about organising a relief committee. I gave my own contribution and collected a fund from the town and the district. Hearing of the riot and the subsequent arrests, Shaikh Abdul Majid and Barrister Abdur Rahman came to Larkana from Karachi to offer help. I engaged Barrister Abdur Rahman for the defence of the victims. In Larkana they stayed as my guests and my house situated on Empire Road became the headquarters of the Defence Committee for the Mussalmans of Larkana. I sought an interview with the Commissioner in Sind, Hudson, and put the entire matter to him. The Commissioner realising the seriousness of the incidents in Larkana appointed a special magistrate and Hamid Ali was replaced as Collector by an Englishman Mr. A. S. V. Acott."[1]

The Hindu activists supported by the officials were very annoyed at the role Khuhro was playing in saving the Muslims and tried to involve him in the cases as instigator of the riot. The D. I. G. Police appointed a special D. S. P. to investigate the complaints but there was no basis for it and nothing came of it. The Defence Committee succeeded in getting most of the arrested people freed except ten leading citizens who were committed to the Sessions Court. Khuhro engaged Bevan-Petman, one of the most reputed Barristers practising at Lahore to defend them. Funds were collected to defray the expenditure and eventually all the accused were acquitted by the Sessions Court.

Khuhro's reputation soared with the Muslims of Sind as a result of his championship of the victims of Larkana riots. He became so popular that even Muslim policemen used to sing of his exploits during their duty hours at night. Throughout Sind he became famous as a courageous politician and champion of Muslim rights.

At the same time it was clear that the Hindu extremist organisations like the Shuddhi and Mahasabha movements were bent upon stirring up communal trouble. In this case they had got hold of a woman who had been married for more than fourteen years and had several children. She was bribed and threatened into abandoning her home and testifying against her husband which resulted not only in personal tragedy for her household but started the first communal riot in Sind. This was the beginning of the strife between the two major communities in Sind and the incident was followed by trouble in other towns, creating hatreds which would encourage divisiveness in the province and end in complete polarization between the communities.

The activities of the Hindu extremist organisations continued unabated. They organised themselves for a confrontation with the Muslims. Hindu households were armed and young men were trained for combat and taught to use arms. The atmosphere was charged with hostility and the failure of the extremists in Larkana was regarded as a defeat which had to be avenged. The tactics of the communal organisations were to create tension with displays of arms and militancy and if this resulted in provoking communal incidents then there was vociferous newspaper propaganda depicting Hindus as victims of *jat* or 'uncouth' Muslims. Cases were then brought against the 'rioters'. In this way the majority Muslim population would remain involved and helpless, especially as the bureaucracy was mostly Hindu and able to influence the higher levels of officialdom.

From 1929 to 1931 there were frequent incidents of violence particularly in Sukkur where the Muslims were in dire need of help and leadership. In May 1929 Khuhro appointed Pir Ali Mohammed Rashdi, an intelligent but somewhat wayward young man as editor of his newspaper *Sind Zamindar* which was published from Sukkur. Under Rashdi's editorship the newspaper became the leading advocate of the Muslim cause and did this very effectively. Sukkur, situated at a key point on the river Indus was one of the major commercial centres of Sind. Hindus were in a majority in the town and much more aggressive in their proselytizing. There was only a very small Muslim middle class since on the whole Muslims lived in rural areas and were very tolerant.

The almost century old British rule had seen the erosion of the traditional social equations in Sind and created raw edges in the relationship of the Hindu and Muslim communities. To a large extent this was the result of the working of the new legal and taxation systems which allowed the *haris* and small holders to fall into debt and what was worse, as a result to lose their land which was the sole source of their livelihood. Those suffering the hardships of the new system found a ready scapegoat in the *bania* and the urban businessmen. The growing power of the latter and their intrusion into agriculture where they became owners of large tracts of land and orchards led to resentments across the spectrum of the traditional rural society. On the one hand the new capitalists lent money to the cultivator at exorbitant rates which almost always resulted in the latter losing their lands and on the other they also controlled the entire commerce of the province which meant that they were the arbiters of both the rate at which the agricultural produce was bought from the cultivator and at which the consumer goods including his own grain were sold back to him. The grower was thus completely at the mercy of the *bania* and frequently forced into debt. This exploitation had the sanction of law. Illiterate and unable defend himself against these sharp practices, the cultivator knew that he was not getting a fair deal from the moneylender and the resentment grew because of the constant threat of losing his land.

There was also the customary Indian religious exclusivism which restricted social relations between the communities and the practice of *chhoot* or 'untouchability' which was not confined to the lower castes of Hindus but forbade socializing and eating with non Hindus. In a majority Muslim province like Sind this was not a problem while the rulers were Muslims because the Hindus were very discreet in their practices of *chhoot*, but once there was a 'neutral' ruler, and they had the economic upper hand, the religious exclusivism came out into the open. The collapse of Non Co-operation and Khilafat movements had unleashed an intolerant mood in India which can only be explained by the use of the religious idiom by the politicians. Reminding people that they were Hindu or Muslim in their public life was not the wisest course to be followed particularly as the revivalist movements, which had been springing up since the 19th century, now seized their opportunity.*

Inter communal marriages were absolutely taboo but there were occasional instances and in the rural areas it was a fairly common practice that lower caste tribal girls were sold by their parents or by middlemen to well off villagers who converted and married them. The *shuddhi* movement therefore not only threatened such households of which there would be at least half a dozen in a big village, but would create communal hatred far greater than the actual number of people affected.

In August 1930 an incident occurred in Sukkur in which Muslims were beaten and injured by militant Hindus. Muslims of surrounding villages poured into the city to avenge the outrage. This resulted in a riot and incidents of looting in the city. The administration, following the Larkana pattern, made mass arrests of the villagers and charged them with the most serious crimes. The police used the most vicious methods to intimidate and punish the suspected people so that there was a public outcry. In this crisis the Muslims of Sukkur turned to the one Muslim leader they felt would come to their rescue and telegraphed

---

* The ordinary villagers who came to the small town bazaars for their everyday needs, clothes, agricultural implements and so on, were treated with utmost contempt by the shopkeepers who were invariably Hindu *banias*. They were quite willing to sell to the villagers but would jeer at their clothes, their accents and their poverty. If they asked for water in the heat of the sub-continental summer, it would be given to them not even in an earthenware cup but would be poured out into their cupped hands. The general term which the Hindus would use to refer to the Muslims was *jat* which colloquially meant a mixture of illiterate and uncouth. All these grievances and slights built up a simmering resentment over the years and could erupt at any time.

Khuhro. The elections for the Bombay Legislative Council had taken place and Khuhro had been re-elected unopposed. Khuhro went at once to Sukkur and with the Larkana experience behind him quickly assessed the situation. He set up a Committee consisting of leading Muslims of the district to collect funds, aid the victims and to organise the defence of those who had been arrested. The Hindus were very vocal in their opposition to this activity on part of the Muslim leadership and most of the members taken on the Committee were scared away but Khuhro remained undaunted. On 28th August 1930, having reached Karachi, he wrote to the Commissioner-in-Sind, G. A. Thomas, describing the Sukkur situation and detailing the police excesses:

"Dear Mr. Thomas,

At the pressing request of Mussalmans of Sukkur I went to Sukkur yesterday to make enquiries into the stories of high-handedness alleged to have been practised by the police officials who are investigating the dacoities in the *mofussil*.

The accompanying statement describes the graphic information of what I learnt there from the most reliable people. I intended to release it for publication in the Press, but as I think it will, if given publicity, have a far reaching effect on the minds of Moslems who might feel very much disturbed and perturbed, I have decided to send it to you first so that you may take the necessary action and thus obviate the necessity of its publication in the open press.

You being a prudent and highly experienced officer, would, I hope agree with me that at this critical moment when feelings are running amok, it is highly desirable that the scandalous state of affairs which is briefly described in the report should be improved in such a manner that it does not attract and agitate the public, which is bound to occur in case these pathetic stories are published in the papers. I greatly dislike this policy and I earnestly request that you will be pleased to consider very carefully and sympathetically the contents of my report and accept the humble suggestions which I have made in the concluding paragraph of it. If you are pleased to take the desired action, I am sure a serious situation will be averted and things will reach a peaceful point without the administration being hampered by the publication of irritating reports."[2]

Khuhro went on to detail the events in Sukkur in the statement he sent to Thomas accompanying the letter:

"Since a week and a half back I have been receiving reports from the local public men of Sukkur giving harrowing stories of the high-handedness, torture, extortion and *zoolum* practised over the people in the *mofussil* by the police and the revenue officers during the course of the investigation of dacoity cases. As I could not fully believe the far-fetched reports I received, I repaired to Sukkur personally, to make full and minute enquiries as to how far the information communicated to me was true. I met the leading people of the town and district, and especially those who had seen the particular incidents of tyranny. After scrutinising all that was placed before me I have come to the conclusion that a great deal of what was brought home to us about the police actions in the *mofussil* is not untrue. There may undoubtedly be some exaggeration, but that is what is bound to occur at the moment of excitement.

It is alleged that the police is beating men and women ruthlessly in order to extort money and in some cases suspects gave confessions under compulsion. Indiscriminate and most brutal beating is carried on to such an extent that some of the unfortunate victims become unconscious. Hair from beards and other delicate parts of the body are pulled out. Clothes are removed from the bodies of women in the presence of their sons, husbands or parents and they are subjected to every kind of cruelty. Arrests are made indiscriminately. The victims are deprived of all their belongings. Money is being extorted. Those who are able to pay are able to escape the brutal treatment, but those who are not able to comply with their wishes are clapped into jail, no matter whether guilty or innocent. The fabrication of evidence in the *mofussil* is not a difficult thing. Great terror and panic prevails. Out of fear women and children have left their homes and hearths and concealed themselves in ponds and pools of water or in nooks and corners of dense forests. Some women have been dragged to jail while their children are screaming outside. This is a brief account of what is going on in the district of Sukkur.

I do not say that those who have committed robberies should not be dealt with, but what I condemn most and I hope everyone would do so, are the *zoolums* which are being perpetrated in broad daylight by some unbridled officers of the police department. I do whole-heartedly sympathise with the Hindus who have suffered on account of dacoities and such other crimes, but I can certainly not subscribe to the cynical idea of allowing the police to become a law unto itself. If the detection of crimes means the perpetration of equally abominable acts of cruelty and callousness, I am afraid there remains no difference whatsoever between the dacoits and the detectors. Both are transgressors of law in as much as one loots the property of people and the other one tortures and extorts, torments and exploits. Both are equally guilty and both deserve the severest condemnation and punishment.

I think it is imperative on part of the Government to put a stop to such a disgraceful state of affairs without any further delay. There is a great deal of anxiety among the people of the district on this account and therefore it is extremely necessary that an Inquiry Committee with a non-official majority should be set up forthwith to inquire into the complaints about the misconduct of the officials who have made detection a source of exploitation and tormentation. Until and unless the Committee is appointed it will be very difficult to restore peace and tranquillity in the *mofussil* and the police would get an encouragement to continue to behave as it has been doing hitherto."[3]

Khuhro described the effects of the situation on the Muslims of Sukkur and suggested the steps the Government could take to ease their fears:

"As to Sukkur town there is great panic and alarm among the Moslems. The mischievous element among the Hindus is fabricating evidence and making machinations to implicate the Moslem leaders. False complaints are being lodged against them and the Hindus are straining every nerve to get the leading Moslems entangled. There is so much terror among the Moslems that those who have actually suffered in the riots, whose relatives have been murdered and those who have sustained serious injuries, are not coming forward to give evidence or make complaints against the Hindus, being mortally afraid of Hindu wrath and revenge.

In view of all these things I would suggest that in the interests of justice and fair play the Government should appoint a committee of inquiry to investigate the complaints of Police tyranny, depute a European Special Magistrate to try the riot cases and those which are connected with the Sukkur affair, and issue a warning to the officers in the district to give up tyranny, and instructions to those who are making investigations at Sukkur to be very cautious in taking steps on the false evidence which is being adduced from time to time by the Hindus and see that they do not allow the Hindus to add to the miseries and misfortune of Mussalmans, by taking undue advantage of their (Hindus) inventive brains."[4]

G. A. Thomas known as god almighty Thomas was an extremely arrogant I.C.S. officer who had served in Sind for many years and was now Commissioner-in-Sind, a post which gave him almost absolute power. He was quite unused to being addressed as frankly and without ceremony as Khuhro was doing. The representative of an Imperial power, he was outraged that a mere native had the cheek to interfere in the what was the basic duty of the rulers – law enforcement. Moreover this interference was by a young man who had been elected to the Assembly – an innovation disliked and resented by most British bureaucrats. Khuhro on the other hand felt that he was doing no more than his duty as elected representative of the Muslims. He was also aware that very few leaders of the community were willing to come forward and risk the displeasure of the Sahibs and that the British bureaucrats were more likely to be influenced by their Hindu colleagues and the Hindu dominated press than by any voice from the Muslim *raiya*. The only other notable leader to come forward was the Khilafat veteran Abdullah Haroon who supported the efforts of Khuhro to get redress for the Muslims of Sukkur.

Khuhro got the full facts of the events in Sukkur and a list of the killed and injured from the Civil Surgeon of Sukkur. He had written to the Commissioner fully aware that any lapse of fact would be used against him and therefore he had been careful that there should be no exaggeration or overstatement in his account. He had also suggested that a European magistrate be appointed and that a Committee of Enquiry be set up – suggestions which, if followed, would calm the situation and assure all parties that justice would be done. Thomas however felt that this was interference in his domain and would not tolerate it. He answered Khuhro's letter the next day in typically arrogant terms:

"Dear Khan Bahadur,

I write to acknowledge receipt of your letter dated 28th instant and enclosure. My advice to you is not to attempt to interfere in matters which are not your immediate concern. While I give you full credit for being actuated by purely altruistic motives, I cannot help expressing the opinion that statements in the press of the nature of the draft statement accompanying your letter are calculated to do an immense deal of harm. So far from tending to create a peaceful atmosphere, in which the investigations into the riots in Sukkur town and dacoities in Sukkur district now in progress, can be carried out, they only serve to exacerbate the communal feelings exciting between the Mohammedan and Hindu communities and to sow the seeds of distrust in those officers of Government who are engaged on a most difficult task.

I have complete confidence in the ability of Khan Sahib Sukhia, who has been specially deputed to enquire into the Sukkur riots, to conduct that enquiry with due impartiality and thoroughness, and also in the ability of the District Magistrate and Police officers engaged in the equally arduous work of investigating the dacoities in the district. Statements of the kind you contemplate making will seriously impede their labours and I must very strongly deprecate such statements being published. I have no intention whatsoever of asking Government to set up a committee of inquiry, with or without a non-official majority, to enquire into the conduct of the Police whilst the investigations are in progress on the strength of such allegations as you have made in your proposed statement.

If in spite of these remarks you persist in your declared intention of publishing this statement in the event of my not acceding to your demands, I shall publish your statement of 28th instant and this reply to it in the press."[5]

Given his arrogance and the probability that this was the first time that a "native", albeit an elected member of the Bombay Legislative Council, had dared to question him it was a very bitter pill which Thomas was not prepared to swallow. A lesser man than Khuhro would have been intimidated by the tone of the Commissioner's reply and backed down. After all he had done his duty and gone to Sukkur at the call of the people there and he had organized a Defence Committee for the victims. He was advised by his friends to be cautious. Sir Shahnawaz Bhutto told him to be careful. The British were still the unquestioned masters and the empire looked impregnable and formidable. No Sindhi politician was in a position to take on the British ruler of Sind.

But Khuhro was not to be deterred. Sir Shahnawaz Bhutto also offered to meet the Commissioner and clear up any misunderstandings that may have arisen. On 1 September Khuhro met the Commissioner to explain the position but found him obdurate. No interference could be tolerated by members of the public. He implied, if not in so many words, that the elected representatives were so much window dressing and ought to confine their activities to the Council chamber and not come out to interfere with the real world of the *raj*. Khuhro gives an account of the interview:

"I was called to the interview by the Commissioner on the Ist September at 12 o'clock. I reached his office a little earlier and sent in my card. I was called in at about ten to twelve. The Commissioner was in an ugly mood and did not even get up to shake hands which ordinary courtesy requires, and more so from an officer of his position. His very demeanour from the very beginning showed that he was already in an antagonistic and prejudiced mood. At the outset he asked me whether I had received his letter in reply to mine re: the Sukkur affairs. I assented and added that I had come to explain to him the intentions which had inspired me to prepare this report and which have unfortunately been misunderstood and even misconstrued by him. I told him most explicitly that my statement did not in any way cast reflection on the District Magistrate, the D.S.P. or Khan Sahib Sukhia, and that on the contrary I entertained a very high opinion about the ability and judiciousness of these officials. I further made it clear to him that what I wanted him to do was to was to go deep into the matter and enquire thoroughly into the stunning and startling reports of Police tyranny and persecution, because the subordinates of the Police and judicial departments were doing all these disgraceful things under the shelter and pretext of inquiry and on the strength of the power that they derived from the higher authorities.

The Commissioner's reply was curt and a most objectionable one. "I don't believe a word of what is written in your statement", he said, "or whether these statements are made by you or anyone else. And I repeat as I have said in my letter that this matter does not concern you at all and therefore I am not prepared to discuss with you." "If you continue", he concluded, "to meddle with these affairs the Commissioner will have nothing to do with you."

I wanted to elucidate the points raised in the correspondence further and also to put the proper interpretation on my statement, but this extreme rudeness and ungentlemanly behaviour towards me clearly indicated that to have more talk with the Commissioner will mean a sheer waste of time. I was, on account of this strange behaviour of the Commissioner, very much disappointed and straight off left the office by the other door."[6]

Khuhro was used to the consideration and courtesy of the Governor of Bombay and to being taken seriously when he wrote to the Presidency government about the problems of the public. He had been able to act effectively in the matter of Larkana riots. He took his duties as public representative seriously and tried to discharge them to the best of his ability. But for the first time he had encountered one of the new breed of mediocre I.C.S. officer, fancying himself part of the ruling class and *ma baap* of the *ryot*. He was jealous of any encroachments on his authority and extremely sensitive about any questioning of his judgement particularly from what he considered to be a jumped up young Sindhi zamindar. He considered that his concerns should be whether he could attend the *durbar* of the Commissioner on his tour and whether he was entitled to a chair at the durbar. He certainly should not be addressing the Commissioner Sahib about methods of keeping law and order and pointing out the shortcomings of the administration.

Khuhro's experience with senior officials of the Bombay Government had led him to believe that he could deal with the officials in an open manner. But such courtesies were not to be extended by an arrogant Commissioner-in-Sind who ruled the province as an untrammelled autocrat. Only two years earlier, Sir Patrick Cadell had been Acting Commissioner and there had been a very satisfactory rapport between him and the public representatives. Khuhro had found him particularly sympathetic, god almighty Thomas was a different kettle of fish altogether.

Joining battle with this virtual despot of Sind was not to be lightly done. The Commissioner was certainly in a position to ruin his career and even get him defeated in elections, and could, in many ways, make life very difficult. But here, as he would at many stages later in his political career, Khuhro put the public interest before his personal comfort and the demands of his career. After considering the position for a few days Khuhro, still at the Carlton Hotel, wrote to the Commissioner on 7th September:

"I acknowledge with thanks the receipt of your letter dated 29th ultimo. From the conversation that I have had with Sir Shahnawaz yesterday, I have gathered that, if I have properly understood him, the delay which I have made in replying to it has led you to the assumption that your letter has satisfied me completely and it is therefore that I have paused to make an early reply. Thus, the very contents of your note and also the attitude adopted by you during the course of the interview on 1st instant have compelled me to vindicate my position by way of making an answer to your letter of 29th. The outstanding feature of your letter and the talk you have had with me is that you flatly deny my representative character, in as much as you think that public matters should not be interfered in by me, as they are not of immediate concern to me. I do greatly appreciate the intention that has inspired you to advise that: 'I should not attempt to interfere in matters which are not my immediate concern', but I am sorry, that during these times when public opinion is rapidly crystallising, a public man and an elected representative of the people, as I have the honour to be, cannot for a moment be expected to act up to such counsels, however candid and friendly they may be, because the acceptance thereof would amount to a clear dereliction of the duty that I owe to my people. When a representative of the people get complaints from persons whose veracity has never been questioned, to the effect that the Police which has never been considered as a saviour and custodian of public honour and property, is responsible for certain criminal abnormalities, it becomes his unshirkable duty to bring those allegations to the notice of the higher votaries of Government, for enquiry and necessary action and the slightest failure in this duty would mean the betrayal of the confidence that he enjoys.

In the present case, whatever I have done, I have done it under a strong sense of duty and strictly according to the dictates of my conscience. I was certainly not actuated by any base motive when I apprised you of the scandalous state of affairs at Sukkur. I am responsible only for the communication of what was brought home to me by the public, and I feel proud that I have discharged my duty quite conscientiously.

I hope you will agree with me that the language, I may be excused if I call it coercive, used in your letter and during the course of the interview was highly unwarranted and one that was not at all compatible with your or my position. I very much regret that you couched your letter in a tone that has greatly injured my feelings, leaving aside your refusal to give heed to the complaints levelled by the public against the Police who are alleged to have played havoc in Sukkur district. A large portion of your letter is full of encomiums showered upon "those officers of the Government who are engaged in a most difficult task." Let me assure you, Sir, that there was absolutely no necessity of giving all these threats or making praise. If I had thought that the publication of my statement would help the cause of my people, nothing could have prevented me from doing so. The fact is that in my much misunderstood forwarding letter I had clearly stated that I myself did not like to publish the report and consequently I had requested you to take the necessary steps directly in the matter and thus obviate the necessity of its publication. But unfortunately you have, to my profound regret, instead of accepting my request for the institution of inquiry, attempted to suppress my statement.

You have evidently misunderstood me when you express that you have full confidence in S. K. Sukhia and others. I have never made any insinuation against these officers and I am prepared to reiterate that I entertain full confidence in these gentlemen. What pains me most is that you are not showing the slightest inclination to inquire into the conduct of your subordinates of the Police and the judicial department, who are alleged to have committed things which, if true, would rend the heart of every human being who hears the pathetic story.

I am sorry I cannot refrain from expressing that I feel greatly disappointed to learn from you that this has no concern with me. I am at sea to understand on what principle your advice is based. If a legislative body sitting at Bombay or Poona has a *locus standi* to consider over matters pertaining to a province which is situated over a distance of 800 miles, I think a legislator belonging to that province has every right to echo the feelings of the public on any matter of urgent importance taking place within his province, for instance the Sukkur affair. Besides as a responsible office-bearer of Sind Mohammedan Association I am duty bound to invite your attention as a head of a constitutional Government, to these serious allegations.

I am further told by Sir Shahnawaz that you have taken exception to the way in which my forwarding letter of 28th August was written. I sincerely disclaim any intention of giving you any threat, and I am satisfied still that it was couched in a most respectfullanguage. It really pains me to hear that you have misunderstood it."[7]

Getting no satisfactory response from the Commissioner even to this explanatory letter and having already failed to make his point of view understood in the interview on 1 September, Khuhro decided to release the correspondence to the press. He not only released the text of the letters but also a detailed report on the cause of the trouble in Sukkur. This was indeed a remarkable occurrence in the annals of British rule in Sind if not in the Indian empire when a young landowner legislator could dare to confront the all powerful Commissioner-in-Sind and hold up his actions to public scrutiny. Khuhro pointed out the excesses of the police and the administration and by implication held the Commissioner responsible. For the British bureaucracy Khuhro was henceforth a troublemaker and not to be trusted. This was the beginning of 'thirties, India was still a stable British Imperial possession and the empire was well and strong. Independence was still a far cry and defiance of the British bureaucracy was not lightly undertaken. Khuhro personally stood to gain nothing from the stand he had taken. In fact he was in good standing with the Governor of Bombay and his high officials. He was an active member of the Bombay Legislative Council and had been awarded the title of Khan Bahadur that very year. He could expect to become member of the Executive Council in Bombay as soon as a vacancy occurred for Sind. But in his determination to get justice for the Muslims of Sukkur he was ready to sacrifice a successful future.

Having gone to the press, Khuhro set about organising public opinion to get justice and to normalize the situation. Seth Abdullah Haroon who was Member of the Central Legislative Assembly wrote to the Commissioner on 16 September pointing out the victimization of the Muslims of Sukkur, enclosing in his letter newspaper cuttings referring to police behaviour. The only newspapers which were giving coverage to the Muslim point of view were the two Sindhi dailies, *Al Wahid* of Karachi and Khuhro's paper *Sind Zamindar* of Sukkur. The Sindhi Hindu press and the Hindu owned English language newspaper *Sind Observer* were virulently anti Muslim and were busy maligning the Muslim leadership active in the Sukkur issue. Their particular target was Khuhro who was referred to as 'Aurangzeb' the Mughal Emperor who was generally regarded as a bigoted Muslim. *Sind Observer* in particular was trying to create differences between the Muslim leadership and trying to sabotage Khuhro's chances of representing the Sind Muslim case at the forthcoming Round Table Conference in London. There was a great deal of bitterness at this attitude of the Hindu press and a letter published in Daily Gazette in August 1930 puts it quite unambiguously:

"The journalist jackals have rallied under the banner of their Major Domo "the Sind Observer" and have strained every nerve of theirs to carry on their nefarious propaganda against the Muslim community in general and its acknowledged leaders and patriots like Khan Bahadur Khuhro in particular....Our young Khan Bahadur, a rising star and an ardent devotee of Islam, who has in his prime of life dedicated his purse and person for the uplift of his community, is a perpetual eyesore to the Editor of the S. O. who has under one or the other false pretext made several unsuccessful attempts to make him an object of public ridicule. To this he has resorted knowing full well that the Muslim community have always cherished a high regard for him which is deep rooted in their minds.... Finding the structure of his concoctions toppled down the disappointed Editor has now hit upon the plan of creating friction between Khan Bahadur Khuhro and Sir Shahnawaz, the distinguished leaders of our community by maligning one and extolling the other, with regard to their nomination in the Round Table Conference. In his issue of the 21st he has indirectly appealed to the Government imploringly that Khan Bahadur Khuhro should not be sent to the R. T. C. because he is a communalist and a separationist and has supported his argument by fallacious and illogical reasons that he will make an unsuitable associate in the R. T. C. The sum and substance of the whole note is that the learned Editor does not like to see the Moslem community represented by one who should place before the conference the numerous grievances of this majority community and urge for the separation of the province from the Presidency which at present is deemed essential for the advancement of the 75% population of this province....

May we ask him where is at all the necessity of sending any Moslem representative to the R. T. C. if he does not fulfil the mission of redressing the political grievances of the Mussalmans of Sind? Why not Mr. Jayakar then should represent Sind and in our opinion an anti-communalist and anti-separationist Moslem representative would be equal to him.

Mussalmans of this province therefore earnestly look to the Government that they are represented by a Moslem leader like Khan Bahadur Khuhro who honestly and sincerely performs the mission with which he is charged."[8]

Khuhro formed a Defence Committee for the Muslims of Sukkur and asked some well-known Muslim lawyers and barristers to prepare the defence of the Muslims arrested under various trumped up charges. On 7 September 1930 the Committee passed a resolution setting up a 'Dictator Committee' "for the purpose of collection of funds, arranging for pleaders, expending the funds and managing the whole defence"

Finding that the Muslims were not easily coerced and that the administration could not get away with the police excesses unchallenged, the Hindu leadership realized that they could not afford a further exacerbated situation since the Hindu population of Sukkur would not feel secure in these circumstances. They sent out feelers for a compromise to which the Muslim leaders responded immediately. Communal friction was a recent phenomenon in Sind and no responsible leader wanted to see it increase. A compromise formula was worked out, Professor S. C. Shahani leading the Hindu negotiating team and the Muslims represented by Khuhro, Abdullah Haroon and Shaikh Abdul Majid worked out a compromise formula and duly released it to the press:

"We the representatives of the Hindus and the Mohammedans greatly deplore the riots that took place at Sukkur, and the gang robberies and other atrocious acts that were committed in the district of Sukkur. It is our firm conviction that events of this kind are greatly harmful to the progress of the country and we express our profound regret at the unhappy and most deplorable happenings in the town and the district of Sukkur. We need hardly say that we fully sympathise with the sufferers.

We view with dismay the situation as we firmly believe that the authorities failed in concerting prompt and adequate measures to avert or intercept the gang robberies and other tragic happenings. We further deplore the conduct of the Police and the Revenue Officers as we are informed that in the course of their investigations a number of them have behaved in a high-handed and atrocious manner, and that in some places the investigation made by them have been perfunctory and in some not started at all.

Under these circumstances we urge the Government that a Committee be appointed by them at once in consultation with us to enquire into the (a) causes of the tragic events, (b) the adequacy and the timeliness of the measures taken by the authorities, (c) the allegations as to the hardship caused to some innocent people during the investigations, (d) the conduct of the Police and the Revenue officials in the course of their inquiry and investigation, (e) the promptness and the sufficiency of the measures taken to bring real culprits to trial and to recover the property stolen or looted, and (f) to concert measures required to remove the political, social, economic and educational defects in the existing situation revealed by the tragic events."[9]

A committee was set up consisting of the most influential leaders of the different communities under the chairmanship of the universally respected Parsi leader Jamshed Nusserwanji Mehta and consisted of three leading Muslims, Seth Abdullah Haroon (or Shaikh Abdul Majid as alternate member), Mohammed Ayub Khuhro and Allahbaksh Soomro of Shikarpur who was well liked and trusted by the Hindu leadership. The Hindu representatives on the committee were Professor Shahani, Lalchand Navalrai (or Chandiram) and Dr. Hingorani. The Committee had powers to co-opt such local leaders 'as they may think proper.' The task of the Committee was:

"(1) To try to restore such stolen or looted property as may be possible to their respective owners.

(2) To consider and determine which cases if any pending should be withdrawn and make a joint recommendation to the Government to that effect and take such steps and make efforts as may be necessary in this behalf and also bring to the notice of the Government such cases as have not been taken up by the authorities against the real culprits.

(3) To do everything that lies in their power generally and take all necessary steps to restore goodwill and harmony among the people and generally to carry out the objects and purposes of the resolutions passed at this meeting."[10]

In view of this agreement the tension in Sukkur reduced considerably and most of the matters were settled amicably. Except in the case of the people charged with the more serious crimes such as murder, Khuhro was able to get a good team of lawyers who succeeded in minimising the damage to the community. This agreement was an object lesson for the politicians that given the will there was no matter that was too difficult for settlement. In another sense also the lessons he learnt from this experience were salutary for Khuhro. He realized that as long as Sind was virtually a fiefdom of the Commissioner-in-Sind there was very little chance for extending the role of public representatives and for implementing autonomy or democracy, even in the limited sense that the Montford reforms had visualized, and that the only way that the role of the representatives could be effective was by making the bureaucracy responsible and accountable, which would be only possible if the legislature could make its presence felt in an autonomous and separate Sind.

For Khuhro the Sukkur events were to add immeasurably to his reputation as the leader who was not afraid to confront the Government and its mighty officials and who was not afraid to champion the ordinary people subjected to the high handed behaviour of the police or other officials. With his reputation considerably enhanced as leader and organizer Khuhro was about to take up a cause which was to be a turning point not only in the history of Sind but was to be the crucial factor in the way the future of the sub-continent was to be decided – Khuhro was ready to be the chief protagonist of separating Sind from the Bombay Presidency.

6

ACHIEVING AUTONOMY FOR SIND

In the autumn of 1930, Mohammed Ali Jinnah, a leading Bombay lawyer and one of the important Muslim leaders in India was in Sukkur to appear for the defence in the notorious "boy in the box" case instituted against Pir Pagaro.[1] The Pir was advised by his close advisers and *murids* (disciples) that he should gain the sympathy and advocacy of Khuhro who was not only a senior legislator but also a courageous politician capable of taking a bold stand even against the colonial administrator's wishes. The Pir sent his senior aide Mohabat Fakir to meet Khuhro at Larkana carrying a written directive to his 'disciples and servants' that Khuhro had been given all the authority to supervise the defence.[2] Khuhro agreed to do as the Pir asked and went to see him when he was brought to Sukkur jail at the start of his case. Pagaro asked Khuhro to meet Jinnah who was staying at the Circuit House on the hill in Sukkur. Khuhro met the Pir at the jail and went to see Jinnah in the evening.

This was the first time Khuhro met Jinnah, although the latter's reputation as the leading champion of Muslim rights in India and a moderate Muslim leader was well-known to him as was his reputation as a leading lawyer. "Jinnah talked politics most of the time, hardly about the case at all-" Khuhro said afterwards. Khuhro stayed in Sukkur for some days and attended the court hearings of Pir Pagaro's case regularly. He and Abdullah Haroon who had come down from Karachi to see Jinnah, both invited Jinnah to a luncheon so that other Muslim notables could meet him and the case for the separation of Sind from Bombay could be put to him. Jinnah accepted the invitation and a lunch was arranged for a Sunday in the Sukkur residence of His Highness the Mir of Khairpur:

"I invited a few leading citizens including Ali Mohammed Rashdi who was editing my newspaper *Sind Zamindar*, Khan Bahadur Pir Baksh Munshi, Retd. Deputy Collector, Abdul Hamid Khan of Old Sukkur, Syed Karam Ali Shah descendant of Syed Masoom Shah, Barrister Abdul Rahman. We also invited about half a dozen businessmen of Sukkur, though not more than about twenty people altogether." noted Khuhro in his recollections of the occasion.[3]

Haroon and Khuhro spoke about the issue of the separation of Sind from the Bombay Presidency and the necessity of bringing up the case forcefully so that autonomy for Sind could be assured in the next instalment of constitutional reforms to be given by the British. Jinnah was asked to take a personal interest in the matter and he said he was very willing to undertake the task. He had already lent his support to this demand from the platform of Muslim League and agreed to take up the issue whenever the opportunity occurred.[4] In his speech at the lunch Jinnah spoke at length about Indian political problems and particularly about the search for consensus on the constitutional reforms and the difficulties in reaching agreement on safeguards for the Muslim minority of India. He gave a resume of negotiations at the Calcutta All Parties Conference where he had made his plea for understanding. He also set out the approach of the authors of the Nehru Report to the demands for Muslim representation and "safeguards". He described the obduracy of the extremist Hindus and lamented the shortsightedness and the lack of generosity of the Hindu leadership including that of the Congress. He gave the example of Zaghlul Pasha of Egypt who, he said, had given the Copt minority of Egypt which was only about 8% of the population, a blank sheet of paper and asked them to put down whatever conditions or safeguards they wanted from the majority community and promised that these conditions would be guaranteed. With this generous action the Copts had been won over to the nationalist cause and supported the struggle against British colonialism. Jinnah's speech impressed his audience greatly and this introduction to the Sind leaders was to prove a very useful prelude to his subsequent political incursion into Sind in the late 'thirties when he came to set up the Muslim League with these very same leaders who would be his most loyal lieutenants in organizing the party in Sind.

In fact the experience of communal discord and the determination of the Hindu extremists to establish their dominance even at the cost of destroying the traditional communal harmony of Sind had disillusioned the Muslim leadership including Khuhro. They were convinced that the only solution was to curb the large and powerful Hindu bureaucracy, which was being obstructive about any genuine action to advance the cause of the Muslim majority especially if it perceived such action to be against the vested interests of the Hindu money lender or affecting their position as officials. The solution was to separate Sind from the Bombay Presidency. In the Bombay Presidency Hindus were in a large majority but in an autonomous province of Sind with its 75% Muslim population the Hindu extremists would become powerless. These circumstances gave new life to the old demand for separation and also produced the new and dynamic leadership which would take up that issue.

Sind had remained more or less independent for most of its long history. Even when it formed part of large empires it always had its own governor and retained regional autonomy. Its rulers whether independent or agents of an imperial government, were guided in their actions by local compulsions. After the British conquest in 1843, Sind had remained a separate province of the British empire under the governorship of Sir Charles Napier for the first few years and lost its autonomy for the first time in history when the British made it part of Bombay Presidency in 1847 and transformed it into a Commissionership. The Commissioner-in-Sind under whom it was now placed, was a unique post with special powers necessitated by the fact that the Presidency capital was hundreds of miles distant by land or by the sea route. Sind was for all intents and purposes a fiefdom of the Commissioner and his officers, a remote connection of little interest to the established bureaucracy of Bombay. In 1868 the Sind Act was passed which entrusted the

Commissioner-in-Sind with many of the powers of the Governor-in-Council and which made him virtually an independent ruler.

With the capital as far away as Bombay it was inevitable that for administrative purposes Sind would be governed almost autocratically by the Commissioner. Thus Sind became a paradise for officials. Here they reigned like medieval princes in splendid isolation, no irksome superior authority to check or question their actions and even if there were issues which the 'Governor-in-Council' had to decide they were heavily dependent on the advice of the local Sind officers. The Governor of Bombay came for a tour of Sind in the shooting season most years and his stately progress up the Indus constituted almost the only supervision of the local authorities. Senior officials of the Bombay Government would come to Sind for about a fortnight in the cool weather, be entertained at hunting and shooting parties and return to Bombay not much wiser about the problems of the province. Thus Sind was subjected to an undiluted form of bureaucratic and paternalistic British rule for over sixty years after the conquest. The fact that Sind was regarded as a prize or special privilege for officials to add to the prestige of their position and enable them to enjoy extra 'perks' is obvious from the fact that serious attempts were made by the Punjab administration to get Sind attached to that province, particularly after the separate administration of North-West Frontier Province had come into being; but these schemes were eventually finally rejected by Lord Curzon who was Viceroy of India at the turn of the century.

From 1847 to 1908, when the Morley-Minto constitutional reforms were introduced into India, Sind was under complete bureaucratic rule. It was only as the principle of representation began to be applied to the government in India that relief became possible. This was particularly the case when Sind began to send elected representatives, albeit from a very limited and circumscribed electorate, to the Bombay Council. For the first time Sindhis were able to put their case at the seat of government and gain the sympathy of their peers from other parts of the presidency. As soon as there was some popular leadership, which in the early 20th century and till his death in 1924 was led by Rais Ghulam Mohammed Bhurgri, the demand for a separate Sind came up. In 1913 the demand was put from the platform of the annual session of All India Congress which met at Karachi in the winter of that year. In his opening address Harchandrai Vishindas, the leading Hindu Congressman and close associate of Bhurgri put his case for separation: "...the Province possesses several geographical and ethnological characteristics which give her the hallmark of a self-contained territorial unit."[5]

Representations were made by Sind political groups to Sir Edwin Montagu, the Secretary of State for India, when he toured India in 1917 on a 'fact finding' mission and he met with delegations of the Bhurgri group as well as the Sind Mohammedan Association, a 'moderate' group of Muslim politicians which had been representing the Muslim point of view since 1885. The constitutional reforms of 1919 did not concede any autonomy for Sind although the problem was brought to the notice of Montagu who in his published Diary of his Indian visit noted–

"The interesting part of the discussions occurred when we came face to face with the separation of Sind. The Sind Provincial Conference which came on behalf of the Congress–Moslem League scheme, wants the abolition of the Commissioner of Sind pending the creation of a special Province. They do not want a special province at present because of the expense. The Sind Mohammedan Association, which is conservative, wants Sind separated as soon as possible and meanwhile the Commissioner kept. *It is undoubtedly true that Sind gives more funds to Bombay than Bombay gives to Sind."*[6] (author's italics)

In the post-World War I period the struggle for separation was at a very low key. In 1924 Ghulam Mohammed Bhurgri died prematurely at the age of forty at the height of his political career. With his death ended for all practical purposes the co-operation between the Muslim and Hindu leaders for the cause of separation. The rise of communal troubles in the 'twenties vitiated the atmosphere for co-operation and caused a change of attitude on part of the Hindu leaders towards autonomy for the province. Now instead of judging the issue from the point of view of better administration, which would bring a degree of democratization to provide the means to improve the lot of ordinary people, they began to think in communal terms. The Hindu leadership, including the long time friend and associate of Bhurgri, Seth Harchandrai Vishindas who decided to oppose autonomy on the grounds that Hindus who were the overwhelming majority in the Bombay presidency as a whole would turn into an insignificant minority in separated Sind. From this time on, the opposition of the Hindu politicians would be bitter and unrelenting.

The struggle for the separation of Sind was fought in three distinct phases.[7] In the first phase the struggle was led jointly by Muslim and Hindu leadership, the chief protagonists being Bhurgri and Vishindas as well as their associates Diwan Gidumal, Shaikh Abdul Majid and others. This phase ended in 1924 with Bhurgri's death and the communal estrangement in the 'twenties. With the break occurring in the leadership and with the new circumstances in Indian politics there was no chance that the kind of joint leadership that had existed could come up again.

In the second phase the struggle was subdued and fought mostly on the All India front in the shape of resolutions at annual conferences. This was the period when the Hindu opposition to separation crystallized. Although some of the most enlightened leaders among the Hindus continued to support separation, a more influential section turned against it and began to raise the alarm about the alleged gloomy future which awaited Hindus in a separate Sind. As a result the All Parties Conference at Calcutta and the Nehru Report itself had to hedge round the issue and give only qualified approval for separation.

The third and final phase of the struggle, the phase in which Khuhro emerged as the most important leader and organiser of the movement, was to be carried on by the Sind leadership as a highly organised and united struggle with help from the All India Muslim leadership which saw the Sind issue as vital for the future of constitutional rights of Muslims in the whole of India.

But before the All India leadership could be convinced of the importance of the Sind problem for the interests of Muslims as a whole, the Sind Muslims had to get their act together and make a coherent case. Khuhro and his friends were determined to revive the issue of separation after it had remained more or less dormant in the post war period. It was brought up occasionally at Muslim get togethers such as the annual Muslim League conferences but inbetween there was hardly any movement in the matter. By 1927 Khuhro had become convinced that the only way to remove the dead hand of bureaucracy was to gain autonomy and began actively to pursue the goal of separation. The first opportunity that occurred was the appointment in November 1927 of the Royal Statutory Commission on Indian Reforms under the leadership of Sir John Simon, popularly known as the Simon Commission, which came to India in the cold weather of 1928 to examine the working of the 1919 Montagu Chelmsford Reforms and the system of "Dyarchy" and to assess the situation for further reforms. The Commission, because of its nature as a British parliamentary body, consisted only of members of the two Houses of Parliament and included no Indian members. There was a great deal of criticism of the lack of Indian representation on the Commission and the Congress Party boycotted the Commission. The Government tried to meet the criticism by nominating local members as representatives from provinces or the Presidency to sit in on the Commission's deliberations in the different provinces. The Congress leadership was not however satisfied by this arrangement and decided to continue its boycott. Similarly the 'nationalist' wing of Muslim League under Mohammed Ali Jinnah also decided to boycott the Commission.

Some important sections of Muslim opinion were however in favour of co-operating with the Commission as they felt this was a good chance of getting their views across to the British Government which in different circumstances would be swamped by the weight of the All India Congress. The Unionist government of the Punjab was also in favour of co-operation with the Commission. Khuhro and his friends who were anxious to put their case to the British Government and were prepared to take all practical steps to secure autonomy for the province, decided that this was a golden opportunity to gain that objective. In fact the non-Congress Hindus were also co-operating with the Commission and appeared in force before it to oppose the separation of the province.

Khuhro galvanised the Muslim leadership of Sind and infused a new spirit into it. The senior leaders at this time were Sir Abdullah Haroon, the Khilafat veteran who along with some others had founded *Al Wahid*, the Khilafat newspaper which became the leading voice of Muslims in the province and Shaikh Abdul Majid, the first editor of *Al Wahid*, also a leading Khilafatist. Both Haroon and Majid represented Sind at all India Khilafat conferences and on the other occasions including the Nehru Committee. Here they gave a dissenting note on the majority report of the Committee set up under Sir Purshotamdas Thakurdas to examine the financial viability of Sind.[8] Apart from these senior leaders, there were Khuhro's contemporaries, Allah Baksh Soomro, G. M. Syed, Noor Mohammed Vakil, Syed Miran Mohammed Shah, as well as his able assistant Pir Ali Mohammed Rashdi, who worked closely with him in organising the campaign for separation. The next seven years were a remarkable example of sustained hard and detailed work in which Khuhro excelled himself. He studied the problem and the case of the opposition both in regard to the Bombay bureaucracy and the Hindu political leadership and came up with an unanswerable case which the British government had to concede finally in the Government of India Act of 1935.

Khuhro recognised that the crucial factor as far as the Government of India and the British Parliament were concerned was the matter of finance – the most important question being whether the new province would be financially viable and if it would be able to pay for itself. If these questions could be answered in the affirmative then it would be much easier to meet the political and other objections of the Hindu opposition. He therefore set about mastering the financial case for Sind.

Khuhro made himself an expert on the whole question of Sind's finances and became an indispensable witness for the numerous committees that were set up to examine the question. He was a tireless worker for the cause, publishing and distributing material, persuading Muslim leaders of other provinces and all India parties to support the case and giving them the material to argue the case. He organised public opinion in the province and bombarded the members of Round Table Conference with pamphlets and telegrams. He fought a well orchestrated and very modern propaganda war to obtain the separation of the province.

The first step in this arduous struggle was to put the case to the Simon Commission. Sir John Simon and his team had landed in India to placards of 'Simon go home'. Congress was boycotting the Commission and so were smaller groups like that of Jinnah and other nationalists. Moderates of all shades were however co-operating in the expectation that the Enquiry would bring increased quantum of self rule and greater autonomy. Sind Muslim legislators and political leaders felt that this was an opportunity not to be missed. There was a tradition in any case of Sind members in the Bombay Council co-operating with the Government benches to mutual advantage and had managed a number of concessions for Sind Muslims as a result.

On 12 November 1928 the Simon Commission began its sittings in Karachi in the impressive newly built red sandstone High Court building. The most important part of its enquiry apart from the working of the 1919 reforms in Sind was to assess the demand for separation and examine its feasibility. The Commission was assisted by a provincial committee consisting of two members, Sir Shahnawaz Bhutto and Syed Miran Mohammed Shah, both Members of the Bombay Legislative Council. The case for separation was put by the delegation from the Sind Mohammedan Association led by Khuhro and assisted by Ali Mohammed Rashdi. He later wrote that compared with the Hindu delegation the Separationists were not well prepared on this their first appearance before a high powered committee. Apart from a short two page memorandum there was no prepared case as such and the arguments and answers came out of Khuhro's own preparations. Khuhro and Rashdi were informed that the Hindu anti separationists were sending an expert team led by Professor Chablani fully armed with facts and figures. Subsequently Rashdi collected all the heaviest law books and gazetteers he could lay his hands on and took a couple of assistants to hand him the books and they all got into Khuhro's car and went off to give evidence before the Commission. The other six members of the delegation were waiting for them. These included Wali Mohammed Hassanally, General Secretary of Sind Mohammeden Association. Khuhro handed over the memorandum of the Association on the subject and then gave evidence as the spokesman of the delegation. He put the case forcefully and argued cogently for separation but was unable in the final analysis to satisfy the Commission.

The case against the separation was put by the All Sind Hindu Association led by Professor H. L. Chablani of Delhi University. Apart from expressing Hindu fears of being swamped by the Muslim majority, Professor Chablani concentrated on the financial aspects of the problem. His main argument was that Sind was subsidized by the Bombay Presidency Government and would not be able to support itself. This was the argument that was most likely to appeal to the British official mind. It was also the argument played up by the Bombay government which was totally opposed to the detachment of Sind from the Presidency.

The final decision of the Simon Commission went against separation saying that the time was not yet ripe for this step. Of the two members co-opted from Sind, Sir Shahnawaz Bhutto agreed with the majority opinion but the young member from Hyderabad Syed Miran Mohammed Shah, advised by Jinnah and Sir Ibrahim Rahimtoola, wrote a Note of Dissent, reiterating the absolute necessity of giving autonomy to Sind.

The decision of the Commission caused great disappointment in Sind but the separationists did not lose heart. From then on the leading part in rallying the forces for the ensuing struggle for autonomy was played by Khuhro. The Simon Commission report had been a setback but he did not allow that to become a problem. He realized that constitutional reforms were bound to come soon and that in view of the Congress boycott the views of the Commission would possibly undergo revision. The exercise of presenting the case to the Commission had provided certain useful lessons. It was apparent that the crucial factor in the fight for autonomy would be the financial condition of Sind and its ability to support itself as a separate province. The battle would therefore have to be fought on the financial front.

To Khuhro with several years of experience as legislator and having to deal with Sind problems and finances in the Council, it was obvious that Sind had more than enough resources to be financially viable. As early as 1917 Sir Edwin Montagu had given his assessment that Sind contributed more to Bombay than the latter gave to Sind. But the picture had been obscured by the Bombay Government which did not keep a separate budget or accounts for Sind. As a result the financial picture of the province was the one the Presidency government chose to show. Khuhro became convinced of this as soon as he began his intensive study of Sind finances. He was determined to get the true picture and to see that this problem did not become an obstacle in the path of achieving autonomy.

Khuhro made himself the master of the facts and figures in fighting the case for autonomy in the propaganda war and the numerous expert committees set up to examine the problem. The Hindus who were opposed to the separation also chose to base their case mainly on the alleged inability of Sind to pay for itself. Hence the fight on both the fronts – the official one in England and India and with the Hindu opposition at home had to be fought on the grounds of financial viability of the province.

Thus by the beginning of 1930 the game was back with the Sind players. Khuhro fired the first shot with his book *Sufferings of Sind* published on 26th May 1930. This book traced the historical background of Sind and discussed its present social, economic and political position, the disadvantages of its administrative union with Bombay, pointing out the distance from the administrative headquarters, the autocratic behaviour of the local officials and the lack of redress for the injustices and problems of the public. He pointed out that even under British rule Sind had been governed separately for some years with Sir Charles Napier as governor and that giving autonomy to Sind would not only re-affirm historical precedent but also improve the administrative efficiency of the British Indian empire – and that this step was long overdue. The book was very widely circulated in India and England as well as in Sind and helped to bring issue back before the public in a very dramatic way.

The Sufferings of Sind had a great propaganda impact and became one of the best known documents of the struggle for separation. The opponents of the struggle denounced the book in strong terms. Professor Chablani tried to counter it by publishing a book of his own *The Separation of Sind from Bombay Presidency (A rejoinder to Khan Bahadur Mohammed Ayoob S. Khuhro's 'A Story of the Sufferings of Sind')*. But Khuhro's book had done its work well and the issue was very much alive before the public and the policy makers.

After the failure of the Simon Commission the British Government decided to solve the constitutional problem of India by reaching a consensus through a series of Round Table Conferences with representation from all major shades of opinion in India. The first Round Table Conference was scheduled to begin in London on 12 November 1930. The separation of Sind was to be one of the issues to be examined at this conference. A sub-committee of the R.T.C. was specially constituted to go into the problem. Jinnah was to be one of the delegates. On his way to London he stopped at Karachi for a short time where he was invited to be the chief guest at a dinner hosted by Seth Abdullah Haroon, Khuhro and G. M. Syed. In a formal Address at this dinner, Khuhro requested Jinnah to advocate the cause of separation in London and Jinnah promised to do so.

The Round Table Conference Sub-Committee on Sind (Sub-Committee IX) was chaired by Earl Russell and its members included the Marquess of Zetland who was later to become the Secretary of State for India, the Marquess of Reading a former Viceroy, H. H. The Aga Khan, the leading Muslim delegate, and M. A. Jinnah.* The Committee was extremely high powered with an ex-Viceroy, a future Secretary of State and top leaders of both Muslim and Hindu communities as well as experts in the field. It was established quite early in the proceedings that there would be determined opposition from the 'die-hard' Hindu lobby, in this case represented by Dr. Moonje, the Hindu Mahasabha leader. The Committee eventually decided that a financial enquiry committee should examine the position of Sind. The crucial factor, as Khuhro had already realized was to be the financial one. Separation was to be contingent on the financial viability of Sind. The question was thus left pending for the next conference to deal with.

In 1931, in accordance with the decision of Sub-Committee IX, Government of India appointed a committee under the chairmanship of Sir Miles Irving to report on the financial position of Sind. The Financial Enquiry Committee informally known as the 'Irving Committee' met at Karachi from July to September 1931. Its terms of reference were:

"With reference to the report of Sub-Committee IX of the Indian Round Table Conference, to examine carefully the probable revenue and expenditure of a separated Sind and the security of the debt on the Sukkur Barrage and also to recommend an equitable adjustment of the financial commitment for which Sind may properly be considered liable."

---

* The other members of Committee IX were Dr. Shafaat Ahmed Khan who was to prove of great help to Khuhro in presenting his case when he appeared as witness before the Committee in 1933, Sir Mohammed Shafi of the Punjab, Sir Abdul Qaiyum from N.W.F.P., Sir Shahnawaz Bhutto and Sir Ghulam Hussain Hidayetullah. The Hindu members were Dr. B. S. Moonje of the Hindu Mahasabha, M. R. Jayakar also an extremist Hindu leader, C. Y. Chintamini, Raja Narendra Nath. Others included Sardar Sampuran Singh, B. V. Jadhav, Sir Pheroze Sethna, H. P. Mody, Sir Hubert Carr and Isaac Foot.

Khuhro gave evidence before this Committee and the others who did so were Abdullah Haroon, Syed Miran Mohammed Shah and Professor Gokhale while the anti separationists who did so were Professor Chablani, Diwan Bhojsingh and Dr. Hingorani. That the divide was not purely and precisely communal was proved by the fact that some prominent Hindu and Parsi Congress men wrote newspaper articles and made public statements to prove that the financial position of the province was strong. Among these were Rewachand Thadani, Rustom Sidhwa, the Parsi Congress leader and Professor Bhateja. The Financial Enquiry Committee however came to the conclusion that a separated Sind would have to start its career with a deficit of Rs. 10,845,000.

The Miles Irving report was submitted to Sub-Committee IX at the Second Round Table Conference in November 1931. Gandhi also attended this session of the Conference as the sole representative of the Congress but there was no consensus achieved on the constitutional issues and the representation of the different Indian communities in the future legislature. In absence of agreement among the Indian leaders the British Prime Minister, Ramsay Macdonald, decided to take the initiative and gave his 'Communal Award' on the basis of which the reforms could go ahead. The separation of Sind and its constitution as an autonomous province was accepted by the government "if satisfactory means of financing it can be found."

To find these means the directive was given:

"We therefore intend to ask the Government of India to arrange for a Conference with representatives of Sind for the purpose of trying to overcome the difficulties disclosed by the report of the expert financial investigation which has just been completed."

Following the suggestion of the Prime Minister, Government of India constituted a conference with the following terms of reference:

"The Sind Conference is being set up in accordance with the undertaking given by the Prime Minister in the course of his statement to the Round Table Conference at the close of its second session on the 1st December of last year. His Majesty's Government have accepted in principle the proposition that Sind should be constituted a separate province *if satisfactory means of financing it can be found*. (Author's italics). The purpose of the conference is to try to overcome the difficulties disclosed by the report of the expert financial investigation made by the Irving Committee last summer. The chairman, having met the representatives of Sind, will report the results of the conference to the Government of India."

Even at this stage therefore the separation of the province was not a foregone conclusion and hung on the question of finances.

The conference opened at Karachi on 25 April 1932 and carried on an intensive study of its subject until 17 May 1932 under the chairmanship of A. F. L. Brayne the distinguished and nonconformist officer who had done so much for the rural areas of the Punjab. There was representation of both the pro and anti separationists. The Bombay government as well as the Indian government were to be represented. Hugh Dow, I.C.S., the expert on Sukkur Barrage finances and a future governor of Sind was on the Committee. The chief spokesman for the separationists was Khuhro and for the anti separationists Professor Chablani.

The Chairman pointed out in his report that the conference was faced with certain difficulties at the outset. The first was that Sind had no separate budget and accounts of its own and as the expert Irving Committee made clear, the figures of actual revenue and expenditure had to be made up by an elaborate and intricate process mainly from the transactions of Sind treasuries. The Accountant General of the Presidency government furnished the conference with a further year's figures of actual and revenue which supplemented the figures for the three years 1927-1928 to 1929-30 adopted by the Committee. The same methods, however, could not be applied to evolve revised estimates for Sind for 1931-32 and a budget for 1932-33, which would have been of great use during the enquiry, particularly in view of the prevailing abnormal conditions of world wide economic depression. The Conference had therefore to depend on such incomplete information as was available.

"The second difficulty" went on the Report:

"is one common to all whose lot it is to attempt to frame financial estimates in the present time of severe economic crisis when all ordinary methods are thrown out of gear and there exists but little certain guidance for the future. This difficulty is particularly felt when an attempt is made to estimate the future position of an immense scheme such as the Lloyd Barrage, the financial results of which have so important a bearing on the future of Sind. The third difficulty was perhaps inherent in the constitution of the Conference. The majority of the twelve non-official representatives of Sind were definitely anxious for separation, a minority were strongly opposed to any change and two members expressed neutrality. The Hindu members, who were opposed to the principle of separation, expressed the view that a decision on that principle had been reached at the Round Table Conference in the absence of any Hindu representative of Sind and that the real meaning of the conclusion of the Sind Sub-Committee lay in the statement of its chairman that if Sind cannot show that it can stand successfully on its own legs, the separation does not take place. The Prime Minister's statement, they feared, would be interpreted as going beyond this.

It was perhaps only natural that, in regard to financial questions into which a considerable range of estimate and conjecture enters, contrary points of approach should lead to differences of opinion, which, however amicably expressed, are difficult to reconcile."[9]

The Conference went into great detail and examined every aspect of the financial condition of Sind present and prospective. The Muslims anxious to secure separation proposed an increase in the taxes on land as a concession, no mean sacrifice seeing that more than 95% Muslim population depended on agriculture for their livelihood, and eventually succeeded in convincing the Conference that an autonomous Sind could be viable. The Chairman brought out the following points in his concluding remarks:

"The task before the Conference was to try to overcome the difficulties disclosed by the report of the expert financial investigation. The main difficulties were bridging in whole or in part of the initial gap between revenue and expenditure at the time of separation and the devising of means to meet both the additional expenditure due to separation and the unavoidable future expansion of net expenditure so far as this could be foreseen. The revenue estimated by the Committee amounted to Rs. 1,8242,00,000 and the expenditure Rs. 2,7982,00,000, the difference being Rs. 97.4 lakhs. These figures exclude the

Sukkur Barrage which is treated separately. The estimate of expenditure included a provision of Rs. 31,00,000. for interest and avoidance of debt and Rs. 16.5 lakhs calculated to be the initial pensionary liability of Sind. These two items are to be transferred from Bombay on the date of separation.

Excluding these items the administrative expenditure in Sind amounts to (Rs. 232 lakhs.) which is still in excess of the estimated revenue by about Rs. 50 lakhs. At the outset it was evident that with ever so limited a field of revenue and reducible expenditure amounting in combination to Rs. 415 lakhs, it would be no easy task to find funds by retrenchment or increase of revenue, to the extent of about one crore of rupees. In the first place drastic retrenchment was likely to prove difficult in expenditure which is mainly incurred on administration and beneficent services particularly in view of the new phase of development in the Barrage era upon which Sind has entered.

Secondly it is unlikely to have much scope for substantially increased revenue in a thinly populated country where the main source of that increase is land revenue any increase of which is confined to a limited field under the settlement system. In this connection it is relevant to note that the income tax and super tax derived from Sind amounted in 1930-31 to Rs. 17,50,000 only of which amount Rs. 12.3 lakhs were contributed by Karachi leaving Rs. 5.2 lakhs for the rest of Sind, which gives some indication of the low degree of industrial development."[10]

Brayne went on to comment on the position of the Hindu members of the Conference:

"The Hindu members of the Conference approaching the problem from the standpoint of opposition to the principle of separation have made little contribution to the task. Their protagonist has endeavoured to prove that the basic figure of deficit given by the Irving Committee was unduly optimistic and that it should be increased by about 26 lakhs. The cost of separation, if Sind is to have at least the ordinary standards of administration of a small province, must, he holds, be at least double the figure of Rs. 11 lakhs estimated by the expert committee. The expansion of expenditure during the next two or three decades must be far in advance of the expert estimate while additional revenue to cover the cost of expenditure is not likely to be forthcoming. No substantial retrenchment in existing expenditure is possible and even the economy of Rs. 12 lakhs already secured ought to be reduced by about half at an early date by restoration of cuts made in expenditure on education and other beneficent services, of new sources of revenue they see no hope save perhaps an income tax on agricultural incomes over a certain limit which would fall on the larger Muslim zamindars.

The basic deficit, including the cost of separation and allowing for additional taxation already imposed and the retrenchment which they accept as permanent would thus be Rs. 138 lakhs compared with 94 lakhs, the comparative revised figure of the expert report. Regarding financial estimates of Lloyd Barrage they adopt an attitude of pessimism. In their view it is unlikely that the estimate of receipts from the sales of land by which amount the Barrage debt will be reduced will be reached and one opinion is that it should be reduced by 25% and the period of recovery extended to at least thirty years. Even the recovery of assessments is in their view not certain and it is out of the question to expect that any improvement in the land revenue by the imposition of higher rates could be affected."[11]

Brayne contrasted the unhelpfulness of the Hindu members attitude with the positive contribution of the pro-separationists: "On the other hand the majority who favour the principle of separation have made a determined effort to show that at least part of the difficulty can be overcome." The pro-separationists put forward proposals which cut down the deficit to about Rs. 30 lakhs. Brayne commented, "Even this net deficit of Rs. 30 lakhs they seek to turn into a surplus by other interest on pre-reform irrigation and unproductive debt to the tune of some Rs. 20 lakhs and claiming for Sind the Rs. 21 lakhs allotted by the federal finance committee without the debit of contribution to federal revenue."

Brayne ended his report by thanking the members whose contribution had been most helpful and useful: "Professor Chablani, Professor Batheja and K. B. Khuhro had made a specially intensive study of the finances and economy of Sind which proved of the greatest value to the Conference and to myself."[12]

Khuhro also contributed an additional note in which a further clarification of the essential majority position was set out. Laying out the basic figures of the financial position of Sind, Khuhro pointed out that there was some room for retrenchment in the cost of administration as "Sind spends nearly Rs. 7 per head which is double of Madras and almost three times of Bengal, and Assam spends only Rs. 4 per head." He also suggested possible new sources of revenue:

"1. On account of tax on Electricity, Transfer of Property Act, New Court Fees and Stamps Act, Sind will get at least 2 lakhs.
2. Due to the imposition of 1 anna cess per rupee of land revenue to meet the extra cost of separation till Sind is sufficiently rich otherwise to meet the cost of administration will give at least Rs. 12 lakhs...
3. Income Tax collected in the Province of Sind will give us as calculated by the Federal Finance Committee, Rs. 21 lakhs. A deficit and a small province like Sind cannot afford to give any contribution to the Federal Government and therefore it will be wrong to take into consideration any contribution from Sind to Federal Government."

Khuhro neatly turned round the argument of those who said that Bombay was subsidizing Sind and that the Province was a millstone round the neck of Bombay:

"4. I am strongly of opinion that Sind should not be made to pay the interest charges for the pre-separation debts. This amount as suggested by Professor Batheja should be charged to Bombay as Bombay will by separating Sind benefit to the extent of about 75 lakhs straight off. According to the calculation of the Federal Finance Committee, Bombay will have deficit of 65 lakhs under the existing conditions if Sind is separated. Bombay is entitled to 322 lakhs as share of Income Tax. Her full contribution to the Federal Government will be 203 lakhs. Thus the net saving to Bombay will be 54 lakhs straight off, if Sind is separated. Bombay can therefore easily bear 21 lakhs of interest charges to get rid of Sind. If Sind continues to hang round the neck of Bombay like a millstone, after the Federal Government is established in India, Bombay will be having a deficit of about 25 lakhs per year in spite of the share of Income Tax as recommended by the Federal Finance Committee and therefore Bombay will be compelled to ask Federal Government for a subsidy of 25 lakhs a year to meet the Sind deficit. To choose between the two certainly Professor Batheja's suggestion of making Bombay pay the interest charges is undoubtedly a clear gain to Bombay Government and a much lesser evil."

Khuhro calculated that if revenue sources were exploited in the light of the suggestions of the Federal Finance Committee in fact Sind would have a surplus of over Rs. 20 lakhs to spend on "nation building" (i.e. health, education, etc.) departments."

In spite of the favourable report made by the Brayne Conference, the hard core anti-separationists continued their vociferous opposition. The Executive Committee of Anti-Sind Separation Conference issued a pamphlet of criticism of the Brayne Report in which the anti-separationist stand taken in the conference was reiterated. In order to publicly refute the anti-separationist arguments which was being publicised, Khuhro issued his refutation of their arguments in a pamphlet, *A Rejoinder to the criticism of the Anti-Sind Separation Committee* which was issued 6 September 1932 and which effectively answered their case and exposed their motives as basically communalist.

The anti-separationists now determined to make a last desperate bid to stop the separation and stepped up their propaganda in India and abroad. The Hindu Mahasabaha party set up an office in London to agitate against autonomy for Sind. The separationist did not have enough resources to set up an office in London so they appealed to the Aga Khan and other Muslim leaders to support their case. On 21 November 1932, from Larkana Khuhro wrote to Sir Mohammed Iqbal who was a delegate to the Third Round Table Conference, to advocate the cause of separation:

"Dear Sir Mohammed,

The Sind Muslims are highly grateful to you, His Highness the Aga Khan, and other Muslim delegates on the Indian Round Table Conference, for taking keen interest in the question of separation of our province from Bombay. I was very glad to find the news published in the *Times of India* that you have expressed to its London correspondent that you will continue to take keen interest in the question of Sind separation by distributing all the literature sent to you in this connection and also by pressing for immediate separation.

I sent in early November by air mail about 20 copies of my pamphlet titled " A rejoinder to the criticism of Anti-Sind Separation Committee" to H. H. Sir Aga Khan to be distributed among the Indian delegates to the Round Table Conference.

I sent directly the copies of this pamphlet to the British delegates too. I have again sent about 40 copies to H. H. Sir Aga Khan and Dr. Shafaat Ahmed Khan, of my latest pamphlet "A convincing case for separation of Sind", which they will receive in early December to be distributed among all the delegates of the Round Table Conference.

I am sending you two copies of it for your own perusal. You will find from these pamphlets how logical is immediate separation from Bombay.

As you know the Sind Azad Conference was held at Hyderabad Sind, on the 15th and 16th instant. It was the most representative gathering that has ever taken place in Sind. I enclose herewith a dozen cuttings of the *Daily Gazette* of Karachi which is an Anglo-Indian paper, to give you an impartial and independent opinion about this conference expressed in its leader, and also the full news about the Conference proceedings including the resolutions passed therein. Pray have these cuttings distributed among the leading members of the Round

Table Conference who are likely to take interest in our problem.

The full text of the main resolution on the separation of Sind, moved by me, was cabled to the Prime Minister, the Secretary of State for India and H. H. The Aga Khan, by Syed Miran Mahommed Shah, the Secretary of the Conference. The perusal of these newspaper cuttings will also make it clear to you that the Sind Muslims do not wish to be hoodwinked by the Sind Hindus by accepting their impracticable conditions, imposed at the so-called Allahabad Unity Conference, which in other words makes Sind separation an impossibility. We emphatically desire that this question be decided on its own merits and that Sind should immediately and unconditionally be separated from the Bombay Presidency and constituted a separate autonomous province.

I would therefore request you on behalf of the Sind Muslims to urge the British Government to separate Sind forthwith. The case for separation, is an excellent one and the financial bogey is a mere pretence to thwart the legitimate aspirations of we Sindhis. In short I might tell you that the Federal Finance Committee have clearly shown ... that with Sind Bombay has at present a deficit of about 155 lakhs. So even if the full share of income tax is transferred to Bombay the latter (Bombay) will yet have a deficit of about 35 lakhs. So the Committee have based their calculations on the assumption that Sind will be constituted a separate province. In that case the Committee shows that Bombay will have a surplus of 54 lakhs if she is allotted full share of the income tax. This clearly shows that it is even in the interests of Bombay that Sind should be separated in order to get rid of her own insurmountable deficit. Besides it should be borne in mind that the cost of separation is only 10 to 12 lakhs and to meet that cost the representatives of Sind suggested some easy taxes in the "Sind Conference" which was held under the chairmanship of the Hon. Mr. A. F. L. Brayne in last April and May and he accepted those suggestions in his report. The income anticipated out of those taxes is much more than the cost of separation. It is therefore obvious that the separation does not involve any extra burden on the Indian tax payer as a whole. Since the Government of Bombay is unable to overcome her deficits without the help of Central Government why to blame Sind? What we ask is that the amount which will otherwise be paid to Bombay, may be paid partly to Bombay and partly to Sind, according to their respective requirements. It does not therefore put any extra burden on the coffers of the Central Government.

I trust you will do all that lies in your power to push forward our most reasonable and legitimate demand.

With all best wishes and regards,

I remain,
yours sincerely,

(M. A. Khuhro)

To,
   Dr. Sir Mohammed Iqbal, M.A., Ph.D., Bar-at-Law,
   Member of the Indian Round Table Conference, London.[13]

The whole of 1932 had seen hectic activity by both the protagonists and antagonists of the "separation" so as to make the strongest case for the Second Round Table Conference to be held in November on which the Reforms that were expected to be announced would depend. On 18 April Sind Azad Conference met at Karachi under the presidentship of Sheikh Abdul Majid. The leading participants in the conference were Khuhro, Haroon, Haji Mir Mohammed Baluch, Syed Miran Mohammed Shah and G. M. Syed who was the chairman of the reception committee. The conference passed a resolution for separation. In the same year 16 September was celebrated throughout Sind as "Sind Separation Day" with great enthusiasm. On 15 November the second Azad Conference met at Hyderabad under the presidentship of Allama Yusuf Ali, (scholar, translator of the Holy Quran). The Conference passed its resolution supporting separation and also set up a permanent body "Sind Azad Conference" with Sir Shahnawaz Bhutto as president, Khuhro as vice president and Syed Miran Mohammed Shah as general secretary. The Hindu communalists retaliated by setting up a Sind Hindu Conference in January 1933 which passed resolutions opposing the British Prime Minister's announcement accepting the principle of separation. On 5 February the Working Committee of Sind Azad Conference met to work out measures to counter the Hindu propaganda. The Committee appointed Pir Ali Mohammed Rashdi to publicize the cause of separation and to counter Hindu propaganda. The final battle in the struggle for separation was being fought.

In March 1933 a Joint Parliamentary Committee was set up in England to examine the framework for Indian constitutional reform. Among the important issues on which the Committee was to give a decision was ofcourse the separation of Sind from Bombay. In April 1933 the Joint Parliamentary Committee requested witnesses from Sind both for and against separation to present their case before the Committee. Khuhro was chosen as the representative of the Muslims of Sind to present their case before the Committee. The Azad conference had however no funds to send a representative to England and so Khuhro had to rely on his own resources.* There was some discussion in the Separation lobby about the desirability of sending someone with Khuhro to lend him a hand in the preparation of the case. Shaikh Abdul Majid himself was keen to go and so was Syed Miran Mohammed Shah who had been of valuable service with his Note of Dissent with the Simon Commission Report. The problem was that Shaikh had no funds of his own and the Separationists could not raise adequate funds. Shah also claimed that he could not raise the necessary money. In a typical letter he put the matter to Khuhro:

"If you assure Ghulam Murtaza Shah [G. M. Syed] that you have arranged Rs. 2,500 he will get you Rs. 500 from A. Rahim Shah in one day. The question is only whether Haji A.Haroon would pay rupees one thousand from his pocket. If he gives the same you must know that the whole amount is arranged. I must further inform you K. B. Nur Nabi was willing to help. So that if you can get one thousand from Seth Haroon, one thousand from Azim Khan (who is still ready to pay) the remaining one thousand you can realize Rs. 500 from Abdul Rahim Shah. But to all these gentlemen you have to write or see them personally. To Ghulam Murtaza Shah also you can write, assuring him of Rs. 2,500. I am writing hard facts to you as I have found them. If you are really serious

---
* Khuhro like most zamindars had little ready cash and had to sell a piece of his land to finance his trip to give evidence before the Round Table Conference.

about your companion you can even avoid taking brother Rashdi and contributing that amount towards the cost of your colleague who will give you as much work as Mr. Rashdi excepting typing and personal attendance and who cares to have a stereotyped typist in preference to a fragile and fair stenographer of London and who would brook an idea of having a male attendant in preference to a romantic figure of a fairy face hovering round about you in your dressing room in London.

Bhutto can tell you how he found Fernandez useless and expensive in London, because you get a better service and cheaper hands in London. So what Mr. Rashdi can do can be better arranged with less expense. Why not contribute that amount towards the expenses of your companion. I don't intend depriving my brother Rashdi of his chances to visit London, but I am only pointing out the solution of the financial difficulty in the public interest and without any additional burden on you."[14]

In the end the financial contributions did not materialize and only Khuhro was able to undertake the journey. As time was short and he had to appear before the Committee on 19 July he arranged to go by air in one of the pioneering commercial flying companies, in this case a French one. These early planes took only a few passengers and flew in stages to Europe. Khuhro was seen off at Karachi by friends and relatives and a number of political workers. The journey to Europe was an adventure in itself.

The plane crash landed in the Iranian desert where Khuhro and another passenger managed to walk several miles to get help and save the situation. On his arrival in England Khuhro sent back the details of his journey to the local papers in Karachi:

"I left Karachi on the 5th by Air Orient Service as I failed to get accommodation with the Imperial Airways. I had to reach London not later than the 15th ...

There were two other passengers with me namely Mr. and Mrs. Dutt. The gentleman belonged to C. P. and his wife is French. She knew only French, whereas Mr. Dutt spoke both French and English. One of the greatest drawbacks of the French Service is that none of them speak English, although they fly right through India. We reached Charbar,* a small town in Persia on the sea coast, at 7.30 p.m. It is about 500 miles from Karachi. We should have landed there as the sun was about to set, but the pilot persisted in dashing to Djask, which was 200 miles further. It was very foggy that evening and after sunset it was impossible to see the land. Ordinarily we would have reached Djask at 10 p.m., but because of the darkness and the failure on part of the pilot to judge the distance properly, he was nonplussed. At about 11 p.m., failing to find Djask he decided to return to Charbar. Having run short of petrol, we had a forced landing in the Persian desert, 50 miles away from Charbar, at 1 o'clock in the morning. While landing the aeroplane crashed, but we luckily escaped by running out of it. That night we had to keep awake for fear of being looted. Early in the morning at six, I, along with two Frenchmen, started in search of some habitation, along with a map and a compass. Even after ten miles walking we could not trace any habitation. After, however, walking another five miles, we were able to come across a dozen wretched huts where we found some Makrani women. They could not understand my Persian as they knew only the Makrani language, a queer mix-

---
* The town was actually Chah Bahar, a small port on the Iranian coast.

ture of Persian and some other Oriental languages. After a great deal of trouble we found one old man who, after some persuasion, agreed to give us his two donkeys as he was unable to secure camels. He gave us his son as a guide to Charbar which was about 35 miles further on. It was a very hot day, the temperature being about 120 degrees [Fahrenheit]. We had to drink very dirty rain water the whole day, which we took with us right up to Charbar, as there is no well in the entire desert of Persia in hundreds of miles. We mostly walked, and sometimes rode donkey, who were too lean to carry us through all that distance, till we reached Charbar at 7 p.m. At Charbar we came to the telegraph bungalow and met the superintendent, who happened to be from Karachi, and he treated us quite nicely and kept us as his guests. We hired six camels there and sent them to the people in the plane with necessary foodstuffs, and with instructions to get them to Charbar along with the kit. We cabled Karachi for a fresh plane which arrived at 12 noon on the 7th but our companions could not reach till 6 p.m. The miserable time that we spent these two days could better be imagined than described. Charbar is a small town with a population of 500 and a Persian army of about 200 soldiers under the command of an officer called the Governor and the Commander in Charge of Civil and Military Administration of the Town. He, I learned, gets a salary of 350 Persian crowns per mensem, equivalent to Rs. 50."

Khuhro's fellow passengers, the Dutts, also sent an account to their home town paper in Jubbulpore in the Central Provinces, which gave Khuhro a rather more heroic role. The paper said that although a plane mechanic and Khuhro had set out–

"The mechanic returned exhausted after having covered 19 miles but the passenger [Khuhro] continued the journey. An hour after the mechanic's return a group of armed men appeared and charging across the desert they surrounded the marooned party. Later that night the Chieftain of the village arrived, accompanied by six men in long black robes. He placed fourteen armed men around the airliner and the passengers were told they must stay there all night. Late the next day a relief party arrived, through the indomitable courage of the passenger, M. A. Khuhro of Karachi, who trudged 45 miles across the desert and rescued the passengers and the crew."[15]

Khuhro described the subsequent journey to England also in his account which was his first to the Middle East and Europe:

"On Saturday we commenced the journey at 6 a.m. and reached Bushire at 4 p.m. with brief halts at Djask and Lingah [Bandare Lengeh] . We did 900 miles that day and spent most of the evening in visiting the city of Bushire which is the biggest Persian port, having trade connections with all important cities of Persia and outside. The day was very windy and had not the sky cleared by 3 p.m., we would have been in a worse plight than the previous one, due to the sandstorm. We passed the night in the Rest House built after the Persian style, and was quite a decent one.

On Sunday morning at 5 we started for Baghdad where we reached at 9 o'clock and soon after breakfast started for Damascus to avoid another sand storm expected that evening. We reached Damascus at 4 p.m. and after seeing the city, left by car for Beyrout which we reached at about 8 p.m. It is about 70 miles by road from Damascus. Damascus is one of the best cities in the East but I prefer

Beyrout port for its climate and environment. This part of Syria is very fertile and well populated. Beyrout port is famous for the export of well-known Syrian and Palestine fruits. The Hotel St. George's where we passed the night is ideally situated overlooking the sea just at the back of it. I can't compare any Bombay hotel with it, as it is much superior all round. I regret the time and the space do not permit me to give a full description of these places."[16]

Khuhro continued his journey to London by a 'seaplane' and describes the journey:

"On Monday we started in a seaplane at 4.30 a.m. and reached Athens at 12 noon and Corfu island at 5 p.m. where we passed the night. The following morning we reached Naples at 9 and Marseilles at 4 p.m. All the time between Beyrout and Marseilles we flew over the Mediterranean sea which was very calm and the weather was very fine and enjoyable. From Marseilles I reached London on the 12th at 7 p.m. by train and was received at the station by Mr. Amjadally, Secretary of the Muslim Delegation as well as a representative of Cox and King's Ltd."[17]

Khuhro put up in a hotel in the Haymarket just off Piccadilly, within easy walking distance of Ritz Hotel where the Aga Khan's suite was the informal headquarters of the Muslim delegation to the Conference. Khuhro immediately got to work to prepare his memorandum and his evidence. In this he was helped by Sir Shafaat Ahmed Khan in whose flat in St.James Court they worked every morning on the material he had brought.[18] They lunched at the flat where the "help" would prepare a light lunch, fried fish or chops and salad. For Khuhro used to seeing English men and women only as high and important officials and members of the ruling class it was a new experience to see them as ordinary workers, house maids, shopkeepers, porters etc. He found Englishmen at home polite and charming – very different from the aura of rulership and arrogance which surrounded them in India.

One of the salutary experiences in this regard was when he went to meet Sir Henry Lawrence at Oxford. Sir Henry a nephew of the famous Lawrences of the Punjab, Henry and John, was Commissioner-in-Sind during World War I. He was a very well liked Commissioner of the old paternalistic school who had worked hard to be fair to the Muslim population of Sind and had tried to give them posts which were due to them. Khuhro had met him later in his career when he was a senior officer in the Presidency and member of the Governor's Executive Council and was particularly sympathetic to Khuhro's efforts to get justice for Sindhi Muslims. On this his first visit to England Khuhro got in touch with Sir Henry who was living at Boar's Hill, Oxford and was invited to spend a weekend with him. Khuhro went up by train and Sir Henry met him at the station. Khuhro found that he was driving the car himself and he said to Khuhro, "Will you sit in front with me or in the back like a Sahib?" Khuhro ofcourse got in the front and was taken for a tour of Oxford and then to the picturesque suburb of Boar's Hill. He found that though the Lawrences had some paid help most of the work was being done by themselves. Lady Lawrence, a niece of Sir Charles Napier the conqueror of Sind, he found a charming down to earth woman who put the young Khuhro at ease though he had tended to be embarrassed when he found her working in the house and even serving up meals at the table.

Back in London Khuhro appeared before the Parliamentary Committee on

19 July and gave comprehensive evidence which proved decisive in getting separation through. Even here the anti separationists did not allow the matter to rest but fought every inch of the way to stop the decision going in favour of separation. The case had been made well however and the political atmosphere was overwhelmingly in favour of separation and so by the end of the Third Round Table Conference the autonomy of Sind was as good as won. Khuhro drafted the statement on behalf of members and office bearers of the Sind Separation Conference at the conclusion of the Third Round Table Conference appreciating the work of all those who had helped the long drawn out struggle and thanking Committee XI and the British government for giving justice to Sind at last.

The Aga Khan who was deeply concerned that the issue be decided in favour of autonomy was very appreciative of Khuhro's performance and said to him, "You are the solicitor for Sind and I shall be the advocate." Many years later when he was in Karachi after the creation of Pakistan, the Aga Khan remembered that he had used these words and said to Khuhro, "The separation of Sind was the foundation stone of Pakistan" and he repeated the compliment he had paid in London. On the conclusion of the Conference he showed his appreciation of the role Khuhro played by sending a telegram to his colleagues in Sind, among them the senior politician Sir Ghulam Hussain who was at this time Minister in the Bombay Executive Council and well-known to the Aga Khan:

"3-8-33

Dear Sir Ghulam,
Khan Bahadur Khuhro came over here on behalf of the Sind Separation Conference to give evidence before the Joint Select Committee. I am glad to say that the impression created by the Khan Bahadur's evidence on the Committee was favourable and we very strongly hope that the declaration of the Government to separate Sind will be upheld by Parliament.

Hoping you are keeping good health.

Yours sincerely,
Sd/- Aga Khan"[19]

The decision to constitute Sind into an autonomous province was made simultaneously with the passing of the Government of India Act 1935 and Sind was duly made a province on 1 April 1936.

Khuhro returned home by ship. The P. & O. ships took about a fortnight and were very comfortable. This journey was the first real holiday for him after years of strenuous activity. Most of the other passengers were British civilian and military officers returning to duty in India after leave in England and were accompanied by their families. There was a great deal of entertainment on board-games, dancing, films and a great variety of food. There was a definite social barrier between the British and the Indians in the early 'thirties. The British were still very much the Imperial masters who laid down a strict code to regulate social relations between Indians and the English rulers. So while Khuhro got on quite well with the English officers he met there was no question of meeting their families except in a very formal way. He found a distinct difference between the Englishman in England and the Englishman abroad. He was however too busy taking in the scene on his first experience of the legendary journey to India with the historic passage through the Suez Canal, the Red Sea, the glimpse of Egypt and of course the novelty of the life on the ship.

Immediately after landing at Bombay Khuhro went straight to Simla to see the Viceroy, Lord Willingdon, and briefed him about the progress on the separation.[20] Lord Willingdon was favourably enough impressed to recommend Khuhro to the new Governor of Bombay, Lord Brabourne, for ministership in his Council the next year when the question of making a change in the Sind seat in the Bombay Executive Council came up. Since 1921 the one seat that was the share of Sind on the Executive Council of the Governor of Bombay had been occupied by Sir Ghulam Hussain Hidayetullah, the most durable office holder in the history of Sind. As Minister for the first few years and then as Executive Councillor he had been in the Governor of Bombay's cabinet for thirteen consecutive years and the Viceroy felt that the time had come for a change, especially as he had to make changes in other provinces and did not want to be embarrassed by this elongated tenure for one man. Hidayetullah, 'a wily old bird' as he was termed by one of the Governors of Sind was a very shrewd politician. Coming from a Shikarpur family recently converted from Hinduism (hence the title of Sheikh), he became a lawyer and started practising in Hyderabad at the turn of century when Hyderabad was the centre of intellectual and political ferment. Hidayetullah was befriended by the powerful Hindu bureaucracy and had entered politics under their patronage. He was chosen as representative of the District Local Board of Hyderabad to the be member of the Bombay Council under the Morley Minto Reforms of 1909. At Bombay he had succeeded in carving out a successful career for himself as an acceptable Sind politician at a time when the most powerful political group in Sind was that of Bhurgri whose politics were firmly nationalist. The Khilafat period saw the rise of Seth Abdullah Haroon another nationalist politician who had vigorously organized the Khilafat movement in Sind. Against these popular and powerful nationalist politicians the government was able to find a number of capable men who could be groomed to act as local collaborators. The most prominent of these was Hidayetullah.

In the words of a social commentator–Hidayetullah "was endowed with great luck... without spending any capital, without enduring any kind of hardship or test and without giving any sacrifice he enjoyed the highest political posts that were possible for a Sind politician."

Ali Mohammed Rashdi, himself an extremely subtle and clever politician and *eminence grise* of Sind politics for many years, made this shrewd assessment of his character:

"Sir Ghulam Hussain always understood the time and never missed an opportunity. He made the right decision at the right time. He never allowed any sign of anxiety or nervousness to become apparent always retaining his composure and appearance of nonchalance. Every evening he would be at his Club without fail and his opponents would become complacent and work more openly against him. When their plans were fully exposed he would strike once and very hard. He operated extremely subtly to get rid of his prospective rivals keeping an affable exterior all the while. His methods never appeared to fail."

He was extremely diplomatic and never made an enemy, always apparently cordial, tolerant and hospitable. In a country where great store was set by the "condescension" (in the old fashioned sense) of the "great", his open house and hospitality was his invaluable and single greatest asset:

"In fact, says Rashdi,"it was through his *dastarkhwan* (table) that he first achieved influence and then kept it. Most importantly, he kept bureaucrats of all descriptions happy and tried as much as possible not to interfere in their dealings. As minister he left most of his work to his trusted officers and devoted himself to meeting people, cultivating influential friends, and keeping himself informed as to what was happening round and about so that he was never taken by surprise. He never showed his annoyance and enmity openly, always kept his cool and never allowed any criticism to get an immediate reaction from him."[21]

As soon as Khuhro had arrived in Bombay in early 1924 Hidayetullah had assiduously cultivated the young man, insisting that he stay in his house whenever he was in Bombay – an invitation Khuhro sometimes took up. He was also available for advice and help on matters pertaining to government and officialdom. Hidayetullah was a convivial man, fond of his evenings at the club drinking with friends, a habit he would continue in Karachi after autonomy when Karachi Club became his favourite haunt. He had many friends among whom he counted not only officials but also businessmen and politicians.

By 1934 Hidayetullah had been occupying the Sind seat on the Executive Council for a good many years. The Viceroy had intimated to the Governor of Bombay that the time had come for a change of face. Hidayetullah had got wind of the way things were going and had already managed to get on the right side of the Governor who asked the Viceroy if he could continue with Hidayetullah in the post. Lord Willingdon expressed his regrets:

"I am terribly sorry that I can't extend Ghulam Hussain and I know you believe me when I say that I am really anxious to do everything possible to ease your work at the beginning. But I may tell you that only two days ago Anderson [Governor of Bengal] sent me a letter to say that Ghuznavi had informed him that I was agreeing to an extension for Ghulam Hussain and Krishnan Nair at Madras and therefore he would like to have an extension for Ghuznavi. You see, I am sure, that if I begin by giving way, I am starting on a slippery slope and, while I do realise your difficulties, you must forgive me if I can't help you in this matter."[22]

Hidayetullah was lobbying frantically to retain his Executive Councillorship and trying every possible avenue. He shrewdly assessed that the two possible replacements for him would be either the well tried Sir Shahnawaz Bhutto or perhaps Khuhro who had just returned triumphant from his visit to England and was not only an experienced parliamentarian by now but also had the backing and popularity in Sind. Hidayetullah had by now won the confidence of Khuhro and convinced the latter that he was his well-wisher and a sincere friend. He now prepared to kill two birds with one stone. He persuaded Khuhro that Lord Brabourne had made up his mind to appoint Bhutto on the Executive Council and as Bhutto was the officialdom's 'yes man', his presence on the Council would hamper the free development of the future province of Sind. After giving Khuhro these high minded reasons for opposing Bhutto, he then hinted that Bhutto's elevation would also adversely affect Khuhro's position in Sind where Bhutto would do his best to outmanoeuvre him. Moreover he pointed out that Sir Shahnawaz's record on the separation issue was not unblemished. He then asked Khuhro to tell the Governor that Hidayetullah should not be replaced in the Council.

In spite of his by now considerable experience in politics, Khuhro was incapable of understanding deviousness. He took politics seriously as a public duty, was deeply concerned with public welfare and had a strong sense of justice. He understood the people and their problems and he had proved that he had perseverance and a talent for detailed work as well as determination to fight to the end. But his greatest failing which would dog him throughout his career was his incomprehension of the motivations of his colleagues and contemporaries. Completely lacking any "machiavellian" qualities he was unable to grasp that others may not be so straightforward. Khuhro displayed at this time a naivety which was the opposite of Hidayetullah's deviousness. At the same time Khuhro had been disillusioned with Sir Shahnawaz Bhutto with whom he had worked closely, first as Deputy Leader of the Sind group of Legislative Councillors in the Bombay Legislative Council where Bhutto had been the Leader of the group, and also as Deputy President of Sind Mohammedan Association of which Bhutto had been President. Khuhro had regarded Bhutto's toeing the Bombay Government line on the separation of Sind as a betrayal especially since he had previously trusted the old man. He now sought an interview with Lord Brabourne and strongly insisted that Hidayetullah be retained as Executive Councillor from Sind.[23]

The Governor quite unused to anything but sycophantic attitudes even from Opposition politicians was utterly taken aback by this frontal assault. Khuhro's intervention made not the slightest difference to official policy. Brabourne was in any case trying his best for Hidayetullah but he did not take kindly to what he considered brash interference in his official responsibility where even the Viceroy was using a great deal of tact. Hidayetullah's cause did not prosper but this episode earned a powerful enemy for Khuhro in the highest echelons of the Imperial Government in India. Khuhro had no inkling that he had offended the all powerful Lord Brabourne. He would continue to make calls on the Governor in connection with his work as well as routine courtesy calls but the latter would not forgive what he considered Khuhro's effrontery and would even warn the new Governor of Sind in 1936 against Khuhro. By making his rash confrontation Khuhro had certainly burnt his boats as far as office in the Bombay cabinet was concerned. The post would go to Bhutto who had played his cards well.

Meanwhile Hidayetullah continued to try his luck. Lord Willingdon wrote to Brabourne on the subject:

"I saw poor old Ghulam Hussain up here when he came for the Economic Conference, and I must say I thought he was rather ridiculous in the way that he took the whole business. He practically sobbed on my shoulder in my room, and told me that I had destroyed his public career, and it was quite impossible for me to persuade him at all that other people were sometimes out of office for a short time, or even for a longer time."

Willingdon went on to suggest Khuhro or Haroon as possible replacements.[24] But as far as Brabourne was concerned Khuhro was *persona non grata* and he would not consider him. Hidayetullah pleaded to be retained as Minister (a step down from Executive Councillor) at least and Brabourne wrote again to the Viceroy,

"Sir Ghulam Hussain is pressing me very strongly to appoint him as Minister when he vacates his seat as Member... As however I feel that if I appoint him a Minister I may be creating a precedent which might cause inconvenience elsewhere I should be grateful for your views on this aspect of the question."[25]

Willingdon replied somewhat coldly:

"Your telegram of 12th instant. Whilst I frankly confess that I do not altogether like your proposal to appoint Ghulam Hussain as Minister I leave the matter entirely to you, and if you consider such a course is the best solution out of your difficulty, I am quite agreeable. Furthermore, I do not think we need worry that such a precedent might cause inconvenience elsewhere owing to the fact that the term of office of a very few Executive Councillors expire before the time when I anticipate the reforms will be introduced into the Provinces. If you decide to appoint Ghulam Hussain I hope he will stand for election at an early date."[26]

Brabourne obviously could not go against such plain Viceregal displeasure and gave in and the Viceroy's personal secretary was able to write to him expressing Willingdon's approval: "The Viceroy, if I may say so, was delighted with you over your not making old Ghulam Hussain a minister. I know how upset he will be and how furious with you! But I hope you will not think me presumptuous when I say that I am sure you did the right thing."[27]

A footnote to this drama of the removal of Hidayetullah and the appointment of Bhutto occurred the next year when the former slipped up and succeeded in annoying Brabourne who hearing of the possibility of Hidayetullah being invited to lunch by the Viceroy protested vigorously by telegram and followed up by a letter:

"I feel I owe you many apologies for having sent you that telegram about your lunch with Ghulam Hussain, but as this has not appeared in any of your earlier programmes, I sent it on the off chance that the whole thing had not been definitely fixed up.

I know for a fact (from C.I.D. and other sources) that he has been particularly poisonous behind the scenes as regarding the Karachi firing episode and had excelled himself in his efforts to have one foot in each camp. On the other hand Shahnawaz Bhutto has played up really splendidly, and I feel that your lunching with Ghulam Hussain would give the latter a considerable leg up in his campaign against the former."[28]

Brabourne was naturally incensed considering that he had put himself out for Hidayetullah even to the extent of almost annoying the Viceroy. He had even recommended him to the Viceroy for the post of President of the Central Legislative Assembly.[29]

But this was by no means the limit of Hidayetullah's ambitions. With Sind as an autonomous province after April 1936 he had much less trouble in gaining the good opinion of the governors of the province and remained in power for most of the next ten years and indeed till he died in 1948 in harness as Governor of Sind.

The association of Bombay with Sind had existed for nearly ninety years when the Government of India Act 1935 severed the connection. Although by the time Sind achieved autonomy the change had become overdue there is no doubt that on balance Sind had benefitted from the connection in terms of political and intellectual sophistication. On the other hand it could be argued that if Sind had been allowed to remain a Governor's province as it had been with Sir Charles Napier, it would have made greater progress in terms of the infrastructure and in evolving a system of revenue administration, a subject of crucial importance in the deeply agricultural country of Sind; and even in the system of education and other areas which would play an important part in the modernization of Sind. In other words if Sind had remained autonomous it would have evolved a system closer to its genius.

As it was serious errors of judgement were made in the initial years of British administration of the province from a sheer lack of understanding of the system and the society. Mistakes were made from which it would take sometime for the country to recover. It was only in the last decades of the 19th century that a revenue system was devised for Sind which suited its peculiar conditions and was not just an adaptation of the *ryotwari* system of the Indian peninsular. These mistakes, the result of a lack of bureaucratic forethought, became an additional hardship for a people undergoing fundamental re-orientation in their lives with the imposition of alien masters with their strange new legal system and innovations in administration.

Given the circumstances of colonial calculations which attached it to a distant, economically and culturally alien administrative region it was fortunate for Sind that the region chosen was the Bombay Presidency, the most advanced and cosmopolitan presidency in India. Here western education had taken root and a system was evolved which included the local languages of the area which were integrated into the education structure. This was adapted by Sind. Here also was the most advanced political elite of India which had initiated the politics of 'association' in India. Congress had been born in Bombay and the great moderate leaders of India, Naoroji, Mehta, Gokhale were all from Bombay. The *savoir-faire* of these men rubbed off on the Sindhi politicians. Respect for the rule of law, the conduct of government at its best in India, a high level of debate in the Legislature and the integrity of public life, were the essential qualities that the Sindhi leaders came to expect from and associate with the British system of rule in Bombay.

In giving up this connection Sind was gaining autonomy which ofcourse was what Sindhis had worked for so hard, but at the same time it was losing a connection which had contributed significantly to its political and cultural growth. For Khuhro Bombay had been his school in politics. It was here that he had his first experience of the working of a legislature, of the cut and thrust of debate, of thinking on his feet and of making a case in the clearest and briefest manner possible. He experienced a varied 'multi ethnic and multi cultural' society which widened his horizons and enriched his personality in ways which would have been impossible if he had been confined politically to his province. Here he learnt to work with a bureaucracy of a high calibre and it was these standards that he expected for the rest of his life. Khuhro saw Sind as continuing the traditions of the Bombay legislature with its principled and moral tone in public life. The crucial difference he saw with the achievement of autonomy was that Sindhis would have a better chance to practice democracy and have their problems solved more expeditiously on their doorstep. He also saw this as the opportunity for the public representatives to control the excesses of the bureaucracy and to have administrations more sympathetic to the public. The achievement of these objectives was to be a more difficult task than Khuhro could possibly imagine.

7

SETTING THE FRAMEWORK

Khuhro, blissfully ignorant of the drama being enacted in the rarefied atmosphere of viceregal and gubernatorial chambers, of the desperate struggle for the Bombay cabinet post and also quite unaware of the repercussions of his interview with Lord Brabourne, continued with the remaining chores of finalizing the separation of Sind. He was euphoric over his tour of England and his good showing at the Joint Parliamentary conference. At home he had been at the forefront of the struggle, and was the undoubted authority on the case for separation, referred to by the public as well as by officialdom. But the public was still concerned about the resolution of the separation struggle mainly because of the unrelenting Hindu opposition and their continuing propaganda. This was reflected in a letter Khuhro wrote to the Aga Khan from Larkana as late as April 1934, several months after his return from England:

"I am directed by the Moslem public men of Sind to wait upon your Highness through the medium of this note and solicit your guidance and advice as to our line of action hereafter with regard to the question of Sind Separation.

The present position about this problem is this: the Hindus have started a most vehement propaganda in Sind; they have held a Conference which has passed a strong resolution against the separation; the Hindu press is publishing most spurious and poisonous material; they have opened an office at London; it is believed that they are trying to enlist the sympathy and support of the members of Parliament for having the measure regarding Sind thrown out and a Hindu delegation is sailing for England in the next month with the object of remobilising their forces at London and securing an adverse report from the Joint Parliamentary Select Committee. And at the top of all this there are the questions of various MPs who have been very often interpellating in the Parliament against the separation of Sind.

This state of affairs is causing grave anxiety to the Moslems in Sind and we require your guidance at this juncture. We are holding a Conference for separation in early May, and if you deem it necessary we might even send a deputation to England to counteract the propaganda which the Hindu delegation might make there. But if you think it would be no use sending a deputation all the way to England then the question would be whether we should open any office in London and if so how is it to be arranged. Besides these points if your Highness is pleased to suggest some other method by which we could conduce to the early achievement of our goal we shall be very glad to carry it out.

I sincerely trust that your Highness will favour us with a reply by Air Mail as early as possible as we would be moulding our policy at the Conference in the light of your instructions.

I attach herewith some newspaper cuttings which will give you an idea of the Hindu movement against the separation."[1]

The Aga Khan was re-assuring saying that the decision had virtually been taken and that this last desperate effort by the anti separationists was not likely to make much difference and therefore opening an office in London would only involve unnecessary expenditure.

The announcement of the separation of Sind and its constitution as an autonomous province was duly made along with the announcement of the new constitution of India, the Government of India Act of 1935. Khuhro felt instinctively that this was the time to heal wounds and to reconcile the people of Sind to each other in the wake of a struggle which might have left a residue of bitterness. He immediately drafted a statement holding out the hand of friendship to the Hindu community and issued it as a joint statement with the signatures of the leading members of the Sind Separation Conference:

"We are immensely gratified to learn that the Secretary of State for India has, on behalf of His Majesty's Government, announced, on the closing day of the 3rd R.T.C. that the latter have decided definitely to constitute Sind into a separate autonomous province. The people of Sind, both Hindus and Moslems–who have the good of their country at heart – owe a deep debt of gratitude to the Government for this act of Justice and we deem it our bounden duty to offer them our heartfelt thanks for it. It is our proud privilege to express that the memory of this unique act of equity and fairplay will be treated by the present generation as well as the posterity as one of its most treasured possessions. We sincerely trust that the Government will fix a coping stone to it by giving us the same rights and privileges which are to be enjoyed by the other autonomous provinces."[2]

The Sind leaders felt that the new beginnings deserved an atmosphere of goodwill and that an appeal should be made to the Hindu political leadership to forget the bitterness of the struggle:

"It was really unfortunate that a section of our Hindu friends opposed the freedom of their country for reasons which everyone could easily understand. But we, as representatives of the majority community, feel glad to assure them that the memory of past will never be allowed to influence our future conduct towards them. We will consider it as a closed chapter and it will be our most sacred duty to give them every reasonable encouragement in all walks of their life, and the day is not far distant when the world would again find both the communities pulling on together harmoniously like the two brothers who have to sink or swim together. Now that everything is over, we earnestly appeal to the Hindu leaders of Sind to let bygones be bygones and divert, hereafter, their attention towards creating an atmosphere of peace and goodwill so that the people of Sind may be able to run the new constitution successfully."[3]

The Sind leaders also felt that the achievement of autonomy deserved a day of celebration:

"While we congratulate the Moslems of Sind for the patriotism they have displayed for having carried forth the cause of their country to a successful conclusion, we would advise them to go still one step further and give open expression to the gratitude they owe to Government. For this purpose we suggest that Friday the 20th of January be observed as 'Sind Celebration Day' when meetings should be held in which resolutions thanking the Government and assuring Hindus of their goodwill be passed. It is hoped that Moslems of Sind will rise equal to the occasion and make it a full success.

Our statement will not be complete without our thanking most warmly His Highness Sir Aga Khan and other Moslem delegates to the R.T.C., and also the Muslims of India in general and leaders like Sir Mohammed Iqbal, Mr. Jinnah and late Sir Shafee and others who have contributed to no little extent to the success of our endeavours.

Before we conclude we express our deep sense of gratitude to Almighty Allah without whose kindness our feeble efforts would never have succeeded."[4]

Even before the actual announcement of the reforms by the Prime Minister, the Government of India had constituted a Sind Administrative Committee to work out the mechanics of Sind as a separate province. The administration as well the infrastructure such as the buildings and offices necessary for the new capital of Karachi and the way in which the services, education, etc. were to be organised in the new province had to be in place for the new province to start functioning. The Chairman of the Committee was Sir Hugh Dow who was considered an expert in Sind finances, especially the administration of the Sukkur Barrage finance. Khuhro and Sir Abdullah Haroon were the Sind Muslim members on the Committee and therefore representing the majority of the people of the province. Sir Abdullah was a highly experienced public man who gave his full support to Khuhro who dealt with the detailed administrative work, the knowledge of which was required for effective participation in the Committee. There was admirable unity of views between the two men, dealing as they were with Dow who was more interested in paring the structure down to its bare bones rather than giving a good working administration to Sind. The Secretary of the Committee was Hugh Trevor Lambrick who was later to become well-known as a historian of Sind.

Dow was an arrogant officer who had a sharp mind but was convinced that he was a member of a superior race carrying the 'white man's burden' in India. He was utterly contemptuous of the 'natives'. Khuhro had already come across him in the Bombay Legislative Council where he had been a Government Whip and an official member. He had often shown open disdain for Indians, remarking that they had been taught to dress and speak by the British and expressed surprise that they dared to criticize the people who had "civilized" them. It was an irony of fate that such a man was not only associated with Sind in connection with the Sukkur Barrage but became Chairman of the Committee to set up the administration of the province and was later to become Governor of Sind. Between him and Khuhro there was a deep antipathy. Khuhro who had excellent relations with, and cordial feelings for, most of the British civil servants particularly men like Sir Leslie Wilson and Sir Henry Lawrence and the last Governor of Sind, Sir Francis Mudie, found himself completely at odds with Dow – a mutual feeling of distrust which resulted in a row during the sittings of the Committee and would have serious consequences for Khuhro later when Dow became the second Governor of Sind.

The terms of reference of the Administrative Committee were to make decisions regarding:

1. The accommodation required at Karachi for Government House, Council Chamber, Secretariat and residence for senior officials of the government.
2. The administrative arrangements that may be necessary to secure effective supervision and co-ordination of the work of the Sukkur Barrage Project.
3. Whether, and if so, what affiliation should be made with existing High Court, University, Medical, Scientific, Veterinary, Forest, Engineering, Agricultural or other institutions in any other province.
4. Whether a self contained cadre should be maintained for the services of all departments ad more particularly for the All India Services.

A questionnaire was circulated widely in Sind among the higher civil servants, intellectuals and leaders of opinion and eventually after a thorough discussion covering all shades of opinion Dow prepared a report on the administrative needs of the new province and projected the cost of the administration. The report gave the cost of the Government House and the Assembly building (14.40 lakhs) and worked out the details of government establishment as well as the cost of the Sukkur Barrage. At the insistence of Dow the costs were kept to a minimum so that some of the essential provisions of the Sukkur Barrage such as the lining of the canals were not covered. Khuhro swallowed the bitter pill of economy knowing that this was the essential condition attached to autonomy but on the issue of a university of Sind he joined issue with Dow.

The question was whether Sind should have a separate university, become affiliated with the Punjab university which some Muslim opinion felt was nearer the cultural requirements of Sind Muslims or remain affiliated with Bombay. The lack of a university had long been felt acutely in Sind and its absence was undoubtedly an important factor in the slowness with which education was advancing in the province. It had been an uphill task for the comparatively recently established and financially starved schools of Sind to match up to the standards of Bombay's well established educational institutions which had along with Madras, the highest educational standards in India. There is no doubt that to a large extent Sind's educational institutions successfully maintained the standards required by Bombay and had been able to produce outstanding scholars, notably, Dr. Gurbaxani, Dayaram Gidumal, Allama I. I. Kazi, Principal Shahani, Dr. U. M. Daudpota, Mirza Kalichbeg, Jethmal Parsram. Some had even emerged from rural schools as for instance Dr. Daudpota. The vigorous cultivation of natural talents owed much to the Bombay system. It was this system moreover which emphasised education in the language of the region and which encouraged the growth of Sindhi as the official language of Sind. In the Punjab on the contrary, the regional language was actively discouraged and the official language adopted by the government was 'Hindustani'. The Sind educators and politicians had grown up in and taken advantage of the sophistication and maturity of the oldest British Presidency in India. Now however they felt that the time for tutelage was over and the special needs of Sind could only be taken care by a Sind university.

Khuhro had been personally involved in the development of education ever since he had entered politics and had been elected member of the legislature at Bombay. He had remained a member of the Bombay University Senate and Syndicate and was also member of the Governing Body of D. J. Sind College at Karachi. He had been very active in getting a due share of scholarships and admissions for students from Sind. He had come to the conclusion that the distance and the alien atmosphere of Bombay discouraged many of the people who might otherwise have gone to the University. At this time the highest education available in Sind were the two or three colleges in Karachi and Hyderabad which were in any case dominated by Hindus – very few Muslims being able to edge their way into them. The examining authority for Matriculation and for higher degrees was Bombay University and although the situation was no longer as bad as in the 19th century when the students had to travel all the way to Bombay to give their examination, which only a few intrepid spirits could manage, it was not conducive to the rapid spread of education in Sind. The spread of education was thus handicapped by a shortage of funds and by the lack of a local university.

It was a cherished dream of Khuhro that there should be a university in Sind. The present changes he thought were an ideal opportunity to establish one and he duly put up the proposal in the Committee. Characteristically he had done his preparations well. He had stretched the terms of reference to get opinions on the need for a university in Sind. He had asked his friends among the educational experts and university teachers like Dr. Gurbaxani the renowned scholar, editor of the *Shah Jo Risalo*,[5] to write in his opinions on the matter to the Committee.

Dr. Gurbaxani wrote a very strong note advocating a university for Sind. He gave as his arguments the fact that

"there are no institutions ... in the world which are situated so far away from the parent university as are the colleges and schools of Sind from the University of Bombay. Such a position naturally acts adversely on the intellectual advancement of the province. The very existence of a university in their midst acts a stimulus in creating an intellectual atmosphere. The absence of such an atmosphere in Sind, in spite of its having colleges and numerous schools for so many years past, far from being a reason against establishing a university is, to my mind, the soundest argument for having one immediately."[6]

He argued further that Sind was very inadequately represented on the Senate, Syndicate, and in the number of Fellows of the University and thus could not exercise any influence on the policy of that University. The needs of Sind were not met and

"we are carried along the current of policies and courses of studies laid down by the University of Bombay primarily in reference to the peculiar needs of Bombay itself or its neighbouring districts." He pointed out the difficulties of the post-graduate students who were required to do exactly what was done at

Bombay and Poona "irrespective of our fitness or equipment for the work undertaken." And yet were Sind free to act in the matter "it could well foster research on lines best suited to its genius, e.g. the history of the province, Oriental languages, its geology, its antiquities, etc., all of which await an army of scholars. In short we must investigate and bring together what could be discovered of Sind, so as to make a contribution to the thought and learning of India. I know of the existence of at least a couple of private collections of invaluable Oriental manuscripts, literary, philosophical, theological and historical which may serve well for the nucleus of a first rate library, even as the collection of Sir Thomas Bodley did in the case of the Bodleian at Oxford."[7]

"Sind", he went on:

"is an old province, perhaps the most ancient in India. It has a history, traditions and a culture of its own. Its soil and stones could be compelled to reveal movements and geological formations of the hoary past. Its races and its language possesses a distinct Oriental bias. All this remains unexplored and no attention paid to the systematic study of Arabic, Persian or Sindhi with all its philological wealth.

A university of our own making for the 'free play of the natural mind' of Sind must quicken our natural growth and impart a wider outlook both to our teachers and young men. To discover, to increase and to diffuse knowledge shall be our main purpose; and if we did that we would soon have an atmosphere in which we could work our political institutions to the real benefit of the people of this province."

To the question whether Sind could be affiliated to any other university if it could not have one of its own he replied:

"If Sind, for any reason, cannot have a university of its own, I would much rather it continued its connection with Bombay, Punjab being the only other university to which affiliation may be sought on grounds of proximity. This move, however will be retrograde, for it is a matter of common knowledge that the University of Punjab in many matters is behind the University of Bombay. Although it possesses the reputation of promoting Oriental culture, it does not give due importance to the critical method of study which is indispensable to the proper development of Oriental research.

I am strongly of the opinion that the sooner we have our own University the better. We shall then be free to develop on the lines best suited to the genius and needs of the people of this province."[8]

Khuhro who had been a student of Gurbaxani and remained a lifelong friend and neighbour, fully shared his views regarding the importance of a university in promoting education in Sind. He stressed the importance of the Committee's recommending the setting up of university as soon as possible. Dow opposed this proposal. His motive may possibly have been to save money as his role on the Committee was mainly to cut down costs wherever possible so that expeniture by the Government of India was at a minimum, but he put his objections in a very offensive way, arguing that a university would be premature in Sind which was too backward a region for such a sophisticated educational institution. He said that he could only see a university in Sind after many years. That at least two educationists from England, 'dedicated to the cause of humanity'[9] should come and teach the youth and create a suitable intellectual atmosphere by setting up schools and thus prepare the ground for the establishment of a university. Khuhro protested strongly at Dow's remarks and demanded an apology on behalf of the Sindhi people but Dow though disconcerted by this reaction from a 'native' was not going to back down immediately. On Dow's refusal to take back his remarks Khuhro staged a walk out – an unprecedented action in a Committee of this kind.

Though in his report Dow did not recommend a university, he felt obliged to remove his remarks and give financial reasons for not putting up a university in Sind. Dow had backed down somewhat in the face of the pressure but he was not to forget the insult he felt he had suffered with the walk out. He would bide his time to get his revenge on Khuhro.

The university, put off by Dow for the present, would be delayed for a good number of years by the outbreak of World War II and it was not till the governorship of Mudie in 1945 that the go ahead would be given. It was eventually be established in 1946. In the intervening years Sind continued to be affiliated to Bombay University, a connection that was at least beneficial in keeping high academic standards in Sind's educational institutions, although it seriously impeded the spread of education in the province.

The other issue which proved to be controversial was whether Sind should have an independent cadre of services. It became apparent quite soon that with the need to keep down the expenses of administration an independent service cadre was out of the question for the time being. The question therefore was whether the connection with Bombay should continue or a new connection should be made with the Punjab, a majority Muslim province, also a province dependent largely on irrigation of the Indus basin, and therefore, it was argued, with similar experience and requirements to those of Sind. The answers elicited by the questionnaire threw doubts on what seemed like an obvious solution. Many thoughtful people gave their opinion that to continue with Bombay would be in the best interests of Sind. In the course of gathering opinion and also in order to get a genuine Punjab opinion Khuhro wrote to a number of Punjab personalities including Sir Mohammed Iqbal who had been so helpful during the Round Table Conferences, for his opinion on these questions:

"8-1-1934"

My dear Sir Mahommed,
You are aware that the Government of India have appointed an Administrative Committee which will make recommendations regarding certain administrative problems incidental to Separation of Sind. The Committee is now holding its sessions in Karachi and I happen to be one of its members. There is a proposal that the Sind Arts, Engineering and other institutions should after separation be affiliated with the University of the Punjab. This demand has been put forth by the Moslems of Sind perhaps as they feel that it will be more economical and beneficial from the Moslem point of view. I would like to know your views in this regard and if possible you may even kindly direct somebody connected with the University of Punjab to send me a note describing the outstanding features of that University on which I may

base my case for affiliation. He may also apprise me of the possible terms on which the University would take up the Sind institutions. I feel that by coming in close touch with the Moslems of the Punjab our people might get a better training. We are also thinking of connecting the Sind cadre of superior services with that of the Punjab but we are told that the Punjab civilians are more autocratic in their outlook and it might be difficult for the people of Sind to manage them. I shall be grateful if you kindly let me know your views on this question as well.

These are two very important points and I hope you will kindly favour me with your views at your earliest convenience."[10]

Allama Iqbal perhaps feeling himself not fully familiar with the points at issue consulted his close friend Allama Yusuf Ali, the great scholar, translator of the Holy Quran and political worker, who had been to Sind a number of times and had presided over the Sind Azad Conference held at Hyderabad only a year earlier. Allama Yusuf Ali sent his thoughtful and well considered views to Iqbal who passed them on to Khuhro with a covering note:

"My dear Khan Bahadur,

I enclose a reply to your questions with which I fully agree. I am glad you sent this question to me. Mr. Yusuf Ali, as you will see, is the best person to judge the matter, and as he happened to be here I thought it fit to consult him. Please note that this letter is meant only for private use and not for publication.

yours sincerely,
Mohammed Iqbal."

Allama Yusuf Ali's letter was the sincerest possible advice he could give, beyond superficial considerations:

"My dear Sir Mohd.,

Here is my opinion on the proposals contained in K. B. Khuhro's letter, which I return for reference.

I would not advise the Muslims of Sind to transfer the affiliation of their Arts, Engineering and other educational institutions from Bombay to the Punjab. Ultimately no doubt Sind will try to have its own university, but for the present, in order to save money, they would do better to keep their affiliation to Bombay. In the matter of

Engineering, Bombay is far in advance of the Punjab...

I would advise our Sindhi friends to have nothing to do with the Punjab University. They could appoint a strong Muslim Director of Education or Education Minister to foster Muslim as well as general education, keep the idea of an independent university before the people. K. B. Khuhro is quite right in his estimate of the Punjab civilians. By their history and training they would be so autocratic that Sind would repent of ever having asked them to ride on its back. Here again for cadre purposes they would do better to remain in touch with Bombay until they can be self sufficient. In the distant future I see Baluchistan's destiny also linked with Sind.

A. Yusuf Ali"[11]

Khuhro had also written to Sir Fazle Husain and Sir Firoze Khan Noon and from both of them he received the opinion that Sind should join up with the Punjab both for university and service cadre purposes. But it was clear that Allamas Iqbal and Yusuf Ali were going beyond mere politics and were advising in the best interests of Sind. With this advice in hand Khuhro opted for keeping the link with Bombay.

With the announcement of the Indian Constitutional Reforms 1935 (Government of India Act of 1935, Clause 46), Sind was to be constituted as an autonomous province. On 23 January 1936 the Orders in Council were announced fixing the date for separation as 1st April 1936.

The struggle for separation had lasted well over twenty years and was a brilliant example of the unity of purpose and consistent struggle by the political leadership of Sind. In the phase of the struggle lasting from 1928 to 1935 particularly, the fight had been relentless and the outcome was by no means certain. In this phase the role played by Khuhro was predominant and without his work and leadership the fight may well have been lost.

With the coming of autonomy and an elected legislature in 1937 Sind had a parliament which was able to devote all its time to the affairs of the province. From 1936 to 1947 in spite of the many problems created by World War II and communal bitterness, Sind enjoyed a new sense of freedom. Many reforms were brought in by the legislature which gave relief to the people and a great deal of work was taken in hand to develop the province in terms of roads and communications including the port and airport facilities. Quite contrary to the expectations of the bureaucracy the Sukkur Barrage debt was paid off during the war years through enhanced prices for agricultural goods and Sind prospered through the extension of irrigation of the Barrage as well as the rise in prices and although much was siphoned off by the Government of India through excessive taxation, surplus funds became available for 'nation building' activities.

There is no doubt that the separation of Sind from the Bombay Presidency and its constitution as a fully fledged province was the most significant event in the process that led to the creation of Pakistan. If there had been no autonomous Sind with its 75% Muslim population, if Sind had continued as part of the huge Bombay Presidency with its multi-racial, multi-linguistic and multi-religious population, the case for partition would have been considerably, even fatally, weaker. Punjab and Bengal had bare Muslim majorities and until 1947 the Punjab had a strong Unionist government which had the support of Hindus and Sikhs and was not inclined to support the demand for Pakistan. Baluchistan, a virtual confederacy of autonomous tribes, was still ruled by an Agent to the Governor General and its reforms were a considerable way off. The North West Frontier Province was given autonomy but its most popular organised party, Khudai Khidmatgar, under the leadership of the 'Frontier Gandhi', Khan Abdul Ghaffar Khan, was firmly behind Congress and remained so till 1947.

The Muslims of the provinces where they were in minority were vociferous in their support of All India Muslim League which acted as their pressure group against the might of Congress and in what was a curious idealistic gesture, they also supported the demand for Pakistan. They were however in a small minority and even in the provinces where they were highly vocal they were only about 20% of the population. Their voice therefore did not carry much weight and was not relevant to the eventual creation of Pakistan. It was the vote of the majority Muslim provinces which would decide the fate of Pakistan and without the unequivocal support of Sind it is difficult to see how the new state could come into being. From 1938 to 1947 therefore the mainstay of the Pakistan demand was the existence of autonomous Sind.

LARKANA MADRESSAH (circa 1912)
Right to Left. Front Row: 2. Dost Mohammed Qadiri. 3. Ghulam Sarwar Qadiri. 4. Kazi Jan Mohammed (Principal). 5. Sayed Subhan Ali Shah. 6. Ghulam Hussain Shaikh, 7. Nawaz Ali (Niaz). 8. Mr. Sadiq Ali. *Third Row*: 1. U. M. Daudpoto. 2. Sardar Wahid Baksh Bhutto. 3. Lutfullah Unar. 6. Ghulam Rasul Phull. 9. Abdul Karim Unar. *Fourth Row: Fourth from Right*, Mohammed Ayub Khuhro.

With first cousin Dost Mohammed (circa 1915).

With Uncle *Wadero* Jan Mohammed.

At a *shikar* camp in Phulloo, Khairpur.

'At Home' in honour of Khuhro on his election victory, with D. C. Larkana and K. B. Shahnawaz Bhutto, 1923.

Music Party by H. H. Mir Ali Nawaz Talpur in honour of Commissioner-in-Sind. Khuhro on extreme left.

Dinner Party by H. H. Mir Ali Nawaz Talpur of Khairpur, Khuhro on the right hand side of the table.

Khuhro's Larkana house (circa 1925).

Members of the Bombay Legislative Council, 1924.

Garden Party hosted by Khuhro in honour of Governor Bombay, Sir Leslie Wilson and Lady Wilson.

Khuhro receiving Sir Frederick Sykes at Karachi Club.

Garden Party hosted by Khuhro in honour of Governor Bombay, Sir Frederick Sykes and Lady Sykes at the Karachi Club, 1932.

Dinner in honour of the opening of the Sukkur Barrage at Karachi Gymkhana, 1932.

Garden Party at Faiz Mahal, Khairpur (circa 1932).

Departure for London by aeroplane, 1933.

The Sind Conference, 1932.

The Sind Administrative Committee, 1933.

BOOK II
(1936–1946)

8

MAKING AUTONOMY WORK

Khuhro said his farewells in Bombay to friends and officials including a sceptical Brabourne and came back to Karachi in time for the inauguration of the new province on 1 April 1936. He was triumphant and optimistic. Not yet thirty five years of age he had a number of major, even heroic achievements to his credit in his dozen or so years in political life. He had worked hard for all of those years to represent his province and his community and had been rewarded with respect and recognition inside and outside the province. He had appeared for the Muslims of Sind at the Round Table Conference Sub-Committee on Sind and had led the fight for separation against a powerful and well organised opposition. He could be excused for feeling that the main political struggle was over and that the path would now be smooth for all the work that needed to be done; the problems of the people would now be solved on the spot by their own representatives working through a majority in the legislature. The next ten years were to be a rude awakening.

His home life was happy. His first wife, a first cousin, had died in child birth in 1930. He had married again in 1933 the daughter of Khan Sahib Mohammed Parial Panhwar of a well-known family of Dadu district. Khan Sahib Mohammed Parial belonged to an early batch of Sindhis who were educated in English and were the product of the Sind Madressah. He entered government service and was Mir Munshi to the Commissioner-in-Sind, Naib Vazir in Khairpur State and then Mukhtiarkar. His chances of further advancement were blighted by his well-known nationalist sympathies and his friendship with Ghulam Mohammed Bhurgri. This earned him the displeasure of Sir Henry Lawrence and he retired from service without achieving the Deputy Collectorship or Collectorship which he could have expected with his record of service and which some of his colleagues did achieve with much less ability but with greater prudence in friendships. Khan Sahib Panhwar was a deeply religious, disciplined and upright person, a conscientious civil servant and a paterfamilias in the manner of 19th century gentlemen. He took a deep interest in Khuhro's career and was extremely supportive throughout the ups and downs in his career. Khuhro's wife, Fatima, thirteen years his junior, was to prove a great support and stay throughout his life and especially during his difficult and trying political career.

Khuhro spent a considerable amount of time in his village and in Larkana dealing with his zamindari work and keeping up with his friends. He continued his interest in the poetry circle with his neighbours the Qadiris and attend *mushairas* (poetry sittings) whenever he was in Larkana. His house was the focus of public interest whenever he was in town. Located in Empire Road, facing the old Gharra canal and the *Kafila Sarai* (caravan serai), it was still almost in open country. This was reputed to be the place where Nadir Shah had encamped during his campaign in Sind in the earlier part of the 18th century.

Every morning Khuhro would go for a ride on the lands. By eight o'clock he would sit on the open terrace in front of the house, with only a small ornamental wall dividing it from the street, and receive visitors and petitioners. Again in the evening he would sit there in the cool of the day with callers which included important zamindars of the district as well as ordinary people who had travelled from around the district and elsewhere to meet him and would know they would be sure to see him. Khuhro had acquired the reputation of being a practical man of few words. He would listen to problems, quickly getting to the heart of the matter and take whatever action was needed immediately. In the early 'thirties there was still no telephone in Larkana so the problem would be dealt with by sending a *chit* to the officer concerned – or immediate orders to the factotum present – or if the problem had to be dealt with in Karachi or Bombay due note would be taken and the matter dealt with at the first available opportunity. If the problem could not be solved, Khuhro would not make promises or hedge about but immediatey tell the person that this could not be done. This kind of bluntness was quite unusual, evasions and circumlocutions being the norm with public men even when the task was impossible. Khuhro did not believe in giving anyone false hopes.

So although he was one of the few people in public life who could be relied on to be of practical help and would do all he could for friend, acquaintance and even foe, he acquired the reputation of being blunt to the point of rudeness. His time was fully organised and occupied, another unusual characteristic in the society in which he lived, so he had little time or appetite for casual socializing. He was regarded with some awe by those who did not know him well.

Khuhro was at this time fairly slim and although not tall had a very authoritative presence. He exuded energy, had tremendous powers of concentration, an incisive mind and wasted few words. His upbringing and status in life had given him confidence as second nature and his already vast experience of political life had re-inforced that basic confidence so that he was one of the few people in public life, in Sind certainly, and even in the sub-continent, who would deal with officialdom on equal terms – a fact not always appreciated by the latter.

While Khuhro was attending the Legislative Council at Bombay he was spending only a small amount of time in Karachi, the provincial headquarters, usually stopping over for official or public business. He did not own a house there and usually stayed at the Carlton Hotel run by an English woman. This was the most convenient hotel for up country people and served the best 'European style' food. After his marriage in 1933 Khuhro had rented a spacious flat in Imperial Man-sions on Kutchery Road but most of his time was spent in Larkana and the village. Now as Karachi became the capital of the autonomous province of Sind, Khuhro felt he needed a house there since he would be spending a substantial part of the time there. He bought a plot of land in the newly developed Muslim Colony, a small area consisting of about fourteen plots one side of a square surrounding a park–the Patel Park – off Bunder Road Extension. This area had been allotted for the use of Muslims officials but well-known public men had also been allotted land to build houses there. Muslim Colony was sandwiched between a much larger Parsi Colony on one side and the vast Amil Colony for upper class Hindus on the other. Khuhro had an elegant small house in the 'thirties colonial style built on his 1,000 square yards facing the park and in due course 124, Muslim Colony, became a very well-known address in the political life of Sind. His neighbours in Muslim Colony included G. M. Syed,"the stormy petrel" of Sind politics only two doors away. Sir Shahnawaz Bhutto at the back, and other well-known political and well placed Muslim bureaucrats and politicians.

In comparison with Bombay, Karachi was a small, quiet, sleepy town. The oldest part of the town – the pre British Karachi were the congested areas of Mithadar and Kharadar as well as the fishing village of Lyari. With the coming of the British the harbour was dredged and modernised and the Napier Mole Bridge was constructed giving direct access from the town to the Keamari harbour. Bunder Road was laid out as the main artery between the harbour and the expanding city. It also was the dividing line between the old city and the British official quarters, government buildings, the cantonement and the Civil Lines. It was further along Bunder Road, off the 'Extension' that the new 'colonies' housing the new middle classes and officials were laid out neatly in squares and comfortably wide streets. A tram went up to Soldier Bazar which served the new colonies. Further along there was the Jail which marked the end of the new Karachi and from where there was the open hilly country side.

When Khuhro started to spend more time in Karachi from the mid 'thirties on, he was still able to give time to his family taking his wife and small daughters out to picnics on the hills after the rains, looking for mushrooms on the hillsides, taking a boat out to Manora island on Sundays or going down to Clifton on a free evening to walk down the Kothari Parade, with the inducement of ice cream at the café at the bottom of the Parade. On the way back to the town there could be a stop at the Café Grand, run by a German couple, with wonderful home made ice cream and cakes eaten out of fine bone china and silver plated tea pots and cutlery. Khuhro had acquired an Austin car which thrilled the children because it had small tables which could be let out at the back where one could put out picnic food. He liked having his children around, taking them in the car even when was calling on official or political business – the children staying put in the car, listening to tall tales and fairy stories from the chauffer or watching the police guard in his little wooden hut at the doors of official residences.

At this time Khuhro's wife was still in *purdah* as were most of her contemporaries. Only a few leading women political and social hostesses like Lady Haroon, Lady Hidayetullah and Begum Tayyabji went about unveiled and certainly no wife of a zamindar could be seen publicly unveiled. Lady Haroon would tease Khuhro's wife saying "Oh Begum Khuhro is in purdah but not from shopkeepers of Elphinstone Street."

Karachi was a clean and comfortable town with a very low incidence of crime and a population of about 400,000. Khuhro's children were enrolled in nearby schools from where they could walk back and forth. Occasionally they would go for a tram ride with a servant up to Saddar and have ice cream at Gulzar hotel at the top of Elphinstone Street or be taken to a film, but usually it was the swings in Patel Park from where they could be summoned easily at meal times. Father's coming home was eagerly looked forward to–there were no regular hours for his work or leisure and quite often he would come and say–"The ministry has fallen today.", the children assuming that the ministry was some kind of mud brick wall which fell down ever so often.

In October 1938 the first son was born to Khuhro after three daughters. It was an occasion for great rejoicing in the family and the whole zamindari. The boy was named Shah Mohammed after Khuhro's father and was followed by another three sons- altogether Khuhro had seven children, one daughter from his first wife and two daughters and four sons from his second wife.

On 1 April 1936 the new Governor of Sind arrived in Karachi. Sir Lancelot Graham was a senior I.C.S. officer but of very mediocre ability. As one of the smallest provinces of India and the most newly formed Sind had no lobby in the Centre to argue for a better officer and thus had to make do with the second best. Sind was extremely unfortunate in her governors and most of the next ten years had top executives who were unable to comprehend the province they were ruling and quite unused to dealing with the delicate task of conducting a fledgling democratic government in a newly self-governing province. A mixture of arrogance and obtuseness Sir Lancelot Graham's shortcomings as Governor were soon to become obvious even to the Viceroy and the Secretary of State. Even before Graham had arrived in Karachi the Viceroy was writing to Lord Zetland, the Secretary of State about the inflated ideas the new Governor had about his position:

> "Lancelot Graham will soon be arriving home, and I think I ought to warn you that he has got somewhat extravagant ideas about the establishment of the Government House in Sind. I think it would be a good thing, if he broaches the subject, if you would impress upon him the necessity for keeping his demands within reasonable limits.[1]

By the time Graham had been Governor for a few years and the Viceroy had some experience of his calibre he was writing:

> "...there is a woolliness of mind about him which makes him a little difficult to deal with; the more so as I do not think that he for a moment suspects that he is anything but a model in regard either to his reports or as to his handling of the province."[2]

For the interim period before an elected government could take over Bhutto, who had been Minister in Bombay was appointed as, Advisor to the Government. An Advisory Council was formed to assist the Governor and Khuhro was one of the members of this Council. The administrative staff of Sind was kept fairly skeletal. Apart from the Governor there was Gibson the Revenue Commissioner, and three other Secretary level officials including Lambrick. The Chief Secretary was a Hindu official, Kripalani, who was on very close terms with Bhutto and according to Graham who himself was very happy with Bhutto—

"Shahnawaz has been very helpful and very loyal to me even at the risk of being charged with being in Kripalani's pocket" and went on to mention the rivalry between Bhutto and Hidayetullah:

"According to Ghulam Hussain Sind is being governed by Kripalani but I don't think that is quite true. I tried to take Shahnawaz and Ghulam Hussain in double harness – but failed..."[3]

Full of goodwill as he was for both the knights of Sind even at this early date of his tenure in Sind, Graham had mysteriously acquired a prejudice against Khuhro which appears from his letter written to Brabourne early in 1937 barely a few months after his arrival in Sind and before really he had any experience of Sind and its politicians and therefore obviously planted in his mind by those opposed to Khuhro. Writing to the Governor about the appointment of a new Collector for Larkana replacing Drew, an Englishman, he says:

"I want to put in a friendly protest against Panjabi sent to relieve Drew as Collector of Larkana... Panjabi has according to Kripalani–a reputation of being an intriguer, of having played the part of jackal to Ghulam Hussain's lion and of having been very intimate with Khuhro. To send Punjabi to Larkana, will if Kripalani's allegations have any substance – be a mistake, it will also be a direct encouragement to Khuhro – *whom Drew has been trying unsuccessfully to break* (author's italics) and direct thrust at Shahnawaz who has most, if not all of his lands in the Larkana District. I feel there is a great deal in this point ...

In brief then I want an Englishman for Larkana, and if I can't have one I should prefer a Muslim to a Hindu and if there's no Muslim to fit the bill I want a Hindu who is not Punjabi. You will realise how difficult it was for Kripalani to put these objections to me – *and I am sure that you would not like to do anything which would make life easier for Khuhro or more difficult for Shahnawaz* (author's italics)[4]

Thus from the start Graham had a prejudice against Khuhro perhaps following from Brabourne's attitude as the letter indicates. This official hostility which had pursued Khuhro through most of his political career while Sind was part of Bombay Presidency would follow him throughout the period of autonomy and then after independence. The major reason for it was Khuhro's refusal to adopt a subservient role to the bureaucrats or to recognize that he had to follow a certain pattern of behaviour as a member of the subject race. Those who did so were eminently successful in gaining official favour and avoiding trouble but Khuhro was impelled to fight for his people and suffered displeasure from on high for doing so.

Khuhro had great hopes for the political future of autonomous Sind. The successful organisation and conduct of the battle for separation had raised the political consciousness of the province and given the Muslim leaders experience of political organisation and an awareness of the issues that concerned the future welfare of Sind. As one writer sums up the position of the Sind Muslim leaders just after the separation of the province:

"Upon the conclusion of the Sind separation movement, the Sindhi Muslim leadership appeared to have reached a pinnacle of political success: they had achieved a broad measure of unity among themselves, they had established close relations with the all-India Muslim leadership and they stood to become the new brokers of power in the new autonomous province of Sind. The question remained: would the Muslim leadership in Sind manage to maintain and consolidate their position of political strength or would they instead prove unequal to the task of shouldering the burden of leadership and responsibility."[5]

Of all the political leaders Khuhro was the one most conscious of these issues, having fought for them for over a decade inside and outside the Bombay Legislative Council. In keeping with his personality and his experience his approach was basically practical. He was not the man to be carried away by the dream of the ideal but he also felt that few problems were impossible of solution. He liked to think of himself as the man who got things done and from his experience of the separation struggle felt that even difficult goals could be achieved with hard work and persistence. He was well aware of the fact that a useful programme could only be implemented through a well organised and disciplined party. In his view the easiest course would be to use the basic consensus that already existed in the Sind Azad Conference structure which had been set up in 1932 of which Khuhro was the Vice-Chairman. Accordingly even before the formal inauguration of autonomy he asked for a meeting of the Sind Azad Conference. The meeting was held in the third week of August 1935 and it was decided that now autonomy had been achieved a new chapter of communal harmony must begin in Sind and that first of all the new party must be organized along non communal lines.

Khuhro also felt that the most important issue and the one that deserved the earliest attention was the rapidly declining condition of the agriculturists. Small landowners and owner cultivators particularly were losing their lands rapidly with the operation of the civil laws. He had spent a good deal of time and energy on trying to get corrective legislation for the plight of the indebted cultivator and now with the achievement of autonomy felt that this must be the priority for the legislature and the administration of the new province. Keeping the Punjab model of the highly successful Unionist Party in view, the meeting decided that the Sind Azad Conference would convert itself into a new political party

"on democratic lines and non-communal grounds to safeguard the interests of the agriculturists in particular and the whole province in general."[6]

These plans and the proposed party was however sabotaged by the personal rivalries which became immediately apparent. In a few days, G. M. Syed threw a spanner in the works by denouncing the SAC meeting as lacking a quorum and accusing Khuhro of trying to dominate it. Not for the last time Syed sabotaged a perfectly reasonable scheme partly because he lacked enough experience of administration or enough appreciation of reality to judge what was possible and what was not. Thus the first attempt to conserve the gains of the separation struggle and turn them into a constructive programme for the autonomous province was shot down in haste. Now the field was wide open and the Sind leaders were free to make whatever bid they could for the leadership of parties.

Shaikh Abdul Majid set up his Sind Azad Party which despite its early enthusiastic organisation was to prove marginal in Sind politics. This was the first party to affiliate itself with Muslim League which Jinnah was trying to organise in anticipation of the new constitution with enhanced provincial autonomy. Majid's efforts to organise his party and to work in co-operation with Muslim League did not prove successful and Muslim League was relegated to the background while parties with a provincial base and interests were able to make reasonable headway.

Khuhro's efforts to get a continuance of Sind Azad Conference having foundered, the most prominent leaders associated with the separation struggle met to try and work out some organisational arrangement for the forthcoming elections.

Times of India reported that Abdullah Haroon was making efforts to set up a party along the lines of the Unionist Party of the Punjab with an agrarian base and along non communal lines. Invitations and a proposed form of constitutions marked 'strictly confidential' had been sent out. Difficulties were anticipated because of the known rivalry between Sir Shahnawaz Bhutto and Sir Ghulam Hussain Hidayetullah on the one hand and the bitter feud between Hidayetullah and Haroon on the other. The proposed meeting was an effort to reconcile the different rivals in the common cause.

Thus it was in June 1936, nearly a year after Khuhro's effort to organise a party that the Sind leaders met at Haroon's house. Among those who attended the meeting were Hidayetullah, Bhutto, Khuhro, Allah Baksh Soomro, G. M. Syed, Miran Mohammed Shah and Hatim Alavi. A party programme was discussed and there was general consensus. Some discussions took place about possible candidates to be fielded by the party. The programme of the party was agrarian oriented reflecting the main concerns of Sind political leadership to redress the indebtedness of the agricultural sector. The party was inaugurated with a splash at Haroon's house where all the important officials from the Governor down, as well as the political leadership were present.

But this attempt to set up a party also foundered as there were too many ambitious personalities involved. The main rivalry being between Bhutto and Hidayetullah both aiming to be the first premier of the province.

After this failure the next attempt to set up a political organisation came at the end of October 1936 when once again a meeting was arranged at Haroon's house and was attended by all the important leaders. There appeared to be consensus and a programme was announced which was essentially the same as the earlier one. Office bearers were chosen with Haroon as party leader, Bhutto and Hidayetullah as Deputy Leaders and Gazdar and Khuhro as Secretaries. At the last minute Sayed Miran Mohammed Shah was taken on as representative of the Sayed group. At this point disagreement arose over the question of the representation of two powerful 'kinship' groups of central Sind.

Sayeds were an important group in the politics of Sind. Well established Sayed families spread over both sides of the river Indus. On the right bank the village of Sann was the headquarters of G. M. Syed, the most important of the political Sayeds and on the left bank prominent Sayed families were established from Nawabshah south and west to Hyderabad and Mirpurkhas. With the achievement of autonomy they came into prominence as an important political group and their natural leader was G. M. Syed who had already established himself as a front ranking politician. Now with the establishment of the new Muslim political party he wanted representation for the Sayed group and the person he nominated was Sayed Miran Mohammed Shah who had played a positive part in the separation struggle by writing the Note of Dissent in the findings of the Simon Commission.

Equally important politically were the Talpurs, the former rulers of Sind and holders of *jagirs*. They were extremely influential in the central districts. The different branches of Talpurs were spread in the districts of Hyderabad, Mirpurkhas or Tharparkar and to some extent in Khairpur. As a group they were inclined to support Hidayetullah and were considered opposed to the Sayeds. Now that Miran Mohammed Shah was nominated as one of the Vice Presidents as a Sayed group nominee it became obligatory that a Mir also become an office bearer. This would also increase the representation of the Hidayetullah group. Khuhro proposed that as offices were being distributed on the basis of different groupings, Sayed Noor Mohammed Shah, representative of the powerful Sayed family of Nawabshah who had been a member of the Bombay Legislative Council and was a supporter of Khuhro, should also get one.

Moreover it was an open secret that Haroon was about to hand over the leadership of the party to Bhutto, a change which was absolutely unpalatable to Hidayetullah. As far as Khuhro was concerned he was able to control any antagonism he might feel for his Larkana colleague and work together with him for a greater cause as he had done in the past, but lately Bhutto had played an ambiguous role in the separation struggle and Khuhro was disillusioned with his politics. On the whole therefore he preferred not to have Bhutto for party leader.

When a compromise could not be reached Hidayetullah left the gathering and together with Khuhro, announced his own party – the Muslim Democratic Party. Hidayetullah, although without a personal political base had gained considerable influence in Sind through his long tenure of power and his diplomatic and political skills while Khuhro ofcourse had a well established political base throughout Sind. The Mir group added its influence from central Sind thus potentially at least a political group as feasible as any other was formed.

It was clear that the precious unity of the struggle for separation was lost, dissolving into rival factions competing for power. The political leaders were accused of lacking any ideological commitment and of merely being interested in office. This charge however was less than fair. The parties as they evolved had definite ideas about the economic and social programmes they wanted to follow. Both the United Party and the Muslim Democratic Party had as their priority the amelioration of the condition of the agriculture of the province and of the rural population, the overwhelming majority of which was Muslim and extremely backward. Thus the aim of both these parties was on the right target as far as the realities of the conditions in Sind were concerned but their methods were unknown. It remained to be seen how far they would be true to their declared aims and how much distracted they would be by their personal and clan rivalries.

The Sind politicians were also criticised for their isolation from all India politics and being mainly concerned with provincial matters. It was certainly true that after the achievement of autonomy the Sindhi politicians who had been playing on the all Indian stage during the Khilafat movement and the separation struggle, confined themselves mainly to provincial interests but there was solid justification for this attitude. After the enactment of the Government of India Act of 1935 and the establishment of provincial autonomy, politicians in India tended to turn away from the Centre and concentrate on trying out the new powers now given to them in their own backyards. That after all was their legitimate first concern – working for the betterment of their own people and attending to matters which had been overlooked in all the years of distant irresponsible government. This was how political life was being arranged in the neighbouring great province of the Punjab where the political and communal harmony achieved under the Unionist Party was the envy of other provinces. In fact Sind tried a number of times to set up a party modelled after the Unionist Party in the Punjab but could not succeed as the social situation in Sind was different . The communal divide between Muslim and Hindu was also the social divide between the rural and urban.

However the minority communities which lacked confidence or political leverage initially looked outside the provinces to all India organisations to weigh in on their side. Thus the Hindus in Sind looked to Congress to support them in local politics and kept the Party alive in Sind in order to use its all India clout in their favour. Similarly All India Muslim League was supported and used by the Muslims of the provinces in which they were a minority mainly the United Provinces, Bihar, and the Central Provinces. Through their overwhelming influence in the organisation and by finding the powerful advocacy of an able lawyer like Jinnah they were able to shape the policies of Muslim League to their taste and requirement which resulted in the resistance Muslim League initially met in the Muslim majority provinces. It was only when the obstacles to their programme became obvious that the Muslims of the majority provinces turned to all India organisations, notably the Muslim League.

Thus on the eve of the elections there were three main parties representing the Muslims of Sind. Although the United Party claimed to be open to both Muslims and Hindus, few Hindus took advantage of that concession. The three parties were the United Party under the leadership of Abdullah Haroon and Sir Shahnawaz Bhutto. The Muslim Democratic Party with Sir Ghulam Hussain Hidayetullah and Khuhro; and the Sind Azad Party of Shaikh Abdul Majid.

The Hindus had their own organisations, some of them owing allegiance to All India Congress and others Sind based such as Sind Hindu Sabha and the Hindu Independents. No Hindu contested on the ticket of any of the three major parties. Elections were duly held at the beginning of 1937. Franchise was restricted to those who paid a minimum land revenue or house tax although it had been greatly extended and voting qualifications had been lowered since Bombay where Sind had sent thirteen members to the Legislative Council, nine from rural and four from urban areas.

The new Sind Legislative Assembly was to be a house of sixty members. In accordance with the Communal Award which became part of the arrangements of the Act of 1935 'weightage' and 'separate electorates' were to continue to be part of the constitution for the time being. Because of the constitutional provision of 'weightage' which gave greater representation to minorities in provincial legislatures at the expense of the majority communities, the majority in Sind which was that of Muslims was effectively reduced in the legislature and made marginal instead of absolute which their numbers warranted. This fact had far reaching implications for the politics of the province. According to population percentage Muslims were entitled to at least 42 seats out of 60, a very comfortable majority. As it was Muslims got thirty four seats, the rest being divided into nineteen general (non Muslim) seats, two European, two landholders, one labour and two representatives of the Chamber of Commerce. A further disadvantage for the Muslims was that while the average Muslim constituency was fixed for a population of 87,353 the general contituency was fixed for the much smaller population of 58,001. Moreover the size of a Muslim constituency was more than double (3089 square miles) that of a general constituency (1495 square miles) and the average number of voters in a General constituency was just over half that in a Muslim constituency.

This considerable cut in the size of its representation was the price that the Muslims of the majority provinces were paying so that the Muslims of the minority provinces should have an inflated representation. The arrangement had been agreed to even in the 1919 reforms so that the Muslim majority provinces had been sacrificing their advantage to enable the Muslims of minority provinces to gain more representation than was their due. At best this arrangement was unsatisfactory because the Muslims of majority provinces lost their strength and were unable to form strong and stable governments and to put through necessary and urgent legislation. They had to spend a great deal of time on political manoeuvrings which could have been spent on solid work. The results in Sind were particularly tragic. Because of the weightage requirements Muslims only had a bare majority and the highly motivated Hindus could easily manipulate a number of Muslim members to form governments of their choice.

Khuhro who had worked in the Bombay Council in a well-knit and loyal group of Muslim members and had worked for separation again with a largely united and dedicated group of politicians for several years at a stretch, was to find this floating number of members a novel and disillusioning experience. His expectation that separation and autonomy would mean concentrating on the programme of social and economic betterment of the backward majority community without the distraction of the affairs of a large Presidency was to come to nought as a new phenomenon of uncommitted elected members made their personal advancement their first priority. The objectives of autonomy were to disappear like a mirage and then to reappear in the shape of Pakistan. But these were to be the experiences of the next ten years and meanwhile there were the elections to be organised.

The method of elections was also changed in the new constitution and the constituencies were no longer multiple as they had been for the Bombay Council. Thus Khuhro was contesting from his constituency of Larkana taluka where he hoped to come in unopposed. However the Shahnawaz Bhutto group expecting that Khuhro would oppose them, set up a candidate against him to keep him occupied in his own election. As a matter of general principle and practical sense

Khuhro avoided as far as he could any strong differences with Sir Shahnawaz and up to 1930 their relationship had been very cordial in spite of the inevitable problems caused by their common Larkana background. The break came with the anti Sind separation stand taken by Bhutto during the Simon Commission enquiry and the damage that was done to the cause of the separation by his toeing the line of the Bombay bureaucracy. Later when Bhutto, seeing the strength of public opinion and the real possibility that separation might become a fact, had changed his stance to pro separation, their political co-operation had been restored. Khuhro however was by then unconvinced about Bhutto's sincerity in the cause and remained sceptical about his motives in public life.

In the elections of 1937 though he was not inclined to support Bhutto he was careful not to oppose him. Bhutto was opposed by Shaikh Abdul Majid who had no background of political work in Larkana and was only known for his reputation as a Khilafat leader. He therefore took a big risk by offering himself for elections against Bhutto who was Advisor to the Governor and had full government support. Larkana thus became the focus for great election interest and excitement with the three leaders of the three parties contesting from there. Bhutto the leader of Sind United Party, Majid the head of Sind Azad Party both fighting Larkana North and Khuhro the deputy leader of Sind Muslim Democratic Party for Larkana East.

Majid started his election work in earnest and won the support of the *ulema* who organised a powerful campaign against Bhutto blaming him for the octroi taxes that had been recently imposed and claiming that he would tax beards next. Processions of ox carts were organised to protest the tax that had been put on goods transported on the carts. Much excitement was generated by the contest. Bhutto sitting in distant Bombay and relying on his cousins and his campaign manager Pir Ali Mohammed Rashdi dismissed Majid's campaign with contempt- "a jackal has entered the lion's den", he is supposed to have commented.

There was no doubt that Bhutto was a powerful and influential figure in the district and had remained so for more than thirty years but during that period his reputation for inaccessibility and arrogance had made him unpopular among the people and even his peers. He had always relied on the favour and support of officialdom but in the elections their backing could not bail him out. The true extent of the opposition only became clear when he arrived in Larkana and found that even the support of his relations was doubtful and some were working actively against him. The elections resulted in a humiliating defeat for him and destroyed his political career. Bhutto found the defeat too much to bear and asked the government to find him a job out of Sind preferably in Bombay as a member of the Public Service Commission. The governor duly sent on his request to Brabourne at Bombay who found the request both incomprehensible and embarrassing as the decision of the Administrative Committee to have a joint Sind–Bombay Public Service Commission had still to be endorsed by the Legislative Assembly but could find no way to refuse it:

"Now as regards S. N. Bhutto. We are perfectly prepared to have him. but from his point of view, it strikes me as utter lunacy because I do not see how, once he has accepted an appointment of this kind, he can ever go back to politics, should he so desire, in the future. I personally feel that appointment to a Provincial P. S. C., should, subject to Section 265 (3) of the Act, be regarded as the end of a man's career, and it strikes me as being absolutely impossible to contemplate that a man who has been a member of P. S. C. should ever have in mind the possibility of becoming a Minister in the future.

I agree with you entirely when you say that if you sent him, he will look a coward. ... all I can say is that I would certainly accept him (though not very gladly, as it may be a little awkward having an ex-Minister) but if I were he, I would most certainly not ask to be sent."[7]

When Bhutto left Sind in the wake of his defeat he left politics behind for ever and spent the rest of his career first as member Public Service Commission and then as *Wazir* in Junagadh State returning to Sind only shortly before independence.

The other major casualty of this election was Abdullah Haroon who belonged to the Memon business community and had nursed the Lyari area of Karachi as a constituency for himself. He had spent money there on charitable works, established orphanages, schools and helped the people of this most disdvantaged Muslim majority district of Karachi in every way he could. But in the election his rival Sardar Allah Baksh Gabole was able to defeat him on the basis of tribal and Baloch loyalty. Haroon although very disappointed did not give up politics and continued to play an active role in the affairs of the province including a major role in the establishment of the Muslim League in Sind. At the same time he did not abandon the people of Lyari but continued his concern and good works in that district.

Although the two leaders of the United Party lost their elections the party as a whole gained more seats that any other in the province with twenty one elected members. The Muslim Democratic Party got three seats and had the support of the four independents as well as the 'Mir group'.[8] The Sind Azad Party of Shaikh Abdul Majid won only one seat and ceased to exist for all practical purposes.

As it turned out the relative party strength had no importance in the formation of the government in Sind. The Governor, Sir Lancelot Graham, knew Hidayetullah from his Bombay days and was keen to have someone who already had some experience of running a government. He therefore used the excuse that both the Leader and Deputy Leader of the majority party had been defeated in the elections and thus he was calling upon the leader of the second most important party to form the government. Since it was in the Governor's discretion to choose the premier he could please himself as regards the choice and duly selected Sir Ghulam Hussain to be the premier of Sind much to the chagrin of the Sind United Party and its new leader Allah Baksh Soomro. However before taking this decision Graham did try to unite the Muslims in one group to be able to form a strong and effective government but these efforts failed because of the personal rivalries of Hidayetullah and Bhutto.

The choice, in the face of the majority won by the United Party was controversial and set a bad precedent for democratic practice in the province. It led the members and the public to believe that the favour of the Governor was the most important factor in the choice of the Premier. The consequences of this and other similar decisions were to distort the growth of healthy democratic politics in Sind. For the moment however Hidayetullah succeeded in forming a government which had the support of the Mir group whose ten members had been allied with the Muslim party group even before the elections. Their leader Mir Bandeh Ali Talpur became Minister in the cabinet as did Mukhi Gobindram who had the support of the Independent and Sind Sabha Hindus. This gave the government the support of about twenty eight members. This number increased substantially quite soon. The Sind United Party put up its own candidate for Speaker in the person of Shaikh Abdul Majid who they felt would be a strong candidate and put them in a better bargaining position. Hidayetullah was however a much wilier politician than SUP gave him credit for and put up Bhojsingh Pahlajani who had been Deputy President of Bombay Council for many years and would automatically get most of the Hindu votes. This strategy was so successful that not only was Pahlajani elected Speaker with the majority of forty over eighteen but Majid himself deserted ranks and joined the government so that only a few members were left with the Opposition. These included Allahbux Soomro, G. M. Syed and Mohammed Hashim Gazdar of the Silawat community of Karachi.

The cabinet had two Ministers who were both coalition partners as well as the Premier thus leaving no room for Khuhro who might legitimately have expected a cabinet seat. He had to be content with being Parliamentary Secretary, a position he accepted with good grace.

Hidayetullah was the political pastmaster but Khuhro was the ablest and most experienced parliamentarian in the House and acted as the chief spokesman of the government. The new government had a programme of legislation which was expected to ameliorate the condition of the rural Muslim population and also to give due share of services to the aspiring Muslim middle class. The legislative programme consisted among other things of the earliest passing of the Land Alienation Bill, Debt Reconciliation Bill, a bill to increase educational opportunities in the rural areas so as to raise Muslim literacy from four to fifty percent in ten years's time and legislation to give fair share of service jobs to the Muslims.

Hidayetullah's government found that in order to pursue this programme it needed all the Muslim support it could get and thus by October through the good offices of Sahibzada Abdul Sattar Jan, Pir Sarhandi, it made a move to reach an understanding with Sind United Party and by 1937 the two parties formed a coalition to be called the Democratic Coalition Party. Khuhro became the General Secretary of the new party and to him fell the task of framing a workable legislative programme and to gain support for it. A number of meetings were held to agree to a programme. It was proposed that a daily paper in the English language should be started to represent the Muslim point of view. Khuhro's correspondence at this time shows the enthusiasm and the seriousness of the government in pursuing its programme. He writes to G. M. Syed the most active member of SUP on 17 November 1937:

"Dear Ghulam Murtaza Shah,
Meeting of the Working Committee of the Democratic Party will take place on Thursday 9th December 1937 at 4.30 p.m. at the residence of Hon'ble Sir Ghulam Hussain Hidayetullah, where the final scheme regarding starting a Daily Moslem

paper and such other matters of importance will be considered. You are requested to attend."⁹

A week later he writes to Syed again:

"You are invited to attend a sub-committee meeting regarding a Muslim paper on 27th instant at my residence at 5 p.m. You are further requested to dine with me the same evening at 7 p.m. after the meeting has terminated.

Yours sincerely
M. A. Khuhro

P. S. Regarding your items (proposals) for Agenda for the meeting on 9th December I will consult the President and let you know. They are too many for one day meeting, as on 9th we have two very important matters to discuss first. Besides on 10th some of us are busy with S. P. C. [Sind Provincial Co-operative] Bank meetings morning and evening. So we shall have to fix some other dates to decide about your proposals and that meeting may last for about three days. I will request Sir Ghulam Hussain to give me some suitable dates for the purpose."¹⁰

The government party's seriousness in accommodating the SUP coalition partners is obvious from the fact that on 4 December Khuhro was once again writing to Syed:

"Dear Shah Sahib,

Many thanks for your letter. I have consulted with Sir Ghulam Hussain with regard to your proposals and it has been decided that they will be taken up after the disposal of other business on the 9th. If, however, that is not possible we shall carry on with regard to your proposals on 10th at 5 p.m. and again on 11th at 5 p.m. i.e. the Working Committee meetings will continue for 3 days each day from 5 p.m. to 8 p.m.

You are therefore requested to please come to Karachi on 9th positively. Your condition that January will be too late for the disposal of your proposals is noted and therefore we desire that your questions should be decided as early as possible.

With best wishes..."¹¹

The Coalition government was thus anxious not to delay any steps or legislation which would better the conditions of the people and fully co-operated with the SUP terms as they touched the general welfare of the province. G. M. Syed the conscience keeper of SUP was in close touch with Khuhro who was actively working on the legislation of the programme. Writing many years later when he was firmly on the other side of the fence from his erstwhile colleagues of the thirties Syed pays a somewhat grudging tribute to this time of co-operation:

"An agreed programme was drawn up for the Ministry to be carried out under the instructions of the Committee and a fairly good progress was thereby made in the course of the next few months. Several meetings of the Working Committee were called and several proposals were adopted some of which were actually carried out by the Government:

1. Exemption of grazing fees from revenue lands.
2. Reduction of grazing fees from forests.
3. Recovery of *Taccavi* (agricultural) loans in easy instalments and reduction,

and in some cases, exemption of overdue interest accrued thereon.
4. Abolition of Commissioner's and Collector's chair *Parwanas*.
5. Abolition of nomination on local bodies."[12]

Unfortunately this unity of Muslim politicians and legislators was not to last long and fell victim to the manipulations of some ambitious politicians. Mukhi Gobindram who had been a very successful minister had to resign due to personal and business reasons and a new Hindu minister had to be found. Hidayetullah and his colleagues favoured Hemandas Wadhwani a lawyer and politician from Jacobabad who it was felt would be able to gain the support of the Hindu members as well being able to co-operate with the Muslims. But here the Ministry came up against the ambitions of one of the cleverest and most manipulative Hindu politicians Sind has produced, Nihchaldas Vazirani, who would prove an extremely destructive and troublesome element in the politics of Sind for the next ten years. Vazirani led the intrigue against the Ministry inciting the Hindus against the proposed legislation telling them that this was specifically against their interests. After the death of the Speaker Pahlajani, Syed Miran Mohammed Shah was elected the new Speaker, this was presented to the Hindu members as a usurpation of their rights, although there was no agreement that this post would go to a Hindu.

The understanding achieved among the two Muslim parties and the Hindu independents also foundered on the restless ambition of some politicians. The Democratic Coalition Party was thus doomed to founder. Vazirani kept up his pressure on the government through the Hindu press particularly in the Sindhi language *Sansar Samachar* and in the English daily *The Sind Observer*. The Government party had tried very hard to counter this campaign by starting its own English paper and keeping in close touch with the coalition partners as the correspondence of Khuhro with Syed clearly shows. Khuhro had found that owning his own paper was extremely helpful in pursuing political aims. This had been proved with the *Sind Zamindar* and *Al Wahid* but also with the neutral *Daily Gazette*, which had done so much for the separation cause. Khuhro was very keen that now that Sindhi Muslims had their own government they should start their own paper in the English language. Writing to Syed on 22 January 1938 he explained these ideas:

"My dear G. M. Syed,

You are aware of the very urgent need of a Muslim daily paper in Sind to ventilate the Muslim grievances and serve other Muslim interests. As we have suffered on account of its absence for a long time, some of the leaders of the Community, including the Hon'ble Sir Ghulam Hussain Hidayetullah and the Hon'ble Mir Bandehali Khan Talpur, have decided to arrange to supply the long felt need and with this end in view a scheme on share basis has been launched, the details of which will be clear to you from the appeal accompanying this letter. If you want any further information on the subject, K. B. Azimkhan, Joint Secretary of the Committee or myself as Secretary of the Committee will be happy to supply...

2. With a view to achieve this laudable object, the Working Committee has decided to sell shares. It has also been decided that the salaried Muslims should be requested to aid the cause at least to the extent of one month's income. I,

therefore request you earnestly to co-operate with us in these our efforts by wholeheartedly contributing your own quota and securing the assistance of your friends and acquaintances. It is the hope of all of us that you will not deny us your wholehearted co-operation and help in this urgent cause of the Community.

3. If need be, the Joint Secretary will make it possible to meet you whenever you desire or find it necessary.

4. A very early response is earnestly requested. I may add for your information that Hon. Sir Ghulam Hussain and Hon. Mir Bandehali Khan Talpur have agreed to purchase shares to the extent of Rs. 3,000/- each and myself of Rs. 2,000/-. The funds are to be deposited in the joint names of Sir Ghulam Hussain as President, K. B. Khuhro as Secretary and Agha Shamsuddin as Treasurer.

Please reply to this direct to K. B. Azim Khan at Hyderabad stating the number of shares you wish to purchase."[13]

All these schemes which were dependent on the continued co-operation of the members soon came to an end. The campaign started by Vazirani motivated by purely selfish reasons found fertile soil in the demoralized ranks of the Congress members. As long as Mukhi Gobindram was Minister he was able to keep the support of the independent Hindu members but as soon as he left and Wadhwani was brought in, Vazirani proved too powerful an opponent and propagandist. He was able to gain the support of disgruntled elements such as the leadership of the SUP, particularly Allah Baksh Soomro, who saw himself as cheated out of the premiership. Thus while the Coalition was busy pursuing its programme with considerable vigour the disadvantages of the 'weightage' clause in the constitution were soon to become obvious for the majority community and were to play their part in destablizing the government.

The Governor felt the rumblings of the Hindu politicians, particularly Nihchaldas Vazirani and writing to Brabourne he explained the situation:

"The general conclusion which I draw from this session is that I have probably got the most effective combination of interests in my Ministry, but that there is not a great deal of faith to be placed in the Hindus, who though not elected on the Congress ticket, show decided leanings in that direction and do not respond the the commands or the appeals of the Hindu Minister. Two of them are openly saying that they are thinking of joining the Congress, because the Hindu Minister has not secured for them from the Muslim Chief Minister the righting of various alleged Hindu grievances."

As regards Soomro's disappointment he writes:

"I had an hour's talk with the Leader of the Opposition the other day and think you may be interested to hear about it. I have noticed that he has been particularly virulent in his attacks on the Ministry ... so I invited him to come and talk to me. He opened up very freely and charged me with retaining in power a worthless Ministry, apparently by my personal influence, and thereby violating the Constitution. This seemed to me a very odd charge and we had a thorough discussion at the end of which I hope I succeeded in persuading him that whatever Ministry is in charge would get as much assistance and sympathy from me as my present Ministry and no more and that doubtless having regard to the highly malicious characteristics of the people of Sind in general, the leader of the future Opposition would make the same charge against me in respect of my second Cabinet as the leader of the present Opposition is now making in respect to my first Cabinet. As I understand the position, my duty is to make the best I can of whatever Ministry maybe in power and I propose to go on doing so. I have ofcourse been told that the leader of Opposition is merely dejected by personal disappointment because he got into debt by spending some 60,000/-[rupees] on his election being then inspired by a sure hope that he would find a seat in the Ministry and would be able to recoup himself for the money sunk in the election. This may or may not be true, but I am very much disappointed with this gentleman because I thought he was one of the better men in the province."[14]

A historian of the period explains the decision of Soomro to 'desert the ranks of the government party'–

"Allah Baksh claimed the decision to defect stemmed from the Ministry's failure to carry out the party's principles and program but the Governor suggested the reasons may have been personal. Graham cited two actions of Hidayetullah that angered Allah Baksh. First of all, Sir Ghulam Hussain had ordered that no contracts of the Public Works Department (PWD), with which Allah Baksh had close ties, were to be awarded to any Members of the Legislative Assembly (MSLA). Secondly the Chief Minister failed to approve an exchange of land to which Allah Baksh was entitled."[15]

Added to the intrigues of Vazirani and the ambitions of Soomro, was the restlessness and impatience of G. M. Syed who insisted that the programme of the Democratic Coalition Party was not being pursued with sufficient vigour. He made up his mind that only a change of government would achieve the results that he wanted. In this he was aided and abetted by Pir Ali Mohammed Rashdi who had been out of the limelight since the defeat of Bhutto and wanted to regain his place in the sun. In G. M. Syed therefore the anti ministry group found their leader. Syed bent on the pursuit of the 'ideal' government started an intrigue against the Ministry. First of all, Syed proposed that the Ministry would be increased to include Allah Baksh Soomro and Nihchaldas Vazirani. A sop thrown to the ruling group was that Khuhro would also be taken on as Minister. Hidayetullah put this proposal to the Governor but was unable to get agreement to expand the cabinet. The result was that the Opposition got the votes of the Hindu members and those Muslim members who were impatient to acquire office to challenge the Hidayetullah ministry.

In fact the Hindu opposition to the Hidayetullah Ministry was not just based on the ambitions of Vazirani for ministership or the insatiable desire of the Congress Party to dominate the government. It was the economic interest of the Hindu capitalist moneylender which was at stake. One of the main planks of the Sind Muslim legislators in Bombay and in their election promises to the people had been to bring in legislation to ameliorate the indebtedness of the Sindhi peasant. For Khuhro this had been a cause since his inception into politics – the heart rending spectacle of dispossessed *haris* outside the Larkana courthouse was part of his personal childhood experiences. It was also the agenda for the assembly of autonomous Sind and the new government wanted to implement the legislation as early as possible. But ofcourse the legislation would strike at the head of the economic position of the *bania* class. Writing his fortnightly report on 20 December 1937 the Secretary to the Government of Sind, Kripalani, mentions a "conference of cultivators" being called by Congress, which, he says:

"has been postponed to 26th and 27th instant to suit the convenience of Mr. Bhulabhai Desai, M.L.A. who will open the conference. Efforts are being made to secure as large an attendance as possible, especially of Muslims. The Conference will discuss, *inter alia*, measures for preventing corruption, the organisation for *haris* and Debt Conciliation and Land Alienation Bills introduced by private members at the last session of the Sind Legislative Assembly.

The local Congress have been occupied lately with determining their attitude towards the first of the above named two Bills. The Bill proposes to make certain provisions for the relief of agricultural indebtedness. The Congress party have decided to express their dissatisfaction with the Bill on the ground that it gives too much *protection to wealthy persons*" [author's italics].

Kripalani should have ofcourse detailed more clearly the Congress objections to the Bills which were not that they gave too much protection to "wealthy persons" but that by giving protection to the Muslim agriculturist they would go against the interest of the wealthy Hindu moneylenders. The conference itself was an anamoly as the Congress, with its almost exclusively Hindu support could not work sincerely for the interests of the *hari* or the zamindar. On the other hand the Hindu Assembly members, both Congress and Independent came together when they found their economic interests threatened and guided by the Congress tacticians, were able to gain the support of the more power hungry as well as the most naive among the Muslim politicians. They also ruthlessly used the `weightage' advantage given to the Hindu minority to throw out any government which could threaten the moneylender interests.

Leaders like G. M. Syed well realised the basic contradiction between the Muslim agriculturist and Hindu moneyed interests:

"Hindu public opinion was aroused against Sir Ghulam Hussain's Ministry and they raised the following three questions to bring it into discredit amongst the Hindus:–

The Muslims had taken advantage of their unity and refused to take in the accredited representative of Hindus on the Cabinet.

The Muslim majority would pass the Debt Conciliation Bill and harm the economic interests of the Hindus to the extent of two crores of rupees.

...Land Alienation Bill would be passed so as to deprive the Hindus in Sind of the right to purchase land in future..."[16]

In spite of the fact that he was fully aware of the nature of the Hindu opposition to the government, Syed continued to be embroiled in the intrigue to destroy it. By the time of the Budget Session of March 1938 arrangements were complete to defeat the government. Secret agreements had been made and members won over by promises of office and favours. Syed relates the episode:

"Thus by the time the Assembly met for the Budget session in March 1938, the small points of difference and dissatisfaction had developed into major issues and this, together with the personal ambitions of some members and inexperience of some and over enthusiasm of others, soon brought about a secret arrangement to break Sir Ghulam Hussain's Ministry with the assistance of the Hindu and Congress groups who had been anxiously looking out for such an opportunity."

Syed then adds:

"I must accept my share of responsibility for the overthrow of Sir Ghulam Hussain's ministry though it was due to my over-enthusiasm and eagerness for speedy realisation of my cherished dreams of having a reconstructed Sind. Experience has, however shown that my calculation was not correct. Lack of practical experience of the working of government machinery, miscalculation of the actual working conditions in Sind and inability to assess others at their true value were some of the factors, and my friends of the Sind United Party were mainly responsible for the failure of my calculations."[17]

In fact it was very naive of Syed and his friends to be taken in by Congress blandishments. Allah Baksh Soomro was enticed by the thought of Chief Ministership which he thought he had been cheated of and Syed by impatience and a misplaced idealism. The secrecy and intrigue also introduced an element of farce into the whole operation. The evening before the budget session Hidayetullah gave a dinner for all the coalition members. Syed and Rashdi debated whether it was ethical to attend the dinner and "eat the salt" of the man they were to betray the next day. Rashdi who had less scruples than Syed insisted that it was necessary to attend the dinner since suspicions would be aroused especially of a man as wary as Hidayetullah.

Later on that night Syed and Rashdi sat conferring with Vazirani at Syed's house, Hyder Manzil. Khuhro who lived only two doors away walked down to see Syed about some minor problem. The servant came in to inform Syed that "Khan Bahadur is just walking in"- Rashdi and Syed felt that on no account was Khuhro to see Vazirani because his suspicions would be instantly aroused. So they pushed Vazirani into the lavatory and told him to sit there till Khuhro had left. Khuhro stayed a short while and left but Rashdi and Syed forgot about Vazirani and went to sleep. About 5 o'clock the next morning Rashdi got up to go to the lavatory and found Vazirani still there. When he saw Rashdi he asked anxiously– "Has Khuhro left? Why was he here so long?" Quick witted Rashdi gave a suitably convincing answer as to why Khuhro had been in consultation with them all night and Vazirani then left to go home.[18]

In the morning the government was defeated on a Rs. 1 cut motion to the utter astonishment of the government party. Hidayetullah shouted "Betrayed, betrayed" but in spite of his last minute efforts to save the government nothing could be done and the ministry resigned on 22 March 1938.

In this entire unsavoury episode it was only Khuhro who came out with an unblemished name and his reputation intact. After the formation of the separate province he had become the member of the Advisory Council – a position well deserved. However when it became apparent that the exigencies of the political give and take and coalition requirements needed sacrifice on his part he made it willingly. As Parliamentary Secretary he carried the load as the Chief Spokesman for the government. When the SUP and the Vazirani group suggested his name as one of three ministers to be included in the expanded cabinet he agreed but was not unduly put out when it did not work out. He remained loyal to his Party and the Premier throughout and after the fall of the government sat in the Opposition with good grace and unimpaired enthusiasm for his work.

Khuhro considered the political intrigue and making and breaking of ministries wasteful of precious time. He could not help comparing the present situation with that of the Bombay Council where the Muslim members had always worked in unison and no persuasion by the powerful and sophisticated Congress (or Swarajist) leadership had been able to break that unity. Khuhro had believed that this unity would continue in an autonomous Sind and it would be consequently easy to achieve the legislation required to improve the condition of the common people. He was in for a rude awakening.

9

ESTABLISHING MUSLIM LEAGUE IN SIND

Allah Baksh Soomro formed his Ministry on 23 March 1938 with the support of Vazirani and his group of ten Hindu Independents, seventeen others including eight members of the Sind United Party, three Europeans and two independents. He also had the support of the Congress members. The Chief Secretary in his official report noted:

"On 18th March 1938, which was the last day for the voting on the demand for grants, the Congress Party moved and carried a cut of one rupee in the grant for 'General Administration', and later on rejected the entire grant. This was rendered possible by the combination of the Congress party, the Independent Hindu party, and eight members of the Sind United Party who resigned from the Ministerial party a little earlier in the day. This brought to a head agitation against the Hidayetullah ministry; and after some hesitation the Ministry resigned on the 21st March 1938. On the same day, K. B. Allah Baksh Mohammed Umar, O. B. E. was sworn in as Chief Minister with Mr. Nihchaldas C. Vazirani and Pir Illahi Baksh as his colleagues in the Ministry."[1]

The main Opposition leadership now consisted of Hidayetullah, Khuhro, Shaikh Abdul Majid and Hashim Gazdar. It quickly coalesced to take advantage of Muslim anger at the removal of a government which had been representing their interests. Jones comments on their attitude –

"..they were bitter that the Allah Baksh forces had fractured the carefully nurtured Muslim unity just to secure office; they viewed as traitorous Allah Baksh's openness with the Hindus and his dependence on them for support; and they were fearful that his Congress dominated program would repeat in Sind the scenario of Congress oppression in the Muslim minority provinces."[2]

Khuhro, Majid and Gazdar decided to mobilize public opinion against the Congress backed government and called a public meeting in Karachi a few days after the formation of the Soomro ministry. The meeting presided over by the veteran politician Majid, evoked a great response and a resolution was passed demanding that Muslim League be organised in Sind to counter Congress machinations. A resolution was also passed characterizing Soomro as a traitor and denouncing his ministry as dependent on the Congress and Mahasabha and against the interests of Sindhi Muslims.

"...K. B. Allah Baksh came down to Sann and tried to induce me to support the principle of the enhancement. I explained to him that it would not be right on his part to expect me to be a party to the enhancement of assessment. But finding him insistent I advised him that the best course for him would be to take the party into confidence and if he could get the majority view to support him in his proposal my personal view need not be bothered about.

I found in the course of my talks with him at Sann that the Khan Bahadur was determined to have his own way and I thought he only wanted me to induce other members to let him enhance the assessment... Soon an emissary in the person of Mr. Ali Mohammed Rashdi was sent down to me by K. B. Allah Baksh and he induced me to accompany him to Karachi... But it appeared later that he had already decided upon the enhancement of the assessment. Only he had kept this fact hidden from the Party and was making an outward pretence of seeking the wishes of the parties that had brought his Ministry into power. Eventually however, Government orders were actually passed, enhancing the land assessment in direct contravention of the decision of the various parties who supported the Ministry.

The result was that the Sind United Party, which had passed a resolution against the enhancement of assessment, was broken up and we had no other alternative, but to walk over to the Opposition benches."[8]

It is obvious Syed did not realise the great damage his divisive politics was having on Sind in the post-separation period. Khuhro however had no illusions about what a Congress backed government would do for the Muslims of Sind and Soomro was now totally dependent on Congress and the Hindu members.

Syed, in an effort to bring about a compromise, asked Sardar Patel and Maulana Azad of All India Congress High Command to come to Sind. Their visit in August 1938 did not succeed in achieving any compromise and they appeared to be reluctant to pressurise a government which was dependent on and subservient to Congress in a Muslim majority province and "instead of improving matters for Sind, the visit of these top Congress leaders let loose the flood-gates of All India controversies upon the soil of Sind."[9]

The ground realities of the situation are summed up by Allan Jones:

"Sindhi Muslims had lost their favoured post-separation position of political dominance by pursuing their penchant for self-centred, personalised politics and in their place their rivals, Sindhi Hindu, had emerged to hold the balance of power in the province's ministerial politics."[10]

The unpopularity of the Soomro ministry among the Muslims in general and its obvious dependence on Congress gave a golden opportunity to Muslim League to organise itself in Sind. Muslim League was not unfamiliar to Sindhis. There had been a branch of the organisation in Sind as early as 1906 and important Sind leaders had been members of the Party including Ghulam Mohammed Bhurgri and Shaikh Abdul Majid. Some attempts had been made to organise the party in Sind particularly by Shaikh Abdul Majid and some Karachi Muslim leaders but these had foundered mainly because of the indifference of the central League leadership and also because it was not seen as relevant to the problems of Sind. Major Sind leaders Majid, Haroon and Khuhro had all known Jinnah for many years and respected him as one of the foremost champions of Muslims rights in India. But the fact that Congress now was making inroads into Sind and that Hindus were relying on Congress to support their cause at the all India level forced the Muslim leadership to think of outside support and this support could obviously come from Muslim League. The activities of Congress in Sind, the formation of a Congress M.L.As. group in the Legislative Assembly and the tour of Congress leaders Vallabhai Patel and the Home Minister of Bombay, K. M. Munshi in Sind in December 1937 to promote the Congress party in the province, particularly in the rural population, had caused concern among Muslims who were not convinced of the sincerity of Congress for their cause.

So far the newly re-organised Muslim League under the leadership of Jinnah had been mainly concerned with getting safeguards and guarantees for the Muslims of the minority provinces. It had made some efforts to gain support in the provinces of the Punjab and Bengal but had not yet turned its attention in the direction of Sind. With the fall of the Hidayetullah Ministry Muslim leaders particularly Khuhro, Haroon and Majid began to try in earnest to bring the Muslim League into the province to counter the power of Congress. In a letter, dated 3rd August 1938, Khuhro wrote to his old friend and mentor Mian Kader who had urged that Muslim League be formed in Sind:

"My dear Kadermia,

Many thanks for your letter of 30 June reply to which was long overdue and I sincerely apologize for the delay which has occurred in replying to your letter. I was, you must be knowing, very busy with the political turmoil in Sind. I fully agree with every word of what you have penned in this your letter. The only course and the honourable course left for the Moslems of India, is to organise a Moslem Political Association i.e. a Moslem League. At first good many Moslems in Sind who were not fully aware of the machinations of Congress minded Hindus, easily fell prey to their poisonous and mischievous propaganda that Moslem League is a communal organisation, controlled by a few ease loving highly placed Moslems and that it had no backing from the general masses. The propaganda of this sort gained footing to some extent in this Province for only sometime. But after the failure of Sir Ghulam Hussain's Ministry, in March last, and the ignoble part that Party [i.e. the Congress Party] played in the downfall of this Ministry, has convinced every right thinking Moslem that Congress is the worst communally minded organisation. Most of the bigoted Hindus who appear sweet on the surface, but are personified hypocrites, have dominated Sind Congress. I have very low opinion of Congress men in Sind. If you were to ask my candid opinion I would much prefer to be an ally of the Hindu Mahasabha than this Congress, at any rate the former are quite clear about their policy and do not attempt to hoodwink us.

Our friends from Sind who have sometimes been coming to Bombay, may have apprised you of the fact that Congress block of only ten in Sind Assembly, whose only constitutional position is to oppose Government, have as a matter of fact been carrying on a duplicate policy and is trying to keep Allah Baksh Ministry in office, in order that such a Ministry should damn it own community and show unreasonable and unjustifiable favours to the Hindu community. Sind offers a very good field for Muslim League propaganda. Me and my colleagues in Sind, have during the last four or five months done considerable propaganda to strengthen the League and I am glad to tell you that we have met with tremendous success. In the next elections we *Inshallah* hope to put up Moslem League candidates throughout Sind and we shall, I am confident, secure a clear majority to form Moslem League Government in the Province. Even now I feel within a month or two we shall have at least 25 out of 35 Moslems as Members of the Moslem League Party, within the Assembly.

I have a great mind to meet Mr. Jinnah and discuss with him about League politics in this province. I shall therefore be much obliged if you kindly let me know his programme for August as early as possible. If he is going to Simla any time during this month, pray let me know so that I may run up and meet him. Sir Abdullah Haroon will even otherwise be there and perhaps Sheikh Abdul Majid will go with me. We propose to invite Mr. Jinnah to visit Sind at an early date and we want to awaken Muslim feelings and do utmost propaganda during his visit, it will serve as an impetus to strengthen the League. I shall be grateful if you kindly meet Mr. Jinnah and apprise him of my views. He knows me very well and I am sure we will have fullest co-operation and help from him. I believe we may even have a clear majority in the Assembly in a few months time to form League Government. I am working in that direction."[11]

The letter with the proposal for an invitation to come to Sind was forwarded to Jinnah who realized that though his earlier rather half hearted attempts in Sind had foundered the time had now come to try again. Not only were there the intermittent contacts with Majid and Haroon who occasionally urged him to take a greater interest in Sind but now there were the details set out in Khuhro's letter in which Muslim League was seen as solution to the problems faced by Sind Muslims. At the same time a letter was sent off by Abdullah Haroon to urge Jinnah to come to Sind as soon as possible painting a rosier picture perhaps than was warranted by the situation:

"I can clearly see that out of 34 Muslim members as many as 27 Muslim members are ready to sign the League pledge. I think there are chances of almost all the Muslim members so doing if the Muslim mass opinion is further stimulated through a provincial League conference which might be organised at Karachi by the end of this month. It may also be necessary to visit some other places in the mofussil and establish a greater touch with the people and win them over to the League side. All my friends are of the opinion that you may preside over the conference and also spend a couple of days in the mofussils for this purpose."[12]

In fact Haroon and Majid had been to Bombay already in June to talk to Jinnah not only about the possibility of re-organising Muslim League in Sind but also to see if pressure could be put on Soomro to carry with him the Muslims of United Party of which he and Haroon had after all been joint leaders, to break with Congress and to affiliate with Muslim League. In the Governor's opinion this was highly unlikely:

"I got from Allah Baksh this morning some rather interesting information on this point. He showed me a copy of a letter written by Jinnah to Haroon with the intention that it should be shown to Allah Baksh. The original was written by Jinnah and it informed Haroon that Sir Ghulam Hussain and Abdul Majid would be ready to combine with Allah Baksh, and support the Ministry as at present constituted, provided that Allah Baksh definitely and publicly identified himself with the Muslim League.

Allah Baksh tells me that he had no hesitation in refusing the offer. He would rather carry on with his present combination of Muslims and Hindus, with the forbearance of the Congress, than identify himself with a fiercely communal institution. What the result will be I should not like to say, but Allah Baksh remains confident, and I incline to think that he is unduly confident."[13]

It was widely expected that Soomro would opt for greater Muslim support and even the Punjab Premier, Sir Sikander Hayat, told the Governor of Punjab that such a development was likely, but they reckoned without the tight strings with which Congress was controlling the Soomro ministry now that they had achieved the virtually impossible in forming a government in a Muslim majority province.

Jinnah, who was faced with Congress ministries in the provinces where the support for Muslim League was strongest, was looking out for any backing he could get to strengthen the position of the minority province Muslims. The deep concern that Jinnah felt was clear from the remarks Brabourne, the Acting Viceroy made in his letter to Lord Zetland:

"Jinnah was if possible even more bitter than usual. He devoted a considerable time to reeling off a long catalogue of oppressive acts said to have been committed against Muslims in various Congress provinces. Most of the examples he quoted were confined to: forcing Muslim children to sing Bande Mataram; the increasing difficulties being placed in the way of teaching Urdu, unpleasant incidents outside Mosques in places where the Muslim population is small; and the efforts being made by Congress to prevent Muslim representatives being elected to local bodies...[he] cannot believe that Linlithgow is not negotiating with the Congress. Suggests keep Centre as it is now; that we should make friends with the Muslims by 'protecting' them in the Congress provinces and that, if we did that, the Muslims would protect us at the Centre'".[14]

The Soomro ministry had started off with high hopes specially so far as the Governor was concerned. He found the Premier "pleasant to work with"[15] and his only complaint was that "he is much under the influence of the Hindu Minister Mr. Vazirani.."[16] Garret, the Acting Governor when Graham went on leave in early August, had a similar opinion of the Ministry: "Nihchaldas is a dominating influence, while the third Minister (Pir Illahi Baksh) commands no respect from either of his colleagues."[17] Most important of all Soomro was willing to introduce the revised rates of assessment which the Government of India had been anxious to impose ever since the province had been separated.

Although Hindu interests were not directly involved in the agricultural assessment problem as they were primarily urban based, the Congress leaders realized that enhancement would make the government very unpopular with the majority of the people and therefore were reluctant to agree to it. The Governor was adamant however. The question of dissolving the Assembly and of the Governor using his special powers had been discussed at the highest level although the Viceroy was very reluctant to use these powers and would rather have the dirty work done by the elected government. Soomro was thus faced with what was practically an ultimatum – raise the assessment or give up the Premiership. He tried desperately to bring round colleagues in the United Party but as G. M. Syed writes, he failed to do so and although he did call a meeting of his supporters they decided against immediate enhancement. Soomro appeared to accept the decision of the meeting but in fact had made up his mind that he would not give up the premiership on this issue and the Governor was able to write to his superiors about the Premier's attitude:

"He assures me that he is not afraid ... and that he is not going to be deterred from pushing through the Revision Settlement of the Barrage areas. He says very emphatically that he has told everybody with whom he had discussions that there has been no question of my overruling my Ministers as there has been no difference of opinion between us, and he is fully prepared to take the responsibility for the new proposals."[18]

The Government Press Note was issued on the 16 July announcing the new rates would come into force in the revenue year 1938-39. Soomro was shrewd enough to know that his main and consistent support came from Congress and that party was not likely to kick against its incredible luck in having a Ministry in the Muslim province of Sind. As for the Muslim supporters of the Ministry, Soomro was sure he could win over enough members through suitable patronage to make a respectable showing of Muslim support. Thus in early August the Acting Viceroy was able to write to the Secretary of State:

"You will see from the papers... that Graham's long drawn out discussions with his Ministers on the question of Assessment are over. The results of his labours are at present being examined by Grigg and the Finance Department and I cannot yet say exactly what they amount to. I think it will turn out that the new rates give us no increase of revenue for the present but will give us a considerable increase when the price of cotton rises... Graham's Ministers, as you will notice, have agreed to the issue of the new orders. In the meanwhile, their supporters are howling around them demanding resignation from the Ministry and Allah Baksh is reported to have resigned from his party. The Congress in Sind have ofcourse, seized this grand opportunity of posing as the champions of a downtrodden and overtaxed peasantry. What the eventual political result will be, I am not at present, going to try to forecast. The Premier's intention seems to be to try to avoid meeting his Legislature as long as possible, in the hope presumably, that the storm may blow over, and the Governor talks of there being no meeting of Sind Assembly until he comes back himself at the end of November."[19]

It was obvious that the Governor short of using his special powers was prepared to do whatever was needed to support Soomro including postponing the meeting of the Legislature till he was able to gather enough support. This action of Soomro split the United Party down the middle and in the face of what was regarded as the Congress betrayal the Muslim leaders turned to Jinnah and All India Muslim League. But it was not until October that Jinnah was able to make time for what was to be a most spectacular conference.

Since April 1938 Khuhro had got his team together and started to organise the Muslim League particularly in upper Sind. He set up branches in the Larkana district and announced a target figure of 10,000 members in the first instance. He had as his "lieutenant" Kazi Fazlullah, the Aligarh educated young lawyer from Nawabshah who had set up practice in Larkana and under the patronage of Khuhro had become an active political worker. He would be `the right hand man' of Khuhro for many years. A public meeting was held in Tajar Bagh in Larkana where apart from other members twenty Municipal Councillors and Local Board members had signed the League pledge, most of them influential men in local politics. He used workers of the former Khilafat committees to leaven the batches of new recruits and thus rapidly activated the "cadres".

Urban Muslims also realized that Muslim interests were not safe with the incumbent government. Mohammed Hashim Gazdar from the Silawat community of Karachi[20] played a leading role in persuading the urban Muslims to join Muslim League. A handicap to the organisation of Muslim League was the opposition of powerful religious parties which had been such a great support for the Khilafat movement as for instance Jamiat-ul-Ulemai-Hind. The appeal of Muslim League in Sind had in fact very little to do with religion and much more with the bread and butter issues of the deprived Muslim masses.

In October 1938 a session of Sind Muslim League was to be held in Karachi. This was to be the founding meeting for the re-incarnated Muslim League under the leadership of Jinnah. Preliminary meetings were held in many of the districts of Sind and almost every district of Karachi, in preparation for the occasion. Arrangements for the reception of Muslim League leaders from all over India were made on a grand scale. All the important Muslim leaders were invited including Sir Sikander Hayat Khan, Maulvi Fazlul Haque of Bengal, Maulana Shaukat Ali, the young Raja Sahib of Mahmudabad, Nawabzada Liaquat Ali Khan, Sir Currimbhoy Ibrahim of Bombay and Maulana Abdul Hamid Badayuni. Khuhro was among the main organisers of the conference, arranging hospitality for the delegates and working on the agenda for the conference and making sure that a substantial number of delegates attended the conference from all over the province.

On 7 October Jinnah arrived by special train at Karachi and received a right royal welcome. An aeroplane was hired to shower flower petals on the train. From the railway station he was taken on a specially bedecked camel cart at the head of a three mile long procession, accompanied by bands playing suitably rousing music, along the major roads of Karachi. Vast crowds turned out to see the procession. The conference started the next day at eight in the evening and continued till 2 o'clock in the morning. "... for its grandeur, majesty and attendance was never equalled in the history of the movement."[21]

The Conference created a considerable impact and this is noted by the Chief Secretary in his fortnightly report,

"The events of the fortnight were overshadowed by the Conference of Muslim League which commenced at Karachi on 8th October and continued till 12th October. A number of distinguished Muslims from various parts of India attended the Conference, prominent amongst whom were the Premier of Bengal and the Punjab, Maulana Shaukat Ali, the Raja of Mahmudabad, Nawabzada Liaquat Ali Khan and Sir Currimbhoy Ibrahim. A rousing reception was accorded to Mr. Jinnah, President elect, on his arrival at Karachi on the 7th October. A number of social functions were organised in his honour and addresses were presented to him by the Karachi Municipal Corporation and Karachi District Board. Scenes of great enthusiasm were witnessed during the session of the conference, an impassioned appeal for Muslim unity and a vehement denunciation of the Congress formed the main features of Mr. Jinnah's presidential address. His sentiments were echoed by most of the visitors from outside Sind, while the local leaders of the Muslim League spoke mainly on the political situation in Sind and attacked the Ministry in very strong terms. The 'frontier policy' of the Government of India, the liquidation of the Barrage debt and the Palestinian affairs were some of the other subjects discussed at the Conference."[22]

Sir Abdullah Haroon as Chairman of the Reception Committee gave the Welcome Address and detailed the major grievances of Muslims in Sind. He referred to the attempts to reach an understanding with the Hindu community and the lack of generosity and accommodation on their part and warned that if there was no change of attitude "it will be impossible to save India from being divided into Hindu India and Muslim India both placed under separate federations." An emotional speech was made by Fazlul Haq the Premier of Bengal urging Muslims to unite behind Muslim League. The Sind audience was thrilled to hear the great Muslim political leaders of India, some of whom were already legends in their lifetime. The Conference ended by passing a series of resolutions about the problems of Sind and then the famous Resolution No. 5 entitled "communal settlement" which put forward the idea of two irreconcilable cultures i.e. two nations. The last part of the resolution read:

"This conference considers it absolutely essential in the interests of an abiding peace of the vast Indian sub-continent and in the interests of unhampered cultural development, the economic and social betterment, and the political self determination of the two nations known as Hindus and Muslims to recommend to the All India Muslim League to review and revise the entire question of what should be the suitable constitution for India."

The resolution was drafted mainly by Shaikh Abdul Majid and Haroon closely assisted by Rashdi. Khuhro was not convinced of the need for this particular resolution and did not attach overmuch importance to it although he went along with the idea of presenting it to the conference out of consideration for the feelings of Haroon who was very keen on it. Although he let it be passed at the session partly because a provincial Muslim League session did not commit him as fully as a resolution passed at an All India Muslim League session, Jinnah was very doubtful about what appeared to him to be an unrealistic and fanciful demand. As a politician and lawyer Jinnah was trained to pursue the art of the possible and a "two-nation" proposal appeared to him to be premature and perhaps even counter productive so he was very reluctant to include it in his all India programme as Haroon wanted him to do. Jinnah avoided the issue of taking the resolution seriously and suggested that the feasibility of the scheme be studied in detail, and that it should be put to him fully worked out before he would be in a position to consider it seriously for the party programme.

Haroon immediately put Rashdi to the task of examining the scheme and the latter took his draft to Lahore where residing in Icchra, he consulted the leading Punjab Muslim writers and thinkers to fill in the details and finalise the embryo proposal.

From these incidental and humble beginnings in Sind the Pakistan proposal evolved so that by the time the Muslim League session came round in March 1940 a number of schemes were ready to be examined by Jinnah and his colleagues. The final shape became the Lahore Resolution which was passed by the Lahore session of All India Muslim League on 23 March 1940.[23]

The Karachi session roused a great deal of enthusiasm in the public as well as with Muslim politicians of Sind. The premiers of the two great Muslim majority provinces of India exhorted them to unite under the flag of the Muslim League. Some of the Sind politicians including Haroon and Syed thought they could use the momentum caused by the session to bring together all the Muslim members under the Muslim League flag and get Soomro to sign the party pledge and thus transform his government into a Muslim League one. Haroon had definitely given the impression in his correspondence with Jinnah that the time was ripe to obtain a majority in the Legislative Assembly. Khuhro was somewhat sceptical about this optimistic attitude. He realised that although some support would be forthcoming from members the power of government patronage was too seductive for others. He also knew that Soomro was in favour with the Governor for having just passed the orders for enhanced revenue assessment. There was no practical reason for him to change loyalties from Congress to Muslim League since his unpopularity among the Muslim masses was not an urgent problem as elections were not due for sometime.

Khuhro, after attending conference left for upper Sind to organise the tour of the interior for Jinnah, leaving Syed and Haroon to do their best to bring about the change of heart in Soomro.

The idea was to get Soomro to sign the League pledge and persuade him to take additional Muslim ministers so that the Ministry would be under the aegis of Muslim League. A meeting was convened on 9 October which was presided over by Jinnah and attended by Fazlul Haq, Sir Sikander Hayat Khan, Allah Baksh Soomro the Premier, Pir Illahi Baksh who was a Minister in the Sind cabinet, Sir Ghulam Hussain Hidayetullah, Mir Bandehali Talpur, G. M. Syed and Shaikh Abdul Majid. Writing notes of the meeting in his own hand Jinnah commented:

"It was agreed that the solid united party of Muslim members of the Assembly should be formed as the "Muslim League party" within the Legislature and all the members who joined the party will become members of the Muslim League and sign the creed and accept the policy and programme of the Muslim League and sign the usual pledge.

(2) In order to facilitate the formation of the new ministry the present Muslim ministers have agreed to tender their resignations and the resignations would be submitted to the Governor simultaneously with the proposal of the leader of the Muslim League party to constitute a new ministry.

(3) That the party meeting of those members who have joined already or agree to join the party of the Muslim League should take place on 12th October at 11 a.m. at Sir A. Haroon's place and those members who are not in Karachi at present to be requested to come down to Karachi there being already 27 members present in Karachi..."[24]

For the role of parliamentary leader, in case Soomro was not chosen, Jinnah noted down four names:

"(1) Khuhro, [ex] Chief Parliamentary Secretary
 (2) Shaikh Abdul Majid
 (3) Gazdar
 (4) Mir Ghulam Ali"
and noted below the names:

"In the absence of your [own, old ?] leader whom would you have."[25]

Obviously experienced and shrewd, Jinnah was not entirely convinced that Soomro would stick to his word and wanted him replaced by another more reliable leader. As regards the major grievance of the Muslims, the enhancement of revenue assessment, the decision was taken in consultation with Jinnah to entrust Sir Sikander Hayat, the Premier of the Punjab with the task of studying the issue and suggesting a solution:

"With regard to the differences of opinion relating to the question of assessment and revenue settlement within the Barrage area the matter to be referred to Sir Sikander Hayat Khan to examine the question and advise the party and the party agree to adopt such attitude course as may be recommended by him in that behalf."

These recommendations were to be put to the party at a meeting fixed for the 12th and that Sir Sikander's proposals would be accepted by the party "as final". The leader of the party was to be elected by a unanimous vote of the party and "in default he should be nominated by Mr. Jinnah and the party would abide by his choice" The personnel of the ministry to be formed would also be on the same principle

"viz. that the party should accept it unanimously and in default the party should abide by the decision of Mr. Jinnah as to the personnel which the leader would submit to the Governor."

This document was signed by Hidayetullah, G. M. Syed, Mir Bandehally, Majid and Pir Illahi Baksh on behalf of the Ministry. It was also decided that the party was to get in touch with other groups provided that such groups were ready to support the programme of the Muslim League.

Thus it appeared that the stage was set for a broad united front of the Muslims in Sind with a Muslim League ministry in the province but this optimism was premature. The Muslim Leaguers had not fully appreciated the determination of the Congress on the one hand and the weakness and vacillation of the Premier on the other. Before the meeting fixed for 12 October could take place Soomro had reneged and written a letter to Jinnah repudiating his agreement using rude and offensive language. It was widely believed that the letter had been dictated by his Hindu colleagues who threatened to leave him if he joined Muslim League. Soomro seems to have come to believe that Muslim support for him would be much less certain than that of Hindu Independent and Congress members. Soomro's statement was published on the day of the meeting which was to decide all the details of the new Muslim League party. He was obviously more confident of keeping his premiership with Congress support than with that of Muslim League since Jinnah had not spelt out that Soomro would be the leader of the parliamentary party. Jinnah was angry and humiliated and showed Soomro's letter to his supporters including Khuhro. The Muslim Leaguers were shocked by Soomro's behaviour and his callous unconcern for the interests of the Muslim majority. Haroon and Syed particularly had pinned their hopes on this conference. As G. M. Syed put it after the fiasco:

"his [Soomro's] supreme desire for the safety of his Ministry being paramount with him, he, as before, considered the support of the Congress and the Hindu groups a more safe plank on which the keel of his Premiership could rest; he was afraid that Muslim support howsoever strong or solid was always risky for the stability of the Ministry."²⁶

The Muslim League war with the Soomro ministry would be unrelenting from now on and it became a point of honour for them that the ministry be brought down as soon as possible.

Commenting on the events Garret, the Acting Governor wrote to Brabourne on 12 October:

"October 12 – the day fully occupied with discussion between Jinnah and members of Allah Baksh's party.

Jinnah pressed Allah Baksh and his supporters to form a League Ministry with six ministers. The names of additional Muslim ministers were discussed but Allah Baksh has kept to the position that the proposed additional Ministers could not have his confidence. Jinnah promised his full support and his personal authority in aid if any of the Ministers should give trouble, Jinnah told Allah Baksh that the Congress party in Sind had wired to the High Command for permission to support the present ministry at all costs and has received the permission asked for.

Allah Baksh saw me in the afternoon and told me that the discussions were to continue and that he with his supporters was unwilling to accept Jinnah's proposals. He says that Jinnah is using every effort to avoid the loss of prestige which he personally will suffer if he fails to secure the formation of a League ministry in Sind. Allah Baksh is not a strong character but his views are moderate and he has scruples about throwing over his Hindu supporters. He is of course under very severe pressure and is much worried, but he will I think hold to his present views."²⁷

Garret, alive to the possibility that the revised assessments would be under threat with a League Ministry, gave him full assurance of support. The two days between the 9th and the 12th had been used by the Sind Congress group to pressurise Soomro effectively. Jinnah was also fully informed about the Congress High Command instructions to Sind Congress to support Soomro in maintaining the *status quo*. After the breaking of the agreement and the formation of the Muslim League parliamentary party under the leadership of Hidayetullah, Jinnah met the Acting Governor on 15 October:

"The conversations at Karachi led by Mr. Jinnah have now come to an end and will be renewed on his return from a rapid tour of Sind.

3. On Saturday October 15th Jinnah asked for an interview. I enquired of Allah Baksh if he had any objection and with his full concurrence I gave Jinnah an interview which lasted for an hour.

4. He claims to have formed a party of about 25 members and to have obtained a large measure of agreement from independent Hindus and Europeans. My Hindu Minister Nihchaldas is ready to join a Muslim League Ministry at any time. Though Jinnah was extremely courteous and restrained, he complained that Allah Baksh had acted unfairly in first accepting Muslim League in presence of leaders like Fazlul Haq and Sikander Hayat and then repudiating his admission on the next day (October 12th).

6. He explained his indignation at the Congress party for giving blind support to any Government which was *not* Muslim League. He stated that the Muslim League did not seek to follow the Congress method of controlling a Ministry from

outside by a Higher Command. Each Muslim League Ministry would be autonomous; and in the event of violation of Muslim League principles the only action to be taken would be expulsion from the League.

7. He argued that if Allah Baksh and his followers had joined the Party there would have been certainty of a stable Ministry. He stated that he had no desire to exclude Hindus, but that he objected to the present position in which the Government of Sind was carried on not by the Predominant Party but by Hindus through a small and unrepresentative section of the majority community.

8. He then referred to the necessity of summoning a session of the Assembly at an early date.

9. My conclusions are that the reasons which led Jinnah to see me are:–
   1. To get an early session while the impression caused by his visit is still fresh; and
   2. To convince me that Allah Baksh is not deserving of Confidence."[28]

The strategy now to be adopted by Muslim League under the advice of Jinnah was to concentrate on the organisation of the party in Sind and to win public support for it which would act as pressure on the members of the legislature. He had assured the Sind Muslim Leaders that by joining Muslim League they were not compromising their autonomy in any way and as he said to the Governor, "each Muslim League Ministry would be autonomous." Jinnah realised that for the moment it was premature to expect that there was enough unity in the ranks of the Muslim members for them to enable them to join together to form a government in the face of the wily tactics of Congress which was able to win over some Muslim members with promises of office and favours.

Jinnah and the Muslim Leaguers now cut their losses and set about to organise Muslim League in Sind. A committee was set up with Haroon as Chairman and Majid as Secretary to set up the basic organisation of Muslim League in the province and elections were held at Haroon's house to elect the Muslim League Parliamentary Party. Hidayetullah was elected Leader, Mir Bandehally the leader of the 'Mir group' as Deputy Leader, Khuhro as General Secretary and Gazdar, Mir Ghulamally, and Nur Mohammed Shah as assistant whips. Every effort was made to establish close co-operation between the parliamentary party and the Muslim League organisation outside the Assembly. The importance of the parliamentary party was considerable because most of the influential and important political personalities were in the Assembly.

Having set up the basic structure of the party, Jinnah set out for his whirlwind tour of Sind. The Soomro ministry had sent out instructions that the tour was to be obstructed and not allowed to be successful. This policy was carried out quite subtly by hints to potential hosts and organisers who on the whole were not prepared to go against the expressed wishes of the government in power. The result was that Jinnah was unable to hold a public meeting except at Larkana where Khuhro and his team had worked hard to make it a success. Khuhro was a sufficiently influential figure in the district for the government opposition to be ineffective and the public meeting was extremely successful. The only other important meeting Jinnah addressed was an "at home" at the residence of Mir Jafar Khan Jamali in Jacobabad. From these small beginnings Muslim League was to grow into the major Muslim party in Sind. By 21 October Jinnah was able to complete his visit to Sind and return to Bombay leaving a suitable inspiring message to his party men in Sind.

The basic task for the Muslim League now was to elect its permanent body and for this purpose a meeting of Muslim League Council was held in late November 1938. This meeting was attended by thirty members of which only five were members of the Sind Legislative Assembly. The meeting was presided over by Khuhro and its most important task was to elect the President of Muslim League in Sind. The contest was between Haroon and Majid, the latter being backed by Hidayetullah who was bitterly opposed to Haroon. The vote was tied and Khuhro put his casting vote in favour of Haroon, who in his opinion would make a more feasible president of the fledgling party. Hidayetullah was much more interested in having a president he could manipulate and saw Majid as filling this role. Khuhro who had been a close associate of Hidayetullah had now begun to distance himself from him since he had shown himself as a single mindedly self serving politician in the period after his removal from office and during Jinnah's visit when efforts to organise the Muslim League party were being made. In the elections for the provincial party offices therefore Khuhro threw his weight behind Haroon. Majid was elected General Secretary of the party.

The first task of the party was to get a session of the Assembly and bring a vote of No Confidence against Soomro. Soomro on the other hand was obviously not very keen on an early session of the Assembly as he knew that he needed to get more Muslim members on his side since if the majority of Muslim members stayed with Muslim League his Ministry could fall. The Congress well aware of the danger did its best to rally opinion behind the Congress backed government by sending its important leaders to tour Sind. Vallabhai Patel came in the fourth week of August, Azad was expected and Acharya Kripalani, a Sindhi himself and a future president of Congress also visited. Their main task was to assess the situation in view of the Muslim League conference and the organisation of Muslim League as well as the near defection of Soomro. Patel had interviews with leading politicians of Sind including ofcourse Soomro and Congress members. Khuhro and Syed met him to protest against the Ministry's policy regarding the revised assessment and also to suggest that Congress was supporting a Ministry which had lost its popularity and acceptance among the people. These arguments did not cut much ice with the Congress leadership which had no intention of jeopardising the Ministry by putting difficulties in its path.

The last few months 1938 saw the visits of not only Maulana Azad and Patel but also Subhas Chandar Bose who toured the interior and Sarojini Naidu who stayed in Karachi for about two days but "attended several public functions at which she urged opposition to Federation and advocated inter communal unity, membership of Congress and adoption of Hindi as *lingua franca*"[29] Yousif Mehrali "a prominent socialist of Bombay" also came and tried to arouse interest in the Congress movement. A 'mass movement' was to be started in Sind by Congress which wanted desperately to be acceptable to the people and to counter Muslim League influence and at the same time to keep the Soomro ministry in power. The High Command wanted to get the revised assessment postponed so as not to alienate public opinion in the province. In fact it was very important for Congress to maintain the Soomro ministry in power because Sind would be the only Muslim majority province to prove its non communal credentials and would also deny Muslim League a government in the province. The dilemma was a very real one and opinion was divided among the top leaders. Soomro was summoned to Bombay to talk to the Congress 'High Command'. He took the Governor into his confidence who told him either not to go to Bombay or to be careful not to accept any conditions which could jeopardise the revision settlement and the re-organisation of the Barrage area. Abul Kalam Azad was quite firm that Congress members should not vote for this legislation but Patel and the Sind Congress were in favour of supporting the ministry rather than risk a purely "Mohammedan or Muslim League Ministry". Soomro came back without definite instructions from the High Command and duly informed the Governor:

"...Allah Baksh saw me today after his return from Bombay. His journey has not resulted in anything as Abul Kalam was present. He declined to go to Wardha [to see Gandhi] on grounds of health. The Hindu leaders were unwilling to over-rule Abul Kalam in his absence.

The position therefore remains as before. The Congress requires the postponement of the whole settlement orders for one year in order to allow time for consideration of objection and for discussion in the Assembly. After that, Government will pass orders modifying the present orders if necessary and lastly Government will discuss their orders with the local Congress before issue.

These demands throw the whole question of Barrage resettlement back to the position it was in July. They go even further than simple postponement for a year...

Allah Baksh assured me that he had committed himself to nothing in his discussions with Gandhi, Vallabhai and other leaders. He is however undoubtedly impressed by his interview with such prominent persons."[30]

Azad appeared to be determined to force a showdown with the government and compel the Governor to use his special powers which might help the nationalist movement in India but would do nothing for the sitting government in Sind. Soomro however was too weak to make a definite stand on the issue and gave the Congress leaders the impression that the matter was still open for discussion although he had given repeated and definite commitments to the Governor that he would not even consider a postponement. Garret comments:

"It is very unfortunate that Allah Baksh has given the impression that he is willing to discuss a matter which is already decided by his Government. It will now remain for Graham to deal with the matter..."[31]

Garret was very disappointed that during the four months Graham had been away the matter of the revised enhanced assessment was still not finally decided by the Ministry and its Congress supporters but he need not have worried as when it came to the question of losing the Ministry or keeping the commitment with the Governor, Soomro opted for the Ministry and the Sind Congress ministers supported him with the blessings of Patel if not Azad.

On his return from home leave Graham was very firm with Soomro:

"I have told him quite frankly that I would rather lose my Ministry than put up with dictation from the Congress." and that "it was preposterous to expect that my Government should postpone the enforcing of the orders for the revision settlement in order to satisfy the vanity of a single Mohammedan [Azad] and thereby improve the position of the Congress *vis a vis* the Mohamedan community."[32]

The Governor agreed to a postponement of the Assembly session while the Ministry lobbied for support among the Muslim members and the session was finally called for 4 January 1939. Muslim League leaders also used all possible avenues of canvassing support for the No Confidence motion they wanted to bring against Soomro. Sir Sikander Hayat sent the important *pir* of Multan, Nawab Murid Hussain Quraishi, who had a considerable following in Sind to come and use his influence on their behalf. As soon as the Assembly met the Muslim League party tabled a No Confidence motion the date for which was scheduled for 10th January for discussion.

The Ministry was in a panic. It could not be sure of its Muslim support and it was also insecure about Congress attitude as the High Command had still not given Soomro an absolute assurance of support on the question of the revision settlement. Soomro was left with the task of gaining support for an unpopular cause without either Muslim League or Congress, as it appeared to him. The only way out of the crisis was to add to the number of Ministers and bribe some of the Muslim members to come in. The man he had been negotiating with was no less than the Leader of Opposition and the Leader of Muslim League Parliamentary Party, Sir Ghulam Hussain Hidayetullah and the Deputy Leader, Mir Bandehali Talpur.

Hidayetullah out of power had been fish out of water. He had been in secret negotiations with the Ministry as Vazirani had hinted to Garret earlier. These negotiations now bore fruit and he agreed to walk over with his friends including the Mir group with Bandehali Talpur. The Governor was privy to these talks and duly notified the Viceroy about the new arrangements:

"...negotiations for a `central combination' ... now appear to have reached a stage at which agreement can be concluded. I have at the suggestion of my Chief Minister had a long talk with Sir Ghulam Hussain, my late Chief Minister and from him I understand that he is so dissatisfied with the attitude of the Muslim League that he is ready to join my Ministry, bringing with him those who are not fanatically devoted to the Muslim League. The consideration for this access of strength of my Ministry is to be an increase in the number of Ministers to five or six.

3. Increase in the number of Ministers is desirable to broaden the base of the Ministry as a whole and to give my Ministers personally a sense of security which would, allow them leisure to formulate and execute a progressive policy instead of leaving them in their present position of tight rope walkers solely concerned with the problem of remaining in office.[33]

Apart from giving the Ministry the leisure to work out a 'progressive policy' the Governor was getting his revision settlement and being saved the use of special powers which would have brought an odour of bad repute to the newly established constitutional reform. Thus the Governor who had found himself unable to oblige the same Sir Ghulam Hussain the same concession he had asked for to save his Ministry a few months earlier, was now prepared to do the needful without blinking an eye:

"4. Both Allah Baksh and Ghulam Hussain assure me that I shall have no further trouble over the assessment. The motion of 'No Confidence' will be moved not in the name of Ghulam Hussain [the Leader of the Opposition] but in that of one of the advanced Muslim Leaguers; and Sir Ghulam tells me that it is his intention to resign with four or five members from the Opposition Party in the course of today or before the motion comes up tomorrow. If that is done I do not think it will prevent the moving of the motion but it will ensure its defeat."[34]

Both Soomro and Hidayetullah told the Governor that the increase in the number of Ministers should not be announced until some date in February when there was to be a short adjournment of the Assembly before taking up consideration of the Budget. For the Governor it was almost imperative to save the Ministry from disaster because otherwise he would have to start all over again with a new government to get the revised assessment accepted or to use his special powers:

> "The position we have to envisage is one in which my Ministers are dismissed on a vote of 'No Confidence' and I am unable to secure a new Ministry except on terms either of postponing – or more probably cancelling – the orders"[35]

The change of sides by a dozen members including two senior leaders of Muslim League left the House gasping for breath and the Opposition was left with only seven hard core Muslim Leaguers, Khuhro, Syed, Gazdar, Majid, Khair Shah, Nur Mohammed Shah and Isran. The No Confidence was voted on 12 January and was defeated by 32 to 7. The Ministry got the votes the Hidayetullah group, Hindu Independent Party and the European members, making obvious the side the Governor was on. Congress, having been spared the necessity of abandoning its principles and of annoying Maulana Azad, remained neutral and thus saved face.

For Muslim Leaguers it was a salutary lesson – the dross had been separated from the gold. It was also obvious that there was no substitute for organisational work and building up public opinion in the province. This had been the strategy used for the separation of Sind struggle which had succeeded so well. There was a crucial difference however. At that time the entire Muslim leadership had been united and a section of Hindu and other non Muslim opinion had been with them. The position was now the reverse. The Muslim League leadership found itself isolated and powerless. The adversary was no longer a distant Bombay bureaucracy and a minority (albeit a powerful and well organised one) in Sind, but the Muslim leadership itself which had become totally divided. The lure of office had proved too strong for most of the elected members. The irony of the situation was that autonomy was supposed to put the control of the provincial government in the hands of the majority community to be used for its welfare, emancipation and for its economic and social betterment. But the incumbent Ministry was a puppet not only in the hands of the minority but faithful servant of the colonial governor doing his bidding even at the cost of the welfare of the people it was meant to serve. It was a bitter outcome for Khuhro and his friends who had expected *nirvana* after the attainment of autonomy. They found themselves even more powerless than before April 1936. But the fruits of autonomy could not be given up so easily. The depleted ranks of Muslim League were determined to save the situation and throw out the Ministry which had inflicted so much damage on the interests of the majority community. Muslims of Sind had to be rallied into an irresistible force. A cause would have to be found and a strategy worked out around it to win back the province. This cause was at hand and had been knocking at the doors of the leaders for sometime. They looked around and found it – Masjid Manzilgah.

10

MASJID MANZILGAH

Masjid Manzilgah was the name popularly given to a complex of buildings on the banks of the Indus at Sukkur* which dated from the time of the Mughal emperor Akbar. This complex consisted of a *serai* (inn) and a mosque, reputedly built by Syed Masoom Shah, Governor of Sind during Akbar's reign. The two domed buildings were situated in what was known as *manzilgah* or camping ground near the banks of Indus opposite the island of Sadh Belo. One of the buildings was slightly larger and more elaborately ornamented and was dated 1589. The smaller of the two buildings, on the western side, had a three domed roof with a larger central dome, was regarded as a mosque by the Muslim population and had a tradition of being used as such. The buildings had been taken over by the British at the time of the conquest during the middle of the nineteenth century and used a residence by its military and political officers in Sukkur, as indeed many of the tombs and other buildings in the conquered territory of India had been used by the British. Richard Burton, the distinguished orientalist who spent his early years in service in Sind reports that "tombs were pierced for windows, furnished with mud verandahs and converted into bungalows by the first military settlers."[1]

One of the early residents of the building had been E. B. Eastwick who came to Sind before the British conquest, in 1839, at the age of twenty-four, and became a Political Officer stationed at Sukkur. He remained here for two and half years and published *Dry Leaves of Young Egypt* his interesting and informative book on Sind at this period. Eastwick, who knew Persian, did a good deal of research and noted down the inscriptions on the historical buildings and tombs of the area. When the buildings were eventually vacated by the officers, they continued to remain under government control. Nothing however was done to repair or preserve the buildings. The official report cited an instance when one of the buildings was even rented out at one time to 'a bania' who used it to store kerosene oil![2]

It had been a long standing demand of the Muslims of Sukkur that the mosque and the *serai* be returned to the community and put to their proper use. This demand was made as early as 1920 and repeated from time to time. It had however

---

* Sukkur, one of the important towns of Upper Sind was situated on the right bank of the river Indus at a strategic as well as picturesque spot. The river was a very wide here with a number of island, the biggest of which was the island of Bukkur with its historic fort and the ancient town of Rohri on the Left bank opposite Sukkur. Sukkur was a river port closely linked with the commercial and financial centre of Shikarpur, a few miles inland.

not been received sympathetically by the authorities at least partly because powerful Hindu opposition was expected as the Manzligah buildings were on the banks of the Indus directly opposite the river island of Sadh Belo where the Hindus had built temples some years earlier. The island had become a favourite place of pilgrimage for them. The Hindu community was numerically as well as financially strong in Sukkur and dominated the Municipality. The views of the community were well-known to the administration which did not want to create a confrontation especially in the charged atmosphere of the 'thirties in India.*

During the struggle for the separation of Sind from the Bombay Presidency in its last and decisive phase after the Simon Commission of findings in 1929-30, the Muslims of Sukkur made a special point of getting a commitment from the leaders of the movement that the buildings known as Masjid Manzilgah would be handed over to them by the Sind government. When Hidayetullah formed the first autonomous Government of Sind in 1937, the demand was put before him by the Sukkur Muslims. But while assuring them that he would take up the matter as soon as he could, in a typically duplicitous manner, he shelved the matter indefinitely. Hidayetullah was experienced enough and shrewd enough to realize that the implementation of this demand would definitely be opposed by the Hindus who formed the majority of the urban population of Sukkur and that the restoration of the mosque could lead to a serious intercommunal problems which would be very difficult for the government to deal with and could even put its existence into jeopardy. Unaware of Hidayetullah's actions the Sukkur Muslims continued their pressure to regain the mosque complex. The demand was presented at the Muslim League Conference of 1938[3] and a resolution passed in favour of the restoration.

In early 1939 the Sukkur district branch of the Muslim League passed a resolution asking the Provincial Muslim League to take up the question of Manzilgah with the government. They particularly asked Khuhro to take up the issue. Khuhro who was Leader of the Opposition in the Sind Legislative Assembly, was ofcourse personally known to the Muslim leaders in Sukkur because of the help he had organised for them in the aftermath of the riots in that district in 1930.[4] The local champion of Muslim rights, the *Sind Zamindar* newspaper, was under his control and his record of courage in the face of government pressure was well-known. The Muslims of Sukkur knew and trusted Khuhro and were convinced of his commitment to their cause. On his part Khuhro felt that the restoration of the Manzilgah was not only worthwhile in itself but that it was a cause which could rally the Muslims of Sind. He promised to bring the matter to the attention of the party and to get it to agree to support it.

During this period Khuhro was making fairly frequent journeys to Delhi not only to discuss matters relating to the Muslim League organisation and to clarify

---

* The communal atmosphere in India had become tense in the years following the Khilafat and Non Co-operation movements in the years following World War I. There had been an intensification of the Shuddhi (purification) movement which aimed to convert Muslims and other non Hindus to Hinduism and had been answered by some Muslim organisation particularly in the Punjab. The tension had spilled over into Sind in the late 'twenties and there had been incidents in Larkana in 1928 and in Sukkur in 1930. In the 'thirties the communal tension had been exacerbated by the political parties including Congress, Muslim League and Hindu Mahasabha.

policy lines with the Muslim League 'High Command', but also in connection with the rights of the landowners in Khairpur State.[5] On 9 March Khuhro left for Delhi on one of these visits and to bring up the problem of Masjid Manzilgah. Khuhro returned from Delhi on 16 March and on the next day, Friday 17 March, a meeting of the Muslim League Parliamentary Party[6] met at Khuhro's house opposite Patel Park in Karachi. In addition to the matters to be taken up in the Assembly the question of Manzilgah was also discussed at this meeting. Khuhro had to make another quick trip to Delhi in the second week of April and on his return on 11 April he wrote to Haroon the President of the Provincial Muslim League, to fix a meeting of the Working Committee of the Provincial Muslim League on 23 April. At this meeting and at subsequent ones leading up to the summer months of June and July, the Working Committee, mindful of the fact that any reluctance on its part would undermine the position of the organisation in the province, voted to support the demand of the Sukkur branch. A delegation was formed to negotiate with the government with Haroon and Khuhro in the lead.

At the time Soomro had become premier he had not only re-opened the Manzilgah issue shelved by Hidayetullah but had also given an undertaking to representatives of Jamilat-e-Ulema-i-Sind* that he would restore the Manzilgah mosque to the Muslims. This undertaking had been given in particular to Maulvi Mohammed Sadik of Madressah Mazhar-ul-Uloom of Khadda in Karachi, a distinguished religious scholar and notable freedom fighter who had played a prominent part in the Tehrik Reshmi Roomal and was a close friend and associate of Maulana Ubaidullah Sindhi.** Soomro had re-opened the matter which had been closed by Hidayetullah but then failed to take any action to fulfil his promise to the leaders of Jamait-e-Ulemai-Sindh, although they had even gone to Sukkur and announced that the mosque would be restored very shortly.[7]

It was clear that a serious crisis was fast developing in Sukkur the repercussions of which would be felt throughout Sind and it was not difficult to work out that the weak and vacillating policy of the Premier was largely responsible for the escalation of the crisis. The Enquiry Committee which was set up in November 1939 under Judge Weston when the crisis was almost over, laid most of the responsibility for the situation developing as it did, on the Premier. The report said that he had categorically stated that he was within his rights to re-open the matter of the Manzilgah even though his predecessor had closed it

---

* Jamiat-e-Ulemai-Sind was inspired by and organised on the same lines as Jamiat-e-Ulemai Hind and was strongly in sympathy with the 'nationalist' cause and with the Congress programme. During World War I the leadership of JUS had worked with the anti British groups including the Sindhi religious school of Pirs of Jhando and Maulvi Ubaidullah Sindhi who took part in a number of conspiracies against the British in India. JUS was thus an organisation which was sympathetic too, if not in actual alliance with the Indian National Congress.

**Maulana Ubaidullah Sindhi was a Punjabi Sikh convert to Islam. A brilliant Islamic thinker and political activist, he spent a considerable amount of time in Sind at the Madressah of Pirs of Jhando Sharif where he acquired Islamic learning and also imbibed his revolutionary ideas. He added the sobriquet of 'Sindhi' to his name in honour of the land where he had acquired his faith and learning. During World War I he took part in a number of conspiracies, the most famous of which was Tehrik Reshmi Roomal or the 'Movement of the Silk Handkerchief'.
Interview with Maulana Mohammed Ismail, the son of Maulana Mohammed Sadik and head of Madressah Darul-ul-Uloom, Khadda, Karachi. December 1989.

The Report further said:

Khan Bahadur Allah Baksh ... says: "Although orders were passed by Sir Ghulam Hussain not to reply to Ithad-i-Millat, and the matter was closed by him, there was nothing to stop me reopening the matter"[8] ...

"Khan Bahadur Allah Baksh reopened the Manzilgah question apparently closed by his predecessor only eleven days after he assumed the office of Chief Minister... without consulting the local officers and at no time during the eighteen months during which the matter remained pending with him did he seek the advice of the local officers. ...It is in fact plain from his evidence and that of the District Magistrate that the latter was regarded as little more than ministerial officer, not necessarily to be consulted or even informed as to the turn of events, to be directed to impose or to cancel orders such as the order under Section 144, Criminal Procedure Code, the primary responsibility for which rests with him, and to be left with substantial discretion to deal with a situation only when disturbance was imminent.

This undoubtedly weakened the general authority of the District Magistrate and I have no doubt (was) one of the causes of the general lowering of the respect for law and order which the disturbances show must have occurred throughout the district."[9]

The enquiry further pointed out the vacillating nature of Allah Baksh's policies when he made promises to Jamiat-ul-Ulema and then failed to fulfil them:

"The connection of ... Mohammed Sadik [of Khadda], President of the Jamiat ul Ulema with the request for assistance in staging Satyagraha has been mentioned. K. B. Allah Baksh states in evidence that the Jamiat-ul-Ulema were his supporters. According to Mohammad Sadik he went to K. B. Allah Baksh in the first week of his Ministry to make representation about the Lauri Haj and his request for a ban on the Haj was granted. He and others of his Jamiat also approached K. B. Allah Baksh concerning the Manzilgah matter about the same time .... He states that K. B. Allah Baksh told him and his companions to go to Sukkur and to satisfy themselves that the building was a mosque. On the 14th April Mohammed Sadik was given a letter to the Collector of Sukkur stating that he and one Hakim Fateh Mohammed desired to view the disputed buildings and asking in the name of the Chief Minister that they should be given facilities. Mohammed Sadik states that they went to Sukkur and inspected the mosque. They addressed a meeting at Sukkur and informed the Muslims at Sukkur that they had been asked by K. B. Allah Baksh to make the inspection, that they were satisfied that the building was a mosque, that they would inform K. B. Allah Baksh accordingly and that the Muslims should await his decision. ... one witness says that they stated that they would get the building restored after their return to Karachi. Another says they stated they had been asked by the Chief Minister to convey a message that the mosque would be restored within a short time. K. B. Allah Baksh denies that he sent any such message, or that he informed Mahomed Sadik and his companions of his personal opinion as expressed in the minute of 3rd April. I find it difficult to believe that the moulvies could have failed to gather the personal opinion of K. B. Allah Baksh before they went to Sukkur.[10]

K. B. Allah Baksh's note of the 12th April states that he had recently inspected the buildings. This note is of interest as it shows very clearly the personal opinion of K. B. Allahbaksh that the building was a mosque.[11]

... K. B. Allah Baksh had committed himself in favour of the buildings being restored to the Muslims more than a year earlier, but in spite of the promises had done nothing."

The enquiring officer gave his opinion that after May 1938 Soomro realised he would arouse a good deal of opposition by the decision to restore the mosque, not only in Sukkur but also in his Ministry, and among his supporters in the Assembly. He preferred to do nothing in the hope that the agitation would die away.[12]

In fact in the latter half of 1938 the agitation did appear to lose some of its force. Maulvi Sadik said in his evidence that after his report to Soomro in April 1938 he approached him from time to time and was given assurances. On one occasion about a year after his report, he said, he was given a definite promise that the Mosque would be restored after three or four days. In April 1939 he wrote to Dr. Mohammed Yamin stating that he had been given assurance by the "Ministry" and that in the circumstances there should be no disturbance or threat of *satyagraha*.

But in spite of this promise the Premier did not give any decision or any indication when he would do so and the reason given for this delay by the Premier was that he was not prepared to do anything under the threat of *satyagraha* which was made in July, although: "It is pointed out that he had taken action under threat of *satyagraha* in other matters, such as Luari Haj and the Om Mandli question." After the renewal of the agitation about May 1939 a number of protests were made by the Hindus of Sukkur but the conclusion of the Enquiry Officer was that:

"The root cause of the trouble is to be found not in the final manoeuvres of the negotiations, but in the long period of inaction, a decision would have avoided the happenings both of October and of November 1939."[13]

Towards the end of June 1939 Haroon and Khuhro met the Premier. He was evasive about the issue and the League representatives left with the impression that he did not have the courage to carry through the promises that he had made. In the meantime the pressure for the restoration continued to mount. The only course now open to the Muslim League was to sustain its pressure tactics. Consequently a Restoration Committee was formed with Haroon, the provincial League president as president of the Committee and Khuhro as vice president. Other important members of the Committee were G. M. Syed and Hashim Gazdar. Pir Ali Mohammed Rashdi was appointed secretary to the Committee.

On 23 and 24 July a widely representative meeting of the Muslim League members, public representatives, prominent citizens, maulvis, lawyers and political workers took place in Sukkur under the presidentship of Khuhro.[14] The meeting regretted the "anti masjid" policy of the government and passed a number of resolutions designed to restore the Manzilgah mosque complex of buildings to the Muslims. The meeting demanded that the Muslim representatives in the Sind legislature withdraw their support from the government if it failed to restore the mosque, and to bring in a government which would do so. Muslim members who did not support restoration would not be elected again. 18 August was fixed as "Manzilgah day" on which day public meetings would be held all over the province to demand its restoration and M.L.As. were urged to withdraw their support of the government. An ultimatum was delivered to the government that if the buildings were not restored to the Muslims, *satyagraha* would be started by them from October 1939. Muslim League district and other branch offices as well as other sympathetic Muslim organisations were asked to recruit volunteers and receive donations of money for which a target of 5,000 volunteers and a fund of Rs. 10,000 was set. A Masjid Manzilgah Committee was set up with Khuhro as treasurer and Agha Nazar Ali, long time associate and manager of Khuhro's Sukkur newspaper *Sind Zamindar*, as Secretary of the Committee.[15]

Although Muslim League had now adopted the policy of 'passive resistance' or *satyagraha* to pressurize the government to restore Manzilgah buildings the idea of this course of action did not originate with Muslim Leaguers. It was actually the Muslims of Sukkur themselves who had threatened *satyagraha* as early as 1937 if the Government of the newly autonomous Sind did not keep the promises which had been made to them at the time of the buildings.[16]

With the decision to offer *satyagraha*, Muslim League in Sind entered an extraordinary and revolutionary phase of its history. For nearly ten years the Muslim leadership of Sind had waged a well organised and tenacious struggle for the separation of the province and the ranks of the Muslim leadership of Sind contained a number of experienced and courageous men who knew both the art of attack and of compromise. These years had also produced a number of determined and committed workers. But never before had they contemplated a course of action which would included defiance of the law of the land. Although *satyagraha* was a new departure for the Muslim politicians and political workers, they had enough manpower to be able to organise it and they had the example of Gandhi's tactics to know how to go about it. The movement for the restoration of the Manzilgah buildings, the adoption of Gandhian tactics of pressure at a time when war was imminent in Europe and when the British government did not want any disturbance in the even tenor of day to day *raj*, was a bold and courageous move. It showed that the Muslim League leadership was prepared to face the wrath of the Imperial government in supporting a popular Muslim cause and at the same time it was capable of uniting Muslims of different shades of opinion under its leadership and able to plan and organise a programme of "resistance". Muslim League was not fazed by the hostility of the government and the powerful bureaucracy, nor by the press under its control. The combined pressure could not divert it from its mission.

Khuhro was now in the forefront of a popular agitational movement. His long association with and knowledge of Sukkur politics and friendship with the Muslim leadership of the town, and his own considerable standing in the town, particularly through the ownership of the newspaper *Sind Zamindar*, which after *Al Wahid* of Karachi, was the most important Muslim newspaper in the province, gave him the trust and confidence of the Sukkur Muslim community and at least in his own view, put the responsibility of seeing the struggle through on his shoulders more than on any other in the Muslim League ranks. The position that he enjoyed in public estimation was given recognition when he was given the presidentship of the crucial meeting of 22 and 23 July which was to set the course for civil disobedience. Khuhro himself felt personally obliged to participate in the 'Restoration movement' for, as a leading figure in the separation struggle he had promised to do all he could for the restoration of the Manzilgah buildings to the Muslims. The failure of the successive governments, including that of Hidayetullah of which he had been a member, had been a disappointing experience. He was determined to do all he could personally at least, to forward the cause of the Sukkur Muslims.

The programme chalked out by the meeting met with wide approval among the Muslims of Sind and put the pro government groups including the *ulema* who supported the government, on the defensive[17]. The July meeting was not determined on confrontation as was obvious from the date set for the start of the civil disobedience movement. The first of October was far enough away to give the government well over two months to take some conciliatory and remedial action.

The Soomro government however failed to take the opportunity to defuse the situation. From the Governor down there was failure to appreciate the seriousness of the demand and of the intensity of feeling among the Muslims. The Governor was in full support of the Sind Premier particularly as he headed the government which had so recently brought in the enhanced tax rates at some considerable cost to its popularity. After the crisis had erupted in November he wrote a long letter in defence of Soomro's role in the Manzilgah crisis to the Viceroy, excusing his indecision and dilatoriness, even going so far as to criticize the report of the Inquiry Committee under Judge Weston which had given the opinion that

"the explosion which began on November 19th was due to the failure over a period of three and half months, to deal effectively with threats to public orders. The Ministry's relations with the Muslim leaders of the agitation in that period were marked by indecision and delay in some measures due to divisions among Ministers themselves."[18]

This failure of perception was clear not only from the vacillation and lassitude of the Premier but also from the fact that the Governor failed to keep the Viceroy informed of the developments in this regard. It was only after the situation had taken a serious turn in November-December 1939 that any urgency appears in his communication. Linlithgow was forced to comment:

"There is a woolliness of mind about him which makes him a little difficult to deal with; the more so as I do not think that he for a moment suspects that he is anything but a model in regard either to his reports or as to his handling of his province."[19]

In fact soon after the start of the *satyagraha* movement in early October the Viceroy sent a telegram to Graham warning him that there were indications that the agitation could assume "more than provincial importance".[20]

Even earlier, in September, the Government of India showed its concern at the lack of adequate information from Sind and the lack of proper preparedness to face the crisis. The Secretary of State and the Viceroy in their correspondence deplored the lack of information regarding the Manzilgah situation from the Governor and the fact that Government of India was not being kept fully informed.[21] As it happened the Government of India was justified in its concern that a serious situation was being allowed to develop at such a critical time. But apart from alerting the Governor to take adequate notice of the situation there was not much it could do. In spite of all the warnings however, quite inexcusably, Government of Sind allowed the situation to deteriorate to the point of disaster.

The 18 August was observed as Manzilgah Day throughout Sind with a great deal of enthusiasm by different political and religious groups. Reports came in to the Muslim League headquarters of the meetings held and resolutions passed throughout the province. The League leaders could now hope that this demonstration of their strength would induce the Government to address the Manzilgah issue. At the same time Muslim solidarity demonstrated by Manzilgah day would serve to impress upon the Muslim supporters of the government that the public was not with them and that the Soomro government was a lost cause. Failing these objectives Manzilgah Day had at the very least shown that there was a conducive atmosphere for the *satyagraha* movement to go ahead in October and preparations for it could be undertaken with confidence. The Jamiat leaders tried to buy time for Soomro but their arguments did not prove convincing[22] and the government caught between Muslim pressure and Hindu opposition continued to vacillate.

On 3 September Haroon and Khuhro again met Soomro and the latter assured them that the Manzilgah buildings would be returned to the Muslims. A meeting of the Restoration Committee was fixed at Sukkur on 16 September to be followed by a public meeting later at night. Khuhro who had just returned from Simla where he had met Jinnah and the Viceroy's staff and briefed them about the situation, wrote to G. M. Syed urging him to make sure to attend the meeting:

"The meeting of the Manzilgah Mosque Restoration Committee has been fixed at Sukkur on 16th instant at 5.30 p.m. In the night at 9 p.m. there will be a public meeting as well, and the meeting may be continued on 17th too. As this is a very important meeting and many important persons in Sind are invited to attend, I shall be glad if you make it a point to attend.

I have returned from Simla on 6th instant and I am going to Larkana this evening. I will be proceeding to Sukkur on 16th morning from Larkana. Arrangements for your stay there have been made there."[23]

By 29 September the Sind Government had still not responded and had taken no action. The Sind Muslim League Working Committee called a special meeting in Sukkur to take the final decision. Writing on 25 September Khuhro urged some caution to G. M. Syed who was ready to leave Sann with his volunteer group with a great deal of ceremony:

"Your letter of the 23rd reached me today. I am afraid you have not known the situation and therefore you will naturally not be in a position to guage the situation properly. Arrangements for *satyagraha* are complete, but we have to decide in the Working Committee of the Provincial Muslim League on the 29th instant at 5 p.m. at Sukkur, as to whether the *satyagraha* should be launched and if so when. The Restoration Committee also meets on the same day. Besides, the Government has issued a communique on this issue, advising the Muslims to allow (themselves) time to think over in calm atmosphere by suspending *satyagraha*, which will also be discussed there. Your presence therefore is most essential and you must make it a point to attend it. The question as to when you and your *jatha* should be directed to offer *satyagraha* will be settled in consonance with the programme that will be laid down on that date. If it is decided to offer satyagraha from Ist October, your *jatha* will be needed by the 5th in any case. Make arrangements accordingly, in advance."[24]

The Government press note Khuhro referred to in his letter had been issued rather late in the day when the arrangements for the *satyagraha* were already complete, but the League Leadership, as is obvious from Khuhro's letter, was prepared to give it fair consideration even at this stage. The press note urged that the *satyagraha* decision should not be implemented and that the Government would soon given its decision on the issue–

"Government have been approached from several quarters for an early decision regarding the Manzilgah buildings alleged to be a mosque and a rest house at Sukkur. Government desire to say that this question is receiving their consideration, and that the matter will be disposed of as soon as may be.

"Government understand that it is proposed to stage a "satyagraha" from Ist of October 1939 with a view to securing the transfer of the Manzilgah to the Muslims. Government need hardly emphasise that a matter of such controversy as the disposal of the Manzilgah should be decided in a calm atmosphere and on a dispassionate consideration of what every party interested in the matter has to say. It is, therefore, the considered opinion of the Government that it is in the interests of everyone concerned that the leaders of the Muslim community interested in this question should not launch satyagraha but should wait for the decision of the Government. And the Government requests all concerned in the matter to create the atmosphere which is necessary for the consideration and disposal of a matter of this import."[25]

The issuance of this Press Note could hardly escape the suspicion that the government was trying to buy time without in fact making any effort to resolve the problem. While it was urging the Muslims to give up agitation it was making frantic preparations to counter the *satyagraha*. Soomro arrived in Shikarpur on 27 September to be near the scene of action. Volunteer groups were getting ready to leave from Shikarpur under the leadership of Wajid Ali Shaikh, a Muslim League worker. The Premier felt this to be an embarrassment for him while he was actually present in his home town and tried to persuade the group leaders not to go but failed to do so.[26] The Sukkur administration imposed Section 144 (forbidding assembly of more than four persons, or carrying of arms) and also Section 42 (forbidding carrying of weapons, sticks and stones, etc.). Enclosing walls around the Manzilgah buildings were strengthened or built anew. Glass fragments were imbedded in the walls and in the grounds around the buildings and police reinforcements were brought into Sukkur. The government awaited Muslim League's decision.

In its meeting on 29 September the Working Committee took notice of the fact that although more than two months had been given to the Government to come to some decision and the Muslim League leadership had twice met the Premier, so far no progress had been made on the issue. The belated press note made no specific commitment and was couched in very vague terms. In view of these facts the Muslim League and the Restoration Committee were left with no alternative but to go ahead with the non violent passive resistence movement.

The preparations for the *satyagraha* were thorough and complete as Khuhro had informed Syed. Following the Congress example, large numbers of volunteers had been recruited and sworn to loyalty and steadfastness. Volunteers from all over Sind had been given instructions as to their duties and divided into groups (*jathas*) which would arrive in Sukkur on given dates so as to avoid an uncontrollable mass of people and confusion. The volunteers gathered at the 'Eidgah Maidan' (Eid festival prayer ground), each group under its own leader, and from here they marched organised in groups, in a procession, shouting slogans, to the Manzilgah buildings, which were a considerable distance away. When they reached Manzilgah on the river bank, the procession stopped and offer *nafl* prayers and the volunteers offered themselves for arrest, each volunteer giving his name as "Mussalman son of Mussalman"[27].

Some volunteers overcome by the emotion aroused by the occasion, scaled the walls of the mosque and when they succeeded in getting inside the building they offered their prayers in the mosque before getting themselves arrested. As each group was arrested another replaced it. Volunteers numbering from three to five hundred had been prepared to offer themselves for arrest each day. The entire exercise was highly organised and disciplined. On the first day 339 volunteers offered arrest and on the second day the number was 550. By the third day the number of those arrested had reached a thousand and throughout Sind *jathas* of volunteers were ready to leave for Sukkur, waiting for their scheduled dates to join the *satyagraha*.[28]

The Volunteers who were camped in Sukkur in hundreds, behaved with unprecedented discipline. The imagination of the province had been caught. People travelled from all over the Sind not only to join but to witness the amazing spectacle of the Muslim *satyagraha*. The newspapers kept those who were not present informed of the impressive scene. They reported that on 3 October Haroon and Khuhro visited the camp and met and talked to the volunteers.[29] It appears that the movement could go on indefinitely. It had an electrifying effect not only in Sind but in other provinces as well. In Lahore, barely two days after the start of the *satyagraha*, a big public meeting was held under the presidentship of Maulana Zafar Ali Khan, intellectual and editor of the powerful newspaper of Lahore, *Zamindar*, where he declared that ten crore (100,000,000) Indian Muslims would offer *satyagraha* in support of Sindhi Muslims.[30]

With the reality of the *satyagraha* before its eyes, the Government backed down. To the surprise of all, on 3 October, the Collector of Sukkur ordered the release of all the arrested *satyagrahis*. Orders were issued to stop all further arrests, the police pickets posted at Manzilgah buildings were withdrawn and Muslims were allowed to remain in occupation of the buildings. Muslim League leaders were triumphant. Their organisation, work, and above all the unity in their ranks, had paid off. The government was in retreat. Their victory was not to be long lived however as this action on part of the government was not to the liking of the Hindus of all shades of opinion. They would soon raise an outcry and put tremendous pressure on the government to withdraw its decision. As G. M. Syed put it:

"But the restoration of the Manzilgah mosque was unfortunately not destined to be so easy and quick an achievement. The short-lived joy of the Muslims was to turn into bitter disappointment, for this unexpected turn in the events was later on found to be merely a subterfuge of the Ministry, calculated only to break up the Muslim *satyagraha* camp.

The impression created at first amongst the people by the sudden surrender of the Government within three days of the launching of Muslim *satyagraha*, was that the Government had at last decided the Muslim claim in their favour and handed over to them the possession of the mosque, through the Collector of Sukkur, but it was soon realised that the Premier had merely evaded the issue for the time being, as he was not perhaps prepared to come out openly in suppressing the Muslim agitation. He never expected that such a huge mass of Muslims would be prepared to come forward in open defiance of the Government and court arrest. It was not possible for Government to find accommodation for all of them in the prisons available in Sind. The Premier resorted to this subterfuge because he thought that it would serve two purposes: he would save himself the odium of having to arrest and imprison thousands of his peaceful co-religionists and also he would be able to gain some more time for decision. He hoped in this way to see the *satyagraha* movement broken up, as he believed that Muslims would find it difficult to keep thousands of their satyagrahis ready for a number of days together and the enthusiasm might also evaporate and thus the whole movement would automatically fizzle out."[31]

The entire Hindu press and opinion, both Congress and non-Congress was infuriated at the apparent capitulation of the Government– "Both the Hindu and the Congress Press carried on a virulent propaganda and kept on goading the Government to oust the Muslims from the Manzilgah premises at any cost..."[32]

The Muslims, while believing that the Government had given the possession of Manzilgah to them had little faith in the consistency of its behaviour and as no formal decision had been conveyed to them, had therefore not disbanded but continued to occupy the buildings. Events proved their scepticism of the Government motives right. From 3 October to 19 November the *satyagrahis* remained in occupation of Manzilgah displaying exemplary self discipline. Not a single untoward incident occurred during this time and no breach of discipline was witnessed throughout; a remarkable feat by any standards and a great tribute to the organisational abilities of Khuhro and his team, which had been mainly responsible for the conduct of the *satyagraha* movement thus far. Khuhro spent every available moment in Sukkur at the same time as calling and attending Muslim League Working Committee meetings in Karachi and travelling to Delhi to consult with Jinnah. On 10 October Khuhro wrote to G. M. Syed urging him to take a more active part in the movement:

"It is surprising that you have not taken any active part in the Sukkur Manzilgah Mosque. You must have read all about the developments from time to time. I want you kindly to come to Sukkur on 12th to meet us there for personal discussion on the latest developments. We will also discuss the communiqué issued by the Government. It is no use to simply send written orders from that distance, but you should give us the benefit of your views personally. I may also call a meeting of the Restoration Committee on the 15th at Karachi or Sukkur so you do kindly keep that date free. If you stay at Sukkur from 12th onward for a few days, as it is very necessary, I will be very thankful."[33]

Syed went to Karachi to attend the meeting fixed by Khuhro and writes:

"About the 15th of October 1939, I went to Karachi to attend a meeting of the Working Committee of the Sind Provincial Muslim League. The meeting had been called to consider the situation and to consider our future line of action in connection with the Manzilgah affair. Be it remembered that upto that time I had not taken any active part in the Satyagraha movement; and, so when I came to Karachi, I was still in a mood to give to the Government any further reasonable extension of time to enable it to come to a final decision."[34]

In fact the Government was under heavy pressure from Hindus of all shades of opinion. The newspapers as well as the Congress supporters of the Government were extremely vociferous in demanding that Manzilgah should be taken away from the Muslims. In taking this attitude the Hindus were being less than reasonable. Just a few months earlier when the Hindu community was involved in the Hanuman Mandir and Om Mandli* affairs the Muslims had not opposed their interests or tried to influence the government against them, treating the matter as strictly between the Hindu community and the government although in the case of Hanuman Mandir, government land had been occupied illegally and a temple built on it. The issue had been decided in favour of the Hindus but the Muslims had not raised any objection.[35] In the case of historic Manzilgah buildings the possession by Muslims was well founded, and there were no Hindu interests directly involved. That the community should take such a hostile attitude showed an intolerance and ill will that was inexplicable and only served to toughen the Muslim attitude.

On 14 October the Sind Governor, under his special responsibility, promulgated an Ordinance investing the Government with special powers outside the ordinary law to deal with Muslim agitation on the Manzilgah issue. This Ordinance was clearly issued in order to intimidate the Muslim leadership as there were enough powers under the ordinary law to deal with the situation. In the Premier's calculation the promulgation of the Ordinance would serve to pacify Hindu opinion to some extent. At this time Hidayetullah, who was Home Minister in Soomro's Cabinet put forward some proposals to the Muslim League leadership. According to these proposals the mosque and the grounds would be opened for the use of the Muslims as a library or for some such secular purpose but not as a mosque. All along Jinnah had been kept in the picture by the Sind Muslim League leaders. Haroon had written to him in early October asking him to talk to the Viceroy.

"Government have shown a woeful lack of imagination and statesmanship. They do not realise that the force they should use against Hitler they are now utilising in crushing their own people."[36]

Khuhro took the proposals to Jinnah in Delhi, staying at Marina Hotel where Haroon was also staying. Khuhro suggested to Haroon that he should return to Sind where he was needed and Haroon promised to go soon. Khuhro went to meet Jinnah at his house, 10 Aurangzeb Road, which was to become a famous landmark in the history of the freedom movement. Jinnah advised acceptance of the proposals and against a fight with the Government on religious issues. He suggested a compromise formula:

---

* Hanuman Mandir was a Hindu temple built illegally on government land in Karachi. When the government tried to end the encroachment Hindus agitated to prevent the resumption of government land. Muslim did not oppose the Hindus and the government was forced to give in to the Hindu occupation.

The Om Mandli affair was a quasi religious scandal. A Hindu 'holy man' Dada Lekhraj had set up an *ashram* or sanctuary, Om Mandli, in Karachi where Hindus women flocked as devotees, much to the horror of the community which wanted the government to interfere and close the *ashram*.

"Government are aware of the extent to which Muslim feeling has been moved on this question of Manzilgah mosque and they are anxious that a settlement should be reached which will meet the reasonable wishes and sentiments of the Muslim community.

The Government therefore hereby undertake to announce their decision within one month from this date and the Restoration Committee agree to suspend the satyagrah and evacuate the Mosque and building pending the decision.

That the Government also undertake to withdraw the ordinance for which there is no need now."[37]

Returning from consultation with Jinnah in Delhi, Khuhro wrote to Syed from Larkana:

"I have just returned from Delhi and shall be proceeding to Karachi by the morning train. Sir Abdullah Haroon is also arriving there on 28th at the advice of His Excellency the Governor General: Mr. Jinnah has prepared a formula which is to be placed before Government for compromise. If Government agree to that, compromise may be reached; otherwise we shall have to push through our programme. Your presence will be very necessary at Karachi therefore kindly reach there on Sunday the 29th at the latest."[38]

Haroon could not reach Karachi for the meeting but other League leaders and the members of the Restoration Committee met at Karachi. The majority of members including Syed, Shaikh Abdul Majid as well as Restoration activists Shaikh Wajid Ali, Naimutullah Quraishi, Pir Ghulam Mujaddid Sarhindi prominent amongst them, refused to accept the compromise suggested by Jinnah and insisted that the Manzligah buildings should be handed over unconditionally otherwise the objectives of the struggle would be nullified. The Restoration Committee thus remained committed to its original aims.[39]

Regardless of the fact that the atmosphere in Sukkur was extremely sensitive, the Hindu Mahasabha held a conference there on 12 to 14 November to which they invited the extremist Mahasabha leader, Dr. Moonje. At this conference a resolution condemned the weak and vacillating policy of the Government on the Manzligah question and called on the Government to take immediate possession of the Manzilgah. The Conference also demanded that Hindu Ministers, Hindu Parliamentary Secretaries and the Hindu Deputy Speaker resign their offices in protest. The press reported Dr. Moonje to have stated that he had received assurances that the two Hindu Ministers would tender their resignations if the Manzilgah was not evacuated by November 17.[40]

The holding of the conference at that time particularly in Sukkur added greatly to the tension. The fact that one of the Hindu ministers attended the conference not only caused embarrassment to the Premier but also brought home to him the threat to the continuance of his Ministry. The Government now saw that the Ordinance had failed in its object of cowing the Muslim League leadership and also in appeasing Hindu opinion. The Soomro ministry was under pressure and lacked a sense of direction. Then on 19 October the Government suddenly cracked down on the *Satyagrahis*. Ruthless action was taken to clear the Manzilgah buildings. Mounted police was sent to remove the volunteers forcibly. Tear gas and lathi charge were used to vacate the buildings. Many were jailed and injured in the operation.

The leaders and main organisers were rounded up and arrested. G. M. Syed who was in Sukkur at the time was quickly apprehended as were the local organisers Agha Nazar Ali Khan Pathan, Dr. Yamin and Niamutullah Quraishi and taken to Hyderabad jail. Khuhro who was in Larkana at the time was detained in his village. A few days later Khuhro's lieutenant Kazi Fazlullah, together with other leading figures Agha Ghulam Nabi Pathan, Shaikh Wajid Ali of Shikarpur and Pir Ghulam Mujaddid Sarhindi, were also arrested and jailed.[41]

Help was sought from the army which did not endear the Governor to the Government of India. In a letter to Linlithgow, Lord Zetland wrote criticising the Sind Government by giving the opinion of the Commander-in-Chief that:

"if the Sind police had been kept up to strength there would have been little need for military assistance".

The fact that the military had to be deployed at Manzilgah after November was not welcome to the Centre which had to be ready for any emergency after the declaration of the war. The Secretary of State wrote to the Viceroy expressing his apprehensions while also deriving some practical lessons from the Sind experience:

The most recent news which has reached me from Sind makes it clear that my appreciation of the state of that province as anything but a peaceful one was only too well founded. The trouble which found a focus in the activities of the Manzilgah Restoration Committee seems to have developed into a pretty (sic) communal outbreak. The use of tear gas seems to have been effective and the success achieved on this occasion gives ground for hope that this may prove to be an effective weapon in dealing with mobs in the event of a civil disobedience campaign...[42]

Linlithgow and the Government of India though unwilling to interfere directly, well understood the situation and this was reflected in the Viceroy's assessment written to the Governor some months later:

"In brief the history of the Manzilgah dispute is that it had proceeded intermittently for some years: but acquired momentum rapidly from about August 1939 owing:

(a) to the efforts of Sind Muslim League to harass the Chief Minister (who refused allegiance to the League) and to overturn his Ministry;

(b) ill feeling between Muslims and Hindus always latent in the Sukkur neighborhood, but fanned into flames by incidents such as the beating of the Pir's son in Sukkur in July, [August actually] the capture of the Manzilgah by the Muslims on 3rd October, the murder of a Hindu saint on Ist November,* and the Hindu Sabha Conference at Sukkur on November 12th to 14th.

The explosion which began on November 19th was due to the failure over a period of three and a half months, to deal effectively with threats to public order. The Ministry's relations with Muslim leaders of the agitation in that period were marked by indecision and delay and in some measure due to divisions among Ministers themselves."[43]

---

* In August 1939 the son of Pir of Bharchundi had been beaten and injured at Sukkur allegedly by some Hindus. It was rumoured that the murder of Bhagwat Kanwar Ram, a renowned religious singer and holy man in October while travelling in a train, was a revenge killing by the followers of Bharchundi. The Viceroy referred to this incident in his letter to the Governor (see above in the text of the Chapter).

The Hindu press was jubilant at the government crackdown on the Muslim occupation of Manzilgah thus further and tactlessly wounding Muslim susceptibilities. The Muslim public was shocked by this sudden turn of events. Some of the leaders of the *satyagrahis* were hurt in the police action including "Dictator"[44] Shaikh Wajid Ali of Shikarpur. Volunteers removed from Manzilgah dispersed into the countryside carrying tales of police brutality and the provocative behaviour of the Hindus.

"Rumours not entirely unfounded, have spread into the *mofussil* that, following the evacuation of the mosque by the Government, the Hindus in the town of Sukkur had begun murdering Musalmans, and that the victims included a Moulvi and his wife."[45]

A number of incidents of violence and lawlessness occurred in and around Sukkur in which not only the town itself was affected but Hindus of surrounding villages were looted and *banias* driven out: Several people lost their lives. Memories were still fresh in Sukkur of the 1930 riots of which the enquiring officer had then reported:

"The riots (in Sukkur Town) were purely communal in character. Feelings between Hindus and Mohammedans which for sometime had not been particularly cordial had been further embittered by Congress activities, and riots were started by a clash between Mohammedans and a Hindu Congress procession. Thereafter indiscriminate murdering and looting took place in Sukkur, and the Hindus had the worst of the exchanges. The news spread rapidly in the District. Mohamedans from the District who had been working as coolies in Sukkur returned to their houses with stolen property, and told of the manner in which Hindus were being attacked and robbed. The rumour started that Government had given permission to Mohammedans to loot Hindus. The idea was an attractive one to Mohamedan cultivators who were heavily in debt to the Hindus. Mahomedans therefore accepted the rumour as true without question."[46]

Judge Weston in his Inquiry agreed with the findings of the Green Report made nearly a decade earlier and said that the reasons behind the 1939 disturbances were basically the same. In the town of Sukkur where out of a population 70,000 nearly 40,000 were Hindus.

"The Hindus have the advantage not only in the numbers but also in wealth. They have a majority in the Municipality; and, in a province where they are a minority community, it is probable, as Muslim witnesses have stated that they make full use of their local majority. Relations between the two communities appear to have been strained for a number of years and the disturbances of 1930 do not seem to have been forgotten.

The Hindus who suffered the more seriously in life, and who alone suffered substantially in property are entitled to sympathy. The situation largely was not of their creation. Their opposition to the handing over of the Manzilgah appears to have been based upon apprehension of injury to their interest ... I do not suggest that a narrow communal attitude is peculiar to Hindus, but as the major community in Sukkur, it may be said that they have major responsibility for creation there of a spirit of reason; and without such a spirit the outlook for the town and for the district cannot be hopeful. As in 1930, so also in 1939 the spark which caused the conflagration was kindled in Sukkur."[47]

The Inquiry made it clear that the "riots" could not be so described and were not planned or pre-meditated:

"Although the disturbances in Sukkur have been termed riots, they were really sporadic outbreaks of lawlessness. In a few cases there are said to have been large bodies of men bent on mischief, but there was no collective and open opposition to authority and in most cases the crimes committed appear to have been the acts of comparatively small numbers. There is little doubt particular person or groups of persons in some cases were responsible for more than one crime."[48]

The victory of Manzilgah rapidly turned to dust and ashes in the mouths of the Hindu community. They were deeply disillusioned with Soomro and laid the blame squarely on his shoulders. Not only had the Manzilgah issue been revived and bungled but in the resultant mess it was the Hindus who had suffered the most in terms of lives and property lost. Hindu opinion, particularly of Sukkur and of Upper Sind generally, turned against Soomro. Hindus wanted a government which could guarantee security for them. Thus gradually their thoughts turned to making some accommodation with Muslim League leadership which commanded the most support among Muslims and had after Manzilgah particularly, gained immense popularity.

Most of the League leadership continued to be in detention for over a month. Khuhro confined to his village spent his time catching up with his *zamindari* work which had perforce to take a back seat during the Manzilgah movement. Now he had time both for Larkana as well as Khairpur matters. From his village Aqil, on the right bank of the river Indus, where he had his family residence, he would ride in the early morning to the protective *bund* on the Indus for his daily walk. The countryside was at its best in these winter months with the mustard fields with their fresh and young stalks (which boiled and salted was a favourite food throughout his life) and the unripened as yet green wheat fields. The recently receded floods had left a rich layer of silt where a scattering of seeds would bring forth abundant crop of chick peas and *saag*, and an early morning ride in the crisp cool air with the water wheels and the bullock carts providing the typical sounds of the Sind countryside, was a perfect recipe for the renewal of the spirit.

But Khuhro with his penchant for work could not allow himself a month of idleness. A good deal of time during this month of confinement were spent in Khairpur on the left bank of the river where his orders of detention did not apply. Quite apart from his own *zamindari* affairs in Khairpur, Khuhro always took a close interest in the problems of the *zamindars* and of the state where he felt that they were subject to the arbitrary and whimsical administration of the rulers. He had already taken up the cause of the Khairpur landowners and cultivators, had organized a Khairpur Zamindari Association and made representation on their behalf not only to the Sind administration but also to the Government of India where he travelled a number of times to meet the Executive Councillor in charge of Native States. During this period of November and December 1939 Khuhro caught up with his work and his friendships in the State. In these days before jeep travel he would ride to the Indus and take one of the beautiful Indus boats across to Khairpur with his horse travelling alongside on a raft ferry. On the Khairpur side the riverine tract running alongside his lands on the right bank of the river was Khuhro *keti*.[49] Here were the vast kacha lands which yearly inundated, yielded fabulous harvests of wheat and pulses and were a sea of yellow mustard flowers in the winter. Khuhro would ride across the land or go on camel back, riding on one of his especially bred *mehri* camels, sitting upright on the richly decorated camel saddle, reading his newspaper, for all the world as if it were a Rolls Royce.

But in this idyllic retreat and with all the activity which the *zamindari* work and the Khairpur affairs generated Khuhro still missed the political cut and thrust. Usually brief to the point of being cryptic in his letters, he wrote to G. M. Syed in some detail about his life in detention:

"I have not heard anything from you ever since the internment of yours and the order of restraint served on me. When I saw you last at Hyderabad on the 20th you were not quite well yet (Syed had been arrested on the 19th while he had a fever and brought to Hyderabad, a journey of 200 miles) I hope you must have regained your health owing to the long felt need of rest having been fulfilled For full two weeks I was on my lands across the river and now I am back in Akil in British territory. According to the order of restraint I have only to live in village Akil in British territory or I can go and live in Khairpur State. The order of restraint is not applicable to me in Khairpur territory as it is outside the jurisdiction of Sind Government. I went there on horseback and crossed the river on ferry boat which is only two miles from my village Akil. The boundary of Khairpur State is less than four miles from Akil village. I hope I will be in a position to meet you before long. With best wishes and salaams to all friends".[50]

Khuhro's detention came to an end on 21 December having lasted just one month. On 9 January G. M. Syed was released from Hyderabad jail and gradually the other leaders were also set free. On 24 December Khuhro wrote to Syed:

"Thanks for your kind letter of 17th. The restraint order against me expired on 21st. I returned from Khairpur State on 23rd and went to Larkana for a few hours. Because of the X'mas holidays it is no use my going to Karachi now. But I will come to Hyderabad on 3rd to meet all you friends and then proceed to Karachi. Sir Abdullah Haroon has come back to Karachi I understand. Mr. Gazdar was at Larkana for two days but as I was in Khairpur territory, I was unable to meet him. I learn that he paid a visit to Sukkur for a few hours and has gone back to Karachi. ...I got a letter from Sir Abdullah Haroon to say that Mr. Jinnah has appointed Sir Karimbhoy Ebrahim and Nawab Sir Shahnawaz of Mamdot to hold an enquiry about the trouble at Sukkur. I hope to meet you soon."[51]

Pre-occupied as they were with the Manzilgah crisis the Muslim League leaders were unable to make a suitable response to the call given by All India Muslim League President to observe a "Day of Deliverance" on 22 December to mark the ending of Congress Ministries in most of the provinces in India.* Most of the leadership and the workers of Muslim League were in jail. Khuhro himself was released just the day before on 21 December and was deep in the countryside of

---

* Jinnah as President of All India Muslim League had given a call for the observance of a 'Day of Deliverance' as the Congress Ministries resigned in the provinces where they had formed governments after the elections of 1936, in protest against the Government of India announcing the participation of India in the war without consulting Indian political opinion. They Day of Deliverance was to pinpoint the alleged injustices suffered by the Muslims under Congress governments. These injustices had been detailed in U.P. particularly by the issuance of Pirpur and other reports.

Sind. So the Governor was able to report to the Government of India:

"The Muslim League Deliverance Day was a poor thing in Sind and actually provoked no excitement anywhere. We told the District Magistrate, Sukkur that he must decide on the facts known to himself whether the celebration should be allowed in Sukkur District and he decided that it should not be so allowed. I have received a letter from him this morning in which he says there was no excitement at all on the subject, i.e. on the prohibition of meetings and processions."[52]

In any case the Muslims of Sind did not feel that they had been "delivered" and were therefore in no mood to celebrate a day of deliverance. The Manzilgah buildings were once again out of their hands. Hundreds of *satyagrahis* as well as the Muslim League leaders, were in jail. Everyday people were being arrested, charged with rioting, murder and looting. The Muslim League leadership was under severe strain. It was confronted with a hostile and revengeful government and the helplessness of the workers and the ordinary Muslim public.

Immediately on his release Khuhro plunged into work. His foremost concern was somehow to save the Muslim public from the punitive steps the government was taking without discrimination. On his way to Lahore to consult with his friends and also seek the advice of Sir Sikander Hayat Khan regarding the problems Muslims faced in Sind he wrote to Syed about the matters uppermost in his mind:

"In Train. 12th January 1940.

I learnt at Sukkur on the 10th that a complaint has been filed against all the members of the Restoration Committee and some others that they got possession of Manzilgah by force. It is under Section 448 and 117 I.P.C. The *Sind Zamindar* press was searched on 8th and all the files of our Committee have been taken away by police.

2. You must be reading all Karachi papers. Did you see the fourteen conditions of Hindus to the Ministry. These if accepted will amount to the complete annihilation of the [Muslim] community in Sind. I therefore issued a brief statement in consultation with Sir A. Haroon, Shaikh A. Majid and Gazdar, yesterday at Karachi, that we have not negotiated with any Hindu or Congress party to form another Ministry, [although] personally I am in favour of it, in the existing circumstances.

3. Have you been watching what a tremendous propaganda is being carried on by the Hindu press in Sind, against me, the leaders of Muslim League party and others who are arrested in Sukkur? They want us all to be crushed. Please read Sind Observer of 11th and 12th January positively.

4. About 1,300 Muslim villagers have been arrested by now in Sukkur and more are yet being arrested everyday. My heart is full, but I need not say anything here.

We will discuss the situation when we meet at Karachi on 23rd. I am informed you are being allowed to come to Karachi for the Assembly.

I am on my way to Lahore on an important political mission and will return to Larkana on the 16th."[53]

The Hindus were putting tremendous pressure on Soomro to crack down on those responsible for the riots and on Muslim League leaders and workers generally. Although there was general disillusionment among them regarding Soomro's uncertain policies and what they regarded as his weakness which had made possible the loss of Hindu life and property, the Congress Hindus were still keen to come to an arrangement with him because they felt they could control him better. However, the Independent Hindu group and the Bhaiband community represented by the Federation of Panchayats, and the majority of Upper Sind Hindus who had been particularly affected by the events, were more anxious to come to an arrangement with the Muslim leaders who they felt had the confidence of the majority of Muslims. Meanwhile Soomro was doing everything possible to regain the confidence of the Hindus. He tried to rush through a Bill applying Frontier Regulations 1872 and 1892 to Sukkur district so that summary action could be taken against those held responsible for the disturbances. This was deeply resented by the Muslim League leadership. Khuhro sent a telegram to Jinnah asking him to intervene with the Government of India:

"Sind Ministry rushing through Bill extending Frontier Regulation 1872 and 1892 to Sukkur District, which Congress and Hindu members support. Speaker Sind Assembly (over) ruled previous sanction. Pray submit our earnest request before G. G. Withhold necessary sanction. Muslim public opinion strongly opposed to this antiquated and repressive measure and majority Muslim members also against it. Hundred of innocent people will be unduly victimised. Allah Baksh Ministry adopting such measures to please Hindus and Congress to retain themselves in office."[54]

On 13 January Jinnah met Linlithgow and discussed the Sind affairs with him. Linlithgow reported to Zetland of the meeting with Jinnah:

"He then touched on the question of Sind. He said he was not yet clear on the rights and wrongs of that matter, but that the Chief Minister had made speeches recently copies of which he would send me, which made the position in Sind impossible if the Chief Minister remained in power. I said I would wait to see the text of them."[55]

As Khuhro's letter of 12 January to Syed had made clear the situation in Sind continued to be extremely tense even with the release of the leaders of the Restoration Committee. The major problems continued unaddressed. There was the question of the possession of Manzilgah, of the people arrested from the mosque as well as the insecurity caused by the subsequent incidents particularly among the Hindus of Sukkur and the rural areas surrounding Sukkur and Shikarpur. The Bhaiband caste which made up the majority of Hindus of Sind, and which was by far the wealthier caste consisting as it did of the business and trading classes, dominating the towns of Sukkur, Shikarpur, Hyderabad, and in substantial numbers in smaller towns, felt disturbed. They were also to be found in the big and small villages of Sind and in the countryside generally, where they were the village shop owners and money lenders. The *banias* felt themselves particularly vulnerable in the midst of a Muslim population which was not only much poorer than them but was also their debtor.

The Bhaiband community was now very anxious to come to a settlement with the responsible Muslims who they identified as Muslim Leaguers. Emissaries went to see G. M. Syed who was recently released from jail and was at his village, Sann. Syed had been a member of Congress early in his career and had good friends among the Hindu politicians, who now went to see him. They asked him to arrange a meeting with Muslim League leaders with a view to reaching an understanding. A meeting was arranged between the prominent *Mukhis* of the Sukkur and Shikarpur *panchayats* and the top Muslim League leaders, Sir Abdullah Haroon, Shaikh Abdul Majid, Khuhro and G. M. Syed, in which there was a free exchange of views between the two sides. The Mukhis expressed a desire to reach a comprehensive understanding and an agreement which would ensure the safety of the Hindu community in Sind. The events of November had come as a shock particularly as they had assumed that a government relying on their support would be able to guarantee their security. Now they had come to the conclusion that they could no longer rely on the Soomro government.

Opposition to Soomro grew in the Hindu community which some of the Hindu groups used to extort further concessions from him as the price for their support. This was particularly true of the Congress group. The Upper Sind panchayats were however insistent that they could no longer accept Soomro as Premier. The Federation of Sind Panchayats appointed a committee and authorised it to carry on negotiations with any party for safeguarding the interests of the Hindu community. These negotiations were fairly prolonged as the *panchayat* committee tried to get the best bargain it could. The main demands of the Hindus were:

1. Appointment of a Tribunal to enquire into–
   (a) causes of the Sukkur riots; and
   (b) to establish if Manzilgah was a mosque.
2. Payment of compensation to the sufferers of Sukkur riots.
3. Non interference with the procedure of law so far as the Sukkur riots were concerned.
4. Percentage of communal representation in services.
5. Adequate measures for the protection of life and property in the disturbed areas.
6. Introduction of joint electorates in Sukkur and Shikarpur municipalities.

While these negotiations were going on, the Sind Legislative Assembly met in a session in February 1940. Speaking of the deterioration of the situation in Sukkur which had led to the riots, Khuhro gave his analysis that the basic cause of tragedy was the indecision of the Government of Sind:

"The chief reason why this trouble arose in Sukkur is the failure on part of the Government to take the right decision at the right time... as long back as June '39, we had made a demand with regard to the question of Manzilgah. The Premier was in office from March '38 and he had taken this question in hand as early as Apirl '38. If he was convinced that it was a mosque and it was a right of the Muslims, he should have announced his decision and handed it over to the Musalmans of Sukkur. He should not have kept them on hopes for so many months. On the other hand if he was convinced that it was not a mosque, he should not have said that he was going to hand over the Manzilgah to the Musalmans.

On this question even the Congress Party made their decision that he should appoint an Imperial Tribunal to take the decision. ..."[56]

The Hindus had given Syed and Shaikh Abdul Majid to understand that they would withdraw support from Soomro and were prepared to form a coalition with a Muslim League ministry but that Khuhro (who was the leader of Muslim

League party in the Assembly and therefore in line for Premiership in any Muslim League or Coalition ministry) should under no circumstances be made Premier as they regarded him as too pro Muslim.[57] Khuhro was sceptical of Congress support and felt that it was unreliable and that the government would be manipulated by it. Syed and Shaikh were insistent however and pointed out that the agreement would be mainly with the Independent Hindus and Congress would not have much of a say in the matter. Khuhro tried to avoid them but they apprehended him at a garden party at the Governor's House which Khuhro was attending and told him that a meeting was being held at his Patel Park house (two doors away from Syed's house) to discuss the matter of the compromise with Hindus and that he would have to be present. Khuhro could not avoid going with them. The proposal they made was that a cabinet should be formed with Mir Bandeh Ali Talpur as compromise Premier, Shaikh Abdul Majid, G. M. Syed and Khuhro as Muslim ministers, and Nichaldas Vazirani and Hemandas Wadhwani as Hindu ministers.

Khuhro agreed to the proposal partly because of the insistence of his colleagues and partly for reasons of safeguarding Muslim interests in the wake of the Manzilgah issue. With the broad areas of agreement reached, the chief *panchayat* members held a meeting at Karachi and asked the Hindu ministers to withdraw from the Cabinet. Somewhat reluctantly the Hindu Ministers did as they were told and came over to the Opposition. Soomro no longer had a majority in the House and after the defeat of a minor amendment he declared on the floor of the House that he lacked a majority. He asked for the adjournment of the House and announced that he would hand in his resignation to the Governor. The House was duly adjourned but the government continued to function for a full month after the loss of its majority.[58]

The period of grace was given to Soomro by the Governor who was anxious to retain him as a pliable and co-operative Premier. Soomro had co-operated fully with the Governor in the matter of assessments and in the war effort even when this was against official Congress policy. The Secretary of State himself had expressed his appreciation of the offer of co-operation: "I caused a communication to be issued from the India Office expressing the appreciation of HMG of the unconditional offer of all the resources of Sind ..."[59]

It was difficult for the Governor to let go of such a useful Premier. He wrote resentfully:

"The intrigue for the removal of the Ministry goes on and in fact little else goes on in Sind at present. It is generally recognised that any other Ministry will have as insecure a seat as the present one, if not worse and the Hindus are moving me to suspend the Constitution because there is no hope of getting a competent Ministry with reliable support.

... I shall be surprised if my Ministry, which seems to be unpopular on all sides, survives the next session and my Chief Minister who was very confident a month ago is not so confident now."[60]

The Government of India itself also found Soomro a congenial Premier. On 21 February Linlithgow wrote to Zetland.

"I was a little disturbed on the very night I left to find the Allah Baksh situation blowing up. As I write things are easier and my instructions to him (Graham) are that he must not accept the resignation of his Ministry until he can make alternative arrangements."

A week later Linlithgow wrote again with a visible sigh of relief:

"Graham's affairs have caused me a good deal of trouble during the last few days; but I am glad to say that all now seems to have gone well, the vote of no confidence, as you will have gathered from the telegram which I have repeated to you, against his Ministry having been defeated by the casting vote of the Speaker, and Allah Baksh having withdrawn his resignation. Let us hope, all will go well."[61]

Seeing the Governor's attitude and the partisanship of the Soomro Ministry in the matter of Manzilgah, Khuhro became even more convinced that it was in the best interests of the Muslim public, now under severe pressure, to remove Soomro. Negotiations were making progress. The Bhaiband community was keen to come to an understanding even though Congress was playing, not a double, but a triple game, by on the one hand telling the Muslim Leaguers that they were withdrawing support from Soomro while simultaneously negotiating terms with him and the Muslim Leaguers and at the same time also advising the Governor to suspend the Constitution. The latter option if it happened to succeed would suit them best because it would dispense with the necessity of dealing with the Muslim elected representatives and leave the bureaucracy, which was overweighed with Amil Hindus, in control and would thus serve their purpose much more neatly than the untidy mess of an elected government.

The Muslim Leaguers were well aware of the Congress thinking but had no option but carry on the negotiations. The plight of the Muslims in the wake of the Manzilgah agitation required a sympathetic government – a necessity which Khuhro with his practical turn of mind and considerable experience in the similar situations, was acutely aware of. If this meant compromising with the excessive Hindu terms then that was the price which would have to be paid. In this regard he had come some way since his 12 January letter to G. M. Syed in which the terms and conditions set by the Hindus had seemed to him to spell the ruination of the Muslim community in Sind. The circumstances in which the Muslims found themselves, the arrests of hundred of workers, the threat of their prosecution for rioting and murder and the likelihood of their being sentenced to death or long imprisonment might lead to despair and disillusionment with political action. A brilliant political move and a successful organisational *tour de force* that the Manzilgah *satyagraha* had been, could rebound as a disaster in the face of the leaders of Muslim League.

These were the problems uppermost in Khuhro's mind when he moved from his earlier point of view to the conclusion that compromise with the Hindus and the formation of a coalition government was the only answer which would assure a healthy political future for the Muslim community. At the same time Khuhro felt that with an overwhelming Muslim majority in the province, there was no long term problem about securing Muslim rights. He had been deeply impressed by the example of Zaghlul Pasha in Egypt which Jinnah had cited in his speech to Sind notables the first time he had addressed them in Sukkur in 1930. That great statesman had asked the Coptic minority of Egypt to write its own terms on a blank sheet of paper and had thus won their support for Egypt's national struggle. On 3 February Khuhro sent a telegram to Jinnah expressing his feelings on the matter and copies to Sir Sikandar Hayat as well as Haroon.

"Muslim public opinion and my Assembly Party strongly favour reasonable compromise with the Congress. League and Congress combined could form stable Ministries in provinces following national programmes ameliorating condition Muslim masses in majority provinces. Allah Baksh Ministry here exploiting disagreement between two parties. Respectfully urge for honourable settlement and save Sind."[62]

The February Budget session of Sind Assembly proved abortive as far as the combined attempts of Muslim League and the Hindu members to unseat Soomro were concerned. But they gathered their forces for another attempt when the Assembly met again in March. In the face of Bhaiband Panchayats's determination get rid of him, Soomro failed to save his government even with the respite given him. The Hindus got Muslim League leaders' agreement on their 21 points. Khuhro was the only one who had serious doubts about the terms but felt that the plight of Sukkur Muslims was desperate enough to require the necessary compromise. Hindus tried to provide for every possible eventuality by insisting that the government appoint a tribunal to enquire into a numbers of matters: whether one of the Manzilgah buildings included a mosque or not; a separate enquiry to establish the causes of the disturbances of November 1939 and those held responsible to be punished; the victims to be compensated with cash; a Consultative Committee to be instituted to deal with situations like the one arising out of the Sukkur riots and with questions relating to law and order with the Premier as Chairman, one Hindu Minister as a member and also the Congress Party Leader as a member. Arms Licences were to be issued to Hindus; police was to be increased in rural areas and more Hindus to be recruited to the police; a 40% share was to be given to the minority in services. Postings of officers in each district to be so made as to have proportionate number from all communities. Further that minority members of judicial, police and revenue departments to be posted in larger number in charge of executive posts in the *mofussil* and 40% posts were to be held by them. Rural affectees of riots (i.e. banias) were to be given government plots if they wished to emigrate from villages into towns.

With Khuhro's previous record in the 1929 riots where he had managed to get free almost all those implicated in riot cases, fresh in their minds, the Hindu negotiators put in a condition that no cases in connection with Sukkur riots were to be withdrawn except those considered by the District Magistrate and Commissioner to be proper ones for reference to the *jirga*. Hindu negotiators also wanted gun licences to be given to *panchayats* and finally that no Bill was to be brought by the Government before the Assembly except with the previous consultation of the parties supporting the government. One of the points was that local bodies elections would be held under the Joint Electorates system and finally that the Government would not be a coalition of the existing parties but would be National Party government. In practice however the members of the new government retained their old party membership as well as becoming members of the new National Party.[63]

On 18 March 1940 the coalition government was formed with Mir Bandeh Ali as Premier. Khuhro became Minister for Public Works. The Premier retained Home Affairs but it was not difficult for Khuhro to persuade him to gain some relief for the Sukkur Muslims who were in fairly dire straits by this time–

"By the time we took over, three Muslims had already been convicted and sentenced to hanging. Cases were pending against two to three hundred who were mostly charged with murder, robbery, arson, looting - all serious crimes. The judge in Sukkur, a Mr. Welles appeared to be unsympathetic to the Muslims. Bandeh Ali was a personal friend but it was difficult for him to take any action overtly in favour of Muslims. I suggested that it would be advisable to change the magistrates in Sukkur and he promised to do what he could. I then went to see Sir Godfrey Davis, the Chief Judge of Sind and told him about the hostile attitude of the judge. Sir Godfrey was an extremely fair and reasonable man. I complained about the attitude of the judge arguing that the sentences were unfair as it was almost impossible to fix responsibility on an individual when a riot was taking place. He listened very carefully and agreed to change the magistrates. He then invited the judge to tea where I was also present and we had a discussion. Subsequently all the Muslims were acquitted of serious charges. The question now remained of those who had already been convicted to hang."[64]

The new Ministry proved to be shortlived due mainly to the changeability of the Muslim members and the unrealistic idealism of G. M. Syed as well as the intolerance of the Congress leaders, but in the brief spell of power, Khuhro did manage to get the death sentences of the Sukkur Muslims commuted and saved their lives. The ire of the Hindus and the officials thus earned was to give him a difficult time ahead.

The Masjid Manzilgah incident was the most serious communal confrontation in the history of Sind before the Partition of India in 1947. The lesson of this incident for both communities was that compromise was the only possible solution for ensuring peace. In the immediate aftermath of the incident this lesson was taken to heart and compromise was achieved. Influential Hindu groups realised that a puppet Chief Minister could not serve their purpose and that an understanding had to be reached with the real representatives of the majority community. This was done and a compromise formula accepted by both Muslims and Hindus which showed generosity and wisdom on part of the Muslim negotiators and a sincere desire for communal harmony on part of the Hindus. That it could not work for long was in great part due to the Congress insistence on not only having a share in the government but in wanting to dominate it. In a majority Muslim province this proved impossible and served only to make permanent the communal fissures by disillusioning the Muslims and putting them solidly behind Muslim League in response to the arrogance of Congress. In spite of the fact that the two communities in Sind from time to time groped towards an understanding and even worked out compromise formulas which could have proved workable given a chance, these attempts failed on the alter of Congress desire to manipulate the government, the failure of the more realistic elements in the Hindu community to fully assert themselves and the lack of a long term vision on part of the majority of the Muslim politicians.

11

THE COALITION GOVERNMENT

The Coalition Ministry with Mir Bandeh Ali Talpur as Premier was sworn in on 18 March 1940. Almost immediately Khuhro left for Lahore where the annual Muslim League session was being held on 23 and 24 March. The situation in Lahore was fraught. Sir Sikander Hayat Khan, the Premier of the Unionist Ministry in the Punjab, had been brought into an uneasy alliance with the Muslim League on the condition that while Jinnah would speak for the Punjab at the all India level, Muslim League would not interfere in internal Punjab affairs. Sir Sikander and his friends had been trying ever since Jinnah had undertaken the re-organisation of Muslim League in 1937-38, to prevent his inroads into the Punjab. So while Sir Sikander was ready to preserve a cordial front and attend the odd Muslim League session, as in Sind in August 1938, he adamantly resisted Jinnah's attempts to organise Muslim League in the Punjab. This was partly due to the fact that the interests of the Muslims of the minority provinces, who were the strongest element in Muslim League at this time and the driving force behind Muslim League policy, were seen to be, if not opposed, at least not in consonance with those Muslims of the majority provinces.

Apart from the Unionist leadership, Jinnah was also having a difficult time getting the Bengal Muslim Leadership to toe the line. In Bengal, like the Punjab except for a few urban Muslims, businessmen like Ispahani etc. there was no sympathy for Muslim League and though Fazlul Haque was ready to come to Sind in 1938 and even to Lahore in 1940, he was not prepared to accept any interference in the politics of his home province.

The Viceroy was in the confidence of Sir Sikander in the matter of his relations with Jinnah, and as could be expected, took a deep interest in the affairs of the Punjab. Writing to the Secretary of State at the end of August 1939 he says:

"Sikander's admirable statement on Saturday last seems fairly effectively to have spiked the guns of Jinnah and the Muslim League, who had met in Delhi on Sunday. I am sending you separately a copy of a personal letter which I have had from Sikander himself. It seems to me pretty clear that relations between Muslim League and the Punjab, Bengal and other important Muslim centres are becoming definitely rather strained and that the chances of a break away are considerable. Zafrulla tells me that he has heard that in the secret meeting of the Muslim League which took place at Delhi Jinnah again begged for *carte blanche* and expressed his readiness to undergo any possible personal sacrifice... that if given a free hand he would bring us to our knees in the immediate future! He has now arrived to take part in the deliberations of the Central Assembly; but I do not propose to make any move to him unless there is an outbreak of war or of some other development necessitating immediate contact with all party leaders."[1]

As early as February 1939 Sikander Hayat had put forward a scheme as his amendment to the Federation scheme in the shape of a proposal for three blocks with greater powers than the provinces which at that point Zetland did not think practicable but events were moving inexorably in that direction as would become clear by March 1940.

But before that, it took sometime to win over even the partial co-operation of Punjab and Bengal for Muslim League. On the one hand Sir Sikander had to "flirt" with Muslim League and on the other he had to keep his Unionists happy and satisfied that his involvement with Muslim League would not affect his policy in the Punjab with its delicate balance between Muslim, Sikh and Hindu interests. The Muslim Leaguers in the Punjab were urban Muslims notably Sir Mohammed Iqbal and Malik Barkat Ali but the rural interests – the Hayats, the Daultanas, the Tiwanas *et al*, were whole heartedly Unionist. At the same time Sir Sikander had also to deal with the unpredictable forces like the Ahrars* and the Khaksars**. The Khaksars, an organisation with the objective of public service but organised along military lines with uniforms, parades and so on which was typical of the Fascist parties of Europe. The organisation gained widespread popularity especially in Sind, Punjab, Baluchistan and N. W. F. P. across the social spectrum, its membership including not only ordinary people from the towns but also landowners. Gradually over the years particularly from 1936 on, a confrontation had been building up between the Unionist government and the Khaksars. In March 1940 eventually Sikander Hayat's government put a ban on Khaksar parades, uniforms and militant displays generally. Allama Mashriqi reacted angrily and summoned a large number of volunteers from all the provinces to hold rallies in Lahore against the government. While Mashriqi himself remained in Delhi he ordered his lieutenant from N. W. F. P. Khushal Khan Jadoon to start the first march with 313 volunteers, (the number of Muslim soldiers in the Battle of Badr, the battle fought by the Holy Prophet), in violation of the ban put by the government.

On 19 March, just a few days before the Muslim League session was due to be held in Lahore, the 313 Khaksars started their march toward the Badshahi Mosque. On the way there was a confrontation with the police and shots were fired in which more than thirty Khaksars were killed and many wounded. Public opinion was outraged particularly as there was considerable sympathy for the Khaksars. The

---

* Majlis-i- Ahrar-i-Islam (1929-47) a break away group from the Khilafatists was largely Punjab based 'nationalist' party which aimed to work for independence and for Muslim causes such as the liberation of Kashmir from the Hindu Maharaja but at the same time worked in close co-operation with All India National Congress in its anti Imperialist campaign.

**The Khaksar Movement (1931-1947) Founded by Allama Mashriqi a brilliant scholar and Cambridge Wrangler who resigned from government service to devote himself to the organisation. The Khaksar movement, with its strong discipline and authoritarain style, was organised along the lines of the Fascist parties of Europe which were much admired by Allama Mashriqi, who was reputed to have met Hitler in 1926.

position for Sir Sikandar was very difficult. In a couple of days the annual session of Muslim League was to start. The Muslim Leaguers of the Punjab particularly Malik Barkat Ali were extremely critical and wanted Sikander expelled from Muslim League. But the latter was able to put his diplomatic gifts and political acumen to good use and survive this serious crisis. On the evening of the 22nd he came to the meeting of the Subjects Committee of the Muslim League where he made a speech explaining the situation and his own position. He spoke with great emotion and ended in tears. The Muslim Leaguers were won over – Jinnah no doubt realising that excusing Sir Sikander at this critical juncture could win his loyalty for Muslim League in a province where headway was proving far from easy.

The Muslim League session took place thus in an atmosphere of tension in Lahore – the venue of the conference was Minto Park in the shadow of the great Badshahi Mosque and not far from the scene of the bloody confrontation. The conference itself was a great success, largely attended and very enthusiastic. On the third day a resolution was passed regarding the incident of 19 October. The resolution expressed sympathy with the Khaksars, called for an enquiry by an impartial committee and urged that the ban on Khaksars should be lifted. Sir Sikander was not mentioned, Jinnah pointing out that blame could only be apportioned after the enquiry had established the facts. However in spite of the supportive attitude of Muslim League, the Khaksar incident in Lahore left a bitter residue in the Punjab which had not yet forgotten the Jallianwalla Bagh massacre. It was only the wholehearted support of the British administrators including the Governor which had rescued Sir Sikander from the mess. At the Muslim League conference his critics were silenced by Jinnah's tacit support and Sikander was able to present his scheme for the constitutional settlement for India which included separate administrative zones to be controlled by Hindus and by Muslims. In fact a number of schemes had been put forward for the demarcation of these separate zones including one by Sir Abdullah Haroon.*

The Muslim League leaders were deeply disillusioned by the behaviour of the Congress governments which had until recently been in power in most of the provinces in India. The arrogance of the Congress leadership made it clear that Congress was the true keeper of the flame as far as the movement for independence was concerned. That its secular credentials as well as its fairplay for minorities particularly, the Muslim community, was beyond question was doubted by Muslim leaders. The suspicion was proved by the example of the United Provinces where, after the elections of 1936 Muslim Leaguers was not accommodated in the Government unless they joined the Congress Party. The United Provinces Muslim Leaguers were thus able to convince Jinnah that there could be no compromise with Congress. The Punjab urban leaders were also against compromise with Congress. In Sind, even though Muslims were a large majority, 'weightage' had reduced their position so that they had become hostage to the blackmail of a few

---

* At the Sind Muslim League Conference in 1938 in response to Resolution 5 which proposed separate Muslim state in India, Jinnah had suggested that the idea be examined for feasibility. In response to this suggestion Pir Ali Mohammed Rashdi had been entrusted with the task of examining the idea. Rashdi had taken himself off to Lahore where he consulted with various Muslim leaders and framed his proposals which were one of the schemes put forward at the Lahore Session of March 1940.

members and Congress could play kingmaker. This had convinced Muslim League leaders like Haroon that the panacea was a separate Muslim state and he remained a strong proponent of the idea.

For a practical man like Khuhro, although a separate Muslim state seemed a far off fantasy, there was the everyday reality of obstruction by Congress and Hindu officers to the recruitment of Muslims in the services and their hostility to any steps which would improve the condition of the Muslims. Khuhro had never made a secret of the fact that his life's mission was the improvement of the lot of Sindhi Muslims so that they could lead a full and honourable life in their own province. Leaders like G. M. Syed, who had strong socialist leanings and who had very close friendships with like-minded Hindus, who liked to think that they were of a *sufi* turn of mind, were forced to conclude that when it came down to a choice between Hindu interests or Muslim interests, even when the former represented the capitalist and latter the exploited poor, the Hindu leaders across the board supported their community interests. In his book *Struggle for New Sind* written soon after partition, Syed records his disillusionment with Congress tactics in Sind and their betrayal time and time again where he fully expected their understanding and co-operation.

In these circumstances the mood of the conference at Lahore, in the wake of the resignation of the Congress ministries, was that of relief and of a general feeling that constitutional safeguards must ensure the position of Muslims in case of future Congress rule. At this time there was no thoroughly worked out position on the status of Muslims in case of independence. The prospects of independence were not immediate. Even after the outbreak of the war in October 1939, as late as December Linlithgow was writing to Zetland:

"After all we framed the constitution as it stands in the Act of 1935 because we thought that the best way – given the political position in both countries – of maintaining British influence in India. It is no part of our policy, I take it, to expedite in India constitutional changes for their own sake, or gratuitously to hurry the handing over to India hands at any pace faster than that which we regard as best calculated, on a long view, to hold India to the Empire."[2]

Britain was now in the middle of a major war in Europe which was soon to spread to North Africa, where Indian troops particularly from the Punjab were engaged in large numbers. The British government was anxious to gain co-operation from Indian political parties and politicians. The Viceroy had set up a War Council in which the Congress had refused to co-operate and Jinnah had also forbidden Muslim Leaguers join but the politicians of the Punjab, the crucial province as far as the British were concerned, fully co-operated in the war effort and its representatives sat on the War Council, doing so in defiance of Jinnah's directive.

The task in hand in March 1940, as far as the Muslim League was concerned was to secure the Muslim position in India when Dominion Status or independence became a fact. How this was to be done was not clear because the requirements of the majority and minority Muslim provinces did not coincide. For the majority provinces, where Muslims did not feel threatened in their own provinces, the fullest measure of autonomy was the objective whereas for the Muslims in the minority provinces a strong central government, a government which could interfere in the provinces to assure their security, was seen as essential. At the same time it was also true Hindus, who constituted the overwhelming majority in India, would certainly dominate the Centre. All his life Jinnah had tried to solve this problem and his demand had been to get a strong enough representation at the Centre to make the Muslim voice effective. In Calcutta in 1929 he had argued for one third representation in the Central legislature and had not been heeded which had led to his famous "parting of ways" with the Indian "nationalists". He had joined up with the Aga Khan and the Iqbal and Shafi group at the Delhi conference and after the fashion of Woodrow Wilson *et al* had issued his "Fourteen Points".

But that was a pre World War II era and before the Government of India Act 1935 had set the theme for the constitutional future of the sub-continent. Now ten years later the most urgent problem was to make the seriousness of the Muslim position clear to the other protagonists. Already the Muslim League leadership had made its position known to the British government. The basic demand of All India Muslim League was maximum autonomy for the provinces* hence it rejected the Federation scheme as it stood and insisted that no constitutional arrangements would be made without the consent of Muslim League the representative body of Muslims of India:

"1. No promise of constitutional advance shall be made without the consent and approval of All India Muslim League.
2. Close liason between Government and Muslim League.
3. Scheme of federation (Act of 1935) shall not merely be suspended but finally abandoned."[3]

Muslim League was thus anxious to establish its "bargain" counter for the day when negotiations would be held in earnest. It had to put forward a programme which would not only produce maximum concessions from the Congress and the British but would also put all the other Muslim organisations, many of which were not at all sympathetic to Muslim League, in a defensive position and with an appeal to the public which would go over their heads. The proposals before the conference had more or less the same theme – the division of the sub-continent into different zones.

At the Muslim League conference, his critics silenced by Jinnah's tacit support, Sikander was able to present his scheme for the constitutional settlement for India which included seven separate administrative zones to be controlled by Hindus and by Muslims. In fact a number of schemes had been put forward for the demarcation of these separate zones. After some hard bargaining between various schemes a small committee was authorised to prepare a final draft for the constitutional proposals to be put forward by Muslim League. Some schemes proposed three sovereign states; all schemes showed determination by the Muslims not to be dominated by the Hindus and to qualify the orthodox democratic principle of majority rule, so unsuited to Indian conditions. The problem of the conflict of interest between the minority and majority Muslim provinces was solved by the tacit understanding that the Muslim majority provinces would have sizeable Hindu

---

* The Muslim League had made provincial autonomy the central plank of its programme as opposed to the Congress which wanted a strong Centre, and this was the main reason that Sind leaders backed Muslim League.

populations and if fair treatment was given to these minorities this would ensure similar treatment to the Muslim populations in other provinces. But this demand for separate Muslim states was actually in the nature of a shadow play, the real aim was to put Muslim League in a position where it could not be ignored in a future settlement for India.

The night of Friday 22 March was spent in discussions in the Subjects Committee which met under the chairmanship of Fazlul Haque of Bengal and the draft of the resolution was finalized. The second open session of the Muslim League conference began at 3 p.m. on Saturday the 23 March under the presidentship of Quaid-e-Azam.

"The *pandal* was crowded to capacity. Khan Bahadur Khuhro, Mr. Abdul Majid Sindhi, and Mr. G. M. Syed, Ministers of Sind were among those on the dais. The *pandal* resounded with cheers of 'Sher-i-Bengal Zindabad' when Mr. Fazlul Haq, the Premier of Bengal, arrived."[4] The resolution which subsequently came to be known as the 'Pakistan Resolution', although there was no mention of Pakistan in it, was presented by Fazlul Haque the Chairman of the Subjects Committee. The famous resolution which was to become the sacred text of Muslim struggle for independence was hardly conceived with such a portentious future in mind. It was hammered out as a compromise between a number of schemes which were presented to the Subjects Committee and it was seen by those engaged in the exercise as pressure tactics to extract as much concession as possible for the Muslims in the future constitutional arrangements of a free India. Fazlul Haque in his speech presenting the resolution emphasised the fact that Muslims were scattered throughout India and not concentrated in particular areas: "even in the Punjab and Bengal our position is not very safe." Efforts were being made to find " a satisfactory solution of this unequal distribution of the Muslim population"[5].

The problem which the Muslim leadership was trying to address was on the one hand to ensure that the majority Muslim provinces had their autonomy and that there was minimum interference from the Centre. This was the stand of the Punjab under Sikander Hayat Khan and was strongly supported by the other Muslim majority provinces. On the other hand the Muslims of the minority provinces could only be guaranteed adequate safeguards if there was a strong Muslim presence in the Centre which was strong enough to have its say in the provinces. It was a dilemma for Jinnah who could not do without the support of the majority provinces but who had all his life fought for strong representation of Muslims at the Centre in order to give adequate security to the minority province Muslims. Jinnah saw the Muslim League party as a strong Muslim party at the Centre speaking for majority and minority provinces alike.[6]

The 'Lahore Resolution' was an "uncompromising version of the Punjab thesis – both in the east and the west the Muslim majority provinces were to constitute 'Independent dominions in direct relationship with Great Britain'. Moreover, the 'various units in each zone shall form component parts of the Federation in that zone as autonomous units.' *This was the assurance which had to be made to the Muslim Politicians of Sind and the N.W.F.P.* Minority Muslims had to be content with unspecified assurances of 'adequate' safeguards."[7]

Notwithstanding all the assurance of the provinces becoming 'autonomous and sovereign' in 'independent zones', the Muslim League leadership well understood that the whole exercise was a 'bargaining counter'. As Ayesha Jalal puts it: "The Lahore Resolution should therefore be seen as a bargaining counter, which had the merit of being acceptable (on the face of it) to the majority province Muslims, and of being totally unacceptable to the Congress and in the last resort to the British also. This in turn provided the best insurance that the League would not be given what it now apparently was asking for, but which Jinnah in fact did not really want."[8]

****

Khuhro returned to Sind from the Lahore conference determined to take up the problems which had long been requiring attention there. The task was not easy with a compromise Premier whose chief characteristic was a weak amiability and who was unable to make a stand even before as muddled a Governor as Graham. Khuhro found him easy to work within the sense that he was a good natured and easy going man and quite amenable to any proposal put forward by Khuhro. Thus, particularly in the case of the Sukkur victims for whom Mir Bandeh Ali was directly responsible as Home Minister, he fell in quickly with Khuhro's suggestions for giving relief to those who were being victimized.

Although the government was a patchwork and not under the discipline of any particular party, it had the potential for success as the Ministers were not pressurised by any power hungry group and could put through a programme of much needed reform. The Ministry included the three most outstanding Muslim leaders of the province, Khuhro, Syed and Shaikh Abdul Majid. It was an excellent opportunity for them to test many of the ideas that they had propogated. The Governor was not used to so much activity and revealed his discomfort to the Viceroy. Writing to inform him of the fall of the Soomro Ministry and the formation of the new coalition government Graham showed the usual obtuseness and prejudice which characterized his dealings in Sind:

"The present ministry was sworn in at a critical time in parliamentary procedure shortly before the end of March and you will remember that we had some anxious correspondence on the subject of getting financial provision for the year. That all passed off quite smoothly, mainly because I had taken the speaker and the leader of the Opposition, my late C. M. into confidence. Both of them had made a series of mistakes in procedure and they were not sorry to have their faces saved by the method proposed by me...

My new ministry consists of four Muslims, three of whom are Muslim Leaguers and the fourth is a traitor to the old Muslim party headed by Allah Baksh; in addition there are two Hindus.

I do not need to go into the details in the change of Ministry except to say that the present Premier assumed office deeply stained with treachery to the late Premier. I have never been able to understand how so incompetent a person as Mir Bandeh Ali Khan was recommended to me by the combination of Independent Hindus and Muslim Leaguers. I presume that the Muslim Leaguers had to accept Mir Bandeh Ali because the Hindus refused to accept a Muslim Leaguer as Premier.[9]

There has never been any real unity in the cabinet since it started to function and I receive almost daily reports of friction and intrigue. Mir Bandeh Ali relies on his status as a representative of the last ruling dynasty of Sind. You have had a talk with him and you will not be surprised to hear that he is utterly incompetent as Minister and, if possible, more incompetent as Premier. He has no capacity for inspiring his colleagues or controlling them and he has been guilty himself of interfering most improperly in matters not within his portfolio."[10]

But aside from Talpur, Graham was contemptuous of all the members of the cabinet. For the benefit of the Viceroy he gave his less than acute observations of the new Ministers:

"My Finance Minister is Shaikh Abdul Majid, a converted Hindu with no property and no interests of corrupt nature but something of the fanaticsm of a convert in the first generation. I like him personally and my Finance Secretary reports of him that he is honestly endeavouring to understand the position and is prepared to accept advice. He is, or recently has been Secretary of the Sind branch of Muslim League but I have never found him tiresome on that account.

Mr. G. M. Syed, a small zamindar in the Dadu District was a somewhat active member of the Manzilgah Committee and was put into jail for months under the Ordinance. He does not appear to bear any malice but neither his colleagues nor I find him an easy person. Not satisfied with starting all sorts of hares in his own department he is everlastingly pushing his enquiring nose into the affairs of other Departments and is quite indifferent as to whether a subject belongs primarily to him or not. I find him rather a strain on my patience and on one occasion I rather lost control at a Cabinet meeting and told him he was talking nonsense. He protested and I withdrew the remarks. We subsequently had a personal heart to heart and he admitted that he had been particularly tiresome that morning and I admitted that I had lost control. We have been rather good friends ever since; but his characteristic has not changed. He has dislike and suspicion of all officials and feels no obligation to support the Government. He is forever creating new Committees and his colleagues,... find him as much of a burden as I do. As an example of his method, I have received from him today a list of thirty subjects, none connected with his Department on which he has addressed notes to the Hon'ble Premier. He complains that they appear to have been sat upon by Mir Bandeh Ali and nobody has seen them besides the Premier.

... Rai Sahib Gokaldas, Minister for Agriculture, a rather solid pleasant Hindu zamindar from Upper Sind, with less education than the ordinary Hindu in politics and more educated than the ordinary zamindar. His subjects are Agriculture and Local Self Government and for the most part he sticks to them. We get on quite happily together and I have no complaints against him.

Nihchaldas, one of my Hindu ministers is already known to you as having been in and out of my ministry for the last 3 years. He is capable and ambitious but beyond his ambition he has no particular axe to grind except the Hindu axe."[11]

For Khuhro the most experienced parliamentarian and administrator in the government, Graham reserved his special ire:

"I think there is shortly likely to be an increase in the friction between him and K. B. Khuhro my P. W. D. Minister, for a number of reasons. In the first place Khuhro is quite shameless in his attempts to secure promotion for Muslims and discouragement in every form for Hindus in P. W. D. Khuhro is probably one of the most dishonest men ever sworn in as Minister. He is entirely shameless as a liar and has no objection to be told that he is a liar. The Secretary Public Works Department and myself are kept very busy endeavouring to prevent corrupt deals on part of this Minister and I am by no means certain that a time will not arise when I shall have to ask you whether in your opinion the material at my disposal is sufficient to justify my dismissing him... I remember being warned by Brabourne before I came here that I should find Khuhro the most dishonest man in Sind; but I was not aware then that I should have the pleasure of having him as one of my ministers."[12]

The incident with Brabourne was costing Khuhro dearly. Graham, a man of poor judgement and susceptible to flattery had been utterly seduced by the deference shown him by the average politician in Sind. Very aware of his exalted position as Governor he could not bear being treated without ceremony as Khuhro was wont to do. With over fifteen years of political and legislative experience, used to dealing with senior officials of the Indian administration and used to the tact and courtesy of experienced proconsuls like Leslie Wilson and Sir Frederick Sykes, Khuhro, unwisely perhaps, did not waste any time on flattering or cultivating Graham or his successor Dow. The result was that in the crucial years of provincial autonomy from 1936 to 1945 Khuhro was severely handicapped in his public work by the active hostility of the powerful governors of the province.

Khuhro had thrown himself wholeheartedly in the struggle for the separation and had provided the crucial material which had convinced the Government of India that an autonomous Sind was feasible. He had been convinced that the majority of Sindhis would have a genuine chance of bettering themselves if their representatives sat in their capital and were immediately responsible to a legislature which they had directly elected. He could not foresee the pettiness of the "civilians" the Government of India thought good enough for Sind. Graham had been proved incompetent early on and both the Viceroy and the Secretary of State were well aware of it but he was allowed to complete his term and he was in turn replaced by Dow, a much shrewder man but one who had no sympathy for the "native". He was not interested in the betterment of the Indian people but was in Sind to serve the interests of the Imperial government, in this case to squeeze as much out of Sind as possible to pay the loan for the Sukkur Barrage.

Khuhro was deeply committed to the cause of Sindhi people. He was a practical man who was always concerned with the problems affecting the lives of the people, of their better government, of lessening their burden and of securing justice for them. In pursuit of these goals he would come up time and again against the bureaucracy which was long used to having its own way and against the top bureaucrat in Sind, the Governor. Unfortunately for the formative period of Sind's autonomy the two governors were second rate men. Graham was quite happy with the less assertive members of his cabinet but resented Khuhro and to some extent Syed:

"My Secretaries find Khuhro and Syed most difficult to get on with. Each of them appears to enjoy snubbing his Secretary and dismissing his notes in a very summary fashion. The only result is that the secretaries bring the papers to me and I have to call on the ministers to justify their notes. I have recently had serious conversation with Khuhro and Syed on this matter and have suggested to them that when they cannot accept the Secretary's proposals they should at least do him the courtesy of discussing the case with him and should make it plain in their note to me that they have done so. In some very controversial P. W. D. cases I have arranged to discuss jointly with the Minister and the Secretary."[13]

The Public Works Department was ofcourse Khuhro's department and he had been pursuing a policy of recruiting more Muslims and of promoting them, in 'affirmative action' sometimes out of turn, so that they could be represented adequately. This policy upset the entrenched bureaucracy which did not want its applecart upset but Khuhro was not an amateur in the conduct of government and could provide the required justification for his actions – an ability which would always earn him the hostility of the bureaucrats. If Khuhro had really been a "careerist" as Dow was to accuse of him being, he would not have risked annoying the bureaucrats and governors of the province. On the contrary, given his opportunities he could have been Minister in Bombay and Premier in Sind. He however chose to do his duty as he saw it at some cost to his 'career'. He had chosen the portfolio of Public Works especially because it had the greatest opportunities for employment of educated Muslims. His years in the Bombay legislature had been devoted to getting jobs and promotions for Sindhi Muslims so that they could have a reasonable representation in the services, and in an autonomous Sind he felt that the time had come to implement the programme he had set himself. If left to routine recruitment and promotion the representation of Sindhi Muslims would not have increased in twenty years and this would be grossly unfair to the majority of the population.

Inevitably this work earned him the ire of the bureaucratic establishment which set much store by its hierarchy and promotions. The two Governors of Sind were not men of vision or imagination and could not break out of their bind and see the problems which men like Frere in the nineteenth century and Sir Henry Lawrence in the earlier part of the century had been able to do. To some extent Sind was paying the price of autonomy. As a part of the Bombay Presidency it was included in the most important province of British India but as the small and remote province of Sind it had now become one of the least important provinces in India and with the least call on its ablest civil servants.

12

POLITICAL SEESAW

In July 1942 Jinnah announced his new 21-member Working Committee of All India Muslim League. Khuhro and Syed were the two members from Sind. In April that year the veteran Sind leader Abdullah Haroon had died and Khuhro became Acting President of Sind Provincial Muslim League in addition to being leader of the Muslim League Parliamentary party and the Leader of the Opposition.

It was a particularly tense summer in the sub-continent that year. The fortunes of war appeared to be going against the Allies what with the continuous advance of the Japanese in the east after Pearl Harbour in December 1941 and fall of Singapore in February 1942. Following the invasion of Burma, there appeared to be a grave threat of Japanese invasion of India. Since its decision to make all the provincial Congress governments resign in 1939, Congress had ostentatiously refrained from co-operating with the Government in the war effort and its leadership had appeared disaffected. There was pressure on the British government from U.S.A. and even China which feared encirclement if the Japanese invaded India, to reach an understanding with the Indian leadership. In March 1942 the British Premier, Churchill, had sent out Sir Stafford Cripps to India with a Declaration that was designed to convince Indians of 'all classes, races and creeds' that India would attain complete self-government as soon as possible after the war.

Immediately after the achievement of peace a representative body was to be set up to frame a Constitution for a free India which the British government undertook to accept subject to two conditions: first any province unwilling to accept the new constitution had the right to opt out and frame a separate constitution with like minded provinces and secondly the Indian States were also to have similar rights. There was to be a treaty between the British government and the Indian Constitution making body covering all matters arising out of the transfer of responsibility from British to Indian hands, including in particular, the protection of racial and religious minorities in accordance with the past undertakings of the British Government. For the duration of the war the British government was to retain 'the direction and control of the defence of India' with the co-operation of Indian leaders. For Congress this meant that no immediate transfer of power was to take place. Moreover the possibility of the Muslim provinces being able to frame their own constitution was anathema to the Congress leadership. The Congress Working Committee therefore turned down the 'Cripps Offer' and Gandhi made the much quoted remark that it was 'a post dated cheque on a failing bank'. Jinnah had been inclined to accept the Offer but in view of the Congress attitude also rejected it on the grounds that it did not explicitly concede Pakistan.[1]

The rejection of the Cripps offer by Congress was, in the light of subsequent events, the throwing away of last real opportunity of preserving the unity of India on Congress terms. If Congress had accepted the offer, Jinnah would have done the same, as he had already indicated to Sikander Hayat.

"Congress – League co-operation in the defence of India might have helped them to iron out their differences and draw closer together instead of drifting further apart. The non-accession clause caused the Congress leaders undue alarm. It was very far from spelling Pakistan, since in both Bengal and the Punjab Muslims were only a bare majority of the population and to get a vote in favour of non-accession, Muslims would have had to be almost 100 per cent unanimous, which they were certainly not in 1942 and might never have been if Congress and the League had worked together for a while..."[2]

The appeal of Muslim League to the Muslims of the majority provinces was not at this point as powerful as it was to become later and it was difficult for Jinnah to get his terms accepted by the British. With the rejection of the Cripps Offer ruling out any understanding with Congress, the Viceroy went ahead and expanded his Executive Council. The 15 member Council included 11 Indian members with Sir Feroze Khan Noon as the representative of the Punjab, the province which was making the biggest contribution to the war in terms of soldiers.

With the war going badly for the Allies and the Japanese steady advance in the early months of 1942 Gandhi was convinced that the Allies would lose India. He made it plain that the British should leave India because as Japanese had no enmity with Indians they would not invade if the British were not present. On 6 July at Wardha, Congress passed a resolution demanding immediate withdrawal of British rule or else 'Congress would be compelled to utilize all its non-violent strength for the vindication of political rights and liberties.' Gandhi remarked: "There is no question of one more chance. After all it is an open rebellion" On 8 August All India Congress Committee confirmed the 'Quit India' resolution. Immediately the Congress leadership was arrested, Gandhi himself being detained in the Aga Khan's palace in Poona. There was a widespread outburst of violence and sabotage particularly of communications such as telegraph, railways and police stations and post offices. The government was taken by surprise and although it coped and brought the situation largely under control, some areas such as Bihar and eastern U.P. were badly affected, so that the eastern border areas were cut off for sometime from the rest of northern India. Muslim League under Jinnah's leadership had been contemptuous of the Congress attempt to, as Jinnah put it: 'to coerce the British Government to surrender to a Congress Raj.'and the 'Quit India' movement was categorized by the Muslim League press as 'undoubtedly the greatest and most unashamed attempt at blackmailing in history.' But this, in Linlithgow's opinion, 'the most serious rebellion since 1857' was largely stamped out within a few weeks.

While the rebellion was at its height in the middle of August, a Muslim League

Working Committee meeting was summoned by Jinnah in Bombay. Khuhro and Syed reached Bombay before 16 August when the Committee was due to meet. There was intense drama in the air. Gandhi was held in nearby Poona and the Congress leadership left outside prison was trying hard to make Indian opinion unanimous behind the Congress agitation. Khuhro and Syed were invited at the house of Krishna Hutheesingh, Jawaharlal Nehru's sister, for dinner to meet Congress politicians. Leading Indian politicians and socialites were present including Mridula Sarabhai. At the table Mrs Hutheesingh put Khuhro next to herself and he was absolutely charmed by the company of the highly sophisticated women who talked politics with ease and conviction. Persuasive arguments were put to Syed and Khuhro that they should get Jinnah to meet Gandhi and at least talk about the problems so that there could be mutual understanding. Syed and Khuhro agreed to discuss the matter with other members of the Working Committee and to take it up with Jinnah. Nawab Bahadur Yar Jung of Hyderabad Deccan was also convinced by the Congress people to try for a rapprochement. Syed talked to the Raja of Mahmudabad, the young protege of Jinnah, and his close friend Hassan Ispahani of Calcutta who was also a favourite of Jinnah. Support was promised by a number of members of the Working Committee but when Jinnah got wind of the move he showed his annoyance and Mahmudabad and Ispahani withdrew their support of the idea. So when Syed brought up the matter in the Working Committee only Khuhro had the courage to get up to second his proposal and there was a deafening silence from the other members who had promised support.

Writing twenty seven years later to Syed, Khuhro recalled the occasion:

"In 1943 [actually 1942] the late Quaid-e-Azam Muhammad Ali Jinnah had called a meeting of the Muslim League Working Committee. At that time influenced by Congressmen you gave notice of a resolution that Mr. Jinnah should be advised to enter into a dialogue with Gandhi who at that time was in detention. Many members of the Working Committee agreed to support you but when Mr. Jinnah spoke and opposed the idea giving his reasons then Mr. Hassan Ispahani, Raja Sahib Mahmudabad, Nawab Ismail Khan and all others withdrew their support and against the wishes of Jinnah Sahib I supported you, although only we two were left."[3]

Syed remembered a dinner at Khuhro's house where apart from Jinnah, Miss Jinnah and Mr. and Mrs. Khuhro, he was the only other person present. Jinnah mentioned the occasion and remarked that he could understand Syed's obstinacy in bringing up the proposal for him to see Gandhi inspite of his explanation for not meeting Gandhi but how was it that Khuhro who he thought was more reasonable, had also persisted in supporting the resolution. Syed speaking before Khuhro could answer, laughingly remarked that Khuhro had been so affected by the charms of the Congress ladies at Mrs. Hutheesingh's dinner that he could not but support the motion.[4]

In fact Jinnah's stand against Congress policy of 'civil disobedience' had been clear and categoric. He had supported the war effort in unambiguous terms. His position was stated in the press: "He calls on the All India Congress Committee to give a lead to the country and divert the mental and material resources from the utility of a mass civil disobedience to war effort:

"The duty of the Government is clear. It must win against brute force and thereby ensure India's place among the free nations of the world. Anyone who stands in the way of a speedy realisation of that objective is no friend of India and must be treated as such irrespective of the consequences."[5]

Jinnah felt that the efforts of Congress notables to influence leading Muslim Leaguers, especially members of his Working Committee were not 'cricket' and was incensed by them. He had the grace however to take the time to give his reasons to Khuhro and Syed for vetoing their suggestion.

By the autumn of 1942 the Quit India movement was dying out. Not all of India had been affected. The rural areas were not involved, the minorities remained aloof and in the opinion of commentators there were no gains for Congress in this movement. Arguably it could be said that the sponsoring of this abortive rebellion in the most dangerous period of the war left a residue of distrust of Congress with the British and the Allies and a determination never to allow the whole of the subcontinent to fall into their hands.

In October 1942 the Soomro Ministry was dismissed by the Governor Sir Hugh Dow after the renunciation of his titles, in accordance with Congress policy.[6] Dow now had the constitutional duty to call the Leader of the Opposition to form the government, but he was not about to call his *bete noire** Khuhro, who was the leader of the Muslim League parliamentary party and the Leader of the Opposition, to become Premier. To avoid doing so he by passed the constitutional practice in an extremely arbitrary manner. He dismissed the Premier but not the whole ministry. He then appointed Hidayetullah, one of the Ministers as acting Premier

---

* Dow had maintained a barrage of propaganda against Khuhro in his correspondence with the Viceroy and also revealed his own deep prejudice in these letters. In June 1942, just a few months before the Soomro dismissal when Khuhro led the Muslim League delegation to him to ask for the removal of the Ministry on the grounds of Martial Law excesses, Dow wrote about the highly uncivil attitude he had taken with the delegation and with Khuhro in particular: "a suggestion from me that I ought to serve an order on K. B. Khuhro to live in the area in order that he might gain first hand information of conditions was by no means received with enthusiasm." (Dow to Linlithgow, 20 Jun. 1942 IOL R/3/1/71) Again when in his capacity as Muslim League Parliamentary leader Khuhro wrote to him to protest against the Premier using his official position to help his brother in the election, Dow although admitting that the charge was quite true blatantly revealed his hatred for Khuhro: "The Premier's tour in connection with the organization of the National War front has... been a great success...Reports from Harries, the Central Intelligence officer, suggested that *the real purpose of the Premier's tour was electioneering on behalf of his brother... who is a candidate for the Central Legislature... There is in my opinion no justification for this reflection* [!! author's italics]... The Muslim League organs have ofcourse made this insinuation and K. B. Khuhro who has not himself raised a finger or given a pie to help the war effort, has written to me to the same effect, and I have given him a reply in which I have 'grudged him no true word about himself'." Dow to Linlithgow 23 May 1942.

Dow was very happy with Allah Baksh who was no mean diplomat. Although ostensibly a Congress supported Premier and bound to carry out Congress policy, the anti war stance of the Congress Party caused problems for Allah Baksh who wanted to keep both the party which supported him as well as the cantankerous Governor happy. Sometimes this involved some disloyalty to the Congress as Dow reports to the Viceroy: "I enclose drafts of two letters, one to M. Gandhi and one to Maulana Azad. These were brought to me last night by my Premier who asked me to vet them for him and to make any additions and alterations advisable. The only addition I have made is para 3 in the letter to M. Gandhi and I have made no alterations in either letter. I handed the drafts back to Allah Baksh this morning and he left me with the express intention of issuing them." Dow to Linlithgow, 27 May 1942 *ibid* Dow was taken with Allah Baksh to the extent that even when his Intelligence officer reported as given above, Dow chose not to believe him.

and asked him to help form another Ministry, while the other cabinet members continued to function as Ministers. It was only a few days later, presumably when Hidayetullah had been able to cobble together a group that the announcement came that the resignation of the Ministers had been accepted. Commenting on the Governor's extraordinary action, G. M. Syed writes:

"...we were amazed to find that Sir Hugh Dow... had called Sir Ghulam Hussain and entrusted him with the task of forming a new Ministry. This was a highly arbitrary and undemocratic step, in so far as Sir Ghulam Hussain, a Minister in the previous Cabinet, did not command at that time the support of a single member, and the man who should really have been entrusted with the task of forming the new Ministry was K. B. Khuhro, the leader of the Muslim League Assembly party which was as matters stood, the single largest group in the Assembly."[7]

Although the Governor was acting against all norms of democratic practice and against the Instrument of Instruction in bypassing the Opposition Muslim League Parliamentary party which had ten members and could expect the support of enough Muslim members as well as Hindu Independent members to be able to form the government without any trouble, Muslim League found itself helpless in the face of the Governor's determination not to have a Ministry under the leadership of Khuhro. The Muslim League party was now in a predicament. On the one hand they had gained relief with the resignation of the Soomro ministry which meant that it was now possible to patch together a united front that would help to form a durable Muslim League Ministry but on the other they could see the advantage of the removal of the pro Congress ministry being lost because of the stubborn refusal of the Governor to follow the constitutional path. The Governor's refusal to call Khuhro was purely a personal vendetta which could not be justified on any political or constitutional grounds although he tried to excuse himself to the Viceroy:

"That Sir Ghulam Hussain was invited to form a Cabinet has been criticised on the ground that his personal following was very small... K. B. Khuhro, who is the leader of the Muslim League Assembly Party, argued that as Leader of the largest Opposition Party, he should have been invited to form a Cabinet. This view was also expressed by Jinnah in a telegram to Khuhro which I have seen... I have paid no regard to these criticism and consider that I was following both the letter and the spirit of my 'Instruction' in selecting Sir Ghulam.."[8]

It was felt in political and public circles in Sind that by not calling Khuhro the Governor had deliberately 'hurled an insult at the Muslim League Party which should have been called to form an Alternative Ministry in accordance with the Instrument of Instructions. Had he done that, an Alternative Ministry would have been formed under the leadership of the League. If ever at all it was necessary to have Sir Ghulam and Pir [Illahibux] within the Muslim League fold, I hope both of them would have gratefully accepted ministerships and signed Muslim League pledges. Majority of Hindus were willing and are still anxious to join hands with the Muslim League and Allah Baksh would have followed the Hindus with his four supporters without his group being given any office in the new Ministry... The whole Assembly would have thus combined together under the banner of the

Muslim League...[but] Our Masters want their own tools and not free men. They prefer individuals to organisations."[9]

Soomro came to see Khuhro twice to persuade him not to join Hidayetullah and that his group as well as Congress would support Khuhro as Premier on condition that it should not be known as a Muslim League Ministry. Khuhro turned down this suggestion although it was an indisputable fact that almost any other Muslim member would have agreed to these conditions to become Premier. Apart from the fact that the determined hostility of Dow would have to be taken into account, Khuhro and his fellow Muslim League leaders were of the opinion that to form a coalition with Congress Hindus would mean dependance upon the Congress support for the continuance of the Ministry. From past experience of the 1940 Ministry they knew that this support could be withdrawn at any time–

"Hindus will demand a heavy price for their support and the League Party was determined not to pay any price in return for Hindu support. Hindus had proved treacherous in the past and they would prove treacherous in the future also."[10]

With this in mind the options in front of Muslim Leaguers were either to continue to sit in the Opposition which would mean that they would sit and helplessly watch the Muslim members, apart from the small hard core, slip away and join whoever formed the new government or support Hidayetullah on certain conditions. On being informed of the position Jinnah sent a telegram opposing the option of joining the government under Hidayetullah:

"Muslim League Party cannot join any Ministry under leadership [of] Ghulam Hussain. Coalition between Muslim League and any Muslim individual or group is contrary [to] our fundamental principles. Unless Governor summons Muslim League Party leader to form Ministry you should not proceed further or participate in formation [of] any Ministry."[11]

But once again the local party leaders felt that they understood the situation better than Jinnah. That it was essential for them to come into power to redress the balance for the Muslims of Sind who had, at best, been suffering neglect during the Congress supported Ministry and to complete the work undertaken during their previous Ministerial stint.

Yusuf Haroon who was acting as the go-between to get Khuhro and Syed to agree to Hidayetullah as Premier, informed Jinnah that–

"Muslim public opinion here strongly favours capturing power considering special circumstances of this province. Failure League supporting suspension of constitution inevitable which Allah Baksh Congress and Hindu opinion anxiously desires resulting Allah Baksh becoming more powerful."[12]

Jinnah was sceptical of the fears of the Sindhis and in his marginal notes on Haroon's telegram writes 'we cannot regulate our policy according to bogey [that] Allah Baksh would get more powerful' and showed his annoyance in the remark 'Expect that for sake of getting three Muslim League Ministers we should sacrifice fundamental principle [of] League policy and destroy league prestige' and that 'if governor suspends it is his responsibility'. He then drafted the text of the telegram to be sent back–

"If Khuhro League leader cannot form Ministry only honourable course remain opposition but support Ministry so long they follow League policy – Cannot agree [to] form Ghulam Hussain Ministry for reasons explained previous telegram. Cannot believe public opinion."*

Khuhro was in a difficult situation. On the one hand there was the question of principle and of the high moral ground that there could be no compromise and on the other the reality that without the co-operation of the Governor it was not possible to get a Muslim League government even when it was in a position to get a clear majority. He felt obliged to make the best of the situation:

"Muslim League [High Command] wanted us to oppose. Ghulam Hussain tried to induce our supporters to form coalition. Yusuf Haroon was the go-between to get me and G. M. Syed to agree. We put conditions: (a) Ghulam and his group would join Muslim League and he would be a Muslim League Premier. (b) Two Ministers out of four from Muslim League. I was to be Deputy Premier and I agreed to Gazdar as the other one at the suggestion of Syed and that we would select our own portfolios."[13]

Khuhro and Syed went to Delhi to see Jinnah. There they met Liaquat Ali Khan, their fellow member on the Working Committee, who advised them that they had taken the right decision but that they should offer their resignations to Jinnah if he thought they had taken the wrong decision. This they did and Jinnah appointed a committee with Khwaja Nazimuddin, Chaudhry Khalique-uz-Zaman, Hussain Imam, Qazi Isa with Nawab Ismail as Chairman, to verify the conditions in Sind. This they did in November - December 1942 when the Committee met members of the Assembly and generally took opinion in political circles. They reached the conclusion that if Muslim League had not formed the Government, the Governor would in any case have carried on without them and that the gain of getting a Muslim League Ministry in place far outweighed other considerations. In January 1943 Jinnah came to Karachi, stayed for about a week and saw the situation for himself. He talked to Hidayetullah who gave an undertaking that he would not betray Muslim League and with these assurances Jinnah left Sind pronouncing himself satisfied. Any doubts he might have had were put at rest when in the same year the All India Muslim League Conference was held at Karachi with great success.

The Muslim League party in Sind went ahead to form a Ministry under the leadership of Hidayetullah who agreed for the sake of office to sign the pledge to Muslim League and to follow its policies. In doing so they were not only going

---

* QAP F/274 p. 269 Jinnah was quite disturbed at the possibility of a rank opportunist like Ghulam Hussain forming a Ministry with Muslim League support. His stream of telegrams were witness to his perturbation. He sent one telegram on 13th October and again another on the next day:
"Your telegram League cannot join Ghulam Hussain Ministry. our Agreeing form Coalition with Muslim individual or group will destroy fundamental principles League policy in Coalition non-Muslims. Only honourable course continue in opposition. Nothing prevents you support any Ministry so long they follow League policy serve Muslim interests. Cannot believe public opinion expects us for getting three ministerships sacrifice Funadamental Principles destroy League prestige credit under slogans capturing power[.] Special conditions Province bogey cry otherwise Allah Bux becoming powerful. Ghulam Hussain Ministry will be puppet ministry like Allah Baksh precarious. No Ministry can exercise power till solid disciplined majority behind it. Refusing commission Muslim League leader and simultaneously holding out threat suspension constitution unless League sacrifices its principles and surrenders to Ghulam Hussain whose past well-known. Governor alone responsible if he pursues this course." quoted in Syed, *op. cit*, p. 90.

against the advice or even orders given by Jinnah but also putting expediency before principle. For Khuhro it was a particularly galling step to take because it was he personally who stood to lose the Premiership which might come his way if only Muslim League support could be maintained. But that was the crux of the matter. The Muslim members were on the whole unreliable as Congress had realized as early as 1938 when they had been able to break the Muslim unity formed under Jinnah himself at the Muslim League conference and Soomro had been wooed away from the League on the very next day following his promises to Jinnah, lured by the offer of Premiership. The fact of life in Sind and indeed in most places, was that the majority of elected members went with the sitting government. So unless the Leaguers were prepared to sit indefinitely in the Opposition with ever declining numbers they had to take what was on offer – and that was Hidayetullah – the chosen one of the Governor. What made office particularly necessary in the eyes of the loyal and consistent Leaguers like Khuhro was the opportunity to implement the agenda that he had been working on since his early days in the Bombay Council – to do something to better the condition of the long suffering Muslims of Sind.*

Judgement on the consequences of this decision for the morale of Muslim League and its subsequent history in the province must still remain reserved even after half a century. For Khuhro personally however it was a bad decision. If he had insisted on Muslim League holding out as Jinnah had advised it was possible that with the growing popularity of Muslim League in the province the pressure on the Governor would have grown to such an extent that he would have been forced to call the Leader of the Muslim League party. This was particularly the case in wartime conditions when in view of Congress rebellion the Government of India wanted co-operation from non- Congress provinces.

Khuhro lost no time regretting the Premiership which has been within his grasp. He chose the portfolio of Revenue and as the senior Minister in the Cabinet, he was in a key position to do something for the majority of the people of the country who depended on agriculture for their livelihood. This meant relief from the heavy taxation under the 'sliding scale' and to get a fair price for their produce. As it was war time not only was there a great demand for food grain but the price in the open market was good. Unfortunately the growers were being deprived of the benefit of higher prices by the policy of the Central government which wanted to keep strict control on the prices so that it did not have to pay high prices for the food to be supplied to the troops. Already by January 1943 the Governor was complaining to the Viceroy that Khuhro was opposing the Government policy on decontrolling wheat.[14] By February he was abusive in his comments:

"K. B. Khuhro, the Revenue Minister is a restless and unscrupulous person who thinks he ought to be Premier and will not be happy till he is Premier. He has a narrow communal outlook and it requires constant watchfulness on my part to prevent him issuing off his own bat orders to which his Hindu colleagues would and have a right to object. He is tenacious in argument and browbeating in man-

---

* Khuhro's reluctance was overcome by the argument used by his fellow Muslim Leaguers that only by being in the government would the residue of those Muslim League activists who were still being prosecuted from the Manzilgah movement. Also this was the chance which might not come again soon to follow up some of the work that had been planned for an autonomous Sind.

ner and quite shameless about his petty dishonesties when he is found out."

Grudgingly he adds: "A very hard worker, and makes plenty of work for others."[15]

Dow was determinedly opposed to the central plank of the Muslim League programme and Khuhro's most important objective in becoming Revenue Minister – the introduction of Land Alienation and Debt Reconciliation Bills which he wanted passed as soon as possible. There were already laws of this kind in force in the Punjab and it was badly needed in Sind. It had been on the Muslim League agenda for a long time. Muslim political leadership as a whole was behind the proposals and the Ministry which had now come into power was determined to get the legislation through.

Dow, the worst kind of intolerant and arrogant colonial official that could be found in the Indian empire, could not by temperament supervise a budding democratic system. Even in his early career in Bombay he had made plain his belief that Indians were a savage lot introduced to civilisation by the benevolence of the British rulers, and he was not about to let the Sindhi Ministers exercise their responsibilities:

"Since I have returned from tour I have had a good deal of trouble with my Ministers, in particular with K. B. Khuhro, over the exercise of my powers to sanction the introduction of Bills. This trouble arises from the fact that my Ministers entirely disregard the Rules of Business and Secretariat Instructions, and a day or two before the Legislative Assembly begins to face me with a series of Bills, rapidly drafted under their inexpert instructions to which they require my immediate signature. These Bills are sometimes very long and highly communal and contentious: they have had no departmental examination and have not been seen before by the Secretaries to Government or by me, and have not been taken in Council as required by the Rules."

Dow obviously saw himself as a schoolmaster dealing with rather backward and careless children who would not dot their i's and cross their t's. Khuhro was ofcourse the recalcitrant 'native' who would not be cowed:

"I have taken the line that I must have a reasonable time to study such Bills and am entitled to have the advice of my officers as well as of my Ministers before coming to a decision; that without actually refusing consent to the introduction of such Bills, I am entitled to delay a decision till I have such advice; and that if this dislocates the Ministry's programme and puts them into difficulties with their political supporters, that is the Ministry's own fault because of the disregard of the rules. I am glad to say that after long discussion in Council and in spite of much bluster by K. B. Khuhro, the Ministers have generally accepted the reasonableness of my attitude [sic] and to the particular Bills in question I have met them in a spirit of compromise."[16]

A part of the package that the Muslim League Party had worked out for the *haris* and *zamindars* was the establishment of some control over the moneylenders and an end to *ex-parte* decisions that had so far deprived the agriculturists of thousands of acres mainly because of the illiteracy and ignorance of the *haris* who did not understand the complicated legal system. Khuhro's agenda as politician and legislator had included legislation to end this injustice since he had first entered the Bombay Council in the early 'twenties and it was now twenty years later that the chance had come to realise the programme. Ironically when the moment had at last come there was the formidable hurdle of the hostile Governor who refused to let the Bills go through even when they had the backing of the majority of the House.

"I have agreed to the introduction of a Bill to control money lending on the Ministers' undertaking that they will move for its publication to invite criticism instead of referring it to a Select Committee as was their intention. A Bill to provide for the postponement of Execution of Decrees has been withdrawn and is being sent to District Officers for opinion"[17]

He offered a sop to the Minister:

"I have agreed to the introduction of a minor amending Bill to scale down the debts of the agriculturists."

The Sind Muslim League Working Committee naturally took note of the failure of the Government to put through the legislation which had been so important a part of their agenda. Dow had his own interpretation of the Working Committee's criticism:

"I understand that the local branch of Muslim League largely instigated by Khuhro took the Ministry to task for not driving these bills through the present Session, and it is perhaps an open secret that it was my attitude which rendered this impossible."[18]

In fact Dow was building up his antipathy to Khuhro to a pathological extent. He had made up his mind that Khuhro was an 'extremist'. Writing of the Sind Ministers going to Delhi to attend a meeting he writes:

"All four Muslim League Ministers are leaving to attend the meeting of All India Muslim League at Delhi during Easter. It seems likely that Khuhro and the extremist section of the provincial Muslim League may try to get Jinnah's sanction for a more militant policy in Sind in opposition of the Premier's policy of conciliation."[19]

Khuhro was also in Dow's opinion mainly responsible for opposition to increase of revenue assessment and also responsible for the entire 'House being against the enhancement of rates'.

It was a fact that Khuhro was pressing ahead with his programme for legislation and improvement of Land Settlement. He made strenuous efforts to keep the revenue rates down and to give the benefit of the enhanced war time prices to the growers as was allowed by the Government in the Punjab where the agricultural sector became prosperous as a result. In Sind Dow made sure that every last pie of the profits went to the Government to pay off the Sukkur Barrage Debt and other purposes so that the agriculturist remained without the benefit of the prices that his produce was fetching. Dow showed by his actions repeatedly that he was interested only in getting as much revenue as possible from Sind without any regard for the condition of the cultivators. In this he came into direct conflict with Khuhro. As Revenue Minister Khuhro was in a position to determine the prices that the Sindhi farmer could expect and the war time demand had raised the prices considerably. Dow had got an agreement from Hidayetullah the Premier that Sind would not change prices as they were at 5 October 1943. Khuhro however had other ideas. He recorded a note for the Premier on 8 November suggesting that maximum prices of food grains should be raised to approximately Punjab levels.

On the evening of the 9th the meeting of the Muslim League Assembly members took place and passed the resolution against rationing. They also passed a resolution closely following the terms of Khuhro's note of the previous day, demanding that prices be re-fixed with reference to those prevailing in the Punjab. As Dow reported it to Wavell, the new Viceroy: " Khuhro took the lead in these transactions; the Premier seems to have put the other [i.e. Dow's] point of view, but was in a hopeless minority. I knew nothing of this resolution about prices when I entered the Cabinet meeting on the following day."[20]

Khuhro had not done his worst yet according to Dow and there was a battle royal:

"Khuhro then sprung his demand that the Government should immediately re-fix prices in accordance with the demand of Muslim League Assembly party of the previous day. After a few stormy passages I flatly refused to allow the matter to be discussed on the ground that I had no notice, no papers on the subject and no time whatever to give consideration to this most important subject. I had to agree to take up the matter at an early date, after Khuhro had noted on the matter and circulated it to his colleagues. This note which must have been already prepared came to me within an hour or two, approved by all the Ministers and demanding a further Council meeting the same evening, a demand to which I refused to accede. The Ministers were leaving for Delhi that evening or the next morning and clearly wished the matter to be *fait accompli* before they left."[21]

Dow thus managed to delay the decision and then before any further step could be taken by the Ministers or the Muslim League party, got the Central Government to issue a direction to Sind Government that they were not to take steps to raise prices or to abolish existing price controls without the prior consent of the Government of India. At Khuhro's insistence the order of the Central Government was sent by Sind Government to be examined for legality, but this could only be a token gesture.

Dow also proved to be very difficult over Khuhro's efforts to get a just and improved Revenue Settlement for Sind which was crucial for the improvement of agriculture and for the long term improvement in the living standards of those earning their livelihood through agriculture, which meant the vast majority of the people of the province. As early as March 1943, less than six months since taking over as Revenue Minister, he had the proposals for the settlement publicised and circulated for public opinion. Dow wrote to the Viceroy in a typically cynical manner:

"There is a lull in this controversy while the proposals are published for public opinion. But Khuhro is very busy with propaganda among the Zamindars and probably a large number of objections to be submitted for his consideration will in effect have been inspired or even drafted by him. He is ofcourse out to keep his own obligations down to the minimum."[22]

In spite of Dow's obvious displeasure Khuhro went ahead in his efforts to keep the rates low. But here again he came across the brick wall of official obduracy, particularly Dow's conviction that he was the expert on Settlement rates and his view would carry in the end. Dow was subject to a peculiar 'mind-set' of the middle grade British administrator in India. His mental make-up was not that of the District Officer – the *ma-bap* of the *Raj* who might champion the *ryot* against the overmighty *sarkar* – or the likes of Dow – sitting in their Secretariat in some far away Headquarters devising means of getting more and more revenues. On the other hand he was not the English aristocrat on Imperial duty who had the good manners to deal with Indian leaders and public men as equals and agreeing to their legitimate demands as for instance the Governors of Bombay Presidency were wont to do. Dow was determined to squeeze the last penny from the cultivator because that would prove his merit as an efficient bureaucrat and if achieving his ends meant slandering the uppity 'native' he would not hesitate to do so. He wrote to the Viceroy with not very subtle derogatory remarks about Khuhro:

"Apart from politics, Khan Bahadur Khuhro's main preoccupation, as one of the biggest zamindars in the richest agricultural tract of Sind, is how to keep the rates in the impending new Settlements down to the lowest possible figure. He has tried wrangling the timetable so as to make the final publication of the new rates before 31st July impossible, but that has been defeated. The session of the Legislative Assembly has now been called for the 24th June and the Settlement proposals are to be considered between the 7th and 9th July. I have thought it advisable to tell Khuhro clearly that the imposition of adequate rates in the Barrage area is a matter in which I consider my special responsibility to be involved, and also of the stage at which if necessary I propose to exercise it."[23] Dow failed to mention that Khuhro did not have any of the newly irrigated lands in the Barrage area.

In his battle for the grower, Khuhro found Dow not only opposing him directly but also sabotaging his efforts by bullying and threatening the other Ministers and putting obstacles in the path of any legislation that was brought in. He made it clear that he would feel free to veto any proposals that did not suit him even if they had the approval of the legislature and the Cabinet. He was quite sure that he could browbeat all the Ministers except Khuhro and perhaps one other:

"As far as I can foresee the position it is only Khuhro and Gokaldas that are likely to press for a considerable lowering of rates. But Khuhro will see to it that the Premier has the life nearly badgered out of him by constant deputations of zamindars and M. L. As, and he may quite likely give way for the sake of peace and quietness. But I do not think there is likely to be any question of the Ministry resigning if I do not finally accept their proposals: Khuhro may try to bring them to this point, but I do not think that even he will persist, for he knows he is not popular with his colleagues and the result might be a reconstituted Ministry from which he would be left out."*

The Viceroy suitably persuaded by Dow's version of the affairs in Sind which reflected a deeply reactionary official attitude wrote back:

"The affair of the Settlement seems to have passed off with very little recrimination and I as certainly amused at your Ministers, with the exception of Khuhro

---

* Dow to Linlithgow, 18 June 1943, Mss. Eur. F.125/99.
  Dow goes on to predict the revenue from the high prices which would be translated into increased revenue for the government and goes on to make a remark which, considering this was still just 1943, calls for some explanation about British plans regarding the creation of Pakistan. He says:"If high prices continue for some years, as they seem likely to do, Sind should be set on its legs financially, and have adequate funds for a considerable expansion of 'nation building' activities. Jinnah will probably realise the implications of this in view of Pakistan and may use his influence with the League organisation accordingly." *Ibid.*

and Hemandas, approving the statement that the consensus of opinion is in favour of your own decision. It is satisfactory that Khuhro's trick in publishing your Minute before the proper date should have recoiled on his own head... It is first class to think that in spite of his efforts your revenue will probably be increased during the present high price period by as much as 2 crores of rupees."[24]

The most serious confrontation between the Governor and Khuhro was on the issue of the Land Alienation Bill which Khuhro wanted to introduce in his first Budget session in March. Dow wrote to the Viceroy about it:

"The most important and contentious Bill of all is a Land Alienation Bill on the lines of the Punjab one: of this the Muslim Ministers are now themselves a little frightened, and have of their own accord withdrawn it for further consideration."

The fact was that Dow had talked sternly to Hidayetullah and to the other Ministers and made it clear that he would not agree to this legislation. He succeeded in getting the Bill delayed but Khuhro was not the man to give up easily and managed to have it sent to a Select Committee by August to prepare for legislation. Dow was not happy about this development:

"A Select Committee of the Assembly has been busy with a Land Alienation Bill and has altered this highly contentious measure in a way which makes it still more obnoxious to the Hindu community.... It appears that 'agriculturists' is to be arbitrarily defined as a man who held land before 1890. Agriculturists who hold less than 100 acres are not to be allowed to sell at all; those with less than five thousand acres can sell only to other agriculturists; and those who hold more than five thousand acres can do what they like."[25]

The fact that moneylenders were Hindus of the Bania caste and the protection given to the agriculturist would prevent further transfer of agricultural land to the moneylenders was used by Dow to give a communal aspect to the proposed legislation:

"These drastic changes intensify the communal aspect of the Bill and during the discussions R. S. Gokaldas [a Hindu member] lost his temper and staged a walkout. I had advised him to ask for the Bill to be discussed in Council before it went into Select Committee but he did not accept this advice and I did not think it proper to insist. The result was that Government went into Select Committee without being committed to any definite policy, and Khuhro siezed the advantage which a packed Select Committee gave him to accept changes which he might not have been able to carry in the Cabinet and would then have been bound to resist in the Select Committee."[26]

Dow would have liked to control the legislation by diluting it in Council where he presided and in Cabinet by getting the weaker among the Ministers to side with him. As it was he threatened his veto:

"I have warned Khuhro that I shall have to consider whether in the altered form the Bill has now taken, my special responsibility for the protection of minorities is not attracted."[27]

Linlithgow wrote back sympathetically obviously realizing that the Governor felt strongly about the matter although he could not have been unaware that similar legislation did exist in the Punjab and other provinces. He wrote:

"I am sorry to hear that a Select Committee of your Assembly is considering a Land Alienation Bill. I can well believe that a Bill of this sort will cause trouble and may possibly attract your special responsibility."

But although Khuhro managed to get the Bill passed in the Budget session of 1944, he left the Cabinet before it could receive the Governor's assent and Dow successfully avoided completing this formality. It would not be until the attainment independence in 1947 that it would go for Consent to Jinnah as Governor General of Pakistan.[28] Linlithgow noted Dow's obvious satisfaction in Khuhro's departure and also the possible advantage it might give him to delay the Bill becoming law:

"In para 2 of your letter of 26th September ... you suggested that Khuhro's departure might have some effect on the Land Alienation Bill. I think that the rest of the Ministry with the possible exception of Gazdar, regarded the Bill without enthusiasm and will not be very agitated if it does not receive assent."[29]

Dow had made certain in any case that the Bill would not easily become law by getting the law department to require the Governor General's consent before it could become law. The Bill, he wrote: "has passed through all stages in the Assembly and has just come up to me from the Legal Department with the advice that it requires submission to the G. G. That advice however only deals with the necessity for reservation under Section 107(2) of the Act, and not with whether special responsibility under Section 52 (1) (6) of the Act... I shall have to decide..."[30]

In having Dow as Governor Sind was very badly served: Apart from the low opinion of the 'natives' that he held and made plain, he actively opposed any improving legislation that the Ministers wanted to bring in using any excuse – a handicap that was certainly not suffered by the Punjab Ministers or in most of the other provinces where similar bills were already part of the legislation. For Khuhro Dow reserved special feelings of animosity and with the refusal of Khuhro to be brow beaten Dow soon came to the conclusion that he would like to be rid of 'this turbulent priest'. Dow's obsession was soon to be translated into the most dangerous crisis of Khuhro's life.

The induction of the Sind Government in 1942 which was the first provincial Muslim League Ministry in India and it obviously called for celebration. Jinnah told the Sind leaders that an All India Muslim League session would be the most suitable way to mark the occasion. March 1943 was suggested by the 'High Command' but Sind leaders felt that they could not produce a suitable show, having just recently come into office. They were facing serious problems with the Martial Law operating in part of the province and the serious floods, with the Indus rising to dangerous levels, which needed immediate attention. Khuhro informed Jinnah of the situation and wrote to Syed on the 17 January with the news:

"I have already replied to Mr. Jinnah by wire on the 10th as well as the 11th. instant after due consultations with our friends here including Yousuf, Gazdar and others, that it was not possible to call the All India session of the Muslim League this year at Karachi or any other town in Sind.

There is certainly no objection in calling the Provincial League session either at Larkana or Nawab Shah or at Mirpurkhas. But Hyderabad would not be the proper place, as it is the headquarters for the Martial Law authorities."[31]

Writing to Jinnah clarifying the position, Khuhro used no frills to decorate his letter and the style in its bluntness must have reminded Jinnah of his own unadorned prose:

"My dear Quaid-e-Azam,

In response to your letter and telegram, I summoned a meeting of the Working Committee of the Sind Provincial Muslim League on the 4th instant and subsequently called an informal meeting of local workers of Karachi on the 10th. The consensus of opinion was found to be that it would not be possible in view of the facts stated here below to invite the All India session of the Muslim League at Karachi or some other place in Sind.

As you no doubt are well aware, the Province of Sind has only recently gone through the ordeal of unprecedented floods that swept over half of the Province. The Hur trouble is another great misfortune which has befallen Sind. The result is that rural economy of the Province in general and of the districts lying along the left bank of the Indus in particular has been dislocated. The promulgation of Martial Law over a greater part of the Province is another factor that has told on the free and unrestricted movements of people and holdings of such huge gatherings as a session of the Muslim League where delegates from all over India are expected to gather in their numberless thousands. As far as holding the session at such inlying towns as Sukkur, Hyderabad and Nawab Shah are concerned, the Martial Law authorities were not prepared to allow us to do so, as they have with difficulty permitted us only now to hold even the elections of our primary branches between the 1st of January and 15th of February. The district elections will be held next March.

As for the session to be held at Karachi, there were innumerable difficulties facing us. Karachi is the most important air-base as well as very important army and navy centre in India. Consequently the A. R. P. restrictions imposed in Karachi are very rigid, in view of which it was impossible to have obtained electrical installations and energy required for the Pandal and other purposes. Besides, there is a serious shortage of food at Karachi and it would almost impossible to get charcoal, wooden material and cloth, etc. for the setting up of the proposed site on the scale compatible with the dignity of the All India session of our League."[32]

Khuhro also put to Jinnah his concerns regarding the legislation he wanted to bring in: "Besides the difficulties ennumerated above, I have had personally to contend with another in my capacity as the Minister for Revenue. The need for agrarian relief is a crying one and I have to see to it that the necessary bills are introduced in the next session of the Sind Legislative Assembly which is due to come off in about a month's time. These bills are important and of far reaching consequences with which the welfare of our masses is linked fast; and, what is more, we are hard pressed by the urgency of relief and rehabilitation of the vast areas ravaged by the recent floods. As I am the Chairman of the Relief Committee, and also am in charge of the Revenue Department, it is my function to tackle this urgent and vast problem of restoring the dislocated economic life of rural people spread over more than half of the area of the Province, for which the Provincial Committee and district committees have been organised."[33] Having recounted this formidable list of problems and programme, Khuhro did reassure Jinnah that the party work was not being neglected: "We are also doing our utmost in spite of these handicaps, to organise the Muslim League in the Province and no opportunity is being left unused for the promotion of the cause of the League.

Khuhro pointed out that Muslim League had been sucessful in getting elected its candidate for the Central Legislative Assembly, Yusuf Haroon, whom Khuhro had strongly backed inspite of the opposition of the Governor, and some Muslim politicians in addition to the Congress:

"Thank God, Yousuf's election has ended so very satisfactorily, he having been opposed and his opponent finding dismal failure looming large before himself thought it wise to withdraw from the contact bearing testimony to the undisputed sway that Muslim League holds in this province, for the promotion of which we have all been doing our best."[34]

Khuhro also assured Jinnah that Sind was only postponing the honour of holding the Muslim League session and that they would look forward to holding the next session in December in Karachi:

"It is our earnest wish and prayer that the next year will be more propitious for us and Inshallah Sind will be in a position to invite the session on a scale that will be in keeping with the grand dignity of the League and in consonance with the traditions of Sind itself as the gateway of Islam."[35]

When the All India Muslim League session was eventually held towards the end of December 1943, it was indeed a very grand affair. Jinnah was brought to the Conference in a huge procession. He was seated on a decorated camel cart, a particularly Sindhi touch, with Muslim League guards in uniform marching along the length of Bunder Road. Thousands of spectators thronged the road to see the triumphal procession and Karachi appeared thoroughly impressed as were the distinguished leaders from all over the sub-continent. His good friend Sir Sikander Hayat was dead but Khuhro had invited all the important leaders from the Punjab including the Premier Sir Khizr Hayat Khan Tiwana. There were also large delegations from Bengal, United Provinces, Bombay and other provinces with the Premiers of Assam, Bengal and Sardar Aurangzeb of North West Frontier Province. Dow wrote his usual cynical comments on the conference to the Viceroy:

"I shall return to Karachi by the 24th and be there over the Muslim League jamboree... I believe the Premier [Hidayetullah] is doing his best to get a large Bengal contingent over, as a counter-poise to Khuhro's Punjabi friends. So Jinnah will again have to decide whether to plump for more food in the bellies of Bengal or more money in the pockets of the Punjab. He will perhaps again have the middle course of abusing the Central Government."[36]

Dow was ofcourse referring to the on-going battle between himself and Khuhro where the latter was trying to secure the best prices for the growers of Sind and may have hoped that the Punjab leaders would support him with Jinnah. It was certainly not clear that Hidayetullah would work for lower prices though he may have given Dow such assurances. Dow's implication that the availability of food in Bengal was affected by the prices in Sind was quite without foundation because the shortages of food in that province – the Bengal famine which was raging at this time – was not due to the high prices for food but to the fact that most of the food was being sent out of India for the war effort and what was left in the country was being hoarded by profiteering merchants.

Khuhro had worked very hard to make the League session a success. He put up a number as personal guests, getting some of his friends to vacate their houses for the occasion. For the Sind League leadership the session was a *tour de force*. Wolpert in his biography of Jinnah describes the occasion:

> "Some 10,000 Muslim delegates gathered in Karachi to attend the thirty first session of the Muslim League that December. When Jinnah entered the brilliantly lighted tent [*shamiana*] he was greeted with thunderous shouts of 'Quaid-i-Azam Zindabad' and 'Conqueror of Congress Zindabad'. He began to speak at 10:50 p.m. on the eve of his sixty-seventh birthday and continued extempore for 100 minutes in English."[37]

Jinnah spoke to a hushed audience whose complete attention while they listened is all the more remarkable because very few understood any English. Khuhro was on the dais alongside with Liaquat Ali Khan and other luminaries including Nawab Bahadur Yar Jung the brilliant Urdu orator and poet from Hyderabad Deccan. After Jinnah had spoken and received prolonged applause Nawab Bahadur Yar Jung was called to come and 'translate' Jinnah's speech. Jung's translation was very free and in a spell binding oration he held the audience in the palm of his hand, laughing and crying and shouting slogans at his will.

Jinnah was obviously not very well but his determination carried him through the strenuous work he had undertaken. At this period Jinnah was spending long period of the summer in Karachi and going to Quetta and Ziarat for holidays presumably for health reasons.

In his speech at the Karachi conference Jinnah had made some feeling comments about his League flock:

> "I get some suggestions which are splendid ones and thoughtful ones and very good too. I get complaints and petty quarrels, which I do not like. But anyhow it is a healthy sign."

He could have been referring to the bickerings in Sind Muslim League where this period was marked by G. M. Syed's efforts to take over the provincial Muslim League and create a Syed group personally loyal to him in control of the organisation. Khuhro who was by far the most dynamic member of the Cabinet, was not only involved in the important legislative work which he had made his special concern but was also very active in the organisation of Muslim League. With the twenty years plus of political work and connections in the province Khuhro had considerable personal following and friends who were recruits to Muslim League and worthy claimants to offices in the party. With Syed's penchant for his fellow Syeds and his firm conviction that only they were suitable for political leadership there was bound to be collision somewhere along the line.

Khuhro had been President of Sind Muslim League since April 1942. G. M. Syed was not a man who could put up with the pre-eminence of someone else for long and began to agitate to displace Khuhro and put in someone more pliable to his dictates. There was no reason to remove Khuhro at first but as soon as Muslim League formed the Ministry, Syed got his chance. He took the position that the offices of Minister should not be combined with those of the party and therefore as Khuhro was Minister he should not also be Muslim League President. Syed sought the intervention of Jinnah in the matter. Particular urgency was lent to the problem in the eyes of Syed by the fact that provincial party elections were to be held in June 1943 and the enrolment of members was taking place. Syed styling himself as 'progressive' and Khuhro and his supporters as 'conservative' was out to take control of the party. In his own words:

"New branches of Muslim League were being formed everywhere, and a brisk competition was going on between the two groups, reflecting the conservative and progressive trends in the organization."

In April when in Delhi along with other Muslim Leaguers on the occasion of the Annual session of All India Muslim League, he wrote to Jinnah complaining in a typically high moral tone:

"There is a general cry that the present Ministry has done nothing :
(1) to bring about the removal of Martial Law
(2) to give relief to the flood stricken people
(3) to stop corruption rampant in most of the Government departments
(4) to ameliorate and improve the social and economic conditions of the masses."[38]

Syed knew very well that his complaints were mostly in the realm of his imagination – that it was certainly impossible for the Sind Ministers to do anything to remove the Martial Law in eastern Sind during the height of the Hur insurrection; that everything possible had been done for the relief of the flood stricken areas, Khuhro himself personally supervising the *bunds* [flood prevention barriers] to see that breaches did not occur; that it was beyond the power of almost any government and certainly of a newly inducted government to do anything effective 'to stop corruption rampant in ... Government departments', or to magically and overnight 'improve the social and economic conditions of the masses'. Jinnah very sensibly pointed out that it was too soon to judge the government on these points.[39]

However when Jinnah arrived in Sind in June on his way to Quetta for the summer break, he agreed that Ministers should not hold party offices and Khuhro had to give up the presidentship of the provincial Muslim League which was then taken up by Syed. On his elevation to the presidentship Syed adopted a hostile attitude to the Ministry particularly to Khuhro who was bringing in the most legislation and who was at the same time very active in party affairs. Syed was busy intriguing in the Assembly to get the members to vote against government proposals and to obstruct its workings in the Assembly and in the Party. Syed was egged on by people who were hostile to the League government for reasons of their own. Ali Mohammed Rashdi wrote to him with more than a touch of mockery:

"Here lies the remains of a pathetic personality, who sought good through evil, who started as a revolutionary but ended as a reactionary and whose contribution towards the affairs of his country was only 'greater confusion'."[40]

In the Party, Syed pursued his aim of appointing his Syed friends and followers. In the provincial Party Syed succeeded in the elections held in March 1944 in getting his friends elected including the key post of General Secretary of the Party. At the time Syed had been appointed President, Yusuf Haroon, the son of the late President of Sind Muslim League, Sir Abdullah Haroon had been appointed General Secretary, but now Syed wanted a fellow Syed in the post and got his way although Khuhro strongly supported Haroon:

"Most of the members of the new Council that elected held progressive and socialistic views. I was re-elected President for the new term and on my suggestion the post of General Secretaryship was given to Sayed Ghulam Haider Shah, instead of Yusuf Haroon."[41]

Syed was being over optimistic in describing his friends as 'progressive and socialist'. They were mostly from the Sayed group and although Ghulam Haider Shah was comparatively better educated than most Sayeds he could hardly justify the description Syed chose to give him. Haroon on the other hand was a senior League worker who had remained in the forefront of the movement especially after the death of his father and with his connections and following in the Party and his family's contribution to it, both financial and political, he had much more obvious claim to the post of General Secretary.

Having packed the Party with his friends Syed proceeded to harass the Ministry bypassing resolutions mostly of a highly impractical nature which he was certainly aware the Governor would not allow the Ministry to carry through. Knowing full well the struggle Khuhro was having to get through a minimum programme: to get the prices of agricultural produce enhanced; to get a favourable Settlement; and to pass Land Alienation and Debt Reconciliation legislation; Syed chose to criticize the 'failure' of the Ministry to carry out the Muslim League programme and of failing to 'safeguard and promote the interests of the masses of Sind.' He chose for his particular target Khuhro and his Ministry for Revenue, a course of action for which he had an obvious ulterior motive. Syed wanted Khuhro out of the Government as he saw him as the most effective rival for power in the Party as well as in the province. If he could not dominate the government, Syed was determined to bring Khuhro down, and if that failed, to destroy the Ministry. Calling a meeting of the Working Committee on 7 July 1944 he levelled a number of charges of neglect and incompetence against the Ministry and then said: "...it is in the interests of the Province and the Muslims of Sind that the Council of Ministers as at present composed should resign."[42]

Jinnah had been aware of the differences that had arisen in the Muslim League organization in Sind. In May, Syed had already complained of Khuhro's 'indirect interference' in the Sind Provincial Muslim League elections[43], although he did not explain how the fact Khuhro's participating in party affairs was 'interference'.

Syed was an extraordinary character, highly emotional, an impractical idealist who combined ideas of a chimerical 'socialism' with strong affiliations to the Sayed community. He was associated with different communist inclined or 'socialist' organisations in Sind such as the Hari Committee which had been formed in the 'thirties. He was a Theosophist as well as a strong traditionalist. In fact he was the perfect embodiment of the woolly idealism which that combination of ideologies suggests. In spite of his aspirations as leader, organisation was not his strong point. He allowed himself to be swayed by his Sayed loyalties and was unable to unite the Muslims of Sind behind him. Instead he spent time in pointless intrigues against the Muslim League government, putting up impossible targets for it to achieve as for instance:'the removal of corruptions from all the departments of the Government.' or overnight 'improvement in the conditions of the masses'. Whenever he decided that these targets had not been met or that a particular colleague was not tractable, he set out to destroy either the individual or the government with no fastidiousness about the allies he might choose for his task. His singleminded pursuit of his chosen target laid him open to the charge of vindictiveness. But at the same time he was willing to admit to the wrong he might have done particularly to his friends and showed a naive willingness to make amends after damage had been done. He was a bad politician and party man but a good and loyal friend. He was an intellectual at heart, delighting in philosphical discussions, necessarily somewhat dilettante, and assiduous in collecting records and writing – one of the very few even among the educated who did so at this time.

Taking over from Khuhro as President Sind Muslim League, Syed, who wanted to put his stamp on the organisation found Khuhro's influence in the organisation intolerable. He also found Khuhro too strong a Minister and too practical an administrator to be dominated by him and to fall in with his fanciful schemes. Khuhro was therefore to be removed. In this scheme he found an ally in Hashim Gazdar, the Home Minister. Gazdar was of Marwari descent and belonged to an old Karachi community. He was a very ambitious man who had come into prominence in the post Separation period.[44] Syed led him to believe that with Khuhro out of the way the Ministry of Hidayetullah would be easily thrown out and Gazdar could then be brought in as Premier with the help of Syed and his friends. To remove Khuhro, Gazdar who was Home Minister and therefore responsible for the police and law and order, was to prove very useful.

By the middle of 1944 the storm clouds were gathering for Khuhro. In the early months of that year Khuhro was travelling by train to Larkana and a well-known Karachi doctor, Dr. Lalwani, was sharing his compartment. Lalwani who was not only a medical doctor but also published the *Karachi Daily*, the only Karachi evening paper and was a keen palmist. During the journey he examined Khuhro's hand and told him that an attempt was to be made soon to take his life and that his chances of escaping death were slim. Khuhro did not attach much importance to the warning but in any case could not have possibly foreseen the way in which the attempt would be made.

13

THE HUR UPRISING

Traditionally every Muslim in Sind has a *Murshid* or Pir.* To be called *be-murshid* or to be without such a spiritual guide was and is, even up to the present day, the worst possible abuse for a Sindhi Muslim. There were numerous Pirs in Sind – centuries old *dargahs*, lesser and greater pirs, all with lesser or greater but devoted following. About a dozen or so of these 'living saints' with hereditary *gadis* were the most important in terms of status and followers. Perhaps the most influential of these were the Pirs Pagara.

The number of Pagaro's followers was the largest in Sind, estimated at the end of the 19th century to be about 200,000. These were spread all over the province but concentrated in Tharparkar and Hyderabad districts with some pockets in Khairpur State. A small number lived in the upper Sind districts of Larkana and Rohri. There was a number of both Muslim and Hindu followers of Pir Pagaro across the Sind border in Rajasthan and even further afield. The Pir himself lived in Pir jo Goth in the Sukkur district. Among his followers were a militant group known as 'Hurs' who had acquired a reputation for a devotion to him as fanatical as that of the historical Assassins of Hasan Sabah of 11th and 12th century Persia.**

The Pirs of Pagaro had a long and colourful history which began when an ancestor Syed Ali Makki accompanied the Ommayed General Mohammad bin Qasim when he conquered Sind in A.D. 711. Sayed Ali Makki settled in Lakki near Sehwan where his tomb is venerated to this day.[1] He was a pious man who attracted a local following. His descendants known as Lakiari Sayeds spread throughout Sind setting up as *murshids* or *pirs* whenever the opportunity arose. The most notable of the Lakiari descendants in modern times was Pir Mohammad Rashid who died in

---

* Spiritual head to guide a Muslim in the path of religion. This was essentially a Sufi concept at variance with orthodox Islam.

**Hasan bin Sabah (circa mid 11th century (circa 1124) born in Qum, a holy city of Iran or Persia, was known as the Old Man of the Mountain. He was according to some sources contemporary of the famous Nizam ul Mulk and of Omar Khayyam and legend has it all three were school fellows. Hasan bin Sabah who controlled the impregnable mountain fort of Alamut in the Elburz mountains, used 'assassination' as a political weapon. His followers were given *hashish* (hence *hashishian* or 'assassins') and a taste of paradise and at his bidding even killed themselves, were used by him to 'assassinate' his opponents. These assassins even made attempts on the life of the great Salahuddin Ayubi (Saladin) and were eventually destroyed by Halaku Khan who invaded Persia with his Mongol army in mid-thirteenth century.

1818. He is said to have performed prodigious miracles and had followers even as far away as Bombay.² He was known as the Pir of the Turban (*pagaro*) and the Flag (*jhandewaro*). In the next generation the Turban and the Flag were to be separated.

Pir Rashid had 13 sons: one of these Sibghatullah had been nominated by his father to succeed him but another brother Mohammed Yasin tried to wrest the succession from him and when he failed, his eldest son set up as the Pir of the Flag in a village which came to be known as Jhandewaro jo Goth (the village of the owner of the flag) in Hala near Hyderabad. Mohammed Yasin's assassination attempt on his brother had stimulated a number of Sibghatullah's followers and disciples to set themselves up as a dedicated group called Farqi Jamaat or Hurs to defend Sibghatullah's title as Pagaro.* There is also a tradition that the Hurs originated with the followers of the Pir who were sent by him to support the *jehad* of Sayed Ahmed Barelvi against the Sikhs in the Punjab in the early 19th century.† Further that the Hurs kept their original instructions as a code for life and thus developed as a specially devoted band of followers of the Pir, and among themselves became a close brotherhood with a way of life which was a mystery to outsiders.

The term Hur was taken from the name of the Islamic hero Hur, a warrior in the army sent by Yezid, the Ommayed ruler, against Imam Hussain, the grandson of the Holy Prophet. He came over to the side of Hussain and died fighting at Karbala. His name came to signify supreme devotion and sacrifice in Islamic history.

So fanatical were the Hurs that even the Pirs themselves found them difficult to handle. Often they would act in what they considered to be the interests of the Pir, without his knowledge and consent. The weaker personalities among the Pagaro pirs were quite unable to control them.

Pir Ali Gohar, the Pagaro at the time of the British conquest had quarrelled with the Talpur rulers of Khairpur when he had told the British authorities about Talpur's fraudulent claim to more territory for the State than was the case.‡ The ill feeling between Pagaro and the Talpur ruler led to an increase in Hur activity and they were in trouble with the Khairpur authorities quite often. This was the beginning of their history of outlawry and banditry. One of their exploits led to charges being brought against the next Pir, Hizbullah Shah, for the murder of a Jhandewara Pir. He also blamed the Hurs for their part in his ordeal. But this only renewed their zeal to avenge their Pir's good name and in doing so committed many mur-

---

* There are other stories about the origins of the Hurs and probably the most convincing in view of their subsequent fanaticism is the one where the then rulers of Sind, the Talpurs, were asked by Sayed Ahmed Barelvi *circa* 1820 to support an attack against the Punjab. The Talpurs, unable to supply resources direct, asked the Pagaro Pir to do so and he chose a group of his supporters who swore unquestioning loyalty. The special instructions that the Hurs were given for Sayed Ahmed's *jehad* against the Sikhs were then subsequently maintained by them as a code for life and thus began the existence of this extraordinarily devoted band of the followers of the Pagaro Pirs.

† Hur tradition claims that a band of five hundred did go to the hills of North West Frontier through Afghanistan but returned only with the loss of one man, which would mean that they were not actually engaged in fighting. Syed Ahmed himself was killed fighting and is buried at Balakot in North West Frontier Province of Pakistan.

‡ Pir Aligohar, the *gadi nashin* at the time of the conquest had originally connived with Mir Ali Murad of Khairpur to draw up documents showing that the Mir who was supposed to be an ally of the Britsh, included in his state areas larger than was actually the case. When the Pir and the Mir fell out between themselves the Pir went to the British and told them of the forgery whereupon not only did the Mir lose the extra territory but also some of his own, as punishment.

ders and outrages. Pir Hizbullah Shah was succeeded by Pir Aligohar Shah in 1890 and during his time the Hurs became an entirely lawless band. They were even banned from the new Pir's village of Pir jo Goth and the Pir's other followers regarded them with fear and dislike. They engaged in dacoities and murders, did not take food or water even from other non-Hur followers of the Pir and did not exchange greetings with them. Their dues for the Pir were collected by their own agents. Hurs led an exclusive life, with secret ceremonies, dressing in blue black clothes, in close brotherhood with each other. It was at this stage that Dayaram Gidumal* described them 'wholly given up to brigandage, regardless of all other ties.' They consider it better now "to reign in hell than to serve in heaven... like Thugs of yore, they have made their evil their good, and rapine and bloodshed their religion."[3]

The area of Sind most affected by Hur activity was the north of Tharparkar district, the Sanghar and Makhi Dandh areas. The latter was the Hurs' primary sanctuary. This was a large depression approximately a hundred and twenty square miles in size which was under water during the inundation season. Immediately to the south of this were areas of jungle while the Sanghar area was well cultivated and had a settled population of Hurs. It was from this group that the outlaws sprang and they would move into the neighbouring jungle and swamp areas when the authorities frequently sought them out. The remaining villages could be relied upon to protect the outlaws and not betray them to the authorities. At that time Sardar Yaqub who was the acting Deputy Collector of the Tharparkar district made a study of the Hur phenomenon and recorded that: "Even the worst criminal expects, as a matter of religious privilege, to receive aid and shelter from all others. It is considered sinful to expose any such criminal, and it is considered a binding religious act to harm those who may be trying to harm or capture him, and to counteract their plans."[4] Hurs took pride in the presence among them of well-known outlaws, the more notorious the more they prided themselves on him– 'recognizsing that the outlaw filled among them an important place...' and when the outlaws were eventually exterminated, a Hur was heard to say, "The country looks now without its charms; everything looks barren, the pleasant *fakirs* are gone, and without them we are nothing more than birds without feathers."[5] Songs were sung about their exploits by folk singers going from Hur village to Hur village and the women would sing of them when gathered together at their festivals.

The administration found itself helpless in the face of the non co-operation of the population and it was not until W. H. Lucas was appointed as Deputy Commissioner of Tharparkar, at the end of October 1895, that any significant success against Hur activity was achieved. Lucas who was to become a legendary figure in the annals of Sind administration** found "the police dispirited, loyal zamindars and baniyas panic stricken and never going out without guards, contributions levied from

---

* Dayaram Gidumal was a noted Sindhi jurist, educationist and writer in the 19th century. He had good relations with his contemporary Pir Pagaro and was consulted by the Sind Government at the time of the first Hur troubles at the end of the 19th century for his opinion on the subject. Gidumal wrote a detailed Note for the government on the subject.

**When the 40s Hur eruption was at its height, Lambrick the Hur Commissioner of the time was told by local zamindars and other people that 'Lucas Sahib had dealt with the matter in one month.' Lambrick was sceptical of this folk story and in fact it was a few months that Lucas had needed to control the situation.

Hindu panchayats, and the Queen's authority openly defied."[6] The policy Lucas adopted was to make the lives of the Hurs so uncomfortable that they would be forced to give up the outlaws in their midst. He began by sweeping away all the outlying 'unauthorized' hamlets and forced the Hurs to live in large villages which could be watched. Makhi Dhand was cleared of graziers and roads were cut through it. Punitive fines for co-operating with the outlaws were strictly enforced and extra police as well as military force was deployed throughout the area. Even with these measures the 'outrages' did not altogether cease. Pressure was put on Pir Pagaro to hand over the outlaws and he tried to convince the Hurs that they should not protect the outlaws. Areas where outlaws operated were taxed for the cost of 'law enforcing agencies', and the people were threatened that no canal water would be given for the cultivation until the outlaws were given up, and they were also threatened with expulsion from the area altogether. In a few encounters with the police and army most of the followers of the notorious Hur leader Bachu 'Badshah' [king], including his chief lieutenant, Piru, were killed. Having lost his most important men, Bachu came in unarmed and gave himself up to Lucas thus ending the two and half year uprising on part of this 'ultra fanatical and criminal sect.'[7]

Although the situation had been saved for the time being the British officials were not satisfied that the problem had been permanently solved. Sir Evan James, Commissioner-in-Sind, expressed his doubts about the future behaviour of the Hurs: "The question remains what measures to adopt for coercing or persuading the Hurs to a better mode of life in the future, and to obeying the Government rather than the Pir. I confess I am in the dark, and not very sanguine as to the future of the Hurs."[8] James gave his opinion that the Hurs were extremely obstinate and fanatical and any incident could set off another incident of violent crime. In fact James was inclined to recommend a special Regulation enabling District Magistrates to fine, banish or confiscate the lands of the 'recalcitrants'. The religio-fanatic' element in their character made them different from the ordinary dacoits and criminals and more akin to Thugs and to Sicilian brigands 'who gave half their spoils to the Church'. The outlaws were not "a mere fortuitous band of refugee criminals but the mature fruit of Hur blood thirstiness and fanaticism." James suggested a number of ways of keeping the Hurs in order for the future: "Sind is non-regulation, so I hope that the ordinary law, administered without too many refinements, may be found sufficient to keep them cowed and check future beginnings of lawlessness."[9]

James also initiated the policy of settling Baluch tribesmen and Punjabi and Pathan settlers in the Makhi Dandh area which was also largely drained to make it into cultivable land: "The importation too, into their neighbourhood of Baluchis, Cabulis and Panjabis, which I shall try and effect when the Jamrao Canal is opened, will help to frighten them into good behaviour, and meanwhile the appointment of a body of Nawab Shahbaz Khan's Bhugtis as a part of the punitive police has been a measure quite in the right direction."[10] In fact a few years later, officers on the spot were admitting that this policy of settlements had actually not succeeded to the extent that had been expected and that the need to suppress the Hurs directly continued. But although by 1896 the long running battle between the Hur dacoits and the administration had been brought to a close and the leaders Bachu and Piru with most of their gang had been caught, the government did not feel sanguine that the danger of recrudescence was over. Although settlements were made on the Makhi lands and police posts were established in the affected areas, the worst fears of James and other officials were realized within a space of two years.

In 1896 Pir Ali Gohar Shah died and was succeeded by Pir Shah Mardan Shah. Over a year later in February and March 1898 the new Pir set out for a tour of the areas with the largest concentration of his followers, in Sanghar and Khipro *talukas*. This tour of Pir Pagaro excited the Hurs very much and the local administration grew apprehensive that some kind of disturbance could occur. The Pir was advised to cut his tour short, which he did, but the fears of the officers were soon realized. Under the leadership of Wassand Kazak a number of dacoities and murders began in May 1898. On the night of 30th June the murder took place of Wadero Mohammed Waris Narejo, a leading zamindar of Sanghar who was well-known for his opposition to the Hurs and who was due to give evidence against some of them within the next few days. Narejo was killed along with his two servants, his house was looted and burnt even though he had taken precautions against such an attack. This murder caused panic among the non-Hur sections of the population in the area. A strong police force was immediately sent by the administration and the local Hurs were fined but with little success.

The Makhi Dandh jungle in spite of being opened up by the Government still gave excellent shelter and the Hurs still created terror in the population at large by murdering anybody they suspected gave information against them. The government attempted to make the Pir himself responsible for giving up the criminals. Some were deported to other areas in the Presidency and many were settled in special areas–precursors of 'concentration camps' – where they were registered and had to present themselves for role-call at regular intervals. The settlements were also subjected to searches from time to time to detect any stolen property or to check if any dacoits had taken refuge there. This was to become known as the famous *lorha* system because of the barbed wire or thorny fences which were used to enclose the settlements – and which was to be used again in the 1940s uprising. The application of the Criminal Tribes Act XXVII of 1871 (amended by Act II of 1897) and the Punjab Murderous Outrages Act No. XXIII of 1867 was amended and extended to the Hurs. The officials, particularly those on the spot, realized that the problems of the Hurs would not be easily solved.

Pir Sibghatullah Shah, the sixth Pir Pagaro, occupied the *gaddi* in 1922 while still very young. His formal guardianship was entrusted to the Vizier in Khairpur[11] who appointed the Government Inspector of Schools, Akhund Rasul Baksh of Rohri as tutor and guardian of the Pir. The tutor was to be his constant companion. The Pir however proved to be a particularly strong and wilful personality quite averse to discipline and as soon he reached eighteen years of age declared his independence by dispensing with the services of the tutor. Soon he acquired the reputation of a man who did not brook any opposition and was determined to rule his flock with full authority. Stories circulated of the death and disappearance of those with whom he was displeased. Strong rumours were also afloat that the Pir had collected arms in his *kot* of Pir-jo-Goth.[12]

Sometime in 1929 a woman complained to the Sukkur authorities that her son Ibrahim Kori was being held prisoner by the Pir in his *kot*. When the woman was subsequently murdered the Sukkur administration decided to raid the *kot* and search the residence within it. As a direct daylight raid could have met with resistence the police decided to use subterfuge to get into the citadel. The local Station House Officer (S.H.O.), a notorious police officer Ghulam Akbar, threatened the non-Hur murids of the Pir who were close to him and got them to agree to open the gates of the main house from inside at a fixed time. At the appointed time, at the dead of night the police posse led by the S. P. [Superintendent of Police] Ray, an Englishman, reached the fort and the gates were opened as arranged, from inside. As was usual in the hot weather the Pir was asleep in the open in the courtyard. The guns he kept with him were removed and the police searched the house. They found a large wooden box in which a teenage boy was being kept prisoner. After that the house was searched and although there was no large cache, a dozen or so rifles and guns, mostly unlicensed and some ammunition was found.[13] The Pir was charged with the "wrongful confinement of the boy Ibrahim", arrested and taken to jail in Sukkur. He was to be brought to trial. The Pir engaged Mohammed Ali Jinnah from Bombay, considered the finest lawyer of the day, to defend him. The Commissioner-in-Sind, G. A. Thomas, appointed Mr. Udharam, the City Magistrate, to try the case in Sukkur.[14]

Just after the case began its regular hearings the Pir got in touch with Khuhro, who noted:

"At that time I was a fairly senior member of the Bombay Legislative Council with some influence with the Governor of Bombay and with other officers of the Bombay government, and had acquired a reputation as an independent minded public man who was not afraid to stand up against the bureaucrats. It appears that Pir Sahib was advised by his close *murids* that he should get my sympathy and support. He sent his senior aide Mohabat Fakir[15] to me at Larkana in October 1929 and asked me to come and see him. I did so immediately. I made a special request to the District Magistrate, a European officer, who allowed me to see the Pir although interviews were banned. I was taken personally by the Superintendent of the jail to the cell where the Pir sahib was confined. The meeting did not take place in the usual room for interviews as it appeared that the authorities did not consider it safe to bring him out to the interview room for fear of attack from outside.

I was very much moved by the plight of the Pir Sahib. He only had bare necessities in the cell, a cot, a chair and a teapoy. He was allowed to order food as he liked as an A class prisoner. He had no complaints except that he was not being allowed to see anyone and was forced to send secret messages through police guards who were bribed by his *murids*. Although the Superintendent left us alone through courtesy, I learnt later that there was some wireless arrangement to overhear our conversation. Pir Sahib asked me to see Mr. Jinnah who had not come to see him in jail and to whom his *khalifas* did not have easy access, to talk to about the case. He also asked me to see the Commissioner on his behalf. In the evening I went to see Mr. Jinnah in the Circuit House on the hill overlooking the river Indus. Mr. Jinnah talked about politics most of the time I was with him and only in passing about the case in which he was being assisted by a local lawyer Mr. Motiram Advani. Jinnah was a very well-known lawyer and also had a great political reputation. His fees in this case were Rs. 500/- a day, a great sum in those days. I stayed in Sukkur for about a week and attended the hearings everyday.

A month or so later I saw George Thomas [the Commissioner-in-Sind] as I had promised Pir Pagaro. Thomas said that he knew that I had met the Pir even before I could broach the subject. He appeared to be quite angry and burst out: "You seem to have sympathy with the Pir but he is a dangerous young man. He is an inhuman tyrant and I will see to it that he is put in for at least ten years." I told the Commissioner that the case was not being tried in a proper manner. The Pir was not allowed to sit in the court and instruct his lawyers on the spot but was kept in jail where the lawyers had to go every time they wanted instruction and the judges did not adjourn the hearing every time the lawyers wanted to see him. In effect the case was being tried in absentia. I realised that there was no way that I could persuade him to be lenient though I thought that the threat of ten years was just uttered in anger. I was very surprised therefore when the sentence was as long as he had threatened. The Pir was convicted to ten years imprisonment and Rs. 2,000 fine. The Pir again asked me to approach Jinnah to file his appeal which I did and Jinnah agreed to do so. The Chief Court of Sind with Sir Godfrey Davis the Chief Justice presiding, reduced the sentence to seven years.

The Pir was sent to Midnapore in Bengal to serve out his sentence. In Midnapore Central Jail he came in contact with Bengali terrorists and became familiar with their methods. He was also politically educated by Hindu nationalists and became sympathetic to All India Congress. These tendencies would become obvious when he returned to Sind at the end of 1936. He was very warmly received by the Hurs as well as by friends and neighbours. Crowds came to see him. Pir Abdur Rahman of Bharchundi who was quite influential in the eastern part of Sukkur district, in Daharki and Ubauro, walked a few miles on foot in the procession of the Pir who was carried in a *maafa* (a covered palanquin). Some two or three months later I went to see Pir sahib and was his guest. Sind had just separated and provincial elections were to take place under the Government of India Act, 1935 and were scheduled in February 1937. The Pir did not take any interest in the elections ... and even before the elections took place he went for *ziarat* (pilgrimage) to the Middle East."[16]

It soon became clear to those near him that the returned Pir Pagaro was a man with a purpose. The Pir believed that he would become the *Badshah* [king] of Sind. Verses by an eighteenth century mystic, Abul Rahim Girohri, were cited to prove that this Pagaro would become King of Sind. The indoctrination he had received in jail had made him into a strong Congress sympathiser. Between 1936 and 1941 Pir Pagaro took steps to consolidate his power politically as also by training a militant force of Hurs. He collected arms and money in readiness for the time that he would take over as the ruler of Sind. Apart from his ideological affinity with Congress terrorists the Pir knew well that Congress was a well organised all India party. In Sind though Hindus were a small minority they were by far the wealthier community and much more powerful than Muslims or Muslim League in terms of their people in the administration, their party organisation and their control of the press. He deliberately set about courting the local Congressmen. He openly expressed strong 'pro-Hindu-cum-Congress views and played to the Congress gallery in every conceivable way', going so far as to interest himself in the reconversion (*shuddhi*) of a Hindu who had embraced Islam. He issued several *farmans* to his followers to wear *khaddar* [homespun cloth], and to avoid eating meat. He was reported to have ordered a *charkha* [spinning wheel which Gandhi had made his own particular symbol], for himself.

The Congress people reciprocated by praising the Pir's policies. He was reported to be fitting up a bus with loud-speakers to propogate for the Congress and to have ordered 10,000 Congress membership forms for the Hurs. He invited eminent Congress leaders to Pir-jo-Goth. The Hindu press also praised the Pir's policy during the Manzilgah agitation, and for his protection of Hindus during the communal riots in Sukkur District in 1939. He gave the Congress leaders an assurance that 'he would nominate Muslims from among his *murids* to contest the next Assembly elections on the Congress ticket' from as many constituencies as possible and offered large sums of money to support the Congress party. He also asked his followers to support Congress candidates in the bye-elections. The Congress Hindus supported his campaign against the police and his attempts to establish a personal rule in Pir-jo-Goth and other Hur areas. The Government was well aware of what was going on. The Chief Secretary of the Government of Sind mentioned the fact in his report to the Government of India:

"In pursuance of its policy of mass contact, the local Congress has of late turned its attention to the Hurs, a fanatical tribe which has long been registered as a criminal tribe in Sind, with a view to keep an eye on its criminal propensities. Endeavours are being made to enlist the Hurs in the Congress fold with promises to obtain a relaxation of some of the restrictions at present imposed on them.

The Congress efforts to enrol members of criminal tribes within the Congress fold have developed in the case of one district Congress committee, into persistent attempts to assist criminal tribesmen against the police."[17]

Pagaro's political clout had increased with the grant of political autonomy and the creation of a purely Sindhi legislature where a number of members needed the votes of the Pir's followers to get elected. The Pir took good care to keep some of the prominent politicians of the province on his side. Hidayetullah, the Premier, had represented the Pir as a lawyer in several cases and it was widely rumoured that the Premier was well paid for his services. Police reports suggested that

"He helped and encouraged the Pir and his followers as much as lay within his means as a Minister, leader and private citizen. Everything that came to his knowledge against the Pir was made known to the Pir with suitable advice."[18]

The sympathies of the Congress supported government of Allah Baksh Soomro were with him in any case as Pagaro had made his inclination to Congress quite clear. When Hidayetullah became the first Premier after the elections, Pagaro persuaded him to abolish the application of the Criminal Tribes Act to the Hurs and have those who had been exiled to Bombay Presidency brought back and end the Hur "settlements".* Pagaro was also allowed to go on an extensive tour of the Hur areas. These incautious policies, particularly in view of the previous experience of the Government with regard to Hurs and its distrust of Pagaro, was due not

---

* There was a wave of crimes by Hurs in 1914-1915 as a result of which the ring leaders were sent out of Sind to 'settlements' in the Bombay Presidency.

only to the personal intervention of Hidayetullah but also to the gullibility of the Governor, Sir Lancelot Graham, who believed that the Pir would be 'loyal' to the Government, a feeling the Pir fostered by making frequent contributions to Government War Fund, as well as to other funds.* The Pir took full advantage of the favourable political climate and made a prolonged seven-month tour mainly to collect money to fulfil his long term objectives.

From 1937 on Pir Pagaro took up the task of building up his power with all seriousness. He ended the influence of orthodox religious forces, the *maulvis*, which were critical of the 'heretical' practices of the Hurs by stopping their propaganda and influence by threat and even murder of the *maulvis* who dared to defy him.[19] Soon the Pir was bold enough to set up what was practically a parallel government in the Hur areas. He levied tax and treated Hur areas as a state within a state. The government was most of all apprehensive about his attempts to raise a private army of Hur *ghazis*. Several thousand Hurs** were reported to have been recruited and were being trained to use arms and were being sworn to absolute loyalty by the Pir. The Pir became even more active as World War II broke out in September 1939 and there were reports of his preparations, collection of funds and arms and the mysterious training camps deep in the jungles on the banks of the Indus. Here in his *keti* the Pir had his camp, and was living there even in the the scorching summer of Sind. Khuhro had occasion to see him encamped in his *keti* the summer of 1939:

> "The Pir was quite friendly with us [Muslim Leaguers] but close to Congress members who often visited him and advised him. He rarely came to Karachi. It was rumoured that he was setting up some kind of militant organisation.
>
> In 1939 the war broke out. I heard the news in Simla and returned to Sind. About this time the Pir had become more active. I had the occasion to meet Pir sahib in the summer of 1939 in his *keti* in Khairpur state. Sardar Kaiser Khan

---

* Graham was an exceptionally gullible man and was completely taken in by the Pir and his friends. The British officials were quite aware of the activities of the Pir but were helpless in the face of the Governor's attitude. The District Judge of Sukkur in 1940-41, A. G. Wells, wrote about his interview with the Governor: " I told him that there strong rumours that France having fallen the Pir believed that his was now chance to become King of Sind and had–I think eight thousand men under arms in a place of his in the forest...

He brushed my apprehensions of the Pir aside–said he had subscribed to the War Fund and that the Hindus of Pir-jo-Goth had given him a gold medal for keeping them safe in the riots. I remember asking him if he had thought of what might have happened to the Hindus of Pir-jo-Goth if they hadn't given him a gold medal.

He also said that the Police had their knife into the Pir and had continued to *shikar* [hunt] him. He gave as an instance of their *zid* [stubbornness] the fact that some years ago when they could not get him any other way they got him under the Arms Act. ... he struck me as obstinately having made up his mind in his favour and that his philosophy was that anyone who gave a cheque for the War Fund of some size must be alright.

Sam Ridley can give you a worse instance this relating to the Pir in which the Pir had stolen someone's land and put up a wall up round it. He ignored an order from Sam to pull it down and instead sent him a cheque for the War Fund. Sam returned it saying he wanted his orders obeyed and not the Pir's money. The Pir then sent it to the Governor who took it like a shot and wrote a letter to Sam pointing out that what the Governor could like the Collector ought...

Extract from a private letter of A. G. Wells to P. Cargill, Feb. 1943, Mss. Eur. F. 208/20.

**According to reports there was a fight in force of approximately eight thousand Hurs fully trained by the Pir of which only a small number actually became functional during the revolt.

Bozdar, who was a member of the Legislative Assembly, asked me to go with him to see Pir sahib to seek his help in the Local Bodies elections. We drove from Sukkur on a very hot day to his camp through the jungle. The Pir was staying in a *landhi* [a structure made of clay and straw, basically a large room with some small rooms leading off it.] Attendants were sprinkling water on the reed matting covering the large openings, so although the temperature outside was about 120 degrees it was quite cool inside and felt like a difference of twenty degrees or more. Pir sahib promised help to Kaiser Khan and invited me to stay with him in the *landhi* which he said more comfortable than electric fans in Karachi. He promised that the temperature would not be more than 70–75 degrees. I said that as soon I was free of the pressing political work (we were busy with the Manzilgah movement at the time) I would avail myself of his invitation. It so happened that I was never able to do so.

In 1939 between June and October I was often in Sukkur because of the Masjid Manzilgah movement. In Sukkur we heard stories about Pagaro's activities. It was being said that he was organising his followers in view of the prophecy that he would become the ruler of Sind. People would convey news to us that some Bengalis had come and were preparing bombs and training the Hurs. Pir sahib, all the while, was in close touch with Congress leaders. In March 1940 Allah Baksh's cabinet was defeated and we came in. I was told that Pagaro did not like it as he was not in favour of Muslim League. But he never openly joined Congress, perhaps he thought that if he joined it openly the Government would get against him."*

While his preparations continued, the Pir took good care to keep on the right side of the Governor with the help of Hidayetullah who was trusted by the Governor. Khuhro who was Minister in the Sind Government of 1940-41 noticed that the Governor was somewhat uneasy about the Pir's reported activities:

"Sir Lancelot Graham learnt about the Pir's activities and send messages to the

---

* Khuhro, Notes K.P.

Wells, the District Judge, Sukkur, in 1940-41, apropos the relations of the Pir with Congress and pro Congress elements mentions his meeting with Graham in November 1940:–

"By that time I had a very strong suspicion that the hot weather murders in Sukkur were the work of the Pir's *murids* and were committed in order to put the Weston Report in the background, prove that the Muslim League Ministry could not keep order and make the return of Allah Baksh possible. I based the suspicion on two things: first, the Pir of Bharchundi who was alleged to behind the thing was a supporter of the League, and these murders were certainly not in their interests. Next they were nearly always committed when a Minister was at Sukkur–as if to draw attention to the incompetence of the Ministry. Next, they were obviously the work of the *murids* of some Pir, and if it was not Bharchundi – he after all never had the reputation of a killer–it was the work of his Pir who was at that very time, like Allah Baksh, flirting with Congress.

My suspicions got what I considered confirmation when, on purpose, I asked Issarsing, if he thought it possible that the Pir Pagaro had anything to do with them. I remember him jumping out of his chair as if he'd had a pin stuck in his bottom and saying, "Oh no Sir, no Sir" and adding that the Pir was a very peaceful citizen. If you have a rack or thumbscrew or two about, I think you might get a lot out of Issarsing.

... talking to John Corin [Secretary to the Governor] out at the back of the old Governor's House either after or before the interview [with the Governor] I pointed out to him that a Minister had gone to Sukkur that day and I bet him a rupee that we should hear of a new outrage in Sukkur in the next morning's paper. We did... Lastly I think I am right in saying that after Allah Baksh got back into power the outrages came to an end." Wells, A. G., Mss. Eur. F. 208/69.

Pir to meet him. Pir sahib usually took Ghulam Hussain Hidayetullah as interpreter. He would appease the Governor with diplomatic manners and give large sums in war funds."

Graham was taken in most of the time but even his gullibility had limits. Officials were persistently reporting that the Pir was definitely organising some big movement and could strike at a critical time. His continuous stay in the jungle also confirmed the suspicions that he was engaged in some secret activity. Khuhro notes the reaction of the Governor to these reports:

"The Governor called him for an interview in January 1941 and asked me to come as interpreter as he suspected that Ghulam Hussain may be giving a different twist to Pir's words as he had been associated with the Pir and also with the Congress ministry in 1939. The Pir as usual talked sweetly and diplomatically to the Governor, made promises and gave Rs. 50,000 as war donation and put the Governor's suspicions at rest."[20]

Graham was quite happy to be re-assured and was soon to have a change of Ministry which was to be much more to his liking, as Wells, one of the British officers at the Government House, said at the time: "My general impression of H.E. was that he thought Allah Baksh a grand fellow. He certainly thought the Pir an injured innocent and said so."[21] This change of Ministry also suited the Pir as Khuhro remarks:

"Meanwhile our Ministry went out and in 1941 Allah Baksh and Ghulam Hussain formed a government. Pir Pagaro came especially to Karachi to help them and he expected this Ministry to be much better for his purposes."[22]

Pagaro was more confident than ever that with a Congress backed Ministry in power and his two close associates Hidayetullah and Soomro running it he would achieve his aims. But his confidence proved to be misplaced. Soomro and Hidayetullah could not withstand the different attitude of the new Governor. Khuhro relates the events at this time:

"Hugh Dow had come in as Governor. He was much sharper than Graham, a die-hard bureaucrat and very arrogant. ... He sent for the Pir in July 1941 and asked him to live in Karachi and not in the jungle. Pagaro agreed and came and stayed in Mir Khuda Baksh's bungalow on Bunder Road. He was there for sometime and then in October he suddenly left Karachi without informing the authorities, in this case Charles Clee, the Collector of Karachi. This move infuriated the Governor. At the same time the Hurs were committing dacoities and murders in Khairpur and Sanghar on a somewhat larger scale than usual. The Pir took the opportunity to visit his Garang Bungalow in Sinjhoro as well as Pir-jo-Goth. The Governor ordered Pagaro to be arrested and brought to Karachi. Sidney Ridley, the Collector of Sukkur and the Superintendent of Police went to Pir-jo-Goth and asked the Pir to accompany them. At that stage they did not tell him that he was under arrest. He was brought to Khairpur and had lunch with Ejaz Ali the *Vizier* of Khairpur. Afterwards he was brought to Karachi. The Pir was arrested at Karachi on 24th October [under Regulation XXV of 1827] and taken by train to Lahore and then by Central Indian Railway to central India and to Seoni jail in Nagpur, as we learnt later. Hur action started immediately after the arrest of the Pir."[23]

Even before the Pir was arrested, on 19th October, the murder took place of his cousin Pir Fatehali Shah along with his bodyguard and a servant who were all 'hacked to death' by Hurs in broad daylight in Sukkur.* There were also some attacks against public property but after his arrest a systematic "guerrilla war" was launched by the Hurs. On his truant visit to his different residences in Upper and Lower Sind, the Pir, was able to give the signal for the start of the insurrection. Targets were chosen carefully to undermine the confidence of the public and damage the government. Government officers and policemen were kidnapped and killed. Government property was destroyed, telegraph and telephone wires were cut, canals were breached, railway stations and police stations were attacked. Government informants were ruthlessly butchered.

The most dramatic exploit of the Hurs was to derail the Lahore Mail, the fastest and best known train of the day on 16 May 1942. The situation became very alarming and by the end of May Martial Law was applied to the eastern districts of Sind. At this time when the Japanese were advancing on the eastern frontiers of India, and Allied armed forces including Indian troops were engaged in North Africa and Europe, the Government of India felt it necessary to deploy a full Division in Sind with General Richardson in charge of the Martial Law administration. It was obvious to the Government that there was a strong similarity between these activities of the Hurs and those of Congress during the Quit India movement.

A government analyst of the Hur movement wrote in 1946 when British rule was coming towards its close and the insurrection was petering out:

"Hur disturbances started in 1941 and which still continue though on a small scale, have many similarities with the Congress responsibility for the disturbances of 1942-3 which took place in Bihar, U.P. and elsewhere in India.

(a) ... by 1941 when the Pir was contemplating the overthrow of the Government he was sufficiently Congress minded because of constant consultations with Messrs. Sidhwa, Lala Menghraj, Jairamdas Daulatram[24] and others. He... purchased *khaddar* worth thousands and distributed it amongst his followers in order to provide a proof of his sincerity to the Congress. He must have consulted Congress leaders of Sind for such a purpose – I do not think this would be denied as it came in the papers in those days.

(b) The aim of both [the Pir and the Congress] was to paralyze HMG in the face of enemy attacks.

(c) In April 1942 Gandhi gave public exposure of the theory which was to crystallize into 'Quit India' movement of 1942. ... Congress Organisation was setting the stage for a mass movement to free India before the resolution [Quit India] itself came to be passed. Hur movement is definitely influenced as the Pir was in close contact with the Sind Congress leaders.

(d) The Hur movement started in 1941 just in the middle of the year–though it became intensely active in 1942 when the essential structure of the proposals for the withdrawal of the British was developed by the Congress."[25].

---

* The Hurs established a pattern that their killings were done in broad daylight in front of as many witnesses as possible in order to terrorize and impress them with their boldness and audacity.

The '40s insurrection had every mark of being well planned and seemed to be used as a blueprint for the very similar Congress revolt of the 1942 and 1943. Lambrick* the Special Commissioner for Hur areas for the greater period of the disturbances, wrote that it was possible that Congress had copied the Hur methods. He pointed out that the Pir had followed certain Congress doctrines and issued orders to his followers to conduct themselves accordingly. This action brought a good deal of publicity. Gandhi was impressed to have a Muslim Pir in a Muslim majority province on his side. But some local Congressmen advised caution that the Pir's activities might have a fallout not quite to the advantage of the Congress reputation. That he was a "murderer and sadist and his followers were criminals"[26] The Pir on his side wanted to get Congress support "with a view to achieving his own megalomaniac plans".[27] The Hurs were very active from November 1941 and "the Congress rebellion ofcourse started in August [1942] and it maybe said that they copied the Hurs...The success of the Hurs' sabotage perhaps encouraged them."[28]

There can be little doubt however that the Pir under Congress influence during his sojourn in Midnapore jail had been given assurances that if at the proper time he could start a serious uprising against the British and help drive them out of India, Sind would be his fiefdom. It was also clear that detailed planning had been done about the preparation of the guerrilla force and its the methods of operation. The Pir had the blueprint and went to work on it as soon as he returned to Sind in 1936. His methods were extremely subtle. He gained the backing of a number of key politicians who could prove useful to him. The Congress supported governments of Sind removed restrictions from the Hurs which had been imposed on them for nearly four decades. He was allowed to undertake prolonged tours of the areas where there were concentrations of his followers, and it was well-known that he was using these tours to collect money to buy arms and to start the training of his followers.

Methods to ensure the absolute loyalty of the trainees were used as for instance, during a parade of the Hur *ghazis* names of two or three would be called out at random and when they stepped out they would be shot dead. At the end of their training *namaz janaza* [funeral prayers] would be recited over them to impress them that their life were solely dedicated to the cause. Training was rigorous and the Pir himself supervised it in his jungle camps. Targets were identified; victims and key installations were selected for the Hur operations. These were railways, telegraph lines, police stations, police officers and other government functionaries. Lists of people to be eliminated were prepared with the Pir's approval and when he was arrested other people were added to the list who the Hur activists identified as having betrayed the Pir although they had been particularly favoured by him. Murders were often committed by the Hurs in broad daylight.

---

* Hugh Trevor Lambrick, I.C.S., was a distinguished officer in the 19th century tradition of scholar officer. He made a deep study of Sind, its countryside, its history and traditions and wrote a number of books on the history of Sind. He also wrote a fictionalized account of the Hur insurrection of the '40s, in the tradition of the 19th century *Confessions of a Thug* where he was personally involved as the Hur Commissioner for most of its duration and during which he became familiar with its organisation and its motivational force. His book *The Terrorist* gets inside the skin of a Hur fighter and is a unique account of the Hur movement.

The most important person killed by the Hurs during the uprising was Allah Baksh Soomro the ex-Premier, in May 1943. Soomro though initially sympathetic to the Pir had passed the Hur Act during his period of office. The Pir was put under house arrest during his Ministry. Soomro expressed his determination to deal severely with the Hurs at two meetings he held in connection with the war fund tour in the summer of 1942. He expressed these sentiments on 10 May 1942 at a meeting in Mirpurkhas in the Durbar Hall in the presence of about three hundred important people of the district. Seth Sitaldas Perumal, M.L.A. from Tharparkar, was murdered by the Hurs on the same day that Soomro had addressed the meeting in Mirpurkhas and where Seth Sitaldas had also made an anti Hur speech. On 12 May at Nawabshah at a meeting attended by about three hundred or so people Soomro held the Hurs responsible for the Seth's death and vowed to destroy them. He said that he was bringing in the Hur Act (passed 20 March 1942) and would do whatever it took to crush the Hurs. He said clearly that the Pir was responsible and he would never allow him to return to Sind.

The Hurs never forgave him for these statements and just a few days later, acting on a report that he was travelling on the Lahore Mail, they attacked it between Tando Adam and Uderolal stations, some distance from Hyderabad. In fact Soomro had boarded the train at Karachi accompanied by Nihchaldas Vazirani, a Minister in his cabinet, but Jam Jan Mohammed, a Sanghar zamindar and M.P.A., who was a close and trusted follower of the Pir and who knew of the Hurs' plan, came to Hyderabad station and induced Soomro to leave the train pleading some urgent reason for him to interrupt his journey. Vazirani remained on the train. The murder of Soomro was the specific reason for the derailment of the train by the Hurs. Immediately after the derailment the Hurs attacked the First Class compartment in which the Premier would be expected to travel. Here they found the son of Hidayetullah who was killed by them. Vazirani saved himself by hiding in the train lavatory. The train was then perfunctorily looted and the Hurs escaped. Soomro was thus saved by a hair's breadth on this occasion. He was not to be spared for long however and was shot while driving in a tonga in Shikarpur on 14 May 1943 less than two months after Pir Pagaro was hanged in Hyderabad jail on 20 March 1943.* Soomro was

---

* Interview with Mangrejo, nephew of the assassin of Allah Baksh Soomro, Larkana December 1992. In the view of the Hurs Soomro's betrayal was compounded by the fact that he was ostensibly pursuing the Hurs with uncalled for zeal. It was reported that on 10 May 1942 while encamped at Mirpurkhas he made a speech in which he referred to the Hur troubles and urged the zamindars to have the courage to denounce them to the authorities and not to be intimidated. Soomro continued to be rash in his public statements. *The Times of India* wrote in an editorial note (16 May 1942): "That the fanaticism of the Hurs has not abated with the passage of time is shown by the murder attributed to them by the Sind premier, of Seth Perumal, a Hindu member of the Sind Legislative Assembly. K. B. Allah Bux made it clear that this was a vindictive crime, committed in the hope that the Sind Government would be intimidated into releasing Pir Pagaro from jail. If this was the motive, its perpetrators will be sadly disillusioned by the *Sind Premier's blunt statement that the Pir Pagaro's sentence must run its course and that, so far from yielding to threats the government will take the sternest possible action to prevent a repitition of such crimes*"

The murder of Seth Perumal Sitaldas illustrates fully the ruthlessness of the Hurs and their inability to put up with any real or supposed denigration of the Pir or any suggestion of disloyalty. Seth Perumal (Sitaldas) was actually a friend of Pir Pagaro and "was on close terms with Hurs supplying them with money, arms, etc. He had Hur mistresses and the Pir made no objection as Sitaldas was

no longer Premier at the time of his murder but his death shows the consistency and deliberation with which the Hurs were pinpointing their victims.

The situation had become so serious by April 1942 that the Viceroy had to call a meeting to consider the situation in Sind. The Governor of Sind, Sir Reginald Maxwell, the Home Member of the Viceroy's Council, Sir Henry Craik, Political Affairs Member, Resident Punjab States, Political Agent Jodhpur State and Sir John Thorne from the Public Affairs Department, as well as officers from the Defence Department attended. The Viceroy felt that it was still a matter for the police 'perhaps calling for a force like the Black and Tans'.* Governor's rule (Section 92 A, Government of India Act, 1935) was considered and rejected because the Ministers were not hindering the operation but if the elected government were removed it would 'enable them to disclaim responsibility and put the whole blame on executive officers.' It was decided for the time being that although there would be a military presence it would remain in the background. The troops in Sind could only be spared for two months more.** Air assistance for reconnaissance purposes might also be necessary. A special officer, (Lambrick) had been placed on duty at this point for three months to make a survey of the problem. Makhi Dhandh was to be cleared as soon as the report of the survey was received. Police and other assistance from other provinces was also discussed as were different methods of maintaining the prestige of the Government in the face of this challenge. The Governor as the man whose opinion carried the most weight, suggested that the Pir should be removed from India. In the meantime, the Governor discussed the possibility of legislation of a Hur Act by the Sind Assembly failing which an Ordinance might have to by issued by him.

The situation deteriorated much more quickly than the Viceroy's conference envisaged. By the time Lambrick took charge as Civil Commissioner in charge of Hur areas in April 1942, Hur terrorist activities were in full swing. The Hur Act (Act I of 1942) had been passed on 20 March by the Sind Legislative Assembly in a secret session. Martial Law was in place but the activities of the Hurs continued unabated. On 14 March 1942 the Ghulam Rasul Shah, the Nazim of Khairpur police, a very senior officer and a relentless pursuer of the Hurs, was murdered. On 16 May the Lahore Mail was derailed, an attempt was made on an Express train near Ghotki in northern Sind and on 8 September Hurs fired on the Down Bombay Mail near Chhor on the Rajputana border. Other senior police officers were attacked and killed, a Deputy Superintendent (D.S.P.) camping in an Inspection Bungalow in Tharparkar district was shot. The Hur operations began at the head of Jamrao canal and extended on both sides of Dhoro Naro. The areas particularly

---

useful. On 10th [May] he went to meet the Premier[Allahbux] at Mirpurkhas and returned home on the same evening as he had an appointment with some Hurs, Imam Bux Sanjrani, Nuro Wassan and others. He left the village at 9 p.m. with a bodyguard of three men and a go between. He met the Hurs and told them that the Premier had told him that the Pir would not come back under any circumstances and that the Government would not be intimidated by anything that Hurs could do and therefore not much could be done to help the gang. Suddenly the Hurs attacked him and the party and killed him and two of his bodyguards. Lambrick to Clee, Chief Secretary to Government of Sind,12 May 1942, Mss. Eur. F.208/48 .

* 'Black and Tans' were a notorious police or 'security' force used by the British in Ireland to crush the resistence of the local population.

**'Martial Law' would be imposed in eastern Sind just two months later.

terrorized were the *talukas* of Sanghar, Sinjhoro, Shahdadpur. Rohri district first saw the occurrence of sabotage of telegraph wires, trains and breaching of canals which spread elsewhere. Perceived enemies of Hurs, both humble and important, were ruthlessly cut down.

Writing in May 1942 the Executive Engineer of Mithrao Canal said:
"Conditions in Sanghar taluka are such that the P.W.D. [Public Works Department] administration has virtually ceased to exist. My superior staff are unable to do any outdoor work... The policy of the Hurs is to make it impossible for anyone who is not actively helping them ... to stay in the tract... I may explain here that the Hurs are apparently working to a definite scheme. I was informed in March that they had a time-table and that unless the Pir was brought back to Sind by the 27th of March they intended to take action against the Government servants and prevent them from carrying out their duties, either by physical or moral intimidation. If this did not succeed, their next intention was to sabotage canals by breaching them and preventing them from being repaired by prohibiting zamindars from giving labour. This was to start one month after 27th March and Khipro was duly breached in accordance with this scheme... "[29]

The tactics of the Hurs succeeded so that there was no cultivation in these areas except by Hur *haris*. The zamindars and cultivators were sufficiently intimidated that they supplied Hurs with food shelter, money and even on occasion, ammunition. The morale of the Hurs was kept up by the special *khalifas* or deputies of the Pir who exhorted the Hurs in their secret camps, as one witness testified:

"Waryam (Khaskheli) used to address these gatherings and ... he told them that they must not desert the Pir now that he had been arrested and they must be content to live away from their families. They must create trouble especially for Muslims who had failed to help the Pir both during his last imprisonment and on this occasion. He exhorted them to loot and murder. He said that the Government (*sarkar*) would have to quit and the Kingdom would then be Pir's."[30]

On 31 May 1942 Martial Law was was imposed in the eastern districts, in parts of Sukkur district, in the whole of Nawabshah, the whole of Khairpur State, parts of Tharparkar and parts of Hyderabad district. Various possibilities were considered for the suppression of Hur terrorism including the traditional one of an appeal by the Pir to control his followers. But by this time it was clear that the Hurs would not take any *Farman* (order) issued by the Pir seriously as he was in prison and would consider it as having been given under duress. Plans were considered to remove the Pir permanently from Sind and send him to Kenya or Secheyelles or even Abyssinia. It was finally decided that he should be tried and hanged in the hope that this would cut off the rebellion at its head.

In November 1942 Khuhro, then Revenue Minister, had gone to Delhi in connection with some official work and in the course of his meetings with the members of the Executive Council the matter of the Hurs and Pagaro came up. Sir Reginald Maxwell, the Home Member of the Viceroy's Council and Sir Robert Thorne of the Public Affairs, both said that they could not understand the delay by the Martial Law authorities in sending up *The* (Pagaro's) case when the G.O.C.

had such full powers. Maxwell asked Khuhro if the Government of Sind had yet applied to the Government of Central Provinces to have the person of [the Pir] made over to them as this was not the concern of Government of India.*

The Hur troubles had not decreased in the months after the imposition of Martial Law and its extension to the Right bank of the Indus was considered. It was decided that the extension of Martial Law eastwards to Rajputana was unnecessary but that as Hurs under pressure on the Left Bank would have drifted to the forests of Larkana on the Right bank, where there were some small settlements of Hurs of Mangreja and Nareja tribes (in the Ratodero *taluka* of Larkana), Martial Law should to be extended to the Right Bank. Subsequently Martial Law was extended to Upper Sind in the Sukkur district and to the Right Bank towards Larkana.

To begin with the Muslim League leaders did not react strongly against the extension of Martial Law. Khuhro could see that the unlawful activities of the Hurs had taken a more serious turn and that the Hur Act had not been effective. In his discussions with both the Sind government officials and with the Government of India officials at Delhi, he had taken a position of supporting extrordinary measures against the Hurs. The Muslim League as a party had no sympathy for Pagaro who had made no secret of his close ties with the Congress. Haroon as President Sind Muslim League had been clearly in favour of Martial Law but soon difficulties arose as the heavy hand of Martial Law became apparent. Opposition to it then arose in the Muslim League ranks. This was the first experience that the people and the politicians had of military rule and the ruthlessness and the thorough-

---

* Commissioner of Police *Memo*, 20 Nov. 1942, Mss. Eur. F. 208/25. F. Young, the Commissioner of Police reported the conversation he had with Khuhro who was passing through Sukkur by train from Delhi to Karachi on 19th November 1942:–

"1. He said that he had been to Delhi and had seen Sir Reginald Maxwell and Sir Robert Thorne. They both told him that they could not understand the delay on the part of the Martial Law authorities in sending up *The* case when the G.O.C. had such full powers.

2. He asked me if the Government of Sind had yet applied to the Government of C.P. to have the person of P.P. made over to them, as those officers had said it was not the concern of the Government of India. I said this was not a matter I could discuss with him on my own.

3. He [Khuhro] hoped that Martial Law would soon come to an end on the east side of the river where he considered there was no necessity for it.

4. He said that there was considerable criticism of the Martial Law authorities particularly in the following details:

(a) Delays in cases being put up. Considering that the G.O.C. had unlimited powers, it was not understood why cases were so long delayed.

(b) He could not understand why Martial Law authorities require so many magistrates. ...

(c) Special stress regarding failure to give publicity to our efforts. When I mentioned our recent successes by the 8/13 Punjab Regiment against Dodo's gang and Ali Mohammed and Pavri's raid, he said nobody had heard of them. I also mentioned the number of people killed in the round up by 8/13 on 4th August 1942 and in the Jinhar battle by the Indian Air Force. He seemed very surprised at these details not being given publicity–(In this I fully agree with him).

(d) He also hoped that the Martial Law authorities had found out how many innocent people had been wrongly run in by the police.

5. I explained the situation with regard to dacoities as far as I thought it desirable to do so. He made many enquiries as to my own future and generally adopted line of direct interrogation which was rather difficult to meet and I had to plead the defence of secrecy.

6. He informs me that Mr. Jinnah had agreed to the two Muslim League ministers remaining in the ministry on certain very easy conditions"

The last reference was to the new Ministry which had come into existence after the dismissal of Allah Baksh Ministry.

ness of its operations, and it took them sometime to realise its consequences. Muslim League therefore re-acted slowly and less strongly initially than Congress where reaction came not only at the local level but even from Gandhi.

Only a few days after the imposition of Martial Law, on 8 June 1942 an 'all parties' conference was called, mainly by the Hindu leadership, at Karachi. Apart from the cross-section of Hindu leaders some Muslim leaders also participated including G. M. Syed. A fanatical Leaguer at this stage of his life, Syed was also against the civilian advisers of the Martial Law authorities, but mainly for personal reasons.* The meeting was very critical of Martial Law and even though it had only been in place for a week. There were already accounts of the "harsh treatment of the civil population by the Military" and Lambrick was the subject of bitter criticism. The meeting decided to start an 'atrocity' campaign against the Military and the Police – "six pages of grievances and accounts of atrocities have been drafted by Mr. G. M. Syed and will be placed before the Working Committee of Sind Muslim League tomorrow".[31]

Muslim League leaders themselves were not too keen on the hasty condemnation of Martial Law, although some members of the Working Committee were sympathetic to the Pir and were pressing for a resolution in his favour. The Working Committee which was highest decision making body of Muslim League in Sind, confined itself for the time being to constitutional procedure and in the months following Martial Law examined the legality of its imposition and the possibility of going to court against it. It also appointed some members to report on the excesses of the Military administration. On 14 September 1942 the Working Committee met at Khuhro's house to consider the situation arising out of the imposition of Martial Law.

Khuhro's feelings were somewhat ambiguous towards the imposition of Martial Law. He had been shocked by the Hur atrocities and the murders of govern-

---

* Rashdi who knew Syed intimately and was close to him explains his strong opposition to Military action:
"He wrote twice to Sir Abdullah Haroon perhaps in December or January during the last winter [1941-2] – maybe even in November–that Hurs were after the life of all Leaguers... He had further urged upon Sir Abdullah to take steps to save people from Hurs. He had approved of the draft representation to the Viceroy. The change in his attitude, which later on estranged our connections, about the Hurs came in by about the month of February this year. We had our Council meeting in the last week of February. On that occasion he came to me and discussed with me certain urgent things. What were these urgent things? – *"That poor Hurs had promised him that they would no longer harm Mussalmans as they had found that their enemies were the Hindus. That the Hurs had assured him about the safety of the life of all Leaguers including myself. That the Hurs had told him that hereafter they would see the ministers who had taken monies from them and yet done nothing for them."* On the basis of these assurances Sayed advised me to forgive Hurs and take a statesmanlike view of their future activities."
Rashdi pointed out that Syed had opposed the draft statement on the Hur question which had put up before the Committee and got the portion about Pir Pagaro deleted. Rashdi claimed that Syed was involved with the Hurs through his relations and also through his Khosa *murids* who lived on the banks of the river near his village of Sann. Rashdi also pointed out that he had previous experience of Syed's 'mental aberrations' – "You all know that when I was conducting the Muslim case before the Weston Court of Inquiry into the causes of the Sukkur disturbances the greatest problem before me was to explain why G. M. Syed had made – in the presence of disinterested witnesses like Mr.Jamshed Mehta and Abdul Samad – the statement that he had planned the murder of 200 or more Hindus through the Manzilgah agitation scheme." Progs. Muslim League Working Committee, 14 Sep. 1942. IOL Mss.Eur.F.208/60.

ment officers like the Nazim of Khairpur and of civilians. It was rumoured that his own name was on the list prepared by Pagaro. The object of the Pir was perhaps not just to eliminate his enemies but also those who could prove an obstacle to his eventual rule in Sind. Khuhro was well aware of the menace of the Hur 'troubles' and the administrator in him wanted to have the problem dealt with as effectively as possible. He had therefore supported the actions of the government against them and not opposed Martial Law. In his discussions with the government both in the province and at Delhi he had pressed for firm action. On the other hand he had been nurtured on the principle of the 'rule of law' and the ideals of democracy which had been the lode star of Indian politicians particularly in a sophisticated presidency such as that of Bombay.

Khuhro's entire political life had as its *raison d'etre* the belief that democracy and elected legislatures, and governments authorised by these legislatures, were the legitimate upholders of law, responsible for the government of the country and for the maintenance of law and order. This was his first experience of Martial Law. He could not quite understand the position of a military commander as the supreme arbiter of the province in which there was a duly elected government. At the Working Committee meeting he voiced some of the doubts and the puzzlement he felt. Reporting his talk with the Governor on the subject of Martial Law he said:

"I might tell you, his mentality is hopeless. He has told us that the proclamation of Martial Law was valid because the Ministers had asked for it and the Law member of the Government of India and the Viceroy had agreed to the proposal. The Governor declines to call even a session of the legislature on account of the fear that we might take advantage of the freedom of discussion there we have there and expose the Martial Law authorities. *He only magnifies the powers which the Military Administrator has to extend Martial Law or issue orders of any nature thereunder.* The Martial Law Administrator, he said–by way of an illustration–, could reduce a senior officer like Mr. Holt from Collectorship to Assistant Collectorship and instal a junior of his over him as Collector, and yet nobody can ask for his explanation."[32]

As a practical man and an experienced administrator Khuhro recognised the need for strong and determined action to stamp out the Hur outbreak. He was also aware of the terror prevailing in the Sind countryside. He himself had built protective walls built around his village and guards were posted day and night. Villages were on the alert throughout Sind and the news or rumour that a party of Hurs had passed near a village was enough to strike terror in the area. No small zamindar or *khatedar* or the even a *kamdar* of a big landowner dared turn away a *khalifa* or even a party of Hurs in need of food or a night's stay. Khuhro with his *zamindari* on both sides of the river, and within Khairpur state, was well aware of the realities on the ground. But at the same time Pagaro was a historic name in Sind. Khuhro's own uncle had become a *murid* of Pagaro. As a child Khuhro had seen the Pir's camp near the Khuhro *zamindari*, the Pir being carried in his *maafa* by eighteen men travelling at an immense speed across the countryside from one camp to another, the awestruck public watching at a respectful distance. For a Sindhi, even one not connected in any formal way with the Pir, his arrest and imprisonment was something of *lese majeste*. So although Khuhro considered himself an emancipated man, impatient of superstition and his religion free of *pirimuridi*, he was, not ununderstandably, concerned about the fate of the Pir himself.

Moreover a few months had passed since the promulgation of Martial Law and some of its shortcomings had become apparent. Khuhro pointed out some of the problems in his presidential address in the Working Committee of 14 September:

"[Martial Law] has been unduly extended. It has already miserably failed. It has brought no return to the people for the enormous sacrifice of civil liberties that they have made....The Nazim (Superintendent) Police, Khairpur was telling me the other day that the Military people do not mean business. They cannot go without car-loads of rations following them, and surely the Hurs are not going to wait at one place, by the time this military caravan reaches them.... Police has been plundering people. Military people have been killing innocent men. Mr. Judge, D.S.P., Sukkur has given them approvers against Pir Pagaro and yet they have taken no steps against him. They have reduced water level in the canals with the result that cultivation has been affected to the extent of several lakhs of acres. This was exactly what the Hurs themselves wanted and which they have got done through the Military. And then who is going to foot all this bill? *Zamindars* have fled from their places out of fear. Their *haris* have deserted fields. There have been unnecessary evacuations on mass scale....Hatchets and other implements which are required for cultivation purposes have been snatched away."[33]

In view of the economic and political consequences of Martial Law which were affecting the province, the problem facing a politician like Khuhro was obviously difficult. The Hindu press and the Congress was taking a very pro Pir and pro Hur line portraying them as nationalist freedom fighters. Muslim League could not afford to be seen to be lagging behind particularly when the people involved were Muslims. Faced with this problem Muslim League took the line that the Government was unjustified in taking a tough line against the Pir when Gandhi, who after all had launched a nation wide revolt, was being treated with kid gloves, living in the Aga Khan's palace and receiving every courtesy while the Pir was in a jail in central India and with the prospect of being hanged. Khuhro and G .M. Syed had consulted Jinnah about the advisability of going to Court against Martial Law but Jinnah's advice was that:

"We should not go the Court of law at this stage; we should first see the Governor and ask him to withdraw Martial Law;"

If the Governor did not agree to do so , Jinnah would write to Viceroy and Secretary of State and get an interview with the Viceroy to put the case to him:

"All that he (Mr. Jinnah) wants is a comprehensive case against the Martial Law and the way in which it has worked."[34]

It was obvious that Jinnah fully realised the dilemma of the Sind Muslim League leaders – that the government was bound to respond strongly to the Hur uprising and that there was no love lost between Muslim League and Pagaro. At the same time the Muslim League could not acquiesce in the harsh measures being taken and the discrimination they had for a Muslim spiritual leader in comparison to Hindu Congress leaders. They also had to register their disapproval of non democratic actions of the government in imposing Martial Law and also to bring to the attention of the Government of India the hardship that was being faced by the ordinary people of Sind. The formula offered by Jinnah was designed to take care of these problems facing the Sind leaders.

In January 1943 Pir Pagaro was brought back to Sind to be tried for 'waging war against the King Emperor.' He landed secretly at the Bolari war-time air strip near Kotri and was taken to Hyderabad jail. The Pir was kept under strict security and his cell was wire tapped. The Pir asked repeatedly to see Hidayetullah, the Premier, whom he considered a friend and whose advice he wanted at this critical time. He also wanted Hidayetullah's assurance regarding the defence counsel the government proposed to appoint and help to get Jinnah to come as his defence lawyer.[35]

Perhaps disappointed at Hidayetullah's response the Pir asked to see Khuhro who was given the message by the Governor:

"The next day Dow sent word to me to see him and he told me that Pir Pagaro when he landed at Bolari was asked if he wanted anything in particular had told the army officers, 'I want to see Mr. Khuhro.' The Governor told me not to see Pagaro as he had to be tried under Martial Law and `might talk to you about matters which may involve you'."

With the Governor ruling out a meeting with the Pir it proved impossible to see him. Khuhro managed however to send a message to the Pir through a police officer and was told that the Pir wanted him to engage Jinnah as his defence lawyer. The Pir also wrote a letter in his own hand to Khuhro for this purpose.* Khuhro got in touch with Jinnah immediately telephoning a friend in Bombay who passed on the message but Jinnah declined to come giving his reason that he could not trust the Pir "who is politically anti Muslim League and has throughout, after his release, been in close contact with Congressmen". Pagaro also sent his own man who offered Jinnah a big fee but Jinnah declined.[36]

By February the Pir was under trial. The Martial Law authorities offered him a panel of lawyers and he selected Dialmal Lalwani–a top criminal lawyer at that time in Sind, although initially he had been reluctant to accept Dialmal as he suspected that he was being foisted on him by the government. He wanted Hidayetullah to declare before him personally that Dialmal was 'genuine'. Hidayetullah did not come to see him and eventually Pagaro accepted the lawyer. The ability of the lawyer in this case was irrelevant as the authorities had already decided to 'secure his execution'.

In November 1942 when Martial Law had been in force for about four months Lambrick, the Civil Adviser to the Martial Law authorities, had prepared a *Note* which spelt out the problem of the Hurs and came to the conclusion that there was

---

* The official translation of the letter written by Pir Pagaro to Khuhro:
"   786
[the numbers signifying 'In the name of God the Compassionate, the Merciful.']
                        18-1-43
Kind friend in whom *darvishes* can have hope of great respectability, Mohammed Ayub Khuhro–may you remain safe.
After compliments may it be known to you that the Military Commander has permitted me to engage Muhammad Ali Jinnah. I shall be able to pay his fees completely, if I am given some facility. At this time it would be in accordance with your religion and your goodness that you should listen to my call. That is your duty. I wish you peace and happiness.
                        Signed, Sibghatullah Shah
                        Pir Pagaro   [*ibid*]

no alternative but to execute the Pir in order to establish peace in Sind. He advised that the trial should be by Court Martial to ensure speed and conviction which was essential in view of the provincial and international situation. The Hur troubles had to be considered against the background of the War. He pointed out that the frustrations of dealing with the Hur menace, which showed no signs of abating had created ill feeling between the different government agencies such as the military and the police and even among the British officials in charge of these agencies. It had become imperative therefore to deal with the problem at its source i.e. to eliminate the Pir. Lambrick was categorical in this respect:

"It is impossible to eradicate the Hur movement so long as the Pir Pagaro is alive."

He drew up a detailed plan as to how the trial was to be conducted and what kind of evidence was necessary as well as the Martial Law Regulations that would be necessary to promulgate. Consequently the authorities had come to the conclusion that:

"The Hur movement is not only a social and economic curse of long standing for the province of Sind but today it is fraught with the greatest dangers, looking to the international situation. The Pir is a traitor to the people of Sind, to the British people and to all the decencies of life. There is no good element in the country that will grieve, that will not enjoy the death of the Pir. Now how to secure his execution?"*

Lambrick's plan for the trial of the Pir including the evidence to be brought against him was largely followed during the trial which took place inside the Hyderabad jail. For the substance of the case Lambrick and Cargill, the Deputy Martial Law Administrator, relied heavily on the help of Pir Ali Mohammed Rashdi, a distant relative of the Pir himself.

Rashdi had come to the attention of the government in connection with the Pagaro problem when he had written to the Governor in 1941 about his apprehensions about the Hurs and the Pir himself.** Dow forwarded the letter to the Viceroy with the caveat–"He is himself a very crooked customer, but has more brains than most of the Muslim Leaguers in Sind". Dow also pointed out that Rashdi wanted to discredit the Ministry. In fact Rashdi, who had played a significant role in the Manzilgah enquiry for the Muslim League side and was still a member of Muslim League Working Committee, was working with the Martial Law authorities and was increasingly distrusted by the Muslim Leaguers who suspected him of having truck with Congressmen as well as being an informer of the government. In his representation to the Governor, Rashdi pointed out that he was a cousin of the Pir and his name appeared on the 'Black list' of the Hurs. He asked for adequate police protection as "it would not have taken me very far if one or two policemen had been posted at my door only to assist the invaders in locating me".[37]

---

* Lambrick, *Note on the Hur Movement*, Mss. Eur. F. 208/16.

**Writing to the Governor, Sir Hugh Dow from his *Moslem Voice* office on Rambaugh Road, Karachi on 22 Oct. 1941 Rashdi put in his claim for the *gaddi* in a long and cleverly persuasive letter and followed it up with subsequent letters pursuing his own and his brother's claim until he was finally told on behalf of the Governor that the claim would not be considered. *Vide* correspondence of Rashdi with Governor and Lambrick. IOL, Mss.Eur.F.125/99, Mss.Eur.F.208/20.

Rashdi traced the history of the Hurs and the Pir himself:

"The death of the previous Pir, in 1925, places the gang under the guidance of a most godless pervert who, within the very first four years of his regime, plans a number of murders and hoards up a huge armoury."

Rashdi went to recount the conviction of the Pir and his association with the Bengali terrorists and his subsequent organisation of an 'army of *ghazis*'. His systematic removal or 'neutralisation' of his opponents – 'The murderers get Advocates of Sir Ghulam Hussain's standing influence and resources to defend them', his appeasment of Hindus–'He sends Rs. 1,500 to Mr. Sidhwa (leader of the Congress Assembly Party) to buy him *khadi* [home-spun material], as if that rare and scarce material could not be secured through any other agency'. After making a damning case against the Pir, Rashdi suggested dealing firmly with the menace emphasising that there was a dire threat to the peace of the country– 'Surely, it cannot be assumed that there does not exist any peril to peace or 'Good Government', when and where His Majesty's subjects are being killed like flies."[38] The campaign against the Hurs had used Rashdi's services and now at the time of the Pir's trial the Martial Law authorities could not have found a more suitable person to frame a strong case against the Pir.

Later when Rashdi was asked for a suitable reward for his services – his own or his brother's installation as Pir Pagaro – or when that failed, to get some recognition for his services through a title and some land, he was warmly supported in these endeavours by Lambrick who wrote an enthusiastic testimonial on his behalf:

"The abolition of the Gadi of the Pir Pagaro is the most essential step towards relieving Sind from a danger which otherwise would have grown greater every year. Abolition of the Gadi was made possible only by the prosecution and execution of the late Pir. The successful prosecution of the late Pir was, I believe, made possible by very largely owing to the efforts of Syed Ali Mohamed Rashidi, but Mr. Cargill is much better qualified than I am to pronounce on this, as the Syed was working with him constantly for several weeks before and during the trial. ... I believe that Chief Administrator of Martial Law wrote officially that his services far surpassed those of any other private individual."[39]

Although Pir Pagaro realised he was up against it he put up as good a fight as he could. Dialmal was an excellent lawyer and made the best case he could. He gave a list of defence witnesses which among others contained the names of the ex-Governor, Sir Lancelot Graham, Hidayetullah who was now Premier, Khuhro now Minister for Revenue in the Cabinet, M. H. Gazdar, the Home Minister and Nihchaldas Vazirani the leading Hindu politician and Member Legislative Assembly.* He had also summoned his leading followers and confidantes who were important landowners of Sanghar and Tharparkar regions, Nawab Jam Kambho Khan, M.L.A., Khan Sahib Din Mohammed Junejo, Khan Bahadur Mohammed Hayat Junejo and Khan Sahib Sardar Dadan Khan Lund. But government pressure was exerted to prevent any evidence in favour of the Pir. Most of those summoned did not have the courage to appear in the Court. Some of those who did appear as defence witnesses actually gave evidence against him and these included

---

* Dow wrote of the trial: "Richardson is satisfied with the way the Pir's trial is proceeding. Dow to Linlithgow, 22 Feb. 1943, Mss. Eur. F. 125/99.

some of his closest associates. A well-known story concerns two landowners who were close friends and followers of the Pir. Although summoned as defence witnesses they offered to give evidence against the Pir on condition that a screen was placed between them and the Pir because they claimed they could not stand up the ferocious look in his eyes.

The Governor had already warned Khuhro not to see the Pagaro or do anything which could be construed to be in his favour. Khuhro true to the manner in which he had conducted his life, acting according to his conscience in spite of strong pressures from outside, decided that he would give evidence as honestly as he could. He was asked to give evidence mainly as a character witness gave straightforward evidence and he says:

"I appeared before the Tribunal consisting of two military officials. On my right was a frosted glass screen. Apparently the Pir was sitting behind it and hearing everything that was being said about him. I gave two statements before the tribunal which were on the whole in favour of the Pir."[40]

The Pir based his defence on the plea that he was not responsible for the 'misdeeds' of the Hurs. That they had reacted to the disrespect shown to the Pir's family when his residence was searched and destroyed and his family forcibly removed from there. His defence lawyer summed this up:

"Hurs became rebels not because the Pir wanted to be a king but only because acts of sacrilege were committed by Government servants... which were such that their religious allegiance to their Pir and to their God demanded of them to do, if they ever would attend [attain] salvation."[41]

Further the Pir argued that various people were antagonistic towards him and had given him false evidence to the authorities about him. He cited the Pir of Bharchundi who was annoyed about Pagaro's evidence which led to the prosecution of one of his followers for the assassination of the famous Hindu spiritual singer Bhagat Kunwar Ram. The Pir also claimed that the Muslim League was against him because he refused to join them in the Masjid Manzilgah agitation. Ghulam Rasul Shah [the Nazim of Police in Khairpur] and his friend Ahsan Ali had a grudge because Ahsan Ali had lost a land dispute with him. He also gave reasons for Rashdi's enmity against him. He claimed that it was because he held decrees against him to pay back a debt amounting to thousands of rupees.

The Pir was at pains to distance himself from responsibility for the activities of the Hurs. As he said:

"this war of Hurs is something in the nature of the old Mahomedan Wars under the Islamic banner [very similar to] carrying on ...a crusade. In neither of these were the prophets in any way responsible. For the Hur the Pir is more than a prophet, the magnificence of the Pir and his entourage, his durbar and his surrounding, his pomp and glory are all facts relevant to the main issue. These will explain why names are registered, why Mukhs are appointed, why Furaq is different from Salim, why a special code governs the Hur and how is it that the frantic follower stakes his all in the name of the Pir."[42]

In March 1943 the Pir was convicted and hanged in Hyderabad jail. His body was shown to his main *khalifas* and then taken away to buried in some unknown place.

The Hur problem did not disappear with the death of the Pir and was only gradually brought under control. By the time Martial Law was lifted at the end of 1943 a full Division of the army had been deployed in Sind and paratroopers had been used in the desert, the first time such troops had been used in the sub-continent. But even then, by September 1944, Dow was writing of his government's difficulties with the Hur remnants:

"My ministers are naturally disappointed that the vigorous measures taken against the remnants of the Hurs since the raising of the Martial Law a year ago have not yet been crowned with complete success and are beginning to realize that it is a long term problem."[43]

The government decided to continue Lambrick as Special Commissioner with a Criminal Tribes Settlement Officer with the rank of Collector. New *lorhas* or Hur concentration camps were set up. At this time there was a notorious outlaw called Rahim Hingoro who was 'credited' with two hundred murders, a thousand dacoities, a hundred cases of kidnapping and a loss of lakhs of rupees of crops burnt. These 'exploits' were no doubt exaggerated but were an indication of what the Government was up against. Rahim Hingoro was not caught until 1952 and while in jail in Hyderabad his wife or paramour led a daring raid to rescue him which nearly succeeded. Hingoro climbed up a rope but fell back into the jail compound when he tripped over the electrified wire at the top of the wall. The Hur problem continued for a few years after independence but gradually petered out as their leaders like Hingoro gradually got rounded up.

The question of the Pir's successor after his death in 1943 began even before his trial. One insistent claimant was Rashdi who wrote a letter to the Governor as early as 22 January 1943 but by 15th February Dow's secretary informed Lambrick:

"This is to inform you that Ali Mohammed Rashdi has been told that in no circumstances would Government consent to his attempting to succeed to the Gadi of the Pir Pagaro should it fall vacant."[44]

The Government sounded out the opinion of the followers and associates of the Pir about the advisability of filling the *gadi* after his death. Most of the people consulted said that the *gadi* should be left vacant–'they want no more Black lists.'[45] After the death of the Pir, his property, which was valued at the total of Rs. 18,14,000, was taken over by the Government of India which undertook to pay for the education of his sons who were to be taken to England.[46]

Rashdi continued to persist in trying to get some reward for cooperating with the Martial Law authorities during the trial of the Pir. He tried both for a title and for a grant of land. There was some prospect of a title–* but that did not materialize probably because Dow, cynical as always, did not recommend it. Rashdi felt that he had been badly let down and blamed the dichotomy of authority between

---

* Rashdi writing to Cargill after the trial was over mentions his hopes: "Regarding title business, I shall be grateful if you see to it that it is expedited and that it is treated as a special case. If things are delayed it may not synchronise with the other affair and I shall suffer the disgrace I have been trying to avoid. I am anxious to know what H.E. wrote to G.O.C. about it. Did he mention my name specifically? That is the point I am anxious to know, because that will assure me of H.E. sticking to his promise, and give me an inkling of his mind. *If my name goes along with others there will be delay at every stage and besides the thing will lose its force, uniqueness and grace....* In recommending me for a title you will kindly see that it is a 'title' which is consistent with my services, my seniority in the public life, and the object in view. It should not be in the nature of a joke. I have had enough of jokes already." Rashdi to Cargill, undated [circa Feb./March 1943], Mss. Eur. F. 208/20.

the British and the elected Ministry. He did try to strengthen his case by pointing out that land grants had been made on nominal *malkana* to "Government supporters such as Sir Shah Nawaz Bhutto, late Mr. Allah Baksh, K. B. Jaffar Khan Buledi, Nawab Amir Ali, Osman Soomro and others."[47] and that such a grant to him went against the grain of his erstwhile comrades:

"Khuhro has turned down my papers regarding Barani land. He told me last night that I had served Martial Law and British officials and that therefore I had no claim on the Ministers. Quite true, I did things which were contrary to their wishes. I am glad H.E. also agreed with Khuhro for all practical purposes. It seems we have a state of anarchy in the province; one does not know whom to serve – the Ministers or the executive. I think this is the last way to enlist people's support for government purposes... From the same circles I have learnt *last night* that I had been recommended for some title by your goodself but that those papers also had met with the same fate thanks to the intervention of the Ministers. I was told: `I needed a lesson which has thus been taught to me – they wanted to bring home to me the fact that my future lay with them rather than with the white Bureaucracy.' These are the actual words I am quoting. They further said others were getting rewards in Durbar in the end of November."[48]

Rashdi was undoubtedly putting words in Khuhro's mouth since even he as a powerful Revenue Minister could not have vetoed any rewards that the British Governor had chosen to give. Rashdi was presumably trying to impress upon Lambrick that by his loyalty to the British he had incurred the hostility of Ministers like Khuhro and this deserved some reward. Lambrick himself at this time was keenly aware of the role Rashdi had played in the case against Pagaro and had urged the Governor to give him a title and money – "some Rs. 20,000 net- which should enable him to purchase at least 100 acres of fair class irrigated land."[49]

The Pir's sons were sent out of Sind first to other provinces but then to England to live with a tutor and go to university eventually. The *gaddi* was restored a few years after independence in the early 'fifties and the eldest son of Pir Sibghatullah Shah, Shah Mardan Shah became the seventh Pir Pagaro.

14

IN THE SESSIONS COURT AT SUKKUR

Although Khuhro had not insisted on becoming Premier of Sind and had been ready to sacrifice his own personal interests and ambitions in the interests of his party and community, he was seen as the most dangerous contender by his fellow politicians, particularly those Muslim politicians who had ambitions of their own and saw Khuhro as the main obstacle in their path. Hidayetullah was well aware that he was Premier by fluke and by the grace of the Governor. He had no real base in the Muslim League Party. Jinnah whom he had done his best to win round would only tolerate him as long as it was strictly necessary in view of the Governor's bias and because of the need to have an ostensibly Muslim League Ministry in Sind. He also knew that as long time leader of the Parliamentary party, Khuhro felt it was his right to be Premier and knew that he had been deprived of this post because of the prejudice of the Governor. Khuhro was also the most active and hard working Minister who had an agenda of reform for the province and was using his time as Minister of Revenue to solve the long standing problems. As far as Hidayetullah was concerned all this activity was causing problems with the Governor. If Khuhro could be got rid off not only would his life be easier and quieter but he would also be rid of his most dangerous contender for Premiership.

This was also the period when the differences between Khuhro and G. M. Syed had surfaced concerning the organisation of Muslim League in Sind. Khuhro had succeeded Abdullah Haroon as President after his death in April 1942. Subsequently he had given up that post when Jinnah had ruled that no Government Minister could hold a party post. Syed had succeeded him as President of Sind Provincial Muslim League. Khuhro had however played a major role in the organisation of Muslim League and had a great deal of influence in it. He had his friends and followers in all the districts in Sind who were important members of the Party. When Syed took over he wanted to re-organise the party along his own lines and fill his own men, in most case fellow Sayeds, in the key posts. Soon there was open friction as Khuhro resisted the displacement of the old Leaguers who had been with the party since its inception in 1938.

Syed although conspicuously eschewing office, wanted to control the Ministry through the Party which would be under his exclusive control as a powerful president. He tried to establish his control of the Ministry by issuing directives and then passing critical and condemnatory resolutions against the Ministry. Jinnah was forced to intervene and induce Syed to moderate his stand.[1] Syed retired hurt but licking his wounds and looking round for revenge. He felt that his discomfiture had been due to Khuhro and that he must be got rid of. Once Khuhro was out of the way it would be quite easy to deal with Hidayetullah. In Gazdar, the Home Minister, he found a co-conspirator and then looked around for an opportunity.

Undoubtedly the most serious enemy that Khuhro had was Dow, the Governor of Sind. The history of the antagonism between the two went back to the time when Khuhro had been member of the Bombay Legislative Council and Dow a Bombay bureaucrat whose duties as Government Whip in the Legislature brought him into contact with the elected members. His arrogance and racist outlook had been obvious and had annoyed the Indian members who came across him. An efficient and hard working officer and with some knowledge of Sind through his association with the Sukkur Barrage administration, he had been appointed Chairman of the Sind Administrative Committee which was to set up the administrative framework for autonomous Sind after the reforms of 1935. Khuhro had been one of the two Muslim members on the Committee. He had a number of confrontations with Dow during the proceedings the most serious of which had been over the question of a university for Sind to which Dow had objected and had made offensive remarks about the fitness of Sindhis for such an institution. Khuhro had strongly objected to his behaviour and had staged a walk-out.[2] Dow had apologised but was not a man who could forgive or forget what he considered an insult from a mere Indian politician. This grudge he made obvious during his tenure as Governor both in his intolerance of Khuhro as Minister and politician and also in his carping criticism of Khuhro in his correspondence with the Viceroy. An opportunity offered itself–an opportunity which offered a real possibility of getting rid of Khuhro, if he played his cards ruthlessly enough.

On 14 May 1943 in broad daylight while he was riding in a tonga with a friend in his home town of Shikarpur, Allah Baksh Soomro, the ex Premier of Sind, was assassinated by two Hurs, Kasim Mangrejo and Ali Mohammed Rajpar, who were seen by the bystanders and later identified. There was no question in the public mind that the deed had been done by the Hurs for motives of revenge. Only a few months earlier when Soomro had been Premier, he had openly threatened to teach the Hurs a lesson in a public meetings at Nawabshah and Mirpurkhas.[3] But although the motive for the murder was clear to the people generally, rumours were deliberately circulated that the murder was politically motivated and that it was perpetrated by Muslim League politicians. The press, largely Hindu owned, was particularly strident in publicising these stories. As soon as it was known that one of the known assassins Kasim Mangrejo was from a village bordering on Khuhro lands, the way was clear for Khuhro's enemies, particularly Dow, to pursue his vengeance.

As the most high profile Muslim League leader in Sind, Khuhro was cast as the unforgiving Muslim out to get the Quisling Soomro and to clear the way for himself as Premier. That the theory did not fit the facts did not worry Dow unduly. That *Khuhro was not the Premier and not a rival of Soomro and did not stand to gain from his death*, appeared not to concern those engaged in the conspiracy. As early as March

1944 when the police had not yet built up any reasonably adequate case against Khuhro and the main witness who was supposed to be the link between Khuhro and the murder had not yet been arrested and his evidence was not available to the police,* Dow was writing to the Viceroy:

"It is almost certain that the Government will weather the [Budget] session, but there is general expectation that it will be followed immediately by some reshuffling of portfolios and the replacement of at least one of the Ministers. Khuhro is generally cast for the role of victim: the failure of his prices campaign has left him looking a little ridiculous, his militant communalism is always a disturbing element, and his suspected complicity in Allahbux' murder case may prove the decisive factor."[4]

The I. G. Police, Ray, an Englishman, who had been dealing with Hurs for a long time had been given the task of making a case implicating Khuhro in the murder. As the Sessions Judge who tried the case was to remark:

"Mr. Ray states that the whole investigation in the case was conducted by him personally. It is a fact that he held all the identification tests himself, prepared all the *mashirnamas* himself, and recorded the statements of practically all the witnesses in his own hand."[5]

The Inspector General of Police for the province of Sind was surely displaying excessive diligence even for the case of a man as important as Khuhro!

The group of Hurs who had assassinated Soomro were arrested and brought to trial. Apart from the actual assassins Mohammad Kasim Mangrejo and Ali Mohammed Rajpar, the group included Kasim Mangrejo's nephew Kamal, and four others.** The murder case was tried before a Special Tribunal and the judgement was given on 26 February 1944. The three main accused freely admitted that they had committed the murder and were sentenced to death and the remaining four to life imprisonment. All the appeals were rejected by 22 September 1944. Khuhro's name came up in the evidence in connection the Hur party crossing his *kacha* lands in the pursuit of their errands. The mention of Khuhro's lands was enough for police officers in charge of framing the charges against Khuhro to use as a peg on which to hang the whole case against him.†

The Hur assassins were sentenced to death but then an offer was made to them by the authority of the Governor that if they gave evidence to implicate Khuhro in the murder their death sentence would be commuted to life imprisonment.[6] Ray

---

* The leading witness in the case against Khuhro, Mohammed Khan, who was made 'approver' and on whose evidence the case was supposed to be based, was arrested on 25th October 1943 and the other star witness Daresh who was Khuhro's *kamdar* and who was supposed to be the link between the murder and Khuhro, was arrested nearly a year later on 19th September 1944.

**The Hur party which killed Soomro consisted of the organiser of the group Kasim Mangnejo, his nephew Kamal, Wali Mohammad Kharal, Abdullah Rasulbux Noonari, Abdul Haq Karimbux Bhayyo, Kambar Bahadur Kasai and Ibrahim Motayo Kasai. Mangrejos lived in the village of Drabhi near Khuhro's *zamindari* and farmed lands around some of their own and and some of them were *haris* on Khuhro lands. Kasim and other Mangrejos often crossed Khuhro lands on their various errands.

† It became clear afterwards that attempts had been made by the authorities to get the main assassins to implicate Khuhro but they had refused to do so. Rajpar especially had been taken out of jail even after his sentence and rejection of appeal, to meet the I. G. and other police officers in the hope that he would give evidence against Khuhro but all these attempts failed and the police had to rely on some other members of the gang.

himself examined the witnesses, Rajpar and Kasim and the latter's nephew Kamal. Obviously if either Rajpar or Mangrejo testified against Khuhro this would make a strong case. Eventually both Rajpar and Kasim Mangrejo were hanged without the police being able to get their testimony implicating Khuhro.[7] The gang members whose evidence the police was able to manage were Mohammed Khan, a member of the assassin group who was later recruited as a police spy; Kamal; Wali Mohammed Kharal, a Hur *hari* on Khuhro's *kacha* lands, through whom Khuhro's *kamdar* Daresh was supposed to have got in touch with the Hurs; and Daresh himself, as the link between Khuhro and the Hur assassins.

Khuhro was uneasily aware of the conspiracy against him. Initially he had dismissed the rumours that he was the intended victim of the conspiracy and had carried on his work as Minister regardless. But gradually he became aware that he was indeed the target. Sind was rocked with rumours that the assassination was politically motivated; that it was the work of Muslim Leaguers and as the most prominent Muslim Leaguer, Khuhro was responsible for it. Every wild rumour was printed with delight by the Hindu press and made the work of the conspirators easier. A son of Daresh, Hussain, was wanted in a dacoity* and the son and father were absconding. The police had decided that Daresh, with his son involved in a dacoity, was the most likely man to be made main witness against Khuhro and were trying hard to find him. By September of 1944 there was no longer any doubt of the seriousness of the situation. Daresh was arrested by the police on 19 September 1944 and after a few days in police custody was ready to give a statement implicating Khuhro.

Khuhro's brother Mohammed Nawaz, who was looking after *zamindari* affairs and living in the village Aqil, was arrested. Khuhro went to see the Governor who wrote with malicious satisfaction to the Viceroy:

"Khuhro has been to see me in a state of perturbation. At the moment he is not on good terms with Gazdar the Home Minister, and although he was a little coy about making some definite request, he was clearly hoping that I could be induced to interfere. He no longer has any such hopes."[8]

Even at this stage Khuhro did not suspect the Governor of being the instigator of the conspiracy. He assumed that the Premier and the Home Minister were out to get him because he was a possible rival. Without support from the Government of which he was member and with open hostility from the Governor, Khuhro had no option but to resign which he did on 26 September. He was arrested immediately afterwards and taken to Sukkur. Writing to Jinnah after his acquittal in August the next year Khuhro was still unsuspecting of the Governor and laid the responsibility for the conspiracy solely on the shoulders of the Ministers:

"The Premier as the head of the Government was in a position to protect his colleague i.e. myself and was expected to see that I was not left at the mercy of the I. G. P., who was, after all, subordinate of the Government of which I was a member. Nothing could have happened without his knowledge and approval. In view of the fact that I was a member of Government the decision whether the case was fit to be sent up should not have been left to the I. G. P. Government ought to have consulted its law officers, the Advocate General, and the

---

* This was a major dacoity known as the Bhumbhatpur dacoity as it had occurred in the place of that name.

Remembrancer of Legal Affairs, and decided after a full scrutiny of evidence on police records, whether the case was such as had reasonble chance of success. ... In every case where the evidence is weak and of doubtful nature, police invariably obtain legal opinion of the Government pleader in the District at least, before putting the case in a court of law. But no such precaution was taken in this case."[9]

In his memo to Jinnah Khuhro detailed the extraordinary conduct followed in prosecuting him:

"I was arrested nearly two months before even the police case was ready to be proceeded with in the Court. I was arrested on 26th of September and the prosecution side was ready to proceed with the case only on the 21st of November 1944. Even the final *challan* was not presented to the Court earlier than 10th of November and the adjournment was obtained by the police upto 21st November. This the Government could easily have avoided, for the police could not have disregarded Government directive.

I was called upon to resign merely at the advice of the I. G. P. The Premier could easily have managed that I was not thrown to the wolves in such an unseemly manner. While the Premier promised to speak to the Governor on my behalf, I have reason to believe that he did nothing of the kind.

The police officers committed all sorts of excesses, manufactured false evidence, coerced witnesses to swear falsely against me, intimidated my friends and sympathisers, and in fact created a reign of terror in Larkana and Sukkur districts to my prejudice.

The committal proceedings were ordered to be held inside the Jail, with a view to frightening and coercing the prosecution witnesses to give suitable evidence for the prosecution..."[10]

Not only was the conduct of the police out of the ordinary in the matter of the arrest and the trial but the Governor took special pains to appoint a special prosecutor who was paid unusually high rate of fees to prosecute the case:

"The Government gave exorbitant and unconscionably high fees to the Special Public Prosecutor appointed at the bidding of the police... For example Mr. Partabrai the ex-Advocate General of Sind, who used to get only about Rs. 2,500/- per month as an A. G. was allowed one thousand per day or part of a day which he spent out of Karachi, for this case. This was absolutely unprecedented, as in equally important trials such as that of late Sardar Wahidbux Khan Bhutto in 1928, the Ali brothers trial in 1921, or in late Mir Ghulamullah (M. L. A.)'s trial, counsels never got more than Rs. 200 per day."[11]

Khuhro did not know even after the trial, that the inspiring force behind the whole matter was Dow himself who had got the I. G. Police, a fellow Englishman, not easily amenable to 'native' pressure, to manufacture the case through specially chosen officers and to organise the whole framework of prosecution including the appointment of the Prosecuting Counsel. Writing to the Viceroy about ten days after Khuhro's arrest Dow reveals his deep personal interest in the case:

"It will soon have to be decided who shall prosecute in the case and also who shall try it. Both are questions of some difficulty. Ordinarily the Public Prosecutor for Sind would be in charge of the prosecution but he is a slim gentleman recently appointed, after much disagreement in the Ministry, as a reward for long services to my Premier of a kind no one would wish to specify too closely. He has in fact been the Premier's jackal and no one would trust him very far perhaps the Premier least of all. The first assistant public prosecutor is an Anglo Indian of reputed honesty, who conducted the case against those of Allahbux's murderers who have already been condemned; but he is not very bright and might be entirely outclassed by any first rate lawyer briefed for the defence. The I. G. of Police will, I believe press for the employment of Coltman from Bombay, but my ministry will probably feel that going outside the Province to engage an eminent man may savour to the public of vindictiveness and an undue desire to secure conviction."[12]

Eventually however in order to make sure that prosecution was in able hands Dow decided to appoint Partabrai Punwani the experienced ex Advocate General:

"I have therefore taken it on myself to decide the matter and have sanctioned the I. G. P.'s proposal to employ Mr. Partabrai Punwani lately Advocate General as Prosecuting Counsel."[13]

Dow was certainly very anxious to secure conviction and indirectly admitted as much, putting the blame on the 'Hindu press' for giving him 'credit':

"The Hindu press is exultant but at the same time anxious to give the Government no credit. The `Sind Observer' has been particularly unscrupulous, asserting that it was only my personal intervention at your express direction that led to the investigation being pursued with vigour..."[14]

Ray was leaving no stone unturned in his efforts to make a plausible case. Ghulam Akbar the police officer who had been concerned in the Hur problem and had worked closely with Ray in prosecuting the Hurs and had built a reputation for ruthlessness, was promoted as D. S. P. over the heads of about half a dozen officers and put in charge of Sukkur District and the case. He was assisted by a notorious officer, Inspector Ghulam Hussain, who played the most important part in concocting the case. Officers were transferred from Larkana district in case they were sympathetic to Khuhro. Hidayetullah had at first promised Khuhro's friends that he would give a fair and independent judge to try the case and had even promised that the case could be sent to another province where the atmosphere would be less biased and there was a greater chance of the trial being fair.* But Hidayetullah did not keep his word, perhaps he was unable to withstand the pressure of the Governor who was determined that the full power of the Government be used to prosecute the case.

After his arrest Khuhro was taken to Sukkur where he was produced before the District Magistrate of Sukkur, Parpia, and the police took a remand of fifteen days. Khuhro made an application for bail to the District Magistrate but it was rejected. The question which was exercising Dow's mind was who should be the judge to try the case. Although anxious to secure conviction which he thought would much easier with a Special Tribunal, he did not want to appear openly biased and was keen to maintain a smokescreen of impartiality. He wrote unctuously to the Viceroy:

---

* The judges who were regarded as being fair Judge O'Sullivan, Mr. Weston who was the judge in charge of Sukkur riots at the time of Masjid Manzilgah, Mr. Bhavdakar and Mr. Kapadia. The judge who was eventually appointed was Paymaster, not a career judicial officer, who conducted the case in a manner hostile to Khuhro.

"It will also have to be decided whether Khuhro has to be tried by the ordinary courts or by a Special Tribunal under the Hur Offences Act. Those who have already been convicted for this murder were tried by a Special Tribunal, and I am told the Inspector General will press for this. My Ministers are anxious that Khuhro should have a fair trial and have at least by implication argued that this can only be secured by having the case tried by one of the two European judges of the Chief Court."[15]

Khuhro himself saw that with the powerful forces working against the only chance he had of a fair trial was if there was a strong independent judge and this could be only possible if the case was tried outside the province. Failing that he would have liked to have Sir Godfrey Davis, the Chief Justice of Sind, in whose independence he had faith. Dow was not about to oblige however and without his agreement Hidayetullah did not have the courage to make the decision. Khuhro's lawyers made an application to the Chief Court of Sind for the case to be transferred out of Sukkur to the Sind Chief Court because they feared that lower court, particularly in Sukkur, would not give him a fair trial:

"...that circumstances make it necessary in the interests of justice to pray that the case if at all tried in this province should be tried by the learned Chief Judge or by the Hon'ble O'Sullivan. J."[16]

Khuhro lawyer, Dingomal, argued that Khuhro was 'a well-known Muslim politician' and 'a prominent supporter of Muslim League. As such he had always been strongly opposed by the Hindus of Sind and was regarded as their 'inveterate enemy'; that the Sukkur District was notoriously communalist and had seen a lot of communal strife in the past; that the Sessions Judge of Sukkur was a member of a club at Sukkur and another at Hyderabad both of which were 'Hindu institutions' or in other words had largely Hindu membership; that the main topic of discussion at these clubs was Khuhro's trial:

"Owing to political animosity there has been ceaseless propaganda against the applicant and the press of this province has transgressed all bounds of propriety in the manner of its comment on the case."[17]

Dingomal contended that all these factors were calculated to affect the mind of the Sessions Judge at Sukkur and therefore work against the possibility of Khuhro's getting a fair trial. Justice O'Sullivan however ruled that it would not be possible for the Session Judge's mind to be affected by these factors and dismissed the application.

The Sessions Judge of Sukkur, Paymaster who was originally a member of the Civil Service and had opted for the judiciary and was later to revert to Civil Service, was to try the case. During the course of the trial he made his lack of sympathy for Khuhro amply clear but the weakness of the case was proved when even this hostile judge had to had to pronounce the case unproven.*

Khuhro's arrest caused a great sensation not only in Sind but in the whole of

---

* Although Paymaster acquitted Khuhro he made some gratuitous remarks regarding Khuhro: "Finally, whether K. B. Khuhro is or is not fit to play any part again in the political life of this province, is not for me to say, and is no business of a Court of Criminal Justice. All I can say is that the trial has not completely cleared him all suspicion of complicity in the crime." By these remarks Paymaster not only revealed his prejudice but incidentally proved that the case was so weak that even a judge as hostile as Paymaster had to acquit Khuhro.

India. Although the real perpetrators of the conspiracy were the Governor and the Muslim colleagues of Khuhro, Muslim public opinion saw the matter as a Hindu conspiracy. This was given further strength by the mindless and emotional Hindu press propaganda against Khuhro and headline speculation in both the English language as well as the vernacular press taking for granted that Khuhro would hang. This kind of virulent propaganda united the Muslim public behind Khuhro which felt that Khuhro was being victimised because of his fearless championship of the Muslim cause. Every child in the province was told by the parents to pray for Khuhro's release and include his name in every prayer.[18] For many people this inclusion of Khuhro's name in their prayers became such a habit that it continued for years after the trial.

Khuhro was lodged in Sukkur District Jail which was situated near the older British official buildings on the hill. His brother was given a cell next to him where he soon busied himself with arbitrating disputes among the prisoners and generally acting as a *zamindar* on a busman's holiday. Khuhro himself was fully occupied in consultations with lawyers and overseeing the defence case. Khuhro was at his best when facing adversity and his courage and stoicism held him in good stead. He faced the refusal of bail and committal to Sessions Trial quite calmly, meeting each setback with renewed determination. The matter of choosing the lawyer to fight his case required some consideration. Khuhro toyed with the idea of asking Jinnah to appear for him and even sent a telegram requesting Jinnah to appear for him. Jinnah telegraphed back his regrets explaining that he had given up his practice and had not appeared in court for five years but sent a message advising that an experienced criminal lawyer with local knowledge would be much better. He also recommended Somjee, a well-known criminal lawyer of Bombay. Somjee was brought in at one stage in the trial at Jinnah's advice but dealing with witnesses proved to be difficult even for a top lawyer like him without the detailed knowledge of local politics and conditions. Khuhro retained Dialmal Narainsing Lalwani, the best criminal lawyer in the province who had also appeared for Pir Pagaro and would prove a brilliant defence lawyer in this case. Dialmal, though little known outside the province was in fact one of the most able criminal lawyers in India and handled the two most celebrated cases of the period, the Pagaro and the Khuhro case.

One of the earliest visitors Khuhro had in jail was one of his bitter opponents at this time, G. M. Syed. Writing to Jinnah on 4 October Yusuf Haroon mentions the fact:

"When I was away to Bombay, Mr. G. M. Syed was at Karachi and then left for Sukkur to meet Khan Bahadur Khuhro in Jail. I have heard that Mr. Syed has made up his mind to help Khan Bahadur in his trial."[19]

Syed had come to Khuhro to say *mea culpa* and ask forgiveness. He admitted to Khuhro that he had conspired with Gazdar to remove him from the cabinet and had promised Gazdar Premiership, but he said that his intention had only been to remove Khuhro from power and not to put his life at risk. Syed said that he would now do everything in his power to help Khuhro. Knowing well the mercurial and emotional nature of Syed and also his basic honesty, Khuhro could not hold any grudge and readily forgave him.[20]

In the trial Syed gave good supportive evidence showing that there could not possibly be any political rivalry between Soomro and Khuhro and that personal relations between them were good. He said that after Soomro's dismissal the chances of his returning as Premier were almost non existent and that therefore there was no question of his being a potential rival to Khuhro. Also Khuhro had the support of Muslim League members and Soomro the support of Hindu and Congress members, so they were not vying for the same support. Also that it was Hidayetullah who had been called to form the Government after Soomro's dismissal and not Khuhro who had Jinnah's as well as Syed's own support. The question of any personal or political motive for Khuhro to get rid of Soomro did not arise. He also admitted in his evidence that he was politically close to Gazdar and against Khuhro and that the Inspector in charge of the case (Ghulam Akbar) was a close friend of Gazdar.[21]

The prosecution built its case on the assumption that Khuhro regarded Soomro as the most important obstacle in his path to become Premier and by removing him from the scene expected to gain that high position and that he used Hurs to achieve that end. The witnesses they brought to prove the case were in two categories: the politicians to give evidence for motive and secondly the Hurs who had conspired to murder Soomro and with along with the Hurs was included Khuhro's servant *kamdar* Daresh, who was supposed to be the link between the Khuhro brothers and the Hurs. Daresh, 'a weak and frightened man', was vulnerable to police pressure because his son was wanted in a major dacoity. He had been absconding to avoid arrest and torture when he was assigned this new role as key witness in this case.[22] The police arrested him and soon got his 'confession' and on 10 October 1944 he was pardoned.

Failing to get the actual assassins to co-operate and give the required evidence, the police had got its two 'approvers' on whose evidence the whole case rested. One was Daresh and the other Mohammed Khan, a nephew of the famous Mohbat Fakir, who had been part of the conspiracy to murder Soomro and who subsequently had joined the police as a spy. Mohammed Khan had also been granted a pardon after giving the required evidence. Prosecution witnesses also included Kamal Mangrejo as 'approver'. There were also a number of corroborative witnesses to prove the conspiracy and the movements of the Hur party.

The politicians and public men to prove the political motive for the murder included Sir Shahnawaz Bhutto who had been specially summoned from Bombay but whose evidence did not go against Khuhro, K. B. Maula Baksh Soomro the younger brother of the late Allah Baksh, Mohammed Usman Soomro a friend of the Soomro brothers, R. B. Kundandas, advocate, Sayed Hyderali Shah and Sri Krishna Lulla, advocate. To counter the prosecution's allegation that there was bitter rivalry between Khuhro and Soomro the Defence brought some eminent politicians including G. M. Syed, Yusuf Haroon, Khan Bahadur Ghulam Mohammed Wassan, a leading zamindar of Sanghar and Tharparkar area who was a target of the Hurs and a close friend of Khuhro. Evidence was also given by Haji Shahnawaz Pirzada, an intellectual, writer and poet who had personally witnessed Soomro's threats against the Hurs and the Pir. It was felt sufficient by the Defence to get the evidence of the public figures only in the Sub-Divisional Magistrate's Court and not repeat the evidence in the Sessions Court as it was already available to the Court.

The committal proceedings were held in the court of M. H. Sufi, I.C.S., the Sub-Divisional Magistrate of Shikarpur who examined the key witnesses. The Defence brought most of its witnesses to this court in the hope that the weakness of the case would induce the examining Magistrate to throw out the case at this stage. This was a vain hope however. It would have been difficult for any committing magistrate to throw out a case as widely publicised as this one–particularly one in which the I. G. was taking such a deep personal interest and the government itself appeared to be concerned. Although he found that the case was fit to be sent to the Sessions, and in the prevailing atmosphere it was perhaps impossible to find otherwise, Sufi gave an assessment of the the evidence which pointed to the basic weaknesses of the case which in fact were eventually to destroy the government case:

"Daresh gives an account of the conspiracy almost as if it came about accidentally. Khan Bahadur Khuhro does not summon Daresh himself but Daresh happens to arrive at Akil village. The Khuhro brothers sent the other servants out of the room ask Daresh to send for some Hurs through Walu [Wali Mohammed Kharal, a Hur cultivator on Khuhro's *kacha* lands.] and get Allah Baksh murdered. Daresh replies calmly that yes he will go and make arrangements for the murder. He does not show surprise or discomfort. Khuhro brothers do not give any detailed or important instructions, nor do they promise any reward. It looks as though Khan Bahadur Khuhro instructs Daresh:'"Go and pick a couple of carrots from Walu's field and bring them for me because I like them.' After Daresh's departure there is no evidence that Khuhro brothers took any interest in the furtherance or completion of this conspiracy or that they met Daresh again, although Walu is supposed to have said to him once: 'Work is going according to plan and with God's will, be completed soon.' But even then Daresh does not acquaint the Khuhro brothers with the progress of the conspiracy."

Sufi went on to point out that even after the murder the Hurs or Daresh show no particular anxiety to get a reward although Khuhro's tour record shows that he was in Larkana a number of times after the month of May. If the Hurs had done the murder for a reward it is inconceivable that they would have waited so long for it or accepted a refusal but the record shows that to this date the Hurs have not got any money. The Prosecution alleges that Daresh went into hiding because he was involved in the murder *but Mr. Ray's Diary shows that Daresh was in hiding after the Bhumbatpur dacoity.* [author's italics] Sufi said he would not go into the details of the contradictions in Daresh's evidence but he concluded:

"the biggest weakness of his evidence is that there is a strong atmosphere of accident around his evidence and as I have said earlier that this unorganized and easy, picking carrots from a field type of conspiracy does not impress me as genuine..."[23]

The case was committed to the Sessions Court and the hearings started in the court of Judge Paymaster on 26 March 1945 at Sukkur. The case was to be heard for nearly three months. Khuhro his brother Mohammed Nawaz and three others were accused that between the months of October 1942 and May 1943, along with 'approvers' Mohammed Khan and Daresh they engaged in a criminal conspiracy to murder Allah Baksh Soomro–

"which murder was committed in pursuance of the said conspiracy of conspiracies by Kassim son of Mohammed Baksh Mangrejo and you thereby committed an offence punishable under Section 120-B read with Section 023 I. P. C."

Section 109 was also applied to the case. The actual assassins Mangrejo and Ali Mohammed Rajpar had been tried in early 1944 and had already been executed. The Prosecution story was that Khuhro and Soomro had been political rivals and that Khuhro bitterly hated the latter and was determined to get him murdered and that he formed the intention to do so around December 1942. For this purpose he determined to use Hurs. Khuhro owned certain *kacha* land called Keti Khuhro to the east of the river Indus and his *kamdar* for these lands was Daresh. Wali Mohammed Kharal a Farqi Hur of Pir Pagaro was a *hari* on these lands and was known to be friendly with other Hurs. That Khuhro visited Larkana on tour from 25 December 1942 till 3 January 1943. That sometime during this period Khuhro went to his village Aqil. That the *kamdar* Daresh had come to Aqil to pay his respects. That on this occasion Khuhro and his brother Mohammed Nawaz told Daresh that Allah Baksh Soomro was their mortal enemy and that he should ask Wali Mohammed Kharal to get the Hurs to kill him and that they would reward the Hurs approximately Rs.10,000 to 12,000. That Daresh subsequently set up the conspiracy and that Soomro was murdered at his say so.

The key witnesses brought by the Prosecution on whose evidence hinged the entire connection with Khuhro, were Daresh the *kamdar* and Mohammed Khan, a police spy, who was stated to be in the conspiracy from the beginning to the end. According to the judge: "Mohammed Khan impressed me as a fairly sharp and intelligent but not a particularly truthful witness."[24] Mohammed Khan's story was contained was in his confession though he did deviate from his original story to some extent later. Paymaster gave a summary of his story:

"He is a young man aged about 25 years, and is originally a resident of Bhiri village, in Sinjhoro Taluka... The whole of his evidence must be read most carefully... In about August or September 1942 Mohammed Khan had gone to see his paternal uncles Achar and Sumar in village Lakhi Tar in Khairpur State. He stayed with them there for four or five months. He then received a message from his maternal uncle Mohbat Behan, who is the chief henchman of Pir of Pagaro. He thereupon went to village Masur-ji-wai, in Naushahro Taluka where he met Mohbat, Ali Mohammed Rajpar, Sono Sanjrani, Miandad, Majnu Behan, Karim Baksh Janvri alias Redho or Radio, and Wali Mohammed Kharal. They all stayed there with Issan Dahiri, for two or three days after Mohammed Khan's arrival. From there they all went to Bhogi village in Khairpur State, at a distance of 20 to 25 miles, and stayed there with Mewo Chang for a day and a night. They then went to Ali Mohammed Rajpar's village, near Mehrabpur Railway Station and spent a night and a day there. They used to travel secretly at night on foot. From Ali Mohammed Rajpar's village the gang went to Khuhro's Keti, which is in Khairpur State, and stayed there for 2 or 3 weeks in Wali Mohammed's *landhi*. On the second day Wali Mohammed brought Daresh to them, and Daresh repeated the famous words, viz. "K. B. Khuhro says Allah Baksh is his mortal enemy, and you should get him killed for him."

All the members of the gang agreed to get Mr. Allah Baksh killed and it was therefore in Keti Khuhro that the conspiracy was first formed in about the second half of January 1943. It may be noted that it is Mohammed Khan's version that all the way from Masur-ji-wai till the gang arrived at Khuhro's Keti he never knew the purpose or object for which the gang were heading towards Khuhro's Keti. Mohammed Khan explains that he merely followed his uncle Mohbat about from place to place without asking any questions. Mr. Partabrai [the Prosecution Counsel] explains that it is possible that Mohammed Khan merely wanted to get farther and further away from the areas in which Martial Law had been proclaimed. To continue, Mohammed Khan says that they then crossed the river in a boat with Wali Mohammed Kharal, arrived near Phulapoto village at night, and there met Kamal and one Ramzo. From there the party went to village Panjudero, distance of about two miles from the Bund, and spent that night and the next day there in the house of Mehardil Chhajro and Imambux Khatti who both live together. From there Kamal took them to Drabhi village which is 3 or $3\frac{1}{2}$ miles from Panjudero, and they stayed in the jungle for 8 or 10 days. Ramzo left to inform Kassim and did not return. From Drabhi jungle the party went to Nim village, and spent a night and a day there with one Yar Mohammed Nunari. They then left for Ahmed Brohi's house near Jagan village. On the way at Khirthar wah which is 12 to 14 miles from Nim village, Kassim joined the party with a mare, which was given to Mohbat to ride.

The party stayed at Ahmed Brohi's house for 8 to 10 days and were joined there by Illahoo Chandio, Tajoo Chandio, Isso Mangsi, Ibrahim Kasai, Ali Baksh Khoso and Kabir Kasai. Then Kassim and Kamal went and fetched Abdul Haq Bhayo who was required to identify Mr. Allah Baksh. On the next day Abdul Haq left with Kamal, Kassim, Ali Mohammed, Sono, Miandad, Tajoo, Ilahoo, Isso Mangsi and Ibrahim Kasai so that he might point out Mr. Allah Baksh to the others. They all returned on the evening of the same day having not been wholly successful. On the next day Suleman Khoso arrived inviting the party to stay in Bilawal's house in Garhi Bhutto. From Ahmed Brohi's house the party first went to Kabir Kasai's house at Khuda Baksh Brohi's village near Jagan and stayed there for about a week. They then went to Bilawal Khoso's house at Garhi Bhutto where accused Allahrakhio Kasai, Karim Baksh Shaikh and the others joined them. There was then further talk of the murder of Mr. Allah Baksh and accused Allah Rakhio left to fetch one Osman Bhayo who lived near Shikarpur and knew Mr. Allah Baksh, so that he might point him out to the rest of the gang. He however returned unsuccessful. Then some of the party went to Kot Lashari while accused Karim Baksh took the remainder to Khahi and made arrangements there for their lodging. Some of those who had left for Kot Lashari joined the remainder subsequently at Khahi. From Khahi accused Allah Rakhio took Kamal, Kassim, Ali Mohammed and Miandad to Shikarpur to show them Mr. Allah Baksh. They returned on the second or third day. After a few days Sono Sanjrani, Miandad, Ali Mohammed, Kamal and Kassim left for Shikarpur, soon after midnight, to kill Allah Baksh. They returned at noon after having accomplished their object. The gang then left Khahi, spent a day and night at Ibrahim Kasai's house which is about twenty miles from Khahi and then came to Drabhi jungle. Here the approver Mohammed Khan states that he parted company from the other conspirators and made his way to Nawabshah... he joined the Police after coming to Nawabshah."[25]

Paymaster felt that the long detailed story of the wanderings of the Hur party and the account of staying in different places over several districts of upper Sind was probably true as it would have been difficult even for a clever young man like Mohammed Khan to make it all up and that it certainly appeared that he was a member of the conspiracy to kill Soomro. But at the same time,

"There are several reasons why Mohammed Khan would not appear to be a wholly truthful witness. He does not appear to be a witness who has genuinely and sincerely repented his past misdeeds and made up his mind to come out with the whole truth, and nothing but the truth. It may first be pointed out that he kept the whole story a complete secret from the police, even though he was himself serving as a police spy for a period of five months from the end of May 1943. He was not seized by remorse even when he heard of Mr. Allah Baksh's murder. He came out with the truth for the first time only after his arrest, upon being questioned by Mr. Ray. He obviously did so to save his own skin... Of course an approver is admittedly a person who wishes to purchase his own life at the expense of others."[26]

This witness was also a known *'Badmash* i.e. bad character'. The Judge felt that there were a large number of discrepancies in his evidence and it was untrustworthy and could not be relied on to implicate Khuhro.

He also discredited the evidence, the 'confession' of Kamal, the assassin Kassim's nephew:

"It is admitted even by the prosecution that Kamal's statement was almost wholly false and was a series of fabrications from beginning to end."[27]

As Kamal was supposed to be one of the key people on whose evidence the connections with Khuhro was supposed to be established and he said that he had himself heard Daresh telling the Hurs that Khuhro wanted Soomro killed, a vital link of the prosecution case was broken. Kamal's 'confession' was needed by the prosecution to show that Daresh's name first came up in it. But as the Judge pointed out: "Daresh's name was already known to the Police, in another connection."[28]

The judge agreed with the Defence Counsel that it was evident from the confessions of Khan Mohammed and Kamal that a false case was being tutored from the very beginning against the Khuhro brothers and that both confessions contained the same admitted falsehoods thereby showing that they must both have been tutored to utter them. The judge also showed that the fact that the assassins did not bother to come and claim the promised reward after the murder although there were several opportunities as Khuhro was on tour in Larkana several times during and after May 1943 and Daresh was shown as approaching Mohammed Nawaz as late as July 1943 and was easily put off by him and when he supposedly asked Khuhro, as late as 4 October for the reward he was not given anything. The Judge pointed out that these witnesses having given 'confessions' subsequently changed their stories a number of times- "It is clear that Mohammed Khan is prepared to invent and exaggerate to any extent in order to help out the prosecution."[29]

Having pointed out the serious weaknesses in the evidence of these key witnesses, Paymaster turned to the main witness on whose evidence the whole case of Khuhro brothers being instigators of the murder conspiracy rested. Daresh was one of the *kamdars* for the *kacha* area. He was an 'elderly' man who 'looked about 55 to 60 years of age. He had been released and pardoned after giving his evidence implicating the Khuhro brothers. The Judge found him 'a rather timid and not wholly straightforward old man...His evidence is not wholly consistent either with his confession or with the evidence of the other approver Mohammed Khan. It is also not wholly natural on certain points." There had been suspicious delay in recording of his statement by the I. G. P. and the Judge remarked: "I do not say that Daresh was necessarily tutored by anyone during this period. But there was opportunity for such tutoring."[30]

"Daresh had not been given the opportunity to pick out the other `approver' Mohammed Khan at the identification parade. There was a great deal of doubt about his date of meeting the Khuhro brothers at Aqil about which his statements at different times varied. The Defence argued that there was an air of casualness about Daresh's whole story regarding the incitement by the Khuhro brothers at Aqil–

"which is entirely unnatural, even supposing for the sake of argument that the Khuhro brothers had been confirmed criminals with several previous murders to their credit, Daresh's story is that the Khuhro brothers met him by mere chance at Aqil. They did not send for him themselves. It is difficult to explain why, if they had wanted to get Mr. Alllah Baksh murdered, they did not send for Daresh themselves, or why K. B. Khuhro did not send for Daresh at Larkana."[31]

Paymaster recounted the story given by Daresh:

"Daresh 's story is that when he went to the bungalow in the Miris [the building which contained grain stores] the Khuhro brothers without any preliminaries told him straight off that Allah Baksh had got to be murdered. Daresh continues that he did not utter one word of protest nor express the least surprise, but at once agreed to approach Walu to do the job. This behaviour on the part of of a timid old man such as Daresh appears to me to be entirely unnatural. Daresh goes on to state that after the Khuhro brothers told him about the grave and heinous crime that had to be got committed they immediately afterwards passed on to discuss ordinary matters regarding cultivation with him, for one or two hours. This would also be most unnatural behaviour. It is also difficult to understand why neither Daresh nor the Hurs demanded any money in advance from the Khuhro brothers towards their expenses. Daresh admits that he was so bankrupt that he could not pay Wadhio even Rs. 8 that he owed him for the maund of wheat."[32]

The judge went to discuss in detail the evidence of Daresh and to point out the inconsistencies and contradictions in it and concluded:

"... I conclude that Daresh is not a particularly honest, sincere or reputable witness... There is no independent evidence at all to corroborate his story, that the Khuhro brothers incited him at Aqil to get the Hurs to murder Allah Baksh. It is true that, even without any corroborative evidence regarding the incident at Aqil it would be sufficient if it were proved that Daresh set the conspiracy in motion at Keti Khuhro and fed and looked after the Hurs there. For, it could be argued that Daresh *must* have been acting on behalf of his masters because he did not even know Allah Baksh himself and certainly had no reason or motive to contrive his death. I have however held above that it is not even proved that the conspiracy originated at Keti Khuhro or that there was any conspiracy there at all."[33]

In fact there was no independent and impeccable evidence to validate the 'approvers' 'confessions'. The evidence of the 'approvers' was not borne out by Khuhro's tour diary which was maintained as he was Minister or by his Travel and Daily Allowance expenses. Paymaster concluded that there was also no reliable evidence to show that Daresh had absconded for some months at the behest of the Khuhro brothers but was doing so due to the dacoity in which his son was involved and in which the police was likely to arrest him. Paymaster also showed in detail that the other witnesses who were to corroborate circumstantial evidence were not able to do so. He detailed the main items of evidence against Khuhro and concluded that there was no credible or material evidence against him and therefore the case was not proved.

In the end the Judge dealt with the evidence regarding motive. The prosecution had presented some politically prominent personalities to give evidence for motive including Sir Shahnawaz Bhutto and Maula Baksh Soomro. However their evidence could not prove motive for the murder:

"It is ofcourse true that the evidence of motive is one circumstance to be taken into consideration against the accused. When it is shown that the motive on the part of the accused was very strong indeed, *and that no one else had any alternative motive* to do the deed, and then motive might form a very strong circumstance indeed against the accused. This is however admittedly not the case here."[34]

The Judge analysed the evidence that the prosecution had offered to establish motive which was wholly political in nature and where the main witnesses were Sir Shahnawaz Bhutto and K. B. Maula Baksh Soomro and held that the evidence of former merely proved general political rivalry over a long period between Soomro and Khuhro. That both were ambitious politicians and were on opposite sides for most of their lives on both public and Local Bodies. But at the same time he quoted Sir Shahnawaz also admitting that:

"Till 1937 i.e. as long as I was in Sind, I used to see that accused K. B. Khuhro and the deceased Mr. Allah Baksh used to visit each other socially and dine with each other. Their social relations were outwardly good. Since 1937 I have lost touch with Sind affairs...".

For Maula Baksh's evidence he commented:

"The evidence of K. B. Moula Baksh (Ex. 130), brother of the deceased Mr. Allah Baksh is to a large extent hearsay. It shows general political rivalry between K. B. Khuhro on the one hand and Mr. Allah Baksh on the other. The fact of this rivalry is so general, public and notorious, that I could even take judicial notice of it."[35]

Evaluating the evidence of these as well as the other witnesses brought in to establish motive, Paymaster gave his opinion that: "the evidence of motive as against K. B. Khuhro is not particularly strong." But added to the weakness of the motive argument against Khuhro was the fact that there was an alternative and this argument was accepted by Paymaster. The Hurs had motive sufficiently strong to carry out the murder without any promise of reward. The history of Hur crime showed that it was on committed – in hot blood out of revenge and not for a reward'. The murder had been committed in broad day light near a Police station and the assassins had taken great risk of being caught. It was not a well planned, calculated and deliberate murder such as a murder for reward would be. It was also a fact that Hurs had very little regard for law and order and very little fear of consequences. That the Hurs had a very strong motive for murdering Soomro was in Paymaster's opinion fully borne out by the facts and by the record.

Soomro was Premier from March 1941 till October 1942. Pir Pagaro was deported in October 1941 at his orders, first to Karachi and then to Nagpur in Central India. Towards the end of 1941 the hedge of the Garang Bungalow was set on fire and the bungalow searched even though it was occupied by the ladies of the Pir's family and his young sons. Khemchand, a *mashir* at the search was murdered by the Hurs soon afterwards as an act of revenge. The Hur Act was introduced in April 1942 again by Soomro's Ministry. Seth Sitaldas, M.L.A., was murdered by the Hurs in May 1942.

"In this connection Allah Baksh went to Mirpurkhas and made violent speeches against the Hurs threatening to cut them down at all costs and proclaiming that he was not afraid of them. Mr. Allah Baksh made such speeches at Nawabshah and other places also."[36]

On 16 May 1942 the Lahore Mail was derailed by the Hurs and a large number of innocent people were killed and injured.[37] The civil administration broke down and on 1st June 1942 Martial Law was introduced. The Pir 'Kot' was bombed and destroyed by the Military. In February 1943 the Pir was tried at Central Jail in Hyderabad by a Military Tribunal and on 23 March 1943 he was executed. Paymaster gave his opinion that the Hurs were well aware of the events:

"The news [of the Pir's execution] was kept secret for some time but was made public after about a fortnight. Prosecution witness Mohammed Khan admits that Mohbat was literate and used to read out newspapers to the other members of the gang. Soon after the Kot Lashari dacoity the Hurs must have come to know, in about the beginning of April 1942 that the Pir had been executed. Mohammed Khan admits that he did come to know about this. The Hurs must have been at Khahi at about this time. It is possible that the gang after collecting at Masur-ji-wai and after going to various places in a northward direction to escape the Martial Law, had stayed at Jagan and then at Garhi Bhutto. At Khahi they learnt about the Pir's execution which drove them to a frenzy, and the murder of Mr. Allah Baksh was then planned for the first time, and was soon after carried into effect."[38]

Adding all the facts and the circumstances together, Paymaster concluded:
"I think Mr. Dialmal has satisfactorily established his contention that the Hurs had a much stronger motive for the murder of Mr. Allah Baksh than K. B. Khuhro. I conclude therefore that not only is the evidence of a motive against K. B. Khuhro not particularly strong but that there was a far stronger alternative motive on part of the Hurs."

There was therefore no option for the Judge but to exonerate Khuhro:
"To sum up, the above items of evidence do not even cumulatively prove beyond reasonable doubt that K. B. Khuhro was a member of the conspiracy."[39]

The judgement was delivered on 3rd August 1945. The day before Khuhro had given instructions to his younger brother that food should not be brought to the court that day and that his effects should be taken away from the jail. Whichever way the judgement went he would not be occupying that cell any more. He was quite calm and sustained by immense faith. He had noted that the attitude of the

Judge had not been favourable to him but at the same time he was well aware that the Prosecution had not been able to prove its case. However there could not be any certainty about the outcome of the case particularly when the government was clearly unfriendly and the atmosphere as charged as it had been during the whole period of the trial.

Outside the court a large crowd of sympathisers had gathered many of whom had come specially to Sukkur to hear the verdict. The crowd had been held back at some distance below the hill on which the court was situated. Among those who were thus not allowed near the court were several M.L.A.s like Sardar Jaafar Khan Burdi, Agha Badruddin Durrani, Agha Ghulam Nabi Pathan, the General Secretary of the Provincial Muslim League and Khan Bahadur Ghulam Mohammed Khan Wassan. Khuhro and his brother were brought to court by car and appeared to be unworried. Khuhro was wearing white *shalwar and kameez* and a red Turkish fez. At about quarter to nine the Khuhro brothers and their lawyers went into the court where Khuhro appeared calm and impassive. He spent the next few minutes talking to his lawyers. At nine o'clock the judge entered the court and immediately started reading his verdict of acquittal. Yusuf Haroon who was present in the court rushed to embrace Khuhro and congratulate him as did others who were present.[40]

The news reached the crowd within seconds. The public broke through the police cordon and rushed to the court. Soon the news spread throughout Sukkur and a crowd estimated at ten thousand surged towards the court to greet and congratulate Khuhro. A huge procession formed and went to a local saint to give thanks. Khuhro then went to the jail to thank the staff for their consideration during his stay there. Garlands of roses were brought to him by the thousand and his friend Wassan garlanded him with a necklace of gold guineas. Workers of the railway workshop came out and joined the procession forcing the workshop to close. By now the crowd which had swelled to over twenty thousand turned to Masjid Manzilgah where with Khuhro, they offered prayers of thanks. Yusuf Haroon addressed the crowd welcoming the release of Khuhro and hailing it as a great blessing for the Muslims of India.

Khuhro thanked the people for their great affection and support. He said that in jail he had received thousands of letters and telegrams from all over Sind expressing their faith that he would be released and praying for him. He promised that he would dedicate his life to the service of the people. Delegations arrived led by Sardar Jafar Khan Jamali from Jacobabad and Shaikh Wajid Ali from Shikarpur to congratulate him. After meeting his friends Khuhro went to Larkana by car where the population turned out *en masse* to greet him, processions forming in different areas of the town converging at his house. After two or three hours he left for Ruk station to catch the train for Karachi.

All along the route big and small stations were crowded with people who had gathered to see and greet Khuhro. No matter what the time of the night the people of towns and villages made for their nearest station with bands, drums and *shahanais*. Throughout the 4th of August people of Sind were rushing to the stations in the hope of seeing Khuhro whether or not the station was on the route of the train regardless of the time. If it was not the right train they formed a procession with the bands and paraded through the towns and villages. These processions and *jalsas* to celebrate Khuhro's release took place throughout Sind for the next several days.

At about 12 o'clock in the afternoon of 4 August, delayed for over an hour en route by the public, the Lahore Mail arrived at the Karachi Cantonement Station carrying Khuhro and his party. At the station people had started gathering since the early morning. Taxis, Victoria carriages and tongas were not charging fares from people coming to the station. Apart from the ordinary people the representatives of religious, professional and workers' organizations were all present at the station. The Premier, Hidayetullah was there with his entire cabinet as was the President of the Provincial Muslim League, G. M. Syed and even the ex Home Minister Gazdar. Newspapers carried the lists of the most distinguished people present at the station as well as the detailed accounts of the scenes at the station and the procession which took Khuhro home.*

Volunteers of Sind Muslim Students Federation and Muslim National Guards took charge of the crowd at the station. The people insisted on carrying Khuhro on their shoulders and eventually a compromise was reached and he was brought out of the station on a chair. A procession was formed with the bands of the different organisations in the lead followed by musicians with *shehnais* and drums and then the Marwari community with their particular ethnic music, Pathans dancing the Khattak dance and Sheedees of Karachi doing their rythmic and energetic dances. In the leading Victoria carriage Khuhro was seated with Hidayetuallah, the Home Minister Mir Ghulam Ali, and G. M. Syed. The next car carriage carried Mrs. Khuhro accompanied by Lady Nusrat Haroon and these were followed by a long procession of cars, carriages, tongas and people on foot including the heaviest parliamentarian in Sind, Gabole and Dr. Khan, both of them dancing all the way. The National Guards under their *salar* the youngest Haroon brother Saeed, marched along shouting slogans and keeping order and seeing to it that there was no untoward incident. The procession vending its way past Frere Hall and Saddar and then Bunder Road ended up at Khuhro's Patel Park house at about 3 o'clock in the afternoon.

The same evening there was a big public meeting at Eidgah Maidan. Originally the meeting had been called to explain the results of the Simla Conference to the people but it became a welcome meeting for Khuhro with hardly a mention of the Conference. Speech after speech was made welcoming Khuhro's release and declaring it as a triumph of truth and victory of the Muslim cause. The police was severely condemned for manufacturing a false case of such serious implication.

---

* Those present included: The Hon'ble Sir Ghulam Hussain Hidayetullah, the Premier of Sind, the Hon'ble Khan Bahadur Mir Ghulam Ali Khan Talpur, Home Minister, the Hon'ble Syed Mohammed Ali Shah, P.W.D.Minister, the Hon'ble Haji Pir Illahi Baksh, Minister for Education, Mr. G. M. Syed, President, Sind Provincial Muslim League, Mr. Mohammed Hashim Gazdar, ex Home Minister, Mr. Syed Ali Mohammed Rashdi, Secretary Muslim League Action Committee, Haroon brothers, Rais Ghulam Rasul Khan Bhurgri, Makhdum Nawab Ghulam Miran Shah of Bahawalpur, Sardar Bahadur Kaiser Khan Bozdar, M.L.A., Sardar Ali Gohar Khan Mahar, M.L.A., Agha Shamsuddin Barakzai, Mr. Mohammed Yusuf Khan Chandio, Parliamentary Secretary, Dr. Khan, Municipal Councillor, Khan Bahadur Allah Baksh Khan Gabole, Parliamentary Secretary, Mr. Abdul Aziz, Advocate, Kazi Abdul Rahman, Chief Editor, *Al-Wahid*, Maulvi Abdul Ghafoor Sitai, Editor, *Al-Wahid*, Khan Bahdur Babu Fazal Illahi Sahib, Mr. G. Allana, Sayed G. Bukhari, Communist worker, Kazi Mujtaba, Communist worker, and Mr. Misquita, Worshipful Mayor of Karachi and others. *Al-Wahid* 5 August 1945.

After G. M. Syed and Yusuf Haroon had spoken, Khuhro made his speech thanking the people for their unstinting support. He spoke of the hundreds of prisoners he had met in the jail who had been put there under Defence of India rules and of whom at least two thirds were innocent. He urged the Government which was supposed to be a Muslim League government, to look into the matter carefully and remedy the injustice. Khuhro talked about his time in jail and the thousands of letters he had got from the public encouraging and supporting him. People had prayed and made *manats* at the tombs of saints for him and he could not ever forget that. Jail, he said, had given him the opportunity to study the Holy Quran and Islamic literature and given him a deeper understanding of religion and life. He said that he was determined to fulfil his duty to the people of Sind and to the Muslims in general and that he felt that his time in jail had been an opportunity to appreciate and assess not only religion but his own duty in life.

In fact the eleven months that he spent in jail at this time when he was forty three years of age had a profound influence on his life. Until now Khuhro had been a formal Muslim observing formalities of his religion in a casual way. In jail he studied the Quran and the Commentaries and was deeply affected by his studies. For the rest of his life Khuhro continued his study of the Quran and his efforts to understand Islam. He was very careful about his observance of prayer and never missed any till the end of his life. Khuhro had never stinted charity which had been part of his life as a *zamindar* and an educated man but now he allocated part of his income for charity, giving scholarships to students and to institutions of public welfare, apart from his *zakat*, which he spent exactly as required by religion. This aspect of his life was extremely private and though friends and acquaintances did notice his punctiliousness about prayer they did not see any difference in his enjoyment of social life or his 'Westernized' style of life.

As the speeches in the public meeting and comment in the press showed, the politicians and the public laid the entire blame for the concoction of the murder case on the police. In its editorial on Khuhro's release even *Al-Wahid* which could have no reason to spare the top officials of the government including the Governor made the 'native' police and Hindu officials and press almost entirely responsible:

"It was the Hindu press which from the beginning directly and indirectly and without any proof sought to lay the blame on Khuhro's shoulders. With the backing of this press propaganda Khuhro's political enemies hatched a conspiracy that somehow Khuhro should be involved in this murder case so that if he is not hanged he should at least be in deep trouble and excluded from political life."[41]

The myth of the fairness of the British officials was so strong that even the press could not imagine the complicity of an Englishman:

"We are only astonished at one thing that an English officer of the Imperial Service, which Mr. Ray is, was taken in by a subordinate officer like Ghulam Akbar, to put Khan Bahadur Khuhro through this trial on such flimsy evidence."[42]

Muslim opinion in Sind and outside was strongly for enquiry against the police officials who were responsible for framing the case but in spite of the fact that the elected government was that of Muslim League no such enquiry was ordered and the interest in the matter of some exalted power became apparent when these officials were actually promoted, a fact which Khuhro mentioned in his letter to Jinnah:

> "As soon as I was acquitted by the Court of Sessions, Ghulam Akbar was promoted as D. S. P. over the head of about half a dozen officers who were senior to him, and was placed in charge of the Sukkur district. Inspector Ghulam Hussain, another police officer who took the most conspicuous part in concocting this false case against me, has been placed in charge of Shikarpur Division."[43]

No one looked up to see Dow pulling the strings however and the politics of Sind continued to be poisoned by mutual suspicion and bitterness. It was Dow himself who indicated in a curious and roundabout way that the evidence against Khuhro had been false. Writing in September 1945 to Lord Wavell, whom he had not spared diatribes against Khuhro throughout his governorship, he appears to be shifting the blame for the conspiracy away from himself. The subject of the letter was Mohbat Behan, the *khalifa* of Pagaro who was one of the main instigators of the murder, Dow says:

> "...Mohbat Behan is one of the absconders wanted in connection with the murder of Allah Baksh, the late Premier. I do not pay great regard to the report...that he has made a statement implicating the late Home Minister, Gazdar. If the report is anything more than election propaganda, it would seem that Mohbat Behan has taken the Khuhro case to heart, and hopes to gain free pardon by implicating someone more important. It is true however that my Premier [Hidayetullah] was greatly excited by these rumours, and asked for a special interview with me. But by the time he arrived, he would do no more than make vague insinuations about his fear that high police officers were concerned in spoiling the case against Mohbat Behan. He gave me the impression that he knew more about the truth than, on second thoughts, he was willing to confide in me, and that he feared that Gazdar, with his back to the wall, might reveal things which both he and Sir Ghulam are in present conditions agreed to be better covered up."[44]

Perhaps Dow was trying to deflect the suspicion of conspiracy away from himself to Hidayetullah and Gazdar. But the implication is clear that the Khuhro case was the result of a Byzantine conspiracy and it was better that no further enquiry was made into it.

It was only after the departure of Dow and the arrival of a new Governor in Sind that finally Khuhro got an inkling of the truth. Sir Francis Mudie came to Sind at the end of 1945, a man not instrinsically obtuse like Graham or vicious like Dow but a comparatively wise and tolerant officer with experience of Indian politics. He developed a rapport with Khuhro and an appreciation of the latter's basic integrity and talent. He hinted to Khuhro without going into details that it was in fact Dow who had been the prime mover in the case against him. Writing to the Viceroy in early 1946 after the elections in Sind, he said:

> "When I saw that it was likely that Khuhro would become a Minister, I examined carefully into the judge's order acquitting him of murder *and have no doubt that the evidence against him was false*... He strikes me as capable, with a strong mind of his own..."[45]

15

WORKING FOR FREEDOM

Khuhro's acquittal on the 3 August 1945 came after the victory of the Allies in Europe in May earlier that year and just three days before the atom bomb was dropped on Hiroshima forcing surrender by Japan on 2 September to General MacArthur. The world had changed and the era of the Cold War was coming in as well as the second unravelling of world empires in the twentieth century. Although Lord Linlithgow, the Viceroy of India, had declared as late as December 1939 that:

"It is no part of our policy ... to expedite in India constitutional changes for their own sake, or gratuitously to hurry the handing over to India hands at any pace faster than that which we regard as best calculated, on a long view, to hold India to the Empire."[1]

But by the end of the war it was clear that the British would leave as soon as agreement could be reached about the form freedom would take in India. The elections in England had thrown out Churchill the hero of the war, and had put the Labour Party under Clement Attlee in power. The British were anxious to get out of India. They no longer had the heart or the will to hang on to the Empire. The exercise of disengagement was about to begin when Khuhro came back on the political scene.

Khuhro was now the undisputed hero of Muslim Sind and of Muslim League. His ordeal had succeeded in uniting the Muslims of Sind as never before and of convincing them that anyone who had their welfare at heart could not be tolerated by the Hindus be they of the Congress or any other variety. According to the views of a pro Congress observer:

"The Muslim League which had failed to make an appeal to the Sind Muslims now became as popular as the Congress organisation in the rest of India – the liberator of the Muslims from the `tyranny of the Hindus and Hindu Congress'. In the whole of Sind there never had been more than a few hundred members of the League all these years. Thanks however, to the war on Khuhro by the `Hindu press' the League membership in Sind swelled to hundreds of thousands."[2]

The Khuhro trial had widened the gulf between the two communities considerably and time was running out for any rapprochement.

At the same time the year that he had been absent from the political scene had seen a most unedifying spectacle of political intrigue and rivalry between the Syed group and Hidayetullah over control of Muslim League and of the Ministry. The intrigues had started as soon as the Ministry had been sworn in, in October 1942 and centred around Syed's ambitions to control the organisation of Muslim League and to be the power behind the throne of the Sind government. Khuhro was one of the casualties of this intrigue but after his exit the struggle between Syed and Hidayetullah became more direct and much more bitter. Immediately after the resignation of Khuhro, Syed called a meeting of the Muslim League Assembly Party, to select a new Minister. Hidayetullah realising that a nominee of Syed would be thrust on him cancelled the meeting. He wrote to Jinnah to complain:

"The position has now become very difficult as Mr. G. M. Syed wishes to establish a Sayed Raj here, and wants me to appoint a Sayed as Minister. We have a Sayed as Speaker, and Pir Sahib whom they count as one of them and Mr. Gazdar is Mr. Syed's ally, as you know already."[3]

Hidayetullah asserted that it was his right to select his own Minister. He accused Syed and Gazdar of intriguing with non-Muslims. More to the point he complained:

"He is the nominated president of the Provincial League, and he has nominated his whole Council. You can very well realise what he can do with a council so constituted who are everything to him."[4]

And again:

"You know very well that Mr. Syed does not like me. After getting rid of K. B. Khuhro, he and his friends wish to get rid of me too.... He wants to have his own Raj at any cost."[5]

The charges and counter charges continued to fly to Jinnah. Syed in his turn accused Hidayetullah:

"... it is not unlikely that the Premier of the so-called League Ministry may form a new Ministry under a different label."[6]

After a delay of some weeks Hidayetullah appointed Mir Ghulam Ali Talpur as Minister instead of Syed's nominee Mohammed Ali Shah of Darbelo. The fight became even more bitter and intense when the question of the bye-election of Shikarpur came up on the death of the sitting Muslim League member. Hidayetullah wanted his son Anwar to be given the Muslim League nomination whereas Syed's candidate was Agha Ghulam Nabi Pathan of Sultankot. The Parliamentary Board had a majority of Syed's supporters and Pathan was nominated but his position was weak. The deceased Muslim League member from this constituency, Khan Bahadur Sadhayo had been elected mainly by the influence and efforts of Khuhro and the election would not be so easy now with Allah Baksh Soomro's brother Maula Baksh in the field. Syed realizing that the position was hopeless withdrew Pathan and put in another candidate without consulting the Parliamentary Board. The outcome of the continuing conflict was the election of Maulabaksh Soomro. The confrontation came to a head with the removal by the Premier of Gazdar from the Cabinet. Jinnah refused to interfere leaving the choice of his Ministers to the Premier.

This was not the end of the matter however as in the next bye-election which was in Tando Mohammed Khan in Hyderabad district, the story was repeated with different candidates of the different Muslim League groups, except that in this case the Ministerial candidate won. The loser in any case was Muslim League as the official Muslim League candidate, nominated by Syed, was defeated. Syed issued a long press statement in January 1945, throwing aspersions on Hidayetullah's principles and his loyalty to Muslim League. By early 1945 the breach was out in the open and the whole country was aware of it and as Syed himself said, the affair:

"had become a major scandal throughout the country, causing immense damage to the prestige and reputation of the entire organization."[7]

In February the Muslim League 'High Command' sent Qazi Isa the Muslim League leader from Quetta, to bring about a compromise but the differences were too serious for him to deal with. Jinnah summoned Syed to Bombay where he spent three days explaining his point of view. Jinnah then sent Liaquat Ali Khan, the General Secretary of the Party and two members of the Working Committee, Nawab Ismail Khan and Chaudhri Khalique-u-zaman, to solve the dispute but they too had to go back without anything to show for their efforts. Syed went ahead with his efforts to throw out the Ministry and on 24 February the Ministry was defeated on a cut motion by twenty five votes against nineteen. The Governor however gave another chance to Hidayetullah to save his government, which he, a past master at wheeling and dealing, was well able to take. He got Maulabaksh Soomro, the new non League member from Shikarpur, to join the Cabinet and gained the support of other non League or 'Nationalist' Muslims for himself.

Syed complained to Jinnah about this, sending him some explanatory telegrams, but Jinnah was convinced that Syed was following a policy which, by forcing a League Ministry to go outside for help, was not serving the Muslim League cause at all. He took strong exception to Syed's actions:

"...you have adopted unconstitutional methods have lent yourself to unworthy intrigues, playing into the hands of enemies, have let down your leader and party to which you belonged, thereby you have already damaged our cause and the prestige of the Muslim League. You have precipitated a crisis, have broken party dicipline, caused a split, shaken the solidarity of Sind Muslims notwithstanding your assurance to me at the conclusion of our Bombay talks and against my advice..."[8]

Syed was furious at what he considered Jinnah's backing of Hidayetullah who while

"professing to be a loyal member of the League, could afford to defy and break its discipline by admitting a non-Leaguer in his Cabinet and still earn the benediction of the League president while I had brought down upon my head the wrath and open denunciation of Mr. Jinnah..."[9]

In fact Hidayetullah had given an undertaking to Maulabaksh that he would stand by him even if Jinnah did not like his inclusion or if he insisted on his joining Muslim League -

"In case Mr. Jinnah or the League high command does not agree in this coalition, I shall not call upon any of you to resign and compel any of you to sign the League pledge. In that case I shall remain with you and stick to this coalition."[10]

In the face of Jinnah's attitude Syed backed down and agreed to compromise with Hidayetullah with the result that Hidayetullah went back on his word to Maulabaksh and removed him from the Cabinet making up the difference by taking Syed's candidate Mohammed Ali Shah as well as two representatives of the Hindu Independent party. The crisis was resolved for the time being and "Sir

Ghulam Hussain breathed a sigh of relief and protected by the Governor and the Quaid-i-Azam, he could only see ahead of him a long stretch of smooth sailing and unchallenged authority at the helm of the Sind Government."[11]

Syed had given in for the moment to the pressure from Jinnah but he had not really surrendered. In June 1945 he held a meeting of the newly elected Council of Muslim League which was packed with his supporters. He brought in Shaikh Abdul Majid who had left Muslim League and formed an Azad Muslim group to try and fill the gap left by the death of Soomro and, it was said, to try for the post of premiership on the same basis. But his plans failed as Maulabaksh made a more credible substitute as the brother of the late leader of Azad Muslims. Shaikh was appointed Chairman of the Committee of Action by Syed, who also welcomed Rashdi now no longer taken up with Hur affairs. In the meeting of the Council held on 3 and 4 June the Council passed several resolutions some of which struck back at the 'High Command' for "divesting the Provincial League of all their inherent powers of control and supervision over Provincial Assembly parties and Ministries." This was ofcourse Syed's response to Jinnah's attempts to control his imposition of authority over the Ministry. A similar situation had created differences between Syed and Khuhro in 1944 and again when Jinnah had come firmly down on the side of Hidayetullah, but interestingly it was also a battle which would be continued by Khuhro against the Centre in the post partition period.[12]

Syed also realised what had long been obvious, that the Central organisation of Muslim League was dominated by members from Muslim minority provinces and that their interests did not necessarily reflect those of the Muslims of the majority provinces. It appeared that a 'showdown' between the President of the Provincial Muslim League and the 'High Command' was inevitable sooner rather than later.

On his release therefore Khuhro came upon a Muslim League riven by a serious split within the province and a looming confrontation with the Centre. At the same time the fate of India was hanging in the balance, waiting upon the settlement between Congress and Muslim League and the good will of the retreating Imperial power. Wavell had summoned the Simla conference in the June 1945 to discuss the formation of the Viceroy's Council which would include representatives of all the major parties. In the end the conference could not succeed because of Jinnah's insistence that all Muslim members of the Council should be nominees of Muslim League and although Lord Wavell was willing to go along to some extent he insisted that a Unionist Muslim from the Punjab be included which, in view of the relationship of the Unionists with the British and the services that the Unionist government had rendered in the war, was understandable. This suggestion was turned down by Jinnah and the Simla Conference was deemed to have failed. Events were rushing towards a denouement however. Elections were due to be held in early 1946 and this was the last chance for Muslim League to make a showing if it wanted crediblility and a say in the negotiations for independence.

Jinnah arrived in Karachi on 28 August. Khuhro was at the airport along with other Muslim League leaders to receive him. Jinnah warmly embraced him and remarked:

"Thank God you have been released with honour to serve your people".[13]

Jinnah was well aware that Sind was at this time the only province in India with a Muslim League government and was very anxious that Muslim League should win a clear majority in the elections scheduled for early 1946 and form a government in the province which would enable him to base his demand for 'Pakistan' on the cornerstone of Sind. Khuhro's popularity was naturally a great asset for Muslim League particularly with the elections in the offing and the split that was threatening Muslim League unity and effectiveness in Sind.

One of Jinnah's the first tasks was to see to it that some kind of compromise was achieved to prevent the debilitating infighting. He proposed a Parliamentary Board with representation from all groups. The anti Syed groups were agitating for a parallel Muslim League to bypass the Syed dominated body. *Al Wahid*, the influential Sindhi newspaper was strongly advocating such a course. It was common knowledge that Yusuf Haroon was a keen supporter of this idea. Haroon had been a protege of Khuhro who had supported Haroon's candidature for the post of General Secretary of Sind Muslim League and also for membership of the Central Legislature on his father's death. The Parliamentary Board was set up in September and consisted of Hidayetullah, Mir Ghulam Ali Talpur, Pir Illahibux from the Ministerial group and Syed Khairshah and Agha Ghulam Nabi Pathan (General Secretary) and G. M. Syed himself (as President) from the Syed group. On his release Khuhro had been immediately taken on to the Parliamentary Board. Syed was not entirely happy with the composition of this Board as his supporters would no longer be in a majority but accepted it "for the sake of solidarity in Sind League"[14] It was however improbable that Syed would go along quietly with the decisions of the Board.

Jinnah left Karachi to go to Quetta for his holiday and on 1 October the Parliamentary Board started its meetings in Karachi to award the tickets. From the very start there were serious differences between the other members and the Syed group. The candidates for the districts in which Syed was not directly interested were selected unanimously mostly at the suggestion of Khuhro, but when it came to the central districts of Sind there was a critical situation. Seeing that he was being outvoted on certain seats, Syed adjourned the meeting *sine die* although the other members protested against this step. The members who did not agree with Syed's action then moved to Khuhro's house two doors away and discussed what was to be done next. A telegram was sent to Jinnah jointly by Hidayetullah, Pir Illahibaksh and Mir Ghulam Ali as well as Khuhro declaring the postponement "illegal, unconstitutional and high-handed" and further that "he desired his favourite Sayeds by allowing tickets in Tharparkar and Hyderabad districts" to them rather than to candidates who had a reasonable chance of winning. Failing to get his way in the Board, Syed was planning to call the Muslim League Council meeting which was packed with his own supporters. Syed sent his own telegram to Jinnah demanding that the members opposed to him be removed and other members be appointed as nominated by his Council. Reporting to Jinnah on 3 October Khuhro wrote:

"The work of the Parliamentary Board was going on smoothly and Larkana, Jacobabad and Nawabshah candidates were chosen unanimously. But the trouble arose over Hyderabad and Tharparkar Districts candidates. The trouble unfortunately is that all the candidates in these Districts were either favourites of Mr. G. M. Syed, or K. B. Mir Ghulam Ali Khan and Hon'ble Pir Illahibaksh. According to the convention agreed upon by us we wanted to issue tickets either by unanimous votes or by overwhelming majority. This convention was followed in the above-mentioned Districts, i.e., Larkana, Jacobabad and Nawabshah Districts. But it was not possible to do so in Hyderabad and Tharparkar Districts as there were three Ministers on one side and three including Mr. G. M. Syed on the other. It made no difference which side I voted as the voting in all cases, so far as these districts were concerned, would be 4 against 3 and in such cases, and according to the convention the matter was to be placed before the Central Parliamentary Board for decision.

Mr. G. M. Syed, however, suddenly adjourned the meeting inspite of the fact that 4 voted against the adjournment and 2 voted for the adjournment. It was really unfortunate to have caused this trouble when it could easily have been avoided by the Chairman by referring such contentious matters to the Central Parliamentary Board for the final decision. In any case the decision of the Central Parliamentary Board would have prevailed.

I am however glad to learn from Nawabzada Liaquat Ali Khan in reply to my telegram that the Central Parliamentary Board will be coming to Karachi on the 12th instant and that the Working Committee of All–India Muslim League is to meet at Karachi on the 14th instant."[15]

Khuhro felt that Syed's instransigence was due to the influence of Gazdar who had his own grievances and had so far been frustrated in finding a larger role for himself, and also Rashdi who realising that Muslim League was in the ascendant had decided to re-join it. He wanted to get the Muslim League ticket for the Central Legislature while at the same time keeping links with the Congress leadership in Sind.[16] Khuhro gave his views on the subject to Jinnah:

"Mr. G. M. Syed has acted very wrongly by causing the rift which could have easily been avoided but Messrs. Ali Muhammad Rashdi and M. H. Gazdar are at the back of it. Mr. Rashdi wanted to bring about the disruption in the League circles at the instigation of the Hindus... He is their hireling and agent who will utilize every opportunity to misguide Mr. Syed and thus cause trouble in the League circles. But your presence will help considerably in surmounting the difficulties created by our enemies. The situation is such that only the Central Parliamentary Board should deal with two districts specially, Hyderabad and Tharparkar Districts after obtaining advice from us here at Karachi and in important cases they could consult you at each stage."[17]

Jinnah wrote back with dire warnings:

"I do hope that the Central Parliamentary Board will be able to successfully handle the matter. All I can say is that the only issue before us is Pakistan versus Akhand Hindustan and if Sind fails, God help you".[18]

What he meant perhaps was "God help Pakistan" because without Sind lining up behind Muslim League there was no hope at all of even beginning a case for Pakistan.

Before Jinnah could arrive back from Baluchistan or the Central Parliamentary Board could meet, Syed had called a meeting of his Provincial Council. Here he expressed his lack of confidence in the Sind Parliamentary Board and nominated a committee of five to advise the Central Board. The League Parliamentary Board which consisted of Liaquat Ali Khan, Nawab Ismail Khan and Mr. Hussain Imam announced three days later that in view of the disagreement in the Provincial Parliamentary Board it would allocate all the thirty five tickets for Muslim seats in

Sind. In its first series of meetings the names of twenty four candidates were decided. In Upper Sind there was not much difference of opinion and where there was any difficulty, Khuhro's advice prevailed. In Sukkur North West, Maulabaksh Soomro, the 'Azad Muslim' candidate was very strong and as the local Muslim League candidates, Ghulam Nabi Pathan and Nabi Baksh Mohammed Hussain were not considered strong enough to win against him, it was proposed that Khuhro should contest from this constituency. It was however eventually not possible to do this as Khuhro was needed to canvass for candidates throughout the province and could not afford to be tied down to one constituency. His opponents, also fearing this, tried to pin him down in Larkana as Dow noted:

"... still under Nihchaldas' subtle advice, the idea is that Rashdi should join the Congress, and should stand as an anti League candidate against Khan Bahadur Khuhro who has a very safe seat in Larkana district. Nihchaldas admitted to me that Rashdi had no chance, but the idea was to keep Khuhro enclosed in Larkana, instead of having him free to stump the country on behalf of more shaky League candidates."[19]

Regarding the Shikarpur election and the Congress strategy Dow wrote:

"The only really strong anti League Muslim candidate is Khan Bahadur Moulabaksh in Shikarpur, and the Congress are most anxious to secure his return as the only possible Premier in an anti League combination. The original idea of the League was to put up Khuhro against Moulabaksh as the only candidate likely to defeat him; meanwhile Khuhro would put up in his own safe seat a stooge, who would resign in his favour if Khuhro were defeated in Shikarpur. But with Rashdi up against him backed by Congress money, a stooge would have a poor chance, so it looks as if Nihchaldas will succeed in tying Khuhro down to Larkana so that Moulabaksh's success in Shikarpur will be assured."[20]

In fact when it came to the crunch Rashdi did not contest against Khuhro who came in unopposed and was able to campaign for the Muslim League candidates in the province.

In Nawabshah where there were five seats, three were allocated Syed's nominees, Sayed Khair Shah in Nawabshah East, Pir Qurban Ali in North West and Sayed Mohammed Ali Shah in Nawabshah North. In Nawabshah West there was a contest between Syed's nominee Sayed Hassan Baksh Shah and Ghulam Rasool Jatoi who was backed by the rest of the Parliamentary Board. Jatoi was assessed to have a better chance of winning. Syed also had his own candidate for the Talpur stronghold of Tando Mohammed Khan in Hyderabad District. Here the Talpur candidate was Mir Hussain Baksh Talpur but Syed wanted a fellow Sayed, Qabul Mohammed Shah who had already been defeated by the former in a bye election when both had contested as independents, although even at that time Qabul Mohammed Shah had G. M. Syed's support. Khuhro supported Mir Hussain Baksh as obviously the winning candidate. Similarly in another constituency (Hala) Hyderabad North, Syed insisted on backing a Sayed, Baqadar Shah against Makhdum Ghulam Hyder Quraishi who was a sitting member and the most influential candidate in the constituency. It was also well-known that Sayed Baqadar Shah was "quite capable of retiring from the contest at the last moment and he has done it on every other occasion".[21] Taking the realistic view Khuhro and others supported the Makhdum.

In Sukkur South East there were three candidates including K. B. Agha Nizamuddin and Pirzada Abdus Sattar who had recently joined Muslim League. Both Khuhro and Syed were in favour of giving Pirzada the ticket as they felt he had a better chance of winning. For Tharparkar North however there was a very serious contest between Khuhro and Syed candidates. Nawabzada Liaquat Ali reported:

"This is a constituency where there is a serious dispute between Mr. Syed and the others especially Mr. Khuhro. There are two candidates K. B.Ghulam Mohammed Wassan, who according to Mr. Khuhro and others has 75 to 80% chances of success against Sayed Ghulam Hyder Shah who is the other candidate. Mr. Khuhro and others all support Wassan. Sayed Ghulam Hyder Shah is a favourite of Mr. Syed and Mr. Syed regards him as a protege of his and he is a pet of Mr. Syed. Sayed Ghulam Hyder Shah is a young man and is an LL.B. student. All the influential people, it appears, have given assurance to K. B. Wassan to support him."[22]

Although Syed had candidates against those favoured by Khuhro or Mir Ghulam Ali Talpur and other Muslim League leaders in at least four other constituencies, the decisive one as far as he was concerned was Tharparkar North. When the ticket for this one was awarded to Khuhro's man Wassan, and although Khuhro had gone as far as he could with Syed conceding whatever he considered was within reasonable limits,[23] the latter refused to accept this decision.

In fact the Central Board had gone a long way to accommodate Syed in the two districts and the difference were finally narrowed down to two seats, that of Rashdi versus Yusuf Haroon for the Central Legislature and of Ghulam Mohammed Wassan in Tharparkar North. The Central Legislature ticket was awarded to Haroon but as Rashdi himself put it:

"I was not too upset. I knew that the sticking point for Syed would be Hyder Shah and for Khuhro, Wassan. This would be the decisive encounter and that Khuhro would get the ticket for his man. This would give us the chance to get into the fight again. I sat in the outside room waiting while the meeting went on and sure enough Syed came out white with fury saying,` the ticket has been awarded to Wassan'. I immediately told him that that mattered not at all and was he not the President of the provincial Muslim League. He could award his own tickets."[24]

The final list of tickets was announced at a public meeting where G. M. Syed and his supporters were not present.

Rashdi knew his man and Syed, the most stubborn of men, liked the idea of issuing his own list of candidates. That evening Rashdi and Nihchaldas Vazirani met at Syed's house opposite Patel Park and drafted a statement for him to issue to the press. Syed summoned an urgent meeting of his Council to consider the situation after the selection of the candidates by the Central Parliamentary Board. Liaquat Ali Khan advised Syed strongly to reconsider his actions and either accept the majority view of the provincial board or accept the Central Board's decision but Syed refused to accept this advice and says of the Central Board's attitude: "... they directed their fury at me and held me personally responsible for this direct contravention of their authority."[25]

On his return to Karachi Jinnah summoned Syed for a meeting to thrash out the problem. Jinnah reminded Syed that they were facing a serious situation just before an election which could be decisive for the fate of Muslims in India and that personal feelings would have to be put aside to work for a common goal. Jinnah knew the elections in Sind were crucial for Muslim League's position in a situation where he could still not be sure of Punjab and Bengal. Jinnah also emphasised that the Central Parliamentary Board was empowered to override the decisions of the Provincial Parliamentary Board. Jinnah reminded him that a good proportion of the tickets had been allocated to his nominees in the two districts but Syed was adamant:

"This was not just a parting of ways, but the prelude to a full-fledged tussle that was to became inevitable."[26]

Syed resigned from the Muslim League Working Committee and announced his own list of candidates who would stand as members of the 'Sind Muslim League'. He also proposed to reconstitute the Working Committee of the Provincial Muslim League. A number of his followers including Ghulam Nabi Pathan parted with Syed at this point and stayed with the official Muslim League, Pathan continuing as General Secretary. Syed got advice from Muslims all over India to sacrifice his personal feelings and remain within the League discipline but was not persuaded.

For Khuhro this was a difficult situation. During his trial Syed had made genuine gestures of reconciliation and had stood by him. Khuhro and Syed were long time political associates, usually on the same side although there was a vast difference in their mental outlook. Khuhro had a clear agenda, was steady in his political behaviour, believing in justice and the rule of law and was convinced about preserving the best aspects of traditional society. Syed on the other hand was a self proclaimed idealist who appeared to be able to reconcile several contradictory ideas: a deep attachment to the traditions of Sayed fraternity and a belief in their innate superiority at one extreme and at the other his belief in and flirtation with socialist ideas and dreams of revolutionary programmes. He saw his fellow Sayeds in the vanguard of the progressive agenda even though most of them were steeped in the deepest conservatism.

Syed was deeply emotional and an extremist. For many years Jinnah was his hero and ideal. He wept openly when he heard of an attempt on his life and was willing to do anything for him. But when he broke with Jinnah his hero became for him the worst enemy and a despicable character. Those who knew and understood Syed's character, like Rashdi for instance, could play expertly on his sentiments and get whatever tune they wanted from him. Khuhro regarded Syed as a political disaster, his so-called 'progressivism' a thin veneer. Here was a man with strong prejudices and an impossible and impractical idealism which he used as a Damocles' sword for successive governments. But Khuhro loved and respected him as a friend perhaps far more sincerely than that sentiment was reciprocated.[27] Long time neighbours with close social and political associations that they had, Khuhro did not want to break with Syed. As far as possible he wanted to accommodate Syed in giving out tickets except in cases when to agree with him would obviously be a disservice to the Muslim League cause. Syed however decided that he would rather give up the party than his candidates.

Syed issued his list of candidates but continued to be President of Provincial Muslim League. The elections for the Central Legislature were due to take place in November 1945 and the Muslim League candidate was Yusuf Haroon. Syed was however openly supporting Rashdi and touring Sind to canvass for him. He did not make any public statement of support for the Muslim League candidate and it was reported to Jinnah in letters from the public that:

"The Syed party... are eagerly working for Pir Ali Mohammed Rashdi carrying on false propaganda against Muslim League and Khan Bahadur Khuhro, whom we trust as the only unselfish and enthusiastic Leader of the Muslim community in Sind."[28]

Khuhro made a concerted effort to awaken Syed to his responsiblities as President of the Party. Writing to him on the 16 November with less than ten days left for the election he urged Syed strongly to support the League candidate:

"You know that the prestige of the Muslim League in Sind is at stake in the election to the Central Legislative Assembly for which the Muslim League ticket has been allotted to Mr. Yusuf Abdoola Haroon. I have observed that so far there has been no official statement issued by you as the President of the Provincial Muslim League calling upon the Muslims of Sind to support the League nominee Mr.Yusuf Haroon. You are well aware that the contest between Mr.Yusuf A. Haroon and Mr.Rashdi who is standing in defiance of the decision of the Central Parliamentary Board is very keen. The success of the Muslim League candidates in Provincial Assembly Elections depends largely upon the result of this particular election.

It is therefore your moral as well as official duty to strain every bit of your energy for the success of Mr. Yusuf Haroon. I have done my best for the success of Mr. Yusuf by touring along with him and separately in all parts of Sind and by meeting the voters and influential persons in each district and calling upon them to support the League nominee, *Mr. Yusuf A. Haroon*. It is also expected that you and your friends and prominent Leaguers in Sind should do likewise.

Surely as the President of the League organisation in Sind, our organisation expects from you the same support to the League nominee. There is hardly a fortnight between now and the polling day.

I therefore request you to devote your entire attention from now on to the electioneering work of the League nominee for the Central Assembly. Let it not be said that we failed in our duty at a time when the Muslim League High Command expected us to be up and doing. I also pray issue a public staement as quickly as possible supporting Yusuf Haroon and calling upon others to do the same.

I hope this personal appeal to you as the President of the Sind Provincial Muslim League will not go unheeded and you will please let me know early what steps you are taking to help the organisation of this election."[29]

The election results were declared on 4 December and Haroon won the seat from Sind. All the Muslim seats in the Central Legislature were won by Muslim League immensely strenthening its position as the genuine representative of the Muslims of India. The provincial elections were due to take place in early January and the position was very difficult for Muslim League in Sind with its President openly at war with the official candidates causing extreme confusion in the rank and file. The major burden of electioneering was carried by Khuhro who had to be everywhere and provide counsel and comfort to the workers and office bearers alike, in the whole of Sind. Khuhro kept Jinnah informed of the course of the campaign and the difficulties in the different constituencies. His communications were always positive, putting forward problems which needed Jinnah's help and suggesting ways which could help the course of the campaign, whether it was getting the help of some Pir or that of Khan of Kalat in influencing voters.[30]

Eventually on 20 December the Central Parliamentary Board withdrew the League tickets from Syed's candidates. A week later Syed resigned from the All India Muslim League and announced his decision to fight the election on a separate platform of Sind Muslim League. He issued a long and bitter statement calling the Muslim League leadership reactionary and accusing it of helping vested interests:

"When they are questioned if it is for men like Sir Ghulam Hussain that we are asked to secure Pakistan, we are snubbed..." and that Muslim League policies were being controlled by Muslims of minority Muslim provinces and against the interests of the Muslims of the majority provinces and were essentially against the interests of the masses: "in Congress there was some hope; in the League there is none."[31]

Syed put up 11 candidates and forged an alliance with Congress which also supported him hoping to break the appeal of Muslim League. Congress was rumoured to have sent large sums of money to support the opponents of Muslim League and it certainly sent some of its biggest guns to gain support. Jawaharlal Nehru and Sarojini Naidu for example toured Sind. Congress hoped to win all the 22 Hindu and General seats. At the same time all the anti League groups came together to oppose it. A Muslim Board was formed with Maulvi Mohammed Sadiq (of the Khadda Madressah in Karachi) and the 'Baluchistan Gandhi' Abdus Samad Achakzai which put up 15 candidates. Maulvis of Jamaat-i-Ulemai Hind as well as others came in their numbers from other provinces to preach against Muslim League. They were joined by Khaksars of Allama Mashriqi and other 'Nationalist' Muslims to 'bury Pakistan in Sind'. With one hand tied behind its back in the person of a hostile President, a divided Working Committee as well as an organisation split down the middle, League fought back largely in the person of Khuhro. The only certain seats were in some pocket constituencies.

Finally on 2 January the Central Committee of Action having "carefully considered the statement dated 26 December issued to the Press by G. M. Syed ..." decided to remove Syed from the Presidentship of Muslim League and expelled him from the party. Gazdar, the Vice President was made Acting President and "in view of the fact that elections to the Provincial Legislature are in full swing," a Committee was appointed with a few prominent Leaguers "to take immediate charge of the election work in the province."[32]

Khuhro now officially in charge of the campaign, and himself elected unopposed in Larkana East, was free to work for the Muslim League candidates throughout Sind. Without the damaging friction and divided loyalties hampering his every step, the campaign went much better. He however refused to go into Syed's constituency to work against him. Khuhro was mindful of the personal relationship and political association which went back nearly two decades and also the fact that unlike most other fellow Muslim politicians, Syed had had the courage to acknowledge his mistakes and stand with him in the murder trial. Khuhro therefore declined requests which came even from the 'High Command' to campaign against Syed.

The results came in by the middle of the month with Muslim League winning 28 out of 35 Muslim seats, the best ever result for the Party and a brilliant victory. Syed won just four seats including his own and there were three independent Muslims some of whom could be expected to join Muslim League as it was likely to form the government. Congress won all the Hindu seats and with four others had 22 members in the Assembly. Congress and the Syed group immediately formed an alliance so in spite of the good showing of Muslim League in the elections, its position in the Legislature as the majority party was not secure.

An alliance or 'Coalition' as it was called, was formed between the Syed group, Independent Muslims and Congress. Syed and his group would continue to style themselves as the advance wing of the League and have Pakistan as their ideal but with certain conditions, mainly that there was a separate existence of 'Nationalist' Muslims outside Muslim League who stood for a joint struggle with Congress. It would also introduce the joint electorate system in the local bodies elections. The 'Coalition,' "would carry out the constructive programme of the Congress as enunciated in its manifesto."[33]

Both Azad and Patel came to Sind to try and get the 'Coalition' to form the government which appeared quite feasible as there was a very narrow margin between it and the League and in view of past experience the new alliance could expect to wean away some of the League members. The final position was Muslim League with 28 members, the Coalition also with 28 and four neutral members including 3 Europeans. One of the Independent Muslims came over to Muslim League but it was only with the support of the Governor who brought his considerable weight over to the side of Muslim League that the Muslim League Ministry could eventually be formed.

The new Governor, Sir Francis Mudie, who had taken over on 15 January, was very supportive of Muslim League though if this was his own predilection or instructions from above was not clear. He tried to persuade Syed to reconcile with Muslim League but without success. Muslim League itself was in a dilemma about the leadership of its Parliamentary Party. Of the six member Committee nominated by the Central Parliamentary Board to run the election campaign, Khuhro was the only one with influence in the whole of the province. Three members, Haroon, Gazdar and Alavi were confined to Karachi, Pathan had till the last moment been with Syed and Mir Ghulam Ali was limited to the Talpur circle so it was Khuhro who had run the entire election throughout the province.

The tradition in Sind was that the leader of the Parliamentary Party was elected and the majority of the elected members supported Khuhro for Premiership. Khuhro himself felt that he had earned the right to the job. He had stood aside once if not twice in the past in the interests of the Party. This time the successful election for Muslim League would have been difficult, to say the least, without his efforts. He felt that he had the programme which he could put through as Premier and win Sind for Muslim League at a forthcoming election on the basis of that record.[34]

But Jinnah was well aware of the fickle nature of most of the Muslim members particularly Hidayetullah. The elected Muslim Leaguers gave their support in writing for Khuhro but even so Jinnah asked him to stand aside as otherwise Hidayetullah might leave the Party. He was promised that when the situation was not so critical he would be given the Premiership. Khuhro had to be content with this assurance although he had offers from the Coalition. It was difficult to imagine any other member of the Assembly turning down these offers, but Khuhro would not betray his party – a fact well understood by Jinnah.

The Governor called Hidayetullah to form the Muslim League government which was only possible with the support of the European members who were instructed by the Governor to do so. Apart from the Premier there were three Ministers with Khuhro as the Senior Minister in charge of Public Works and Revenue. Two seats were kept vacant for Hindu Ministers as had been customary in Sind governments hitherto. This time however all the Hindu members were under Congress discipline so although the Premier tried hard to get some Hindus to come in he could not succeed. In fact the Coalition Party was quick to move a No Confidence motion against the Government as soon as the Budget session started. The Ministry was very precarious with just a majority of one and the Muslim members, as was their wont, used this fact to blackmail the government.

Realising that it would be difficult to keep the support of the members if they were offered jobs by the other side Khuhro and Hidayetullah tried to pre-empt any blackmail by trying to get an understanding with the Muslim partners of the Coalition. Syed went to see the Premier and offered to come to an understanding with the Muslim League leadership. Both Hidayetullah as Leader and Khuhro as Deputy Leader of the Parliamentary party sent a telegram to Jinnah advising some compromise. They gave their opinion that it was in the interests of the party and the province that the expulsion order against Syed be removed and he and his friends be re-admitted to Muslim League:

"Syed and followers willing join League provided ban removed. Situation demands their entry. Muslim public also anxious settlement. Kindly wire approval."[35]

The answer from both Jinnah and Liaquat Ali was that the ban could not be removed unless Syed "surrendered unconditionally" and "express regret for defying League discipline and decision, assure complete loyalty in future. Only then question of removal of ban can be considered." – a condition which had no chance of being fulfilled.

The No Confidence motion was defeated by 30 to 29 votes but the narrow vote gave a chance to the opportunists. Just before the end of the session Mir Bandeh Ali announced his revolt. He told the Governor that he was crossing the floor. Khuhro comments,

"I went to see him in his flat on Bonus Road where I found N. A. Faruqui, the I. C. S. officer, trying to persuade him not to cross the floor. He would not budge however and the next day he was sworn in as Minister."[36] Seeing the success of this maneouvre, another member elected on the Muslim League ticket, Pirzada Abdul Sattar next threatened to cross the floor. Khuhro relates the incident: "The Governor asked me to persuade him not to do so and that he would be made Minister after the Budget session. I went to see him at his house but he flatly refused. I took him to the Governor who told him also to wait until after the Budget session but he refused the Governor also and was then sworn in. The notification was withheld until after the Budget which was passed the next day."[37]

The Budget was finally passed and the Ministry could now get down to business. In the new reshuffled cabinet Hidayetullah was anxious to keep Khuhro as powerless as he possibly could. He did not want him to have Revenue, the portfolio that he was particularly keen on as he wanted to introduce some reforms. Mudie informed the Viceroy of the problems in distributing the portfolios:

"Khuhro was the main difficulty. When we had four ministers, he had both PWD and Revenue portfolios. I wanted him to keep PWD as he has got drive and ability and the scheme for the Lower Sind Barrage wants a lot of pushing. Khuhro wanted Revenue. The reason he gave was that he is interested in Agricultural credit, which is true, and he wanted to introduce certain bills in the next session of the Assembly. Ghulam Hussain on the other hand did not want Khuhro to have Revenue as he said it gave him too much power. In the end I left PWD with Khuhro, Revenue to Pir Illahi Baksh, Land and Agriculture to Bandeh Ali, Public Health and Education and Local Self Government to Abdul Sattar -"[38]

Khuhro however did not allow such a minor matter as not having the portfolio to stand in his way. He felt that the planned legislation for the welfare of the agriculturists should go through in the Muslim League Ministry, Mudie reported:

"The Ministry particularly Khuhro are very keen to introduce Bills dealing with rural credit at the next meeting of the Assembly and we had the first meeting of the Cabinet on this subject yesterday."

Mudie also showed how intolerant and unfair the attitude of Dow had been on the question of the Land Alienation Bill on which he had such battles with Khuhro and for which, when it had been passed, he had eventually refused assent:

"Your Excellency will remember that the Assembly passed a Bill restricting the transfer of agricultural land from the agriculturist to non-agriculturists. Dow however refused assent. I am not sure that I would have done so as the Sind Bill was far less communal than the Punjab Alienation of Land Act, though the principle involved in it is the same. I told the Ministers that Dow having refused assent, I could not give it to another Bill based on the same principle i.e., dividing the population into agriculturists and non-agriculturists."

Khuhro, keen on getting his legislation, discussed the issue with Mudie and a compromise solution was worked out:

"The Committee of the Cabinet has now agreed to a Bill drawn up something on the lines of a Bill passed by Congress Government in the U.P. It will still ofcourse be controversial because the moneylending interest is strong and the object of the Bill is to prevent the moneylender getting the zamindar or cultivator in his power by overlending or charging too high an interest. But it should go through."[39]

For Khuhro life was not easy in the Cabinet. He was keen to use his power as Deputy Leader and Senior Minister to push through legislation and gain the long time objectives, not only of easing the situation of the agriculturist but also getting a fair share of services for Muslims. But Hidayetullah, afraid that Khuhro was out for his job, was busy hindering any action Khuhro wanted to take. Mudie noted the difficulties:

"There is a good deal of friction within the Cabinet. Sir Ghulam has been ill with flu and is not quite right again. Even when well he is really past hard work. He has difficulty in keeping his team together and, in particular, in managing Khuhro who is itching to step into his shoes, as he probably will do sooner or later."[40]

There was a difference of opinion between the two on the matter of promotion for Muslims on a quota basis. Khuhro argued that Muslims were almost unrepresented at the higher levels and it needed extraordinary measures to get them there. In this he was able to get the support of all the Ministers except one. Hidayetullah who knew he might have to rely on the Hindu vote to retain his Premiership vehemently opposed the idea:

"Now all Ministers except Sir Ghulam, have demanded that the ratio be applied to promotion... It is not ofcourse that the Ministers don't recognize the objections to applying the communal ratio to promotions. It is simply that first and foremost they want a Muslim Raj with most of the high officials Muslims. Things like efficiency come later. Any argument that what they want would be unfair to the Hindus in the services is countered by the argument that the present position in which the great majority of the higher officials are non-Muslims is unfair to the Muslims in a Muslim province."[41]

The long struggle to get adequate representation for Sindhi Muslims had resulted in great sensitivity among Sindhis regarding the issue of locals and outsiders. When the Government of India wanted to induct ex-servicemen in the civilian departments claiming that it was a step to further Indianize the services, the Sind Ministers strongly objected:

"... regarding recruitment of war service candidates... Various arguments were put up, but the real thing was that the Ministers didn't want non Sindhis – they could not tell me the name of a single Sindhi commissioned officer. I tried to get them to agree to examine the list of candidates to see whether there were any that might be suitable for the Service that we are contemplating to replace the I. C. S., recruiting to which I presume is ended, except possible for the war service candidates. I got a little support from Khuhro but was strongly opposed by Ghulam who called Khuhro a communalist, which is true, but, on this occasion unjustified."[42]

In fact, inspite of his reputation for promoting the fortunes of Sindhi Muslims and his work for autonomy, Khuhro was very far from being a communalist. The driving force, the motivation, in his life had been a strong sense of fair play which he exercised as much in favour of Hindus as Muslims. The Hindu officers were quite aware of this and the Khuhros relations with Hindu politicians, business men or officials were always excellent. It was the fear that he would be difficult if not impossible to manipulate that had kept the Hindu politicians strongly opposed to Khuhro becoming Premier, an opposition which more than any other factor had been responsible for excluding him at least in 1940. On his part Khuhro had never played along with the bureaucracy just because it was powerful. He had never hesitated to oppose it, at some cost, if it meant fighting against what he considered gross unfairness. The feeling was strong in the Muslim population of Sind that it was high time that their rights were considered. It was already ten years since autonomy and the political consciousness of the people had grown considerably.

The fundamental constitutional problem as far as Khuhro was concerned was the problem of 'weightage' which deprived the Muslim majority of its effectiveness. The majority was artificially reduced and in a House of 60, Muslims had only 35 members in spite of an approximately 75% population ratio. The result had plagued Assemblies throughout the period of autonomy. With such a narrow difference any member could blackmail the government to get favours in return for his vote. With a more secure majority obviously this kind of blackmail would have been much more difficult. The position had been made much worse with the split in the party. With the results of the elections in, Khuhro had immediately realised the implications and had publicly stated as early as February that 'weightage' should be abolished. Apart from Sind, the majority provinces of Bengal and Punjab also suffered from this provision. The experience of ten years of an autonomy limited by the Draconian powers of the Governor, had made the public aware that unless there was real power with the Assembly, not subject to the Governor's veto, effective reforms could not be introduced and the electorate was becoming disillusioned with democracy. There was therefore the widespread feeling among Sindhi leaders that Sind should gain a much larger amount of autonomy as soon as possible and that the elected Assembly should truly reflect the composition of the population. This idea was ofcourse not far removed from the proposals of the Lahore Resolution and the Sindhi leadership in Muslim League felt it was foregone conclusion in the light of the League programme that they were fighting for complete autonomy after independence, for a federation of "constituent units which were autonomous and sovereign".

The climate of opinion in India in the spring and summer of 1946 was conducive to the thoughts of the politicians turning to and concentrating on fundamental constitutional issues. And for Muslim League in particular their election triumph of earlier that year had made them feel more confident. The party carried all the Muslim seats of the Central Assembly and out of 495 provincial Muslim seats under the separate electorate system Muslim League got an impressive 446, wiping out the Unionists in the Punjab and gaining a majority of Muslim seats in all the provinces except the North West Frontier Province.

The Labour government in Britain was felt to be sympathetic to the Congress and also, unlike Churchill, was ready to give independence to India and was preparing the way for the devolution of power. On the 19 February there was a naval mutiny in Bombay followed by one in Karachi. About two hundred people were killed in the rioting and demonstrations but the uprising was not backed by the political parties particularly the Congress Party. Patel advised the mutineers to surrender with the result that it soon fizzled out. But it was a further reminder to the British that dismantling their hold on India was more than ever essential.

On the same day as the outbreak of the naval mutiny, 19 February, the British Government announced that a Cabinet Mission would come to India to assess the political situation and work out the ways and means to give it independence. Lord Wavell had already proposed that an Executive Council, with representation from all the main parties in India be set up and that a preliminary conference should be convened to decide on how the constitution making body should be formed. However by the time Wavell was ready to put this plan into action the British Cabinet was already taking charge itself and had nominated the Cabinet Mission.

The most dominating personality among the three Ministers in the Mission was that of Sir Stafford Cripps, the austere socialist pundit who felt he was something of a specialist on India and who had already come out with the Cripps Proposals in the middle of the war. Although Pethick Lawrence was the Secretary of State for India, it was Cripps who actually made Government policy on India and now dominated the Mission. The third member of the Mission was A.V. Alexander. Its task was to try to bring the leaders of the principal Indian political parties to agreement on the two issues: first, framing the constitution for the self government of India and secondly, to set up a new Executive Council or Interim Government. Although the Congress and Muslim League's proclaimed objectives were contradictory, it was hoped that working together would help them to come to a solution which could save the unity of India.

The Cabinet Mission spent two weeks in India and held discussions with a wide spectrum of people. As Deputy Premier of Sind and member of the Muslim League Working Committee Khuhro was ofcourse interviewed by the Mission. He recalled that during the interview all three members, Lord Pethick Lawrence, Cripps and Alexander were present and the discussion centred round the viability of Pakistan of which Sind was to be a vital ingredient, as well as alternate proposals which would be acceptable to the Muslims.[43]

At the end of the Mission's intense and widely varied discussions no consensus could be reached so the Mission decided to put forward its own proposals for the consideration of the Indian politicians. Their main proposal was that there should be a loose federation with a three tier constitution. The three tiers were to be the existing provinces at the bottom and that these provinces would then form three groups at the second tier. At the third tier there would be an All India Union. The Union was to have three subjects, Foreign Affairs, Defence and Communications. It would have powers to raise finances for these subjects. All the other subjects were to remain with the provinces.

A conference was called at Simla to consider the proposals but failed to reach agreement. Congress did not like the idea of provinces grouping together at the second tier. Jinnah wanted a weak Centre which would not have any power to raise taxes and was holding the Pakistan card in reserve. Congress was not prepared to accept such a weak Centre. Nehru, a doctrinaire socialist saw an independent India as a field for his socialist experiments, centralized planning and Five-Year Plans. His vision of India precluded strong provinces and a dependent Centre.

Still without a consensus from the Indian parties the Mission issued a Statement on 16 May laying out its proposals which purported to be a compromise between a full sovereign Pakistan and the Congress demand for a strong Centre.

The Statement proposed the three tier solution which it had come up with earlier. They proposed a Constituent Assembly to work out the details which was to be elected by members of the Provincial legislatures. This would divide into three sections representing the three groupings of the provinces which the Mission had decided on. There were the six Hindu majority provinces, the three Muslim provinces of Punjab, Sind and N.W.F.P., and the two Muslim majority provinces of Assam and Bengal. These groupings were very favourable to a Muslim minority in India but were an obvious source of dissatisfaction to Congress.

The Statement fell far short of what the Muslim League rank and file had been led to expect. Even so the Muslim League High Command formally accepted the proposals and did so by saying this was the 'first step on the road to Pakistan.' Confused by what they considered a serious climb down by Jinnah and the 'High Command' was subjected to a great deal of questioning from the rank and file.

Jinnah was inundated with telegrams asking what was actually happening. But in Sind there was relief that a solution had been found which would concede as much as the Muslim majority provinces could hope for. The Statement appeared to be the best solution given the situation which had deteriorated considerably since the late 'thirties and certainly since 1942 when the Cripps proposals had been made. But it did not appear that the Indian political leaders had the wisdom or the foresight to give and take, to suffer some loss of face for the sake of the future of the subcontinent.

The unyielding and rigid attitude of Congress was clear from the remarks of Vallabhai Patel in a letter to Vazirani. Declaring that 'we will hear no more of that mischievous cry of Pakistan' he also ruled out 'grouping'of the provinces: "I feel certain that the Muslims of Sind as a whole will not like to be ruled by Punjab and have a capital in Delhi for the Union and one at Lahore for the Group... The Cabinet Delegation cannot and should not coerce any province to go into a group against its own will, although it has freedom to opt out later."[44]

Khuhro had been elected to the proposed Constituent Assembly, by the Sind Legislative Assembly as one of the three Sind representatives, for 'framing a new constitution for India'.[45] Well aware that most constitutions could be worked if the will was there, he found himself greeting the 16 May Statement with relief. He knew that the Mission's proposals particularly for the three provincial groupings, with their two to one Muslim majority in the two groups, should be firmly supported, since Congress would be certain to sabotage any arrangement which they saw as disadvantageous to the Hindu majority. On 4 June Wavell gave his personal assurance to Jinnah on behalf of the Cabinet Mission that

"we do not propose to make any discrimination in the treatment of either party; and that we shall go ahead with the plan laid down in the Statement as far as circumstances permit if either party accepts; but we hope both will accept."

Khuhro who spent most of June in Delhi, on call for Working Committee meetings, was hoping that Jinnah would accept the offer and in private meetings urged as much.

The Muslim League Council met on 6 June in Delhi and formally accepted the Statement, at the same time expressing the hope that it would eventually lead to Pakistan. In fact this was the first public admission by Muslim League and Jinnah that they would accept something less than Pakistan. Congress however continued to delay its acceptance. In the absence of this acceptance the Viceroy announced the Ministers he would take into his Cabinet. These included six Congress Hindus, five Muslim Leaguers and one each from the Sikh, Parsi and Indian Christian communities. Muslim League thus did not get its demand for parity. The announcement also said that in the event of either of the two main parties not coming into the Coalition the Viceroy would go ahead and form the government with the parties that had accepted. At this point when it looked as if the formation of the Interim Government would go ahead, Congress accepted the Statement of 16 May but refused to enter the Interim Government. The Mission then decided that if Congress would not enter the Coalition it would not be formed and that negotiations for it must begin again, a clear violation of the announcement that even if one major party refused to come in the Coalition arrangements would stand. The Mission declared that in a short time elections to the Constituent Assembly would be held and the Viceroy would make fresh efforts to bring an Interim Government into being. Muslim League felt utterly betrayed.

Jinnah was well aware that there were informal contacts between the Congress leaders and the British government both at home and with Cripps in India, but was helpless to do anything.[46] Congress had by far the greater clout in sub-continental politics. This was not politics of principle but *realpolitik*, reflective of the two parties' relative position in the country. That the Congress leadership was more interested in gaining points rather than real agreement was a misfortune which could not be cured. Jinnah was certain that the Congress had not accepted the Statement in good faith and that there was a good deal of ambiguity and disingenuousness on their part. This was proved correct in a very short time.

The Mission left India on 28 June with the impression that they had at least got an agreement on the main constitutional points of the 16 May Statement but their hopes were soon to be belied. On 6 July, just over a week after the Mission had left both Patel and Azad changed the ground rules of the Statement. They said that provinces must be free to decide from the very start whether or not to join the grouping that had been laid down by the Statement. Then on 10 July, Nehru now President of All India Congress went still further saying Congress had only agreed to go into the Constituent Assembly and nothing further, and later at a press conference he said:

"What we do there [in the Constituent Assembly] we are entirely and absolutely free to determine. We have committed ourselves on no single matter to anybody."[47]

With regard to the grouping clause he remarked that there would probably be no grouping at all.

Though for the discerning observer the resiling of the Congress from its previous position could not come as too much of a surprise the proposed provincial groupings would mean that two of the three sub-federations would be Muslim dominated in a sub-continent where three quarters of the population was Hindu, it was at least something of a betrayal of its avowed secular position and a retraction of its given word. This repudiation of proposals so painstakingly arrived at and their acceptance by parties received with so much relief, sent shock waves through the country not only among the Muslims but other minorities and the Indian States. Fears of a Congress totalitarian *raj* swept the Muslim population and their faith in the power of the British to impose a fair settlement was deeply shaken. On 25 July the Muslim League Working Committee met at Bombay and on 29 July the Muslim League Council meeting passed a resolution withdrawing its own acceptance of the Statement of 16 May and announced that it would resort to 'Direct Action as and when necessary' to force acceptance of the Pakistan demand.

Wavell realised that this return to the demand for Pakistan was a weapon to secure better terms for Muslims and intimated as much to the Secretary of State but Muslim League was up against Congress leaders who lacked foresight and generosity and only understood hard bargains. They were ready to use the steam roller of the majority community to deny the assurances of security that the minority communities so desperately wanted. Congress now certain that the British had no desire or will to stay on and that Lord Wavell was on the way out, felt that it was in a strong position to enforce its own terms and that no concessions need be made to Muslim League. This was the attitude of Nehru in 1937 on the morrow of the election results and this again was the attitude of the Congress now that he was President of Congress.

On the 6 August Nehru was invited to form the Interim Government. The Congress Working Committee accepted the offer. Nehru invited Jinnah to join the government but with so little on offer as compared to the Cabinet Mission proposals he had little option except to refuse. In marked contrast to the attitude displayed to Congress, the Viceroy went ahead with the plans to induct a Cabinet under Nehru even without Muslim League participation. Although Muslim League had been offered five seats in the Cabinet in the previous arrangement and Wavell wanted to continue that precedent, Nehru agreed to only three Muslim seats one of which was given to a 'Nationalist' Muslim and two left in reserve for Muslim League. On 2 September the new Cabinet took office including members of minorities except for Muslim League.

For Muslim League the situation had deteriorated even further. While negotiations were going on about League's participation in the Government disaster occurred from another direction. It had been decided by the Party to observe 16 August as 'Direct Action Day' as a form of protest. But although Jinnah had urged the Muslims to stay calm and use the day for 'peaceful reflection' the outcome of the day, as Gandhi had found on many previous occasions, could not be predicted or controlled. In Bengal the Muslim League Premier, H. S. Suhrawardy declared a public holiday. Early in the morning the riots started with looting, arson and murder and continued for four days resulting in 5,000 killed, 15,000 injured and over 100,000 homeless. Among those killed, wounded and rendered homeless were both Hindus and Muslims although the latter were reported to have started the trouble. The 'goondas' and criminals were largely active and the blame for the riots was laid at the door of the Muslim League Premier, Suhrawardy... "undoubtedly too much latitude was given to the rioters on the first day and there was an unaccountable delay in calling in the troops and imposing a curfew."[48]

The Bengal riots and killings were to set a deadly precedent, with an immense loss of goodwill which would make reconciliation impossible and would cost India its unity. Bihar was to follow Bengal with riots in which thousands of Muslims were killed and made homeless and so the events spiralled out of control. Above all with this outbreak the moral position of Muslim League was greatly weakened and Congress got an opportunity to crack the whip. Patel's comments summed up this situation:

"The Muslim League tried its programme of direct action in Calcutta and to their great bewilderment they have found out that two can play at the game although it may be started by one. The poor Muslims in Calcutta have suffered terribly and the League discredited itself by their doings in Calcutta. If they follow the same method of arson, loot, murder and anarchy, they may be able to inflict hardship on the non-Muslims but eventually that way will without doubt lead the League organisation to ruin and destruction.[49]

Although Wavell tried to persuade Congress to soften the terms regarding the grouping of the provinces and keep them as proposed by the Cabinet Mission and agreed by Muslim League, he could not succeed. Congress insisted on its own terms which meant that there were no assurances regarding the provinces meeting in sections or groupings. The Congress position was that each province had the right to decide whether to join a group or not and they were supported by the powerful Sikh community of the Punjab which did not want to be stranded in a 'Pakistan'. Wavell went so far as to threaten that he would not call the Constituent Assembly but he was not backed by the British Government. It was clear that Congress had no intention of working the Cabinet Mission Plan as it was but to put its own interpretation on it. Muslim League had no options left now. Its bluff of 'direct action as and when necessary' had been called and now it was left with no cards to play. Informed Muslim opinion was extremely anxious that events were passing them by and that the constitution for a free India might come without Muslim League participation. In Simla on a visit to the summer capital in connection with the Sind–Punjab water dispute, Khuhro, an unrelenting realist, who could see the ground slipping away from Muslim League, sent a telegram to Jinnah urging acceptance of the terms:

"In view of the Viceroy's conciliatory statement giving definite assurances regarding strict adherence to proposals of 16th May and particularly provinicial and group constitutions and no decision possible on any major communal issue unless majority Muslim members agree and also giving reasonable assurances regarding functioning and personnel of Interim Government – I earnestly request you summon Working Commitee at Delhi early date to review latest political situation and consider whether modification of Bombay decision desirable. Yourself may further clarify doubtful points with Viceroy at Delhi."[50]

He followed up the telegram by writing to Jinnah on 26 August, expressing his anxiety about not missing the opportunity and urging Jinnah to get into the government and the Constituent Assembly so that Muslims would be part of the constitution making process and to disregard the short term vexations in order to gain long term objectives:

"My dear Quaid-e-Azam,

I have this day sent you a telegram, copy of which I enclose herewith confirming it. I do hope you will kindly come over to Delhi and review the entire situation and get in touch with H.E. the Viceroy. It will be a good thing if you could kindly convene a meeting of the Working Committee at Delhi, as soon as it maybe convenient to you. I am only anxious, as many others are, that our case may not go by default.

Hindus may, in our absence, frame the Constitution of their own liking and it will be difficult for us later on to get it changed.

I am here in connection with the Sind – Punjab water dispute and I hope to go back to Karachi on Thursday or Friday at the latest."[51]

Nehru had sworn in his coalition government on 2 September and lacking assurances Jinnah had refused to go in at that point. But Wavell once again made an effort to get Muslim League to join, a development to which Khuhro was referring in his telegram and letter. It was obvious that if Muslim League did not take this opportunity, it may be left out of the process of constitution making altogether. The British Government lacked the will to insist on the Mission proposals. Nehru was not keen on having Muslim League representatives in his government so the Viceroy's offer was the best Jinnah could expect at this point. So although he had not got parity or assurances on groupings the only way out for Jinnah was to come into the government on whatever terms were available. On 26 October Muslim League members took office as Ministers in the Interim Cabinet.

The announcement of names by Jinnah caused a good deal of surprise and heart burning in the top ranks of Muslim League. The choice of Liaquat Ali Khan was fairly obvious and Nishtar, who although not regarded as a front ranker, was from a majority Muslim province albeit one in which Congress was in power. But the nomination of Chundrigar who was not a front ranking Muslim League leader and little known in top Muslim League circles, caused a good deal of surprise. Also the name of Ghazanfar Ali Khan, whom Wavell characterized as 'a rather irresponsible sort of buccaneer' from the Punjab, did not spring immediately to mind as Central Cabinet material.

Khuhro was in Delhi in connection with the meeting of the Working Committee and recollected that Khwaja Nazimuddin, a leading Muslim Leaguer and ex Premier of Bengal, and Nawab Ismail Khan from U.P., were both shocked and disappointed not to be included. Khuhro and Daultana, the young Oxford educated recruit to Muslim League from the Punjab with his very beautiful and newly married wife, took both of them for a drive to the Qutb Minar for consolation.[52] Mudie, the Governor of Sind, had strongly recommended Khuhro to Jinnah as good Minister material for the Interim Government but Khuhro himself was not aware of this and quite undisturbed at not being one of the five. One Muslim League nomination was Jogendra Nath Mandal the scheduled caste member whose inclusion would definitely annoy Congress and indicated that genuine co-operation between the two major parties was still illusory.

The lack of calibre of the Muslim League nominees to the Interim Cabinet meant that 'Congress can always make dialectical rings round them and appear reasonable and moderate.'[53] But more seriously for the long term it also meant that they had to rely heavily on the Muslim members of the Central civil service who were thus able to acquire a great deal of influence over these politicians. Subsequently these members of the central bureaucracy of India would become extremely powerful in Pakistan some of them being taken up as Ministers of the Central Cabinet and who from their past had no commitment either to democracy or even perhaps to Pakistan and whose influence would work to the detriment of democracy in Pakistan.

The joining of the Interim Government by Muslim League was greeted with palpable relief by the people particularly the Muslims. The country was experiencing some of worst communal riots and killings at this time. The killings in Calcutta had been followed by killings in other districts of Bengal particularly Noakhali, in Bihar and in Bombay. The public hoped that the Coalition government would be able to handle the situation and bring about communal harmony. The efforts of the government and the fact that there was a Coalition partnership between the different communities did bring about peace for a while but its continuance depended on the ability of the Congress and Muslim League to reach a reasonable working arrangement for the time being and a genuine understanding in the long run. The only way that Muslim League could strengthen its bargaining position was by consolidating its position in the Muslim majority provinces. At the moment Punjab had a Congress Unionist coalition, N.W.F.P had a Congress

Government, Bengal had a deeply troubled Muslim League government and Sind a shaky Muslim League government. Faced with this bleak scenario Jinnah had somehow to strengthen his position. At this moment Sind was utterly crucial to Muslim League strategy. The Muslim League position in Sind had to be secured at all costs as otherwise the field was wide open for the Congress.

****

It was clear to the observers of the scene that the Muslim League Ministry in Sind was very precarious indeed. It had survived the Budget session by giving in to blackmail by at least two aspirant Ministers and there was every prospect that any future session of the Assembly would bring more trouble. After a number of delays a session of the Assembly was called on 11 July to elect the Sind members for the Constituent Assembly. Even on this occasion there were two defections from the Muslim League parliamentary group and it was rumoured that three others were on the verge of deserting. With the Opposition now definitely in a majority it gave notice of a No Confidence motion which the Government would not be able to face. But the Governor came to the rescue by proroguing the Assembly on the grounds that the special session was only concerned with the election of the members for the Constituent Assembly and could not entertain any other business.

The Governor put off the Assembly for the month of Ramadan but had to summon it to consider the Supplementary Demands which he did for 5 September. The Ministry expected trouble which it got. There were a large number of members coveting Ministries and who could not possibly be accommodated. The Opposition could make promises to all the members who crossed over. When the Assembly reconvened on 5 September it was found that even with the support of the European members, the Government was short of one vote. The Speaker resigned to vote with the Government but when the Deputy Speaker, Ms. Jethi Sipahimalani, resigned as well to vote with the Opposition there was a complete deadlock as neither of the parties could afford to give up a member to preside over the House. With the rush of members, anxious for Ministerships, over to the Opposition, there was no hope of a stable government. Although there was a case for the Governor asking the Opposition to form a government it was probable the same game would have continued with that Ministry as well. With this state of affairs the Governor took permission from the Viceroy to dissolve the Assembly and go for another election.

The election due to be held in December 1946 was absolutely critical not only for Muslim League in Sind but for Muslim League strategy in the difficult and delicate negotiations which were taking place to decide the future of India. Congress was also fully aware of the importance of thwarting a decisive League victory in Sind. The split in Muslim League and the defection of the Syed group had been a stroke of luck for Congress who had nearly gained Sind. As a result if now Sind could be denied to Muslim League there would be no weapon left in the armoury of Jinnah and it would seal the fate of provincial groupings or 'Pakistan' or whatever else Jinnah wanted. Already Congress had spent money to get the No Confidence motion through but without the desired results.[54] Now with new elections no effort was to be spared to achieve the majority and defeat Muslim League.

With the prospect of a second election within the year the position for Muslim League had not changed in any significant way. The burden of elections would still have to borne by Khuhro, the only League leader with province wide influence and a mass following. The other 'names' of League leadership, Haroon, Gazdar and even Hatim Alavi, who had a prolific correspondence with Jinnah, were confined to Karachi or as the Premier Hidayetullah, to the limited, though powerful, circles of the Governor's court. So apart from the tribal and kinship seat of the Talpurs and some of the Sayeds, the responsibility lay on Khuhro's shoulders. Muslim League tickets were awarded to more or less the same people who had them in the last election. The Sind Parliamentary Board recommended tickets should not be awarded to those who were so ready to betray the party but Mir Bandehali had already been pardoned by Jinnah and in the end Syed Nur Mohammed Shah of Nawabshah was also awarded a ticket with the recommendation of Khuhro. Against G. M. Syed the candidate chosen by the Central Board was Kazi Mohammed Akbar.

The Central Parliamentary Board was relying heavily on Khuhro for advice regarding the distribution of tickets as well as the organization of elections. Yusuf Haroon had been nominated President of Muslim League and he was considered to be a loyal supporter of Khuhro. The situation was certainly not to the liking of Hidayetullah who was anxious to re-occupy the post of Premier and knew that Khuhro would be a serious rival for that position. Hidayetullah lost no opportunity to complain to Jinnah about Khuhro and to see that Khuhro did not get too close to him. This anxiety took some very petty forms as for instance when Jinnah had agreed to stay with Khuhro in Karachi during his visit in November 1946, Hidayetullah wrote to him complaining that Khuhro 'was hobnobbing with G. M. Syed and is opposing me. He is really an enemy of the League.' He asked Jinnah to stay with him and when Jinnah said that he had agreed to stay with Khuhro, offered him the old Governor's House for his stay to induce him to change his mind.

The elections were scheduled for 9 December and the results for Muslim League were expected to be better this time round as public feelings ran high in its support. But there was still the question of Syed and his followers whose coalition with the Congress had proved such a headache for the League Ministry. Jinnah asked the Sind leaders to see to it that Syed and his group should lose their elections and sent his troops in the shape of students of Aligarh university to make propaganda against Syed. Student workers and imported orators, however good and devoted could not be expected to obtain the desired result and once again it was the Governor and the bureaucracy under his control that was to make the crucial difference. Mudie asked the officials to see to it that certain key seats were won by Muslim League including that of Syed and Mohammed Ali Shah of Nawabshah. In this latter district the District Collector, a Punjabi I.C.S. officer Masud, created a legend in high-handedness, harassing the supporters of Mohammed Ali Shah, threatening to put them in jail as *'badmash'* and he "actually went and took statements of a few irresponsible men and got Abid Shah [a supporter of the candidate] arrested, handcuffed and taken through the bazar of Nawabshah with a rope round his waist."[55] Official pressure certainly won this seat for Muslim League and that for Hidayetullah's son in Thatta where Government interference was also quite blatant.[56]

Open interference also took place in the constituency of Syed himself, but it was doubtful if it could have succeeded outside a few seats and luckily for Muslim League it was able to make a very good showing on its own elsewhere. Jinnah had asked Khuhro to personally go into the constituency of Syed but Khuhro expressed his inability to do so. For Khuhro who had always gone along with Jinnah's wishes even when they went against his own judgement, this was a matter in which he felt strongly. Whatever Syed's differences with Muslim League and political differences with himself, Khuhro was not about to make himself part of a crusade against Syed who he felt had stood by him in his time of need. Jinnah had urged Khuhro in the election held earlier in 1946 that he should campaign against Syed in the latter's constituency but Khuhro had refused on the grounds of personal friendship. This time too, although Jinnah himself who had been in Karachi the last two weeks of November, had to be in London for discussions with the Cabinet, he specially sent Miss Fatima Jinnah twice to Khuhro's house with the message that he should go into Syed's constituency. But even under this pressure Khuhro excused himself. Khuhro firmly believed that his refusal to work against Syed had earned him Jinnah's annoyance which cost him the Premiership after the election.[57]

The election results favoured Muslim League overwhelmingly. It obtained 83.9% of the Muslim vote compared to the 60% vote it had got in the January election and won 34 out of 35 Muslim seats. Congress won 18 general Hindu seats making up to 21 with one woman, one Labour and one Commerce and Industries seat.* Khuhro was certain that in this new Assembly with its Muslim League majority, he would be able to get the Premiership and at the meeting of the Parliamentary party he got 25 out of 34 votes. But once again he was asked to stand down by Jinnah. Commenting on the situation Syed wrote:

"In the new League Assembly Party, K. B. Khuhro was a hot favourite for the Premier's post in the new government. He was backed by more than 25 members out of 35. But Mr. Jinnah who was at that time sojourning in Karachi, as a guest of Mir Bundehali Khan, saw to it personally that the old regime was reimposed on Sind. Shaikh Ghulam Hussain Hidayetullah, bereft of his title of Knighthood... but still the hero of many a battle, continued enjoying undisturbed the Premier's gadi basking under the patronage of the Governor and the blessings of the League President."[58]

Khuhro himself felt that this was quite unfair considering the number of times when sacrifice had been required he had stood down so that Hidayetullah who chose to blackmail Muslim League, should become Premier. He must have had some thoughts that by joining the Opposition with his close supporters, he could have the Premiership even at this stage. After all both the majority Muslim provinces of the Punjab and North West Frontier Province were not with Muslim League. But even if he had some stray thoughts Khuhro believed too strongly in his cause to betray it at this moment. Jinnah sugared the pill by promising that he would be the first Premier of a free Sind. Jinnah's decision about the Ministry was made on 3 January, delayed in order to allow the resentment at the decision to die down somewhat. Sind was the only province where he was in a position to nominate the

---

* The Election Results showed: Muslim League–34. Congress–19 (+1 Labour, 1 Commerce and Industry), European–3, Jamiat–2.

Ministers and he fully savoured the task. Khuhro was given the Public Works Department and the additional department of Post-War Development which would require a great deal of work, a sop to the disappointed Khuhro perhaps...

"Jinnah announced his decision about the Ministry on 3rd January. I do not know why he took so long, but probably he wanted to allow time for the excitement caused by Khuhro's attempt to supplant Ghulam Hussain to die down. The only departure that Jinnah made from the proposal which I gave him on the 21st was the allotment to Khuhro of `Development' in addition to P.W.D. He consulted me by phone before doing this. I think Khuhro will accept the position and not try to oust Ghulam Husain again, especially if he is allowed some scope as Minister for Development."[59]

Mudie detailed the other appointments in the Cabinet:

" 'Home' has now been given to Bandehali who is stupid but honest. The Karachi Daily described him as innocuous. I don't think that he'll cause any trouble. ...The great thing is to keep it [Home Department] away from Ghulam Ali [Talpur], who when he was Home Minister, acted in a completely arbitrary and illegal way... I also got the Medical and Education portfolios away from Pirzada Abdul Sattar, who is extremely idle. He has now got Revenue, where all the work is done by the Revenue Commissioner."[60]

Khuhro's temperament did not allow him to dwell on his grievances and he met the new challenges with his usual determination and energy. The work of the last Ministry remained incomplete and with the track record of the Ministries in the past Khuhro knew that speed was of the essence in getting things done. With the Development Ministry as well as Public Works, Khuhro had the crucial tasks not only of post-war development but also to present the Sind case for the waters of the Punjab rivers and Indus for which Sind as the lower riparian needed to have a hard bargainer. He could not expect however that the Sind Government under Hidayetullah would give the kind of backing that he would need in these difficult and delicate tasks. However never the one to shirk a job Khuhro brought up his plans in a Cabinet meeting as early as he could:

"I had a long Cabinet meeting on the 20th at which we got through a good deal of business, though I had to postpone one or two items on one excuse or another till the atmosphere might be more favourable. The majority of the Ministers seemed to think that certain proposals regarding the organising of Development work gave too much power to Khuhro who is Development Minister now. I think however, that I'll get them through in the end. It is important to keep Khuhro fully employed, as otherwise he may start intriguing against Ghulam Hussain again. Also he is extremely able and can get things done."[61]

The obstructionist attitude of his colleagues continued to hamper Khuhro throughout. Some of this hostility was undoubtedly due to the Premier's fear of being supplanted and of the feeling of jealousy for a more able colleague but it was also true that Khuhro invited hostility by his impatience of his fellow Ministers. He was apt to work on problems which strictly speaking were not his particular concern but where he felt action was necessary and overdue. There were complaints from Ministers that if he wanted certain matters dealt with he would expect the concerned Minister to put his signature to a Note drafted by himself. Some Ministers as for instance when Mir Bandehali, would go along but some of them resented what they considered an infringement of their territory and there were many enemies of Khuhro to play upon their resentment. Mudie, the most sympathetic Governor he was to work with in Sind, understood Khuhro better than most and had as early as October 1946 given his opinion to Wavell that Khuhro would be better away from the political infighting of Sind:

"... Khuhro is of a peculiar temperament, with very few personal friends ... I think it rather a pity that Jinnah did not select him for your Council. He is an excellent administrator and would have done well in Delhi removed from the intrigues and personalities of Sind."

The Centre could possibly have been an appropriate field for the exercise of his full talents, but Khuhro never sought a position in the Centre for himself and only held one Central Ministership, the last of his career. Khuhro saw his own role as Premier of Sind, in a position to be effective and to put through the agenda he had made for himself from his earliest time in politics. For the field he had chosen for himself, a province where to get full support he had to flatter and cajole and to cater to the egos of provincial politicians, Khuhro did not have the required gifts of diplomacy and guile. He was congenitally unable to flatter or be sycophantic, the lack of qualities which had served him ill both with Governors and with colleagues. He had an ill concealed contempt and impatience for his less able colleagues largely because of the fact that he knew very well that principles had very little to do with their politics and that they would sell the cause of Sindhi Muslims for a mess of potage or a ministership without hesitation. Time and again he had seen a government which could have done some good for the people voted out because some members, usually Muslims, had been bought with a ministership. Khuhro was unwilling to waste time on tact and diplomacy and compromise for legislation which could vitally affect the public good. He felt that he carried the burden for passing the legislation which would make a significant difference to the welfare of the people who he felt trusted him. He could not bring himself to pander to the sensitivities of colleagues who dragged their feet in the active pursuit of these objectives. Mudie remarked on this point:

"We had a cabinet meeting yesterday, marred by personality clashes. The feeling against Khuhro is very strong at present. He interferes too much in other Ministers' Departments. On the other hand, he is about the only one that can get things done. I quite like him but he is generally unpopular."[62]

The question of prohibition was brought up by the Minister in charge of Excise and Taxation but was strongly opposed by Khuhro who although a complete teetotaller himself considered Prohibition impractical and a loss to the government:

"Our new Minister... signalized his appointment by announcing that his policy was prohibition. But I hope to put a stopper on that. Both Ghulam Hussain and Khuhro are strongly opposed to prohibition, the former on principle and the latter on practical grounds."[63]

But apart from these diversions there was serious matters to attend to. The Government brought in the Sind University Bill in April. Although it was not his particular charge, Khuhro had been interested in the establishment of a University in Sind since before the separation of Sind and it was on this matter that he had quarrelled bitterly with Dow when working on the Administrative Committee in 1934. Dow had opposed the immediate establishment of the University and made some disparaging remarks and Khuhro had walked out in protest. In 1940 the 'National' government of the post Manzilgah period had appointed a committee to examine the University question and a Report had been prepared laying down the general principles and requirements of Sind University but obviously its establishment would have to wait till the end of the War. Mudie indicated some of the passions that raged round this issue:

"The controversy over this Bill has been so long and so bitter that nothing but the Act and the whole Act will satisfy the League at present."[64]

Having passed the University Bill the Government went on to pass the Sind Primary Education Bill which took primary education out of the hands of the Local Bodies and put the financial responsibility on the Government. The Government hoped that this would enable it to get ahead with compulsory primary education.

The Sind Rural and Land Transfer Bill was pending since the last Assembly, but Khuhro had got through the Sind Landholders Mortgage Bill to fill the gap for the Land Alienation Bill and the Debt Reconciliation Bill both of which had been thwarted by Dow. Mudie was much more sympathetic and although he had pleaded inability to pass the two Bills on the grounds that he could not reverse the decision of this predecessor, he had suggested the Credit and Transfer Bill as replacement. The difficulty of getting through public welfare legislation in a colonial setting was fully illustrated by the problem the Ministry faced in getting even a comparatively sympathetic Governor to get through legislation passed by a convincing majority in the House. Unwilling to appear to veto long awaited and popular legislation, Mudie sought the help of the Central Government:

"This Bill was introduced to deal with cases in which land had been mortgaged by conditional sale, and the sale set forth in a written document and the conditions being agreed to orally. In such cases it is said that the Bania often repudiates the oral agreements. The main provision of the Bill allows a zamindar to apply to the court for a declaration that the transaction is a mortgage not a sale, in which case contrary to ordinary law, he is allowed to give oral evidence, which is at variance with the sale deed. There is a similar provision to the Deccan Agriculture Relief Act but the present Bill goes rather further. The Muslim zamindars, who are the backbone of the League, are very insistent on the Bill and the Hindu zamindars, most of whom are strongly opposed. Some of the latter have gone to Delhi to see what can be done about it. The Bill will have to be reserved for your assent. My personal opinion is that though some of the provisions of the Bill may be difficult to put into practice, the principle is alright. Political difficulties will arise if assent is withheld. When I send up the Bill, I will send up a memo from the leader of the Congress Party in the Assembly asking that assent be withheld with a note giving my own views."[65]

The Sind Rural Credit and Land Transfer Bill, though less satisfactory for the Sind agriculturists than the Bills which had not received assent from Dow, was eventually passed by this last Assembly of colonial rule. But until the end Sind continued to receive the big stick whenever it sought relief for the people. Tax was levied at the punitive sliding scale which creamed off all the benefits of high prices. In comparison with prices in the Punjab which were at market level with the profits going to the grower, in Sind the Central Government could always have its own way. Mudie made a feeble protest:

"The Sind Government feel that they have been done down by the Government of India which has refused to raise the minimum price in Sind to the Punjab level. The higher price allowed in the Punjab has naturally excited the envy of the Sind zamindar... There is a good deal in the Sind case, that Sind has been badly treated in this matter... In the end I got the Ministers to accept the Government of India decision `under protest' which will doubtless be conveyed."[66]

Khuhro as Minister in charge of Public Works was concerned with the building of the Lower Sind Barrage and connected with this was the dispute between Sind and the Punjab about the division of the waters of the Indus and the five Punjab rivers. The problem was an old one which had come into being with the expansion of irrigation in the Punjab, particularly with the development of the Canal colonies in the 'twenties which meant taking extra waters from the rivers flowing down to Sind. To offset the effects of the increased irrigation upstream the Lloyd Barrage at Sukkur had been built which had rationalised the use of water and greatly increased the acreage under cultivation. The Punjab however wanted to increase its usage of water and came into confrontation with Sind over the historical rights of the latter over the waters of the Indus river system. Khuhro had been in close touch with this problem throughout his legislative career, first while the Barrage was being constructed in the late 'twenties and early 'thirties and again particularly when he was Public Works Minister in 1942.

During this period the question of the sharing of the waters was occupying the minds of both the Punjab and Sind governments. Khuhro had got the services of Coltman, the well-known Bombay lawyer who had worked for him in the Sukkur riots of 1928, to represent Sind before the Rao Commission. After long and tortuous negotiations an agreement was finally reached by 1945. According to this the Punjab canals had first claim on the waters of the Punjab rivers and no claim on the waters of the Indus. On the Indus supplies (i.e. the total of all the rivers flowing down into the Indus, Sind's share was 75%. Thus out of a total of 103.3 MAF Sind's share was 48.74 MAF and Punjab's was 48.33 MAF. The Rao Commission had given the opinion that to get the desired level of water which was necessary for the needs of Sind, two additional barrages would have to be built on the Indus. The Sind Government wanted the Punjab to bear at least part of the cost of the construction of the barrages. The principle was accepted by the two governments and it was to finalise this agreement and to decide the financial arrangements between the two governments that Khuhro went to Simla in July to meet his Punjab counterpart Nawab Muzaffar Hussain Qizilbash.[67] The Punjab Government agreed to put up 15% of the costs of the barrages to be built. The agreement was a triumph in terms of the share of waters with the undivided Punjab and remained the working agreement between the two provinces.

The war years 1939–1945 had meant the stoppage of development schemes in India. Sind had suffered particularly in this regard as it had initiated important schemes just three years earlier after the separation of the province. After the end of the war in 1945 Government of India had given the go ahead to the provinces to take prepare comprehensive plans for the development of the provinces. The Sind Government put together a consolidated plan for the development of the province under the aegis of the Ministry for Post-War Development which was looked after by the Premier himself. In January 1946 Khuhro was given this Ministry in the newly formed cabinet.

When Khuhro took over as Minister for Post-War Development the Government of Sind had already issued a blueprint for the development of the province.[68] This scheme was reasonably but cautiously worked out by the officials and was bit too tame for Khuhro. In his view the most glaring omission was the lack of any plan to develop an industrial sector in Sind. The Sind Government plan which was put before Khuhro gave reasons why Sind should not be developed industrially.: "Conditions in Sind do not favour heavy industrialization on any large scale development of cottage industries. Cheap power which is one of the essential requisites of heavy industries is not available in the province...Industrial development however depends on policies to be adopted by Government of India for India as a whole. Therefore the schemes for Industries Department do not contain any scheme for development of a major industry."[69] The plan did say that there was possibility of developing industries based on oil seeds, good quality salt, wool, cotton, wool and cement. Khuhro however felt that Karachi as a sea-port and major airport of the sub-continent was situated very favourably for take off as an industrial centre. He felt that there was enough potential in the province and with the development of an industrial area with a proper infrastructure Karachi could attract a good deal of investment.

In this he was fully supported by Mudie. Khuhro retained a well-known town planning consultant from England, Lt. Colonel Swayne Thomas, to make plans for greater Karachi which included a large industrial site which was to be called Sind Industrial Trading Estate. Khuhro also made provision for government funds to be given as loans to encourage entrepreneurs. The city was thus all set for a prosperous and orderly growth.

****

Since the elections of January 1946 and then the arrival of the Cabinet Mission events had been moving fast at the all India level and Khuhro found himself travelling to Delhi and Simla practically every month. By this time there was a regular air service between Karachi and Delhi and Khuhro was able to use it for his frequent journeys to Delhi. The Indian capitals of winter and summer in the years of 1946 and 1947 offered an stimulating mix of political, constitutional and social activities. There were the frequent Muslim League Working Committee meetings for which he has to spend several weeks at a time in Delhi. Then there were negotiations and meetings with members of the Interim Government, the first national government India had had for two hundred years. In addition there were matters connected with administrative affairs which Khuhro had to attend to as Minister. At the same time there was an exciting social life around the political leadership of India which was gathered in the capital at that time. Everyone knew that history was being made and felt themselves to be the arbiters of the future of the sub-continent.

The departure of Lord Wavell had brought the glamorous Mountbattens to Delhi. Lady Mountbatten had already been a visitor to Karachi in connection with her war work and Karachi was also the first stop for the Viceregal couple on their arrival in India on 19 March 1947. Khuhro was present at the newly rebuilt

Mauripur airport along with the Governor and the Premier for the arrival of the new Viceroy. Khuhro recalled that the Mountbattens had a cup of coffee with them and talked for about an hour showing no sign of fatigue after their journey. Edwina Mountbatten, his wife, very plainly dressed, was very gracious and friendly.

Through the summer, autumn and winter of 1946 and the spring and summer of 1947 Khuhro flew back and forth from Delhi and Simla. Along with the hectic schedule of meetings and negotiations were the tea parties and the dinner parties at the homes of politicians and princes. Muslim Leaguers could not compete with the number of vivacious and charming hostesses that Congress could produce but it was fun enough to go shopping with Pyari Isa, dine with the Noons, Sir Feroze and his young and beautiful European wife Viqarunissa, go to parties at the Roshan Ara Club, where among the resplendent Punjab and Sind landowners and Bengal and U.P. nawabs were the few 'out of purdah' Muslim League women – Begum Aizaz Rasul, Zari Sarfraz and the lively Shaista Ikramullah.

Although the events of these months were exciting the political developments were essentially depressing. Ever since the Bengal holocaust, the Hindustani plains of the subcontinent were sinking ever deeper into a mire of blood. Gandhi and Liaquat Ali had made pronouncements predicting a civil war. There was no spirit of co-operation and the Hindu and Muslim political leaders were busy scoring points off each other. The Interim Cabinet was divided into two camps 'each functioning under separate leadership and each attracting to itself its own supporters from among the civil servants and building up its own exclusive area of power.' While Congress was being obdurate, refusing to see any merit in the Muslim League point of view, waiting for forced surrender and quite blind to the disaster looming just ahead, Jinnah took refuge in the stonewalling tactics he knew so well. It was obvious that India was being sacrificed to the mediocrity of its leadership which did not have the imagination to be generous or to take the long view. Congress 'swayed by the Gujerati [or *bania*] mentality of its leaders, i.e. that of a trader driving a hard bargain.'[70] or of Jinnah, ill and perhaps at the end of his tether, hoping something would give.

When Wavell had persuaded Muslim League to join the Cabinet, against the scarcely concealed wishes of the Congress leadership who felt that the Muslim League Ministers would form a 'King's party', it had been hoped by both the Viceroy and Nehru that Muslim League would come into the Constituent Assembly and be party to the framing of a constitution for a free India and that it would rescind its decision made at the Council meeting of 29 July to reject the Cabinet Mission Plan. Jinnah's consistently held position was that Congress must accept the fundamentals of the Cabinet Plan and its interpretation as made in the 16 May Statement. Unfortunately the Attlee government 'both cowardly and dishonest' according to Wavell, backed down under Congress pressure and would not insist on its own interpretation for fear of offending Congress. Wavell was of the view that the British Government could get an agreement from both the parties if it remained firm and even threatened to impose a plan of its own if all else failed. He wanted the British government to announce the date of British withdrawal, suggesting January 1948 in advance and make a phased retreat from the sub-continent leaving, if necessary, provinces in control of their own affairs.

Watching the speed with which events were moving behind the scenes, Khuhro and the Sind leaders could hardly believe that the British were planning on such an early departure. The seriousness with which the details of the constitutional negotiations were being pursued by the political parties and the British Government gave the appearance of concerned and responsible negotiations. Khuhro felt that there was time for thorough arrangements to be made and that Jinnah was playing his cards slowly and cautiously just because there was enough time and there was the will in the other parties to persuade and cajole the Muslim League to get its agreements in terms which would be better for 'Muslim India.'

Mudie reported to Wavell in February 1947 a conversation between a British General and a Sindhi politician:

"About a fortnight ago, General Boucher who commands the Airborne Division, was travelling in the train with a Muslim, who... must, I think, have been G. M. Syed, and was treated to a long tirade on how the British were letting down the Muslims by deserting them. I had other indications of the same feeling during my tour in Upper Sind. There is widespread, though not as yet vocal, feeling among Muslims that they should openly declare that they are on the side of the British and want to remain within the Empire. I have recently been approached on this point, by an ex-Communist and ex-Congressman, who has recently joined the League and by Khaliquzaman* when he was here about a month ago on some business."[71]

Even making allowances for the Governor's prejudice and the tendency of the people to play to the egos of the rulers, there is no gainsaying the fact that the ordinary people and even their leaders were bewildered by what appeared to be voluntary withdrawal by an Imperial power whose authority had not been challenged by anyone except a few 'babus'. For the Sindhi public this was certainly an extra-ordinary idea.

With his fellow citizens Khuhro also felt that the first concern of Muslim League was to get the best terms from the Congress which would be possible if the British played fair. It appeared that Cripps, etc. were in favour of Congress but Wavell at least appeared to be unbiased. Khuhro was all in favour of going into the Constituent Assembly with 'reservations' or whatever it took because he believed that co-operation and negotiation was likely to be much more productive in the long run than negativism. But at the same time he would go along with whatever decision Jinnah took because he firmly believed that Jinnah was an expert negotiator and his objectives were the same.

Muslim League leaders understood that the demand for Pakistan was definitely 'a bargain counter' and none of them could visualize a Pakistan entirely separate from the rest of India. The Pakistan plan had never been worked out or discussed in detail in Muslim League meetings, there were no special committees appointed after the adoption of the Lahore Resolution of 1940 to spell out what was meant by Pakistan and as late as 1947 Khwaja Nazimuddin had to confess that no one in Muslim League knew what Pakistan meant.[72] Any attempt at a serious discussion of the issue was evaded by the 'High Command' as Khuhro himself experienced when he tried to discuss it with Liaquat Ali on a visit by the latter to Karachi: "In Liaquat's very presence, Khuhro asked how, if Pakistan was conceded, they pro-

---

* Chaudhry Khaliquezaman-prominent U. P. politician and Muslim Leaguer.

posed to run it. He [Liaquat] opined that partition would harm Muslims although in public he always defended the League's demand for a partition of India. He was honest enough to admit in private that Pakistan was only a bargaining counter."[73]

Khuhro was happy that Muslim League had joined the Interim Government; he was keen that it should go into the Constituent Assembly and was disappointed when Jinnah decided that it would not.[74] He felt that no opportunity should be lost to work together with the other parties who certainly could not be wished away, so that some mutually acceptable arrangement could be arrived at. This had been his experience in a long political career and even out of the fire of Sukkur in 1939 the Sind Muslim leaders had been able to get potentially the most workable government in Sind in the form of the 'National Party' government. But that was not how the events on the all India scene were shaping up and from the sub-continental corner of Sind Khuhro and his friends watched helplessly.

In the last week of November 1946 Jinnah had arrived in Karachi for a prolonged stay. Karachi with its moderate climate, excellent civic administration and unpolluted air was considered something of a health resort in India and Jinnah, exhausted and ill wanted to rest and to be in the only province in India which was securely in Muslim League hands. During his stay in Karachi at the old Governor's house which was put at his disposal, Jinnah met his party men informally and spent time with them. He was frequently a guest at Khuhro's house,* especially at lunch requesting his favourite dish, fried pomfret fish with tartar sauce or alternatively *surmai* or *ladyfish*. The conversation was largely concerned with the approaching freedom of the sub- continent which at this point was still expected to be at least a couple of years away. The Interim Government and the strategy of the Muslim Ministers was discussed but Jinnah never brought up Pakistan as a serious possibility even as late as the winter of 1946. The Muslim League leaders were convinced that some solution on the lines of the Cabinet Mission proposals and the Statement of May 16 would be worked out for a free India.

It was from Karachi that Jinnah flew to London on 1 December accompanying the Viceroy and other delegates to discuss the constitutional developments with the British Cabinet. The meetings lasted from 3 to 6 December but they proved inconclusive Jinnah flying back to Karachi on 22 December after spending a few weeks in London.

Events moved swiftly after the second election of 1946 in Sind which took place in December. Wavell was being replaced as Viceroy by Mountbatten. Wavell had personified patience and caution and had given the impression that there was time enough for bargaining and that the forbearance of the departing British would last long enough for a fair settlement in India. In fact this was the premise on which Jinnah had based his strategy but it turned out to be seriously mistaken. On 6 January 1947 the All India Congress Committee passed a Resolution to accept the Cabinet Mission proposals regarding grouping of provinces with the proviso that this would not involve compulsion of any province, and would not compromise the rights of the Sikhs in the Punjab. It stipulated that a province or a section of a province would continue to have the option to exercise its choice in accord-

---

* Khuhro was living at this time in an official residence which was later to be occupied by the first Prime Minister of Pakistan and is at present the State Guest House in Karachi.

ance with wishes of the people. The Muslim League Working Committee meeting in Karachi on 31 January however decided that the qualifications in the Congress acceptance of the 'grouping' clause nullified the purpose of the 16 May 1946 Statement and that it would not rescind its July Resolution rejecting the Cabinet Mission proposals. With this decision the Cabinet Mission Proposals were finally dead.

The Labour government wanted to get out of India as quickly as possible. On 20 February 1947 Attlee announced June 1948 as the date for the departure of the British from India and also announced the removal of Wavell and the appointment of Mountbatten as Viceroy. This was an ultimatum to the Indian political parties that an agreement had to be reached by this date or the British would give up power in any case:

"...whether as a whole to some form of Central Government for British India or in some areas to the existing Provincial Governments, or in such other way as may seem most reasonable and in the best interests of the Indian people."

One of the main purposes of this declaration was obviously to concentrate the minds of the Indian leadership on the practical matter of finding a constitutional solution but at the same time it was clear that there would be no more tea and sympathy for those who felt themselves getting the short end of the bargain. For Muslim League this was an unhappy augury, as its best hope lay in long and patient negotiations. A precise time-table cut the ground from under its feet. With a British government bent on appeasement and a Viceroy and the Congress leadership mutually charmed with each other, Congress sensed victory and made its intentions clear. The pronouncements of its leaders made it obvious that they wanted partition and on their own terms. They would not consider conceding any safeguard that Muslim League was asking for and were prepared for the division of Punjab and Bengal. The Union Powers Committee of the Constituent Assembly interpreted the three common subjects of the federation in a way almost to deny all substance of autonomy to the provinces. Nehru and Patel made it clear to the Viceroy that Congress would not tolerate a 'Pakistan' at the Centre as that would mean giving parity to that entity. Jinnah could have 'a truncated and moth eaten' Pakistan and go his own way. Jinnah tried every way he knew how to keep the negotiations going and get some guarantees of autonomy and share of power at the Centre for the Muslim 'sectors' but he could not succeed in the face of Congress obduracy. Any serious consideration of the events leading up to 14 and 15 August 1947 makes it clear that although paying lip service to the unity of India the Congress leadership, Patel, Nehru and Gandhi, wanted and precipitated partition along the lines that it occurred. Impartial historians have to agree with Ayesha Jalal that "It was Congress that insisted on partition. It was Jinnah who was against partition."[75]

Unfortunately for India the man sent out as Viceroy with full powers was vain and shallow with the most superficial acquaintance of India. It has been proved beyond doubt by historians that Mountbatten was only interested in getting as much personal kudos as possible from the situation by making a quick and 'successful' withdrawal from India without adequate thought for the consequences. He was shrewd enough to understand that he would have to get the confidence of the Congress leadership for this purpose and that the Muslim League position was so weak that he could bulldoze it if necessary. Rather than concede any genuine provincial autonomy or give the option to the provinces to form different 'groupings' the Congress had decided to accept partition which would give as little as possible to Pakistan. This would in reality not be a partition but a mere breaking away from the mother country of a few peripheral areas which, poor and unsustainable, would be likely in a short time, perhaps a few years, to rejoin the mother country.

Jinnah's objective, as always, was to gain a reasonable amount of influence at the Centre, parity perhaps, for the Muslim majority provinces. These provinces were to remain as they had been in British India with substantial minorities of Hindus, Sikhs and other communities and thus a balance would be achieved between the different groupings and Muslims would be assured of a certain amount of security. To avoid the partition, which was becoming inevitable given the attitude of the Congress, Jinnah tried different tactics. He agreed to let Suhrawardy, with the Hindu leaders like Sarat Bose, to try to keep Bengal united. In May 1947 he also demanded that if partition went through there should be 'a corridor' to link the two wings of Pakistan. This demand could not be taken seriously but it certainly was an indication that Jinnah did not consider negotiations to be at an end and that his options were still open.

But all these tactics were futile in the face of the secret negotiations which Mountbatten was holding with Nehru and even Patel. The proposals he was giving to the British government for approval were at their behest and Jinnah was not even shown these proposals until it was too late for his views to be taken into account. The June 3rd (1947) Plan, the blueprint for partition and British withdrawal, was brought back by Mountbatten after consultation with the British government and was shown to the Indian leaders on 2 June with a view to announcing it the next day. Jinnah said he could not agree to it unless he discussed it with the Muslim League Council. Mountbatten refused to give the necessary time and said he would take the responsibilty on himself for the Muslim League approval. It has to be said that if Jinnah had any reservations about it he had no business to connive at it and 'nod his head' when Mountbatten looked at him for approval.[76] Having taken this line of least resistance it was too late afterwards to make other legalistic points and objections. Mountbatten had spotted the weaknesses and ruthlessly exploited them.

Mountbatten announced 15 August 1947 as the new date for the departure for British, more than nine months earlier than the previously announced date of June 1948 and just about nine weeks from the date of the announcement. In this unbelievably brief period the entire transfer of power and the establishment of the two new states was to be completed, entailing as it did the division of assets, the division of the army, for the bureaucrats to exercise their options and then engage in the task of setting up at least one administration from scratch.

The new state of Pakistan had to find a capital, a government and start functioning. The two major provinces of Bengal and Punjab had also to go through the exercise of partition and as a result face unprecedented communal violence and the biggest cross migration history had as yet witnessed. The new states would start functioning even before they knew what their boundaries were and as it happened there would little that could be done about the demarcation by Pakistan at least, once the award had been made by the Boundary Commission. There was no question but that it was a scuttle and an abdication of responsibility to the minorities in the sub-continent.

The Muslim League leaders in Sind were certainly not expecting Pakistan until the momentous announcement of June 3 and had no clear idea of what it was going to be. The response to the Plan was muted and the reaction even among the Hindus of Sind was slow. Even the most perfunctory discussion about the functioning of the new state had not taken place when Jinnah summoned Hidayetullah and told him that Karachi would be the temporary capital of the new state. Hidayetullah agreed and even fell in with the idea that the Sind government should move to Hyderabad. It was up to the Governor to register his protest at the untenable idea:

"Ghulam Hussain, when in Delhi, agreed that the temporary capital of Pakistan should be in Karachi and for some inexplicable reason said the Sind Government would move to Hyderabad, which is impossible as Ghulam Hussain must have known – we cannot provide reasonable accommodation there even for district officials. Both the Federal and Provincial governments must, therefore, be in Karachi and this can only be done if Malir Cantonement is evacuated by the army. Jinnah is now saying that it is the Sind Government that must go to Malir. I had a Cabinet meeting last night and the line that the Sind government are to take is that Karachi must be taken as including Malir and so there is no question of their having gone back on their word and the transference of the Sind Government to Malir is impossible.

The Pakistan government wants to bring 4,000 clerks in addition to officers. To turn 4,000 clerks, mostly Hindu, with their wives and family members out of their houses in Karachi and to put in their places 4,000 Muslims, mostly from Punjab and the U.P., in one month, is administratively impossible, except under war conditions. Even to attempt to do so would be political madness. So, unless the Ministry have changed their mind, we are sending a reply by special messenger today to say that Pakistan Government must go to Malir, though we are prepared to accommodate Federal Ministries and swells like that in Karachi."[77]

Mudie's letter was just an indication of the tip of the iceberg as far as the problems that would be faced in setting up the new administration. As Minister for Development and for Public Works and after 14 August as the Premier of Sind, Khuhro would have to face them almost single-handedly. The euphoria and the unreality of the weeks between 3 June and 14 August was tempered by the sheer hard slog that preparing Sind for the flood of refugees and the establishment of the new Central Government entailed. But the work was no hardship because it would help the realisation of freedom, the culmination of a career of over a quarter century. Khuhro had had similar feelings of euphoria on the eve of the separation of Sind but he hoped that this time there would be no betrayal. Khuhro hoped that Pakistan would be a dream come true, he did not expect any aspects of nightmare.

Sind Members at their last session of Bombay Legislative Council, 1935.

Khuhro, formal portrait in London, 1933.

Begum Fatima Khuhro, 1933.

Eldest daughter Khadija and youngest grandchildren.

Khuhro with daughters Hamida and Rashida.

Khuhro with sons Shah Mohammed and Shah Zaman.

All India Muslim League Working Committee, Bombay 1942.

All India Muslim League Working Committee, Bombay 1942.

Muslim League meeting at 'Seafield', Karachi, October 1938.
Left to Right: Khuhro, Yusuf Haroon, Mir Bandeh Ali Talpur, Sir Sikander Hayat and M. A. Jinnah.

Jinnah with Sind Muslim League Leaders.

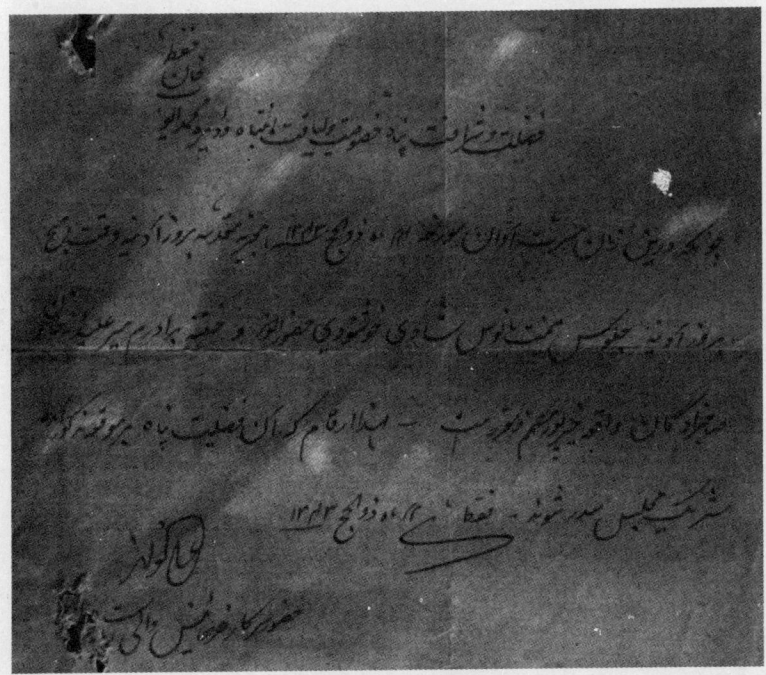

Letter from Pir Pagaro to Khuhro from Hyderabad Jail, 1943.

Farman of Pir Pagaro.

Invitation (in Persian) from Mir Ali Nawaz Talpur.

Khuhro with friends and colleagues, 1946.

Jinnah with Muslim League Leaders.

Jinnah at the Sind Legislative Assembly building, 1946.

The first Eid prayers after Independence, Karachi, August, 1947. Khuhro on left of Jinnah.

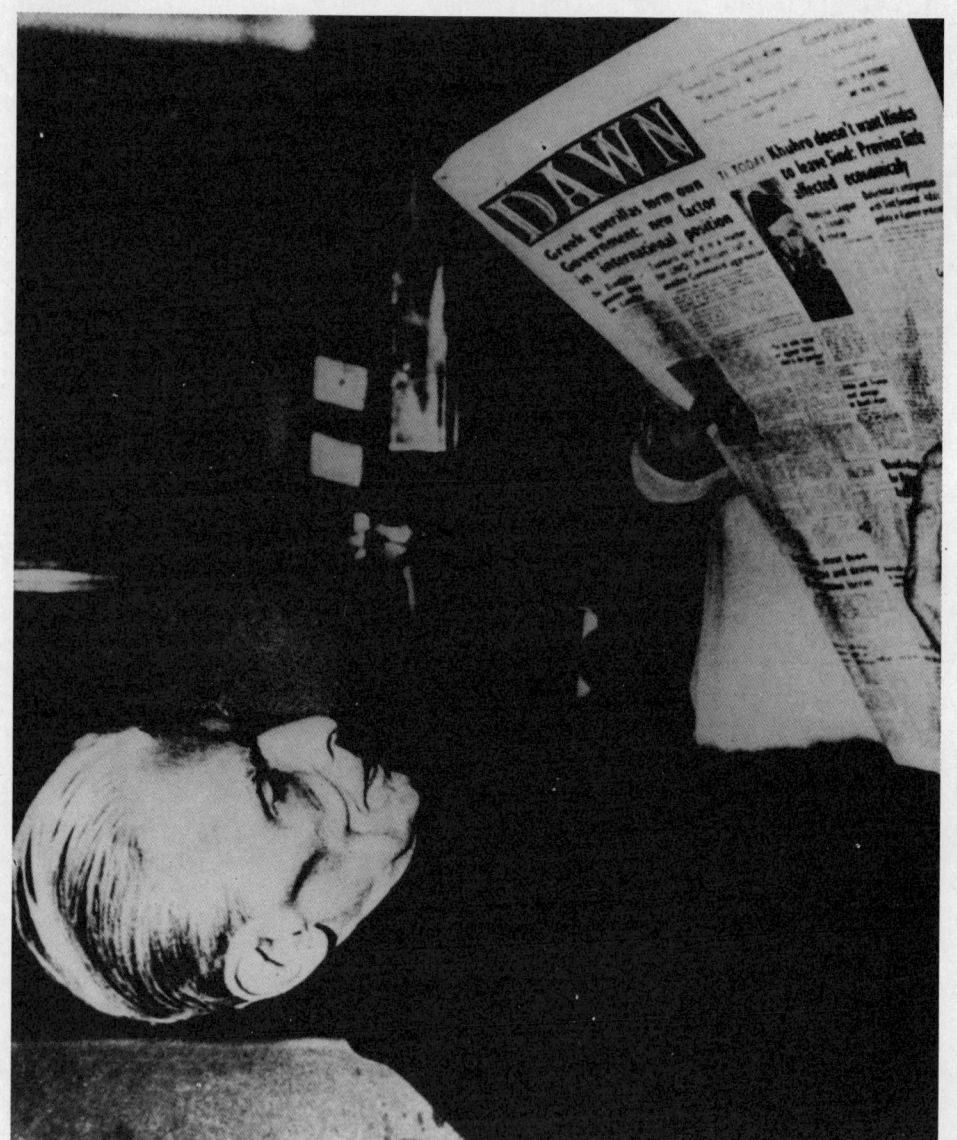

Quaid-e-Azam reading a news story about Khuhro in Dawn.

BOOK III
(1947–1980)

16

PREMIER OF SIND

14 August 1947 was the day fixed for Pakistan's independence. Mountbatten, the last Viceroy of India, was to fly down to Karachi to hand over power to the new state. Coincidentally this was Khuhro's 46th birthday and he was to be the first Premier of Sind in independent Pakistan.

Jinnah soon to be officially titled Quaid-e-Azam had already arrived in Karachi on 7 July and had been greeted enthusiastically by large crowds excited at the prospect of independence and that their tiny provincial capital was to become the capital of the new state. The Constituent Assembly of Pakistan, the body that was not only to frame the constitution of the country but also to act as its legislature in the interim, met for the first time on 11 August in the semi circular Sind Legislative Assembly chamber. The elegant but comparatively small chamber was choc a bloc with the sixty nine members[1] occupying their benches, officials and visitors crowded every space and were eagerly thronging the visitors gallery. Miss Jinnah and other notables sat in the distinguished visitors gallery along with such diplomats as had arrived already in Karachi. Jinnah was sitting in the Speaker's chair. The first task of the Assembly was his unanimous election as its President.

Khuhro filed one of the seven nomination papers for Quaid-e-Azam as President of the constituent assembly and he then made one of the few congratulatory speeches on that day. He recalled the Lahore Resolution of 1940 which many at the time had considered a dream but now seven years later without any bloody war and without any serious sacrifice Pakistan had been achieved. He paid tribute to Jinnah's sagacity and unparalleled statesmanship. Khuhro then went on to say that the primary task of the Constituent Assembly was to frame a constitution and which he was sure "under the guidance of Mr. Jinnah would be such as many would envy."[2] His was the only speech which mentioned the absolute priority of this issue. On the next day the Assembly conferred the official title of Quaid-e-Azam on Jinnah. It also set up a Parliamentary Committee for Fundamental Rights with Khuhro as one of the members.

The Mountbattens flew in on the afternoon of 13 August. They were received at the airport by the Sind Governor and by Khuhro as the next Premier of Sind, and were driven to the Sind Governor's House which now housed the Pakistan Governor General. There they were greeted by the Quaid-e-Azam and Miss Jinnah.

Khuhro managed to find time to attend the official functions that day including the airport reception and the banquet at Government House, which he attended with his wife but he was spending every minute he could, overseeing the transformation of Karachi into the capital of Pakistan. He was also handling the problems concerned with the terrific influx of refugees and numerous other crises. The next morning the transfer of power ceremony took place in the Sind Assembly Hall. This was simple but impressive and over in an hour. Pakistan was now a fact. The Mountbattens did not participate in any of the celebrations but flew back to Delhi straightaway. The Pakistan Government had managed to organise an impressive number of events including a military tatoo to celebrate the independence and the founding of Pakistan but Khuhro was too busy even to take his children to that.

When Jinnah had decided in June to be the Governor General of the new state, it had caused some surprise in League circles as they understood that the Governor General would be a figure head in the constitutional dispensation of Pakistan and Bharat. It had been considered at one point that Mountbatten might be Governor General of both Pakistan and India. But when Jinnah decided to take the position himself the situation became constitutionally quite ambiguous and would become even more confused as he proceeded to preside over cabinet meetings and acted as the effective head of the government.

For the post of Prime Minister Jinnah had chosen Liaquat Ali Khan, his long time aide. Liaquat Ali was a suave courtier well able to disguise his own ambitions and fall in with whatever Jinnah decided. The rest of the Cabinet was almost the same as the Muslim League nominees in the Interim Cabinet about whom Wavell had been so scathing. The two new members were old colonial civil servants, Ghulam Mohammed as the Finance Minister and Chaudhry Zafrulla as Foreign Minister.

The Central Cabinet was in place and the new capital chosen by Jinnah but that was the limit of the arrangements that had been made by the Central Government. The entire burden of the actual practical stages before independence on 14 August was left to the Government of Sind. It was Khuhro, the Premier of Sind who was thus the key figure in this crucial formative phase of Pakistan's existence.

The decision to locate the capital of Pakistan at Karachi had been taken only a few weeks before the inauguration of the new state. Chaudhri Muhammed Ali, the soon to be Secretary General of the new administration had set out the lack of choice available. Bengal which had a Muslim League ministry was ruled out because the province itself had to build a new capital at Dacca. Other provinces in the western wing of the country were also rejected for different reasons. He reported that,

"In West Pakistan the only province which had a Muslim League ministry was Sind... Karachi is a – 'a clean modern town with a mild climate; it had a fine harbour and an airport which provided ready means of communications with East Pakistan and the outside world. It was also the birthplace of the Quaid-e-Azam though this was not the reason for the selection of Karachi."[3]

Used perhaps to the limitless resources of the Finance Department of the Government of India, Chaudhri Muhammed Ali had little comprehension of the problems that would be faced by choosing to set up the capital in one of the smallest provinces of British India where the burden of this immense task would fall on the

Government of Sind. The decision to make Karachi the capital posed Khuhro with his toughest assignment yet. As PWD Minister it was Khuhro's responsibility to get not only residential space for the '4000 clerks, 200 peons and their families' but office space for the Ministers, bureaucrats and their departments and to do this within two months. The Pakistan government insisted on being accommodated in central Karachi and was not prepared to go anywhere like Malir, just where there were plenty of wartime buildings and barracks available.

The Government of Sind decided to sacrifice the open space around the High Court and offered their own Government House, their Assembly Building as well as their Secretariat. The Sind Government moved to Napier Barracks then considered almost outside the town. Khuhro had his office as Premier in a small annexe behind the Barracks. The Sind Assembly sat in its Chamber when the Constituent Assembly was not sitting. Eventually Sind Assembly would hold its sittings in a school building on Bunder Road which was quite inconveniently distant from the Premier's office in Napier Barracks.

The barracks and houses that had been built for the use of the armed forces on Bunder Road and the Lines area as well as elsewhere were put at the disposal of the incoming government. With the war experience of building army barracks behind them, the PWD department undertook the job of putting up as many buildings as possible in the short time available.

Khuhro spent most of the twenty four hours available each day on this urgent task in the two months before independence. Sind was a solvent province and had an adequate development budget for its immediate needs but providing a capital of the new state was certainly not within its means and the new Government of Pakistan had few funds of its own. But miraculously the buildings were ready by the time the Central government arrived in the middle of August, once again proving Khuhro's exceptional organisational capacities.*

The search for houses for the Central grandees sometimes turned into a farce as when the wife of the prospective Prime Minister herself looked for a house in Karachi. Her first choice was that of the house of the Chief Justice of Sind but the wife of the Chief Justice would not hear of it. Her second choice fell on one of the grander houses of one of the Ministers of Sind, in this case the one occupied by Mir Ghulam Ali Talpur who also refused to oblige. In the end Khuhro offered to give up his house and move to a smaller house usually occupied by the Collector of Karachi.[4] The Finance Minister of the new government Ghulam Mohammed was offered an elegant town house which belonged to a Parsi family but was situated a little bit on the unfashionable end of a fashionable residential road and was rather ungraciously accepted. A separate house could not be found for his son in law which remained a sore point with the Finance Minister. All this fuss about the 'suitability' of houses caused much surprise to Khuhro who had expected a some-

---

* The Central Government, despite the fact that it took over Karachi from Sind within the year and named it the permanent capital of Pakistan, continued to function from the temporary 'huts' which the Sind Government had built in the space of two months from June to August 1947. For the next twenty years till its departure from Karachi in the 60s only one shoddy building was put up by the Central Government. No other city in the country at that time could afford the capacity and space to absorb the function of temporary capital. Tughlaq House... was a landmark as perhaps the only permanent building or structure built by the Federal Capital Administration..."I. A. Zafar, *The News*, 22 Jun. 1993.

what different spirit from the founders and policy makers of Pakistan at a time when the ordinary citizens were facing incredible hardships, their trains being held up and massacres on both sides of the border – the thousands of people caught up in the cross migration could count themselves lucky if they could arrive at a refugee camp.

Khuhro was thankful that the Ministers were accommodated, the offices completed. Even Chaudhri Mohammed Ali admits that the job had been done,

"By August 15, somehow or other, shelter had been found for the thousands of families that poured into Karachi, and office accommodation for every ministry and department had been found or hastily constructed."[5]

It would have taken a very humble bureaucrat and politician indeed not to be dismayed on arrival in Karachi at that time. It was a small provincial capital of a mere 400,000 people and they would have quickly compared their situation with that of their counterparts in India working in the splendour of the newly constructed Lutyens buildings in New Delhi. The resources of the Sind government would seem very scant by comparison and many of the incoming bureaucrats and politicians were not slow to criticise their hosts.

Khuhro was nominated for Premiership of Sind after independence on 15 August by the Sind Muslim League Assembly Party. The election for the leadership of the Party took place despite an earlier undertaking by Jinnah to Khuhro that he would be made Premier of Sind after independence. Just before independence when Khuhro was on one of his visits to Delhi, Liaquat Ali Khan invited him to lunch at his house and confirmed that the Jinnah's promise made after the elections of December 1946 would be honoured and he would be nominated Premier of and that Hidayetullah was being made Governor. Khuhro felt that the latter nomination was unusual as in no other province was a local politician being made Governor and also the relations between himself and Hidayetullah were strained which could make things difficult, but he did not protest. That evening, at a reception at the Delhi Club Jinnah told Khuhro that he had been approached by Pirzada Abdus Sattar who wanted to be made Premier. Khuhro was surprised at this as he had understood that the decision had already been made that he should be Premier and it was on this understanding that he had stood down in favour of Hidayetullah in January. However he now replied that he would not interfere and that the Assembly Party could decide.

Back in Karachi Khuhro called a meeting of the Assembly Party on 15 August as Deputy Leader of the Parliamentary Party. Hidayetullah had already been sworn in as Governor that morning and Khuhro was therefore *de facto* Leader of the Assembly Party. Khuhro asked Liaquat Ali Khan to depute a nominee to supervise the election of the leader so that there could be no future allegations of unfair elections. I. I. Chundrigar was sent by Liaquat Ali to preside and Khuhro was elected unanimously.[6] There was no other nomination. The Muslim League members of the Assembly had already decided that Khuhro would be the Party leader and Premier of Sind. Chundrigar then asked Khuhro to choose his cabinet but Khuhro took the unusual step of taking a ballot for the three ministers. Mir Ghulam Ali, Pir Illahi Baksh and Kazi Fazlullah, the latter Khuhro's protege from Larkana, were elected. The Cabinet was sworn in the same evening. Khuhro had been scrupulous in following this procedure for selecting his Cabinet as he did have the right to put up the names of his choice and with his strength in the Assembly Party could have his choice easily endorsed. As it happened this method of selecting his cabinet would prove a costly mistake.

Earlier when the membership of the Constituent Assembly was being decided, Khuhro nominated Pirzada and Gazdar for the representation from Sind in the Constituent Assembly where the full strength of the Sind contingent was five. In July Khuhro had been given the option of Central cabinet membership but it was also made known that if Khuhro did not take up the offer no other name from Sind would be acceptable.[7] Khuhro decided that he would not give up the chance of the Sind Premiership with the opportunity of pursuing his well thought out programme for the Province. He did not therefore accept the central cabinet post which would have meant abandoning Sind at this crucial point in history. It was not in his nature to leave unfinished business even though preferment and a much easier life would have resulted for him on taking a central Ministership.

When the Pakistan Cabinet had been announced no name had been included from Sind. This caused great surprise and when this omission had not been rectified for two months the Sind Muslim League Assembly Party met under the chairmanship of Khuhro to discuss the issue. The result was a strongly worded statement by the Sind Muslim League Parliamentary Party, which said it

"viewed with deep dissatisfaction the fact that the province has no representation in the Pakistan Central Government while some provinces have dominant representation. As such Sind has no voice whatever in shaping the policies of the Pakistan Government."

The Party expressed its

"considered opinion that in the federal structure of Pakistan every federating unit should have equal voice both in the legislative as well as in the executive. In absence of such provisions small provinces like Sind, N.W.F.P. and Baluchistan will be converted into vassals of the bigger provinces of Pakistan"[8]

This statement obviously went beyond a mere demand for a Ministership for Sind in the Centre and emphasised the smaller provinces' claim to equal rights with the bigger provinces in the Federation. The Sind leadership was very much alive to the issue of autonomy and the rights of the provinces in the new state. In the years ahead this would become the most thorny issue in the constitutional history of Pakistan. The statement had the desired effect and a Ministership was immediately offered to Sind. Khuhro nominated Pirzada Abdus Sattar for the post.[9]

Khuhro was himself being closely consulted by Jinnah. Every morning Khuhro had a meeting with Jinnah when the latter was in Karachi to apprise him of the latest developments, the number of refugees, the border with India, the state of law and order and so on. Karachi was rapidly becoming a vast refugee camp and Jinnah was extremely worried about the mass exchange of population which was taking place and the bloodshed that accompanied it. He had expressed both his apprehensions and the fact that such a calamity had not been anticipated by him.

In fact Jinnah told Khuhro categorically that he expected to retain the minority communities in Pakistan. They were to be re-assured that they were safe so that they were not tempted to migrate. He made it absolutely clear that the presence of minorities in Pakistan and their security was the only guarantee for the security of Muslims in India. Jinnah emphasised this point repeatedly and gave Khuhro to understand that he must take every step necessary to prevent Hindu migration from Sind, the only province with a sizeable Hindu population. Jinnah was anxious that Pakistan was not seen as a religious and exclusive state. He was reported to have said when asked if Pakistan would be an Islamic theocratic state, "What does this theocratic state mean. I do not understand."[10]

Khuhro fully agreed with Jinnah. Hindus, he felt, were an essential part of the society and economy of the province and he could not see any reason why the violence of the Punjab or the North Indian provinces should spill over to Sind which had no history of such problems. He was in for a rude awakening. The first signs of impending trouble appeared when the Congress leadership in the shape of Acharya Kripalani, the Sindhi born President of All India Congress for 1947, arrived in Sind on 2 August 1947, just a few days before independence. He had toured extensively ostensibly to explain the Partition plan to Sindhis but privately gave it to be understood to the Hindus that Pakistan could not last and they should make a temporary migration which would cause immense problems for the new state. They could return in triumph once the state had collapsed. Khuhro knew of this move and hastened to counter it. He was also aware that as refugees from India arrived in ever greater numbers the Hindus of Karachi and Hyderabad were being intimidated and harassed by them to vacate their houses and their lives made increasingly difficult so that they would be forced to migrate.

The months after Partition were very difficult. Reports of massacres on both sides of the border in the Punjab were coming in all the time. On 21 August riots occurred in Quetta of all unlikely places, in which about thirty people were killed and over forty injured. These reports put a great deal of pressure on the Sind Government. At the same time there were a number of incidents of armed robberies in the interior where some wealthy Hindu traders were the victims. These disturbances were dealt with by Khuhro very firmly. Law and order was being strictly kept. Khuhro, while dealing with the problems of the capital and government matters in these extraordinary times was also touring the province constantly to keep a personal eye on what was happening.

The volatility of the situation was obvious and on 4 September in the wake of a particularly tragic case of communal violence in Nawabshah the Provincial government found it necessary to impose a curfew in certain areas. The Nawabshah incident which happened on 1 September was the first serious case of communal violence to occur in Sind during this period and it was no accident. The railway authorities reported that on 1 September the 55 Up Mixed train which left Nawabshah at 11.40, was derailed at mile post 77 between Nawabshah and Shafiabad at 12.5 hours. An armed mob attacked the Sikh refugees in the train killing 11 men and 4 women outright and injuring 17 others.[11] Khuhro who was in Hyderabad at the time took prompt action to restore peace; he summoned the Collector to answer for the incident and conferred with the minority leader Professor Ghanshyamdas Jethanand who led the Congress Assembly Party and Dr. Chimandas, also a prominent Congress leader, to discuss the situation.

The Collector, Masud, who had come to public attention at the time of his high-handed actions during the elections of 1946, was still posted at Nawabshah. He was an I.C.S. officer at a time when this label meant almost untrammelled power. Moreover he knew that the new Government of Pakistan had retained the authority to post and transfer I.C.S officials and that he was responsible to the Central authority and therefore could afford to defy the Provincial Government.[12] The invulnerability of this I.C.S. officer had already been demonstrated when the complaints of major Indian political figures against him in 1946 had gone unheeded and he continued in his post. Now when Pakistan had become a fact he still felt he could do as he wished. Nawabshah was home to a large Sikh community and Masood's policies resulted in their exodus thus making 'room' for an overflow of the East Punjab refugees. He was not concerned that this was against the express and explicit policy of the Sind government.[13]

The train incident of 1 September sparked off other incidents of looting against the Sikhs but the Government of Sind took stern action to suppress the violence. Apart from the immediate measures an Ordinance was also passed for the maintenance of public safety. On 5 October Khuhro applied the Safety Ordinance to five districts of southern and eastern Sind including Karachi, Hyderabad, Sukkur and Nawabshah, to which the most heavy immigration was taking place by sea and air and from the Rajasthan border and even from the Punjab. But panic had set in and despite the fact that military protection was provided the migration of Sikhs and Hindus continued from Nawabshah.

In Karachi and Hyderabad there was another alarming phenomenon. The new arrivals were entering and occupying houses where the owners, particularly Hindus, were still living, and throwing out the owners. On the one hand Government had to requisition houses where it could with minimum inconvenience to the citizens and on the other it was having to safeguard the citizens against this cruel harassment. Khuhro set up a Committee of retired Sind officers for the

> 'purpose of preventing illegal occupation of vacant premises in the city and regularizing their occupation with instructions to avoid putting Muslims and non-Muslims in the same blocks with a view to preserving communal harmony."[14]

In consultation with H. S. Suhrawardy the ex Premier of Bengal who was at this time working with Gandhi to stop the communal violence, Khuhro set up a Peace Board under his own Chairmanship with Yusuf Haroon, Shaikh Abdul Majid, Professor Ghanshyam and Kumari Jethi Sipahimalani as members and G. Allana and M. P. Tahilramani, the latter a good friend of Khuhro, as secretaries of the organisation. The Board was to devise ways and means to maintain peace in the province and to remove the causes of the exodus of the minority communities. The aims and objects of the Peace Board give a good indication of the apprehensions of the Hindus of Sind in the weeks after Partition. They also give a valuable insight into the thorough way Khuhro grasped the essence of a problem.

The detailed aims of the Board were first, to devise ways by which lawless elements in the Province could be kept under control. Secondly to see that the life, honour and property of the minority community are protected and the community is saved from coercion, harassment and intimidation. Thirdly to devise measures necessary to maintain the normal economic life in the province. Fourthly to create the psychological atmosphere and necessary conditions which would discourage the exodus of Sindhis from Sind. Fifthly to rehabilitate refugees on a well organized basis and in accordance with a properly conceived plan and programme. The Board also set up sub-committee under Sardar Mohammed Baksh, a senior civil servant and with a number of Hindu members, to redress grievances of the minority community.

A key element in the resettlement and absorption of refugees in Sind was their dispersal throughout the province. Khuhro knew that not only was it very difficult for a few towns to take in the influx but could see from his experience of Karachi and Hyderabad that unbearable tension was being created from the large and chaotic influx. If the refugees could be settled throughout the province in co-operation with the local population the problems could be minimised. Also with dispersal it would be easier to find work for the refugees and with proper work they would not crowd the camps and get used to handouts. Khuhro ran special trains to take the refugees to the interior and visited the refugee camps in Karachi and Hyderabad to persuade the inmates to follow this plan. The newspapers reported the efforts that were being made:

> "The urgent need for resettling refugees on the land or absorbing them in some trade or employment was emphasised by Mr. M. A. Khuhro, the Premier of Sind at the Regional Employment Exchange this morning... when he visited the exchange to inspect the work being done there in connection with securing employment for refugees who are pouring into Sind in large numbers."[15]

Khuhro asked the officers to put the incoming refugees into different categories for employment purposes so that they could be made self supporting and be absorbed into the social fabric as soon as possible and not have to depend on hand outs. Mr. Nazir Ahmed, an I.C.S. officer, was appointed Refugee Settlement Officer to carry out the work of settling the refugees in a manner so that they need not be a burden on the state.

But there was a lot of opposition to this policy from the refugees themselves. Dawn reported on 21 October:

> "Mr. M. A. Khuhro, Premier of Sind paid a visit to Hyderabad (Sind) on Sunday last where he spent a very busy day conferring with the Collectors of Hyderabad, Thar and Parkar, Nawabshah and Sanghar on the question of relief and resettlement of the Muslim refugees who have come in thousands to Sind. He was satisfied with the work being done in all the districts. Though he was grieved to learn that most of the Muslim refugees in the Bholari camp and in Hyderabad were very unhelpful and refused to do any work so as to become earning members of society. He desired all officials and non-officials to explain the real position to the refugees and make them useful citizens of Sind and induce them not to rely only on being fed and housed at public cost."[16]

As it happened, after the removal of Khuhro from office in 1948 this policy was abandoned. From then on the officers in charge relied largely on the allotment of evacuee property among the refugees. The policy of allotting plots and money among the refugees sowed the seeds of future corruption and 'something for nothing' attitude in the refugee population.

The Sind Government was in charge of customs on Sind's borders because the Centre whose responsibity it was had not enough trained manpower. Liaquat Ali had reports that Muslim refugees coming to Pakistan were being deprived of their possessions and robbed at Delhi and elsewhere. Evading taking any hard decisions himself the Prime Minister sent an officer, Hasnie, Joint Secretary, Ministry of Economic Affairs to Khuhro to ask him to pass a law and to take action at the provincial level to prevent Hindus leaving Sind from taking substantial amounts with them. Khuhro should perhaps have hesitated to fall in with the demands of the Centre which was obviously passing on a matter of its own responsibility to the Government of Sind, but he obliged and had an Ordinance passed to maintain law and order and to prevent the smuggling of arms, ammunition, gold etc. The implementation of this law naturally led to excesses on part of the officials which Khuhro had to make special efforts to allay. On 21 October Dawn reported that

"the Premier personally inspected at Hyderabad station the searches being made of the luggage of the Hindu evacuees migrating from Sind to Jodhpur, Bombay etc. He gave instructions personally to the Government officers conducting the searches to be more liberal in allowing the Hindu evacuees to take away their personal effects, the main object of the search being to stop merchandise in bulk being sent out of Sind without a permit.

He examined the heap of articles [taken from the passengers, and told the officers] that they should have allowed most of these articles to be taken away by the passengers as they were mostly stray pieces of silk cloth or wool for knitting. The Hindu public present at the station platform expressed gratitude to the Premier personally for his liberality and kindness to the evacuees."[17]

Back in Karachi Khuhro was given a civic address on 23 October by the Karachi Municipal Corporation where he set out his belief in basic democratic institutions and reiterated his life-long commitment to them. Beset by the most pressing problems and chaos barely held at bay, Khuhro re-assured himself and others present that there was an order beyond the present turmoil. He paid tribute to the most senior local government of the province:

"It is no small satisfaction to me to watch your corporation administer this great city."

He then went to recall the history of local self government in the sub-continent:
"Historically local self-government institutions have been the bedrock of representative democracy and at once the beginning and the bridge leading to parliamentary government. It was in the laboratory of local self-government that the Anglo Saxon race evolved and perfected this instrument of government by the scientific method of trial and error. Perhaps it was what one may call the divine tactics of history which brought about the fateful association of that race with the sub-continent of India for neary 200 years in order that democratic self-governing institutions could be planted in our soil. These institutions have now taken root and we have begun to understand their mechanism and to operate them on our own and no longer under the eye of our English taskmasters."[18]

He also emphasised the importance of local bodies as an essential training ground for politicians to learn the art of politics:

"In the task of fitting our people for self-government and training them to work the complex and delicate machinery of parliamentary democracy, our local self-government institutions and in particular this corporation play an invaluable part. Many of our future parliamentarians and popularly elected representatives will, I hope, learn, digest and assimilate the theory and practice of parliamentary institutions. Thus also will Sind and Pakistan at all times produce democratic leaders who can successfully confront the current crises which overtake the world from time to time and thus meet the challenge from forces of reaction and fascism which are always ready to capture power in order to destroy freedom and democracy and plunge the world into war and chaos. With this hope and prayer I once again thank you, your workshop and your councillors of the Corporation of Karachi for the great honour you have done me in presenting me with the civic address before such a distinguished gathering this evening."[19]

On that evening however he made what was, in view of Pakistan's later experience, a prophetic statement:

"Our own future, the future of unborn generations and the destiny of our country as an independent state will in no small measure depend on our capacity to work these institutions successfully should we be tried in this respect and found wanting we shall fall victims to the tyranny of dictatorship."[20]

Soon Khuhro was on tour again, this time taking with him Sri Prakasa the respected senior Congress politician who was High Commissioner for India to Pakistan, to try and re-assure the Hindu population and persuade them not to emigrate from the province. He and the High Commissioner travelled extensively in the province making speeches and reassuring Hindus so that by the end of the tour "a good and cordial atmosphere had been created."[21] Khuhro was very surprised when on his return Liaquat Ali Khan reproached him: "Our High Commissioner cannot get out of Delhi and you are taking the Indian High Commissioner on tour". Khuhro patiently explained the necessity of reassuring the Hindu population especially as some of its leaders had been advising them to leave. He reminded him that it was Quaid-e-Azam's policy to see that the minorities were safe and happy, if only to secure the safety of Muslims in India.

In the first week of December Khuhro was invited to attend a conference in connection with Kashmir in Lahore where the Prime Ministers of India and Pakistan were to meet on 8th December. The Maharaja of Kashmir had been delaying the accession of the State to Pakistan. In October tribal *lashkars* had crossed over from N.W.F.P. into Kashmir and fighting was raging in the state. The conference in Lahore was abortive as Nehru did not agree to any compromise. Khuhro who was staying with his old friend Sir Francis Mudie now the Governor of West Punjab, was approached by officers in charge of *Razakars* (volunteers) to visit the camps in Rawalpindi and assess the situation to see what help the Government of Sind could give. Liaquat Ali Khan who was perhaps anxious that his government's involvement in this operation was known to as few as possible, did not like the idea of Khuhro going to Rawalpindi but could not stop him. Khuhro went to Rawalpindi, saw the camps and arranged to send a special train of weapons, food and other supplies to the *Razakars*.[22]

Mudie had his own agenda for Khuhro and took him to see the Ferozepur and Walton refugee camps. Khuhro was very much affected by the plight of the refugees there but could not possibly accede to Mudie's request that he take 300,000 refugees into Sind. Khuhro refused the request pointing out that Sind, one of the smallest provinces of the sub-continent was having to house not only the entire Government of Pakistan but also taking in refugees at the rate of a thousand a day from the Khokhrapar border in addition to those who were coming in from Bombay. The resources of the province had been stretched to the limit. Mudie was a good friend of Khuhro and he did not like refusing him but Khuhro knew that the demanding and difficult situation in Sind would be unbearably exacerbated if more refugees were taken in.

This would not be the end of the matter however and in February Liaquat Ali was writing to Jinnah that the Joint Refugee Council had decided to send a lakh of refugees to Sind from West Punjab, "We are anxious that Sind should absorb as many refugees as possible."[23] Khuhro however refused again pointing out that it would be impossible for Sind to absorb them without adequate support from the Centre which had so far not funded any refugee expenditure. He re-iterated that this was not something that could be done lightly and without preparation. The fact was that the peace in Sind towns was extremely fragile. There had been trouble even in the Punjab, especially in Multan, where large numbers of unsettled refugees were creating problems. The provincial government of the Punjab was failing to deal adequately with the refugee influx so that the Quaid-e-Azam asked Liaquat Ali to stay in Lahore most of the early months of 1948 to oversee the refugee work. He also set up a small Committee of Ministers under his own chairmanship to deal with urgent problems as they arose.[24]

In December 1947 Khuhro felt that he had the situation in Sind largely under control and wrote to Sharma, the influential Hindu editor of the important Karachi newspaper, the *Daily Gazette*, on the minorities issue:

"On several occasions, I have proclaimed from public platforms that the considered policy of my Government is to persuade Sind Hindus not to leave their native land in panic. I have given them every assurance of the security and sanctity of their life and property. I can proudly claim to have honoured these assurances fully in observance. My Government have also assured the Hindu equality of rights as our fellow citizens of Pakistan and that they will not be discriminated against in pursuing their lawful avocations in services, trades and callings. We are most anxious to keep our Hindu nationals with us as a most essential element of our political and social life. I am glad to be able to claim that the Hindu exodus has now spent its force and even many of the evacuees who had taken panic flights are now returning to us in ever increasing numbers. These are obvious signs that Hindus do have confidence in our sincerity of purpose in the matter of protecting them against the depradations of the criminal and anti-social elements amongst our refugee influx. I hope you will give thought to the contents of this letter and will believe me when I say that I consider the presence of Hindus as essential to the prosperity and greatness of Sind and Pakistan."[25]

Khuhro's efforts to maintain peace had been successful up to this point even though mass migration into the province was in progress. Everyday ships carrying refugees docked at Karachi. The Khokhrapar crossing was open and refugees were streaming in from there. There was great sympathy for the refugees at this time and the public voluntarily provided as much food and shelter as it could. Khuhro himself wrote in his note at this time

"Officers were appointed to settle people in the interior of Sind with some thought to how much Karachi could absorb. We left doors open in Sind for refugees with full public consensus on the issue. There were some highway robberies. Hindu merchants were being robbed in towns like Ratodero. I put all that down with a strong hand."[26]

The victimisation of Hindus and Sikhs had largely been controlled by constant vigilance. The administration ensured that the Hindus in Karachi were not victimized and deprived of their houses and property and that evacuee property was allotted in a fair manner. Efforts were being made to disperse refugees to avoid an unbearable burden on the cities of Karachi and Hyderabad and that the inevitable tension should not be too great.

This delicate balance which had been achieved by so much hard work was soon to be disturbed however. Khuhro's success depended not only on his own mastery of administration but also because he had got together a team of civil servants on whom he could rely to carry out their orders. That chain of command proved to have some very weak links. One such link was the Collector of Nawabshah. There were, in fact, more interests to be served in disturbing the peace of Sind. Khuhro sent his letter to the *Daily Gazette* on 25 December. He could not have guessed that within a fortnight the bubble would burst.

The Nawabshah disturbance in September had caused a loss of confidence in the minority population there and subsequently large scale migration took place from the district. The Sind Government did all it could to make the departure of the Sikh community as peaceful as possible. Trains from Nawabshah arrived at Karachi full of Sikh emigrants for onward evacuation by sea. The Government was providing police security to the evacuees while they were temporarily housed in the Sikh Guru Mandirs of Karachi to await ship space.

Khuhro was in his office on 6 January when news came of riots in Karachi. At 11 o'clock the Secretary of the Peace Board, Tahilramani rushed into Khuhro's room to tell him that the Sikhs who were in the Guru Mandir were being killed by men armed with knives. Khuhro relates that he:

"I tried to get the D.I.G. Police, Kazim Raza but he could not be found so I instructed S.P. Sharif Khan to cordon off the Mandir and save the people. About an hour or so later Tahilramani came rushing back again and said that the people were still being killed and the police was doing nothing about it. The D.I.G. was still not available. I found out later that he had been with the Chairman Port Trust where he had gone ostensibly to attend some meeting but had delayed returning to his office. It transpired that the police guard had not gone to the Cantonement Station to protect the Sikhs and the police appeared to be scarce and indifferent to the situation in the town. It also appeared that the police did not intervene to stop the riots. At 12.30 p.m. I left the office went to the trouble spots. I saw for myself that mobs of refugees armed with knives and sticks were storming the temples and many of them had got inside the Guru Mandir. The S.P. Police was outside and told me that he was helpless as he only had ten policemen armed only with sticks and they were outnumbered and were unable to stop the rioters."[27]

Khuhro who had gone to the riot areas with one guard, a chauffeur and a gun, felt that he had no option but to intervene personally. He asked his guard to aim his gun and himself fired into the rioters. The sight of the Premier himself firing was enough to put an immediate stop to the attack on the Guru Mandir and the mob melted away.[28] By this time general rioting had broken out in the city and shops were being looted. Khuhro toured Karachi with Sharif Khan and used his pistol on a number of occasions and thus brought a temporary halt to the riots but it was not easy to get the situation under control:

"I had got guests for lunch but I rang my wife and asked her to make my excuses and give them food. She told me that Quaid-e-Azam had telephoned several times and had been very anxious about the trouble and was asking about him `Where is Khuhro, tell him to talk to me'"[29]

Khuhro got in touch with G.O.C. General Akbar Khan at about 1.30 p.m. and the latter said he would send the troops in by 3 o'clock. The army arrived under the command of Brigadier K. M. Shaikh. Khuhro himself remained touring the city constantly till about 8.30 that evening by which time he felt that calm had been restored.

It was also time to give a detailed report to Quaid-e-Azam:

"I came home and after a hurried dinner went to see him at about 9.30. He was pleased to hear that the situation had been brought under control. His words were, 'Good, you have taken firm action. Stop the riot any how. These refugees have blackened my face. Only two days ago Sir Zafrulla said in the United Nations that there is no riot or disturbance in Pakistan and there are several riots in India including three or four in Delhi.' I told him that I had already stopped the riots and I would see to it that they did not recur. After seeing Quaid-e-Azam I again went on a tour of the city and at 12 o'clock that night at Garden Police Station I had a conference with General Akbar Khan and Brigadier Shaikh. I told them that I suspected that riots would start again in the morning and that if necessary the army should be prepared to shoot the rioters on sight. The next morning by 10 or 11 when I was again patrolling the city armed with a gun and my P. S. Agha Shahi carrying a pistol. I was told that riots had started but after two or three people were shot the riots stopped."[30]

Khuhro was on hand personally to attend to the complaints of the victims of the riots. Several Hindu officers and prominent citizens who were in the riot areas telephoned him and he sent special transport to take them to safe areas.[31] These firm measures worked,

"Within three days riots were completely under control. We saved many lives. Not more than 10 or 15 people were killed although there was a certain amount of looting."[32]

Khuhro had not only shown exceptional personal bravery during this episode but he had proved once again his grasp of a situation which he had followed up with clear sighted, practical means of resolution. Khuhro had shown his effectiveness as an administrator in a way no other contemporary did in the sub-continent at that time.[33]

As soon as the situation had returned to normal Khuhro took the Quaid-e-Azam and Miss Jinnah on a tour of Karachi to see the situation for themselves:

"On 8th or 9th January I took Mr. Jinnah and Miss Jinnah for a drive in the city and showed them that everything was normal. Jinnah very much appreciated the quick restoration of law and order."

Not so the Prime Minister however,

"After the riots ended about the 9th or 10th I went to see Liaquat Ali Khan in connection with some matter and he said to me,` What sort of Muslim are you that you protect Hindus here when Muslims are being killed in India. Aren't you ashamed of yourself. You have even killed some Muslims.' I was very surprised but I replied that it was my foremost duty as administrator to keep the law and order and protect the citizens no matter of what religion."[34]

Khuhro succeeded in recovering stolen property and having killers and looters arrested but later had to release most of them because of pressure from the Central Government.[35]

In February a session of the newly formed Pakistan Muslim League was held in Khaliqdina Hall in Karachi with the agenda of re-organizing the party and electing office bearers. This session was presided over by Jinnah and he paid a rich tribute to Khuhro, 'Khuhro is the most efficient Minister I have seen.' Khuhro was given a standing ovation at the meeting. Some weeks later Jinnah invited Khuhro and his wife to a private lunch at Bahawalpur House in Malir where he and Miss Jinnah used to spend their weekends. There were no other guests present and Jinnah was unusually open and frank in his talk. He was extremely cordial and complimented Khuhro on his dealing with the Karachi riot and told him categorically, "you are the best administrator I have." Jinnah went on "I have a very high opinion of your administrative ability. You are better than most of my Ministers. Only Zafrulla and Ghulam Mohammed are competent the rest are useless." Khuhro responded by asking him, "What about the Prime Minister?" Jinnah replied, "He is average the rest are below average." As the Khuhros were leaving Jinnah and Miss Jinnah came out to see them off, a most unusual gesture for Jinnah; he remarked, "Ghulam Mohammed is coming to see me about Karachi. I believe you will not agree to hand it over."

Jinnah's remarks came as no surprise to Khuhro who was only too aware of the differences that were building up between the Central Government and his own Government of Sind. Khuhro, as Premier of Sind had been dealing with one of the most critical moments of history in the sub-continent and Sind unprepared and with very limited resources, found itself in the eye of the storm. Apart from preparing Karachi to receive the Central Government and its hangers on, accommodating the massive flood of refugees and maintaining law and order in a highly volatile situation, the Sind government also met the financial demands of a Central Government unable to pick up its own bills.

But more tellingly there were the idiosyncratic requirements of Central Ministers and bureaucrats who frequently felt that they were being thwarted by Khuhro. With no working experience of the democratic system, the Central bureaucrats in particular had never experienced a situation where their wishes were not instantly obeyed. In the provinces however there had long been the cut and thrust and the compromises of democracy. The situation was clearly impossible for any Sind government which wanted to retain any semblance of autonomy and to put the interests of the people first. It was also a bitter pill after the euphoric expectations of independence.

Khuhro increasingly felt that there was no appreciation of the effort the Government of Sind was making and the sacrifices that were being made by the people of Sind who were not only welcoming the refugees with open arms but whose province had to postpone many programmes of development in order to meet the needs of the Central Government which had arrived penniless in Karachi.

Instead of helping with the law and order situation and co-operating to defuse the tensions which increased with each batch of refugees, the Central Ministers had actively encouraged and even instigated the breach of peace in the city. There were other problems also where they were less than helpful. The building of offices and other accommodation had been done by the Sind Government at its own expense. The enormous cost of taking in refugees and settling them was also being borne by Sind and on top of that the Punjab Governor had asked him take in refugees to the tune of 300,000. The Punjab, a far bigger and richer province, he claimed, could not afford to look after them. The attitude of regarding Sind as a legitimate milch cow was plain to see and Khuhro wanted no more of it.

Soon after the arrival of the Central Government the Finance Minister Ghulam Mohammed had asked for a loan from Sind. The Indian Government had promised to hand over 60 crore cash balances to Pakistan but these had not arrived so Sind should give over its own reserves to Pakistan for the time being in order to meet immediate expenses. Khuhro explained that he had deposited the Sind money with the banks and that he could not possibly hand over the province's money in this irregular manner. He advised Ghulam Mohammed to get his money from India from where it was due. The Finance Minister complained to Liaquat Ali Khan who asked Khuhro to come and see him and:

"Liaquat Ali made an emotional appeal, 'This is your government. How can we starve here. We cannot even pay the salaries.' I said that we had already spent a good deal of money and were continuing expenditure on refugees. We had handed over our offices and done whatever else we could. On his insistence however I agreed to hand over our reserves of 30 crores at 3%."[36]

There was also a clash with the Central Government over the allotment of houses in Karachi. The Government of Sind had appointed Controllers to allot houses that fell vacant because of the exodus of Hindu owners as well as other accommodation that became available. This was being done by sharing it out between the immigrants and the locals on basis of need which the Sind Government considered a fair allocation of available accommodation. Liaquat Ali Khan and Ghulam Mohammed however insisted that all the accommodation must be given at their say so and moreover that forcible occupation of houses by certain elements should be condoned. This Khuhro was not prepared to do and so the Central authorities looked around for ways in which they could take over the control of housing in Karachi.

Unfortunate unpleasantness occurred between the Prime Minister and the Sind Premier when the former demanded more water for his official residence to be used for lawns and waterfalls in his garden. At a time when Karachi had to subsist on well water from Dumlotee and most houses used pebbles rather than lawns and when hundreds of thousands of people were pouring into the city, Khuhro felt that the demand was just too much and rejected it when the Municipality referred the matter to him. Liaquat Ali Khan was very annoyed and said to Khuhro in a public reception, "In Karachi the Prime Minister of Pakistan cannot even get water without your permission." Khuhro patiently explained the position which he felt should have been obvious and he had not liked to refuse the request but had no option.

Another more serious clash between Khuhro and the Prime Minister occurred when some Defence Ministry officials informed Khuhro that they understood that the Prime Minister had agreed to hand over to India some six sabre jets which were parked at Mauripur airport although India which had to hand over large amounts of stores, tanks, armour and 60 crores of cash, was not ready to do so. They appealed to Khuhro to do what he could to stop the planes from leaving. Khuhro responded immediately to the seriousness of the situation and ordered the I.G. Police to throw a cordon round the planes to stop them being flown out. He then went to see Liaquat Ali Khan and informed him of his action and that the planes should not be allowed to go until the Indian government had fulfilled its obligations. Liaquat Ali Khan said that Pakistan must fulfil its part of the bargain. Khuhro however did not make any commitment to the Prime Minister and left. Khuhro comments:

> "About a month later, in November, Liaquat Ali hosted a reception for some foreign dignitaries. He confronted me on the occasion saying that I was interfering in the function of the Central Government and that it was not my job as Chief Minister of a Province to interfere in the administration of Defence which was entirely a Central subject. I told him that I was doing this in the interests of the country and we must see that at least part of the agreement was implemented by India. What we had to give them was not even 10% of what India had to hand over to us so as far as I was concerned commonsense suggested that we should go slow and see how the Indian Government responded. Liaquat Ali insisted that I should withdraw the police and not interfere in Central affairs. After this I withdrew the police. I was informed by the Deputy Defence Secretary that the planes were taken over immediately by Indian pilots who were heard to say within the hearing of some Pakistan Air Force oficers that they would use the planes to bomb the 'so-called army of liberation and then these fools will realize the blunder they have committed."[37]

The Prime Minister became increasingly frustrated and was determined that Karachi was removed from the administration of the Sind Government and put under the control of the Central Government. For this he prepared the ground carefully. First of all Jinnah who had formed a good opinion of Khuhro's abilities and administration was to be alienated. He was persuaded that Karachi was his birthplace and should be directly under Central control; that it was not befitting his status that his capital should be administered by a provincial government and be dependant on it. He was also told that it would be impossible to take over Karachi if Khuhro was Premier and would subsequently have to be removed. Khuhro, only four to five months into his Premiership, was in a very vulnerable position. His position was not improved by his reluctance to descend to the same dirty tricks as his enemies. He felt strongly that his work should justify him and that his constitutional position was also strong enough to withstand his enemies. In this he greatly underestimated the attempts to undermine him. A press campaign was started against him by Altaf Hussain, the editor of *Dawn*. The newspaper was used to vilify Khuhro and accuse him of all manner of wrongdoing mostly by innuendo and unsupported accusations. He was accused of being unfriendly to the Pakistan government. A campaign of dis-information was launched. Throughout 1948 *Dawn* carried on its anti Khuhro war hoping that some of the mud would stick.

At the same time no stone was left unturned to turn Jinnah against him. One such attempt was to tell Jinnah that the Quaid-e-Azam Fund was not able to met enough donations because Khuhro's Premier's Fund for refugees was attracting all the money. As a result Jinnah wrote to Khuhro in late December 1947, asking him to wind up his Fund. Khuhro wrote back explaining the problems faced by the Sind Government in the settlement of refugees and the lack of co-operation from the Centre:

"I would like to place before you the background and the earlier history of the Premier's Fund for your information. In fact soon after I took over as Prime Minister of Sind on 16th August 1947, I found that a lot of Muslim refugees had started coming to Karachi and Hyderabad owing to the general massacre of Muslims in East Punjab and in some of the Indian States – like Bharatpur, Alwar, Patiala, Jodhpur, Udhaipur, Jaipur and Bikaner. Soon after that Ajmer refugees started coming to Hyderabad by train, and many people from the ports of Kathiawar, Bombay Presidency, and some of the other provinces began to pour in by sea.

Even before the partition of India, we had refugees from Bihar who had sought asylum here because of the massacres that took place in that Province towards the end of 1946 and early 1947. The Government of Sind had already incurred a good bit of expenditure in constructing huts for them at Karachi. As the killings in the Dominion of India gathered momentum, we found the refugee problem assuming such stupendous proportions that we felt we could not cope with it with our comparatively slender financial resources. So I rang up Mr. Ghulam Mohammed, the Finance Minister, and told him that as the refugee problem was the primary responsibility of the Pakistan Government, 50% at least of the total expenditure incurred by us on the resettlement and rehabilitation of refugees ought to be paid by them.

In early September, my estimate was that we would be spending about 20 lakhs of rupees within 6 months or so over this problem. I therefore decided to raise 10 lakhs of rupees by public subscription from the people of Sind. I requested Mr. Ghulam Mohammed to pay the remaining ten lakhs. Although Mr. Ghulam Mohammed did not definitely commit himself, he gave me a hopeful reply and the next day, when I called a meeting of the leading citizens of Karachi at my place, I explained the position to them. It was decided in that meeting, to open a Fund, called 'Premier's Fund' for the resettlement and the rehabilitation of Muslim refugees who were coming in an almost destitute condition and were thus placing a heavy burden on the Government of Sind which had to provide them with food, clothing, shelter and employment and even with bullocks and agricultural implements to settle them on lands.

In order to launch a vigorous collection campaign, I called a conference of District Officers at Karachi and asked them to invite people to give donations for the Fund and I also issued an appeal through the press to the public of Sind to contribute generously to the Premier's Fund. During my tour in the beginning of September in different District and Taluka headquarters, I repeated my appeal to the people to contribute liberally towards this fund. The collections really started in November and December when Zamindars and agriculturists had secured their income from the Kharif crop. A target of 10 lakhs was fixed for the whole province and the quota of contribution was fixed for each district and Karachi city after taking into consideration its contributing capacity.

Soon afterwards the Quaid-e-Azam Fund was started and the Governor of Sind was put upon the Committee in charge of it. His Excellency the Governor formed his own Committee for Sind, on which I was invited to serve. I informed the Governor that I had no objection to closing down my own Fund, and handing over our collections to the Quaid-e-Azam Fund, provided a certain amount of cash was placed at the disposal of my Government for ready expenditure by Collectors on refugees who were continuing to pour into Sind at an alarming rate. But as nothing transpired and no promise of a cash balance for ready and emergent expenditure was held out to me I had perforce to permit the Collectors to pursue their collections to my Fund in order that they could draw upon it for expenditure in their respective districts. Up to now nothing has been given from the Quaid-e-Azam Fund for the resettlement of refugees, although the Sind Government have had to establish camps at Bolari, Hyderabad, Karachi and at other District Headquarters throughout the Province. But for my Fund which enabled the Collectors to draw upon the cash balances thus collected, the Government of Sind would not have had ready money to spend in setting up these camps at very short notice...

I have not been correctly reported when you have been informed that I had given out that the Quaid-e-Azam Fund would be spent on the relief of refugees only for the Punjab. What I had said was that as the Punjab refugee problem has assumed colossal proportions compared to what Sind was faced with it was to be expected that the lion's share from the Fund would go to the Punjab. But I had contended that even then Sind had to face a very serious refugee problem and required a vast amount of money for solving it satisfactorily, and therefore I had no option but to continue collections to my Fund especially when nothing had either been given or promised to the Sind Government from the Quaid-e-Azam Fund. The Chief Secretary to the Government of Sind had under my instructions officially asked for help from the Quaid-e-Azam Fund, but so far no reply has been received.

However, I would like to assure you that I have no objection to closing down my Fund, and I am instructing all the Collectors to wind it up within their respective districts and to send the amounts so far collected by the end of this month, after deducting the expenditure incurred by them on the refugees so far, whatever balance remains will be transferred to the Quaid-e-Azam Fund. But as we have been required to take over a lakh and half of refugees from the Punjab immediately, and over and above this Muslims from the Dominion of India, specially from Ajmere and Kathiawar ports, who continue to pour in by land and by sea everyday, we shall be requiring an appreciable sum of money to draw upon for our day to day expenditure. I might point out that we are still receiving about 1,000 to 1,500 refugees daily by sea and by land. In the circumstances we would require at least 5 lakhs to be placed at our disposal immediately for emergent expenditure and as need arises we shall be asking for more financial help. In making donations from the Quaid-e-Azam Fund, I would request you to bear in mind that Sind should not be treated as a minor affair in this matter, and should be given a considerable share from the Quaid-e-Azam Fund for expenditure on refugees, especially when this problem can by no stretch of imagination be considered the responsibility of Sind Government in the sense in which it is of the Government of West Punjab. ...

I may respectfully point out that I am very much in touch with the refugee problem as it is being dealt with under my personal supervision. The arrangements at various places in Sind, and the collections for the Premier's Fund have been carried out under my instructions. But ofcourse I am not quite so conversant with the complexity of the refugee problem in other provinces, particularly in the West Punjab, because I am not a member of the Committee which has been set up to administer the Quaid-e-Azam Fund. Sind is represented on this Committee by His Excellency the Governor, who is not in direct touch with day to day administration of the Province. Hence I am afraid he is not in a position to inform himself of the nature of the situation facing this Province."[38]

Khuhro knew very well that the enquiry from Jinnah was the result of mischief making by the Governor who had flung various accusations about him to Jinnah and he hinted as much in the letter as he also pointed out the lack of co-operation from the Central Government in the matter of help for the refugees. Khuhro's bluntness would not have gone down well with Jinnah who had by now acquired demi-god status but Khuhro was not used to obfuscation when it came to matters of public interest and therefore deliberately painted the whole picture for him.

Jinnah was to get a sharp reminder of the abilities of the Sind Premier only two days after he recieved the letter on the 6 January when the riots broke out in Karachi but by this time it must be assumed he had already agreed to the plan to remove Karachi from the control of Sind Government.

Early in the third week of January 1948 a Cabinet meeting was called in the Governor General's House which Khuhro was also invited to attend. This was not an unusual procedure as Khuhro was invited quite often to attend Central Cabinet meetings. But he had been warned by Pirzada that the subject of the Centre's take over of Karachi would be brought up. Jinnah was presiding over the meeting. Liaquat Ali Khan made a speech that the Central Government could not continue to live under the shadow of the Provincial Government.

'The Central Government is sitting here like strangers. We have no power, everything is sanctioned by the Provincial Government especially Mr. Khuhro who controls the city. We are nothing in Karachi. If I want a gardener I have to refer to Mr. Khuhro, if I want water for my garden I have to refer to Mr. Khuhro. He is everything, we are nothing.'

He said further that the Sind Government must move out of Karachi. Compensation for Karachi could be discussed and given to Sind,

'Go make your capital in Hyderabad or somewhere.'

Khuhro was stunned at the venom of this attack and particularly by Jinnah's attitude:

"Jinnah sat silently throughout and did not defend me at all."

This desertion was particularly shocking coming so soon after Khuhro had been so highly praised by Jinnah for his courageous and effective handling of the riots in Karachi only ten days earlier.

Khuhro robustly responded pointing out that provincial governments administering a capital city was not unprecedented. For over a hundred years Calcutta, the capital of British India was administered by the Government of Bengal which shared the capital and Simla which was the summer capital of India was under the control of the Punjab Government. It was right and proper that the administration of Karachi should be with the Sind Government. There was no need for the Central Government to interfere. In any case he would have to consult his government before making any reply. The Cabinet decided to form a committee consisting of three Central Ministers I. I. Chundrigar, Raja Ghazanfar Ali and Ghulam Mohammed to talk to the Sind Government about making Karachi the permanent capital of Pakistan.

Khuhro circulated a note in the Sind Cabinet regarding the Central Government demand. He attended the first meeting of the Central Committee where the Central Ministers decided to resume the function of Customs. It was also decided that the Sind Government should hand over the Rent Control and House Allotment functions to the Central Government. Ghulam Mohammed nominated his personal secretary to take charge of House Allotment.

Khuhro was convinced that the Centre was unjustified in its demand to take over Karachi and that the move was unjust, unprecedented and a poor reward for all that Sind had done for Pakistan and the Central Government. He wrote a long note to the Prime Minister reminding him that the Central Government was only temporarily in Karachi according to Quaid-e-Azam's own commitment and therefore there was no need for the Sind Government to move out. He re-iterated his argument that Calcutta had remained the capital of the Indian Empire for nearly two centuries and that during that time the city had remained the capital of the Bengal province and been administered by the Government of Bengal. Also that the summer capital of British India, Simla had been administratively under the Government of the Punjab. With these examples available there was no necessity for Sind to move its capital. Meantime the Central Government could go ahead and build its own capital. The Sind Government also went through the exercise of working out a compensation figure for Karachi which came to Rs. 60 crore (Rs. 600,000,000) for the buildings alone. Eventually when the question of compensation was discussed with the Central Government it would only agree to 30 crores. But even this reduced figure remained only on paper and no compensation at all was paid then or later.

By the end of February the Committee had met a number of times and an extensive correspondence had taken place between Khuhro setting out the Sind position and Chundrigar setting out the Central Government position. The Sind Government said that,

"a serious difference of opinion has arisen regarding the terms of reference of the official committee. Mr. Chundrigar desires that it should examine in detail a proposal to shift the capital of Sind from Karachi. The Government of Sind, with the full support of the Assembly, is entirely opposed to this course and sees no reason why it should be considered. "[39]

Khuhro had every word he wrote fully approved by his Cabinet colleagues. He knew he was up against a formidable opponent – the full force of the Central Government with the backing of the Quaid-e-Azam himself. The news that the Central Government wanted to take over Karachi was known after the Cabinet meeting in the middle of January and there was a strong reaction from Sindhis. On 21 January newspapers reported the demonstrations of Sindhi students in Karachi:

"The Sind Muslim Students Federation on Tuesday launched its campaign against the proposed move to separate Karachi from the rest of Sind. About 800 Muslim students drawn from various colleges in the city staged a demonstration at the residence of the Sind Premier, Mr. M. A. Khuhro in the morning.
The demonstrators submitted their demands which besides opposing the separation of Karachi from the rest of the province, urged the Sind Government not to admit any more refugees from outside. They also demanded that Sind Muslims should be given preference in Government service and should be encouraged in taking to trade. The Premier addressing them said, "The Government of Pakistan has not yet officially written to us about the separation of Karachi from the Province of Sind, but the Sind Government will not yield to this move at any cost. We will see that Sind is not deprived of its rights."[40]
As the news spread the feelings in Sind ran high. The Sind Assembly as well as the Sind Muslim League Council passed strong resolutions against the proposal. The Council in a meeting on 2nd February passed a strongly worded statement:
"This Council of the Sind Provincial Muslim League while placing on record its amazement and alarm at persistent reports that Karachi city and its surrounding areas are to be taken away from Sind Province to form a separate area to be centrally administered by the Pakistan Government, deems its sacred duty as the accredited mouthpiece of Sind Muslims and also a well wisher of Pakistan, to place on record its emphatic protest against such a move, and in view of the following reasons and facts, earnestly urges upon Quaid-e-Azam Mohammed Ali Jinnah, both as the constitutional Head of the State and as the chosen head of the Muslim League organization to be pleased in the best interests of all concerned to disapprove such a move, for the following reasons:
Firstly, Karachi has been a natural and a corporate part of Sind since centuries and is now its nerve centre, economic, commercial, industrial, educational and cultural entity of the Province and any attempt to deprive the Province of its nerve centre will completely strangle the life and growth of the Province.
Secondly, such a move will not only be a flagrant violation of the express provisions of the Pakistan resolution passed by the All India Muslim League at its Lahore Session in 1940, according to which the territorial integrity of every unit constituting Pakistan is guaranteed but it will constitute a serious breach of faith with the people of the Province but for whose unequivocal and clear lead, the ideal of Pakistan would have remained an empty dream.
Thirdly, such a move is fraught with grave consequences inasmuch as, on the one hand, it will be an ill recompense for the spirit of Islamic brotherhood and generous hospitality shown by Sindhi people in welcoming Pakistan Government and doing everything possible in the cause of those lakhs of their Muslim brethern who have migrated to Sind not only from various areas of the Indian Dominion but also from several areas of Pakistan itself.
Fourthly, such a move is likely to prove a grave menace to the growing spirit of unity among Pakistan Muslims, as the natural and legitimate urge of the people of the Province to safeguard their vital interests will be exploited by those anti Pakistan forces which have lain low on account of the sincere and solid support that Sind Muslims have hitherto unreservedly given to the cause of the Muslim unity above everything else.

This Council further calls upon all its accredited representatives and constituents especially the Sind members of the Pakistan Constituent Assembly, the Sind Ministers and Members of the Sind Legislative Assembly, the district and primary branches of the Muslim League and indeed every well-wisher of Sind and of Pakistan to do everything in their power, to resist this unjust, impolitic and unwise move."[41]

A few days later on 10 February, the Sind Legislative Assembly passed a Resolution on the issue:

"This Assembly records its apprehension and alarm at the contemplated move of the Pakistan Government to remove the city of Karachi from the control of Sind administration and to place it under its own immediate jurisdiction as a centrally administered area. This House, therefore, resolves that Karachi must not be handed over to the Central Administration at any cost and further to call upon the Leader of the House and his Cabinet colleagues to bring home to the Government of Pakistan that such a step would not only cripple Sind economically and politically, but would also constitute a flagrant contravention of the Pakistan Resolution at Lahore in 1940 which emphasises the sovereignty and the territorial integrity of the autonomous units constituting Pakistan, not to speak of the violence which it would inflict upon the loyal and patriotic sentiments of the people of the Province towards their own independent State of Pakistan."[42]

The Assembly included the 'Pakistan Resolution' to remind the public and the Central authorities of the basic commitments that had been made to the provinces to win their support for Pakistan:

"It is the considered view of this Session of All India Muslim League that no constitutional plan would be workable for this country or acceptable to the Muslims unless it is designed on the following basic principle, viz., that geographically contiguous units are demarcated into regions which should be so constituted, with such territorial re-adjustments as may be necessary, that the areas in which Muslims are in majority, as in the North Western and Eastern zones of India, should be grouped together to constitute `Independent States' in which the constituent units shall be autonomous and sovereign."

For Khuhro the mandate was clear. He had to oppose the Centre's scheme to take over Karachi. For him it was not a question of defying the revered leader but of following democratic norms which had guided his whole political life. He was acting in the best interests of the province and people whose welfare had been entrusted to him. If this meant that he had to take on the Central Government he was prepared to do it. Almost any other man in his position would have hesitated and weighed the pros and cons for himself personally. He knew that Jinnah thought highly of his ability and that he would be able to enjoy a career of great privilege and power if he went along with the Centre's wishes. It must have caused him some hesitation to defy the man who had just achieved a rare feat in history, an independent country, albeit with some help from his friends and indeed his enemies.

But Khuhro knew that the idea did not emanate from Jinnah, no matter how enamoured he appeared to be of it and that the motives of the initiators of the move were certainly not of the purest. Mean motives had been behind the scheme and not least to do with the control and disposal of the rich pickings of evacuee property and settlement of immigrants in order to create a constituency for the displaced Ministers. Khuhro was only too well aware of this background. For who could know more than him the value of Karachi to Sind. He had struggled for the separation of Sind from the Bombay Presidency and had been deeply involved with the building of Karachi as the capital of the province. He knew well the cost of each brick and the thought and hopes that had gone into each building of this city, the 'nerve centre' as he called it, of Sind. Although they may never have visited it, he knew that even the remote villagers of the province were proud of this shining city which was their capital and which was the symbol of autonomy achieved and independence gained. He could see no reason at all as Sind was prepared to share its capital for as long as the Centre wanted to remain there, that the control of it should be taken away from the provincial government. For his convictions he was prepared to do battle no matter who and how powerful the adversary.

The Prime Minister asked Khuhro to a meeting in his office on 6 February and suggested that a Committee consisting of Pakistan Government and Sind Government officers be set up to

"examine the administrative, financial and other implications of making Karachi the permanent seat of the Government of Pakistan in addition to its remaining the Capital of Sind."[43]

Khuhro sent the names of his team which included the Chief Secretary Booth and the Secretaries for Finance, P.W.D., Local Self Government and Home to Chundrigar asking him to nominate the Centre's men. Chundrigar immediately disagreed with Khuhro's understanding of the situation:

"I must, however, point out that the statement in your letter that Karachi is to remain, in addition, the Capital of Sind is not in accord with the decision of the joint meeting. The correct position is that ... Karachi should be the permanent seat of the Government of Pakistan. The questions whether Karachi should also continue to be the Capital of Sind, or whether the Provincial Capital be shifted to some other place and Karachi converted into a Centrally Administered Area were left over for further consideration... It was also agreed that these two issues should be dealt with at a joint meeting of the Ministers of Pakistan Government and the Government of Sind, and in the event of disagreement, the matter should be placed before the Quaid-e-Azam for final decision."[44]

Khuhro wrote back refuting the claims made by Chundrigar that there was any agreement on the shifting of the Sind Capital from Karachi:

"With reference to your second paragraph, I must point out that as far as I and my colleagues are concerned, there was no agreement on any of the points mentioned by you.

In view of the very clear mandate given by the Sind Legislative Assembly (a copy of the Resolution is attached), I regret that I cannot agree to instruct the officers of this Government nominated on the Committee to discuss the shifting of the Capital of Sind to some other place. I hope, therefore, that discussion will be confined to the first of the two main terms of reference given in your letter."[45]

The Central Minister assured Khuhro that the
"report of this Committee will not commit either the Government of Pakistan or the Government of Sind to its recommendations. The participation of your officers in the work of the Committee will be without prejudice to your contentions, of which we are aware. The decision on the material points will be reached by a joint meeting of the Ministers of the Pakistan Government and the Sind Government... and the matter in dispute will be placed before the Quaid-e-Azam for his decision."[46]

Khuhro re-iterated his stand:

"I suggest that we agree to defer discussion on the question of shifting the capital of Sind from Karachi until the Committee has explored the implications of the Capital's remaining here."[47]

The Central Government it appeared, was reluctant to confine the discussion of the Committee to 'the implications of the Capital's remaining [in Karachi].' and wanted to get the Sind administration out of sight as soon as possible and so Chundrigar tried once again to get Khuhro's commitment to get all the points of the Central agenda discussed by the official Committee citing an 'oral commitment', "Will you now confirm in writing what you told me on the 17th instant that the Committee may examine all the terms of reference and give a fact finding report?" Khuhro was no amateur in spotting official ambivalence, replied in clear and unambiguous terms explaining at some length the implications of what the Central Government was asking for:

"Thank you for your letter of the 20th February. I am sorry if I gave you a wrong impression in our personal conversation on the 17th. I have already made it clear in my letters of the 14th and 19th February, which were written in consultation with my Cabinet colleagues, that my Government is definitely opposed to any discussion of the proposal to shift the capital of Sind from Karachi. Unless detailed discussion in the official committee on the first of the issues proposed by you leads to the conclusion that Karachi should not continue as the capital of Sind, and the reasons in support of that conclusion are fully weighed by my Government, such discussion is premature and unnecessary. I must observe that no reasons for the proposal to compel us to shift our capital have yet been advanced in any quarter.

2. Moreover discussion on the proposal would further exacerbate public feeling in the Province, which has already unfortunately worsened owing to loose talk about the amputation of our capital. This would render more difficult the establishment of friendly relations between the local population and the immigrants, refugees and others – a problem which is already a source of anxiety to my Government.

3. Assuming that it is finally decided that the permanent capital of Pakistan should be in Karachi, the Sind Government will co-operate most willingly to remove any difficulties there may be in the way of free operation of the sovereign Government here, as soon as the difficulties are pointed out. The Official Committee will go into this in detail. I see no reason to suppose that the removal of such difficulties will entail shifting the provincial capital elsewhere. It must be obvious without my going into any detail, that the practical difficulties of such a move would be enormous and its permanent results on the life of the

Province catastrophic.

4. I would earnestly request you to appreciate the position of my colleagues and myself, as Ministers responsible to an Assembly which has so recently given its unanimous vote against the proposal. If you will approach the matter in a generous and accommodating spirit, I am convinced that a solution of all difficulties can be found which will provide for both Governments exercising full authority in their respective spheres in Karachi, and will avoid the wound to the feelings of the people of Sind which the amputation of Karachi would inflict.

5. Lastly, in order to put a stop to the unfortunate and damaging public agitation which has arisen I would appeal to the Pakistan Government to issue a statement that while consideration is being given to the measures necessary to define the special relationship between the Central and Provincial Governments in respect of the administration of the city which is the capital of both, there is no intention of compelling the Sind Government to move elsewhere. This step will do something to counter the bad feeling which has arisen, and which may, if not checked, seriously affect the orderly resettlement of refugees in this province."[48]

As Khuhro pointed out in this and a previous letter the news was out that the Central Government wanted to sever the very head of Sind by taking its capital. There was a wave of anger in the province and an agitation started among the students. After the first demonstration in Karachi which was reported on 21 January a series of processions and demonstrations were held at the houses of Ministers and even at the Governor General's House. The demonstrators shouted slogans against the head of the state and a black flag was hoisted on top of the Leslie Wilson Muslim Hostel right opposite the Governor General's House. Jinnah was put out by this *lese majeste* and called Khuhro specially to complain that his younger brother was leading the agitation. In fact Khuhro's youngest brother Ali Gohar was living in the Leslie Wilson hostel and was one of the students participating in, though by no means the leader of the 'agitation', but these complaints were certainly an indication of the unease that Jinnah felt during these months.

There had been long standing differences between the Governor Hidayetullah and Khuhro and it was understood by people who knew both such as the ex-Governor Mudie that the juxtaposition of the two would produce a difficult situation. Khuhro could have made life easier for himself if he had gone along with Hidayetullah's quirks but Khuhro was a strict administrator who did not tolerate lax behaviour in the carrying out of public affairs. Various situations arose between the two, for example the Governor had demanded Rs. 2,00,000, a large sum of money at the time, for the decoration of the Governor's House to which Khuhro could not agree under the circumstances then prevailing in the country. He sanctioned Rs. 75,000 and pointed out that Ministers were only given Rs. 25,000 for the purpose. At an early stage of Khuhro's Premiership Hidyetuallah also sent Permanand Kundanmal the Advocate General of Sind, a personal friend of his, to see Khuhro with a message that Khuhro should oblige the people that were sent by him. Khuhro knew that the people who had to be obliged had probably paid for the favours and this would certainly tarnish the reputation of his administration so he refused to do as he was asked. Hidayetullah was resentful at not getting his way and waited for an opportunity to get back at Khuhro. However he knew that he needed to act carefully since Khuhro had support within the Sind Assembly and Party and also at that time the confidence of Jinnah.

By April 1948 however, the situation was ripe for Hidayetullah to strike. He came to an understanding with two of the Ministers, Mir Ghulam Ali Talpur and Pir Illahi Bux that if either of them was made Premier they would take the Punjab refugee overflow and hand over Karachi to the Central Government within three days. They set about getting signatures for a no confidence motion against Khuhro. For this purpose both of them toured Sind to sound out the members but they could not muster any support and reported failure. Hidayetullah took the two Ministers to Jinnah to discuss the problem. Jinnah was reported to have said to them, "I am prepared to remove him but you work out a plan whereby I can do so." The Advocate General Wasim gave his opinion that the Governor of Sind had no power to dismiss the Chief Minister if the latter enjoyed the confidence of the Assembly.

Well aware of the Governor's hand behind the problems in his Cabinet, Khuhro wrote to Jinnah on 22 April, appealing to him as a fair arbitrator:

"My dear Quaid-e-Azam,

As you are well aware, an unfortunate controversy has arisen between two of my Cabinet colleagues, Pir Illahi Baksh and Mir Ghulam Ali Talpur, and myself. These gentlemen have come out with public statements expressing their want of confidence in myself as Premier of Sind and have even gone to the length of openly attacking me for the manner in which I have been carrying on the Government of this province.

2. Whatever may be the rights and wrongs of the matter, the fact that two of my Ministers have openly revolted against me as Premier, has confronted the province with an unfortunate state of affairs. According to the way that Government is carried on in Sind and Pakistan, not to speak of Great Britain and the Dominions on whose constitutional pattern the governance of this country has been based, the Cabinet system of Government can only function effectively, if at all, provided there is political homogeneity in its composition and collective responsibility in its working. These two conditions are absolutely fundamental to its successful working as it is essential that it must function as a unit, not only towards legislature but also towards the Governor.

3. The activities of my two colleagues during the last few days have disrupted the political solidarity of my Cabinet and have destroyed its sense of collective responsibility. Pir Illahi Bux and Mir Ghulam Ali Talpur have gone to the extent of writing behind my back to the Governor, openly disassociating themselves from certain of my actions in the transaction of Government business and have not even hesitated to go back on certain unanimous decisions taken by the Cabinet – decisions to which they themselves had formally and solemnly subscribed.

4. As these two Ministers have openly revolted against my leadership as Premier, and have by misguided counsels disrupted the political solidarity of my Cabinet and destroyed its basis of collective responsibility, it has become very difficult for me carry on the Government of the province if they remain in my Cabinet. Constitutional propriety clearly demands of them that they should

resign office when they have such differences of opinion with me and lack of confidence in my leadership. But as they have chosen to flout constitutional practice and procedure, as has indeed been demonstrated by their repudiation of the principles of the political solidarity and collective responsibility of the Cabinet, I have no other option but to advise His Excellency the Governor to remove them from office, if they persist in refusing to hand over their resignations. Only thus will it be possible for me to restore the functioning of my Cabinet on a proper constitutional basis.

5. I need hardly emphasise that according to well established conventions of the constitution and authoritative usage throughout the British Commonwealth, it is the constitutional right of the Premier to choose his colleagues and to drop any Minister whom he finds unwilling to accept the obligations and discipline which he owes to his Premier. As I command overwhelming support as Premier – both in the Muslim League Assembly Party and in the Legislature as a whole, it would be incumbent on the Governor to accept my constitutional advice and act upon it.

6. I am writing this letter to apprise you of the state of affairs brought about by the actions of my two colleagues and I most respectfully request you to direct the Governor of Sind under section 51, sub-section (5) of the Constitution Act to remove the Pir and also the Mir from office, if they persist in their refusal to hand over their resignations. I wish to replace them by other persons who are willing to accept my political leadership and whose confidence I command, so that the political solidarity and collective responsibility of the Government, which has so rudely been shattered, may be restored and Government may be carried on as smoothly as before."[49]

Khuhro felt, as this letter showed, that he could depend on Jinnah who had a great reputation as a constitutionalist and for being a man of principle but there was no immediate comfort from that direction. Khuhro assumed that Hidayetullah had support from powerful forces at the Centre to take the steps he was taking but was still not certain of the level of that support. Besieged as he had felt with all the manoeuverings to get him out of power Khuhro made a tactical blunder. Hidayetullah issued an order about a week earlier changing portfolios and taking away the charge of Home Affairs from the Premier. He had obtained the opinion of the Advocate General that the Governor had the right to re-assign portfolios. The Chief Secretary referred the matter to Khuhro asking if the order was to be implemented. Khuhro was advised by Kazi Fazlullah, a good friend, colleague and a lawyer himself, to agree to the change as this might defuse the situation. Khuhro allowed the change to be gazetted but the situation was far from defused. Khuhro wrote to Jinnah who he hoped would be a fair arbitrator but the formality of the address itself and the nature of the letter was an indication of the distance that he now felt between himself and Jinnah whose guest he had so recently been at a private meal and who had lavished so much praise on him only some weeks before:

"Your Excellency,

I beg to invite your kind attention to the following:-

1. I am the leader of the Muslim League Assembly Party in Sind, and hold, by virtue thereof, the office of the Premier of the Province. I was elected as such,

unanimously, eight months ago and continue to enjoy full confidence of my party. This is evident from the fact that as lately as February last the Party and, later, the Legislature had unanimously passed a vote of confidence in me. Ofcourse, the Budget presented by me and the Legislative measures brought forward by my Government were also passed.

2. Your Excellency will recollect that, in accordance with your instructions, the Muslim League Assembly Party had appointed a Standing Committee, which is elected by the Party every year, for advising the Ministry, from time to time, regarding administrative matters. This Committee met on 21st and 22nd March last to discuss among other things certain complaints which it received against the working of the Civil Supplies Department, of which Hon'ble Mir Ghulam Ali was the Minister in charge. The Committee had invited both Mir Ghulam Ali Khan and myself to attend its meetings, but both of us were unable to do so. The Committee eventually passed a Resolution criticising some aspects of the working of the Civil Supplies Department.

3. As soon as Mir Ghulam Ali Khan learnt about this resolution he issued a press statement holding me responsible for the criticism contained in the above resolution. I was at the time away at Lahore. On my attention being drawn to this statement, I issued an explanatory press note correcting the wrong impression under which the Mir Sahib appeared to have issued his statement.

4. On my return to Karachi, I met my Hon'ble colleagues, Mir Ghulam Ali Khan and Pir Illahi Baksh, (the latter having by now joined hands with the former, and issued a press statement of his own equally vehemently criticising me.) and as a result of the frank talks that we had, the misunderstanding was removed and the Mir Sahib issued a fresh statement, the following operative part of which is specially noteworthy:–

"I, therefore, sincerely regret that in the course of my press statements issued in this connection, I should have brought in the name of the Premier, who is the leader of our party and enjoys our full confidence, into this controversy."
Following this, I took the controversy as closed.

5. But four days later, i.e. on 6th of April, the two Hon'ble Ministers, to my great surprise, undertook a tour of Sind for the purpose of fomenting a rebellion in the Party against me. Pursuant to that object, the Pir Sahib also summoned a meeting of the Party in his capacity as the Deputy Leader and fixed it for 14th April. The phraseology of the notice for the meeting, as issued by the Pir Sahib, itself reflected a rebellious mood on their part. Indeed, the Assembly Party having already been regularly summoned and fixed for 30th April, for the purpose of straightening out the difference between the Standing Committee and the Mir Sahib, there was no need whatsoever for a separate Party meeting being called on his own by the Pir Sahib. The subsequent averment of the Pir Sahib that the meeting called by him was an 'informal affair' intended to 'thrash out certain important matters' is belied by the very wording and form of the letter of invitation issued by him. In the course of their aforesaid tour, the two Ministers did everything in their power to disparage, to lower me in the estimation of the party members, and to drive a wedge between me and the party.

6. On 14th April, the meeting called by the Pir Sahib came off and was attended

by only 8 members (including the two convening Ministers themselves), although the total strength of the party was 37. These eight persons dispersed without reaching any formal decision. Indirectly it showed that my position within the Party continued to be unassailable.

7. Finding their plan miscarrying, and despaired of response from Party members, the two Ministers issued a joint statement on the next day condemning me over again openly and on the basis of certain imaginary assumptions. To this I issued a rejoinder couched in most conciliatory terms, being on my own part unwilling to widen the gulf. A comparative study of both these statements will give Your Excellency an idea as to the respective moods in which the two sides were. My statement, however, only brought forth two further statements from them, more violent and vituperative.

8. On 14th April, I received a letter from the Governor, desiring me to see him. For reasons of health, I could see him only on 16th when His Excellency told me that he had decided to redistribute portfolios. Without conceding that he could do so except on my advice, I pleaded with His Excellency to give me his proposals as also to enable me to consult my Hon'ble colleagues and tender my advice on this matter. Fuller details of what transpired in the course of this interview are embodied in the confirmatory letter which I addressed to him.

9. Disregarding my pleadings, the Governor passed an order the same afternoon (16th instant) reallocating the portfolios and had it issued under the signature of his own Secretary. This order when communicated to the Chief Secretary evoked a note from the latter. Thereafter, the Secretariat of the Governor directly got a Gazette Extraodinary published embodying the said order of the Governor.

10. In the afternoon of the same day, I requested the Governor not to rush the matter through and and asked him to enable me, instead, to consider the matter along with my colleagues. As His Excellency did not appear to be in a mood to accede to my request, I sent him another letter on the following day tentatively acquiescing in the position created by him, pending the result of my representation to His Excellency the Governor General. Naturally, I directed the Chief Secretary meanwhile to enforce the Governor's order.

11. My humble submission now is that the Governor's order, re-allocating the portfolios contrary to my advice, deserves to be withdrawn, and that, in view of the following grounds, Your Excellency will be graciously pleased to issue a directive to him to the effect under the provisions of Section 51 of the Pakistan (Provisional Constitution) Order, 1947:–

(a) Both constitutionally, and, from the standpoint of democratic conventions and usages, it is the privilege of the Premier to arrange allocation of portfolios. The advice so tendered by him is virtually binding on the Governor.

(b) Unless such a privilege is enjoyed by the Premier, it is impossible for him to maintain homogeneity or cohesion in the Cabinet or ensure its smooth working. No Premier can effectively discharge his responsibility to the Legislature or to the country unless he has a free hand in the matter of distribution of work.

(c) It is the Premier who is responsible and answerable to the Legislature regarding all matters pertaining to the administration. He can possibly render no account to the Legislature regarding those branches of the Administration in the allocation of which to the Ministers concerned he has no hand. The position in the Legislature as a result of an imposition as this from the Governor, would become grotesque in the extreme.

(d) It undermines the position of the Premier in that he having no hand in the distribution of work, his colleagues would not owe to him that measure of responsibility which they must, if the Cabinet is to work smoothly.

(e) Even during the pre-Freedom days, no Governor, in these matters, had ever imposed his will on his Premier. If that was the position under the old dispensation, whereunder Governors enjoyed 'special responsibilities, individual judgement and individual discretion', it is highly inappropriate and inexpedient on the part of any Governor, in the new setup, to arrogate to himself and exercise and make a fetish of powers and functions which even the old Governors never deemed it fit to avail themselves of.

(f) This order of the Governor affords an encouragement to the rebel Ministers, who normally deserve removal from office by reasons of their behaviour alluded to above, to persist in their defiance of the Premier who represents the choice and will of the Party as a whole. At any rate, it could not conduce to the ensuring of better relations between the two Ministers and the Premier, setting as it does a premium on discord and intransigence.

(g) There is no precedent in the annals of any democratic country in which a constitutional head may have acted in this manner, in the matter of allocation of work, *vis-a-vis* his Premier.

(h) The grounds on which the Governor has based his order are also unsustainable. The two grounds he has given are: 'expeditious despatch of work.' and 'more harmonious working of the Cabinet.' The one is untenable, because neither had he any premises for holding that the government work was not being carried on expeditiously nor could he reasonably maintain that Pir Illahi Bux or Mir Ghulam Ali Khan were more efficient or more energetic than those colleagues of theirs whose portfolios the Governor has transferred to them. The other ground, I am afraid, is so transparently incorrect that it hardly calls for any comment. Rather it is just the other way about. In the course of his conversation on the subject with me on April 16th, the Governor had referred to yet another ground, namely, that there were complaints against the Supplies Minister, Mir Ghulam Ali Khan, and therefore he intended to divest him of that portfolio. But what baffles the imagination is that the very same Minister has been later invested by him with the portfolios of Revenue and P.W.D., both of which are decidedly more delicate and important. It sounds like rewarding a delinquent for his delinquencies, and subjecting the other branches of the Administration also to the same bout of mismanagement.

(i) Even supposing that the grounds given by the Governor did hold any water – although I strongly maintain that they did not – the requisite relief could not come through the Governor but through the Legislature and the Party to which alone the Premier was answerable regarding the good government of the Province. In this case the Governor has, unluckily, assumed powers and functions which were altogether foreign to his office and lay exclusively within the province of the Legislature. In other words, it infringes on the powers and privileges of the Legislature and brings into being a new institution more potent than even the Legislature itself. This, besides envisaging an unworkable arrangement, is liable to lead to greater friction between the various parts of this triangle and overlapping of powers and functions.

(j) So long as a Premier carries the Legislature with him and enjoys its confidence, the Governor cannot override his advice or create any situations for him which may stand in the way of his properly discharging those responsibilities which he owes to the Legislature. In this case, I have had a vote of confidence from the Legislature sitting in regular session as also from my Party, as lately as February last. Even now a motion of confidence signed by an overwhelming majority of the Party members is awaiting formal adoption at the meeting of the Party due to be held on the 30th instant. Such being the position, the Governor, I am afraid, cannot draw any adverse conjectures of his own as to the working of my Government, much less proceed in their light.

12. While requesting Your Excellency to issue a directive to the Governor in the terms of my prayer in paragraph 11, I also submit that Your Excellency will, in the interests of good government of the Province and harmonious working of the Cabinet, supplement your directive with an additional instruction to the Governor to dismiss Mir Ghulam Ali and Pir Illahi Bux on the basis of, inter alia, these grounds:–

(a) That they have been guilty of gross misconduct in that they have issued public statements disparaging me – their Premier. This has undermined the prestige of the Party, of myself as the head of the Cabinet, and of the Government with which they have been associated. A reference to Appendices B,D,G, and H will convince Your Excellency of the gross impropriety they have been guilty of.

(b) They have disrupted the solidarity of the Cabinet and made its smooth working difficult.

(c) They have carried on a campaign of vilification against me throughout the Province in the course of their recent tour.

(d) They have spread wild rumours as to the backing and encouragement they claim to be in the enjoyment of both from the Governor and from some members of the Pakistan Cabinet. These rumours are definitely designed to strain the relations subsisting, on the one hand, between the Governor and the Premier and, on the other hand, between the Provincial and the Central Governments. In this formative period, situations such as these cannot be countenanced.

(e) They have been trying to disrupt the Party and demoralise Assembly members and the public at large by abusing the new powers placed at their disposal by the Governor.

13. Lastly, I sanguinely hope that Your Excellency will be pleased to vindicate the prestige and the position of the Premier, in disregard of the fact who he is, safeguard the interests and privileges of the Legislature, help the growth of happy conventions consistent with modern notions of democracy and prevent springing up of undemocratic precedents which will only tend to make the task of every Premier everywhere difficult."[50]

Khuhro had appealed to Jinnah on the basis of constitutional practice in a parliamentary system, to 'safeguard the interests and privileges of the legislature, help growth of happy conventions consistent with the modern notions of democracy' and which he assumed Jinnah believed in and which with his respect for law, would be his first priority. He pointed out the evil effects that were likely to ensue if the constitutional norms were ignored and the Governor was allowed to arrogate to himself powers which did not belong to him and that this action, 'infringes on the powers and privileges of the Legislature and brings into being a new institution more potent than even the Legislature itself.' Later events in the province and indeed the country would prove these words to be prophetic.

Hidayetullah meanwhile went ahead, now with Home Affairs out of Khuhro's hands, to frame cases against him with the co-operation of pliable police officers and some co-operative civil servants.

The continuing efforts of two renegade Ministers to get votes against Khuhro met with failure and on 25 April the Governor and the two Ministers met Jinnah and told him that they were helpless. Jinnah told them that they would have to suggest some way of removing Khuhro, preferably a constitutional way.[51] He called Khuhro to see him and told him that both the Prime Minister and the Governor were complaining about him and that he should resign for the time being and stay away from politics for about six months- 'go abroad or sit quiet and I will summon you back'. Meanwhile an Inquiry Committee would be set up to examine the complaints against him. Jinnah said that he was prepared to make a commitment to bring Khuhro back as Premier after six months and that Khuhro should trust him. Jinnah dictated a note to his Personal Secretary in Khuhro's presence. Khuhro told Jinnah that he was prepared to resign but would not accept conditions. Jinnah told him that he should take the note and think it over and reply within twenty four hours. Khuhro went home and talked it over with Daultana who was staying with him who also agreed that the conditions in the note were untenable. Khuhro wrote back to Jinnah that he was prepared to resign but that he could not accept the conditions that had been put to him.

On 26 April Jinnah telephoned Khuhro who was in his office and said to him, 'Khuhro you are dear to me. I don't want you to go. You are one of my best administrators and I want you to be there to secure the country. It is only a question of six months and then I will call you back. No harm will come to you if you do as I ask.'

Khuhro told Jinnah that he was ready to resign and that he was already clearing out his office in anticipation of his accepting the resignation. Khuhro wrote his resignation and sent it. He finished clearing his office and was lunching with some guests at his house when the Governor's Personal Secretary, was announced. He had brought the letter of dismissal.[52] Khuhro received the letter at the table, glanced at it, put it down and went on talking with his guests.[53]

Pir Illahi Bux was sworn in as Premier and within twenty four hours orders regarding the hand over of Karachi to the Centre and the bringing in of surplus refugees from the Punjab were passed. Collector Masud went specially to Lahore and brought back two trains of refugees to Nawabshah.

Khuhro clarified his position in a press statement which was published the next day, though not all the papers carried the bold and defiant declaration:

"No one can doubt that in my eight month tenure as Premier of Sind I have discharged my responsibilities towards the people of Sind with utmost integrity and have striven for their welfare with all the strength at may command. At the same time I have left no stone unturned in serving the people of Pakistan as a whole. The success of my administration in dealing with the extraordinary and highly volatile conditions of the past several months is there for all to see and no other province in the whole of the sub-continent has a better record. I had expectations of a better reward than the one I have received. I have however no regrets at my conduct during this entire period. Whether in or out of office I intend to work for the rights of the people of Sind and for safety and security of Pakistan without any reservation."[54]

Khuhro went to give the details of the crisis including the fact that he had laid the entire situation before the Quaid-e-Azam who had responded that no matter how strong or justified Khuhro's stand was he should resign at this time. Khuhro said that he made it clear to the Governor General that he was directly responsible to the Legislature and that the Ministers who felt unhappy with his government could move a motion of No Confidence which would decide the fate of the Ministry. This was the correct constitutional procedure which he was in no doubt Quaid-e-Azam was aware of.

"I made clear my willingness to immediately call a session of the House for this purpose... It is a fact that as recently as February last the Sind Legislative Assembly passed a unanimous vote of confidence in me and since then there has been nothing to change that position. But in spite of my strong position constitutionally, in keeping with Quaid-e-Azam's desire I was ready to resign and in accordance with that on 26 April I sent my resignation to the Quaid-e-Azam.

All my legitimate and constitutional demands were rejected and last evening the Governor (ignoring my resignation) sent me an order of dismissal. At the same time he announced that he would appoint a tribunal to examine the charges (not yet framed) against me but not against any of the other Ministers or the Governor himself. The irony is that the tribunal would be appointed by the self same Governor."[55]

The action of the Governor in dismissing a Premier with a clear and overwhelming majority in the Legislature was absolutely illegal and unconstitutional under the law then prevalent. Later laws would be brought in giving special powers to the Governor General which would allow the Centre to bring in and throw out provincial governments at will and in turn Central Governments would themselves be thrown out undemocratically. The foundations for these tragic events which would eventually strangle the infant democracy of Pakistan were thus laid at the very birth of the state within eight months of independence

Khuhro's detailed exposition of the situation in the letters he wrote to Jinnah are key documents to understanding the pressures and tensions that local grass-roots politicians were feeling from the Central leadership. This leadership was largely composed of civil servants from the old Government of India. They had mostly held positions in peripheral departments and lacked experience at the centre of power. They assumed the mantle of the British rulers with delight and alacrity and felt that they were replacing the Raj. But while the British rulers of India owed allegiance to a higher ideal – that of the British Raj – the Empire, the new rulers of Pakistan would have no higher allegiance than to themselves. They had little understanding of their new country and because they rarely sought the people's electoral backing, they felt no allegiance to them. Democratic practices which bind elected representatives to the people were completely unknown to them. It was a recipe for disaster and Khuhro was the first victim of their machinations. A democratically elected, immensely popular and experienced politician had been removed from the Premiership of a province within eight months of independence. It was a crushing blow for Pakistan and an extraordinary situation for Khuhro himself.

17

UNDER SIEGE

On 26th April 1948 Khuhro was dismissed from the Premiership of Sind. A Special Court of Inquiry was specifically set up without reference either to the Sind Cabinet or the Sind Legislature.[1] It was an entirely new procedure devised, it would seem, to remove Khuhro from holding public office for a considerable time.

It was barely eight months since independence and Khuhro had made the difficult step from opposing the imperial power to nation building with consummate skill. He had almost single-handedly managed to prepare Karachi for its new role as the capital of a new country. He had dealt with the enormous problems in the wake of the partition of the sub-continent and departure of the colonial power and now he was being laid low. It was a situation full of irony for Khuhro, a most faithful Muslim Leaguer and as he would consider himself, soldier for the cause of Indian Muslims.

At this stage, in April 1948 Khuhro was an elected member of the Sind Assembly. He had been voted to that position a mere four months previously and had then been elected unanimously by the Parliamentary Party to be Premier of the province. He was enormously popular within Sind. He was a man who got things done. He was trusted by the people. And yet his enemies were determined to see him out of politics for the forseeable future although there was no precedent in a post-colonial democracy or indeed any democracy for the removal of an elected incumbent politician.

In the next three years the powers that were ranged against Khuhro would try three different ways to remove him from politics altogether. First they set up the Special Court of Inquiry to try him on no less than 62 charges, all of them relatively minor relating to his eight-month period as Premier. Then there was the criminal charge brought against him for supposedly sequestring a printing press for use in the *Sind Observer*, a newspaper which he controlled, and finally in 1949 the notorious law known as PRODA was introduced to intimidate politicians in general and to remove Khuhro from active politics. But even this extraordinary abuse of democratic processes failed to quell Khuhro. In each case he marshalled his facts and arguments with meticulous detail and fought fiercely against the shortsighted and relentless forces who were intent on bringing him down. It was a remarkable display of courage in adversity.

The Court of Inquiry presided over by the Chief Justice of Pakistan, Sir Abdur

Rashid and Justice Shahabuddin from East Pakistan, started its hearings in early June, sat for six months, and finished its proceedings in early December. It started with a long statement by the Prosecuting Counsel, Parmanand Kundanmal, a close friend and confidante of Hidayetullah, the Governor of Sind. The statement was a compilation of charges framed to cover practically every administrative action Khuhro had taken in his few months of office, a case of flinging a lot of mud hoping that some of it would stick. Government officials were brought in as witnesses and it was obvious that they were under pressure to try and incriminate Khuhro. But in the absence of independent evidence it was to prove impossible to establish the more serious charges of maladministration and none at all of corruption.

The 62 charges related to alleged maladminstration in which were included all actions relating to and dealing with the emergency situation in the province from 13 August onwards.[2] These included charges relating to appointments made by the Premier without reference to the Governor and sometimes it was alleged, against the advice of the civil servants. Further charges related to the posting of government officers, administrative decisions either accepting or rejecting the recommendations of bureaucrats regarding appointments and administration, allocation of houses even to such eminent public figures such as Haji Maula Baksh Soomro, M.L.A. and to a Secretary of the Sind government. There were charges relating to the levels of rent fixed for houses allocated in Karachi, giving of *taccavi* loans to respectable zamindars and here again the name of Maula Baksh Soomro was cited as well as that of Khan Bahadur Haji Fazul Mohammed, M.L.A.; of having a minor case withdrawn against Mir Jaffar Khan Jamali, an important Muslim League supporter since the early days of its organisation in Sind and a man who had defied the government of the day to invite Jinnah to his house for a meeting during his tour of Sind in 1938; condoning of some and punishment of others, in fact all possible matters of ordinary day to day administration were brought up as charges against Khuhro.[3]

The recurrent theme of the prosecution counsel was that Khuhro had ignored the Governor. The main instigator of the Inquiry against Khuhro was Hidayetullah who had set up an office in his house to frame the charges and to conduct the case against Khuhro himself.

On 30 September Khuhro made his statement to the Court of Inquiry. Khuhro knew that he had to tread carefully in his defence statement. The whole intricate story of his removal from office and the complex web of intrigue that had preceded it was not clear even to Khuhro at this stage. He was, however, sure of the way the case had been framed and who were the immediate instigators of it. He was also very clear on the way that he had run the administration, the nature of the crisis and the pressures under which he had worked during his premiership. His statement before the Court laid out a clear and convincing picture of the period of partition in Sind and he laid bare the history of the political rivalries and jealousies that had motivated the old man, Hidayetullah, who had become the catspaw of Central authoritarianism.

His statement before the Court of Inquiry ran to approximately 17,000 words or about 33 pages of text. It was prepared by him personally from careful examination of his own papers and notes and with such official documents as he could command. The case roused intense public interest and was fully covered in the newspapers. The court was full everyday it sat and Khuhro was imperturbable and calm throughout the proceedings. The case could be seen simply as an old fashioned dog fight between two politicians but there were deep seated constitutional principles at stake. Khuhro spent much of his defence spelling out these principles. The most important one was the position and power of the Provincial Governor and in particular his relations with the Premier and Cabinet. Khuhro's point was that Governor was merely a constitutional and titular head of the government and that the Premier actually dispensed power.

But to begin his statement Khuhro traced the politics of Sind since the separation from Bombay in 1935; his initial close alliance with Hidayetullah and the gradual disillusionment with the old man especially after the latter's abandonment of Muslim League for the sake of a Ministership in an anti-Muslim League government. He particularly concentrated on the elections of 1946 and the fact that he had the confidence of the House after both elections but had stood down from the contest for Premiership in at the specific request of the Quaid-e-Azam. That Hidayetullah was unable to reconcile himself to the fact that his days of Premiership were over and was determined to punish Khuhro who had dared not to pander to him. He pinpointed Hidayetullah as the vengeful spirit behind the prosecution case:

"The 62 charges framed against me betray a desperate attempt on the part of Shaikh Ghulam Hussain the Governor of Sind to justify his malicious and wicked report which he made against me to the Quaid-e-Azam and on the basis of which he secured the assent of the Governor General to my dismissal from Premiership ... the old gentleman has girded up his loins, established the prosecution office in his own house, used questionable methods for constraining all and sundry to give suitable evidence and spent all the resources of the province to compass my ruin and political death"[4]

Khuhro argued that the only legitimate way to test the charges against him was by summoning him before at the bar of the House of which he was member and leader:

"Had the Governor entertained the least respect for constitutional law, and had his conscience been clear, he should have summoned the assembly session and there arraigned me at the bar of that tribunal. *That was and is the tribunal of the people in all democratic states.* The charges relate to the discharge of my duties as a Minister and these had to be considered primarily by the electorate through their representatives in the Assembly. But the Governor dare not face the people or invite their verdict."[5]

Khuhro characterized the charges as entirely malicious: "Disregard for accuracy, harshness of diction, rashness and falsity of allegations, suppression of truth and suggestion of falsehoods, are some of the prominent features of the blue book containing the charges framed against me... Behind this ill-will there is history. The ill-will is both potent and deep rooted and its causes are personal."

The statement went on to trace the political history of the previous ten years giving an account which summed up the key factors of this period and Khuhro's understanding of the situation in the province:

"Sind was constituted a separate province and in 1937 got its first popularly elected Ministry. At that time there were two political parties in the province, led by Shaikh Ghulam Hussain Hidayetullah and the late Mr. Allah Baksh respectively... I was in Sir Ghulam Hussain's party.... It was our party that formed the first Ministry ... Though sufficiently senior and having a substantial number of followers, I did not press my claim for a place in the Cabinet because the interests of Muslim unity demanded that I keep out and make room for those who, but for this temptation might have switched over to the other side..."

Describing the salient features of the way party politics and democracy had functioned in Sind since the attainment of autonomy in 1936 and the distortion of democracy which had occurred through the opportunistic and self serving role of Hidayetullah who had used the Muslim League organisation or thrown it aside and even damaged it as suited his purpose. He himself had been a friend and colleague of Hidayetullah, but had been disillusioned when the latter had abandoned Muslim League, deserting his position as Leader of the Opposition and of the Muslim League Assembly Party, for the sake of a ministership. Khuhro had then been elected to these positions and led the fight against the anti-people policies of the government. He also described the two elections of 1946 in both of which he had the support of the majority of Muslim League members and both times he had stood down from Premiership on the appeal of Mr. Jinnah who had asked him to give up the Premiership to Hidayetullah as otherwise the latter would join up with the opponents of Muslim League and Pakistan. Khuhro quoted a statement of Hidayetullah when he was Minister in a Congress backed Ministry. Hidayetullah had said:

"In Sind I have always been opposed to the Muslim League and I continue to be of the same view. Nowhere in India has there been a Muslim League Ministry. Every Muslim majority province has a mixed Ministry running with the co-operation of all communities and classes. Therefore it is stupid and opposed to practical politics to keep beating the drums of Muslim League."[6]

Khuhro pointed out that although he had sacrificed his claim to Premiership at least twice in favour of Hidayetullah the latter was not appeased. After he had been elevated to Governorship of Sind, Hidayetullah resented a position which would constitutionally deprive him of the power he had enjoyed as Premier. The position of the Governor in an independent country was in any case one of a titular and ceremonial head rather than that of a powerful colonial governor with 'special responsibilities'. Khuhro summed up the changes that had occurred in the constitutional position of the Governor after independence and the relative positions of the Governor and the Premier:

"... the Cabinet is the Executive authority in the province and in that Cabinet the Premier is the predominant authority. The Premier presides over the Cabinet and superintends and co-ordinates the work of all departments. The Premier assumes responsibilities for all the activities of his colleagues. He appoints those colleagues and can require their resignation though in the exercise of both these powers he is controlled by the opinion of his party in the Assembly. The Cabinet is chosen by the predominating party in the legislative assembly. It consists of men who have agreed to a definite political programme. These men are a group of ministers who hold various portfolios. They have agreed to pursue a common policy under a common chief, the Premier: convention prescribes that the Cabinet must always agree. If disagreement manifests itself on any except insignificant points of policy, either the Cabinet or the dissentient Minister must resign. In no case may a Minister disavow either expressly or by implication the policy of his colleagues so long as he remains in the Cabinet. Generally the Premier combines with his position the office of the Finance Minister and other offices.

The aforesaid is the constitutional position which I claim to have held. *The contention of the Special Counsel appears to be this – that in spite of our having become a free nation we had to be governed by the secretaries.* He is rudely shocked to find that the erstwhile ruling Bureaucrats should have been allotted their proper place in this democratic government. He is amazed to learn that it is the Premier who is the chief executive and that it is the Premier who has to pilot the State. He is impelled to denounce the capacity of the Premier to lay down policies and to insist on these being carried out. He grows hysteric on realizing that the Governor is a mere titular head retained as a vestige of the inglorious past and that in the new constitution a governor will have no nook to stay in.

I most respectfully submit that this true position of a governor created a revolt in the mind of Shaikh Ghulam Hussain who would fain revert to Premiership if it were possible for him to rally the legislature round himself. ..."[7]

Khuhro continued with a comparative analysis of the constitutional provisions which existed before the 'Independence Day' and which came into force after that date.

"I shall confine myself only to such aspects of this great change as relates to powers, functions, and responsibilities of Provincial Governors and Ministers, or regulate the mutual relations of these two institutions. The idea, indeed is to bring out in relief the lines of demarcation which separate the old from the new order of things.

Before August 1947, Provincial Governors enjoyed the following powers:–
1. Individual judgement .
2. Discretion.
3. Special responsibilities
4. Appointment and dismissal of Ministers and Dissolution of Assembly.

In the first field the Governor could overrule his ministry in respect of such proposals as emanated from the latter. In the second field he could take the decisions without even consulting his ministry in respect of such proposals as emanated from the latter. In the third field he enjoyed powers for protecting and safeguarding the interests of Services, Minorities, etc. The fourth field covered his inherent powers which were necessary to maintain a system by which to shape ministries.

As a natural corollary of his having been invested and saddled with so many powers and responsibilities the Governor, relying on Government of India Act, 1935, presided over Cabinet meetings, to enable him to have proper insight into the working of the administration so that there was no covert encroachment on his own preserves; he even held the power to frame,"in his own discretion" the Rules of Business. But, although, constitutionally and statutorily so fortified was their position, Governors of the pre Independence period, conventionally, invariably followed the advice of their ministries even with respect to such matters as fell within the field of their 'Discretion', 'Individual Judgement' or 'Special Responsibility'. This was being done evidently with a view to encouraging the growth of democratic ideas. In other words, their effort was to act as far as possible as *unmeddlesome constitutional heads*."[8]

Khuhro described the relative position of the ministry in the colonial era:

"As to the position of ministries, suffice it to say that everything which did not fall within the gubernatorial fields, described above came into the purview of their powers. That is to say, with regard to those matters they `tendered' their advice to the Governor who was bound under the constitution, to abide by it except in such cases as according to him came within the ambit of any of his special powers. That, however does not mean that the ministers had no voice in respect of matters falling in the last category. As has been stated in the previous paragraph even about these matters the ministers were consulted by Governors and save in certain very rare cases, this consultation always led to the ministerial advice being abided by."

and then went to describe how it changed in an independent and democratic dispensation:

"In consequence of coming in to force of the Independence Act and the Government of India Act – as modified by the Pakistan Adaptation Order – the entire former constitutional position underwent a vital and revolutionary change. The Parliament having accepted the principle of giving freedom to the people, in the truest sense of that term, divested the governors of all the powers they held in the previous constitutional set up. Freedom complete and unabridged was being conferred on people who had to exercise it through their own chosen representatives, the ministers and anything repugnant to that object had to be dropped out. For example the Governors who were mere employees of the Governor General and drew no sanctions from the people, had to be relegated to a secondary position namely that of a nominal constitutional figurehead. The British Parliament while revising the Constitutional Act, had therefore to alter the very original structure of the relevant sections so as to omit terms like 'Discretion', 'Individual Judgement' and 'Special Responsibility'. Whatever power which apparently now rests with the Governor it is his duty to exercise according to the instructions of the Governor General vide Section 51, Clause (5) if the Act...

"... In the House of Commons the Attorney General, while speaking on this new Independence Act, had observed:

"After the appointed day (i.e. 15th August 1947) the Governor General will act constitutionally on the advice of his Ministers." (Hansard: 14 July 1947, p. 127). If that was to be the position of the Governor General, under the new dispensation, how could his inferiors, the provincial governors, arrogate to themselves wider and greater powers than even him. This would be illogical and grotesque. That no more than such is the role of the Governor will also be apparent from a consideration of the Constitutional laws and usages of the other Dominions of the British Commonwealth."[9]

Having delineated the constitutional position of the Governor and the Premier after independence, Khuhro went on to describe Hidayetullah's obstructive and difficult behaviour after he had been appointed Governor. The elected government of an independent state needed to conduct its affairs in the spirit of a truly independent representative government. 'Every system and every piece of procedure had to be remoulded in order to conform to this new pattern.' Khuhro started by bringing the Rules of Business in line with the new constitutional position:

"A start had naturally to be made with the Rules of Business which governed the entire gamut of office procedure. Provisions which were till then necessary in order to ensure proper fulfilment of the special responsibilities and due discharge of his duties by the Governor had to be excluded; because under the new conditions his role was to be a different one; namely that of a purely constitutional head. Formerly even these Rules of Business had to be finally framed by the Governor `under his discretion'. Under the new Act, however, he had lost his discretion even in that matter."

However when the changes made by the Cabinet were sent up to the Governor he 'regarded them as the very first challenge from me to his powers'. He resisted giving his consent and had to be persuaded that he could not constitutionally do so. But he created enough problems so that even when the Revised rules were agreed to by the Governor,'the rules remained defective – the bad drafting of Rule 16 being due directly to the higgle-haggling of the Governor.'

Khuhro then detailed the procedure followed in the pre-independence and post-independence periods with regard to the sending up of files to the Governor:

"In the post-independence era the constitutional position of the Governor having changed and he having lost all his former powers the files had to go to him merely in order to keep him informed of the general trends of administration, none of the orders on the files being delayed pending his concurrence. The last word in every matter rested with the Ministry.

After August 15, I followed this procedure. The files kept going to the Governor, in the ordinary way, without issue of orders being held back. Shaikh Ghulam Hussain apparently acquiesced in it. In any case there is nothing on record to show that he disputed the constitutional appropriateness of this procedure till a particular stage."

Khuhro pointed out that the displeasure of the Governor came out in the open when certain personal favours he wanted done were not agreed to by the Ministry. He wanted his son to be made Parliamentary Secretary, an object he achieved as soon as Khuhro went out of the Government. He demanded a much larger sum of money for the redecoration of his official residence that was customary for the Governor's residence. The Governor also wanted to make a deal with the Government to lease some land he had bought on terms unduly detrimental to the Government's interests. Khuhro turned down all these demands and won the bitter hatred of the Governor.[10] The Governor himself tried to arrogate to himself the powers that had been enjoyed by the colonial Governors although he had no basis for such a claim. Hidayetullah then started an intrigue in the Cabinet itself with two of Ministers who had ambitions of their own. The two Ministers went on a tour of Sind to try and drum up support so that a motion of no confidence could be moved against the Premier. They failed to gain any support from the M.L.As. in this attempt: "Only a month earlier the Assembly party as well as the legislature had passed unanimously resolutions reiterating their faith in and reaffirming their loyalty to me, as leader of the party and the leader of the House."[11]

Hidayetullah who, during the April 1948 crisis[12], had made a commitment to the Quaid-e-Azam that he would find a constitutional way to remove Khuhro, was desperate. Khuhro described his continuing efforts which could hardly be characterised as constitutional:

"The failure of the two Ministers' mission now compelled the desperate Governor to throw off even whatever little mask he had till then worn. In the hope and belief that if I am divested of my portfolio of Law and Order and... Pir Illahi Baksh invested with it probably the scales may be tilted in favour of the new plan... No arguments legal, constitutional or procedural, could prevail. Even the ground that he could not effect any such changes except on the advice of the Premier fell flat. An hour later his Secretary walked into the Chief Secretary's room armed with an order changing the portfolios. The Chief Secretary, naturally could not accept and enforce orders of that kind unless they came to him through the proper channel, the Ministry." On the Chief Secretary's refusal to follow this unconstitutional demand the Governor had his orders published in a *Gazette Extraordinary*. As Khuhro commented, `in order to maintain the appearances of my Government' he told the Secretariat to follow the orders regarding the change in the portfolios, 'my intention being to lodge my protest with the Governor General and seek redress through him...'.[13]

The Assembly and the Party meanwhile continued to express their faith in Khuhro's leadership:

"While this was going on, 23 members of the party out of its 35 effective members, published a joint statement reaffirming their faith in me and asked for a meeting being held to pass such a resolution formally. In pursuance of the requisition and in view of the new developments the Secretary of the Party fixed a Party meeting for April 30, for the purpose of formal adoption of a resolution of confidence. This created grave apprehension in the mind of the Governor that if this meeting was allowed to take place and nothing was done to push me out of office previously, his entire plot would have aborted."[14]

In order to forestall the Assembly resolution which he could not stop, the Governor adopted another tack. He used the Law and Order department to frame charges against the Premier. He set up an office in his official residence to make up the case. He summoned officers of the Government and coerced them to give evidence and pressurising them by suspending the officers who did not co-operate. He then approached the Governor General to dismiss him before the date of the Assembly meeting and institute a Court of Inquiry against him. Khuhro argued with the Governor General pointing out that the Governor was acting against accepted constitutional practice in countries based on the parliamentary system:

"I took the following position before the Governor General:

a. Governor's charges were ex-parte; I had not been apprised of them; my explanation had not been taken.

b. Dismissal of a Premier who enjoyed the confidence of the legislature and through it of the country on the basis of such accusations would be constitutionally highly inappropriate;

c. The Governor, if he believed his charges were genuine, should follow the constitutional and regular procedure namely, that of having the charges referred to the legislature to which alone was he responsible and which alone he could render accounts and which had kept in readiness its own machinery (the Committee of Privileges) for meeting such contingencies.

d. Appointment of a Court of Inquiry behind the back and over the head of the legislature whose creature I was, to examine accusations against the Premier, constituted a most arbitrary proceeding, unheard of in the annals of democratic institutions.

e. Dismissal of a Premier before even those so-called charges were established would amount to trying a man only after he has been hanged.

f. Even if these charges had any substance in them I should be furnished with their copy and my explanation should be taken thereon prior to any action being taken.

g. A party meeting had been already called and a regular session of the legislature could immediately follow, and the Governor through the two rebel Ministers could get a no-confidence motion moved against me on the basis of these charges. Constitutionally that alone would be a normal and regular way of dealing with such a situation.

68. ... I request [the Governor General] that if I had to be sent out it would be in the interests of justice and consistent with good conscience and equity if the scope of the proposed inquiry were widened so as to bring under scrutiny the actions and behaviour of my accusers also, so that the Court of Inquiry may be in a position to give its verdict after getting a balanced and comprehensive view of the entire picture. Indeed this implied that the other two Ministers must also be subjected to the same inquiry and the Governor himself. None of these reasonable prayers however prevailed."[15]

Khuhro made a water tight case against the untenable position taken by the Governor and cast doubts on the role of the Governor General himself. He recounted how instead of parading the differences in the government in public he chose to rely on the Governor General to correct the situation as his constitutional position demanded. He could not be aware that the Quaid-e-Azam had his own agenda. In fact as long as Hidayetullah had felt that Khuhro had the confidence of the Quaid he dared not object to his diminished position but as soon as he realised that he was in a position to serve the interests of the Centre he pounced on Khuhro. The game was on to divide and rule the provinces and the foolhardy knights of democratic practice and provincial autonomy of which Khuhro was the foremost exponent, were the target.

Khuhro then turned to his own role in the period after Partition and of his conduct in the face of the immense challenges that faced him as Premier of Sind during one of the biggest upheavals that history had witnessed:

"... the unprecedented upheaval which followed the establishment of Pakistan and which involved the unorganised and panicky flight of millions of people to and from Sind. I had not only to straighten out the complications which had marred the smooth running and effectiveness of the adminstration during the previous regime, but I had also to face the new conditions. In other words I found myself called upon to discharge this colossal task with the aid of a weak and degenerated administration which had been unable to record any achievement even during the previous normal times.

It is necessary, at this stage to throw some light on the various aspects of the duties which devolved upon me in consequence of the new upheaval;

a. The new State of Pakistan having decided to make Karachi its capital, arrangements had to be made for its reception, for housing its personnel, and for maintaining law and order and public utility services in a tolerable state of efficiency.

b. Owing to the disturbances in the neighbouring territories (Punjab on the East, Quetta on the North, and Rajputana, Bombay, Gujerat, Kathiawar and Ajmer on the south east) Sind became not only an asylum for the uprooted Muslim population of these places but had to function as a transit camp for the fleeing multitudes which kept moving in and out through the openings it had on the other Dominion.

c. This provided the criminal population with an opportunity to start its depradations with greater violence and ferocity, the administration of law and order having never been known even before that, for its capacity to meet any situations even of lesser intensity. By the way of illustration it may be mentioned that previously when about 500 or 1,000 Hurs had taken into their heads to defy it, the Government could not cope with them and had to yield its place to Martial law administration for a whole year. Robberies, dacoities, murders, attempts at murders, hurling down of human beings from running trains now became the order of the day, the old and the new population having found in it an invaluable opportunity to settle old and new scores with the Hindus – their mutual relations having been none too happy during the previous several decades.

d. There was breakdown in communications. Owing to the exodus of the Hindu staff, railways, posts and telegraphs fell into disorganisation. A Government for making itself effective, depends on proper working of communications. When communications are disturbed and disrupted the helplessness of a government needs to be experienced to be fully realized.

e. The same was the state of other departments which were directly under the purview of the provincial administration. In Sind in spite of my best efforts the ratio of Hindus in the services had never fallen below 60%. Now if 60 per cent employees of a government suddenly go out or lose interest in their work or come to be suspected of doubtful loyalties, the position of the Government must in the very nature of things become unenviable.

f. The temper of the refugee population which had arrived here, – it having passed through intense suffering at the hands of the Hindus in their original-country, – was not at all conducive to the proper maintenance of law and order. This point does not need to be emphasised because a comparative study of conditions here and elsewhere during that period should amply prove that whereas the conditions everywhere were uniformally tense and unhelpful, Sind had come out of them with the least possible damage to the people and to its own reputation.

g. In the misery of the people the corrupt officials and their underlings had seen a rare chance for enriching themselves. With increased daring they had swooped upon the people and created a state of unmitigated administrative anarchy.

h. Running of Refugee Camps and housing of those who had descended on the capital and other important towns in the province not in thousands but in hun-

dreds of thousands, caused further headache to the administration. Looked at in the context of the fact that on account of war neither the capital nor our towns had been in a position to have any new building plans during the past ten years, the seriousness of this problem should not become difficult to realise.
i. The possibilities of influx of new population consequent upon the establishment of Pakistan had during the previous one year given rise to a new but heated controversy on the basis of Sindhi vs non-Sindhi. During the time of Sir Ghulam Hussain violent propaganda had been carried on by both sides, the Sindhi side having received special stimulus on account of Mr. G. M. Syed's party which having sustained defeat at the hands of the Muslim League a year earlier had now identified itself completely with it. The daily *Qurbani* which was the mouthpiece of this party had been allowed to add fuel to this fire. When I took over I found the situation so tense that at one time open conflict and disturbances between the two sections of the population seemed imminent. The Sindhi element in the ministerial party felt so keenly in terms of provincialism that no minister could take a firm attitude in such a delicate matter without running the risk of one day-finding himself thrown out of office. It was with a view merely to saving his own skin that Shaikh Ghulam Hussain had not been able to muster courage to arrest development of that canker even though at that time it was only in its early formative phases. It fell to my lot now to ban *Qurbani* and take firm action to put down this movement."[16]

Khuhro went to detail the problems that arose over the disposal of property of the emigrating Hindus, of accommodating the incoming refugees, of preventing grabbing of houses and property and the myriad problems which he could only hint at in his necessarily brief Statement:

"The period preceding and covering my premiership was period of profound revolutionary change in the country. The conditions obtaining in the new State became formidable. An effective proportion of the population changed its loyalties. There were enemies outside and saboteurs within – all intent on wrecking the State. The province was being drained of its wealth and denuded of even the barest essentials of life. The refugees came in, in lakhs. We were threatened with utter disorganisation. There was a wave of crime and there arose an anarchic defiance of law and order. My Government had to battle against enemies on all fronts. Our resources were taxed up to the breaking point. As the Premier of the Province, I had to play my role and to justify the trust reposed in me by my people."[17]

Khuhro summed up his constraints in a eloquent paragraph:

"These were the problems and difficulties to face which I was called upon, from the very first day of the tenure of my office with the help of services which had been inured to an easy life during the previous eight years and for which strict control or vigilance from the top now meant positive discomfort. Naturally this gave rise to discontent and a feeling of resentment amongst them. But it was unavoidable and the risk had got to be run if the province had to be taken out of the crisis. What was more depressing was the fact that two of the four ministers in my cabinet had also been used to the old ways and had failed to grasp the spirit of the new times. Therefore in the midst of upheaval it was not possible for me to depend upon their intellectual or physical resources."[18]

Khuhro had achieved this in spite of the inadequate government machinery and the lack of co-operation from some of his colleagues and above all from the Governor, as well as the lack of understanding from the powerful Centre:

"Encompassed by these unfortunate circumstances and subjected to a number of handicaps I had to meet the challenge of these abnormal events, unknown to the history of the province... How far I succeeded in my mission is indicated by the present placidity in the Sind conditions which is due only to my labours."

But he could not help adding:

"It is a different thing that I have received a reward just the opposite of what it should have been. But there is nothing extra ordinary about it. The number of the sincere workers of the Muslim community who had been let down and betrayed is a legion. In the galaxy of those pathetic figures I am probably the smallest man."[19]

Khuhro made a plea which could well have echoed the historical figures who despite their great achievements have been brought down by lesser men:

"I do not deny, but plead guilty to the charge, that in the face of the facts enumerated above I had not always followed the usual red-tapism or rules of business; at times I might have even drawn more upon the services than they had been used to giving under the previous Premiers. But it was unavoidable in view of the peculiar nature of the situation which was being contended against. When an evil assumes the terrific velocity of a cannon ball it is a bad administrator who imagines he can arrest it by moving in a dog-cart."[20]

Khuhro pointed out that his leadership and his administration had the complete confidence of the people of the province and of their elected representatives – his colleagues:

"The Sind Legislature whose creature I was, and to which alone till lately I thought I owed all responsibility, had taken cognisance of the manner in which I had run my administration and after mature consideration given me a renewed vote of confidence, passed unanimously and couched in terms of utmost generosity. No other Premier in the entire constitutional history of this province had been the recipient of such and honour at the hands of the legislature. Why the Assembly had taken that unusual step to indemnify and give a note of credit to me, its nominee, the Premier, was because having charged me with the duty of fighting an abnormal situation it wanted to let no grass grow under my feet. This happened in February 1948, and implied that all actions of the Premier till that day stood indemnified. Indeed, it was on account of such a firm attitude on the part of the legislature that the Governor did not dare to approach it against me and has followed a most novel and unheard of procedure to hit me."[21]

Khuhro thus laid out his argument and his protest at the treatment he had been subjected to. He argued that he had become Premier at a time of uprecedented crisis in the country. A crisis which warranted not only unusual capacity in the leaders by way of ability and dedication but also which required initiative and great skills of crisis management. That the quality of the crisis demanded instant decisions and extraordinary measures, quite out of the experience of the officials who ran the day to day administration of the province. This was the situation which could so easily have got out of control as indeed it did in the Punjab, and other area particularly of northern India. As Khuhro explained so graphically the situation was kept under control practically by sheer force of will and an administrative *tour de force*. That certain short cuts had to be taken in this crisis was just so much power to the course. The Sind Legislature recognised this by its vote of confidence and its praise of the Premier in February.

Khuhro pointed out that constitutionally he was within his rights and that the Independence Act had given him as the elected Premier the powers which Premiers of the colonial period did not enjoy. This was strictly within the democratic paradigm but unfortunately it won him the enmity of the Governor who had till lately himself been the Premier of the province. The Governor frustrated at his powerlessness undertook the task of bringing down what he considered to be an overmighty Premier. In this he chose his moment well. Khuhro had just fallen foul of the Central authorities who chose not to see the effectiveness of his exercise of power, but only the extent of that power, which they considered again as curtailing their own. They were anxious to lay their hands on the riches and potential of Karachi by hook or by crook. They gave the go ahead to the Governor do their dirty work even when it meant clear violation of constitutional norms. Khuhro detailed the constitutional position which justified his stand, in documents addressed to the highest authority in the land, but these were ignored and the constitution violated by the forces determined to get him out.

Khuhro backed up his argument not only by the pleading of constitutional justification and the extent and seriousness of the crisis on the successful management of which depended the safety and indeed the continued existence of the country, but also described the context which had shaped his political career and had brought him to power at this crucial stage – a career which had been characterised by sacrifice in the interests of the community and the national cause and had at no stage exhibited any sign of self aggrandisement. In this context the charges that had been brought appeared frivolous and trivial and that is how Khuhro wanted them treated by the Court of Inquiry.

Khuhro went through the exercise of answering the charges one by one. The civil servants, particularly those belonging to the provincial service had been coerced and threatened with suspension or reversion. A number of them took refuge in forgetfulness and the defence had to get their corroborative evidence only after getting records. Khuhro cited the names of some of the senior officers whom he had trusted as men of integrity: "I accuse them of having denied certain things which they knew full well and having knowingly attempted to create wrong impressions on the Court."[22]

Some of the charges dealt with the alleged interference of the Premier in the portfolios of other Ministers, an odd charge to bring against the person who as he pointed out was the Head of the Government and the Leader of the Party and ultimately responsible for the conduct of his government. First Khuhro explained the duties of the Premier according to the Constitution and the Rules of Business:

"Alleged interference in the work of other Ministers i.e., Pir Illahi Baksh and Mir Ghulam Ali is also an accusation levelled at me. It is admitted that in certain respects I had to interfere for the sake of purity of administration and proper maintenance of the law and order and decent standards of administration which every Government worth the name should maintain.

The Special Counsel, accused me in his opening address that I interfered with these two Ministers who had of late become the pets of the Governor. But he conveniently forgot that I being the Premier of the Province and thereby Head of the Government, the Leader of the Party in power and the Leader of the House and the Legislature to which I am responsible for the proceedings of the Ministers, it was my duty to interfere when I was legitimately required to do so. He also forgets that in addition to being the Premier, I was also directly in charge of the Finance Department and the Department of Political Services and the General Department. All the files therefore in which any kind of expenditure is involved or all such files where the Services are concerned (e.g. promotions, transfers, postings and punishments) I must see. Rules 12, 14, 17, 18, 19, 20, 23, 24, 25, 25a, 26, 27, 28 are the Rules of Business which give powers to Finance Department and P.S. and G.A. Department with respect to various subjects mentioned therein and I controlled these departments. These departments give a very wide field for exercising authority and control over other Departments. All important cases therefore are submitted to the Premier who also happened to be in charge of the Departments of Finance, P.S. and G.A. In addition all important matters of Policy and all Legislative measures cannot be decided upon unless and until the Premier has seen the papers and expressed his opinion. The Premier may place all these cases before the Cabinet or may decide finally as he deems fit.

It might be reiterated that the Premier as the Head of the Cabinet is answerable to the House of the Legislature. There being the Government based on joint responsibility, if any Minister is censured by the House or if the financial demands of a Department in charge of another Minister are negatived by the House the Premier has got to tender resignation of the whole Cabinet and he must own the responsibility, unless the Premier before the actual censuring of his colleague by the House or rejection of funds, has taken place, has called upon him to resign and has reshuffled his Cabinet. This will be the proper course for any constitutionally minded Premier of a Provincial or Federal Government."[23]

Having explained the constitutional position Khuhro then described his actual experience with the recalcitrant Ministers.

"...I had at times to overrule my colleagues to keep the administration at a proper high level. I would like to quote a few examples how it was necessary for me on occasions to interfere and overrule some of my colleagues in the interests of purity of administration."

Khuhro pointed out that in most cases his 'interference' had directly dealt with the prevention of smuggling of essential food and other items from Sind and Pakistan at a time of national crisis when the country was dependent on the food being produced in the province:

"It had been proved from the evidence of the official witnesses – for instance the Assistant Director of Food and Civil Supplies Department (Mr. J. G. Kharas) has said – that I did interfere and cancelled the orders of Hon. Mir Ghulam Ali Khan who allowed lot of permits to a certain favourite zamindars of his in Badin and Tando Bago talukas of Hyderabad districts and one or two of Tharparkar district to take rice from Hyderabad district to Tharparkar which district is on the border of Kathiawar and Rajputana States. Similarly some favourites of his were allowed to sell rice from their husking mills in Sukkur district by sending to other areas. This directly contributed to the shortage of food grains in Badin, Tando Bago, Mirpur Mathelo and Ubauro talukas, and this very materially contributed towards smuggling of foodgrains from the surplus province of Sind. In spite of my having created special post of Anti-Smuggling Officer in the grade of Superintendent of Police stationed at Hyderabad with a number of Dy. S.Ps., Inspectors and Sub-Inspectors to assist him. The grain was being smuggled out by permit holders. It has also been proved that my colleague ordered a number of permits for various articles which were in short supply in Sind to be issued to individuals to take away all these things out of the province. I ordered all these to be cancelled and thereby prevented black marketing in various types of essential goods in Karachi and the province."[24]

Khuhro also showed by quoting examples that his 'interference' with the departments of his colleagues as for instance in Law and Order was to prevent gross miscarriage of justice:

"The interference in Law and Order went to this extent that Mir Ghulam Ali ordered a Sub-Inspector to arrest certain people under Public Safety and produce them before the District Magistrate of Hyderabad to be kept in jail for six months. When the District Magistrate, Mr. M. H. Sufi brought this fact to my notice I directed him to go into the history of the conduct of each person and release them at once if they were innocent."

Instances can be multiplied to amplify my stand that the tendency of the two disgruntled colleagues of mine had all along been to grind their own axe and that my presence in the Cabinet was a checkmate to their schemes." Khuhro quoted the evidence of the I.G.Police to show that the two Ministers misused their powers and he could not do otherwise but prevent that as far as he was able:

"The evidence of Mr. Pryde as to what had happened at Tando Mohammad Khan after my dismissal and the indications available in the forest records would afford patent instances of how my colleagues grew restive under my gaze, but in obedience to the orders of this Court, I feel bound to refrain from giving a schedule of their misdeeds and inequities lest I be blamed for circumventing the rulings of the Hon'ble Court."[25]

Ending his Statement Khuhro once again reminded the Court of the circumstances in which he had the charge of the high and ultimately responsible office in the key province of Sind and the exigencies of the situation which governed his conduct:

"In concluding this part of my statement I beg leave to state that in my time I used the Sind Maintenance of Public Safety Law against bad characters who participated in the crime wave that rose from September 1947 onwards due to the exodus of Hindus on a large scale.

After the partition of the country, that is after 15th August and incoming of a large number of refugees everyday provided ample opportunity to commit robberies in the daylight and dacoities on high roads for these bad characters. The crime figures produced by Mr. Pryde would show that the crime increased systematically from September to December and the nature of the crime that was on the increase was dacoities, robberies and house breakings. The general round-ing up of bad characters in the Province had the desired effect: this type of crime assumed normal position after January 1948 as the direct result of the strong action against bad characters under my orders."[26]

Khuhro then went to refute each charge in the context of the Statement he had made. The last days of the Inquiry were taken up by the arguments of the Defence Counsel and the Prosecuting Counsel's counter arguments. The Prosecution argued that the evidence of its witnesses was reliable.

"The Chief Justice, however, replied that he had grave doubts about their reliability. Finally the Prosecution asked the judges to include in their verdict some statement as to the undesirability of entrusting Khuhro with public office in the future. This the judges naturally refused to do."[27]

The Court of Inquiry ended its sittings on 3 December exactly six months after it had started. The expectation was that its findings would be given in about a month's time.

****

While Khuhro was busy with the Inquiry and the court case the scene had changed in Pakistan. On 11 September Quaid-e-Azam had died and had been succeeded as Governor General by Khwaja Nazimuddin, the Muslim League leader from Bengal. Hidayetullah had died in the same month and been succeeded as Governor by Justice Din Mohammed, a Punjab lawyer who had been member of the Boundary Commission. And by December the focus of political interest in the country was back on Khuhro. It was a spectacular comeback well reflected in a political report from the High Commissioner for the United Kingdom:

"All the other local events during the period under review have been thrust into the background by the somewhat spectacular return to politics of M. A. Khuhro."[28]

The report was referring to the elections of Sind Provincial Muslim League, which on the same evening as the Inquiry had ended its sittings, had elected Khuhro as its President.

"On the evening of December 3rd, some seven hours after the closing time for nominations, Khuhro was nominated for the Presidency of the League and the other candidates withdrew. The latter included Syed Ali Akbar Shah, who had previously been regarded as the Illahi Baksh Ministry's candidate. The following day this person issued a statement that he was not prepared to be labelled as the Ministerial candidate, and that no one was better fitted to lead the party than Khuhro."[29]

Khuhro was elected President of Sind Muslim League on 5 December and made a conciliatory statement which emphasised the priority of the nation's defence. In terms of provincial priorities he pinpointed the welfare of the mass of the people and refugee rehabilitation. He also talked about the settlement of the Kashmir issue: "every citizen of Sind must realise that the liberty of Kashmir is ultimately the liberty of Sind."[30]

While the people of Sind thus welcomed Khuhro back into politics the forces which had been working against him were none too pleased. Altaf Hussain the editor of *Dawn* was particularly virulent in his attack. He blamed the Sind Provincial Muslim League for 'running the grave risk' of electing a man who was facing charges in a Special Court of Inquiry and followed it up by various unfavourable reports and comments on Khuhro. These attacks were part of the carefully orchestrated anti Khuhro campaign he had been waging through the medium of *Dawn* ever since Khuhro had developed differences with the Centre and which would continue during his period as editor of the newspaper.

The election of Khuhro was also taken badly by the sitting government of the Province under Pir Illahi Baksh who was discomfited by the withdrawal of his first candidate for the presidentship and the decisive defeat of the second. He announced a boycott of the remainder of the League elections and threatened to set up a rival Muslim League at Hyderabad. This move did not attract any support and in any case Pir Illahi Baksh was soon up to his neck in trouble regarding his own election to the Sind Legislative Assembly.

As newly elected President of Muslim League Khuhro set about drawing up a programme of action for the Party and for the Muslim League government in the Province. These included two resolutions against the conduct of the Ministry. (1) The first condemned the gross and widespread misuse of Government's extraordinary powers and (2) the second called on the Government to suspend action on the transfer of the provincial capital to Hyderabad until the Assembly had an opportunity to discuss the matter.

Khuhro was firm that the Sind Assembly must have a chance to discuss the whole issue of moving the capital. Khuhro was well aware that the Government of Sind would have to face not only the lack of an adequate infrastructure but also the enormous expenditure that would be required in a situation where the Centre showed no signs of coming up with the compensation that had been promised.

The Muslim League Council also promised to work (3) for the removal of illiteracy, corruption, black marketing and smuggling of food grains.(4) It was supportive of the national policies on defence, Kashmir and (5) also announced its full intention of doing all it could to remove the growing distrust between Sindhis and the refugees and (6) a promise that "the civil liberties of the people shall be safeguarded by encouraging the growing and reasonable demand of the public for the right of free expression of views, and preventing unwarranted inroads upon the liberties of the people by misuse of executive authority."

This programme of Sind Provincial Muslim League indicated that Khuhro continued to think in broad strategic terms.

****

The course of the Inquiry had convinced the public that the charges were on the whole frivolous and that Khuhro was bound to come out of it exonerated. It was rumoured that the Court of Inquiry "will censure Mr. Khuhro mildly and then be shelved."[31] It was also clear that Khuhro's political base was secured and that public confidence in him was not shaken particularly as the successor government had a dismal record in contrast with which Khuhro's decisiveness and strong administration stood out as an example of how a government could be conducted. Hence there was a great deal of speculation about his return to power through an understanding with the Centre whose acquiescence was seen as necessary for getting the office of Premier. The process of acquisition of supreme power by the Centre was well on its way in Pakistan.[32]

The findings of the Court of Inquiry were submitted to the Governor General at the end of December 1948 but it was not till after March 1949 that they were made public. There was a good deal of speculation about the findings and the delay that was being made in their publication. The fact was however that there was no serious charge proved against Khuhro and no legal provision to remove him from taking part in elections or holding office. It was also clear that with his base continuing strong and his popularity enhanced rather than diminished. Khuhro could return to power in no time at all unless his enemies at the Centre could come up with some new strategy.

The Prosecuting Counsel in his closing arguments had wanted the Court to include in their verdict some statement as to the undesirability of entrusting Khuhro with public office in future. The judges categorically refused to do so and they also cast doubts on the reliability of the witnesses that the prosecution had produced. No charges of corruption or any other misdemeanour were proved against Khuhro and the Inquiry suggested that he had taken shortcuts and failed to follow due procedures in some cases. It was expected that these charges of 'maladministration' would bring some strictures from the court but no further and that Khuhro would resume his public career. Liaquat Ali, however, was not prepared to let the matter go. He did not want Sind under Khuhro's control and the only way to prevent that was by passing some special legislation under which he would be disqualified from holding public office.

Because the case before the Inquiry had lacked credibility and Khuhro's exoneration appeared likely, as soon as the proceedings of the Inquiry were ended the Government brought up a criminal charge against him that he had used his position as Premier to allow the Sind Observer Press in which he was a shareholder to acquire a Linotype Printing press which had been imported by the Government of Sind but for which it had no longer any use. This case was an obvious one of harassment and Khuhro was able to clear his name successfully from the High Court. The 'Linotype' case as it came to be known, started proceedings immediately after the end of the Inquiry and in August of 1949 Khuhro was exonerated by the High Court. The British High Commissioner reported back to his Government:

"Popular enthusiasm at the acquittal was tremendous. Khuhro was garlanded in the Court room with flowers, and wreaths of gold coins and hundred-rupee notes. Chaudhri Khaliquzzaman and Yusuf Haroon, as well as the other Sind Ministers, called on him at his house to congratulate him. The Sind Government observed a half holiday ...indeed his reception after the acquittal was that of a public hero not of a disgraced politician."[33]

In January 1949 the Central Government tried the third of its strategic options to remove Khuhro from the political scene. The Public and Representative Officers (Disqualifation) Act or the notorious PRODA was especially framed and passed by the Constituent Assembly with a special provision was made for it to apply retrospectively to Khuhro. PRODA was perhaps the first legislation of its kind in the democratic world to be used to victimize politicians who could not be got rid of in a democratic way through elections. It was a masterstroke by the mandarins of the Central Government who had little faith in the people of Pakistan and were only interested in gathering power into their own hands. PRODA became a handy weapon for them to beat down politicians from the different provinces, be they from Sind or Bengal or even from the Punjab, if they tried to assert themselves or their provinces or if they were perceived to be a threat to the designs of the overmighty centrists. This sword of Damocles would distort the politics of Pakistan and irretrievably damage the process of democracy in the country. As one commentator puts it: "The weakness of the government was shown by having to bring on the statute book Public Representative Officers Disqualification Act to bring under check erring or assertive politicians. Liaquat's political limitation was betrayed by his frequent tendency of equating Muslim League with the nation...[which] was inconsistent with the changed position of the League as a political party. The failure to tolerate and appreciate the role of the opposition cast long shadows."[34]

With PRODA, including its special retrospective clause, in his hands the rumour was that Liaquat Ali Khan wanted Khuhro disqualified from politics for ten years, the maximum period provided under PRODA, even though no serious charges were proved against him. It was assumed by the public that the ten-year provision had been provided to keep Khuhro out for that period of time. On 22 March 1949 a Notification of the Governor General was published in the *Gazette of Pakistan* that under section 3 of PRODA Khuhro was disqualified for a period of three years from being 'chosen as a Minister, Deputy Minister or Parliamentary Secretary ..., a member of the Constituent Assembly, the Legislature of the Dominion, the Federal Legislature, any local body or local authority, and also declared him ineligible for holding any office of profit under the Crown for a similar period."

Khuhro immediately announced that he would contest the Governor General's order and go to court to have PRODA declared *ultra vires*. Khuhro had very good grounds for his case. He filed his suit by August and was to be heard in October. Working closely with his old friend Dingomal Ramchandani, whom he retained as counsel, Khuhro set out his case for the Chief Court of Sind. Khuhro contended the G.G.'s order on the grounds that

"it was beyond the law making powers of His Excellency the Governor of Sind to set up a Tribunal for Inquiry into the allegations made against a Minister, having regard to the scope of legislation provided in the Provincial List of the Seventh Schedule of the Government of India Act of 1935 as amended by the Pakistan Provisional Constitution Order, 1947."

This argument which he had made in the Inquiry hearings had been overruled by the Special Court and he had faced the proceedings under protest. Khuhro submitted that sometime in February 1949 'The Public and Representative Offices (Disqualification) Act 1949' had been passed by the Constituent Assembly. Khuhro contended that the disqualification order was illegal and inoperative 'inasmuch as the Public and Representative Offices (Disqualification) Act 1949, is or was unconstitutionally passed and is *ultra vires* and of no legal effect, being beyond the law making powers of the Constituent Assembly.'

Khuhro had a profound understanding of the constitutional issues involved and was able to argue his case on a number of levels. First he argued on the basic constitutional issue of whether the PRODA law was sustainable in itself and secondly that it was technically illegal as well. He argued first that—

"(a) Under Section 8 of the Indian Independence Act, 1947 the powers of the Legislature of the Dominion, shall for the purpose of making provision as to the constitution of the Dominion, be exercisable in the first instance by the Constituent Assembly of the Dominion and until other provision is made by the Constituent Assembly, the Dominion shall be governed in accordance with the Government of India Act as adapted or modified by the Governor General of Pakistan in accordance with Section 9 of the said Act and that any provision of the Government of India Act which operated to limit the power of the Legislature of the Dominion, shall have like effect as a law of the Legislature limiting for future the powers of the Legislature, unless and until other provision is made by the Constituent Assembly under Section 8 (1) of the Indian Independence Act, 1947.

(c) The Constituent Assembly therefore has two fold functions to perform, First, to frame the constitution of the Dominion.
Second, to act as the Central or Federal Legislature.

(d) As Constituent Assembly, it has power to frame the constitution of the Dominion and may amend, alter or modify the provisions of the Government of India Act or the Independence Act, but as Federal Legislature its Legislative powers are limited to the exercise of powers as are contained in the Government of India Act as adapted by the Pakistan (Provisional Constitution) Order. The law making powers of the Federal Legislature contained in the Seventh Schedule of the Provisional Constitution Order do not empower the Constituent Assembly to enact any law, like the Public and Representative Offices (Disqualification) Act, as no entry therein can cover its pith and substance. The Constituent Assembly has passed no measure to amend or modify the Seventh Schedule in this behalf."

The second ground on which Khuhro based his argument was that the Act had not had the Governor General's consent which was mandatory for all laws passed by the Constituent Assembly:

"(e) Every Bill passed by the Constituent Assembly must be assented to by the Governor General, in His Majesty's name under Section 32 of the Government of India Act and Section 6 (3) of the Indian Independence Act. The Public and Representative Offices (Disqualification) Act was not presented to the Governor General for assent, nor has it received such assent and is therefore not in force.

The third ground which Khuhro argued was that the Act was applied retrospectively to him and that the Tribunal which examined him was not framed under PRODA:

"(f) Under Section 3 of the (PRODA) no order of disqualification could be passed against the person sought to be disqualified unless he was found guilty;
(i) By the Federal Court or a High Court moved in this behalf by an order of the Governor General or a Governor,
(ii) or a Tribunal set up *in this behalf* by the Governor General or a Governor.
The plaintiff was not found guilty by Federal Court or a High Court, but he was found guilty by the Special Court of Inquiry, which was not a Tribunal set up in this behalf, that is to say, for the purpose of (PRODA), which was not in existence when the Sind Special Court of Inquiry Ordinance, 1948 was issued and which again was issued for the limited purpose, namely, whether the plaintiff's dismissal from the office of the Premier of Sind, was justified or not. The report of the Special Court of Inquiry, which was a secret one, it is submitted cannot be

made the basis of Disqualification under the Public and Representative Offices (Disqualification) Act, 1949.

(g) The provisions of the (PRODA) could not be given retrospective effect and applied in the case of the plaintiff.

(h) The Sind Special Court of Inquiry Ordinance, 1948, itself was illegal and *ultra vires* as at the time it was promulgated, the Governor of Sind had not Legislative power under Seventh Schedule to the Government of India Act as adapted and no circumstances existed under Section 88 of the said Act to promulgate the same. (i) The said Act further was not passed by His Excellency the Governor with the aid and advice of his Cabinet as required by the Rules of Business but on his own initiative which constitutionally he could not do and said Ordinance therefore is of no effect.

The plaintiff therefore submits that he is entitled to a Declaration that the Order of Disqualification passed against him by His Excellency the Governor General under Section 3 of the (PRODA) mentioned above, disqualifying him for a period of three years for being or being chosen as Minister ... or to hold any office of profit under the Crown, is inoperative, illegal and *ultra vires* and further that he continues to be the Member of Sind Legislative Assembly and the Constituent Assembly of the Dominion of Pakistan. The plaintiff is further entitled to an injunction restraining the defendants from acting over the Notification of H.E. the Governor General ... to regard the plaintiff as disqualified by virtue of Section 3 of PRODA or from taking steps to fill his seat on the Constituent Assembly or on the Sind Legislative Assembly ..."[35]

On 20 March 1950 the Chief Court of Sind presided over by Justice Constantine, passed an order declaring the Order disqualifying Khuhro as "inoperative, illegal and *ultra vires* ", and ruled that Khuhro continued to be a member of the Sind Legislative Assembly and of the Constituent Assembly of Pakistan. There was a wave of jubiliation throughout Sind and Khuhro was received with an enthusiastic ovation in the Sind Legislative Assembly which was in session when the Order of the Chief Court was announced. At this time just two and a half years after independence in August 1947, the Courts were still independent enough to deliver judgements which were known to be against the wishes of an overweening Prime Minister and the Assembly of Sind could show its independence and enthusiasm at Khuhro's exoneration even though the government of the day was against him. This integrity in both public life and the courts was not to last long in Pakistan and the Centre's determination to destroy Khuhro, the symbol of provincial independence and defiance, was to play a considerable part in the destruction of these institutions.

Some weeks later, in May, Khuhro was in Thatta to perform the inauguration ceremony of a steamer ferry that was to ply between Thatta and Sujawal when he received a message that he should see Liaquat Ali Khan the same night as soon as he returned. The Prime Minister was due to leave for a visit to U.S.A. Khuhro drove to Karachi and met him at 11 o'clock that night. Liaquat Ali made no bones about being put out by the judgement and told Khuhro that he was sending Yusuf Haroon, the incumbent Sind Premier, to Australia as High Commissioner but that he, Khuhro, should not take the Premiership of Sind for at least a year. The Prime Minister said that he would agree to his nominee instead:

"You have won in Court against me but we will go in appeal against you in Supreme Court. But if you drop the idea of Chief Ministership for the time being you can come in later."[36]

In fact Liaquat Ali was bluffing as Khwaja Shahabuddin, the Minister of Interior, told Khuhro afterwards and showed him the files to prove it. The Central Government had been given the legal opinion that an appeal was not likely to succeed. Khuhro who had a clear majority in the Assembly, suspected that Liaquat Ali was not being entirely truthful but he realised that if he became Premier it would result in further damaging tactics from the Centre. He was not, at this stage, anxious to renew hostilities with the Prime Minister. He agreed to support a compromise candidate for Premiership. Khuhro was learning the hard way where the real power lay in Pakistan.

18

DISILLUSION

In October 1949 while he was still working on his submission to the Sind Chief Court Khuhro flew to Saudi Arabia with his wife to perform the Haj pilgrimage. He had long wanted to go but only now found the opportunity. He needed the spiritual experience and the consolation of this great pilgrimage and the renewal of spirit which it bestows so as to face the trials and tribulations which lay ahead. He was to go again for Haj some years later but this was his first experience and was to make a deep impression which would remain with him.

This was a time when the journey to Saudi Arabia was still something of an undertaking. Khuhro's elder sister had been to *Haj* in the early 'thirties. The journey then had been made by ship from Bombay to Jeddah and from Jeddah to Makkah and Medina on camel-back in caravans with the constant fear of attack by robbers. In 1949 the road from Jeddah to Makkah was motorable but the Khuhros travelled to Medina by a cargo plane which had been specially provided with seats for a few passengers. The cities of Makkah and Medina were still largely as they had been in the 19th century. Medina had a charming railway station which terminated the railway built by Sultan Abdul Hamid II. There were some elegant Ottoman buildings, including the pavilions of the Harmain Sharif which had been rebuilt by Sultan Abdul Majid

The precincts of the Holy Kaaba were only partially paved and the paths leading up to the holy Kaaba were interpersed with gravel where the pilgrims dried their white cotton shrouds which had been washed with the holy Zamzam water. The ground between the two hillocks where *sai* was performed – commemorating the place where Hagar had given birth to Ismael and had run to and fro looking for water to give to her newly born child – was still an unpaved street with shops along it with local people going about their business among the pilgrims. The houses were old fashioned: the more prosperous citizens living in Turkish style houses with elegant wooden balconies and there were also a large number of ageless adobe houses which the Khuhros hoped were much as they had been in the Prophet's time. Makkah and Medina had not changed for centuries. In a few brief years, indeed when Khuhro went next in the early sixties, the towns had changed dramatically because of oil money and the prevalence of aeroplane travel.

Although he was not in office the Saudi government offered its hospitality to the Khuhro who, mindful of the etiquette of *haj* which requires the pilgrim to pay his own way, refused. During the Haj King Abdel Aziz ibn Saud camped in Makkah and invited distinguished visitors to dinner with him. Khuhro was happy to be the King's guest every evening while he was in Makkah. Khuhro was also included in Ibn Saud's party for the ritual cleaning of Kaaba from inside when it was opened during the Haj. He was given a small broom for the purpose which he retained as well as the piece of the *Ghilaf* of the Kaaba which he was given when it was removed and replaced with the new one which Egypt sent annually.

Dining with Ibn Saud every evening was a memorable experience. Khuhro who admired the great Saudi warrior who had defeated the Hashemites who were generally considered Imperialist stooges by the Muslim world, welcomed the chance to see and meet him. The *dastarkhwan* was laid on the ground and there would be a varied assortment of people present. Khuhro noticed St. John Philby, the nonconformist and even eccentric Englishman who was close to the King at that time and was always present. He talked more than almost anyone else there. Ibn Saud was about seventy at this time and not in very good health. He was to die about four years later, but he had a tremendous presence even then and conducted proceedings with great dignity and grace. Khuhro's conversation with the King was necessarily limited as he had no Arabic and the King did not speak English. The King however was very interested to hear from Khuhro about the independence of Pakistan.

The Khuhros returned home on 20 October and he immediately filed his appeal against PRODA in the Chief Court of Sind. The High Commissioner for U.K. reported to the Secretary of State for Commonwealth, "With Khuhro away on Haj – he has just returned – there was little political activity during this period."[1] But now renewed in spirit after the Haj, Khuhro faced the future with even more than his customary courage. It would take a few months before he was free of the PRODA shackles but during that time his influence or stature in Sind were undiminished. The Central Government was not at all pleased.

Whether in or out of office, Khuhro dominated politics in Sind in post independence Sind from 1947 to 1958 until democracy was summarily dismissed by General Ayub Khan. Khuhro's role in the freedom movement, with his position in the All India Muslim League and his pre-eminent position in the leadership of Sind, he had every expectation that after independence he would have a reasonably uninterrupted period in office as Premier and that he would be able to put into effect his political programme. He thought that with independence the last hurdle in the struggle for Sindhi emancipation which started with the separation of Sind from Bombay Presidency, would be overcome. He assumed that a provincial government under his leadership would be able to work singlemindedly to put through the reforming legislation for which the people of Sind had waited so long. He had reason to feel confident of this because he had the support of most of his fellow landowners and he was a revered and genuinely popular figure with the Sindhi people who saw him as their undaunted champion, particularly after his acquittal in 1945. Never before had there been in Sind a successful power politician who was also a popular hero.

These expectations of Khuhro were completely belied as the events of the first year after Partition proved. Even with the support of the entire Sind Assembly and the Muslim League Party Khuhro was forced out of office within months of independence. The next few years would show that though he continued to be the unrivalled leader of Sind, fully supported by the people as well as the party and with the majority behind him in the Assembly, he was unable to achieve power for anything but short periods of time. Even when he was Premier, however briefly, it was to be at the pleasure of the Central Government who made and broke provincial governments as they saw fit. The irony was that the achievement of Pakistan, which had been a fight for the autonomy of the provinces to free them from the colonial yoke turned out to be more of the same. As far as the people were concerned the solution for their problems lay in more autonomy and Pakistan had promised that not only in 1940 but subsequently in 1941 where Quaid-e-Azam had himself reiterated the resolution which included 'autonomy and sovereignty' for the constituent units. People expected Pakistan to be the culmination of autonomy and the continual expansion of self government which was after all the practical definition of 'freedom'. The despotic grip of the Pakistan Government proved to be more real, more enveloping and more oppressive than any British colonial lasso, which at least was couched in technical euphemism and the language of law. The colonial rule of law, however misused, was replaced by the naked tyranny of unprincipled men.

Hence the next few years would be spent by Khuhro in increasing disillusionment. The Centre perfected a cynical game to keep control of the provinces and Khuhro realised the hollowness of democracy as it was being practiced in Pakistan. He saw the Centre act in a similar manner in East Bengal. In N.W.F.P. the democratically elected majority government of Dr. Khan Sahib was dismissed within eight days of the creation of Pakistan. In the Punjab Liaquat Ali Khan played Mamdot and Daultana against each other in a masterly manner. When at last Daultana had the required majority in the Assembly, in January 1949, Liaquat Ali advised the Governor General to dissolve the assembly and impose Governor's rule (Section 92A).* Thus the mighty province was brought under the direct control of the Centre for the next two years and the elections not held till March 1951.

For Sind the tension was more acute because the Central government was physically present in the province. Khuhro's entire political philosophy was based on the premise that adequate autonomy for the provinces of India was natural, desirable and essential. A Province was where people lived: each province had its own particular identity and logic for development. It was the duty of democracy to work towards the welfare of the people and the improvement of the conditions of their lives. Khuhro wanted to preserve the best aspects of the traditional society of

---

* Apparently as early as August 1948 (just about three months after he had got rid of the Khuhro government in Sind) Liaquat Ali Khan had wanted the imposition of Section 92A in the Punjab but Sir Francis Mudie, then Governor Punjab, had advised that democracy be given another chance in the province and the Provincial Assembly got a respite of four months.

The Daultana group in the Punjab was generally perceived to be supported by Liaquat Ali Khan and when Daultana was elected President of Punjab Muslim League, but this support of the Prime Minister turned out to be chimerical as when Daultana garnered enough support to become Premier the rug was pulled out from under him.

Sind and to remove any injustices and hardships which people suffered. His was a very practical approach to the problems of society and the management of government.

It was only gradually that he realised that the political reality of the newly independent Pakistan was very different not only from the expectations of the ordinary man but also from the kind of political framework he was used to working in under the British, where some respect at least was paid to the letter of the law. Thus an increasingly disenchanted Khuhro fought unceasingly against the diktat of the Centre, manoeuvring ceaselessly to avoid the big stick but more often than not finding himself at the receiving end. Khuhro was the primary and the most important target for those forces in Pakistan who wanted to crush the incipient democracy and the cherished autonomy that the people of the sub-continent had fought for so long.

Khuhro was just 46 years of age when Pakistan came into being. He was at the height of his powers. He had already proved himself one of most able administrators in the sub-continent. He should have had the opportunity to make a vital contribution to the development of Pakistan. In fact he lasted less than a year as Premier for the first time and he managed to become Premier twice more, but he was only Chief Executive for less than three years in all. He spent more than a decade 'disqualified' to hold office through a series of rogue 'laws' such as PRODA and EBDO which had been specially devised by bureaucrats and central politicians. What should have been the best years of a massive contribution to his country and to the province of Sind were thus cruelly wasted.

Throughout the first decade of independence Khuhro retained his support in Sind whether in or out of power. He had dared to defy the Quaid-e-Azam on the issue of Karachi. He had been dismissed from the Premiership of Sind. A Court of Inquiry had been conducted against him. A special law to disqualify him from holding public office or from taking part in elections to the Legislatures had been passed. But nonetheless the party and the public continued to support him. This was much to the bewilderment and embarrassment of those at the Centre.

Pakistan, realised, was a very different country from the one expected by those who had been in the forefront of the freedom struggle. The levers of power had found their way into the hands of those who had played no part in the freedom struggle, had never contested elections or had any first hand acquaintance with the people they were now governing. Their primary concern was to keep power they had so fortuitously acquired and they did so by whatever means necessary even if that meant destroying the legitimate heirs of the freedom struggle who were the democratically elected representatives of the provinces: the people who had raised political consciousness, prepared the ground for the achievement of freedom and provided the basis for Pakistan.

This new ruling class kept itself in power by delaying the making of Pakistan's constitution; and in the meantime systematically destroying the establishment of stable government in the provinces. They successfully destroyed the most able provincial politicians by playing one group off against another and when this failed inventing PRODA to keep them in line, with the threat of the Governor's rule thrown in as well. Specially favoured sections of the press were used to further this ruling clique as the legitimate government of Pakistan. Dissidence was equated with treason and Pakistan was portrayed as a country continually under threat from disloyal elements. The grounds for the usurpation of power by an illegitimate clique of second rate politicians and overmighty bureaucrats was laid in the very first years of Pakistan.

Khuhro in common with the other workers for freedom and the achievement of Pakistan, had assumed that the new state would reflect a certain austerity commensurate with freedom from colonial rule, and would be led by men who approximated as nearly as possible to principles and conduct set by the founders of Islamic polity. Thus there was astonishment when the new head of the state, government ministers and high officials slavishly followed British Imperial protocol and aped Mughal court extravagance. The new government surrounded itself in Viceregal formalities: aides-de-camp, military secretaries, was inaccessable to the public, had a secretive mode of government and followed an excessively extravagant lifestyle.

The activities of this ruling class which encompassed ministers and the top cadre of civil servants gave no clue that Pakistan was a newly born, poor, mutilated state with enormous problems which could hardly afford to pay its employees let alone indulge in any extraneous extravagance. There was a constant rounds of garden parties, ladies in the latest French chiffons or flowing silk *ghararas* (a *Nawabi* court dress with trailing skirts) and men in formal dress. Pakistani government ministers, officials and diplomats mingled nightly at receptions and dinner parties. The Prime Minister's wife was the leader of a fashionable society, setting the tone with clothes and entertainments reminiscent of the great days of the Mughals and the Oudh court circles. Begum Liaquat Ali Khan showed concern too for the under privileged but much in the manner of a Lady Bountiful. She organised *Meena Bazaars* along the pattern of the Mughal court 'fairs.' Stalls were set up by locals and diplomats. Folk dancers and entertainers of all kinds were included to set a scene reminiscent of Arabian Nights. Incredulous Karachi watched as it was transformed from an squeaky clean sleepy provincial capital into a city where an insouciant and extravagant lifestyle was led by the rulers and their *begums*.

Khuhro made an occasional appearance at official functions but was too busy to be sucked into the social round and was ill disposed to take part in the intrigues which went on at these gatherings. To some extent that went against him as he was usually unaware of the court intrigues that went on behind his back. It was an atmosphere very alien to and quite different from that of the serious and focussed struggle of the years before independence. The veterans of the movement for the separation of Sind; and of the years leading up to the realisation of Pakistan were unbelieving spectators of the manoeuvres taking place before them. Those at the Centre took more and more powers to themselves and in doing so deliberately reduced the power and resources of the Provinces.

****

At a time when India was forging ahead with the framing of its constitution, Pakistan was dragging its feet. A sound constitution is an essential prerequisite and a necessary framework for nation building and providing the basis on which a society can prosper and flourish. But those at the Centre weaved and ducked this responsibility deliberately using a series of diversionary tactics to put off the day.

An Objectives Resolution for the constitution was produced soon after independence. This set out the stages of constitution making–the first of which was the work of the Basic Principles Committee. But this did not produce its report until the later part of 1952.* This proved to be a shallow exercise which served little useful purpose. However, it did introduce the religious factor into the constitutional process.

The Objectives Resolution had made somewhat pious and vague references to Islam:

"Whereas the Muslims shall be enabled to order their lives in the individual and collective spheres in accord with the teachings and requirements of Islam as set out in the Holy Quran and the Sunnah."

This affirmation of Islamic ideals was hardly necessary in a state which was overwhelmingly Muslim. However it skirted the issue that there were a varied mix of sects and *firqas* which co-existed peacefully but could be roused to frenzies of intolerance under certain circumstances – as the history of Pakistan would witness. It was no secret that there was no agreed system of *shariat* in the Muslim world which could be used as a reference point for the constitution makers. Nonetheless the Basic Principles Committee attempted to expand the meaning of Islamic ideals into a series of religious provisions it wanted included in the constitution. These provisions were of such a general character that they could, and would be used not only by vested interests like the religious parties but also by unscrupulous rulers who twisted their meaning to their own devices. Thus a Pandora's box of controversy and religious conflict in Pakistan was opened which created an atmosphere of sectarian intolerance.

For all of its existence the Muslim League, despite its name, had been a 'secular' organisation concerned with the economic and political rights of the Muslim community of India in contrast with the 'Islamic' and quasi-Islamic parties of which there were a large number many of which had been in the forefront of politics in the 'twenties. These were more focussed on religious concerns and were opposed to Pakistan considering that it would narrow the field of activi-

---

* The Objectives Resolution was meant to be merely a pious affirmation of Islamic ideals but was at best unnecessary in a state which was overwhelmingly Muslim but where there were a varied mix of sects and *firqas* which co-existed peacefully but could be roused to frenzy of intolerance under certain circumstances – as the history of Pakistan would witness.
It was also no secret that there was no agreed system of *Shariat* in the Muslim world which could be used as reference point for the constitution makers. The Objectives Resolution served only to open a Pandora's box of controversy and religious conflict in Pakistan and created an atmosphere of sectarian intolerance.
The unctuously pious and vague sections of the Objectives Resolution were the following:
"Whereas the Muslims shall be enabled to order their lives in the individual and collective spheres in accord with the teachings and requirements of Islam as set out in the Holy Quran and the Sunnah;" This section was then defined by the Basic Principles Committee in a number of recommendations which laid down the Islamic ideals to be followed. These provisions were of a general character which could and would be used not only by vested interests like the religious parties but also by unscrupulous rulers who had merely to follow the guidelines laid down by the Basic Principles Report to harass the people of Pakistan.

ties for the Muslim *ummah*. While Pakistan was a distant dream, the 'Islamic' parties were bitterly opposed to it in principle but once achieved they lost no time in taking their place in the country's political life. Liaquat Ali's delaying tactics gave them the chance they wanted. With the Report of the Basic Principles Committee asserting Islam was an essential foundation of the constitution they could claim that 'Islamic ideals' underpinned the very existence of Pakistan.

Only in 1956 was some sort of constitution finally cobbled together which formally regularised the Centre's powerful role and the Provinces (by this time only two) with much diminished influence.

The central government established control over the economic and financial resources of the country with, it turned out, little regard for the requirements of the people. They decided from the start that industrialisation was the best way forward and devised policies which were consequently at the expense of the rural areas and agricultural economy on which the majority of the people relied. Industry which had been a provincial subject since 1935 was transferred to the Concurrent list. Prices of agricultural produce were kept down in order to 'encourage' the industrial sector. Labour costs were lower as food prices were kept artificially cheap. New industries were also encouraged by special tax breaks. However little else was done to implement and foster new industries so this policy failed to deliver much needed revenue and resources for the Government and country.

The first budget announced by the Finance Minister Ghulam Mohammed in 1947 allocated 70% of the total revenues of the Central Government to the Armed Forces. He admitted that this was money which would be better spent on the social and economic development of the country. The provinces were hit badly by this budget. Their share of taxes was cut substantially and they were in addition, divested of the right to collect the sales tax. The provinces which had been badly disrupted by the Partition were now deprived of their means of recovery by a reduction of their resources. Their autonomy was further eroded by the take over by the Centre of other financial controls. Their development programmes were also drastically cut.

The Central government took no notice of the protests of the provinces which were led by East Bengal. In these first few years it calmly established wartime controls over the production and distribution of various commodities – thus opening the way for patronage and corruption. The Centre set up a profileration of committees which would control every aspect of the economy.

On the eve of taking over as Chief Minister for the second time in March 1951, Khuhro registered his protest against Central Government policies. Speaking in the Constituent Assembly he said

"the large surpluses this year and next year were mainly due to the enhanced cotton export duty. Out of the total quantity of 14 lakh bales exported from Pakistan every year about 5 lakhs came from Sind and Khairpur. But in the matter of grants to the provinces provided in this year's budget Sind had not been fairly treated and had been allocated only one crore."

Although there were complaints from other provinces as well that they had not received fair portions of the grants, Khuhro maintained–

"but my complaint is that the worst sufferer in this respect is the province of Sind...Sind [is] the most heavily taxed province. In the case of jute East Pakistan got its share of export duty but Sind received nothing as its share of cotton export duty. The incidence of taxation in Sind was about 14% as against 10% in the Punjab and only 2 or $2\frac{1}{2}$% in East Pakistan. Therefore Sind deserved a larger amount of grant from the Centre. The proper approach to the problem should be that those from whom taxes are realised should benefit at least equally."[2]

Squirming under the heavy hand of the Centre Sind was also the most deprived province in terms of its share of revenues. In the same speech Khuhro pointed out that Sind had not so far received compensation for the loss of Karachi which had taken place three years earlier and which had been promised by the Quaid-e-Azam. This compensation amounted to at least Rs. 50 crores and of which

"At least four or five crores should have been provided in the next year's budget of the Pakistan government so that Sind could start building its new capital."[3]

The revenues which the Centre sought to control were, in the absence of other sources, derived mainly from agriculture. This was the backbone of the economy and also the most deprived sector in terms of infrastructure and social welfare. Khuhro had felt that with the achievement of Pakistan the agricultural sector would benefit. Majority rule would be confirmed and without the obstructions put by the colonial governor there would be no hindrance to the welfare legislation for the rural sector. The picture that was taking shape in Pakistan was the very reverse of these expectations. By 1950 Sind was still waiting for the Governor General's consent to the Land Alienation Bill which had been refused consent some years earlier by the colonial regime!

The arrogance with which the Centre treated the Provinces turned into downright foolishness when they turned to foreign affairs. They embroiled Pakistan in a mess in Kashmir and in unnecessary and frivolous attitudes regarding states such as Junagadh and Hyderabad. When India took over Hyderabad State in October 1951 Pakistan perceived it as threat against itself and immediately ordered expansion of its defence forces. It was painfully obvious that Pakistan was in no position to support a large defence establishment and that if it opted to do so, it was apparent even by the time the first budget of the country was announced, that it would be at the expense of the people of the four provinces of Pakistan. The policy makers at the Centre were constitutionally incapable of sympathising with the people of Pakistan and their priorities and policies made that very clear.

East Pakistan suffered spectacularly at the hands of the Centre from the beginning with the Quaid-e-Azam's disregard of Bengali sensitivities by his declaration that Urdu would be the only State language. The Centre also imposed its own people as Ministers. Khwaja Nazimuddin as the Premier had hardly any support. He was forced to implement the Centre's unpopular diktats. The 1954 elections with the rout of Muslim League and the victory of the Jugtu front was proof of this unpopularity. In Sind the situation has received less sympathy from Pakistan historians but was if anything more tragic than that of East Pakistan.

For Sind the day of bitter disillusionment with the Centre's thirst for absolute power came with the Centre's unilateral decision to take over Karachi in the face of the unanimous opposition of the Sindhis. The pride of Sind, the city which had been built as the provincial capital with its hard earned resources only ten years earlier and was at the time of Pakistan's creation one of the best loved and cared for cities of the sub-continent was summarily taken over by the government to which Sind had given refuge and for which it had spent all its savings. Sind government had given a sincere welcome and space to the capital of Pakistan in Karachi, moving out of its offices and secretariat and into army barracks. The understanding had been that the Pakistan government would in time build its own capital either in and around Karachi or elsewhere more centrally in Pakistan. But the behaviour of the Central government after its arrival in Karachi particularly its takeover of the city in the face of the united opposition of Sind showed the machinations of the Centre at its most ruthless. Its total disregard of the Province's anguished outcry at loosing its capital served to illustrate that the Centre would stop at nothing to achieve its aims. Even Quaid-e-Azam sided with the Centre against the democratically expressed wish of the people and government of Sind.

The resolution severing Sind's links with Karachi was moved in the Constituent Assembly on 22 May 1948 at 5 o'clock. The Centre had chosen the timing with some cunning–the debate was called at the last minute on the last day of the Assembly's session. The result was that only two Sindhi members–Khuhro and Gazdar–out of four managed to be present. But they put up a spirited showing against the cynical Central politicians who knew full well their powers to thwart and suspend the democratic wishes of the people.

The debate well illustrates the widely different attitudes and approaches of politicians from the Centre and the Provinces. Khwaja Shahabuddin the Minister of Interior moved a Resolution in the House:

(a) that the capital of Pakistan shall be located at Karachi;
(b) that all executive and administrative authority in respect of Karachi and such neighbouring areas which in the opinion of the Central Government may be required for purposes of the capital of Pakistan shall vest in and or shall be exercised by or on behalf of the Government of Pakistan and the legislative power shall vest in the Federal Legislature; and
(c) that notwithstanding anything in any law for the time being in force, the Government of Pakistan shall proceed forthwith to take such steps and adopt such measures as may be necessary to give effect to the purposes of this motion.

Gazdar stood to oppose the resolution and to express the wishes of the elected members of Sind. He read out the Resolution passed in the Sind Assembly–

"This Assembly records its apprehension and alarm ... that such a step would constitute a flagrant contravention of the Pakistan Resolution passed in 1940 which emphasises the sovereignty and territorial integrity of the autonomous units constituting Pakistan."

Gazdar said prophetically,

"Sir if you do not want to make democracy a farce, if you do not want tracking towards absolute dictatorship, you should have respect for the feelings of the people of Sind... we do not want to give up Karachi."[4]

The unanimously passed Resolution of the Sind Provincial Muslim League under Khuhro's presidentship was also read out.

Liaquat Ali replied to the debate in a supercilious and patronising vein saying that Gazdar was suffering from high blood pressure or 'only a slight nervous excitement'. Thanking the Government of Sind for the 'the assistance they had given when Pakistan came into being' he said with doubtful sincerity,

"It never was, it never is and it never will be the desire of the Pakistan Government to do any harm or injury to the people of Sind. We shall see that their interests are not prejudiced in any way...Pakistan Government would make financial adjustments with the Sind Government and the the Government of Sind would not lose a single penny from the revenues it was getting from Sind, including Karachi, at present."

When Khuhro who was well aware of the financial situation remarked,"Look to your budget" Liaquat Ali rebuked him saying unctuously and meaninglessly, "Governments did not look to their budgets, but to their credit. If the coffers of a government were full of gold and the Government had no credit at all the gold was not worth a handful of sand." Making another snide comment at Gazdar he said, "Mr. Gazdar remarked that we were robbing the Sind Government. Our standards of morality are higher than his.[!] The Pakistan Government will never be guilty of any immoral deal with the provinces,[!!!] and the strength of the provinces is the strength of Pakistan." With supreme irony and implied contempt for the people of Sind, he concluded "that everyone who had breadth of vision would realise that it was ultimately Sind and its people who would benefit by Karachi becoming the capital of Pakistan...If Sind's people did not realise it today, the future generations would bless this Assembly for having selected Karachi as the capital of Pakistan."[5]

At the same time he refused to give Mian Iftikharuddin the assurance he asked for that the people of Karachi would continue to have the right to democratic representation:– "he wants an assurance to a few educated people that they would be allowed to fight the elections for the Sind Assembly... the future constitutions of Pakistan would be framed by the Pakistan Government but by the Constituent Assembly of Pakistan and it would decide the future of administration in Karachi."[6] The Resolution was duly passed.

In these early days of Pakistan the public spirit was still undaunted. The President of the Sind Muslim Federation, Mohammed Shafi Ansari immediately sent off a telegram to the Governor General at Ziarat where Jinnah was staying, protesting against the Resolution rushed through the Constituent Assembly:

"Humbly submitted Sind MLAs will never accept compromise or arbitration over Karachi's separation. Kindly reject Constituent Assembly's Resolution as opposed to united will and opinion of Sind and its representatives..."[7]

The Sind Muslim League Assembly Party then passed a Resolution on 12 June which said that it:

"...most emphatically records its disapproval of the resolution of the Pakistan

Constituent Assembly who, in utter disregard of the wishes and sentiments of the people of Sind, carried the resolution and thus banged the door of amicable settlement between the representatives of Sind and Pakistan governments disregarding the historical, geographical and social link between Karachi and rest of Sind and has thus paved ground for unrest and dissatisfaction among the people of Sind which this Party considers impolitic and inopportune. Further, this meeting conscious of dire necessity of strengthening and building up Pakistan and securing solidarity of all Provinces for this purpose at this most critical period notes with painful regrets that the action of the Constituent Assembly is sure to weaken Pakistan's solidarity by creating discontent in entire Province of Sind. In view of the above, this Party earnestly appeals to the Pakistan Constituent Assembly through the Government of Pakistan to revise their decision and allow the administration of Karachi to remain in the hands of the Provincial Government to whom the territorial integrity and Provincial autonomy was guaranteed by the Lahore Resolution as well as by the Pakistan Constitutional Amendment Act."[8]

In order to implement this Resolution this Party nominated a Committee from the members of the Assembly

"to wait on the Quaid-e-Azam, the Prime Minister of Pakistan and the Minister of Interior, in this connection, and report to the Party the result of their negotiations where upon the Party will decide its future course of action".

The delegation consisted of Mohammed Hashim Gazdar who was member of the Constituent Assembly as well as the Sind Assembly, Kazi Fazlullah, Kazi Mohammed Akbar, Agha Ghulam Nabi Pathan, Haji Ali Akbar Shah and Haji Ali Mohammed Mari."[11] The delegation had already met Prime Minister Liaquat Ali Khan on Sunday 13 June but had not had a satisfactory discussion. Liaquat Ali had been quite unhelpful and rumour immediately spread that he had made insulting remarks about the Sindhi people and their culture. These rumours persisted and became part of the folk legend regarding the attitude of the Centre towards Sind.

On 21 June the delegation met the Quaid-e-Azam at the Government House at Ziarat. The meeting went on for two and a half hours – a long time for the sick Jinnah and an indication of the seriousness of the subject. The delegation placed before him the point of view of "4,000,000 Sindhi Muslims:

"We discussed with him all aspects of the question-administrative, economic, political and educational – and tried to impress upon him the various implications and likely repercussions of the proposed separation move...We suggested building a new Karachi in the vicinity of the present City to accommodate the Capital of Pakistan. Along with other suggestions even this did not find favour with the Quaid-e-Azam."[10]

The delegation however stood its ground. These were still days when public representatives believed in their democratic rights. The maximum concession they could make even to the great Quaid himself was that Karachi should accommodate both the Central and Provincial capitals. But Quaid-e-Azam would not agree to this:

"In spite of protracted discussions, we regret we are not able to make the Quaid-e-Azam agree to the point of view of the people of our Province. Accordingly we are returning to Karachi to apprise the Sind Muslim League Assembly Party of the trend of these discussions and it will be up to the Party to decide their future course of action in the matter."[11]

The fact that the Province's united opinion had no weight as far as the rulers of Pakistan were concerned was made absolutely clear by the imperious cast of statement of the Quaid, implying as it did that the elected legislators of Sind did know not what was good for them and that

"There was a great deal of confusion of thought and it was obvious that the real facts, condition and the situation was not fully appreciated or grasped... and [if] the leaders would not fight for the shadow but the substance – namely to secure from the Pakistan Government fullest compensation by financial adjustment, – and from now onwards fix upon a suitable place for their own capital, prepare a proper scheme and plan, and build it up it would be the best and the most beneficial course for them to adopt."

The Quaid-e-Azam threw in a sop to the summary rejection of the Sind standpoint saying soothingly that all this change over would take a few years and that the Sind Government was not to be thrown out immediately:

"Neither the Pakistan Government nor the Sind Government can immediately quit Karachi. The Pakistan Government will undoubtedly define and demarcate immediately an area which they think should be centrally administered...but there will be no immediate dislocation...it will have to be done gradually."[12]

The Sind Muslim League Council then met to continue the fight and declared its faith in Khuhro's leadership. Khuhro thoroughly disillusioned with the Central leaders decided that the Sindhis would register their protest. He appointed a Committee of Action and declared 2 July "Karachi Day". Mass demonstrations were held throughout Sind. Nothing Sindhis could do however was to affect the Central Government juggernaut.

On 23 July 1948 the Governor General exercising his powers under subsection (1) of Section 290 A amended the Constitution (Indian Independence Act 1947) and made a law to be known as Pakistan (Establishment of the Federal Capital) Order, 1948. This law purported to have been promulgated in implementation of the resolution passed by the Constituent Assembly on 22 May.

The question arises that since the amendment to the constitution and the order demarcating the boundaries of the new capital were made by an Order of the Governor General why did Liaquat Ali Khan feel it necessary to get a Resolution from the Constituent Assembly? A convincing argument is put forward by a recent commentator[13]

"If an executive order were issued without there being some form of sanction of the Assembly in its support, it was likely to give rise to a public reaction against it. Such a reaction could assume serious proportions and it might not remain confined to the Province of Sindh. Therefore it would be useful first to approach the Assembly. But then the procedure adopted should be such that the matter was not publicised before it was brought to the Assembly and in the House there should be as little discussion as possible. This dual object could not be achieved if a regular Bill was to be introduced. Therefore the only option was to bring the matter to the Assembly in the form of a resolution.

But a resolution could also receive undesirable publicity and a debate on it could also be quite long. Something had to be done to meet these two possibilities. As far as the fear of publicity was concerned, this problem was solved by keeping the matter a secret and bringing it to the House with a very short notice to the members. And it order to ensure that there was no long debate, a suitable day and a suitable hour were chosen for moving the resolution."[14]

The Constituent Assembly had been in session from 15 May and was due to end the session on 22 May. The Resolution was moved on the last day towards the end of the session at 5 o'clock in the evening. "The time was chosen not without care"[15] It was so chosen as to give the least time for debate or for Sindhi members to talk to their colleagues from other provinces and lobby for their point of view. Many of the members, particularly from East Pakistan had already left. The opinions of the province and of the people directly affected were ignored and the Resolution bulldozed through.

Two most important matters however were left unaddressed. First the question of the area that was proposed to be taken over for the use of the capital and secondly the amount of compensation to be paid. As it happened the Central Government acted in bad faith on both issues. With regard to the first question the calculation of the town planning experts had been that the total requirement for a new capital of Pakistan was approximately 800 acres in all. Government buildings for an Assembly building and its Secretariat were estimated to take 200 acres; residential buildings for Ministers, government employees and foreign embassies, etc. would take approximately 600 acres.[16], but the actual area which was taken over for the capital was 566.81 square miles![17] Karachi which had been so far regarded as the 'provisional' capital was now termed the 'permanent' capital although the constitution had not yet been framed and it was the prerogative of the duly elected assembly under duly framed constitution of Pakistan which would have the right to designate the capital of the country.

Liaquat Ali Khan had his own motives for wanting the separation of Karachi from Sind and also for the extraordinarily large amount of territory that was taken from Sind. He was uncertain of his political position in Pakistan.[18] He had been elected from East Pakistan and although he could probably get a seat from there or from the Punjab, he was dependent on the support of East Bengalis or Punjabis for that seat and the members from the five provinces for Prime Ministership. He was not sure that he could get it. His actions were therefore directed towards making certain of an electoral seat for himself and as far as possible getting compliant members who would support him. For the first objective what better than to be elected from Karachi demographically engineered to make a suitable electorate for him. To achieve this end Karachi had to administered directly by the Centre and under his control – a control which had to be established whatever the means:

"If we take an overall view of all the executive and legislative measures that Mr. Liaquat Ali Khan took during this early period of the history of Pakistan which came to an end with his tragic assassination, it would appear that the single main object towards which his policies remained directed was how to perpetuate his rule. For this purpose he had chalked out quite a comprehensive plan under which all those political leaders and movements which could be potential challengers to his political future were to be humbled... Mr. Liaquat Ali Khan did not have much regard for whether or not his actions, in this direction were legally or morally justifiable."[19]

To achieve the second objective, that is to get support from the Assembly he had to crush any leadership that was independent-minded. He considered all those politicians who were effective and had popular support as a threat. Apart from Khuhro his most spectacular target, he removed Khan Sahib from the Frontier province and Mamdot from the Punjab who became another PRODA victim. The twin strategies were thus well underway by the middle of 1948. The machinery of PRODA was to get rid of the 'turbulent priests' and the 566.81 square miles of federally administered territory of Karachi was ample to return not only Liaquat Ali Khan but a number of his loyalists as well.

There remained the question of 'compensation' to be paid to Sind for the expropriation of its capital. The Quaid-e-Azam himself had emphasised that Sind would be fully recompensed financially and had advised the Sind Parliamentarians' delegation that

"if the Sind Government and leaders would not fight for the shadow but the substance, – namely to secure from the Pakistan Government fullest compensation by financial adjustment...would be the best and most beneficial course for them to follow."[20]

Sind was however, badly short changed. Apart from the cost of Sind Government buildings and directly owned property which Khuhro estimated at Rs. 50 crores in 1951[21] there was the vast area which would be developed into real estate, the taxes lost to the province and not least the cost that Sind was putting in to build the Lower Sind Barrage which was to provide the water-supply for Karachi. Matters would work out quite contrary to Quaid-e-Azam's rosy picture of 'fullest compensation' and the assertion that:

"Financially, the building up of the capital would cost not lakhs but crores of rupees, and the Sind Government had neither the finance nor the machinery to undertake the administration of Karachi in all its various aspects."[22]

As it happened Sind was not to get even a fraction of the loss it underwent. A committee set up to compound the amount of compensation due to Sind fixed it at 600 to 800 hundred million rupees in 1950.[23] Sind received altogether 6 million rupees as compensation![24] The successive governments of the province continued to ask that the compensation be paid as promised but to no avail. This was the limit of the compensation paid from the time of the takeover in 1948 to the time it was handed back to Sind after the break up of One Unit in 1970. In all its time in Karachi the Pakistan Government did not build one substantial or elegant building in Karachi, just one or two tawdry structures were put up in the vicinity of the beautiful stone buildings built by the autonomous Government of Sind before partition, filling up the carefully preserved open spaces of the Sind capital.* The money that was saved on Karachi would eventually go to build the new capital of Islamabad.

But even more tragic than the fate of Sind's premier city, was the fate of

---

* In spite of the tall claims made by the Prime Minister that Pakistan Government was better able to maintain Karachi, spend money on its development and pay back compensation to Sind Government as well it delayed building even the essential housing required for its employees as witnessed by the Governor General, Khwaja Nazimuddin's letter to Liaquat Ali Khan: "I have more than once spoken to you about the urgent necessity of building residential accommodation for officers, particularly the clerical establishment... From enquiries made by me I have come to learn that very little progress has been made about building the new Capital..." Governor General to Prime Minister, Government of Pakistan, 16 Jan. 1949. QAP.

democracy at the hands of the Centre. Since the Reforms of 1919 democratic elective politics had been in practice in Sind as in other provinces of India. The politicians of Sind were experienced parliamentarians and had links with their electorates not only on a traditional basis but also on the new grid of electoral constituencies. For over a quarter century therefore there had been a working system which linked together the people and their representatives with a vested interest in the federal system and in provinical autonomy. The representative and democratic system in Sind was thus strong and self confident on the eve of Partition in 1947. Events since then had reversed the previous gains in a catastrophic manner.

The actions of Liaquat Ali Khan and Jinnah when they took over Karachi, openly disregarding and riding roughshod over the democratically elected legislature; the representative government of Sind and the clearly expressed public opinion of the province fatally injured the democratic system of the country. It was clear to the powerful bureaucrats of the 'steel frame' of the British Empire that with the political leaders in the centre destroying those in the provinces that they too could benefit. The uncertainty in the provinces, the delay in the constitution making, the postponement of elections in the country, the failure of the central leadership to re-organise Muslim League after independence, the evasive tactics of the Prime Minister who faced chaos in the country and so turned to foreign affairs to bail him out and give himself semblance of authority. This all showed the bureaucrats all too clearly that power was ready to fall into their hands.

Social disorder in the provinces reflected the increasing disillusionment and discontent. Even before Liaquat Ali Khan was assassinated on 16 October 1951 power was slipping from his hands into those of the two institutions left intact by the British imperial power – the bureaucracy, the army and their handmaiden, the intelligence services.

What did all this mean for the badly bruised politicians of the provinces? They were learning, perhaps more slowly than need be, that their expectations of democracy and autonomy were quite illusory. The new dispensation required that for survival they must go along with the central requirements without fuss and without high-minded questions about constitutional or democratic niceties. If they did so there were immense rewards to be had but woe to them if they did not comply. Occasional bursts of spirit would lighten the sky of Pakistan as for instance when in 1954 the Jugtu front won the elections in East Pakistan but the central puppeteers saw to it that the old 'Shere Bengal' did not last too long. He was soon dubbed traitor and sent home. On the whole the darkness was unrelieved. In Sind no chance was to be given for any party to win elections which did not fall in with the central diktat. When Khuhro formed his Sind Muslim League and fought elections in 1953 the Central interference was able to manipulate most of the seats for their own nominees.

In the few years that followed Partition, it became increasingly clear to the politicians that assertion of democratic rights was not a rewarding activity in Pakistan. In the absence of organised public opinion, no matter how strong the largely inarticulated opinion and sentiment of the people may be, for political leaders to make brave stands for issues was as pointless as the boy who stood on the burning deck 'when all but he had fled.' Survival in public life meant compromise with those who called the shots or else forced oblivion. For Khuhro whose every breath was politics this reality sank in gradually. The political drama in Sind and Pakistan between August 1947 and October 1958 was a bitter and object lesson in death by torture of democracy – a child of tender years in the provinces that made up Pakistan.

19

DEALING WITH AN OVER MIGHTY CENTRE

In February 1949 Pir Illahi Baksh, after only ten months in power after he had replaced Khuhro as Premier, was disqualified by the election tribunal and had to vacate his seat in the Legislature. As Premier he still had a grace period of six months to get himself re-elected to the Assembly but although handpicked by the Centre the previous year, he had quickly lost favour.* The Governor of Sind at this time was Justice Din Mohammed of Boundary Commission fame. He called Pir Illahi Baksh to the Governor's House and presented him with an already typed copy of resignation which the intimidated man signed immediately.

Pir Illahi Baksh had done his best to win favour with the Central Government, handing over Karachi immediately, taking in as many refugees as were decreed by the Centre and generally falling in with their demands. When for example Khwaja Shahabuddin, the Central Minister for Refugee Rehabilitation toured Sind in November 1948 and later announced unilaterally the numbers of refugees to be taken by Sind and the measures to settle them, the Sind Premier who accompanied him "seems to have remained a silent spectator throughout the tour."[1] It would be difficult to imagine Khuhro allowing himself to be sidelined in this manner. But apparently all this subservience and obsequiousness was not enough.

In his anxiety to please the Central authorities the Sind Premier alienated the Sindhi cultivators. The High Commissioner for U.K. reported, "Sind *haris* agitate that refugees are being settled on land which was taken from them by Hindu moneylenders by illegal means."[2] The Central Government in contravention of the civic rights of its own citizens also declared invalid *bona fide* sales of property by Hindus to local Muslims so as to get as much property as possible declared 'evacuee property' and to dispose of it as they wished.

The unwillingness of the Centre to help the the Sindhi people in any way was obvious. Legislation to improve the conditions of the indebted *haris* such as Sind

---

* Pir Illahi Baksh although chosen specially by the Central Government to replace Khuhro, perhaps because he was seen as weak and manageable, quickly lost favour with the puppet masters and for several months before he was removed in February a 'virulent' press campaign was conducted against him again led by Altaf Hussain of *Dawn*. As the British High Commissioner reported back to his government," Dawn has carried on its campaign against the Sind Premier with unabated venom."(HCR, 5-11 Nov. 1948, L/P&J/5/331).

Land Mortgage Restoration Bill, which had been passed by the Sind Legislature before Partition had not been given the Governor General's assent. There was sufficient uncultivated land which could have been allocated to refugees but very few of them were farmers. The Central Government was more concerned that well developed orchard land be declared 'evacuee property', to give to the favoured few among the refugees as 'compensation'. The poorer refugees were on the whole urban artisans or petty civil servants who had no wish to go to rural areas although Khuhro had tried to disperse them in the rural areas of Sind. It was only the East Punjab refugees who came into Nawabshah and some parts of the left bank lands who wanted to work on the land and who were quite capable of developing uncultivated land and did so when given the chance.

To further tighten its control over Karachi's assets the Central Assembly passed the Sind Rent Restriction Act which gave the administration of Karachi power to allot space in *partially vacant houses* [author's italics] and discretionary powers to declare 'vacant' parts of 'large houses occupied by a small number of people'. A measure which was quickly open to abuse–

"... the minorities for their part have little hope that it will be applied in a non discriminatory manner. The opportunities for corruption and favouritism which will arise are obvious."[3]

All this was being done at a time when Khuhro was being investigated for 'maladministration', for taking administrative measures far less tyrannical and unjust than the ones which the Central Government was announcing everyday!

At the same time the Centre was impatient that the Sind government move out of Karachi. Pir Illahi Baksh was anxious to comply but he had only Rs. 200,000 to spend and he was not getting any compensation for Karachi. In the end the Sind Government employees resisted as there was nowhere for them to live in Hyderabad. The Sind Provincial Muslim League under Khuhro's presidentship also told the Sind Government that the move would not be tolerated. The matter was postponed for the time being. The Centre was meanwhile busy taking over the assets of the Sind government, as for example the Sind Industrial Trading Estate (SITE) which had developed by the Sind Government as part of its post-war development for Karachi and on which considerable resources had been spent, was taken over by the Centre.

Mir Ghulam Ali Talpur was very keen to become Premier after the Pir Ministry was removed in February. He was trying hard to gain support among the Assembly members as well as currying favour with the Centre. Liaquat Ali however had his own candidate for Premiership – Seth Yusuf Haroon. A young man of just 32 years of age with a suitable pedigree as Sir Abdullah Haroon's son, Yusuf was completely without Ministerial experience. He was a businessman without any deep understanding of or influence in the rest of the province. But from the Pakistan Prime Minister's point of view he was ideal – easy to influence and 'guide'.

Liaquat Ali decided that the Assembly party meeting to elect the new leader should be held in Hyderabad in the third week of February and nominated Mian Mumtaz Daultana who was President of the West Punjab Muslim League, to preside. He also sent his right hand man, Altaf Hussain, the editor of *Dawn*, to Khuhro to ask him to support Yusuf Haroon. The support was asked for a trial period of six months extendable for another period of six months. He also offered to accept

Khuhro's nominees for all the positions in the Sind Cabinet. Khuhro, who in any case was not going to support Mir Ghulam Ali, agreed to back Haroon who had been regarded as one of his men in Muslim League before independence and whom he had supported for election to the Central Legislature in 1946. Haroon was subsequently elected Leader of House and formed the government taking two nominees of Khuhro, Kazi Fazlullah and Syed Noor Mohammed Shah as ministers, but Liaquat Ali opposed the third name on Khuhro's list, Agha Ghulam Nabi Pathan.

Haroon made no pretence of being independent of the Prime Minister. He had daily meetings with him and referred to him in practically every matter. The situation was highly unsatisfactory from every point of view since the requirements of the Centre and the province rarely coincided. Khuhro and other Sindhi politicians were naturally not happy with the situation but were wary of taking action as the threat of Governor's rule (Section 92A) which had been imposed in the Punjab in January, was ever present. Sindhis were not allowed to forget it, since every newspaper under the Centre's influence was constantly demanding its imposition in Sind.

Haroon was immediately faced with a financial crisis in Sind for which the Centre's policies of squeezing the province were in a large measure responsible. Speaking during the Budget session he painted a bleak picture:
"a deficit of nearly two crores of rupees this year [1949] no cash balances, no prospect of recovery in the future, broken bunds, undependable canals, neglected roads, no nation building plans, no policy of retrenchment and no credit in the money market."[4]

Haroon pointed out that with the loss of Karachi a major source of revenue had been lost to Sind and the low taxable capacity of the Sind rural population to which was added the burden of refugees made the positon of the Sind Government almost impossible. An Emergency cess (rate) was imposed nevertheless on land revenue, threatening further poverty for the rural population. It was hoped that the Centre would pay some of the compensation that was due from it and give some share of the revenues it had sequestered from the province. Khuhro gave assurances of his support for a solution to these grave problems through a Muslim League Working Committee's resolution expressing confidence in the Ministry and pledged support so long as "the present Ministry would faithfully carry out the programme of the Muslim League."[5]

An example of the high handedness of the Central Government was exposed when the question came up in the Budget debate of the expenditure incurred on the Special Court of Inquiry which had been instituted to examine Khuhro. There was a heated debate in the provincial legislature when the members opposed the sanctioning of the expenditure by the provincial Government when actually the tribunal had been appointed without the knowledge or approval of the Sind Cabinet. Eventually the Premier had to admit that although the Sind Government had had no say in the matter at this stage there was no alternative to voting the demand as the expenditure had already taken place.

The Sind Assembly also pinpointed the problem of province's search for an alternative capital showing a strong consensus of opinion that the Provincial Government should refuse to incur any expenditure on the building of a new capital until not only the amount of compensation due to it from the Centre had been definitely decided on, but a substantial advance payment had also been received. The Assembly also showed its concern about the dual control that was being exercised by the Central Government on the settlement of refugees in the province, a control moreover for which there was no adequate financial backing.

The Budget debate reached consensus that retrenchment in government expenditure was necessary to meet the difficulties of the province. A Retrenchment Committee was set up under the chairmanship of Hashim Gazdar to give suggestions for economy in government expenditure. This Committee presented its report a year later when Haroon had been replaced as Premier by Kazi Fazlullah. The report was given to Khuhro for evaluation and suggestions. In a detailed commentary on the suggestions of the Committee Khuhro showed his mastery of financial detail and his comprehensive knowledge of administration. In his summing up Khuhro gives a clear picture of the Sind finances some three years after Partition:

"The Retrenchment Committee have very briefly dealt with this subject... and have given only one page to it. The Committee have rightly pointed out that because of the loss of Karachi without proper financial adjustment, the Provincial Government has been very hard hit. For more than a century the Provincial Government have been spending considerable sums of money to develop the city of Karachi. This was the only really modern city in the whole of the Province. The Assets and Liabilities Committee which at the earlier stages was called the Administration of Karachi Committee, and which was appointed in the year 1948, showed in their preliminary report that (the *annual*) loss of revenue due to handing over Karachi to the Centre would come to 60 lakhs (60,00,000) and ultimately a crore of rupees. I gather from the Finance Secretary that on the basis of actual realisations of 1947-1948, the estimated annual loss comes to more than one crore. Besides even after allowing for the realisations from excise duty within the city of Karachi, the net loss in the Excise revenue due to the exodus of Hindus comes to 40 lakhs a year. In addition Sind loses 70 to 80 lakhs of rupees annually due to not getting her share of $12\frac{1}{2}\%$ of income-tax realisations that Government of India used to pay to this Province. Sind Province used to get at least 75 lakhs annually for the post war development schemes. That ofcourse did not help the general revenues of the Province nor was it intended for covering up any deficits, but the payment of the amounts did enable the Provincial Government to incur expenditure for the general development of the Province. So far the Provincial Government have not received development grants from the Centre on anything approaching this scale. I may also mention here that during the war period Government of India gave about 40 lakhs of rupees annual grant for the purpose of the expansion of the police force. It may be argued that the war is over and therefore there is no case for such a grant, but it should not be forgotten that the conditions in this country have actually been worse after Partition than they ever were during the entire war period. Several lakhs of people migrated from this country and several lakhs have come in a most disorderly manner. The Provincial Government have spent considerable sums of money in settling these so far and that too not with much success.

Now I wish to make certain observations with regard to the steps to be taken for augmenting the revenues of the province. In the first place the Provincial

Government should arrive at a proper settlement with the Government of Pakistan regarding payment of compensation, both Capital and revenue, for the loss of Karachi, as soon as possible. If the Sind Government is to get a fair deal from the Central Government on this point, most of our worries will be over. The Sind Government should also try to secure a share in the Income tax and proper share from the Sales tax realisations."[6]

Khuhro also suggested that the Central Government pay at least 50% of the expense of the Border Police for which it was proposing to pay only 30% as

"the border police will be doing semi-military duties and the protection of the border and defence of the country is entirely a central subject."[7]

While out of power Khuhro was closely involved in the affairs of state, studying most of the problems faced by the Government of the province and giving it the benefit of his long experience in politics and administration. He gave advice when asked for as in the case of the Retrenchment Committee. But he also set down the guidelines for the Government so that they would follow through the resolutions of the Sind Provincial Muslim League the ruling party of which he was President.

Conducting the affairs of Sind in these difficult circumstances, with Liaquat Ali breathing down his neck and the Sind Legislature angry at the policies of the Centre being thrust at them, Yusuf Haroon had to make a choice sooner or later. In November 1949 he chose to come down on the side of the Prime Minister. He dropped the Ministers from his Cabinet who had been the nominees of Khuhro. Khuhro then gave him notice to call the Assembly and face a motion of No Confidence. At this Haroon lost his nerve and agreed to compromise. In January 1950 he reshuffled the Cabinet again taking three nominees of Khuhro as Ministers – "a pointer, perhaps to a weakening of the Centre's position *vis a vis* Khuhro since last February" as the British High Commissioner observed.[8]

Liaquat Ali Khan knew that the Sind Assembly was not properly cowed and a weapon had to be found to do that. This he found in the threat of 'agrarian reform'. He set up a committee of the Central Muslim League to go into the question although it was clearly the purview of the provincial administrations. His motives were doubtful as the British High Commissioner reported home:

"The moving spirit behind the setting up of this committee was Liaquat Ali Khan himself, and there is no doubt that he is using his influence over Yusuf Haroon to the full."[9]

It proved difficult for the Prime Minister to continue this ploy as Haroon's position remained uncertain. In May 1950 when his two terms of six months were over, Haroon resigned as Premier and took the post of High Commissioner to Australia. The motives behind the "agrarian reform" now became clearer.

Sind agriculture had for centuries been dependent on a scarce and essentially migratory population for the cultivation of land. For thousands of years the yearly inundation of the Indus provided fertile land. The cultivators had to move from their villages during the floods and then return to wherever the river had left the land rich with silt. Villages were therefore by and large temporary and makeshift, easily dismantled and easily re-assembled – a phenomenon that in the nineteenth century, Napier had been astonished to see and failed to understand. Colonial revenue officers spent over half a century before they devised a system suitable to the conditions of Sindhi agriculture.[10] Later an expensive irrigation system was introduced when the remarkable Lloyd Barrage was built at Sukkur in the early 'thirties. Most of this was paid for by the Province. The taxes to do so were punitive and prevented any accumulation of capital by the agriculturists, a process which was taking in the Punjab at that time.[11]

Since a *perennial* system of irrigation had been introduced the reform of the land tenure system was needed and the Sind legislature had taken steps to do this as early as 1941. A Bill was drafted in 1942 on the lines of Bombay Act XXIX of 1940 but was put in cold storage as the colonial government had its hands full with the World War and the Hur rebellion in Sind. Khuhro who was Minister for Revenue in 1943 instituted a Committee to study the problem but the Committee proceedings were halted when he left the Government in 1944. A report was published in 1945 but had already become obsolete. In March 1947 the Government of Sind appointed Hari Enquiry Committee under the chairmanship of Sir Roger Thomas, Adviser to Sind Government on Agriculture. The Committee submitted its Report in December 1948. The Report described in detail the practical difficulties which arise when tenancies need to be moved around because of insufficient water supply.

The Act, based on the Report gave hereditary rights (Tenancy Right) to *haris* who had cultivated at least four acres of land for the past three years for the same *zamindar*. Where however the system of shifting cultivation was prevalent, a *hari* who had cultivated different pieces of land for the same *zamindar* annually for the last three years would be granted cultivating rights also.*

The Act also gave the *hari* a more equitable share in the produce of the soil. The Act took account of the difficulties caused by the scarcity of cultivators (*haris*) in Sind by providing for termination of Tenancy Rights under certain conditions including compensation.[12] In introducing the Act the Government of Sind felt that it met "the reasonable demands of *haris* and provide the best solution to grant of Tenancy Rights in consideration of the practical difficulties which hedge the problem."[13]

The real problem in Sind, unlike for instance in northern Indian provinces like the United Provinces of Agra and Oudh, was not scarcity of land but shortage of manpower:

"In other provinces the principle problem is that of peasant villages with their heavy pressure on land and uneconomic holdings. This does not apply to Sind."[14]

The Royal Commission on Agriculture in India giving details of the situation in Sind reported:

"The problem of the consolidation of holdings was investigated but it was found that the evil of fragmentation does not exist in Sind to any large extent and that large areas of land are still available,...."[15]

The Report and the Act dealt fair handedly with the most important problems of the *zamindar* and the *hari*. Vested interests in the Central Government however were not willing to let it rest. The Prime Minister and the central bureaucracy

---

* The *hari* or the cultivator in the context of land tenure in Sind is defined by the Royal Commission on Agriculture in India as "a tenant who pays rent usually on a share basis, the share being half the crop on flow land and one third of the crop on lift land. He is, as a rule, financed by the landowner himself, who also directs what is to be grown and how it is to be grown, while the *hari* provides his own men, bullocks and implements." In the Punjab the tenant had to pay half the assessment (i.e. Government revenue dues or tax) but in Sind the tax was paid entirely by the *Zamindar*.

were intent on creating unrest in the province. From the first they sought to sabotage the *Hari Report* through their own tried and tested bureaucrat Mr. Masood, Collector of Nawabshah who was a member of the Committee. He adopted a very belligerent and unco-operative attitude from the beginning. He hardly attended meetings but proceeded to write a 'Minute of Dissent'. This did not concern itself with the terms of reference but was a diatribe on the iniquities of the *zamindar* and their supposed penchant for women and an idle life; their cruelty towards the cultivators whom they treated like 'slaves'; the evils of absentee landlordism of which there could have been hardly any example in Sind at this period! He then wrote a essay on Islamic history and his opinion of the rights of 'peasant proprietors' in the Holy Quran of which he also said, "Barring a few exceptions, the precepts of the Quran in this regard have not been practiced by the Musalmans throughout the Islamic history."[16]

Was Masud doing this by himself or was he pushed? The way the press took up the Masud 'Note of Dissent' was certainly a pointer that some prompting had taken place. The intellectully challenged Pir Ministry in one of its dimmer actions did not at first publish the Masud's Note so that rumour gathered that it was a charter for the *haris*. This allowed the Central authorities to make massive propaganda mileage out of it. The Chairman of the Enquiry Committee, Sir Roger Thomas, commented mildly on the Masud phenomenon:

"The promised Minority Report by Masud has been received by the Government. The first part of it is concerned with the alleged indiscretions of the Chairman! (I once handled a wasp's nest which I found easier than handling Masud in the Committee). His recommendations are concerned with nationalization of land and abolition of *zamindari*. These subjects were outside our terms of reference."[17]

Although the recommendations of the Report were duty enacted by 1949, the anti Sind lobby was not satisfied. The press kept up its propaganda for months, siezing every opportunity they could for Sindhi politician bashing. When in a speech at a Rotary Club meeting in March 1951, Khuhro made an off the cuff remark in his usual blunt style that, "the problem of *haris* does not exist in the province it exists only in some newspaper offices" the press of Karachi went up in smoke. Full page articles were written denouncing Khuhro and quoting the Masud Note in full.[18] Khuhro was depicted as a die hard 'feudalist' and maligned constantly. This propaganda to malign Khuhro and other Sindhi politicians was just one aspect of the game plan to undermine and destroy all provincial leadership and local democratic initiatives.

The press was used to conduct similar campaigns in other Provinces. *The Evening News* of Karachi's reporting on 9 December 1950 is a typical example:

"The N.W.F.P. Government's Act abolishing Jagirdari does not touch the main land problem and means little to the hard pressed cultivators. In West Punjab the unhappy legacy of the past remains although reactionary circles opposing change sometimes attempt to show that Punjab, being a land of peasant proprietors, the land reform problem is not so acute as it is in other provinces. This is already an illusion..."[19]

The attacks on Sind though were much more virulent than on the other provinces and these took on added strength when Khuhro became Premier for the second time in March 1951.

Khuhro's position on agricultural management in Sind was well thought out and not at all undermined by the consistent barrage of abuse and criticism. In April 1951 just a few days into his Premiership he answered the major attacks on the system of agricultural management in Sind through the editorial of his newspaper *The Sind Observer*:

"A section of the local Press has, since sometime, taken upon itself the task of advocating the cause of the Sind Haris *amicus curiae*. But unluckily because there exists no direct contact between the advocates and the clients, sometimes some of the arguments advanced happen to be uninformed and unintelligent. Besides, on occasion, these zealous advocates, in the exhuberance of their emotions and in their anxiety to produce quick results, have been mixing up various issues which only tended to prejudice the very cause they are out to advance. For example, very often one found them simultaneously attacking zamindars, criticising Mr. Khuhro, supporting the Sind Haris and demanding greater political rights for the refugees. An unwise and tactically wrong approach as that exposed their very own intentions to serious suspicions. In any case it provided the other party in the controversy with a ground to allege that this entire solicitude for the welfare of the Haris was inspired by a desire to uproot the local zamindar, break the political power of the local population, and enable the new settlers to dominate Sind's political scene in the future. Personally we do not subscribe to this view; some of the critics of Sind's agricultural system are definitely inspired by highly altruistic motives... What however cannot be gainsaid is that even this section of the critics had not approached the problem from the right angle.

It is hardly conducive to the cause in view attacking Mr. Khuhro or the landholders of Sind without trying to understand their viewpoint. Not only is it unfair but even from the point of view of results it is not likely to lead them anywhere."[20]

In his usual concern for facts he carefully detailed the rationale behind the land tenure system and the prematurity of the demands for the abolition of the *zamindari* system as follows:

"Firstly, there has been so far no economic survey in Pakistan which might sustain the assumption that the Sind *Hari* is not getting a fair deal from the owners of the land, or that he is being robbed by the latter, or that he is not receiving what, consistently with the principles of equity, he is entitled to, or that he is not better off than his opposite number in the rest of the Pakistani provinces, or that unless the *zamindar* is wholly liquidated the condition of the *hari* can never be ameliorated.

Secondly that the entire present approach to the problem is based on ignorance, hearsay and wrong premise.

Thirdly, that Pakistan's economy depended wholly on agriculture and that therefore one must not try to trifle with, or disturb or disrupt the existing system till at least the whole matter has been scientifically studied and alternative means of keeping up the national economy have been properly developed.

Fourthly, that there was no analogy or comparison between the *zamindari* in Sind and the *zamindaris* elsewhere – say in East Pakistan-; there was a world of difference in the very nature of the tenures on which land was held in the two provinces.

Fifthly, that the position of the Sind Zamindar *vis-a-vis* his land was quite different from the position of the East Bengal Zamindar *vis-a-vis* his holding. The Sind *zamindar* in relation to his land stood in the same position in which an industrialist stood in relation to his factories. Both had acquired their respective properties by investing money and both deserved to be treated alike. You cannot reasonably liquidate one and patronise the other. If agriculture is to be nationalized, whether by direct or indirect means then, the same procedure ought to be adopted in the case of other means of production also.

Sixthly if the industrialist was a useful member of society because he contributed towards the augmentation of national wealth then the Sind *zamindar* too claimed the same place. The Sind *zamindar* paid more than Rs. 7 crores per annum to the State although the population of his province was about 10 lakhs only. As against him the East Pakistan *zamindar* paid only about a crore and half even though the population of that province was nearly four crores.

Seventhly that even as it is, the *hari* in Sind has acquired through the latest Sind Tenancy Act more rights and privileges than were enjoyed by his counterparts in any other province of Pakistan. In the Punjab nothing whatsoever had been so far done for him; the same hundred years old laws and rules operate to this day. In East Pakistan there had been no reforms in the sense they are sought to be enforced in Sind. The very struggle to abolish the old system of Permanent Settlements had as yet produced no tangible results. In the N.W.F.P. also all that had been done was the tenant had been given security of tenure for a brief of period of five years only and that was all. As against that Sind had already given to the *hari* permanent and hereditary rights of tenancy; he had been guaranteed 50% share of gross income; he, as a matter of right, could receive interest free loan from the *zamindar*; he could also get seed-*taccavi* from him free of interest; he had been rendered completely immune from forced labour and from all kinds of exactions; under the law he enjoyed perfect equality with the *zamindar* in a court of law and can have his claim adjudicated upon judicially.

Eighthly in Sind the pressure of population on land is much less than it is in the rest of Pakistan provinces and consequently here there is more land available than could be cultivated by the *haris*.

Ninthly, in Sind no scheme of agricultural development can proceed if the institution of *zamindari* is abolished. Would it be possible to build say, the Kotri Barrage at a cost of Rs. 30 crore (which had been raised by way of a loan) if all the lands to be commanded by it are a *baksheesh*.

Now, whether one agrees or not with the *zamindar,* in all that he says one cannot legitimately take up the attitude that a decision must be summarily pronounced against him, here and now without even his points being properly examined. In fact it is there where the trouble has been arising. Our contemporaries have been sometimes found jumping to conclusions without meeting any of these points in a judicial and dispassionate way. In economic matters at least such should not be the attitude of a responsible press."[21]

This closely argued exposition of the age old system of agriculture in Sind has all the hallmarks of Khuhro's attention to detail, his passion for the truth and the conscientous way he approached political dissension. His was not the approach of emotional rhetoric and unsubstantial half truths even in such a matter where his own livelihood was under discussion. Khuhro was genuinely mystified about the storm had arisen over the question of land tenure.

But all the while Liaquat Ali was planning much more drastic action than harassing *zamindars* to fulfil his ambition of being the unchallenged master of all he surveyed. In April 1949 the U.K. High Commissioner reported to his government his assesment of the real motives behind the manoeuvres and intrigues of the Pakistan Prime Minister:

"A pliant and submissive Sind is an important factor in Liaquat Ali's plans for the amalgamation of Western Pakistan."[22]

Although this plan or its details were not widely known, political circles were aware that a scheme was being hatched by Liaquat Ali and his associates. There was a great deal of suspicion about the motives of the Central Government and rumours were rife that plans were afoot (even as early as 1949) to amalgamate the provinces in West Pakistan and form a single administrative unit. The Working Committee of the Sind Provincial Muslim League under Khuhro, took serious notice of this report and passed a resolution in the last week of March 1949 condemning the idea of the amalgamtion of provinces as likely to deprive the people of Sind of their right to manage their own affairs.[23]

On 18 April 1949 a conference of Sind Provincial Muslim League opened at Larkana. This was the first of nine such 'full' conferences, one to be held in each district of the province to acquaint the public with their programme. This conference passed a strong resolution of protest against any proposal to amalgamate the provinces of West Pakistan into a single unit. The Conference was attended by Khwaja Shahabuddin, the Central Minister for Refugee Rehabilitation and Sardar Abdur Rab Nishtar. Nishtar presided over the conference, trying to impose 'Central Government control', for which he and Shahabuddin had been deputed to the conference 'to prevent the passage of violently Provincial conference.'[24] Nishtar had to face the outrage of the Sind Muslim Leaguers in the Subjects Committee which was presided over by him and where the resolutions were being drafted for the conference, the "uproar became so great that the meeting passed completely beyond Abdur Rab Nishtar's control.[25]

Other grievances against the Centre were also brought up. The Subjects Committee had drafted resolutions asking the Central Government to declare the proceedings against Khuhro void and to withdraw his disqualification from public office. After much effort Nishtar managed to get the resolutions protesting against the Centre's treatment of Khuhro withdrawn for the time being... "but these victories cost Nishtar hours of heated debate, and will not have improved relations between the Centre and the Province."[26]

There was much resentment also of Khwaja Shahabuddin's speech in which he criticised the settlement of refugees in Sind–

"Shahabuddin was called a dictator by the Sind speakers who followed him, and criticism of the Central Government, which was accused of ignoring Sind, of making the Province the `first target of encroachment' and of attempting to destroy provincial traditions, and culture reached a pitch where Nishtar was forced to intervene and appeal to speakers to refrain from making remarks likely to create dissension in Muslim League ranks."[27]

The strong feelings of the Sind Muslim Leaguers were reiterated at the subsequent Muslim League meetings in the province.[28]

The Central leaders were reminded of the promises made at the taking over of Karachi, 'that Sind Government would not lose a penny from having to leave Karachi, and that Sindhis would continue to receive preference in recruitment to Karachi's services'. These commitments had been totally reneged. In fact Sindhis were being removed from or rejected by the Karachi administration. In April 1949 the Karachi Administration gave details of officer strength in the Karachi police in reply to a Lahore newspaper's accusation that the force was being recruited exclusively from U.P. and that Punjabis were being excluded. The figures given by the administration revealed that out of 177 officers only 28 came from Sind. This revelation clearly substantiated the complaints by Sindhi politicians that with the separation of Karachi, Sindhi claims for recruitment to the services had been ignored. The nature of the new dispensation was clear from the harassment to which the Press Reporter who filed this item was subjected to by the Police so that the matter had to go up to the Deputy Minister of Interior.[29]

The Sind Provincial Muslim League under Khuhro's leadership was an extremely active organization, hammering out a programme for the welfare and the economic betterment of the province and making every effort to achieve its objectives through the democratic channels of the Muslim League government. But it also showed concern for national and international affairs.[30]

In February 1951 Khuhro entertained Al Haj Amin-el-Hussaini, the Grand Mufti of Jerusalem, who was in Karachi to attend the Motamar-e-Alam-e-Islam meeting. Presenting an address of welcome to the Mufti Khuhro emphasised the need for unity in the Muslim world. He referred to the immense problem of Palestine refugees saying that

"the people of Pakistan could well appreciate the colossal problem of providing relief to the countless victims of human vindictiveness... But if Pakistan could not do as much as it would like in this connection it was merely because its hands were already full with the same problem facing it on a scale absolutely unique in human history."

Khuhro announced a personal donation of Rs. 7,000 to the Palestine Fund and the Grand Mufti donated £50 to Pakistan Refugee Fund to which Khuhro also donated Rs. 3,500.[31]

In 1951 Liaquat Ali Khan took over as President of the Pakistan Muslim League, although the Quaid-e-Azam had as far back as 1942 laid down a policy that party office was not to be held by those who held public office. Khuhro had given up the presidentship of Muslim League when he became a Minister in early 1943.[32] Now following Liaquat Ali's example, provincial Chief Ministers also took over as heads of the provincial Muslim League parties. Khuhro who had been re-elected President in September 1950 with great enthusiasm and given the power to nominate all his office bearers, now had the way open to him to become Chief Minister. Since Khuhro's first stint as Premier of Sind, Prime Minister Liaquat Ali Khan had decreed that only the head of the Federal Government be designated Prime Minister or Premier and all heads of the Provincial Governments be called Chief Ministers.

Khuhro assumed the office of Chief Minister of Sind on 25 March 1951 nearly three years after his removal as Premier on 26 April 1948. It was a measure of the Centre's power that although his disqualification under PRODA had been removed by the Chief Court of Sind in March 1950; he had been President of Sind Muslim

League and had the support of most of the members of the Sind Legislative Assembly, he had to wait until the Centre had agreed that he take office.

Even before the findings of the Special Inquiry Court were submitted to the Central Government and long before the decision of that government was announced the Sind Muslim League Council had elected Khuhro President of the organisation in December 1948. He had stood down from the Presidentship to await the outcome of the Inquiry which exonerated him. In 1950 he was re-elected to the Party post. In fact his leadership of the Muslim League party remained unaffected by any action the government took against him during that time and he had remained throughout this period the most powerful figure in Sindhi politics.

Khuhro became Chief Minister at a time when massive problems were facing Sind. Resources had been depleted and were pitifully low now that Karachi was under Central control. Administration had been weak in the absence of Khuhro's firm hand. In addition, there was the distinct possibility that Central control through the imposition of Section 92 A would be invoked.

In his second term although there was not much love lost between Liaquat Ali Khan and Khuhro, there was a tacit truce which allowed Khuhro to work without too much overt interference. At this time Liaquat Ali's position had weakened in the Central Government with a parallel strengthening of the bureaucratic elements in the Government. Within six months of Khuhro becoming Chief Minister, in October 1951, Liaquat Ali fell prey to an assassin's bullet. After that the camouflage of civilian and democratic control of Pakistan became more transparent than ever.

Khuhro started off his premiership with his usual aplomb although the Centre and its henchmen were "inclined to postpone the killing of the fatted calf."[33] but even *Dawn*, a powerful newspaper which was generally regarded as the spokesman of the Prime Minister and was virulently anti Khuhro, admitted that the

> "thing which stands most to his credit is his adherence to the Muslim League through fair weather and foul. He also possesses that now-a-days rare quality in politicians and administrators which goes by the name of 'dash'."[34]

Having guided the previous Kazi Ministry from the Party Committee Khuhro did not need to make any radical changes in the policy of the Government. He praised Kazi "for having cleared off the old Augean stables" and drawing up ambitious schemes for financial improvement of the province. He looked forward to the completion of the Lower Sind Barrage "which is bound to usher in a new era of prosperity in the Indus valley".[35]

Khuhro himself took charge of the Information portfolio "with a view to establishing close contact and complete harmony between the masses and the representatives of the people. Without mass contact and without the fullest public confidence and co-operation we can make little headway."[36]

Khuhro spelt out his programme of agricultural improvement, which included the rapid implementation of the Tenancy Act. His other policies were to encourage industry and to provide an improved communications infrastructure. He wanted also to further the spread of education in the province.

He reminded the Central Government that Sind was still waiting for the money due to it and without which it was not possible to carry out any of the urgently needed nation building schemes for the Province. He declared that his Government "shall see to it that, as time rolls on the common people who look to us with expectations are not disillusioned." This included an industrialisation programme in Hyderabad, where an industrial estate was set up to solve the unemployment problem.[37]

Khuhro made refugee rehabilitation one of his main priorities. He set out the situation with his usual acumen:

"facts and figures bear out that this Province has gone a long way in resettling the lakhs of refugees who came over to Sind. The new schemes of satellite towns which await implementation will hardly leave any room for genuine grievance."

But he advised the refugee leaders to adopt a more reasonable attitude:

"our problems are their problems... and if a proper attitude of mind is developed and an unbiased approach is made to the entire problem then there would be no difficulty in solving it."

And he reminded the refugees that they had duties as well as the rights and privileges they were demanding,

"I assure my refugee brothers that if they, while claiming all kinds of rights give proof positive that they realise their duties and their obligations as well, they will always find in me their greatest supporter."

He appealed to these new Sindhis not to create a

"new sect of their own but to merge themselves with their fellow Sindhis and enjoy in common with them all that the land has to offer to its people."[38]

He was deeply concerned that the refugees be properly absorbed into the society of Sind. He had witnessed the way that the Centre was handing out free plots of land which many allottees would immediately sell and then apply for another. Khuhro wanted the permanent settlement of refugees to be done as fast as possible so that the drain on State resources would cease. He pushed ahead with the building of the satellite town of Latifabad outside Hyderabad and laid down the rationale for the payment of the houses which was based on the capacity of people to pay by making easy instalments and insisting that free distribution was not encouraged.

At this time a number of refugee organisations had sprung up in Sind which were demanding that Assembly seats be reserved for refugees. Khuhro set his face against this demand as he felt this would divide the people into 'watertight compartments' and prevent the assimilation of the immigrant population–

"The refugees had come over to Sind to settle permanently in the Province and were not birds of passage."

He promised however that special care would be taken to guarantee their representation.[39]

The influx of vast numbers of immigrants was causing problems which were not confined to finding them houses and employment. On 23 October, some months before Khuhro took over the administration of the province, a rumour spread in Hyderabad that a Sindhi had kidnapped a Muhajir boy. This quickly led to a riot situation with a confrontation between a mob of refugees and the police. The mob was led by some 'mischief mongers' who were responsible for together a crowd of people which they would not let disperse. A "Abdul Qayyum Kanpuri and others of ilk by means of the grossest exhortations induced tazia-wallas and akhara-wallas to go to the Police Station." The mob surrounded the Police Station and started stoning it and the policemen there. They would not listen to the reasoning of the police or of the District Magistrate and when the police fired warning shots they intensified their stoning. Some shots were fired from a near by building injuring a number of people so that the police was forced to fire into the crowd which resulted in some injuries and deaths.

There had been no incident of violence in Hyderabad during Muharram for several years and this one was a clear case of wilful mischief making. The newspapers published exaggerated reports of killings which greatly added to the tension. The Government reacted swiftly by setting up an enquiry and publishing the results immediately. The findings of the enquiry cleared up many doubts about the deteriorating law and order situation in the urban areas of Sind. In this particular case fantastic rumours had been put about that Sunni boys were being kidnapped by Shias for the purpose of sacrifice. As the Report put it:

"There is no evidence that there was any Shia-Sunni tension at Hyderabad before or during the ten days of Muharram. In Hyderabad the Sunnis themselves take out *tazias* as they have done always in the past."[40]

The Report pinpointed the causes of the deteriorating law and order situation in the city:

"Refugees who cross the Pakistan-Bharat border at Khokhrapar and its neighbourhood find Hyderabad a convenient rendezvous. Some move on to the interior but others remain at Hyderabad, without the police having any opportunity of knowing who these people really are. In these circumstances it is but natural that some bad characters should find their way into Hyderabad City. ... There can be no doubt that most refugees still feel unsettled and are apt to lend a willing ear to men who style themselves leaders and politicians. In these circumstances it is easy for pushing adventurers and mischief mongers with some ability to take and exhort unsettled refugees to assume the role of leadership and to make approaches to Government authorities ostensibly in the interests of the refugees but hardly ever without the background of self interest to serve.The good unsuspecting refugees thus become an easy prey. To serve their own self interest, such men try to overawe the resisting and inconvenient District Authorities into compliance."[41]

Khuhro was well aware of this kind of problem and had come across it in his first term as Premier. He now had to clear up the aftermath of this incident. He assured help to the families of those affected[42] but at the same time he was anxious that there should be no repetition of such incidents. He kept a tight grip on the situation by frequent visits and personal supervision of the district administration.

He took time off in April from work to give a dinner in honour of the Prime Minister and Begum Liaquat Ali Khan at Karachi Club of which he had been elected President that year. Most of the political and social elite attended. The dinner was followed by music where the main singer was Ustad Manzoor Ali Khan, then in his twenties and already the most accomplished classical singer in the province and also a most innovative singer of the classic *Kaafi*, particularly of Shah Abul Latif's poetry. Khuhro who had a great love of Indian classical music since he was a young man and a frequent guest at the musical functions of Mir Ali Nawaz Khan, the Talpur ruler of Khairpur in the 'twenties. Throughout his life Khuhro took the opportunities to hear the great singers of the sub-continent and though rare these days it was a favourite form of relaxation for him.

****

By the time Khuhro became Chief Minister in 1951 the rot had already set deep into the political system of the new country. Khuhro soon became aware that even colleagues in his own Cabinet were paying court to various czars in the Centre or the Governor of Sind intent on the fast track to power. Kazi Fazlullah was put out at no longer being Chief Minister and egged on by his supporters sought the favour of the Governor. Mir Ghulam Ali, long time candidate for Chief Ministership was seeking the support of Ghulam Mohammed, the powerful Finance Minister. The Governor saw an opportunity provided by this in-fighting to impose Governor's rule in the province and backed a PRODA application against Khuhro which was filed by Mir Ghulam Ali and Kazi Fazlullah. Khuhro's supporters then filed an application against Kazi and Ghulam Ali. This intrigue and counter intrigue did not have the support of Liaquat Ali Khan who was treading carefully. He was preparing to remove Nazimuddin and Khwaja Shahabuddin and get rid of the overmighty Finance Minister Ghulam Mohammed. He got Daultana to talk to Mir Ghulam Ali and when that did not work told the Governor that he did not want PRODA applications encouraged and instructed him to dismiss the application against Khuhro. The Governor had not yet taken the action he was told to do when Liaquat Ali was assassinated on 16 October. When later he did dismiss the PRODA application against Khuhro he left loopholes for its future use against Khuhro if required.

The power scene changed in Pakistan after Liaquat's death. In what must be described as a *coup*, a secret conclave of bureaucratic power brokers assumed the mantle of ruling Pakistan, the chief of whom was Ghulam Mohammed the Godfather of the bureaucrats. The others in the group included Chaudhry Mohammed Ali, Nawab Mushtaq Gurmani and Khan Qurban Ali Khan. Iskander Mirza, Secretary Defence, was soon to be inducted into the inner circle. This group decided how offices were to be shared out. Nazimuddin became Prime Minister and Ghulam Mohammed himself the Governor General who thus assumed a prime position to manipulate the affairs of the state unhindered by a pliable Prime Minister.

Just a couple of months after Liaquat Ali's assassination the Governor of Sind, who had developed ambitions of his own and felt that he would get Central support for Section 92A, asked Mir Ghulam Ali to renew the PRODA application against Khuhro and also had one put against Kazi Fazlullah. There then followed a rush of applications under PRODA against all the major politicians which suited Governor Din Mohammed very nicely. He had one or two charges perfunctorily investigated and then referred them to a Tribunal. Meanwhile Prime Minister Nazimuddin felt he could also fish in the troubled waters of Sind and backed Mir Ghulam Ali, a great favourite with him, for Chief Ministership. But Nazimuddin's support was not of much use with the Governor determined to get power himself. Din Mohammed was able easily to out manoeuvre Nazimuddin and get his own way. With all the possible candidates who could command support in the Assembly being investigated under PRODA the field was clear for him and he asked for the resignation of Khuhro and "when the Assembly would not support a replacement Ministry he dissolved the assembly"[43] and imposed Governor's rule in the Province on 29 December 1951.

Din Mohammed's reign was not to last long however as very soon he fell out with the Prime Minister who understood a little belatedly that he had been outwitted in the matter of Section 92A. Din Mohammed was removed and Mian Aminuddin who was related to Nazimuddin was appointed Governor of Sind. The new Governor was just as determined as the old to rule without the fuss and bother of an Assembly and a Ministry. He recommended disqualification for all the politicians under PRODA Inquiry. On 26 January 1953, all the politicians under inquiry were disqualified.

Khuhro was disqualified for six years. He was shocked at this disqualification which had been based on a couple of untenable charges and issued a statement expressing his outrage at the shameless butchering of the democratic process:

"The news about the order of the Governor General disqualifying me for a period of six years on the findings of the Tribunal appointed under PRODA was a great surprise to me, particularly after I have gone through the report of the Tribunal. Out of the seven charges referred to the Tribunal by the former Governor of Sind Mr. Din Mohammed I have been fully exonerated on four."

One of the charges related to a period when Khuhro was not even Chief Minister when it was alleged that he had influenced the then Chief Minister Kazi Fazlullah to cancel "the detention orders of Hashim Mari, directly or indirectly."

The charge under which Khuhro was found 'guilty' was that at the recommendation of senior politician and Assembly colleague, Maula Baksh Soomro, a tribal chief Sardar Khan Khoso had been transferred to Hyderabad jail as the facilities in Jacobabad were not adequate. Sardar Khoso had been charged with the murder of his kinsman Sardar Azizullah Khoso. It was alleged against Khuhro that he had deliberately interfered in the investigation by sending the Deputy Inspector General of Sind Police (D.I.G.) to see to the case instead of the Inspector General Sind Police (I.G.). Khuhro pointed out that he had not stopped the investigation which continued right until the time he went out of power and that it was not necessary to send in the I.G. Police who after all was in charge of the entire province and in sending the D.I.G. Police of Sind he had deputed the second most senior officer of the province and that in terms of investigation of the case this would not make the slightest difference. This routine administrative decision could hardly be construed as maladministration:

"one thing is clear that the investigation of this crime alleged against Sardar Khan was carried on right upto the end of February 1952 whereas I resigned my office on 18th December 1951 and Section 92A was promulgated on 29th December 1951; and H.E. the Governor was in charge of the administration, and the case against Sardar Khan was withdrawn in the end of February or early March, 1952 after consulting the Advocate General as there was no evidence against him. This Deputy Inspector General of Police, according to the Chief Secretary and the Inspector General of Police, the two Government witnesses, was a very competent investigating officer in Sind and even the then Governor who was wholly and solely in charge of the administration in January and February 1952 did not replace him. No one in fact complained to the Governor or the Inspector General of Police that the investigation was not being properly conducted by the Deputy Inspector General, throughout the period of more than three months."[44]

Khuhro pointed out that, in contradiction of the charge laid against him, the I.G. was kept fully informed of the investigation and that it was quite unnecessary for the I.G. to be personally involved in a single investigation: "Is it good administration, may I ask, to pin down the Inspector General of Police, who is the head of the entire police administration of the province, to one case in a District in Sind when he has far more pressing calls on his time..."[45]

Khuhro put his case against the PRODA to the public:

"I now leave it to the people of Pakistan to judge for themselves, whether such an order disqualifying me from public life for a long period of six years on the basis of these flimsy charges is at all justifiable? The inference that it is a clear case of political victimisation is therefore irresistable. Unfortunately in this country today justice is not evenly meted out but that there are different standards of justice for different sets of people: those who may happen to be friends and favourites get one kind of treatment while totally different treatment is meted out those who are *persona non grata* with those in authority."

Khuhro described the disastrous and demoralizing consequences of PRODA on the democratic politics of Pakistan: An analysis which was to be completely vindicated by the subsequent history of Pakistan:

"Thus PRODA, regarded as a sample of unique legislation peculiar to Pakistan, would appear to be a fraud on democracy, a law passed to defeat the purposes of law. It has brought about and will continue to bring about demoralisation in this country's administrative set up. If it has not been used against other Ministers, it is not because no case exists for its operation, but simply because it has not as yet been found worthwhile to do so.

No administrative initiative is possible if every Minister is kept perennially worried about a possible action under this Act. And that is precisely why no appreciable progress for these years in this country has been registered in the matter of securing social justice and administrative efficiency.

In its actual working the position amounts to this: no Minister of a government, Provincial or Central, can exercise his own judgement in the course of his duties and functions as a minister responsible to his people through the elected provincial legislature. No democratic country particularly of a federal type has ever conceived such a law where the mere constitutional head of the provincial administration in his discretion can put up his ministers on trial before a tribunal nominated by him and before doing so call for their resignations, on a mere application of any five persons...This state of affairs is not obtained any democratic country in the world."[46]

Khuhro was still the President of the Sind Provincial Muslim League and still the most influential politician in Sind but he now knew that survival in politics was not ensured by the confidence of the people and legislatures but by being on the right side of those who wielded the real power and that in Pakistan's case these were not elected by the people of Pakistan. Nazimuddin was desperately clinging on to the Prime Ministership but his well-known vacillation and lack of grip was useless in the face of the powerful machinations of such masters of the craft as Ghulam Mohammed. The Prime Minister barely understood the situation and seemed oblivious of the forces that were sweeping Pakistan along the road to authoritarianism.

The Ahmadiyya riots erupted in Lahore and Ghulam Mohammed and Gurmani advised Nazimuddin to go there and dismiss Daultana, the Chief Minister of the

Punjab. Towards the end of March 1952 Daultana resigned and Martial Law was imposed in Lahore, by, it appears, the unilateral action of Iskander Mirza without prior consultation with the Prime Minister. It was a deathly blow to the democratic process. Nazimuddin however still failed to understand where his strength lay and what were the forces he had to fight against. He went on playing the game of intrigue and counter intrigue and helped to create a situation which would play into the hands of the bureaucratic power brokers who ruled Pakistan.

Nazimuddin had been elected President of Pakistan Muslim League in December 1951, following the precedent set by Liaquat Ali Khan who was both Prime Minister and President Muslim League. He was now in a position to wreck the Party as well. On his return to Karachi he ordered elections in Sind where he now tried to displace Khuhro from the leadership of the Party. He tried to put his own man as leader and also to distribute the Party tickets through the Central Parliamentary Board. Khuhro resisted this and walked out of the party meeting where the game was being played. Khuhro ignored the list of the Central Parliamentary Board, especially in cases where their candidates were less likely to win. At this point Nazimuddin removed Khuhro as President of the Sind Provincial Muslim League. Khuhro then moved the Chief Court of Sind to grant him a stay order against the action of the Prime Minister. His plea was that the meeting of the Council of Pakistan Muslim League which had elected Nazimuddin President was unconstitutional, hence his election as President of the Party should be declared null and void and a permanent order passed to prevent Nazimuddin interfering with the affairs of the Sind Provincial Party.[47]

Members of the Sind Assembly as well as Party members were being openly manipulated from the Centre not only in Sind but in the other provinces as well. In N.W.F.P. Qayyum Khan had refused to recognize the tickets being given by the Central Parliamentary Board. He refused any interference from the Centre and would not allow anyone including a senior politician like Suhrawardy, into the province even for electioneering purposes. He threatened to arrest anyone who came on charges of disturbing the peace. Nazimuddin however acquiesced in this situation and recognized the members backed by Qayyum as official .

By now Nazimuddin had fatally weakened himself and gave the bureaucratic cabal a wonderful opportunity to pounce. On the night of 17 April telephone lines to the Prime Minister's house were cut. As Nazimuddin was leaving early the next morning to go on an election tour of Sind in support of the Central candidates, he was summoned by the Governor General. When he got to the Government House he found the other Ministers already there with Ghulam Mohammed presiding over a meeting. Nazimuddin was told that he was unfit to be Prime Minister; that his administration was very poor and that he was being dismissed. The only Minister who protested was Nishtar with the result that he was also removed from the Cabinet. Mohammed Ali Bogra the Pakistan Ambassador to U.S.A. had already reached Karachi and was now installed as Prime Minister.[48]

The *coup* of 17 April revealed clearly the state of power politics in Pakistan. There was barely the thinnest of facades of parliamentary government. Power was in the hands of a group of senior executives from the Punjab who had passed beyond the rank of civil servants into a decision making inner circle. The politicians – West Pakistan landed aristocrats and East Pakistan middle class professionals who had been active in the Pakistan movement were being out manoeuvred by the powerful instruments of colonialism – the civil service – and just below the surface but as yet hardly visible was the army. The long term aims of this inner cabal were now in the open. They wanted to ensure that their writ was law in the western wing of the country and that they were unhampered by public opinion. They also wanted to ensure that the majority from East Bengal was kept in place by various devices administrative and eventually constitutional. With Bogra as the figurehead Prime Minister, the power clique was predominantly Punjabi with Ghulam Mohammed, the Governor General at the top. Chaudhry Mohammed Ali, the erstwhile Secretary General, and Finance Minister in Nazimuddin's Ministry was retained in that post, and Nawab Mushtaq Gurmani, perhaps the most astute member of the circle was Minister of Interior.

With the removal of Nazimuddin the policy of the Centre did not change towards Sind where it was found essential for it to have its own nominees in power. In the provincial elections Khuhro fielded his own candidates in some of the constituencies but with blatant interference from the Centre he won only half a dozen seats. This time the candidate selected for Chief Ministership was Pirzada Abdus Sattar, who had been the Sind Minister in the Central Cabinet since 1947 and was trusted by Ghulam Mohammed. The Governor asked Pirzada to form the Ministry in May 1953 without going through the formality of calling the Assembly to elect the leader and therefore his majority was not tested.[49] Six Ministers were installed in his cabinet, including a nominee of the Mir group as well as Ali Mohammed Rashdi and Kazi Akbar.

By the beginning of 1954 differences in the Ministry came to the surface. The Superintendant of Police of Larkana refused to obey the orders of Kazi who was the Home Minister and said he would only obey the orders of the Chief Minister. Kazi together with Rashdi asked Pirzada to transfer the S.P. but the latter refused to oblige. The two Ministers then came to Khuhro and said they would co-operate with him to remove Pirzada. Khuhro although under disqualification still had a following in the Assembly. Kazi Fazlullah also joined the group. Khuhro called a meeting in Kazi Akbar's house in Hyderabad where about 80 members out of a House of about 110 attended. Members were most unhappy with Pirzada and complained bitterly that he would not take any decisions and kept most matters pending.

The month of March was spent by the Opposition in the province trying to prove to the Centre that it had a majority. Meetings, signatures and deputations to the Prime Minister were being organised everyday but to no effect. It appeared that the opinion of the majority of the House carried no weight with Governor General Ghulam Mohammed. This was not ofcourse a surprise to Khuhro who had been through it all before. Khuhro then telephoned Prime Minister Bogra that he wanted to bring a deputation of Sind Assembly Members to meet him. Khuhro took 75 of them to see the Prime Minister which proved that Pirzada had no support and should be removed.

The Assembly was meeting for the Spring Budget session and the Supplementary Grants had still to be passed. Pirzada felt that he could not sustain his majority and adjourned the House without attempting to pass the Supplementary Grants. The Opposition asked the Governor to re-convene the House as otherwise all expenditure would be illegal. Bogra told Pirzada that he would have to face the House and pass the Budget. Finding himself in a tight corner Pirzada went to Ghulam Mohammed who obliged. To the surprise of everyone the next day the Governor, Habib Rahimtoola, prorogued the Assembly without getting the Budget passed and Pirzada continued as Chief Minister.

Pirzada now set about trying to win back support. Kazi Fazlullah was already negotiating with him and was ready to change sides at a price. Khuhro went to see Kazi at the Palace Hotel where he was staying, to persuade him not to betray the alliance. Kazi showed Khuhro a letter he was writing to Prime Minister Bogra offering co-operation to Pirzada and demanding ministerships for two nominees of Khuhro's and two of his own. Khuhro refused his offer saying that he could not possibly betray the members who had trusted him. He asked Kazi to remove his name from the letter and left convinced that Kazi was going over to the other side. Kazi came to terms with Pirzada who then raised the number of his Ministers from six to twelve in order to retain support. But in spite of the unprecedented number of Ministers Pirzada did not have the courage to call the Assembly.

Khuhro felt that time had come to mend his fences with the Pakistan Muslim League. He asked Bogra to recognise Sind Muslim League which Khuhro had separated from the parent body during Nazimuddin's time. Bogra realising that this was the only way to ensure a Muslim League presence in Sind readily agreed. He called a meeting of the Pakistan Muslim League Working Committee and got them to recognise Sind Muslim League and Khuhro was put on the Central Working Committee.

Meanwhile a few weeks later the struggle for power at the Centre between the 'Punjabi group' and the 'Bengali group' was to take another turn. Elections had taken place in East Bengal in March 1954 where Muslim League had a trouncing and the United (Jugtu) Front made up of a number of different parties had won an overwhelming majority. The veteran leader Maulvi Fazlul Haq was leader of the alliance and was due to form the Provincial Government. The new leadership was soon in Karachi where Khuhro gave a dinner in their honour and entertained the men who were to be so important in the next few years in Pakistan and who were potential allies for Sind – among them Fazlul Haq, Suharawardy, Maulana Bhashani and Hamidul Haq Chowdhry.

The defeat of Muslim League in East Bengal posed some serious problems for the Centre. Not only would the United Front form the government in the province but the composition of the Constituent Assembly would have to be changed and the Central Cabinet as well. The Centre with its palace politics and penchant for arranging matters without reference to the Constituent Assembly or the electorate was duly alarmed. Threatened with the collapse of its carefully constructed power structure, the central clique acted to resist any changes that might reduce its power. They made it clear at an early stage that no change would be made in the Central Cabinet or the composition of the Constituent Assembly.

The representatives of East Bengal in the Constituent Assembly had lost their *raison d'etre* as (except the minority members), they were from Muslim League which was now reduced to a small group in the Provincial Assembly. The Muslim League members of the Constituent Assembly were asked not to resign. The newly elected members from East Bengal were given the pacifier that the Constitution of Pakistan would be ready soon and that general elections would be held by May next year! The Central Government was buying time to sabotage the new order in East Pakistan. The making of the East Bengal Government was delayed by the Centre carefully exploiting the differences between the different groups of the United Front. They orchestrated a press campaign against Fazlul Haq accusing him of being a traitor after he visited Calcutta where he reportedly made some ill judged remarks. Eventually on 13 May Fazlul Haq formed the government of East Bengal. On 15 May there was a serious riot among the workers of a jute mill. On 30 May a little over two months after the elections and a only fifteen days after he had formed the government, the Fazlul Haq Ministry was dismissed and Section 92A was imposed in East Pakistan. Iskander Mirza a newly emerging 'tough' member of the inner coterie was sent as Governor. The immediate danger to the power of the coterie was thus averted but again at a heavy price for the future of democracy in Pakistan.

In the meantime events were building up to a crisis in Karachi. By the middle of September 1954 the Prime Minister announced that he was ready to go ahead with the framing of the constitution. He was however under pressure from some of the colleagues closest to him, particularly Fazl-ur-Rahman a fellow Bengali and the Sind Chief Minister Pirzada Abdus Sattar. They wanted to drastically reduce the powers of the overbearing Governor General, Ghulam Mohammed, who despite a stroke which had left him with speech impediment, had been running the government at his whim and fancy and threatening PRODA against any politicians he took against. The position of the Prime Minister was that of a lackey, merely taking orders in all matters of administration. The group which now included Hashim Gazdar from Sind and Maulvi Tamizuddin the Bengali Speaker of the Constituent Assembly, decided to act secretly and swiftly. But before doing so it was essential that PRODA was repealed. This step was essential to pre-empt the Governor General who it was strongly rumoured, was about to institute PRODA proceedings against as many as 22 people including those who were active in the repeal of the Act.[50]

The first bill to repeal PRODA had been introduced in the Constituent Assembly three years previously in 1951 by Hashim Gazdar in order to remove the disability from Khuhro and included the retrospective clause to give relief to those like him who had already suffered under the Act. This Bill had failed because of strong opposition from the Central Government but it was revived now and was passed on 20 September 1954. But the repeal was selective. Politicians under disqualification were not given relief and even those under Inquiry at the time were not to be included. Pirzada moved the amendment to the Bill which provided that:

> "This repeal shall not affect any penalty, forfeiture, disqualification or punishment already incurred or awarded under the said Act or any reference pending before any Court or Tribunal on or before September 1, 1954."[51]

As one historian remarks, "The first part of this amendment maintained the disqualification of the three former Sind ministers (Pirzada's rivals) and the second part permitted proceedings to continue against Mr. Daultana."[52] Similarly Hamidul Haq Chowdhury was to kept out of politics in East Bengal.[53] This unjust discrimination robbed the action of its veil of virtue and revealed the fact that the politicians who ostensibly wanted to return powers to the Constituent Assembly were only a bunch of men with self interest as their chief motive.

The anti Ghulam Mohammed group then hurriedly passed a bill which also stood in Gazdar's name and which had not been supported by them in 1951 when it had been introduced. This was to make certain amendments to the constitution to curtail the powers of the Governor General–

"1. that the Governor General shall in all cases be bound by the advice of the Cabinet.
2. In the future, no person shall be appointed prime minister or a minister unless he is already a member of the Constituent Assembly.
3. The Cabinet shall have joint responsibility and a motion of no-confidence against a minister is one against the entire cabinet. The bill was rushed through within 18 hours."[54]

Meanwhile Ghulam Mohammed who was an ill man was resting in Abbottabad where Gurmani, the Interior Minister and member of the Punjab inner circle, sent him an urgent message to come to Karachi. Bogra had, immediately after finishing the business in the Assembly, left for a visit to the U.S.A.

Khuhro who had been watching the mysterious goings on and the strange compromises that had been made to patch together a constitution for Pakistan, and who found the motives of the men who had repealed PRODA with such obvious malice, extremely suspect, issued a statement showing his distrust of a document that they might produce. He pointed out that the constitution which was being prepared by this Constituent Assembly would throw the country into disorder and confusion. He demanded that the Assembly be dissolved and a new one be elected on the basis of adult franchise:

"As has been established through its own recent deeds, our nearly nine year old constitution making body is now definitely in an advanced state of decomposition. It has passed laws which should do little credit to any civilised body of men. It recently deemed proper to repeal PRODA but those four or five victims of this bad law against whom it could be said to have been misused, were denied the benefit of this repeal.

The so-called new constitution which it has made, is again brimful with the bacili of disintegration. It will now be a misnomer to call it an Islamic Constitution, nor will this state emerge as the Islamic Republic after passing such a ridiculous constitution."[55]

Khuhro immediately set about to get his own PRODA disqualification removed as well as of those who still remained under it. He talked to Gurmani pointing out that the repeal of PRODA had obviously been partial and unfair and that he and the others should also be given relief. If it was a bad law it was a bad law for everybody. Gurmani suggested that Khuhro should make the application to the Governor General. Khuhro consulted some lawyers as well as Abdur Rab Nishtar who helped draft the petition for him, arguing that Khuhro and the others should have the benefit of the repeal of the Act. Khuhro sent the petition to the Governor General, who though no friend of Khuhro, but seething with anger against the group in the Constituent Assembly, immediately granted the plea and removed the disqualification from Khuhro. Others also benefited from the acceptance of

Khuhro's petition.*

The Governor General's order was 'a stinging rebuke to the Assembly'. It noted that the orders of disqualification had been retained although the law itself under which they had been made had been condemned as bad. "If it had been misused, there could be no justification for the continuance of penalties."[56]

Meanwhile Ghulam Mohammed had been making preparations for a counter-attack against those he felt had betrayed him. He sent a message to Suhrawardy who was in a hospital in Zurich, asking him to co-operate and gave a promise that he would be made Prime Minister at a future date.[57] Suhrawardy issued a supportive statement saying that the Constituent Assembly had ceased to be a representative body and that a new assembly should be elected. He argued that provincial autonomy should be increased in the new constitution and that East Pakistan would support the proposal for the unification of West Pakistan. During this time Ghulam Mohammed had sent for Justice Munir and warned him that the Assembly was to be dissolved and that he should not give judgement against the dissolution to which he readily agreed.[58]

With endorsement from Suhrawardy and flanks covered by Munir's promise of co-operation, Ghulam Mohammed was ready to put his plans into action. General Ayub Khan, the Commander in Chief, was consulted and kept fully involved as was Major General Iskander Mirza, at that time Governor of East Bengal and a key man in the group. Both Ayub Khan and Mirza had gone to the U.S. with Bogra and now accompanied him back. Bogra terrified of what was in store, first went home to meet his close advisers and was then summoned to the Governor General's House.[59] He was kept there until three in the morning and made to sign the dismissal of his cabinet. The Constituent Assembly was dissolved and a new Cabinet announced. Bogra suitably cowed was kept on as Prime Minister and his new Cabinet included Mirza as Minister of Interior, Ayub Khan as Minister of Defence, Chaudhri Mohammed Ali as Finance Minister, Mir Ghulam Ali Talpur and Syed Amjad Ali, the Punjabi businessman, in other senior positions. Dr. Khan Sahib of the *Khudai Khidmatgar* Party an older brother of Khan Abdul Ghaffar Khan, was brought into the Cabinet as was Suhrawardy as Minister of Law some weeks later when the latter returned to Pakistan.

Political power was now completely in the hands of Ghulam Mohammed and his cohorts. He now moved against those who had conspired against him with their constitutional amendments a month earlier. He told Bogra to remove from public office those responsible for the intrigue against him in the Constituent Assembly. Pirzada, the Chief Minister of Sind had been prominent among these and Ghulam Mohammed was particularly bitter about him as he had gone out of the way and had the Sind Assembly prorogued when he was in trouble and could not get a majority. Further, even when the Budget had not been passed, he had al-

---

* Notwithstanding the Governor General's order freeing Khuhro and others from the PRODA disqualification, the Chief Court of Sind decided issued a *writ* of *quo warranto* nullifying the Governor General's decision and taking the view that the Governor General was not competent to reduce the period of disqualification under PRODA. Khuhro went in appeal to the Federal Court which decided on 17 October 1955 that not only the Sind Chief Court had no jurisdiction to issue the *writ* but that as PRODA was not law as it had never received the assent of the Governor General, the disqualification under that law was void. (Federal Court Bench consisting of Justice M. Munir, Justice M. Shahabuddin and Justice M. Sharif, Judgement of Federal Court, delivered at Lahore, 17 Oct., 1955).

lowed him to run the government and carry on with government expenditure illegally. He had also allowed him to double the size of the Ministry to 12 ministers instead of the previous maximum of six, in order to get a majority. Now Ghulam Mohammed was determined to teach Pirzada a lesson. Pirzada realised that he had put his position in jeopardy. Attempting to salvage the situation, he had issued a press statement supporting the new regime immediately after the *coup* on 24 October welcoming the action of the Governor General. It was too late however.

The Governor of Sind, Nawab Mamdot, asked Pirzada to call the Assembly and pass the long overdue budget, knowing that Pirzada could not command a majority and would have to resign. Pirzada refused to do so. The Centre decided that the Governor should insist on the resignation of Pirzada if he did not call the Assembly and he was to be dismissed if he did not obey. Gurmani talked to Khuhro, who confirmed that he had a majority in the House, and asked him to be ready to take over as Chief Minister.

Gurmani told Khuhro that the One Unit scheme was being brought in as a necessary prerequisite for a constitution for Pakistan. The Generals were behind the One Unit idea and Ayub Khan was in the Cabinet to push for this particular project. The Government was armed with legal advice as well as agreement from East Bengal, led by Suhrawardy. He also told Khuhro that the Centre wanted the co-operation of all the governments of West Pakistan including that of Sind. Khuhro demurred. All his life he had been a strong advocate of provincial autonomy and he firmly believed that provinces inherited by Pakistan were the true embodiment of not only the cultural diversity and linguistic wealth of Pakistan but were also the most economically viable and homogeneous units that could be administered. He was not persuaded that the formation of One Unit was a good solution to the constitutional problems of Pakistan but he was told categorically that there was no other option and that the Governor General had the power to impose the One Unit. He was told that the province of West Pakistan was to be declared within two months at the latest as Ayub Khan was insisting that the date for it be expedited. Khuhro therefore knew that his sojourn as Chief Minister would not be prolonged, that in fact it would be less than two months. His sense of duty came to the fore as he realised that at least he would be able to help the province in a practical sense by making certain that its essential interests were safeguarded in the amalgamated province.

Pirzada's dismissal was announced on 8 November. On the morning of the 9 November Mamdot sent for Khuhro who told him that he had the support of over 70 members in a House of over 110. Khuhro was himself not a Member of the Assembly at this time but was in a position to get himself elected and constitutionally he had six months in which to do so. Mamdot asked him to form the Government immediately. Khuhro was sworn in for the third time as Chief Minister with a cabinet of five, the other four ministers were Maula Baksh Soomro, Kazi Akber, Nur Ahmed Shah and Ali Mohammed Rashdi. The task before them was urgent, to work fast to get as good a bargain for Sind as possible in these difficult circumstances where within months it would be absorbed with the other regions of Western Pakistan to form a single administrative unit–West Pakistan.

20

AUTHORITARIANISM TRIUMPHANT

The idea of One Unit had been floating around for sometime. It had surfaced during Liaquat Ali's time in 1949 when it had been considered as a means of crushing the political leadership in the smaller provinces. It had at that time been roundly condemned by the Sindhis, particularly the Sind Muslim League, the major political party in the province, under Khuhro's leadership. Although not heard of again for a few years, it remained an option for the ruling Punjab group which was now in control of Pakistan. After the victory of the United Front in East Bengal, the ruling clique, consisting as it did of the Punjab and N.W.F.P. army and bureaucracy axis, became very anxious to avoid an unpredictable East Pakistan majority in a newly elected Assembly, particularly under a new constitution. One Unit was the solution for those who could not come to terms with the 'din of democracy'. Ayub Khan takes the responsibility for the idea himself when he says that he worked it all out on the 'warm night' of 4 October 1954, in London, when he sat down and wrote down a document to solve the ills of Pakistan.[1]

The men who were occupying positions of power in the civil service and in the armed forces were constitutionally incapable of understanding the way democracy worked. So far no chance had been given to the politicians to work democracy. This had been amply demonstrated by the events leading up to 1954. The struggling plant of democracy in the provinces had been well and truly crushed and it had never even been planted in the Centre. Ayub Khan illustrates the self-satisfaction of the bosses in the army and in the bureaucracy and their patronising, even contemptuous, attitude towards politicians. He claims that he joined the cabinet of Bogra to act as 'buffer between the politicians and the armed forces'! He also joined it to see the One Unit through. Obviously he had not understood the democratic concept that politicians were representatives of the people who were independent and sovereign; and that the army was merely their servant whose function was to defend the country from its external enemies. The bureaucracy showed even less understanding of democracy as when Ayub Khan reports that Chaudhry Mohammed Ali, the quintessential bureaucrat turned Prime Minister, said to him, "Why don't you take over and save me from this business?"[2]

By the time of Ghulam Mohammed's *coup* in 1954 a constitution for the country had still not been produced, and it was now more than seven years after independence. Delaying tactics had run out with the completion of the two drafts of the Basic Principles Committee report. The ruling clique were only concerned to produce a constitution which would leave them holding the reins of power. A federal democratic constitution would give power to Bengal and the smaller provinces, who could combine together to spell destruction for the clique and even keep the Punjab in helpless isolation. This was the worst case scenario and it was constantly before the ruling clique.

The solution was to prevent the Bengalis from being in a majority position in any future parliament and also to prevent the 'ganging up' of East Bengal with the smaller provinces of West Pakistan. And this done by the concept of 'parity' and One Unit in West Pakistan. There would be the same number of elected representatives between the two wings of the country. With these two arrangements in place the ruling clique felt that a constitution could be cobbled together which would enable them to maintain the balance of power acceptable to them. Obviously the key to the success of this scheme was the acquiescence of the Bengali politicians. The newly elected Bengali politicians had already had a taste of the big stick when the government of Fazlul Haq had been summarily dismissed within a few weeks of its induction when Section 92 A had been imposed. The 'western'[3] strong man, Iskander Mirza had been made Governor of East Bengal. East Bengal politicians realised quickly that although democratically they were entitled to power, they could not enjoy it without the consent of, and compromise with, the ruling clique. The clique had named its price-parity and One Unit – and the Bengali politicians decided that they were prepared to pay it especially as they were promised 'maximum autonomy' as a reward. The interests of the smaller provinces of West Pakistan were not really considered by the Bengali politicians. The decisive factor in the acceptance of the constitutional formula was the active connivance of Bengali politicians and this they gave.

Just after the dissolution of the Constituent Assembly in October 1954, Suhrawardy had issued a categorical statement linking One Unit with maximum autonomy. When he joined the Cabinet on his return in December he was given the Law portfolio and became responsible for the drafting and passage of the One Unit Bill in the reconstituted Constituent Assembly. When Suhrawardy left the Cabinet in the summer of 1955 and Fazlul Haque took his place, the same commitment was made by him.

The Cabinet constituted by Ghulam Mohammed in 1954 contained the men 'who called the shots' in Pakistan at the time, as well as the puppets who were needed to camouflage the exclusive nature of the power group. The core members of the group were Ghulam Mohammed himself, General Ayub Khan the Minister of Defence as well as Commander in Chief, 'General' Iskander Mirza now the Interior Minister, Chaudhri Mohammed Ali, the second most powerful man of the bureaucracy, now Finance Minister. Others included M. A. H. Ispahani of the business family from Bengal and Ghulam Ali Talpur, the token Sindhi. Ghulam Mohammed and Mirza were able to persuade Dr. Khan Sahib, a decent but gullible politician and close friend of Mirza, to join the Cabinet, thus defanging the dreaded Red Shirts.[4] Dr. A. M. Malik, Habib Ibrahim Rahimtoola till recently the Governor of Sind and a few more including some Bengalis, completed the Cabinet of thirteen. Gurmani was given the key job of Governorship of the Punjab, a crucial position with the One Unit in the offing.

There appeared to be no important opposition to the scheme which was by now public knowledge. Some of those who had supported the curtailment of the Governor General's powers through a constitutional amendment had already somersaulted into the camp of the Governor General.[5] January was the deadline by which One Unit had to be in place. All the provincial assemblies had to pass their resolutions in support of One Unit before that date. It was ofcourse possible for the Centre to bypass the provincial assemblies altogether as they had been given the legal opinion, endorsed by Suhrawardy, that there was provision in the Government of India Act 1935, section 290 that the boundaries of provinces could be changed by the Governor General. This interpretation of the section was too wide and in actual fact the Governor General had limited power which could only be exercised in case of differences between provinces. The ruling clique decided however that they would rather have the provincial assemblies pass resolutions in favour of One Unit, so that public opinion was seen to be on their side.

A few days after Khuhro had taken over as Chief Minister in November 1954, the Prime Minister called a meeting of Central Cabinet members, all the Chief Ministers of the provinces of West Pakistan and A.G.G. (Agent to the Governor General) Baluchistan, Sardar Bahadur Khan. Bogra said that it was very difficult to frame the constitution and that it was essential for good administration that One Unit was set up in West Pakistan.[6] Most of the talking was done by Gurmani and Chaudhry Mohammed Ali, explaining why One Unit was considered necessary and making it clear that the move had already been decided on, and that the Central Government had the power in any case to do the needful. They urged that the Chief Ministers get the resolutions passed in their respective assemblies. Khuhro pointed out that the move would be very unpopular but he was not supported by any of the other Chief Ministers. Sardar Abdur Rashid volunteered to get the resolution passed in the Frontier Assembly first[7] and he was followed by Chief Ministers of Khairpur, Bahawalpur and A.G.G., Baluchistan, who said that they would get the resolutions passed. However, surprisingly, it was Sir Firoze Khan Noon, the Chief Minister of the Punjab, who raised objections saying that such a move would bring a bad name to the Punjab which would be blamed for aiming for a greater Punjab and that he could not agree to it. He was however brushed aside by Gurmani and others from the Punjab. Khuhro was told that if Sind objected it was on its own. Khuhro said that he would need to talk to his cabinet and that Sind would wait till all the other provincial assemblies had passed the resolution before it would consider doing so.[8]

Khuhro consulted with his colleagues and they discussed every aspect to decide what their course of action would be. It had been made very clear to them that One Unit was definitely coming – 'the generals want it' as Gurmani had put it. Khuhro had himself seen in the meeting with the Central Ministers, that no other province was prepared to resist. East Bengal was fully supportive of One Unit. The question was whether Sind was in a position to go it alone and risk the wrath and the combined might of the other provinces and the Centre. Khuhro had already been there with the separation of Karachi. He had seen how, even with full support of the public and the political forces of the province, and with a comparatively independent judiciary at this early date after partition, resistence was useless. Was there any point in pitting the strength of the province against the Centre? Experience as well as judgement after bitter years showed that there was not. He and his colleagues knew that the Centre would find another man to carry through the resolution. Khuhro and his colleagues came to the reluctant conclusion that the best they could do for the province was to bend and let the storm pass over. They decided to set certain conditions which were vital for the welfare of Sind and try to get them accepted. They decided to talk to Ghulam Mohammed and Gurmani, who were experienced enough and political enough to be flexible in their dealings with politicians from sensitive provinces.

The terms and conditions were carefully considered by Khuhro and his colleagues, discussed with Gurmani and then presented to Ghulam Mohammed. These were:

(a) To provide constitutional safeguards for Sind;
(b) that the income from the province of Sind to be spent on it;
(c) Government jobs in Sind to go to Sindhis and to be overseen by Sind's representatives;
(d) Agricultural land which was shortly to become available after the completion of the Lower Sind Barrage to be given to local landless cultivators and to permanent inhabitants of Sind of local or refugee origin.
(e) Surplus land only if any left over, to be sold off as Government decides;
(f) Quota for Sind to be fixed in the Central services;
(g) Adequate funding for Sindhi language and culture for which Sind government had allocated initial amounts;
(h) Reasonable share for Sindhis in Defence services;
(i) No law to be imposed on Sind against the wishes of the majority of its members.
(j) The share of Sind in the Indus system to be safeguarded.
(k) Maximum autonomy to be given to the provinces and the Centre to keep only three subjects, i.e. Defence, Foreign Affairs and Currency.[9]

This list reveals the political acumen and farsightedness of Khuhro in realising the very real dangers that One Unit would present to the welfare of the people of Sind who would be in a minority in the new set up. At the same time he was aware of the helplessness of the province to resist the will of the Centre. He had tried to do that once and failed. He was now trying to make the best of a bad bargain.

These terms were accepted by the Central leaders. Khuhro in his speech on the bill in the Central Assembly detailed the agreement reached with the Centre. The crucial question was how these terms would be honoured and who would see that they were? This ofcourse would be the responsibility of the elected representatives in the West Pakistan Assembly and of the Sind Ministers in the West Pakistan cabinet. The smaller provinces were to get 'weightage' that is, more parliamentary seats in the 'One Unit' Assembly than their populations warranted. The Punjab would have 40% of seats although its population was 56%. With this weighted representation in the Assembly and in the proposed West Pakistan Cabinet, it was assumed that the promises made to Khuhro and his colleagues would be honoured.

On 22 November Bogra announced that One Unit would come into being by 1 January 1955. Mir Ghulam Ali Talpur was Speaker of the Sind Assembly but he also became a Minister in the second Bogra cabinet. Khuhro considered it was incompatible to have a Speaker who was also a Central Minister. Iskander Mirza, one of the key figures of the central clique tried to bring about a rapprochement between Khuhro and Talpur. The meeting took place at a lunch given by Sayed Wajid Ali where Iskander Mirza, General Ayub Khan, Talpur and Khuhro were present. Talpur put forward terms for his support of Khuhro which included two Ministers in the Sind cabinet. Khuhro offered to take one Minister but objected to two as he did not want a larger and unwieldy cabinet which would also be more expensive for the province. Khuhro was not keen to accommodate Talpur as he remembered only too well Talpur's betrayal in his first term as Chief Minister.

According to the promise made by Sardar Abdur Rashid at the Cabinet meeting in November 1954, the N.W.F.P. provincial assembly was the first provincial Assembly to pass the One Unit resolution on 25 November. This was followed by the resolutions by *jirgas* of the tribal belt as well as of the Frontier states. On 29 November the Punjab Assembly passed its resolution, quickly followed by resolutions of Bahawalpur state, Khairpur state, Baluchistan Quetta Municipality, the Shahi Jirga of Baluchistan and Baluchistan States and of the Karachi Municipal Corporation. During this period Khuhro was carefully watching the process noting that there was no sign of resistance. Finally the turn of Sind came.

On 11 December the Sind Assembly met in Hyderabad and the resolution in favour of One Unit was passed by 104 to 4 including all the members of the Talpur–Pirzada group. The members who voted against the resolution were Rais Ghulam Mustafa Bhurgri, Abdul Hamid Khan Jatoi, Shaikh Khurshid and Pir Illahi Baksh. Pirzada himself stayed away from the session. The vote went smoothly as the pro-One Unit groups in the Assembly such as Talpur and the Ministerial group constituted a majority and Khuhro, unlike Sardar Rashid in the Frontier, was not interested in a unanimous vote. There was no vocal or organised opposition in the province. G. M. Syed, who was the only important leader opposed to One Unit, had long been marginalised in Pakistan politics, having left Muslim League before independence. His views were considered eccentric and his opposition was taken as an individual idiosyncracy and not as any real reflection of public opinion. His activities had in any case been pre-empted by the Central Government in Karachi who had arrested him and kept him in Karachi jail.*

The provincial legislatures' approval was, in fact, a mere formality, as work on the implementation of the plan had started long before the legislatures had endorsed it. The circumstances were reflected in the announcement the Prime Minister made on November 22, when the Punjab and Sind had still not voted. He said that the ideal form of government would have been a unitary system,[10] but in Pakistan the facts of geography made this 'unsound, inexpedient, impolitic and improper'. The next best alternative, he said, lay in the formation of a unified

---

* The Resolution approving the formation of One Unit was passed thus with only a few votes going against it. There was no mainstream opposition in the province. Khuhro, realising the problems that could arise as the result of this merger of the provinces, had done his best to safeguard the interests of Sind. But a few years later, Khuhro would find himself the target of propaganda as the 'man who had made One Unit'. This propaganda erupted in the late 'sixties during the dictatorship of Ayub Khan and became more virulent as the time for elections approached in 1969. The purpose of this propaganda was obviously to malign Khuhro enough to affect his position in the elections and the instigator of the propaganda was Zulfiqar Ali Bhutto who wanted to clear the field for himself in Sind.

West Pakistan, which would (i) save expenditure on administration; (ii) speed up the economic development of West Pakistan; (iii) provide a bright future for hitherto 'neglected areas'; and (iv) simplify constitution making by placing East and West Pakistan on an equal basis. The measure would destroy provincialism and strengthen the integrity of Pakistan. "To bring about such 'a psychological change', it was proposed to organise provincial representation in such a way as to eliminate the fear of provincial domination and to reassure regional susceptibilities of language and culture."[11]

On 16 December the Governor General issued an order establishing a council with Gurmani as its chairman which would devise a system for the administration of West Pakistan. As Chief Minister of Sind Khuhro was one of the members of this council. The council finalised its report in February 1955.

Suhrawardy who was Law Minister at this time announced that a draft constitution had been prepared by the Central Cabinet. In March 1955 the Governor General issued an ordinance under which he amended the constitution to form the province of West Pakistan. But then the whole matter was delayed. Between December 1954 and May 1955 the battle was fought between the Speaker of the dissolved Constituent Assembly and all powerful Governor General. The Speaker of the Constituent Assembly, Maulvi Tamizuddin Khan, had gone to court against the dissolution of the Constituent Assembly by the latter.

The Sind Chief Court had given a decision in Maulvi Tamizuddin's favour and declared the Governor General's decision *ultra vires* but the Central Government went on appeal to the Federal Court of Pakistan where the verdict went in favour of the Governor General. The Federal Court ruled that all laws passed by the Constituent Assembly required the assent of the Governor General thus invalidating the constitutional amendments of 1954 as well as many other laws which had not received the required assent. On April 12 1955 the Federal Court refused to validate the actions of the Governor General. It also ruled that notwithstanding its previous ruling the Governor General now had power to amend the constitution by his own order. The One Unit scheme had therefore to await the approval of a reconstituted Constituent Assembly. The Central Government was also advised that the One Unit decision could be challenged in the Federal Court and that the Act must be passed by the Central Legislature. The resolutions passed by the provincial assemblies were now rendered meaningless and without significance and the responsibility lay with the Central Legislature. A new Assembly was to be constituted with members elected by the provincial assemblies which had ofcourse, unlike the Constituent Assembly, been elected since independence.

Elections for the Constituent Assembly, even indirect ones, were now unavoidable and this created panic among those who knew they would find it difficult to get elected. To ensure election for themselves the Central clique which included Gurmani and Mirza, a method was devised by which instead of the Provincial Assemblies voting as a whole to elect members, would elect them by district; i.e. members from each district of the province were to elect members to the Constituent Assembly so that each member was elected, as it were, by a pocket borough. These indirect elections brought in Muslim League as the biggest group with 33 members, Progressive Party had 2, East Pakistan sent back Krishak Sramik with 16 members, Awami League with 13, Congress' 4 and there were six independents.

Delay in the setting up of the One Unit meant that Khuhro's period as Chief Minister was unexpectedly extended. He now had to summon the Sind Assembly for the Budget session in March 1955. The Assembly had a large group of supporters of Mir Ghulam Ali Talpur. He was at this time, a Central Minister as well as the Speaker of the Sind Assembly. Talpur was not satisfied however as he wanted above all to become Chief Minister of Sind and to this end he tried to create a situation which would make the Budget session impossible. Khuhro was aware of this and in December had asked Prime Minister Bogra to get Talpur to make a choice between his Ministership and the Speakership. Khuhro went ahead with arrangements for the election of another Speaker and even announced the date but no resignation arrived from Talpur. In early March Khuhro again reminded the Prime Minister that Talpur had not resigned and was drawing salaries from both the Central Government as Minister and Sind as Speaker which was clearly illegal. Khuhro got no clear answer from Bogra so he went to the Governor General and informed him of the problem. He also told him that Talpur was intriguing against him and was likely to create problems in the session which was to be called shortly. After a few days the Governor General called Khuhro and told him that he had talked to Talpur who was reluctant to resign as Speaker so he had therefore dismissed him from the Central Cabinet. The next day a gazette notification appeared to this effect.

Khuhro summoned the Sind Assembly for the Budget session in the third week of March 1955 at Hyderabad. He was camping at the Circuit House when some three days earlier the Secretary of the Assembly, Shaikh Zafar Ali, informed him that Talpur had arranged for a hundred passes to be issued for the Visitors' Gallery in the Assembly Chamber. At the same time C.I.D. reports came in that some *goondas* from Hyderabad and Tando Mohammed Khan, which was Talpur's home town, were going to be in the gallery and there would be trouble in the Assembly. The game plan as Khuhro learnt later was to start a fracas in the assembly so that as presiding Speaker he could adjourn the Assembly *sine die*. The Governor had apparently given him an understanding that as the Budget session would not have taken place he would impose Governor's rule (Section 92 A) and make Talpur Chief Adviser.

On the basis of these reports the police was ready to proceed against Mir Ghulam Ali. Khuhro agreed that a case should be filed and that Talpur should be arrested and removed from Hyderabad. On 24 March this was done. Khuhro knew the necessity of this action to thwart what was obviously a very thorough plan. He instructed the police to treat Talpur with all possible courtesy. Talpur was arrested and taken in his own car a few miles away to Mirpurkhas in Tharparkar and then onwards in another vehicle to a Rest House in Mithi. After a couple of nights he was brought back to Mirpurkhas and then to Hyderabad where he was kept in the Central Jail. By this time the Budget session was over and a new Speaker Pir Qurban Ali had been elected. Therefore when Talpur's lawyer put in an application for bail on the grounds of his health, Khuhro instructed the Public Prosecutor not to oppose it and Talpur was duly released on bail, although Khuhro was strongly advised particularly by the shrewd Rashdi, not to do so.[12]

Talpur and other opponents of Khuhro went to the Prime Minister and complained that any consequent trial would be unfair whereupon Khuhro asked Firoze

Khan Noon, the Chief Minister of the Punjab, to have the case transferred to the Punjab. But when the lawyers advised Mir Ghulam Ali that the case was strong and he might not be acquitted, he approached the Prime Minister who asked Khuhro to drop the cases against Talpur, Kazi and others. Khuhro obliged, again against the advice of Rashdi. Talpur did not let up his hostility to Khuhro whom he and his friends continued to wilify. As Rashdi pointed out later, if the whole thing was a put up job why did the Mir and the co-conspirators not go through with the trial in a court which was obviously and patently neutral, and win the case on merit, instead of pleading for it to be withdrawn and then shouting from the rooftops that he and the others were being victimized.[13] The opportunity was taken by the opponents of Khuhro, particularly Altaf Hussain of *Dawn* to make all sorts of false accusations including one that Mir Ghulam Ali had been taken on camel back to Mithi and had been deliberately mistreated, a charge of which Mir Ghulam Ali himself cleared Khuhro.[14]

The first session of the newly re-constituted Pakistan Constituent Assembly was held in Murree on 7 July 1955. Khuhro took a house there for the session and went up on the 4th, with his family. Iskander Mirza, was also on the same train as well as Yusuf Haroon and other political leaders. Newspaper reporters were at every station anxious to know what plans were afoot for the country and for West Pakistan. They were keen to know that if Iskander Mirza's friend, Dr. Khan Sahib, was to be Chief Minister of West Pakistan and what was being done about Khan Abdul Ghaffar Khan who was still in detention. Mirza enjoying his pre-eminent position parrying their questions and entertaining the politicians in his Saloon car.

Murree was spectacular that season. It was the only developed hill station in Pakistan at the time and was still the preserve of the upper echelons of the Civil Service and the aristocracy of the Punjab. The turbaned landowners of the Punjab, the Sindhi zamindars with their flowing shalwars kameez, the East Pakistanis in their pyjama-kurtas, the Congressmen in their white dhotis, and the top men of Pakistan smart in their well tailored suits, took their walks on the Mall. Khuhro bought himself some beautifully carved walking sticks and strolled down from his house near Kashmir Point, in the evenings with his family giving his children ice cream and cakes at Sams or Lintotts. The Mall with its two restaurants was like a political salon every evening, with beautifully dressed women, men well aware of their importance, and the usual crowd of hangers on eager to please and be seen. Even the towering *khaddar* clad figure of Khan Abdul Ghaffar Khan, just released from jail, was seen strolling down the Mall.

The days were mostly taken up with the serious business of hammering out a constitution and reaching compromises on who was to take the top posts in the country. The new Punjab Governor's House at Kashmir Point with its breathtaking view across to the snow topped mountains of Kashmir, where Nawab Gurmani was now residing, was the venue for many of the meetings. The Assembly sessions were being held in the more modest premises of the Murree Club. This was the last time the old ruling class of Pakistan would be assembled together and be on display so openly. Never again would the tribal chieftains and Bengali Congressmen, the Punjab chiefs, Sindhi zamindars, the old Parliamentarians, the leaders of the Pakistan movement, gather together in a mood of such self confidence; they were quite unsuspecting of any threat to their position and influence and quite sure that they could produce a viable and acceptable constitution which would serve Pakistan well into the future.

Apart from Assembly work there were continuous meeting at the Governor's House with Gurmani putting the One Unit administration in place. Here differences arose between the Central leadership and the Frontier Chief Minister Sardar Abdur Rashid. Originally Sardar Rashid had been promised that he would be Chief Minister of West Pakistan, but Iskander Mirza, who was now perhaps the strongest man in the Centre, wanted Dr. Khan Sahib an old friend from his Political Agent days, whom he had already taken into the Cabinet and whom he felt he could manipulate easily. The change in the plans was made less than gracefully and there was an atmosphere of secrecy and intrigue about the whole affair. Both Chaudhry Mohammed Ali and Gurmani had given Rashid to understand that he would be made Chief Minister. When Mirza insisted on Dr. Khan Sahib, Chaudhry Mohammed Ali agreed but did not inform the other Chief Ministers. The first time the members of the West Pakistan Administrative Committee knew was when Dr. Khan Sahib suddenly appeared in a meeting of the Committee in Lahore.

Rashid was dropped and he took it badly. At one of the meetings at the Governor's House, after this change of plan had become apparent, Rashid announced his decision to oppose the One Unit plan in the Assembly on the grounds that promises were not being kept. He gave an ultimatum to Gurmani that unless the promised arrangements were kept he would totally oppose One Unit. Gurmani was furious and asked Khan Qurban Ali Khan to dismiss the Frontier Ministry and impose Section 92A. When Rashid spoke against the One Unit Bill in the Assembly he explained his position. At first, he said, he had agreed to the formation of One Unit in the informal meeting with the Central Cabinet at the Prime Minister's House[15] but when they had come out of the meeting he had told Chaudhri Mohammed Ali that he needed a note explaining the reasons why the One Unit was to be formed, so that he could talk about it in his own Assembly. Chaudhri Mohammed Ali asked Daultana to produce a note for him which Rashid claimed, he read in the train on the way to Peshawar and got a clear impression that this was a plan for forming a 'greater Punjab'. However Rashid did not explain to the Assembly why he moved the resolution in the Frontier Assembly, made a speech in favour of One Unit and got a unanimous vote for the resolution several weeks later.

Khuhro's main concern in Murree, apart from contributing to the work on framing the new constitution and working on the administrative framework for the West Pakistan province, was to get assurances on the conditions that had been put for Sind's joining One Unit. Chaudhri Mohammed Ali repeated the assurances given by the Muslim League Parliamentary Party and Suhrawardy who was piloting the bill was very much party to the whole proceedings.

The session in Murree ended by the end of July and the Constituent Assmbly was scheduled to meet in Karachi at the end of the first week of August. But before the House met again a little later than on the due date, there were to be important changes in the power structure. Suhrawardy's ambition, of which he made no secret, was to become Prime Minister. This was the understanding he had been given by Ghulam Mohammed when he had given his support for the October *coup* and for One Unit. Ghulam Mohammed was by now mentally imbalanced and rapidly deteriorating and the ruling clique was changing its mind about the dispensation in Pakistan. It appeared that they no longer wanted Suhrawardy as Prime Minister and they wanted Iskander Mirza who could be passed off as Bengali, as Governor General. A meeting was called at the Prime Minister's house at Karachi, to decide whether Mirza was to be considered from the west or the east wing of the country. Bogra was told that if Mirza opted to be an East Pakistani he would have to go as both the Governor General and the Prime Minister could not be from the same wing. Khuhro attended this meeting to select the leader of the party and decide the province of Mirza's origin. Mirza opted to be considered Bengali and the way was clear for Chaudhri Mohammed Ali to be elected leader of the House and Prime Minister.

Understandably Suhrawardy was upset and sent his lieutenants Shaikh Mujibur Rahman, Abu Hussain Sarkar and Ataur Rahman to Gurmani who was living in Punjab House on Bath Island in Karachi. Gurmani, a key member of the ruling clique and a master of diplomacy, was entertaining Khuhro to lunch that day. He asked Khuhro to stay on for the meeting with Suhrawardy's men after lunch. Gurmani told the Awami Leaguers that the Prime Minister would have to come from the largest party in the Assembly and that Suhrawardy could be number two or Deputy Prime Minister. There was a possibility of Prime Ministership but after sometime.

Gurmani asked Khuhro to sit in on the meeting as he knew that the relations between him and Suhrawardy were strained. Suhrawardy had a small party organisation in Sind and the members of his party had wanted some favours from Khuhro who had not obliged. They had then started an agitation against Khuhro even putting in a writ in the High Court against him which however, was rejected. In retaliation, Suhrawardy in a completely unprecedented move had brought in a resolution in the Central Cabinet that Khuhro should be dismissed. This came to nothing as the resolution was discussed in the Cabinet and all the Ministers voted against it. Bogra wrote a personal letter to Khuhro informing him of Suhrawardy's action. Khuhro was therefore not in favour of Suhrawardy's becoming Prime Minister and backed Gurmani at the meeting. Suhrawardy refused the offer of Deputy Prime Ministership and determined to oppose the Constitution Bill even though he himself had drafted it. He looked to find an excuse for his about face. He told Rashdi that he would target Khuhro in order to oppose One Unit.[16]

The Central Assembly reconvened in Karachi on 8 August with Gurmani again in the Chair but with the scene about to change shortly. Before the House met on the 12 August there was a new Leader of the House, Chaudhri Mohammed Ali, and Suhrawardy found himself Leader of the Opposition, and not as he had been expected Prime Minister. Bogra had been sent off to Washington as Ambassador. Suhrawardy who refused the offer of Deputy Prime Minister was out of the Cabinet and was replaced by Fazlul Haque the ex-Chief Minister of East Pakistan as Minister for Interior.

Khuhro was therefore not surprised when Suhrawardy's five and half hour speech on One Unit was less concerned with the bill and more with the alleged dictatorial policies of Khuhro. In what must have been a tongue-in-cheek speech, hardly expected to be taken seriously, he claimed to have discovered a new 'ism' after Machiavellism and Marxism i.e.'Khuhroism'. Inventive lawyer that he was, Suhrawardy sought, in his clever speech, to divert attention from the fact that the

One Unit Bill was over his own signature and that he was in large part responsible for the drafting of the constitution. This he did by attacking Khuhro with dazzling verbal acrobats. But inbetween the attacks on Khuhro Suhrawardy could not help showing the real hurt and frustration that he felt:

"Now, Sir, the correct constitutional position regarding this is that whereas I may and I do adhere to the principles of the Bill, and considered and do consider the unification of West Pakistan as a measure of integration was most desirable, it does not mean, Sir, that I am compelled to support it in all its aspects even though the circumstances have changed... Undoubtedly some vindictive, spiteful and mean-minded people for whom any action that a person might take must be motivated by personal consideration, might think that I have changed my attitude because I was not elected the Prime Minister or that the promise which was given to me was not carried out..."[17]

In fact Suhrawardy's disclaimer had a strong taste of sour grapes:

"I am very sorry for the honourable gentleman who is the Prime Minister today. The Honourable Prime Minister today has stepped into the shoes of another Prime Minister and I cannot understand what great charm was there in that office..."[18]

The disappointment felt by Suhrawardy was sympathised with by a number of speakers in the Assembly session who pointed out the remarkable difference in his attitude before 8 August and afterwards. It was on 6 August that Iskander Mirza had been sworn in as 'East Pakistan' Governor General and on the 8 August that Chaudhri Mohammed Ali had been selected as 'West Pakistani' Prime Minister.

In his speech on the 'The Establishment of West Pakistan Bill' Khuhro had to perforce to begin by replying to Suhrawardy. He took his cue from that speech to trace the background of Suhrawardy's political career which had many vulnerable spots. Suhrawardy proved too thin skinned to sit through Khuhro's speech which related Suhrawardy's co-operation with the Central ruling clique and his support of One Unit as Law Minister and even earlier. Khuhro quoted writers on Indian and Bengali politics on his career before Partition and the many devious roles he had played at that time as well as in the early years of Pakistan. It was left to Suhrawardy's excitable lieutenants, Shaikh Mujibur Rahman and Zahiruddin to try and interrupt and obstruct Khuhro's speech. Khuhro spoke for about six hours, just a bit longer than Suhrawardy. In a speech which was spread over three days Khuhro not only replied in detail to the charges brought against him by Suhrawardy but more importantly gave the conditions the Sind Government had negotiated with the Centre for entering the One Unit arrangement.

Khuhro gave a detailed exposition of the economy, welfare and position of Sind. He demonstrated the considerable progress the Province was making in education, culture and building up its infrastructure.

Khuhro explained the financial position of Sind. The Province had not only paid back the debt of Rs. 25 crores to the Government of India for the Lloyd Barrage at Sukkur but was also in a position to spend 24 crores on the Kotri Barrage which was just being completed. Sind expected that after meeting the need for forests and other necessary projects such as seed plantations, etc., there would be a million acres at the disposal of the Government of which a large part would given at concessional rates to landless *haris* of Sind. Sind Government had a balance of about

20 crores and its 'financial position was a very happy one', but Khuhro warned

"We do not stand in need of any doles from the West Pakistan Government but at the same time we must realise that the finances of this province cannot be available for expending in other areas because our commitments are very great.'[19]

Khuhro also gave an outline of the development work which had taken place since the achievement of autonomy in 1936, starting from 300 miles of *pucca* roads to 1,100 miles in 1954,

"we have spent no less than 65 to 70 lakhs on hospitals and medical colleges;[20] we have spent 50 lakhs on agricultural college in Tando Jam; we are committed to spend 60 lakhs on the Sakrand College and 20 lakhs on public schools and we are also spending about 25 lakhs on the residential university of Sind."[21]

Khuhro also detailed the allocation for the development of language and culture of the province:

"So far as culture and language is concerned, Sind has done its bit. Our Legislature has passed an Act appointing a statutory body which goes by the name of Sind Cultural Advancement Board to look after the development of Sind Culture. Sind Government has made an endowment of 25 lakhs for the purpose of progress of culture and language of Sind. Another 25 lakhs we have given for the library, art and art gallery and the development of oriental[22] and Sindhi literature and its preservation. It is hoped that in the future set-up, Sind's interests regarding its culture are fully preserved."[23]

Khuhro touched on a subject which was intimately involved in his relations with the Centre–Karachi:

"Sir, Karachi has been a part of Sind ever since Sind was known as a province. During the entire period of British Rule of 100 years, Karachi was the capital of Sind, and whatever even the Bombay Government has spent, it was spent mainly on Karachi towards its buildings and other things. Then later after its separation from Bombay from 1936 onwards, Sind itself had spent a lot on Karachi... Sind has today financial interests of about 96.5 crores in Karachi itself. The cost of buildings which was promised by the Central Government to be given to the Province of Sind was about 96 and odd crores which comprised the cost of land surplus income and other things which have been capitalised. It is a tragedy I think if Karachi is not going to be a part of West Pakistan."

Khuhro spelt out the assurances that Sind needed:

"...there are certain safeguards which must be considered during the course of the passing of the Bill regarding the Province of Sind and for that, methods will have to be devised as to how these safeguards can be fully assured...300 thousand acres shall be reserved for the landless *haris* in the province of Sind. In the rest of the land also, whether it is 6 lakhs or 7 lakhs of acres, the indigenous population must have priority and preference.

...the question of the allocation of water for these Barrages will be the paramount interest of the unified legislature and the Government of West Pakistan should see that the present water-supplies are fully preserved and safeguarded. In the matter of services, I do not want to say much, because the present arrangement by the Administrative Council as far as present services are concerned has been satisfactory. For the future the proposal of the Administrative Council is that as far as subordinate or Class II Services are concerned, the recruitment shall be from within the divisions themselves, but as far as Class I and Superior Services are concerned, it shall be the responsibility of the future Government. The people do want very rightly that the proper ratio of population should be reflected even in the Superior Services..."[24]

Khuhro then turned to the present urgent needs of Sind:

"At present, Sir, the Province of Sind is passing through difficult times. We have suffered losses. Recently we have suffered because of floods and heavy rains and in these areas many of the villages and towns shall have to be re-built and the people shall have to be resettled to bring them back in their homes. For that large sums will be required which ordinarily if Sind were a separate Province it can do it. It shall be the paramount duty of the Government of Sind to give top priority to the rehabilitation of the people of their own province and it should be the duty of the future Government of West Pakistan if it comes before that, that these areas where the floods have played havoc recently are given proper attention and these areas must be given sufficient funds to rehabilitate and rebuild the villages which Sind Government could not easily do from its own resources without any aid from the Central Government."[25]

Finally Khuhro came to the question of the necessity of having a democratic order for the country:

"Lastly, Sir, it is the desire and a very strong desire of the people of all Provinces, and it should be the desire of all the Provinces in West Pakistan who are coming in One Unit that there should be a democratic form of Government. Nobody likes Section 92-A administration and we are one with you the Honourable Members from Bengal, that Section 92-A must go as early as possible and there should be from the very beginning, at the very initial time, even before the appointed day, there must be some kind of a legislature either by direct election or by indirect election. Whatever may be, it is said that a legislature must be there to safeguard the interests of the people and nobody, at least, I for one, and my people shall never agree to have 92A administration in this set up, and Sir, before I close I want to make it clear that the Government, our friends and our party shall have to consider all these things in the interests of the minority Provinces."[26]

It was clear from his speech in the Constituent Assembly that Khuhro shared public apprehensions about possible betrayal of the promises that had been made. He knew that the only way to ensure that these promises would be kept was through a legislature in which the smaller provinces were adequately represented. The Punjab by taking a lesser representation than it was entitled to went some way to re-assuring the smaller provinces that their interests would be safeguarded. But democracy would be the only way to ensure that the promises would be kept. He appealed to Suhrawardy to go beyond his pique and work for the benefit of the country:

"I think Sir that my Honourable friend, the Leader of the Opposition will fully co-operate in seeing that this Bill is passed in a proper form and will see that the interests of the people are safeguarded and that it is not unnecessarily delayed but he will see that the time at our disposal is fully utilised for the benefit of our country.

I would lastly appeal to the Leader of the Opposition that he should adopt a constructive attitude with respect to this Bill. There should be no distinction of this that he is on the Government Benches or on the Opposition Benches. In politics these things very often happen and those who are in power today maybe out of power the next day and maybe in Opposition... As far as the people are concerned, they should be given a democratic form of Government and I agree with him that there should be free and fair elections ... and for that the Constitution must be prepared..."[27]

The debate on One Unit was ended by Gurmani's speech in which he reiterated the assurances and the promises that had been made to the smaller provinces. The Bill became law in the middle of October 1955. An Interim Government of West Pakistan with six Ministers was appointed to administer the new administrative unit. The Ministers were Sardar Bahadur Khan, Khan Qurban Ali Khan, Abdul Hamid Dasti, Chief Minister, Punjab, Daultana and Khuhro. The representation in the Interim Cabinet was thus 60% from the smaller provinces and 40% from the Punjab. The elections for the West Pakistan Assembly took place in January 1956 and Muslim League was returned with a majority. The Chief Minister Dr. Khan Sahib however refused to join Muslim League but the rest of the Ministry was composed of members of the Muslim League Party.

The Government of West Pakistan started functioning. Khuhro had charge of a number of portfolios including Revenue, Industries and Commerce, and Refugees and Rehabilitation. He was also on most of the constitution making committees and had to stay in Karachi working on those and so was not fully conversant with the frictions particularly among the Frontier members in the newly formed West Pakistan Government.

The work of constitution making was going on apace and by 29 February 1956 the task was completed. There was a last minute hitch as Iskander Mirza delayed signing the document until he was given the assurance that he would continue as President after the promulgation of the constitution. He was given that assurance and on 2 March he signed the document and on 5 March he was inducted as President of the Republic of Pakistan.

In the month of March 1956 Iskander Mirza called a meeting at which Gurmani, Governor West Pakistan, Dr. Khan Sahib, Daultana, Colonel Abid Hussain, and Khuhro were present. Dr. Khan Sahib had asked to expand the West Pakistan Cabinet to twelve and he also suggested the names to be included. These included Khuhro's opponents from Sind and Daultana's opponents from the Punjab. It was obvious that these suggestions were inspired by Mirza who was up to his usual game of creating situations of disharmony of which he could take advantage.

Chaudhri Mohammed Ali called a meeting to work out a compromise formula. It was agreed that Dr. Khan Sahib would remain as a non Muslim League Chief Minister but that he would not join any other party or make a new one. He would be a 'neutral' head of government and all other Ministers would come from the Muslim League Party until new elections were held within one year. As Muslim League was expected to come in as the majority party, it was agreed that after the elections the Chief Minister would be from Muslim League. The Prime Minister Chaudhry Mohammed Ali, Khuhro, Daultana and some others signed this agreement.

Meanwhile trouble was brewing between the two Ministers from the Frontier, Dr. Khan Sahib and Sardar Bahadur Khan. The Ministers had already found Dr.

Khan Sahib difficult and idiosyncratic. He did not consider the Ministry as a team and took most of the decisions on his own. He was also extremely emotional. In a typically understated manner Khuhro notes:

"I had not known his method of working as Chief Minister, of the way he ran his government in the Frontier as we had no contact with the Congress Ministry of the Frontier."[28]

For example it was reported while the Chief Minister was touring Haripur in the Hazara District a woman brought a complaint that she was a widow with a small piece of land on which she depended for her livelihood, but that Sardar Bahadur Khan who owned land in the neighbourhood, was taking away her share of the water and she was unable to cultivate her land. Dr. Khan Sahib 'somewhat hasty and emotional by nature', did not bother to make a proper enquiry although in this case his colleague and the Minister for Irrigation was concerned, immediately ordered that the water supply of Sardar Bahadur Khan be reduced.*

This was the last straw as far as Sardar Bahadur Khan was concerned as there had been other differences and between him and Chief Minister. Khuhro and Daultana were still in the middle of negotiations with the President and the Prime Minister about the future set up of West Pakistan. They were with Mirza in the President's House when a telegram arrived for them from Sardar Bahadur Khan that no compromise was possible with Dr. Khan Sahib. When they got to Khuhro's house, where Daultana was staying, there was phone call from Sardar Bahadur for Daultana saying that he and Khuhro should press for a Muslim League nominee to be Chief Minister. If that could be done then obviously Sardar Bahadur Khan had a chance to replace Dr. Khan Sahib. Daultana was at first inclined to agree with Sardar Bahadur Khan but Khuhro argued that such a change in the existing arrangements would cause a serious breach perhaps in the Cabinet but certainly with the President since he was backing Dr. Khan Sahib fully. In any case except for the Chief Minister all the Ministers were Muslim Leaguers and that the present arrangement was tolerable until the elections. Daultana agreed with Khuhro and a compromise formula was worked out with the Centre. The names for the expanded West Pakistan Ministry would be finalised by Chaudhri Mohammed Ali and Governor Gurmani and would include only members of Muslim League.

Sardar Bahadur Khan was very annoyed that his plan to oust the Chief Minister had not worked and he was determined to make trouble. He and Qazi Isa who was General Secretary of the Party began canvassing members from Sind, Frontier and the Punjab against the agreement which had been reached by Daultana and Khuhro. Nishtar who was President of Muslim League was also against Dr. Khan Sahib and wanted to be rid of him. He called a meeting of Muslim League Council on 2 April at Lahore. The meeting met in the Assembly Chamber. From Sind, Pirzada, Kazi Fazlullah and Mir Ghulam Ali's brother came out strongly against the agreement and vociferously demanded a Muslim League Chief Minister. In spite of all the strident opposition from the Frontier Leaguers and the oppo-

---

* It had been rumoured that Iskander Mirza who had experience of working with Dr. Khan Sahib when he was Political Agent in the Frontier knew exactly how to distract him from serious work. Some pathetic looking person would be sent to him to complain that some official had stolen his chickens and the Chief Minister would rush off to right the wrong and punish the guilty official leaving the field clear for the schemes of the Political Agent.

nents of Khuhro and Daultana, the agreement would have been carried with a large majority. Nishtar realising the outcome, adopted an unusual tactic for the voting on the resolution to ratify the agreement. Resolutions were always voted on openly and ballot had only been used for the election of officers of the Party. But on this occasion, at the suggestion of Qazi Isa and Sardar Bahadur on the assumption that members would not like to vote openly against Khuhro and Daultana, the voting was by secret ballot. But in spite of this unusual device the counter resolution of having only a Muslim Leaguer as Chief Minister was carried only by a comparatively small margin.

The result was as Khuhro had predicted a disaster for Muslim League. Iskander Mirza had cut short his tour of Azad Kashmir and was camping in the Governor's House in Lahore waiting to hear the result of the vote. As soon as they heard the result, he and Gurmani decided to formed the Republican Party. They threw an open invitation to defectors from Muslim League to accept Ministerships. Dr. Khan Sahib wrote to Gurmani on the 6 April that he wanted Khuhro, Daultana and Sardar Bahadur Khan out of the cabinet. On the same day Gurmani had already received the resignations of the three Muslim Leagures.[29] A number of Muslim Leaguers who were the most vociferous against the agreement between the Centre and Muslim League now jumped into the Republican Party without even the formality of resigning from Muslim League. Those from Sind included Mir Ghulam Ali's brother, and those like Kazi Fazlullah, Pirzada and Ghulam Nabi Pathan who had declared themselves against One Unit and who at the Muslim League meeting had been the loudest in demanding a Muslim League Chief Minister.[30] Mir Ghulam Ali's brother Ali Nawaz Talpur, Kazi Fazlullah, Pirzada and Pathan were made Ministers. Other prominent Muslim Leaguers like Dasti the ex-Chief Minister of the Punjab, Makhdum Hassan Mahmud the ex-Chief Minister of Bahawalpur also made haste to join the Republican Party and became Ministers. The West Pakistan cabinet was eventually expanded to about 20. Nishtar was very chagrined at being so thoroughly out manoeuvred but it was too late. He was no match for Mirza.*

****

In July 1956 Khuhro was asked by the Prime Minister to lead a Parliamentary delegation to U.S.S.R. This was a particularly important task as the relations of Pakistan with the second super power had not been particularly cordial and Pakistan was considered a firm Western ally ever since Liaquat Ali Khan had chosen to go to the U.S.A. rather than the Soviet Union in 1950. Since then the Pakistan establishment had wholeheartedly embraced the Western camp and its relations with the Soviet Union were formal at best.

The visit included meetings with the Soviet President Voroshilov and also Nikita Khruschev, at that time the all powerful Secretary General of the Communist Party. This was the year that Khruschev had made the revelations about Stalin's excesses against the Soviet people in a secret address to the Supreme Soviet and the first

---

* A historian of the period writes of the creation of the Republican Party: "It came into being mainly because the factions of the Muslim League in West Pakistan could not agree upon the distribution of power and influence. The Punjabis were divided, and the other members wanted to avoid the possibilty of Punjabi domination. The party was formed to give support to one man, Khan Sahib, and to keep out office two other men, Daultana and Khuhro." Callard, op. cit, p. 75.

signs of cracks in the facade of the Soviet monolith had appeared. The Russian landscape that the delegation saw was however as conformist as ever. Everywhere there were the heroic statues of Soviet youth and slogans of *Miry Mir* or 'peace and friendship', perhaps a subtle dig at the 'war mongering' West.

Khuhro flew with his party via Sweden for the visit which was due to last for just over a fortnight. The delegation which included parliamentarians from both East and West Pakistan, reached the Baltic city of Riga in the evening of 19 July. Here Khuhro witnessed his first 'midnight sun' as it stayed bright till late at night with people strolling in the street and the parks. The delegation also ate its first Soviet meal, an enormous feast with black and pink caviar and a variety of Russian pickles as starters—a portent of what was to come. There was also a wonderful variey of bottled juices which were enjoyed a great deal by the teetotallar Pakistanis. Certainly there appeared to be no shortage of good quality food in the Soviet Union as opposed to the impression given by the Western press. But then again the Pakistanis had no real opportunity to see what the common diet was.

On 20 July the delegation arrived in Moscow and Khuhro gave a very friendly reply to the welcome address at the formal reception at Moscow airport:

"For us and for the entire world your country, which in so short a time has been able to make such progress in every sphere is a fine example. The Pakistani Government and people are imbued with an enormous desire to establish close and friendly relations with the Soviet Union. We are very happy to have the opportunity of visiting your great country as members of the delegation of the Pakistani Parliament. This will enable us to see everything with our own eyes and make many personal contacts..."

From a tourist and historical point of view the Soviet Union was spectacular. The Kremlin was crammed with historic buildings which included the palaces of Ivan the Terrible and other early Czars, with their low ceilings and walls, entirely painted with frescoes, the neo-classical buildings and the splendid reception rooms of the post-Peter the Great era. The fabulous collection of artifacts in the Kremlin as well as the holy relics of Lenin were all impressive to the visitors in this period when the Soviet Union was still a mystery to the outside world. The delegation also saw the waxen preserved bodies of Lenin and Stalin in the black mausoleum outside the Kremlin and the Red Square with its curious onion domed basilica. They noted the almost religious awe and respect with which the people lined up in their never ending queues to see the dead leaders in this avowedly athiestic State.

It was in Moscow that Khuhro and his delegation had meetings with Khruschev and Bulganin in one of the beautiful and ornate conference rooms. Both the leaders were very affable, Bulganin smiling quietly and Khruschev ebullient and talkative. Khuhro introduced his delegation which was given a warm and flattering welcome by Khruschev. The meeting went well until Khuhro brought up the Kashmir question. On this point Khruschev absolutely refused to see the Pakistan point of view. He thumped the table and said,"Talk to us again after fifty years."!

From Moscow the delegation went to Leningrad by train, decorated splendidly but in a very old fashioned manner – all gold and plush. Leningrad was in complete contrast to Moscow, grand and Versaillesesque with wide avenues, canals and palaces. They saw the great art collection at the Hermitage with rare western masterpieces as well as modern Russian art. They also saw a ballet at the famous

Kirov Theatre. The delegation had a chance to visit Stalingrad, the scene of the heroic resistence to Nazi armies in World War II, where just one of the ruined buildings had been preserved as a reminder. From Stalingrad they went to Tbilisi, the capital of Georgia and the home town of Stalin, but for the visitors the *koh kaf* of fairy tales. A visit to the sea side resort of Sochi on the Black Sea was also included and gave the Pakistani parliamentarians a chance to see the benefits enjoyed by the citizens of the Soviet State. The town was full of clean and efficient hospitals and the rest homes that all state employees (and everyone was ofcourse a state employee) came for their free holidays. The people on the beach and on the streets seemed carefree and happy, smiling and flashing gold teeth. Seeing and meeting them was quite an eye opener for the visitors whose ideas of the Soviet state and its citizens was based on the Western media's propaganda.

The highlight of the visit for Khuhro and the rest of the delegation was the four days they spent in Uzbekistan, a region so closely involved with their own history, their literature and their religion. The first stop in Central Asia was the major city of Tashkent. Central Asia was almost inaccessable to outsiders and hardly any Pakistani apart from diplomats ever got a chance to visit it. For Khuhro, brought up on Muslim history and Persian poetry it was a dream come true to come within throwing distance of Samarkand and Bokhara. He had requested that both of these legendary cities should be included in their itinerary. The Russian hosts however took them only to Samarkand and not Bokhara which presumably was not a shining example of Socialist progress.

Apart from the visits to industrial complexes and collective farms there was the romance of history. Samarkand, Taimur Lang's city was at this time still 'unrestored' and the magnificent Madressahs like the Shah i Zinda were almost in ruins, just hinting at their former grandeur. But Taimur's tomb, the mosques and other buildings in the slope of the Afrasiyab hill were wonderfully preserved with their matchless blue tile work, mosaics and inscriptions. They also saw the Ulugbek Observatory and walked along the Registan square. The imagination of the visiting Pakistanis could see in these remnants the magnificence of Taimur's court and the work done by craftsmen that he had imported from all over the conquered territories. The story of Hafiz's verse:

اگر آن ترک شیرازی بدست آرد دل مارا

بخال هندووش بخشم سمرقند و بخارا را

حافظ شیرازی

and the reaction of Taimur who asked the poet how could he dare to exchange Samarkand and Bokhara for the mole on his beloved's cheek, came alive for Khuhro who recited the Hafiz verse to his companions as they were walking round the tomb of Taimur.

Before leaving the U.S.S.R., Khuhro made a broadcast on Moscow television and radio expressing thanks for the warm reception that had been given to the delegation and the desire of Pakistan for friendship with the Soviet Union:

"We have seen that the Soviet people desire friendship with us and peace everywhere. Our country and our people also want peace. They want friendship with all countries, with all their neighbours, and especially with your country. I have brought with me a goodwill message from my people and my Government and I am very glad to have brought it to its destination. When we return home, we shall convey a message of friendship from your people and your Government."[31]

While he was still in the Soviet Union, Khuhro heard of the invasion of the Suez Canal by the Anglo French and Israeli forces. This had come in the wake of the nationalisation of the Suez Canal on 27 July. The news of the attack by these big powers on a struggling third world country which was also Muslim, was shocking in the extreme, and on behalf of the Pakistani parliamentarians Khuhro condemned the aggression in strong terms. On his way back home Khuhro stopped for a few days in London which was still experiencing post-war austerity and was much changed since he had been there last, in 1933 in the heyday of the empire. In London he met Hamidul Huq Chowdhury, the Pakistani Foreign Minister who had come to attend a conference on the Suez problem. Khuhro gave him a run down on Russian thinking and public opinion. He also met Daultana who was holidaying in London with his family. Soon Khuhro was back in Karachi.

For Khuhro 1956 continued to be a good year for interesting travel. In October he took advantage of some meetings held in Dacca, for a weekend visit to Calcutta. He took his two daughters Hamida and Rashida along for this visit to the eastern wing of the country. Dacca was still a pleasant but small town, extraordinarily green and tropical for Khuhro's daughters from semi arid Karachi. From Dacca they flew to Calcutta where they were the guests of the Governor of West Bengal, Padmaja Naidu the daughter of the legendary politician and poetess Sarojini Naidu. The Government House was the ex-Viceregal palace modelled on Lord Curzon's ancestral home Kedleston in Derbyshire County in England except that the Government House was much larger. The Khuhros stayed in the wing where the Prince of Wales later Edward VIII had stayed on his visit to India. They were suitably impressed by its understated elegance. They also visited some of the impressive Raj buildings of Calcutta including the National Library housed in Belvedere in Alipur where the Lieutenant Governors of Bengal used to live. The decaying grandeur was everywhere obvious ranging from Regency buildings to the elaborate wedding cake of the Victoria Memorial. Khuhro met some of his old acquaintances including the well-known financial expert B. T. Thakur from Sind who was now living in Calcutta and other local luminaries.

****

At home in Pakistan the situation at the Centre had become very uncomfortable for Chaudhry Mohammed Ali, who was at least nominally a Muslim League Prime Minister. He had assumed a stance of 'neutrality' when the Muslim League Ministry had been thrown out in West Pakistan and had continued by ignoring the anamolous situation whereas a Muslim League Prime Minister he had to see the Party being humiliated. The neutrality stand could not last and in September 1956 he resigned.[32] Iskander Mirza now agreed to a coalition of Awami League and the Republicans with Suhrawardy as Prime Minister although he did not trust him particularly as he was a much abler politician than those he had recently dealt with.

Meanwhile the situation in the West Pakistan Assembly continued to cause headaches for the Centre. Despite the defections and the open ended invitation to members of the West Pakistan legislature to join the Republican Party and become Ministers, Muslim League remained a strong Opposition Party in the Assembly.

In March 1957 the Muslim League leadership talked to the G. M. Syed group in the West Pakistan Assembly, which although small held the balance between the Republicans and the Muslim League. The Syed group agreed to support Muslim League if it supported a resolution against One Unit which Muslim League agreed to do.[33] This was a momentous turn around in Muslim League policy in less than two years since One Unit had come into operation. It appeared that not only the smaller provinces but the Punjab had become disillusioned with the way it was working. Although it had the strong support of the Punjab bureaucracy the politicians were finding that they had to make compromises with the politicians of the smaller provinces on almost every issue. It was a tough lesson in democracy and the bureaucrats of the Punjab were getting impatient. It also showed that in making the decision for One Unit, politicians had really been bulldozed by the single-minded centrists.

When on 20 March 1957 the Assembly met for the Budget session Sardar Bahadur Khan the leader of Muslim League Parliamentary Party challenged the Chief Minister to a vote. Dr. Khan Sahib asked the Speaker to adjourn the Assembly *sine die* and he himself remained absent from the House. The Republicans were very alarmed and Dr. Khan Sahib realising that defeat was imminent advised the Governor to dissolve the Assembly and let him continue in charge of a Caretaker Ministry. Gurmani asked Mirza for permission to dissolve the Assembly and impose Section 193 (Section 92 A in a new guise). Mirza would not hand over West Pakistan to Gurmani however as he wanted to keep power himself. He wanted to suspend the Assembly and told Dr. Khan Sahib that he would be able to resume as Chief Minister after he had built up his strength. The Muslim League demanded that as the Opposition Party with the prospect of a majority it should be called to form the government. Mirza would not agree to these normal parliamentary procedures. On 21 March 1957 he suspended the Assembly and imposed Section 193 for two months, the period would be extended for a further few weeks.

Khuhro issued a detailed press statement criticising the suspension of the democratic government in West Pakistan and exposing the hypocrisy behind it. He also warned the ruling clique against the evil consequences of such an undemocratic step. He said:

"Suspending the democratic form of government and imposing section 193 rule on the whole of West Pakistan, which covers one half of the entire country, coming as it does almost on the eve of the first anniversary of the Pakistan Republic Constitution, tramples on the democratic rights and the intelligence of the people here and abroad. It is indeed ominous for the very future of democracy in this country.

The relevant clause 193 of the constitution lays it down as a condition that before imposing Section 193 the President should satisfy himself that a situation has arisen in which the government of the province cannot be carried on according to the constitution.

In this case there was no question of the President being so satisfied because the Opposition commanded a clear and visible majority and was prepared to form a Government and carry it on in accordance with the provision of the Constitution. That was all the Constitution prescribed and demanded and that was exactly what the Opposition was quite prepared for and was demonstrably in a position to accomplish, and yet it was not given a chance to do so.

How then could the statement that the Central Government was satisfied that the Government of the Province cannot be carried on in accordance with the provision of the constitution be regarded as true and honest. And if that statement is, on the very face of it ruled out where is any legal, constitutional or moral basis left for the suspension of the constitution and replacement of democracy with one man rule?"[34]

Here yet again Khuhro was being prophetic. Khuhro also exposed the excuse that had been advanced that members had crossed the floor:

"The only pretext advanced in justification of this action is that some members had crossed the floor. But how had the outgoing Khan Sahib Ministry itself been installed in power if not through the crossing of the floor by a large number of members quite a few of whom were straight away elevated to the Ministerial *gaddi*? And was not Dr. Khan Sahib's entire Cabinet almost wholly composed of the people who had crossed the floor? Again who today runs and sustains Mr. Suhrawardy's own government at the Centre? Excepting his own original 13 Awami Leaguers, the rest of his supporters in the Coalition are almost all those who had crossed the floor. The so-called Republicans, till yesterday were but full-fledged Muslim Leaguers having been directly elected on the Muslim League tickets. The East Pakistan non-Muslim members till only a year ago constituted but one of the vital constituent elements of the League, United Front coalition.

Now if changes setting in the party position through crossing of the floor implied failure of the Constitution and justified denial of an invitation to the Opposition Party to form a government, why was Dr. Khan Sahib allowed to form the government in April last year, against the decision of the majority party and why is Mr. Suhrawardy's own government in office today? What is unconstitutional and immoral in one case was far more unconstitutional and immoral in previous two cases. But yet that was allowed to happen because those in power wanted it to happen.

Nor does it lie in the mouth of Suhrawardy, of all people, to say, in his Republic Day speech that because there were rumours afloat that the new West Pakistan Coalition was likely to work for changing more provisions of the Constitution, he would not allow such a coalition to assume office.

Is such an approach democratic and appropriate? Mr. Suhrawardy's own party, the Awami League, wanted and still wants radical changes in the Constitution, so that more regional autonomy is conceded to the provinces. Must that Party, on that account, be denied office even though it may be having a majority in the East Pakistan legislature? Mr. Suhrawardy's party at the Centre was most bitterly opposed to the present constitution and to this very creation of One Unit itself last year. It had even walked out of the House when the Constitution Bill was going through the third reading stage as a protest and had even boycotted the celebrations which followed the passage of the Constitution. And yet would it have been right on the part of the President if on that ground he had kept the Awami League out of office even after it had built up a majority for itself in the Parliament?

Frankly the way the Awami League Prime Minister has been forgetting and even violating the principles which he and his party have been consistently professing and profiting by, leaves one deeply amazed. If it is in this spirit and with this intellectual integrity and with this concern for principles and consistency that the oath of allegiance to the constitution is going to be honoured then all one can say is God save this country from Awami League rule."

Khuhro added a warning:

"Nor indeed need the Awami Leaguers feel happy over what they have done. By brazen facedly violating the democratic principles they have released forces of evil of which, who knows, they themselves may some day be the worst victims."[35]

The prediction would soon proved accurate.

Meanwhile the Republicans were able to gather enough strength and in a position to form the government in West Pakistan. Mirza decided however that Dr. Khan Sahib although very loyal to him was not strong enough to withstand the Muslim League opposition and put in Sardar Rashid as Chief Minister. The second Republican Ministry of West Pakistan was sworn in on 17 July and the Assembly was re- called on 14 August. Meanwhile the Syed group (part of National Awami Party), realising that the chances of Muslim League being allowed to form the government were nil decided to co-operate with the Republicans. In return for their support the Republican government of West Pakistan agreed to push through a resolution asking for the dissolution of One Unit, the formation of zonal federations and a higher degree of autonomy for the provinces. On 17 August the Resolution was adopted by 107 votes in favour with Muslim League abstaining. It has to be assumed that a decision to pass a resolution against One Unit could not have been taken by Dr. Khan Sahib, a protege of Iskander Mirza, without a nod from the latter. The most probable motive for Mirza allowing his creation, the Republican Party, to co-operate in passing the anti One Unit resolution was to alarm the military top brass, particularly Ayub Khan, the strong protagonist of the One Unit scheme. This has to be taken in the light of later events as a move by Mirza in a game in which he would bring in a dictatorial regime.

Mirza found this a good opportunity to get rid of Gurmani as Governor of West Pakistan and weaken Suhrawardy whom he considered an old ally of Gurmani. He insisted on the resignation of Gurmani who although the architect of the prevailing set up was forced to resign. He was replaced by a bureaucrat, Akhtar Hussain. Gurmani who was in Karachi at that time asked Khuhro and Daultana to come and see him at Punjab House, his usual residence in Karachi. Here they found Mujibur Rahman and Ataur Rahman, Suhrawardy's lieutenants already present. Gurmani said to the Awami Leaguers that he would resign but that Suhrawardy should be warned that his Prime Ministership at the Centre would not last long. This prediction proved to be true. Mirza did not like Suhrawardy and was afraid that if he remained Prime Minister he would not support him for Presidentship after the elections which were to be held soon.

Meanwhile the resolution against One Unit sent shivers of apprehension in the ranks of the West Pakistan establishment. Ayub Khan landing on a tour of lower Sind expressed to the West Pakistan Ministers receiving him at Bolari near Hyderabad:

"I will see how these people are going to undo the One Unit."[36]

On 23 September Mirza issued a statement saying that despite the resolution in the West Pakistan Assembly the break up of One Unit was not on the cards and that elections would have to take place under the present constitution. On the same day Suhrawardy made a broadcast also backing One Unit. He toured the country making speeches in favour of One Unit. Astonshingly however Mir Ghulam Ali Talpur, Minister in the Central Cabinet not otherwise known for taking independent stands on political issues, particularly if that issue was backed by the highest in the land, came out against Suhrawardy saying that the Prime Minister's arguments were wrong and it was not necessary for the elections to be held under the present constitution. It was obvious that this opposition to the Prime Minister from an essentially 'yes man' had been inspired by Mirza who wanted to get rid of Suhrawardy. Quite understandably the President, who had the power to remove Ministers, took no action against the apparently recalcitrant Minister. The Republican Party which had voted against the One Unit was now said to be against Suhrawardy and showing a lack of confidence in him. When the latter asked for an Constituent Assembly session to get a vote of confidence Mirza told him that he only had the option of resignation or dismissal. Suhrawardy resigned.

Mirza was by now the supreme arbiter of governments in Pakistan whether central or provincial.[37] In West Pakistan by the Budget session of 1958 he had installed his friend Nawab Muzaffar Hussain Qazilbash as Chief Minister thus violating the understanding that the Chief Minister of West Pakistan would be from the smaller provinces. In the Centre he now tried out his bridge companion, I. I. Chundrigar. His aim throughout appeared to be to get a permanent Presidentship for himself. He persuaded the Muslim League leaders that they should form a coalition with the Republican Party and the Krishak Sramik party from East Pakistan. The Muslim Leaguers put up the condition that separate electorates should be restored. Khuhro was present at an informal meeting at the President's House where apart from Mirza there were Nishtar, Chundrigar and Daultana. Mirza promised at this meeting that he would bring about a settlement between the Republicans and Muslim League and also get the separate electorates condition accepted. Khuhro was surprised that no Republicans were present and that Mirza was making all the promises on their behalf.

Nishtar called a Working Committee meeting to discuss the matter. Khuhro was of the view that separate electorates were not an essential policy matter and if this condition was insisted on it would bring about a split. Khuhro argued that Muslim League would be $\frac{1}{3}$ or less of the coalition and that it did not have the majority in the Assembly and as a minority government would be at the mercy of the President. He also pointed out that forming a government under these conditions was not the wisest thing to do.* Daultana and the Punjabi group were anxious however to reach an agreement and Chundrigar sided with them. Khuhro

---

* The party positions in the Assembly at the beginning of December 1957 were as follows:

	Members		Members
The Republican Party	21	Nizame Islam Party	3
Awami League	13	Hamidul Huq group	3
Muslim League	12	Mohammed Ali group	4
Krishak Sramik Party	4	East Pak. Scheduled Caste Federation	2
National Awami Party	4	United Progressive Party of East Pak.	1
The Congress Party	4	Independents	6

The Chundrigar coalition had support of 45 members including four independents and one belonging to the Huq group. The parties included in the coalition were Muslim League, Republican, K.S.P. and the Nizame Islam.

had also learnt from Noon who was a good friend of his, and from Dr. Khan Sahib, that the Republicans were actually against a Muslim League minority government and would not agree to separate electorates. He warned Chundrigar of this but the latter said that it was up to him to decide the matter. Khuhro was very annoyed at the attitude of a man who was being imposed on them by the President and walked out of the meeting which was being held at Chundrigar's house. In fact Khuhro was so disgusted at the shortsightedness of the Punjab group and that of Chundrigar that he told Daultana who was his guest in Karachi that he was thinking of resigning from the Party. The next day, presumably prompted by Daultana, who was a bit shaken by Khuhro's threat, Chundrigar came to call on Khuhro to apologise but according to Khuhro 'our relations were never the same again.'[38]

On 18 October 1957 Chundrigar took the oath as Prime Minister in a coalition Ministry which included Daultana, Yusuf Haroon from Muslim League, Republicans Noon and Syed Amjad Ali, the latter as Finance Minister. The Ministry had the support of the Krishak Sramik party. Khuhro who would normally have expected a seat in the Cabinet, was excluded on the excuse that the Republican Party and particularly Iskander Mirza did not want him. Khuhro quite justifiably felt that this was a lame excuse as Muslim League could hardly be dictated to. Khuhro let Chundrigar and his other colleagues know that he was not happy with the way things were going, but kept on with his duties as President of Sind Muslim League, as well as a leading Muslim Leaguer and parliamentarian, without allowing his annoyance to affect his work.

The Republican Party, as Khuhro had warned, did not stand by the commitment that Iskander Mirza had made on separate electorates and Chundrigar had to face the collapse of the coalition structure based on that understanding. There was an opinion that the insistence of Chundrigar on separate electorate had altogether a less noble motive than Muslim League ideology:

"The process to amend the particular provision dealing with joint electorates was bound to evoke great controversy and defer the General Elections indefinitely and automatically extend the life of the ministry."[39]

To postpone the elections indefinitely was also the dearest wish of Iskander Mirza who was reducing politics to chaos so that he did not run the risk of being replaced as President by a newly elected National Assembly. Hamidul Huq Chowdhury and East Pakistan members of Congress as well as some Awami Leaguers agreed to oppose the move and got the Republicans to go along as well. Chundrigar found that he was not in a position to get a majority when he came to ask for a vote of confidence from the Assembly which he needed to do within 60 days of taking office. He submitted his resignation to Mirza who asked him to form another Ministry but Chundrigar found he could not and on 16 December, after one of the shortest terms on record Chundrigar resigned as Prime Minister. Mirza now asked Sir Feroze Khan Noon to form the government. Noon had the support of the Krishak Sramik party and of the Awami League as well. He promised to hold the elections by the end of 1958.

Khuhro had been attending the Commonwealth Parliamentary Conference at Delhi when he got an S.O.S from Daultana that he should return immediately as Chundrigar was resigning. Khuhro returned just as Chundrigar was due to leave office but before Noon had been sworn in. He made a courtesy call on Mirza on his return from Delhi on 14 January, and was sitting with him in the verandah of the President's House when Noon turned up and said to Mirza,

"We want no more hanky panky- Republicans are in a majority and they have elected me leader."[40]

Mirza was not too keen on Noon as he wanted to choose his own Prime Minister but momentarily he was helpless as even Dr.Khan Sahib refused to see him to discuss the matter. The next day he swore in Noon.

Mirza did not stop intriguing after the formation of the Noon Ministry and began immediately seeing members of the Opposition. East Pakistan members Mohan Mia (Yusuf Ali Chowdhury) and others were encouraged to create trouble for the Government. In West Pakistan also, Mirza was constantly engaged in intrigue. He saw Daultana frequently and talked about removing Noon. He invited Khan Abdul Ghaffar Khan and G. M. Syed secretly to dinner. Khuhro came to know of this meeting through some friends of G. M. Syed. A few days later Khuhro met Mirza and asked him why he had been meeting Ghaffar Khan and G. M. Syed. Even knowing Mirza's penchant for intrigue Khuhro was not expecting the blunt answer he got,

"I want Ghaffar Khan to create trouble in the Frontier Province so that I can create grounds for the dismissal of the Ministry. I am not happy with Noon. I do not want an election. I will bring in Martial Law for a short while and then appoint a ministry of my own choice."[41]

In fact Mirza was being quite open about his dislike of the prospect of elections and of trying anything to avoid them.

****

Khuhro was quite uneasy at the way the One Unit arrangement was being implemented. Practically all the conditions he had negotiated with the Centre were being violated in practice. To some extent this was the fault of the Ministers who were representing Sind in the West Pakistan government for not safeguarding the interests of the province with vigour against bureaucratic encroachments. But on the other hand the bureaucracy seemed to have its own agenda for the amalgamated province and the fact that the agreement was not being carried out was a deliberate breach of trust with the smaller provinces.

The basic understanding that Gurmani himself had repeatedly emphasised that the lower services would be given only to locals was being disregarded and the Punjabi bureaucrats were importing even peons and clerical staff from their home towns in the Punjab. This practice assumed the proportions of a scandal in Sind as did the fact that the promised allotment of 300,000 acres on the Lower Sind Barrage reserved for the *haris* of Sind was kept in abeyance while land was given to army personnel and the civil service.[42] Questions were asked by Khuhro in the West Pakistan Assembly to which evasive replies were given by Kazi Fazlullah the Sind Minister in charge. Khuhro continued to bring up the matter repeatedly in the West Pakistan Assembly as well as the Muslim League meetings both provincial and national. The fact that Muslim League had the previous year agreed to back the resolution to do away with the One Unit appeared to him a commitment to this issue and when the Party backtracked in its session at Dacca in October 1957, it shook his faith in his colleagues, the fellow leaders of Pakistan Muslim League.[43]

On 23 January 1958 the Working Committee of the Sind Provincial Muslim League under Khuhro's presidentship had passed a resolution urging the League High Command to modify its stand on the One Unit issue:

"Whereas the scheme of integration of the provinces of West Pakistan has proved to be a complete failure administratively, economically and politically, resulting in untold hardship and misery to the common man, more so in the smaller Provinces and whereas the Committee while reiterating the earlier resolution on the subject, once again feels duty bound to bring it to the notice of Pakistan Muslim League High Command that the people of the Sind Province are opposed to the continuance of One Unit and in view of their avowed opposition to it, it will be in the interests of the Muslim League organization that its stand on this vital issue is modified so as to be in conformity with the expressed will of the people concerned, namely, the restoration of the province of Sind (Khairpur included) prior to the coming General Election.

Accordingly this Committee strongly urges upon the Working Committee and the Council of Pakistan Muslim League to review the situation in the light of the public opinion crystallised in the former smaller provinces of Sind, N.W.F.P., and Baluchistan and so amend the Resolution passed by Pakistan Muslim League at Dacca, that it does not preclude the possibility of modifying the One Unit scheme by carving out four or five provinces according to the administrative convenience of the people residing in the part of the country or alternatively to have a complete unitary form of government doing away with the provinces both in East and West Pakistan expressed through their accredited representatives in the Provincial Assembly and the National Parliament."[44]

On 14 February 1958 Nishtar died and a few weeks later Qayyum Khan was made President of Muslim League. Khuhro developed differences with the new leader almost immediately. The Council of Pakistan Muslim League met at the end of March in the Khaliqdina Hall of Karachi and Khuhro asked permission to move a resolution to dismantle the One Unit.

"Whereas the scheme of integration of the provinces of West Pakistan has proved to be a complete failure administratively economically and practically resulting in untold hardship and misery to the common man more so to those residing in smaller provinces like Sind, Frontier and Baluchistan and the former states of Bahawalpur, Khairpur and the Baluchistan States Union. This Council of Pakistan Muslim League is of the considered view that the people of smaller provinces are opposed to the continuance of the One Unit and in view of their avowed opposition to it, it will be in the interest of good administration if suitable steps are taken to undo the wrong in conformity with the expressed will of the people concerned.

Accordingly this Council of Pakistan Muslim League strongly urges upon the Government of Pakistan to review the situation in the light of public opinion crystallised in the former smaller provinces of Sind, N.W.F.P., Khairpur, Bahawalpur and Baluchistan and arrange for the creation of four or five provinces in West Pakistan according to the administrative political convenience of the people residing in this part of the country..." [45]

The Resolution was discussed in the Council meeting and had the support of the Bengali members. There was a prolonged discussion in the Working Committee meeting that night. Qayyum Khan who had just taken over as President of the Party, advised the Council to postpone the consideration of Khuhro's resolution till the next Council session which amounted in fact to an indefinite postponement. Qayyum Khan pointed out that at the Dacca session the Council had passed a resolution in favour of retaining the One Unit and therefore 'the office needed notice of this resolution.' He further said that

"In a democratic organisation one cannot shut one's eyes to the controversial matters. I assumed office only yesterday and I have found the contents of this resolution were not circulated for consideration of the members, moreover attendance today from certain areas is not what it should have been..."[46]

Khuhro felt that this attitude smacked of hypocrisy as the Muslim League including its leading Punjab and Frontier members had agreed to support the breakup resolution only a year earlier when it meant their regaining power but would have nothing to do with it when it promised no such advantage. Khuhro and the other councillors from Sind walked out of the meeting in protest.

Khuhro who had soldiered on in Muslim League in spite of the shabby treatment by Chundrigar at the time he became Prime Minister, and had never changed his loyalties since he had joined the Party in 1938 in spite of many provocations, felt badly let down. This was all the more hard to bear as the man who handed out the humiliation was none other than Qayyum Khan whose chequered career hardly bore close examination and who until 1945 was a member of Congress and a bitter critic of Jinnah and Muslim League. It was a matter of public record that having remained a Muslim League Chief Minister of the Frontier province for six years he opposed a Muslim League candidate in 1956. It was ironical that a man whose loyalty had been so changeable should now be the supremo of Muslim League.

Khuhro began to seriously think about leaving Muslim League. He had been offered a Cabinet post by Noon who knew of his differences with the Muslim League leadership, but Khuhro had turned down any suggestion that he might leave the League. However with the recent events in the party he was forced to think of alternatives and he spent some days consulting with friends about his future course of action. Qazilbash, the West Pakistan Premier was very keen that he join the government and spent sometime persuading him to take up Noon's offer. Khuhro had certain conditions for joining the Cabinet. He came to an understanding with the Republican members of Sind that they would jointly form an anti One Unit front. He also told Noon that he would not join the Republican Party but would continue to be a Muslim Leaguer, and if necessary he would detach the Sind Muslim League from the parent body. This he had done once before when he had differences with Khwaja Nazimuddin. By 8 April all the difficulties had been resolved. Khuhro found Noon amenable and felt he could work with him comfortably. In the afternoon of that date he was sworn in by the President and was given the Defence portfolio.

Khuhro announced that Sind Muslim League would hold its Council session in Sukkur in a fortnight's time to decide its future course of action. The central Muslim League leadership was totally taken back. With Khuhro leaving Muslim League one of the strongest pillars of the Party was suddenly removed. In fact Khuhro's loyalty to the Party through every crisis had led the Punjab leadership to assume that no matter how Khuhro was treated he would remain loyal and continue to use his immense influence for the party. Now that Khuhro refused to fall into line on what he considered a matter of principle, the Muslim Leaguers were amazed. Qayyum expelled Khuhro from the Party for a period of seven years.

Khuhro was quite prepared for this eventuality. In his press statement he pointed out that the feeling against One Unit administration was growing very intense in the national parliament as well as the Provincial Assembly which reflected the feelings of the public of smaller provinces. Recalling that the League Council had passed a resolution for One Unit in October last, he said,

"...I had therefore decided to sever my connections from the Pakistan Muslim League at that time and on my way back from Dacca on 11th October I issued a statement to the press at Lahore Airport to that effect, but I was later prevailed upon to hold back my decision till Sind Muslim League Working Committee and the Council had reviewed the position in the light of the latest decision of the Pakistan Muslim League Council at Dacca."

Referring to the formation of the coalition government with the Republicans (the Chundrigar Ministry) Khuhro said Muslim Leaguers understood that the Republican Party would support separate electorates and the law to that effect will be changed as early as possible. As well as sharing power at the Centre an agreement would be reached for sharing power in West Pakistan immediately after the return of the President from his European tour. It was soon discovered that this was not so. No such written agreement was made between the two parties on the electorate issue nor was any verbal agreement reached or even talked about concerning the sharing of power in West Pakistan. This, said Khuhro, caused great resentment among the Muslim Leaguers throughout West Pakistan–

"several people saw me from Sind and sent several letters to that effect and I was from the very start honestly convinced that it was a great mistake on the part of Muslim League Party to have joined the coalition and subsequent events have proved my doubts beyond a shadow of doubt."[47]

Khuhro pointed out that a year earlier Muslim League had been prepared to enter into an alliance with N.A.P. to undo One Unit and that policy had continued as late as September 1957 and when an agreement was reached between the Republicans and N.A.P. Khuhro went on,

"This year in March a fresh agreement was entered into with the National Awami Party to break the West Pakistan Ministry on the basis of a general economic programme. But it was informally agreed by the leaders of Muslim League party in West Pakistan that a resolution demanding referendum on two major issues viz. whether One Unit should be retained or the province of West Pakistan be sub-divided into four or five provinces or that there should be a unitary form of government for the whole of West Pakistan and secondly whether elections should be held on the basis of joint or separate electorates. But to my surprise when my resolution came up for discussion on March 31 in the Council meeting, it was being opposed and ultimately deferred for about three months. The delay in this matter obviously makes its implementation impossible because there are hardly six months left between now and the time when the elections are to be held, viz. November next."

Khuhro asserted his belief that the people of Sind had lost faith in Muslim League's sincerity–

"I am definite that the people of Sind are completely disappointed as far as Pakistan Muslim League is concerned. The results of the coming elections will prove whether I am popular or otherwise among the people of Sind."[48]

Khuhro announced that he would hold a meeting of Sind Muslim League Council in the last week of April in Sukkur and the decision to form a separate the Sind Muslim League would be taken there. He implied that leaving the Pakistan Muslim League was a matter of political survival as he could not have contested elections in Sind with any hope of winning on the PML ticket and it appeared unlikely that they would change their stand on the issue in time to affect the elections. On 28 April the Council of Sind Provincial Muslim League met with Khuhro presiding. It decided to sever all connections with the Pakistan Muslim League and to function as a new party. The main office bearers were appointed and a committee set up to frame rules and regulations for the party. Khuhro was to be the Convenor and one of the main aims of the party was to campaign against One Unit. The PML reaction to Khuhro's move was furious to the point of desperation. Qayyum Khan called him 'Judas Iscariot' and asked

"how could Mr. Khuhro be loyal to the government and the people when he could revolt against *his own* political organisation."[49]

He did not mention the manner in which the party had treated Khuhro. He did not pause to think of his own career. On his way back from Karachi he addressed a crowd at Multan where

"he was prompted to dilate on civil liberties, when he got a pamphlet in which he was denounced for his undemocratic ways during his regime as Chief Minister of the former province of N.W.F.P. The Khan defending himself said that civil liberties were only for the peace loving and patriotic citizens and not for the enemies of Pakistan. He said a Muslim League government would never tolerate the existence of traitors."[50]

As Minister of Defence in 1958 Khuhro was holding one of the most important portfolios of the Government or as Qayyum Khan called it 'the most important portfolio', and not as it was to become in later years, a mere show job. The most crucial decisions regarding the defence of the country were still taken at Cabinet level and for important policy matters the chiefs of all the three arms of the defence forces were invited to Cabinet meetings. In matters concerning a particular service the Defence Minister could consult the head of that service as a courtesy, or take the decision himself. Khuhro invariably consulted the heads of the services in any matter which pertained to the management of their department. He felt that this was the best way to ensure co-operation and a spirit of willingness in the forces, although he ensured, as far as he could, that policy remained the preserve of the political leadership. By 1958 it was already perhaps too late for the politicians to take complete charge of policy relating to foreign and defence matters but to some extent Khuhro felt that a strong and confident political leadership could ensure effective control while treating the armed forces leadership itself with respect. During his tenure of almost exactly six months as Defence Minister that was how Khuhro performed his task.

On the very first day Khuhro took over as Defence Minister, General Ayub Khan telephoned him and invited him to come to Rawalpindi to inspect the establishment there. On 17 April Khuhro arrived in Rawalpindi by air for a two-day visit.

He was received at the airport by General Ayub and the Defence Secretary and was given a guard of honour of a detachment of the Air Force. He then went to visit the Wah Ordinance factory. Khuhro was a guest of Ayub Khan at his official residence and was taken round the GHQ and introduced to senior military officers. Ayub gave official dinners in his honour. Khuhro was impressed by the affability of the Commander in Chief and the professionalism of the army. Just before his departure from Rawalpindi at the end of his tour Khuhro found Ayub Khan visibly upset. He told Khuhro that he had just got the news that the Minister for Industries and Supplies had persuaded the Prime Minister that military supplies including military weapons should be procured through his Ministry. General Ayub said to Khuhro that he was shocked as this arrangement would not work. Ayub Khan asked Khuhro to get the decision cancelled. Khuhro talked to the Prime Minister and told him that the decision appeared to have been taken in haste and was not practicable. Noon agreed to cancel the order and Khuhro worked out a compromise by which a senior C.S.P. officer would be appointed Deputy Secretary in the Defence Ministry to supervise procurement and supplies, etc. This arrangement was accepted by the C-in-C as satisfactory.

After his return from Rawalpindi Khuhro visited the Pakistan Air Force headquarters at Mauripur just outside Karachi where he was received by the Air Force C-in-C, Air Vice Marshal Mohammed Asghar Khan, who briefed him on the work of the air force and also introduced the Chief of Staff, Air Commodore Rabb and the principal staff officers to him.

Some weeks later while Khuhro was in Lahore, Ayub Khan came to see him at 7, Club Road where Khuhro was staying as guest of Kazi Fazlullah, then a Minister in the West Pakistan Ministry. Ayub Khan told Khuhro that his term was coming to an end the following January and he was anxious that Khuhro should get the Prime Minister to settle the question of whether he would continue, and if not that his successor should be named soon. Khuhro put the matter to Noon who was hesitating somewhat as Ayub Khan had already had eight years as C-in-C. But they decided to ask Ayub Khan to apply for an extension which he did, asking for four more years. Noon and Khuhro agreed among themselves to this. Khuhro then talked to Mirza who seemed unwilling to agree and said emphatically that the term should not be extended beyond two years, otherwise he would veto it. It would appear that Mirza wanted Ayub Khan to believe that the politicians were against his extension and thus give him a personal motive for acting against them. At Mirza's insistence an extension of two years was given to Ayub Khan but it is now clear that Mirza had played his game successfully and given Ayub what amounted to a personal grudge against the Ministers Noon and Khuhro. Mirza had succeeded in creating bad blood between the Cabinet and the all powerful Commander-in-Chief.[51]

After the imposition of Martial Law in October 1958 and the arrest of Khuhro soon after, there were a large number of stories circulating in public circles that Ayub Khan was taking his revenge for the way Khuhro had treated him. Among these were tales of how Khuhro had kept Ayub Khan waiting for an hour before he saw him when he came without an appointment, of how Ayub Khan had come to receive him in *mufti* and Khuhro had sent him to change into uniform and come back to the airport. There were stories of how Khuhro refused to stand for any nonsense from Ayub Khan who was regarded as a spoilt favourite of successive Central regimes. There was certainly a modicum of truth in these stories to the extent that Khuhro was a man who did not stand nonsense and took his duties as responsible Minister of Defence seriously. Khuhro was also very matter of fact and almost curt in his communication with the C-in-C, and not concerned to curry favour with the military.[52]

The date for the general elections in the country had been finally set for February 1959 and Noon's Government was going ahead with the preparations. The appointment of the Chief Election Commissioner was the privilege of the President and he had appointed his close friend F. M. Khan, another bridge companion. Mirza sent for Khan and told him to refuse to hold elections in February 1959 with the excuse that there was not sufficient time for the preparations and that he would need at least another year. When the Chief Election Commissioner appeared before the Cabinet he made this plea for time. The Ministers pointed out that there were at least eight months before the date for the elections which was absolutely sufficient time to complete the preparations. Khan then went to consult A. K. Brohi, the constitutional lawyer, to ask him what he should do. Brohi advised him that since his appointment by the President had already been made and the salary was paid by the Ministry it would be better if he kept on the right side of the Ministry and went ahead with the preparations on schedule. After hesitating for some weeks F. M. Khan went to Mirza and told him that he would have to hold the elections as legally advised. Mirza was furious and was casting about for other ways to postpone the elections.[53]

In July Khuhro had scheduled a programme to visit Lahore, Rawalpindi and Azad Kashmir and take the passing out parade at Kakul Academy. He was also invited to spend a couple of days with the President who was holidaying in Nathiagali. Khuhro travelled with his family to Rawalpindi by train. In Lahore the Prime Minister had called a meeting to discuss the threat of a march on the ceasefire line by the Kashmiri leader Chaudhry Ghulam Abbas. During the previous few weeks Abbas had started a movement for crossing the ceasefire line and had collected a fairly large number of volunteers. Noon called a conference at the Chief Minister's office at Lahore to consider the problem and the policy to be followed by the Government on this sensitive national issue. Apart from the service chiefs the two ex-Prime Ministers Suhrawardy and Chaudhri Mohammed Ali were also asked to be present. Chaudhri Mohammed Ali supported the move to cross the line but he was vehemently opposed by Ayub Khan who argued that if the move was supported by the government, India would make it an excuse to make war and Pakistan was not in a position to defend itself. He expressed himself very strongly and even arrogantly saying that if the movement was not stopped he would order the army on the Cease-Fire line to shoot the people trying to cross. He said, "It is for the Kashmiris to fight not for our civilian population to fight."[54] Ayub Khan was ofcourse not accurate in describing the Azad Kashmiris as 'our civilian population' but the enthusiasts were silenced especially as the other heads of services also agreed with Ayub Khan.

Khuhro was met at Rawalpindi railway station by Ayub Khan on the morning of 7 July.[55] After breakfasting with the Adjutant General at the GHQ General Shahid Hamid and Mrs. Shahid Hamid, close friends of the C-in-C, the Khuhros left for

Murree to stay there for a couple of days and then to go up to Nathiagali to be guests of the Mirzas. The day after the Khuhros reached Murree, Ayub Khan telephoned to say that he had been rung up by Mirza with an urgent message to go to Nathiagali and see him. Khuhro said that he was going to Nathiagali the next day as Mirza had asked him to arrive in time for lunch. Mirza was leaving for Turkey for a Baghdad Pact conference soon.

The Khuhros drove to Nathiagali and arrived mid morning at the President's House. As soon as they entered Ayub Khan met Khuhro and told him that he wanted to talk to him privately. They walked out in the garden where Ayub Khan told him that he was called by Mirza to discuss the possibility of abrogating the constitution and imposing Martial Law in the country. Ayub Khan told Khuhro that he felt duty bound to inform him as he was Defence Minister and his immediate boss and it was up to him to find out what Mirza was thinking. Khuhro told Mirza that he wanted to talk to him and they went to his office room. Khuhro confronted Mirza and told him what Ayub Khan had said. Mirza was taken aback particularly at the fact that Ayub Khan had told Khuhro of their confidential talk. He blustered for a time and then told Khuhro that he would never do such a thing as to abrogate the constitution and his talk with Ayub Khan had only been thinking out loud. However, he said, he had grievances against the Ministry and he did not want elections soon. He wanted the Ministry to put them off for a year. He said that he was off to Ankara and Khuhro would be going to London for a conference and when they were all back he would meet with friends such as him and Noon and discuss their differences. In the end he said,"I assure you that I will never take any steps without consulting you."[56]

Khuhro did not wholly believe Mirza but he was re-assured that Ayub Khan appeared unhappy with the idea and he knew that without his help any such action would be impossible. In these early days of the post colonial era there had been no instances of military take overs in recently liberated countries, the *coup* in Baghdad was still to happen and Khuhro whose thinking was always within constitutional limits, could not imagine that military rule or Martial Law could be extended to a whole country. His experience had been that only in small areas like cities could the military come to the aid of civilian authorities. Khuhro had seen Mirza in these spasms of anxiety and excitement before and knew well his penchant for intrigue. It had been clear for sometime that he was the prime mover in creating the disturbed political scene and the quick succession of governments.

After his visit to the Mirzas at Nathiagali Khuhro continued with his tour programme. He visited the 'cease-fire' line in Kashmir and inspected the troops and the defence arrangements in the area. He also presented the awards at the passing out parade at Kakul and inspected other defence establishments. By 16 July Khuhro was back in Karachi inaugurating the first conference of instructors and office bearers of flying clubs in Pakistan.

On 18 July a very important All Parties Conference summoned by the Central Government was opened in Karachi by the Prime Minister to discuss the arrangements regarding the country's first general election. The conference was to be attended by the Central Cabinet Ministers, officers of the Election Commission. Other invitees included delegates of all the parties of any importance and the minorities.[57] The agenda to be discussed in a closed door session included (a) fixing a date by which the demarcation of constituencies of both provincial and central legislatures was to be completed; (b) discussing polling arrangements; (c) discussing arrangements for preserving a peaceful and orderly atmosphere before and at the time of polling; (d) whether elections should be held on the same or on different dates in both wings of the country.

The Prime Minister announced that his government was determined to have a free and fair election according to an agreed schedule and that he wanted to associate all sections of public opinion 'in a vital matter like this' which was the reason for the conference. The conference was informed that the work of sorting the claims and objections to the preliminary voters' lists was almost complete and the final publication of the polls would be done by early August according to schedule.

The seriousness with which the government was pursuing its programme for elections was extremely alarming to Mirza. He and Ayub Khan returned to Karachi from Ankara in the third week of July, the Baghdad Pact conference having been cut short with the news of the blood bath in Iraq. Ayub Khan who was to accompany Khuhro to London for the meeting of Prime Ministers and Ministers of Defence of the Baghdad Pact powers in the last week of July, came to excuse himself pleading work and that he wanted to stay in the country and 'watch possible repercussions' after the Iraqi *coup*. He sent 'his best man', General Yahya Khan to the conference instead. The Prime Minister and Khuhro were in London for the conference which was attended by John Foster Dulles, the U.S. Secretary of State, Harold Macmillan the British Prime Minister and the Prime Ministers and Ministers of other Baghdad Pact countries. Khuhro remained in Europe for about two weeks after the end of the conference, visiting the World Fair in Brussels and returning home by on 22 August. On the way the P.I.A. plane stopped in Baghdad where the Ambassador came to see Khuhro at the airport but was not allowed to meet him.

The political scene in the months of September and October was chaotic. The economic situation was dire. The new president of Muslim League Qayyum Khan was leading a campaign against Mirza personally and accusing him of being the source of all the instability in the country. To a large extent this was true and because the public realised this instinctively Qayyum Khan was able to get massive support. In August when he came to Karachi to address rallies, his reception crowd at the Cantonement railway station was tear gassed. Apparently even the army officers offered to stage a *coup* with Muslim League support to pre-empt the plans to subvert the elections.[58] But although it was obvious that Mirza was unhappy with the approaching elections, it was not at all clear to the politicians to what extent the army officers were involved with him and also how closely they were in touch with the U.S. and other Western diplomats. As Khuhro said he could not imagine a huge country like Pakistan with its two wings a thousand miles apart being under a 'martial law' regime. Even the British had not attempted anything like that at crisis moments like the Quit India movement. In this however he underestimated the combination of the Pakistan army and the skills of the British Indian Political Department in the shape of Ayub Khan and Mirza.

During the summer of 1958 there was instability in the East Pakistan and frequent turmoil in the Assembly which culminated in the Deputy Speaker being fatally injured on 23 September. Mirza was now publicly criticising the working of democracy in Pakistan and advocating 'controlled democracy'. He was also encouraging everything that could alarm the military. Khuhro was astonished when Mirza spoke encouraging words about the strong anti One Unit movement in Sind. In late September Rashdi, who had seen the writing on the wall and prudently retired to the Phillipines as Ambassador, came to see Khuhro and warned him that he had just been to see Mirza and something quite serious was about to happen. He had heard enigmatic references to changes and Supreme Court Chief Justice Munir had been there being asked to co-operate. He warned Khuhro to go slow on the anti One Unit movement. Khuhro, according to Rashdi, poohpoohed any idea of danger from what he cosidered a perfectly legitimate political activity. Rashdi then drove straight to the airport and waited there till he could get the first flight out to Manila.

About this time the Khan of Kalat appeared to raise a banner of revolt against the Pakistan Government. Khuhro had just returned from a tour in the first week of October and went to call on Mirza who appeared to him to be more restless than usual talking at random or so Khuhro thought. Mirza said to him,"Do you know that the army is marching on Kalat to arrest the Khan?" Khuhro asked Mirza who had ordered his arrest and why. Mirza replied that 'It is reported that the Khan has revolted and declared independence. The Ministry might have ordered the arrest." Khuhro had not ordered any such arrest and he had no information of any declaration of independence.

As far as Khuhro knew the Khan had been asking for autonomy and a 'greater Baluchistan' for sometime. Indeed the idea had been sown in the Khan's mind by Mirza himself way back in January of that year when he had invited the Khan to stay with him in Karachi. The Khan had jumped at the idea and had immediately told the most important Baluch sardars some of whom he had summoned to Karachi. Khuhro had quickly become appraised of the situation by Mir Jaffer Khan Jamali an old friend and Muslim League colleague and other sardars from the Sind Baluchistan borders. They had told him that the Khan was in Karachi and was planning a greater Baluchistan which was to include the whole of Jacobabad district, parts of Larkana and Dadu districts and the major part of Dera Ghazi Khan in the Punjab. Khuhro then went to see the Khan who told Khuhro about his idea for a greater Baluchistan and confided that he had Mirza's support. Khuhro had confronted Mirza about this totally unscrupulous behaviour and Mirza did not even attempt to deny it. He said that he wanted to be rid of Noon and create trouble for him so that he could abrogate the constitution and bring in Martial Law for two or three months.

Meanwhile the Khan had been getting support for the idea and by the beginning of October he felt he was in a position to hold a *durbar* to announce his programme. He held the *durbar* at a place called Miri in Kalat state where he made a speech and an address was given to him on behalf of a reception committee welcoming his move. The speech had apparently been written by himself. He also hoisted a flag on the Miri fort.

The Government had then struck to order his arrest. There was no doubt that the orders to arrest the Khan were inspired by Mirza. Khuhro knew that the Khan was a very simple man and to arrest him after this put up job was a clear injustice. Khuhro protested to Mirza about the whole matter. Mirza said, "I am disgusted. You should postpone these elections. You should clear this issue between us otherwise it is no go but that I will have to bring in Martial Law. You people don't listen you are insisting on having elections." Khuhro said "Yes we are going to have elections in February" Mirza said, "But what is going to be my fate? I hear that Vicky Noon* and Shaheed Suhrawardy have come to an agreement that Feroze Noon will be the President and Suhrawardy will be Prime Minister. Vicky says she will come and live in this house. What will be my fate?"[59]

Khuhro explained patiently and with what he thought was eminent reasonableness that this was not a necessary scenario. Even if it were true that Noon and Suhrawardy had come to an agreement it need not be automatically put into effect. In East Pakistan Suhrawardy could have a majority but in West Pakistan Muslim League looked as if it would sweep the polls. Khuhro pointed out that Qayyum was succeeding in reviving public support for Muslim League at least in the Frontier and the Punjab. The Republicans could not win and would not be able to form a government, knocking out at least one half of the combination that Mirza dreaded. Muslim League and the Awami League were an unlikely combination. In any case if he was not made President, Mirza could hope for at least an ambassadorship to the U.S. or the High Commissionership. But Mirza appeared unconvinced.[60]

By this time Mirza's plans were quite advanced and Khuhro's arguments were not likely to convince him to change his mind. Khuhro could not have known that behind almost every disturbing development there was the hand of Mirza. Thus the Peshawar to Karachi march planned by Qayyum Khan,[61] the chaos in East Pakistan[62], the 'revolt' of the Khan of Kalat were all inspired by his 'hidden hand'. At the same time he was busy poisoning the mind of the generals and smoothing the path with the Western Powers for his *coup* in which Ayub Khan was to play a vital but temporary part. The plans for the takeover were about to be executed.

After leaving Mirza, Khuhro went to the Prime Minister and learnt from him that Mirza had told him directly that the Khan had revolted and that the army should be sent in to help the civilian administration to arrest the Khan. Khuhro was very perturbed. He sent for the Defence Secretary to get the details and then got in touch on the phone with General K. M. Shaikh who was in charge of the army at Quetta. General Shaikh told Khuhro that M. H. Sufi, Commissioner Quetta had asked for army support and the contingent had reached Kalat where the Khan had been arrested and was being brought back to Quetta. Apparently some firing had taken place. At the time there was nothing much that Khuhro could do. The next day Khuhro was at lunch with Qazilbash at Mir Ghulam Ali Talpur's house when they heard on the 1 o'clock news that a reshuffling of portfolios had taken place. Khuhro's portfolio of Defence had been taken over by the Prime Minister and he had been given Interior. Mir Ghulam Ali who had the Interior Ministry was now given Industries. This was a great surprise as there had been no hint given to Khuhro that this change was in the offing. Immediately after lunch Khuhro went to see Noon who was resting. Khuhro went into his bedroom woke him up and asked him why had this change been made without consulting him. Noon replied that Mirza had rung him early that morning and told him to make the change at once. He had said, "Khuhro is interfering too much in the matter of the

---

* Lady Vicarunissa Noon was the wife of the Prime Minister and a very intelligent and active woman who took great interest in social work and education.

arrest of Khan of Kalat and has asked for an explanation from G.O.C. Quetta. You must change the portfolio at once." Noon said to Khuhro placatingly, "I have compensated you by giving you Interior."[63] Khuhro was now confirmed in his knowledge that Mirza was behind the whole Kalat fiasco and that there was nothing that he could do for the Khan any more.

The endgame was being played out but the Prime Minister and his Cabinet did not suspect how close the denouement was. On 6 October the portfolios had been changed. About a week earlier some villagers of Mirpur Sakro near Thatta had come to see Khuhro in his office. They had come with a retired S.P., Israr Mohammed Khan as their spokesman. They complained that a large contingent of the army had come into their area and had been firing guns in the day as well as at night which was causing panic in the villages. Khuhro called the Defence Secretary and G.O.C. Karachi, General Sher Bahadur to find out what was going on. The next day General Sher Bahadur came to report that these were just routine annual exercises which were held in different places and that it was only a brigade or two. Khuhro learnt a bit later that a whole Division had been moved from Quetta and brought to Karachi, as it turned out, in readiness for Martial Law.

Khuhro was also informed that Ayub Khan who was due in Karachi a couple of days before 18 October to receive Robert Mcnamara, the U.S. Defence Secretary, whom Khuhro was supposed to entertain to dinner. But on 5 October G.O.C. Karachi informed Khuhro that Ayub Khan was arriving in Karachi on 7 October. On the evening of the 7th Khuhro, although no longer Defence Minister, telephoned Ayub Khan in his saloon at the railway station and asked him to come round. Ayub said that he was just going to dinner with the President but would come the next morning. Khuhro had an appointment to see Mirza that evening. Qazilbash and Mir Ghulam Ali were already with Mirza but he appeared somewhat distracted and the visitors, apart from Qazilbash, did not stay long. Khuhro had a dinner engagement at a Rotary Club dinner at the Beach Luxury Hotel where he went with his wife and daughter. In his speech to the Rotarians Khuhro spoke about the freedom struggle and the problems that had been faced by the independent state of Pakistan. He spoke about the forthcoming elections and the hopes that were pinned on those elections, particularly that the democratic process would get back on the rails and they could concentrate on building up the country.

On the way home at just before midnight Khuhro saw a number of military carriers on Kutchery Road outside the Prime Minister's House and on Victoria Road. On getting home Khuhro tried to telephone the Prime Minister's House but found his telephone cut. The next morning he read in the newspapers that the Constitution had been abrogated and Martial Law declared throughout the country.

21

TARGETED UNDER DICTATORSHIPS

Khuhro spent the day after the *coup* taking a look at this curious creature, Martial Law. He drove around Karachi. There were only a few vehicles on the road and there were military jeeps and armoured cars patrolling the city. He visited Ghulam Mohammed's and Sanaullah, the stores he sometimes shopped at in Elphinstone Street. The shops were deserted and there were only a few people about. He found the people uncertain and subdued. No one knew what to expect from the military take-over. The atmosphere was haunted by the military coup in Iraq which had occurred the previous July and which had been bloody and merciless. After his tour of the city Khuhro went to see Noon who told him the details of what had happened as far as he knew. The ADC of the President had brought him a letter after 11 o'clock the previous night and he had been woken up because of its urgency. Noon asked the ADC to wait for a possible reply but the latter said that a reply would not be needed and went away.

On the evening of the next day, October 9, Khuhro was sitting with Ghulam Faruque, Chairman P.I.D.C. and a friend of Mirza's, discussing the situation when a phone call came from his house that the army had surrounded the house and the accompanying police D.S.P. was asking for him. Khuhro at once returned to his house and was informed by the D.S.P. that he was under arrest.

Khuhro was taken to the Frere Police Station where he was not told what the charges were. A few hours later, just about mid-night the D.S.P. told him that he was being charged with black-marketing a car. This was a bailable offence and Khuhro asked that his lawyer be informed. The D.S.P. told him that he had strict instructions from the Commissioner of Karachi that other 'higher authorities' did not want him released under any circumstances. The next day Khuhro was taken to a City Magistrate at the latter's residence and the police asked for a ten-day remand for the purposes of investigation. Khuhro was put in judicial custody and taken to Karachi Central Jail that evening. Here the Superintendent of the Jail did not know where to put Khuhro and gave him a room in the hospital. The next day the Superintendent got in touch with the District Magistrate of Karachi, Muzaffar Hassan who was unable to say anything. Eventually two days later, on 12 October, the Superintendent came to Khuhro and told him that he was now an A class prisoner and would be given his own room and could get his food from home. Otherwise he was entitled to Rs. 10 a day and a servant to cook the food. Khuhro opted for home cooked food. He was also entitled to some facilities like a table lamp and some extra furniture. G. M. Syed had also been arrested a few days earlier and was in a different part of the jail but Khuhro and he were able to communicate with each other in writing and mostly through the verses of Shah Abdul Latif.[1]

Eventually Khuhro was informed of the charges against him that he had sold a car at a higher price than that fixed by the government. The charge was quite clearly inapplicable since at the time of the sale there was no law restricting the price of second hand cars. The restrictions were introduced only after the imposition of Martial Law. Khuhro was eventually to be fully exonerated by a unanimous judgement of the Supreme Court but before that went through a period of great mental and physical stress which he faced with indomitable courage.

Khuhro was clearly the victim of the regime's desire to show that the politicians were corrupt and dishonest particularly those at the top. The *coup* needed a 'show trial' not only for the public at home but especially to impress Western governments. The world had to be shown the depths of corruption in the parliamentary regime and the new regime was ruthless enough to cold bloodedly plan a false case against someone they knew was innocent.[2]

The case against Khuhro was prosecuted at a time when Martial Law was a completely new experience and no one knew what to expect. The entire country was on tenterhooks. The torrent of Martial Law regulations, reports of the proceedings in Martial Law courts and the terror of the rule of men in uniform had over awed and frightened the people. In these circumstances Khuhro was put in jail to be tried under charges which were untenable under the law and of which, under different circumstances, any common or garden court would have completely exonerated him. But the Special Judge trying Khuhro's case was certainly not made of the stuff which could withstand the fear of Martial Law. Khuhro immediately engaged A. K. Brohi who told him that although the charge was untenable, the courts were so intimidated by Martial Law that he he could not hope to get bail from a lower court and perhaps even the High Court and the case would in all probability have to go to the Supreme Court. This assessment proved to be absolutely correct. By the end of October the case had still not started and Khuhro was denied bail by the Special Judge who was trying his case under Martial Law.

He was also denied bail by the High Court in early November. The case finally started its hearings on 12th December in the court of the Special Judge, Kambar Ali Mirza. Khuhro pleaded not guilty:

"In a brief statement he told the court `it is true that I purchased the car and had sold it outright. But the allegations against me are false. There is no element of black market in the deal.'Clad in a light blue Gaberdine suit, the former Defence Minister stood in the witness box for about ten minutes and quietly listened to the judge reading out the one page accusation against him."[3]

The prosecution's case was flimsy. The witnesses put up by the police were easily exposed[4] and it was clearly apparent that it was a put up job, but even so the outcome was very much in doubt because of the special circumstances surrounding the case.

The proceedings ended on 22 February and the judgement was delivered by the Special Judge on the 26th. On that day the court was packed full and there was a large crowd outside. Even for those who knew that the Special Judge would not dare go for an acquittal and that this was a 'show trial', the verdict was a shock.

Under Martial Law Regulation No. 26, Khuhro was awarded 5 years rigorous punishment and a fine of Rs. 1,50,000 on the charge of selling his Chevrolet car on the black-market. He was given (C) class in jail. Khuhro who knew that acquittal from this court was highly unlikely took the verdict calmly and was unruffled even when he was handcuffed in the court and taken to jail. The Superintendent was in a quandry as to how to enforce this judgement. The jail authorities gave out that Khuhro was ill and put him for the time being in the hospital ward. Three days later Khuhro was given (A) class.

A writ petition was filed in Sind High Court as well as bail application but as Brohi had predicted, none of these were successful. The High Court bench with Chief Justice Kayani and Justice Wahiduddin Ahmed gave a judgement tailored to suit the times when they ruled that the Special Judge had the jurisdiction to try the case under Martial Law and that they had no right to revise the decision of the lower court. But 'their Lordships said that they would make no order as to costs *since we ourselves have been in doubt from time to time while hearing this case as to the correct legal position.*'[5] At the same time the case against Khuhro had been bifurcated and another case of cheating was made out and transferred to be tried in Dadu district. This case proceeded just after the end of the first one and finally on February 1960 Khuhro was acquitted of the charge in this case by an unusually fearless judge, Justice Azizullah Memon, the Special Anti Corruption Judge, Dadu.

Immediately after the High Court judgement Khuhro had filed an appeal in the Supreme Court and had been released on bail at once. On 5 April 1960 a full bench of the Supreme Court consisting of Chief Justice Munir, Justice M. Shahabuddin, Justice A. R. Cornelius, Justice Amiruddin Ahmed and Justice S. A. Rahman started hearing the appeal. The hearing lasted till 11th April. By this time Brohi had been appointed High Commissioner to India and H. S. Suhrawardy was representing Khuhro. When Suhrawardy had come to know that Brohi had left the case he had offered to represent Khuhro and moreover had refused to take any fees. It was a magnificent gesture from Suhrawardy who had more often than not been Khuhro's political opponent and with whom he had at least one historic debating encounter in the Constituent Assembly. Suhrawardy worked hard and argued his case brilliantly.

On 19 April the Supreme Court, in a unanimous judgement, accepted the appeal, quashing the conviction and the sentence by the lower court and held that the entire proceedings before the Special Judge void and *coram non judice*. On the substance of the case it held that there was no independent evidence to support the accusation. The Supreme Court issued what amounted to a reprimand to the Special Judge that he had not mentioned one word on the vital point that no independent evidence had been offered but also that 'he was confirming something that did not exist in law'. In a precisely argued judgement the Supreme Court Bench fully exonerated Khuhro:

"In fairness to the Deputy Administrator [Martial Law], and the Administrator [Martial Law], because it appears that the sentence has been confirmed by him as well, we should mention that from the manner in which the judgement was written by the Special Judge it was impossible for the confirming authority to appreciate the legal and factual aspect of the case or to separate the alleged Martial Law offence from the alleged pre Martial Law black-market deal for which the appellant was admittedly not tried. The Court which tried this Martial Law offence was not set up by the Administrator; nor was the case sent to that Court by the Administrator himself. The jurisdictional aspect of criminal Courts, especially where it raises intricate questions of law was a matter with which he was not supposed to be conversant. Therefore when he confirmed the sentence, he could not have been conscious of the position that what he was confirming was something that did not exist in law or that he was purporting to validate what could not be validated. On the merits apart from the statement of Abdullah Khan who is a pardoned accomplice that the appellant came to his show room on 8th of October and asked him to finalize the deal, there is no other evidence of any act or omission by the appellant subsequent to the promulgation of Regulation No. 26... it cannot possibly be contended that these statements [of other witnesses as well] are admissible evidence against the appellant or that they amount to independent corroboration. And in the absence of such corroboration, the prosecution took a grave risk in separating the charge under the Hoarding and Black-market Order from that under Martial Law Regulation No. 26. An officer of the Special Judge's experience could not be unaware that law requires corroboration of an accomplice by "independent evidence", and that an accomplice's own previous statements or the confession of a co-accused is not corroboration by independent evidence. There was however not one word in the judgement on this vital point for the consideration of the confirming authority.

We accept the appeals and quash the convictions and sentence of the appellant."[6]

The ordeal was over. Khuhro's own steadfast belief in the the tenets of Islam, the conviction that life itself was a trial, had sustained him and he had presented a calm, unagitated and unfazed face to the world even at the moment of deep worldly humiliation. Now the letters of congratulation and good wishes he got from all over the country, from Sind both from Sindhi and Urdu Speakers, from the Punjab, from friends as well as strangers, gave him renewed faith.

****

In April 1959 when he was finally released from jail after nearly six months of confinement and had won the appeal in the Supreme Court, Khuhro was 58 years of age. His domestic life was on an even keel mainly due to the steadfast and patient management of his wife who faced the most difficult situations with unwavering confidence. Their children were being brought up by her almost singlehandedly as Khuhro's political life and zamindari work came increasingly to occupy all his time. In 1957 Khuhro had moved from the official residence which had been occupying on Khuhro Road into the house that he had built in the Civil Lines.* His children were growing up. His daughter had just gone to Cambridge to read History. While Khuhro was still in prison his eldest son Shah Mohammed, who was at Aitichison College in Lahore, had to leave school to attend to zamindari concerns in Larkana. His younger sons were still at school. His arrest and trial gave a chance to Khuhro to become aware of the goodwill and support that he enjoyed in the province and in the country. Letters of concern and prayers poured

---

* Khuhro Road originally known as Scandal Point Road stretched from Lovers Bridge from Queens Road (now Maulvi Tamizuddin Road) to turn into Drigh Road (now Shahrahe Faisal). The road had been renamed Khuhro Road by Karachi Municipality to honour Khuhro as an important freedom fighter. This was changed after the imposition of Martial Law into Club Road.

in while he was in jail. Fakirs and saints from all over the country offered their prayers and predicted his exoneration. Most satisfactory were the letters of support from ordinary people whom he had helped or who had looked to him as a true public servant and their champion all their lives. They and their families had prayed for him when he was being tried under the colonial regime in Sukkur in 1944 and they prayed for him now when the Martial Law regime was trying him in 1959.

After his release Khuhro needed to take his bearings in the unfamiliar situation. Political life as he knew it all his life appeared to be at an end. New parameters were being drawn up for public life in which free association and free speech was threatened. The Press rushed to praise the new regime. It had been an article of faith for Khuhro and his colleagues in the All India Muslim League that freedom from colonial rule would mean a constitutional and democratic system. They did not dream that the military and bureaucracy which they regarded as creations of the colonial power would end up as masters of the country for which freedom had been so hardly won. It was painful in the extreme to see the transports of delight that the newspapers displayed at the forcible crushing of the democratic rights of the people and the apathy and confusion of the people.

Since he had first entered political life in the early 1920s Khuhro had seen his role clearly. He had come into the political arena with certain goals in mind, the attainment of democratic rights for the people of his province with all the accoutrements of rights and benefits that they could demand in a democratic dispensation. In pursuit of this goal he had fought the fight in the Bombay presidency, taken up the challenge of achieving autonomy for Sind as a fully-fledged autonomous province of a federal India, and then had put Sind behind the All India Muslim League and its demand for the self-determination of the Muslim majority provinces. When the colonial power left behind a partitioned India with the states of Bharat and Pakistan, Khuhro had worked indefatigably to make a success of the new state. He had firmly believed that by continuing and completing the process of democracy and by fulfilling the promise made in the Lahore Resolution of 1940, the provinces would enjoy the fullest autonomy and would fulfil the expectations of the people for freedom and emancipation. Even in the darkest period of the machinations by the Central ruling clique he had not lost hope and had joined Sir Firoze Khan Noon's government to see to it that elections took place and democracy was put back on track. This election would have been the death knell of the ruling clique and it had not been allowed to occur. The unthinkable had happened instead and a military bureaucratic coup had taken place.

Now for the first time in his life Khuhro found that there was no political work for him to do. So far whether in or out of office there had been Muslim League work and public work which had taken up most of his life. Khuhro realised instinctively that the political scene had changed fundamentally and that he would find it difficult to come to terms with the changes. There was no room for the kind of independent thinking, leadership and public dealing that Khuhro was used to practicing. His kind of leadership although it had a wide public following and acceptance and indeed popularity, had been rendered obsolete. Now political life depended on proximity to and acceptance by the military dictator.

The 'establishment' of military and bureaucracy was the ruler now. The new breed of politicians accepted this basic fact and tailored its behaviour accordingly.

The fact was ofcourse that the 'establishment' needed a number of tame politicians as a conduit to the public. Pakistan was a multi ethnic, multi lingual and multi cultural state. The public was cowed and confused in the early stages of Martial Law but the fear would wear off with familiarity. Ayub Khan was clever enough to know that he could not use the army to rule directly for any length of time. He needed the 'collaborators' to ease the relationship of the regime with the public at large. For this an army of second rank politicians was to come in very useful. There was any number of politicians who were able to make the transition. For the front ranking politicians of the pre 1947 vintage, of whom Khuhro was a prominent member, the situation was unfamiliar and in many cases completely distasteful.

Initially the restrictions against leading politicians ruled out normal political activity for them. When these restrictions came to an end within four years or so these leaders thought they had found a role in opposing the military dictator and backed Jinnah's sister as symbol of the principles on which Pakistan had been founded. But the ground rules had been changed by the regime which made this election a lost cause. Even with huge public support Miss Jinnah could not win because the electorate was limited and corrupted.* Powerful forces that had been the 'steel frame' of the colonial power had now asserted themselves finally and nakedly against the fledgling democratic forces and won. Khuhro and his colleagues became the victims of this turn of fortune in history. Throughout the years of Ayub Khan's dictatorships and the subsequent Yahya and Bhutto regimes Khuhro would be facing malevolent and vengeful administrations which were bent on making life as difficult as possible for him and those who spoke out.

The military dictatorship would spawn its own brand of politicians. The large majority of these would be the 'yes men' who would do their masters' bidding and collect the meagre crumbs from their table. But there was also the opportunity for the more clever of them to use the situation to make their fame and fortunes. Among these was Z. A. Bhutto who started his career as a young lawyer picked up by Iskander Mirza on the Iranian grid (both Bhutto's and Mirza's second wives were Iranian), and made Minister in the first Martial Law cabinet. He was able to use his position as Minister in the Martial Law cabinets both under Mirza and under Ayub by a clever mix of flattery and hard work to get close to the dictator and get prominent posts in the regime. Along with the favoured position came massive publicity and rare opportunities. As luck would have it Bhutto also came from Larkana, Khuhro's home district. The most dramatic moments in the closing years of Khuhro's political career would be those of confrontation with this most prominent member of the new breed of politicians.

On his release from jail in April 1959 Khuhro had first to deal with problem of 'land reforms' of Ayub Khan which had been announced in early January that year when Khuhro had been still in jail. The authorities demanded that full details of land holdings were to be handed in immediately. He dealt with this while he was still in detention. He was allowed one visit per week when he saw his family and dealt with the *kamdars* who had travelled up from Larkana with copies of the records which were required. He also carried on with the routine *zamindari* work which was more onerous with the death of his brother, Mian Mohammed Nawaz, a few years earlier.

As in most *zamindari* families the family landholdings were difficult to disen-

---
* See below in the Chapter.

tangle. Officials who knew that the regime was hostile to Khuhro, acted accordingly. A good deal of land was lost because of hostile decisions by the officers in charge of implementing the reforms. Even when the matter had supposedly been finalised, regimes under three dictatorships would be revive the question again and again just to harass Khuhro and indeed other opponents of the regimes. Khuhro proved his mettle as a true fighter and for the next 17 years kept on fighting the cases as they were revived again and again.

The Khuhro family lost a great deal of land in the reforms. Others who were in favour of the regime or who had fore knowledge and had taken pre-emptive action by subdividing their land holdings in time. Khuhro gave up land in the districts of Larkana, Khairpur and Dadu and although theoretically (Martial Law Regulation No. 64) those surrendering land were to get compensation somewhere near its market value, Khuhro was given a minimum price fixed for the surrendered land. A mere Rs. 60 per acre where the minimum market price was Rs. 2,000 per acre, and that too in government bonds recoverable in 20 years![7] In fact the compensation was a fiction.

In Khuhro's considered opinion the land reforms were misdirected and quite wrong for the country particularly if crops were to be produced efficiently. The example of Egypt and Iraq was there before the eyes of the Pakistan government. The so-called reforms under President Nasser and the revolutionary regime in Iraq, had transformed these rich agricultural countries from being exporters of agricultural produce to becoming importers of even food grain. Ayub had not consulted the public and his announcement of land reform had a great deal of posturing in it. The intrinsic value of the measure was much less in evidence when they were implemented. In a memo written a few years later Khuhro pointed out the mistaken nature of these 'reforms':

"Land Reforms introduced by Ayub Khan in 1959-60 have in fact done no good to our country. Most of the lands surrendered have gone out of cultivation as *haris* who were given such lands on easy instalments and at a very low rate of Rs. 225/- per acre, payable in 25 yearly instalments, have in many cases failed to pay even such easy instalments and lands have been either auctioned to other purchasers or have been abandoned."[8]

To make the reforms work much more homework needed to be done and local conditions to be taken into consideration. It was Khuhro's considered opinion which he had voiced earlier on several occasions that the matter should properly have been left to the provincial legislatures to work out thoroughly. Moreover the division of land into small holdings was self defeating in a Muslim country where the law of inheritance resulted in a continuous process of reduction in the size of holdings. Khuhro argued that small size holdings were economically unviable:

"Agriculture should be treated as industry. Modern type of cultivation requires machinery like tractors etc. purchased or hired from the government. These are very expensive and so also are fertilizers and insecticides. It is not possible for an owner of 200 or 300 acres in Sind to afford it, to develop his land and to keep it in proper condition. Nor can he easily buy these expensive fertilizers or get his crops sprayed against various diseases. Naturally in such cases either the crops will fail or the output will be low and therefore uneconomic. There should be proper economic holdings and in Sind lands being inferior due to excessive salt, an economic holding will not be less than 500 acres or say 18,000 product units. Land ceilings should only be worked out according to product units. Lands on the Right Bank of the river Indus, generally are not very fertile in districts of Thatta, Dadu, Larkana and also western parts of Sukkur district are inferior in quality. Small land holders are usually promised loans from Agricultural Development Bank or Government Taqavi loans. But these loans bear a heavy rate of interest upto 9% or 10% and besides borrowers have to pay bribes and commissions to bank officials to secure such loans. The result is that in most cases these small *khatedars* are unable to pay back such loans and they are continuously harassed by local officials for recovery of such loans and their cattle and other belongings or even lands are sold to recover these loans. In most cases however loans are not recovered despite all such efforts.

Lands in the Punjab are far better and more productive than those in Sind. Consequently limit of such holdings which is already quite low should be determined according to fertility of the soil in different areas i.e. according to product units.

I may also point out that the Indo–Pakistan sub-continent is being helped by the supply of large quantities of food grains by those countries like the U.S.A., Canada, Australia and West Germany, who have not imposed any limit on their holdings. As against that India will always be in a plight facing acute food shortages because of the holding being too small. Besides in our country there is the Muslim law of inheritance, hence in the next ten or fifteen years there will be an acute problem of small and uneconomic holdings. People will lose interest in lands altogether as they will be quite uneconomic, resulting in most of the areas going out cultivation. This actually happened in Southern India even in the days of British rule, because of the Ryotwari system in Bombay and Madras provinces."[9]

****

In the meanwhile Ayub Khan had started to create a group of people with a vested interest in supporting the Ayub regime. First of all in August 1959 he had promulgated EBDO (Elective Bodies Disqualification Order) Tribunal to disqualify all the leading politicians in the country and approximately 7,000 politicians had been disqualified throughout East and West Pakistan. Khuhro was disqualified on the convenient ground that he had previously been disqualified under PRODA in 1954.[10] As there were no specific charges there was no point in contesting the disqualification. Political parties were banned, their offices closed and their record as well as their funds had been siezed by the time Khuhro was free from the case.

By the end of 1960 the so-called Basic Democracy system was put in place. Elections under this system took place in December 1960. There was massive publicity and for the first time in Pakistan modern propaganda methods were on a Goebellian scale. 'Basic Democracy' was publicised as being 'suited to the genius of the people.' A village or group of villages elected a number of representatives, about 8 or 15 according to population size which became the village council. In towns, committees were formed according to *mohallas* and each chairman of the Committee automatically became member of the municipality. Thus the number of municipal committees was greatly reduced. In Sukkur for example, with a population of nearly 200,000, the number of councillors was only about 15. The Chairman of the Municipality was a bureaucrat who acted as administrator and a number of other officials were also nominated on to the Municipal Committees which meant that the official proposals were always carried no matter how inappropriate they were or whether they had the backing of the people. The system took democracy back to 1895 when the Ripon reforms had first introduced the local bodies which had a mixture of elected and nominated people and an official, usually the European Collector presided. For the Collector, the official Administrator had been substituted but otherwise it appeared that the intervening long struggle for self-government and democracy which had lasted for three quarters of the century had been cancelled and the people of Pakistan were back to the tutelage which had started in the 19th century.

The main function of the BDs as the representatives elected under the Basic Democracies system were called, was to attend meetings whenever any minister or high official came to the city and to listen to his harangue patiently and unquestioningly. Most people of doubtful character got elected, police informers and sycophants or whoever the officials cared to put up or support. No politician contested for BD seats and in rural areas the *zamindars* who would contest the elections for the provincial or central assemblies put up their nominees. Khuhro also put up some of the people from his area who duly became BDs.

The total number of BDs in the country was 80,000, in a country of over 100 million people. The BDs formed an electoral college for the election of the President.[11] The BD system was a great pet of Ayub Khan and those surrounding him took to praising it extravagantly in a bid to gain his favour. They loudly proclaimed the genius of Ayub Khan who had so miraculously associated the people with democracy and that they were now in charge of their own affairs in the villages! One of the foremost proponents of the system was Z. A. Bhutto. Once when the Shah of Iran was visiting Pakistan, so the story went, Ayub Khan asked Bhutto to explain the wonders of the BD system to him. He did so enthusiastically and suggested that the Shah could not go wrong in introducing the system into his own country. The Shah, it was reported, listened politely.

The worst fallout of the system under Ayub was the insidious corruption it introduced. The Government started giving liberal grants to BD committees ostensibly for building offices, schools, roads, water supply etc. Though these were much needed improvements the monitoring was in the hands of bureaucrats without any political oversight. The result was that the local officials who were chairmen etc.of the committees shared out the cash between themselves and the BDs. This was in fact the intention of the government which wanted to create a vested interest in maintaining the regime and were willing to bribe the BDs to do so. No noticeable improvement took place in the villages.

At the same time as the BD system was invented propaganda was unleashed against the existing social system. Ayub Khan needed to legitimise his destruction of the original parliamentary and democratic system and its replacement with army dictatorship. This could only be done if the previous system was depicted as corrupt and pernicious beyond redemption. Traditionally the *zamindar* class had not only been responsible for cultivating the land and producing the resources on which the state had depended for its survival; it was also responsible for keeping the peace, keeping an eye on any mischievous elements in the area and in most cases, arbitrating in case of disputes, deciding the compensations to be paid and when in rare cases it was necessary, handing over criminals to the state. As a result the rate of crime was very low, criminals were known and the matter of their capture simple. It was a society remarkably free from crime–cattle lifting or *crime passionnel* being the major forms in which it was manifested.

The fact that a sizeable number of *zamindars* supported Miss Jinnah against Ayub Khan in the Presidential Elections of 1964 confirmed the regime in its anti *zamindar* policy. It determined to destroy the reputation of this class. Now for the first time in the history of Pakistan a deliberate campaign was launched to malign the *zamindars*, the leaders and respected elders of the rural and agricultural Pakistan, which in effect meant more than 85% of Pakistan. Through the press and film and then through the new and powerful medium of television, through beguiling stories and tales of horror, the *zamindars* were depicted as cruel monsters sucking the blood of the people, raping women and marauding in the countryside. This maligning of all people with influence in the rural areas such as landowners, tribal heads, *Pirs* and so on was to continue and become the stock in trade of the media in Pakistan undermining a stable society without putting anything else in its place. This campaign of vilification led inevitably to friction and the loosening of the ties of society and consequent chaos and rampant crime. The next two decades would amply bear witness to this malevolent policy.

In February 1960 Ayub Khan obtained a vote of confidence from the BDs confirming him as President. This had been managed with careful planning.[12] But the public of Pakistan refused to be satisfied with the BD system and there was a growing demand for political activity in the country. In a country such as Pakistan, with a nearly a hundred years of party politics and more than half century of at least some degree of democratic and parliamentary rule; with one half of the country separated from the other by a thousand miles of Indian territory, it was impossible even for the self-confident Martial Law regime of Ayub Khan to expect indefinite acquiescence. The clamour for political parties to be allowed to function and to play their part in reviving democracy grew. There was increasing criticism of the system being put in place by Ayub. The Field Marshal was ofcourse surrounded by sycophants and yes men,[13] who praised his amazing sagacity and were joined by foreign commentators who compared him to Solon and Lycurgus[14] and advised him that politicians were inherently bad and that the best form of government for the country was centralised or even unitary.

In the end it became obvious even to Ayub Khan that the public was not taken in by the facade of consensus presented by the unanimous vote of the BDs and wanted some genuine political set up in the country. The election held under the system of Basic Democracies in 1959 and 1964 as well as for the national and provincial assemblies in April, May 1962, were partyless and members were elected as individuals. There was a growing public demand for political activity and the revival of political parties. The period of the EBDO ban had been used by the religious parties to extend their influence, as religious activities could not be banned. The 'secular' parties had suffered a severe setback in comparison and this was to have an enduring effect on the political and social atmosphere of Pakistan. At the same time most of the members elected to the Assemblies were connected to the much maligned politicians. It became very difficult for Ayub Khan to control the Assembly members not bound by party discipline and he looked round for some means to remedy the situation. By July 1962 Ayub Khan perforce agreed to the revival of political parties. A Political Parties Bill was enacted allowing political parties subject to restrictions. Ayub also adopted a political party himself.

The party Ayub Khan decided to hijack was the founding party of Pakistan – Muslim League – as his close associates had advised him that he could cash in on the residual goodwill of this party. The convention of the revived Muslim League was held in September 1962 at the newly built Aquarium building at Clifton in Karachi.

The whole show was dominated by Ayub Khan's Ministers and the two Governors. Nawab Kalabagh, the Governor of West Pakistan was the main organizer. It was arranged that only selected people were allowed to speak. The Convention Muslim League as it became known was not at all like the original party. Meanwhile the leadership of the old Muslim League decided to revive the real Muslim League. They met in August 1962 in Karachi and decided to call a Council in Dacca on 22 and 23 October 1962 to form the party which was called Council Muslim League to differentiate it from the Convention Muslim League.

Khuhro travelled from Karachi to Dacca to attend the Council as did Daultana from the Punjab, Sardar Bahadur Khan, Yusuf Khattak and others. Abdul Qayyum Khan the previous President of the Party had not come and Khwaja Nazimuddin who had retired from active politics was persuaded to become President although he was quite reluctant to take on the responsibility. Khuhro who did not have very cordial relations with Khwaja Nazimuddin in the past accepted him with good grace and co-operated with him fully. The Punjab Frontier group however abandoned their support for him within a few months.

By the end of 1962 there were strong differences between Daultana, Sardar Bahadur Khan and Khwaja Nazimuddin. The former wanted close co-operation with Suhrawardy's National Democratic Front. Khwaja Nazimuddin was for keeping the Council Muslim League separate and distinct with its own agenda and not move towards the Conventionists or to the Front.

Between September and December 1964 the second Basic Democrat elections were to take place in the country this time with political parties. The 80,000 BDs were then to form the electoral college to elect the President. In Sind, Zulfiqar Ali Bhutto was put in charge to ensure the election of members who would support Ayub Khan. Khuhro toured Sind exhaustively and was able to win a lot of support. Alarmed at this challenge Bhutto set about applying official pressure. An atmosphere of terror was created. District Magistrates gave the police signed warrants without names to arrest anyone they wanted outside the polling stations. Locally influential people were threatened with arrest. Bogus voting papers were given to people and large scale false voting took place. For the first time in Pakistan rigging and even terrorism were blatantly used in elections. The Opposition candidates sent a telegram to the Election Commission which they released for publication pointing out that the elections were far from fair:

"Elections in Larkana District are being rigged and manipulated at the active instigation of Zulfiqar Ali Bhutto, Foreign Minister who has been in Larkana since nominations for Basic Democracy Elections were filed on fifteenth October and before that date. Wherever Government party candidates are likely to lose in elections he gets false votes put in the box of the Government side candidates through Presiding Officers or Returning Officers.

In several cases truck loads of *goondas* armed with guns hatchets and *lathis* create fight if Government side is losing in election and such voting is forcibly stopped. In some cases elections have actually been stopped. Also there are cases where result on site is declared by the Presiding Officer in favour of Opposition candidate yet the Returning Officer overnight changes and next day Government candidate is declared elected. *Goonda* action and free fight with hatchet and *lathis* is freely resorted to. It is quite clear that the Government dont want to do free and fair elections. They want to defeat Opposition candidates at all costs. It is obvious therefore that the promises and public statements of the President Muhammad Ayub Khan and the Governor West Pakistan are only meant to mislead the public. Why this mockery of fake elections?"[15]

Bhutto was personally presiding over the Larkana elections. He had publicly announced that he would withdraw from his office (as Foreign Minister) if the official party i.e. Convention Muslim League did not get 80% of the seats in Sind.[16] His personal interest was therefore deeply involved in ensuring success for government candidates. Harassment of the Opposition included incidents of actually firing guns on government opponents. The jeep of Khuhro's eldest son, Shah Mohammed was the target of one attack and although he was not in the jeep two of the workers in the vehicle were killed and the driver was hit. In due course Bhutto would perfect the art of harassment and rigging and make it so foolproof so that it would continue to be practiced for the next thirty years.

In the summer of 1964 the candidates for presidential election due early the next year had been selected. Ayub Khan was running for the office and miraculously the Opposition parties made a brilliant choice in Miss Fatima Jinnah. Miss Jinnah had been persuaded with some difficulty to stand. She was a symbol of the nation's longing for democracy and a fitting answer to the first dictator of Pakistan.

For Ayub Khan's elections preparations were carefully made. A great deal of money was collected from industrialists. His Minister for Commerce and Industries told Khuhro that he expected to collect 3 crores from Karachi and 3 crores from the rest of West Pakistan.[17] Most of the money collected was spent in East Pakistan. Even as prominent a leader as Maulana Bhashani was reported to have been heavily bribed.[18] In West Pakistan official coercion made money less necessary. Miss Jinnah made wildly popular election tours in both wings of the country and worked hard inspite of her age. There were some murmurings among her supporters about her acerbic temperament but Khuhro found her quite easy to work with, her blunt style matching his own. In a free vote there was no question that she would have won the election. But the dice was heavily loaded against the Opposition: official interference and propaganda were very strong and sometimes took a farcical form, as for instance when the government cut off electricity when Miss Jinnah was due to speak at public meetings and blacked out or censored her broadcasts on the rare occasions when she was permitted to speak on television and radio. In the circumstances it was impossible for Miss Jinnah to win.

In Larkana where Khuhro was personally overseeing the election as was Bhutto for Ayub, Miss Jinnah got 35% of the vote which was an excellent result under the circumstances. The election was lost but the Opposition leaders, particularly Miss Jinnah, did not let this defeat perturb them. On the 27 of January Khuhro gave a big dinner party in honour of Miss Jinnah at his house, to which all the Opposition leaders as well as well-known Karachi citizens were invited. The mood at the dinner was almost that of victory much to the bewilderment of the official side.

22

INTIMATIONS OF DISASTER

In February 1965 Khuhro got a call from Zulfiqar Ali Bhutto asking for a meeting and asked him to lunch at his house in Karachi. Ostensibly the purpose of his visit was to persuade Khuhro to petition Ayub Khan to condone the remaining 2 years of his disqualification from politics under EBDO. Bhutto painted a rosy picture of how he would ensure that the petition was immediately accepted. Khuhro declined politely pointing out that he had waited out 5 years and could wait for the other two without any problem. There was no question of him filing the petition.[1]

Possibly Bhutto wanted to make points with Ayub Khan by getting politicians to give *maafi namas* as they came to be called but it was more likely that Bhutto was there to show off. At the lunch Bhutto was extremely confident and full of himself. He talked nonstop and told Khuhro that he had advised Ayub Khan to have a one party state like Kwame Nkrumah of Ghana and that all the district officials would be office holders of the party, for instance the Deputy Commissioner would be the local President of the party, the Superintendent of Police would be Secretary, etc. Khuhro was astonished and told him that would be the last nail in the coffin of democracy and the people would never accept it. Bhutto was not talking idly however. When later he became head of state and then Prime Minister he made certain that government servants were sufficiently subservient to the party to behave almost as though they were party members although public opinion proved to be sufficiently strong, even with the years of dictatorship, to make it impossible for him to formally declare a one party state.

At this time Bhutto was Foreign Minister having reached these unimaginable heights in a very short time. He was Ayub's trusted man in Sind. He was a young man just thirty years of age, having started his bar practice in Karachi when he returned from the U.S. and Oxford. He had been taken up to be Minister in Iskander Mirza's Cabinet after the coup of 1958 as the token Sindhi. Here he had worked hard and gained the confidence first of Mirza and then of Ayub Khan when the latter had kept him on in the Cabinet after he had got rid of Mirza. He had taken special care to win the trust of Ayub Khan and was widely regarded as his 'blue eyed boy' and was thought to have a father son relationship with him. At the same time he had cultivated a close friendship with several Generals at the Rawalpindi headquarters when the capital moved there from Karachi in the early 'sixties.

Bhutto was clever enough to realise that advancement in public life in the post military coup period lay in the favour of the military bureaucratic establishment and deliberately chose that path to political power. That this was largely a deliberate choice is illustrated by an incident which Bhutto often related when he was Chief Martial Law Administrator in 1972. When Bhutto had just returned from the U.S.A. his father Sir Shahnawaz then living in retirement in Karachi had sent him to Khuhro to get his advice about getting into politics. Bhutto recalled that Khuhro had told him to join a political party first of all and work for it, fight an election for local bodies and when he had gained enough experience to apply for a party ticket for the provincial or central legislature. Bhutto would laughingly relate this story and remark that if he had taken Khuhro's advice he would still be a local bodies member. This was ofcourse how Khuhro had built his own career and he believed firmly in the due process of democratic preferment.

The contrast between Khuhro and Bhutto could not have been greater. There were however superficial similarities. Both came from zamindar background and from the same district of Larkana but there the similarities ended. Khuhro was rooted in his background and had deep seated principles on which he had based his political career. He was secure in himself and therefore not buffeted about by the fluctuating fortunes of politics. Khuhro understood traditional society which had a healthy concern for the mutual rights and obligations of the different sections of the society and the limits within which each operated. Of corporate loyalties and a belief in negotiation – 'pactism' of the so-called 'feudal' system Bhutto on the other hand had no knowledge or apprehension of how it worked except in the crudest way. These rights and obligations had missed him by as he strove for the narrowly selfish individualism that he had seen in the West and thought of as the only way forward. He belonged to the new breed of politicians par excellence. He had the slightest acquaintance with traditional Sindhi society from which he had been uprooted at an early age. He had spent his life in westernized Bombay and then gone to college in the U.S.A. He aspired to the fashionable shibboleths of the day which meant for him the 'one party state' at this time and would mean 'socialism' later when he fell out with Ayub Khan.

As the military dictator's favourite Bhutto was very powerful. He was using this to establish his power base in Sind and particularly in Larkana. Kalabagh who was considered the absolute ruler of West Pakistan used to say on many occasions that his writ did not work in Sind because that was Bhutto's exclusive domain. Larkana was ofcourse treated as his particular fief.

Bhutto had a streak of jealousy and intolerance which was not suppressed even when he was enjoying such an eminent position in the country. His intolerance was particularly directed against Khuhro as the following incident shows. Khuhro had been the founding President of the Pakistan Indonesian Cultural Association for sometime when Bhutto became Foreign Minister. During this period Brigadier General Roekmito Hendraningrat was the Indonesian Ambassador to Pakistan. He had very cordial relations with Khuhro. President Soekarno was to visit Pakistan in 1963. As Foreign Minister, Bhutto was to receive him at Karachi airport. Khuhro as President of the Pakistan Indonesian Cultural Association was to be at the airport to greet Soekarno and later he was also to have an interview with the Indonesian President. When Bhutto came to know of this he told Roekmito that if

Khuhro was to meet Soekarno the Cultural Association would not get recognition from the Government of Pakistan. Surprised and embarrassed, Roekmito called the Secretary of the Association Mahmudul Aziz and told him of Bhutto's ultimatum. Aziz assured Roekmito that Khuhro was an experienced statesman and would find a way out of the situation. Aziz went to see Khuhro and explained what had happened. Khuhro calmly told Aziz that

"relations between Pakistan and Indonesia were more important to him than his own person. Mr. Bhutto was acting like a child but that was to be expected. However Mr. Khuhro said he could not act in the same manner as Bhutto and he would apologise to the Ambassador that he could not be present at the airport as he would be out of Karachi on tour and that the Vice President Hakim Ahson would be in the receiving line instead."[2]

Thus saving a very embarrassing situation Khuhro went off to his lands and Ahson deputised for him. Khuhro who could not resign while the Indonesian President was in Pakistan had found a way out, but he knew that Bhutto would probably create other incidents if he stayed on as President so he resigned soon afterwards. Sometime after Khuhro had entertained him to lunch Bhutto was to be summarily dismissed by Ayub Khan who had nurtured his career so thoroughly for the previous eight years.

****

During these years from 1960 while Bhutto had been forging ahead with his extraordinary career Khuhro's political activities had been marginalised by EBDO, the regulation instituted by Ayub Khan in August 1959 to disqualify politicians from taking part in political activities. Khuhro tried to take advantage of the atmosphere favouring industry to set up some agro based industry in Sind. He had set up a number of companies and got the capital together from banks which were still private at that time.[3] But every time he approached the government for the necessary permissions he came up against a brick wall. In the end he was told unofficially by the Nawab of Kalabagh, the Governor of West Pakistan, that he was being opposed by Bhutto. If any matter of official high-handedness was brought to his attention Kalabagh would say that he was helpless and that Sind and Larkana in particular were Bhutto's *jagir* and he was told to keep his hands off. In fact Bhutto made no secret of the fact that he wanted to destroy the Khuhro family's influence and ability to be effective in politics. He openly expressed his view that he did not fear Kazi Fazlullah who was also from Larkana, because he was malleable and also he had no children who could continue in politics but because Khuhro had children who could follow him in politics he would never allow them to put in industries which would enable them to have a base for future politics. It appeared that Bhutto's plans to consolidate his base in Larkana district entailed weakening if not destroying the Khuhro family. He did his best to do so while he was Ayub Khan's minister by using the state machinery against the Khuhros.

In 1967 Khuhro, freed to some extent from the laborious work of dealing with the matter of land reforms, decided that he could take time off to go for his second Haj pilgrimage. Khuhro and his wife decided to combine the pilgrimage with a tour of the holy places in Jordan and Iraq. The Haj was in March that year and the Khuhros left Karachi by air on 15 March. There was a noticeable difference in the facilities since their first pilgrimage in the 'fifties. The roads and hotels were much improved since their last visit more than then years earlier. The area of the Holy Ka'aba was fully paved with marble unlike before when it was largely gravelled; the place for *sai* or where Hagar had run to and fro was now no longer a street with shops but an enclosed space covered with a roof. The pilgrimage was performed in comparatively good weather and easy circumstances. Khuhro renewed some old acquaintances including Ahmed Yusuf Zainal Reza in Jeddah. Before leaving Saudi Arabia Khuhro had an audience with King Faisal ibn Abdel Aziz in Jeddah and was invited to dinner by the King. Khuhro was very impressed with the personality of this great leader of the Islamic world. He was fortunate enough to see King Faisal again in Lahore during the Islamic Conference some years later.

From Jeddah the Khuhros flew to Amman on 5 April where they were looked after by the Pakistan Ambassador Nawab Rahat Saeed Chattari and Begum Chattari. On the next day they motored to Jericho and visited the palace of Hasham bin Abdul Malik, the Ommayed Khalifa (724 A.D.). They found Jericho very green and full of gardens. On the 6th they visited Hebron and saw the tombs of Prophet Ibrahim (Abraham), Yacoob (Jacob) and also visited Bethlehem on the way to Al Quds, Jerusalem, which was then under Jordanian control. En route they also visited the tomb of Hazrat Moosa (Moses) situated between Jericho and the Dead Sea. The Khuhros spent Friday 7 April in Jerusalem where they both were able to offer the Friday prayers in Masjid Al Aqsa. They then lunched at the Intercontinental Hotel on the Mount of Olives. The Khuhros also visited the tomb of Mary and the Church of Christ before going back to Amman. On 8 April they flew from Amman to Baghdad reaching there in the evening.

In Baghdad they stayed with Mohammed Salim Al-Radi a member of one of the old families of Baghdad who had been the Iraqi Ambassador to India at the time of the July coup in 1958. Madam Suad Al-Radi was one of the most beautiful and charming Ambassadresses in the Indian capital and was a wonderful hostess to the Khuhros in Baghdad. She came from a family of distinguished Ottoman-Kurd background. One of her cousins, Mahmud Shevket Pasha had been a Grand Vizier in Istanbul before World War I. Her father Munir Abbas was still alive at the time the Khuhros went to Baghdad. The elder Al-Radi daughter Selma had been at Girton College, Cambridge, with Hamida and the families would remain close friends.

The Khuhros visited a large number of religious and historical sites in Iraq including the tomb and mosque of *Piran Pir*, Syed Abdul Qadir Al Gaylani and saw the historic library there. They visited the tombs of Imam Moosa Kazim and Mohammed Taqi at Kazimain. They also visited the mosque of Hazrat Ali, the place he was martyred at Kufa and also his tomb at Najaf. They also visited the tomb of Imam Hussain at Karbala as well the tombs of other Imams, covering about 400 kilometers in one day. The Khuhros also visited the ancient Mesopotamian capital of Babylon, the Abbassid monuments at Samarra as well as the cave where Imam Mahdi was said to have disappeared. Khuhros were thrilled to see all these historical sites many of which were part of the collective folklore and historical memory of the Muslims of the sub-continent.

They also met and made friends with members of very distinguished Iraqi families including the Al-Gaylanis. They visited Al Sayed Yusuf the head of the Gaylani family in his old family house on Mustansir Street on the bank of the river Dajla (Tigris) in the middle of Baghdad city. They dined with Syed Abdul Qadir his younger brother who was the life-time Iraqi ambassador to Pakistan. They were lucky to visit Baghdad at a rare period of calm and stability after the turmoil following the July coup of 1958 and those that would follow in the later years. On 15 April they left in the early morning by P.I.A. for Karachi taking wonderful memories of their fortnight's journey through history.

On his return from Haj and the visits to the holy places of Islam, Khuhro's friends decided to give a reception in his honour in Karachi. Friends from all over Sind subscribed for the reception which was held in Frere Hall gardens to congratulate Khuhro on his second pilgrimage and to hear of his experiences visiting the historic and holy places.

****

The Martial Law authorities since 1958 had made full use of a situation where the provinces were already conveniently amalgamated into One Unit for their easier manipulation. Untroubled by any public opinion and public check on their conduct of the country's affairs they had played havoc with the people of the smaller provinces depriving them of opportunities and treating them as subjects in a conquered land. The Martial Law administrators made notorious decisions in Sind in particular the one made by General Tikka Khan, the Administrator of Zone B (Lower Sind) that the Sindhi language was no longer to be a compulsory requirement for the Matric examination. This at once destroyed the status of the language and its importance as a means of assimilating the different ethnic groups in Sind.

The new regime also overruled the understanding that had been given by the Central Government in 1955 that after the formation of One Unit the land which was brought under cultivation in the Barrage schemes of lower and upper Sind would be allocated to the local cultivators at reasonable rates. Instead large amounts of this land was given to civil and military bureaucrats at nominal rates. It was widely known that whenever the regime wanted to reward any one of its favourites they did so by giving them land in Sind. Similarly another undertaking given in 1955 that lower grade jobs would be allocated preferentially to local people was completely ignored. In fact the opposite was done and clerical or peon positions were filled by people imported from outside the province. It was notorious that the government officers who were mostly from outside Sind, made sure that every job in their charge went to their *graeen* (fellow villager). At the same time development in the province came to a standstill. The problems were compounded because the people had no channel of communication to the rulers. The only Sindhi Minister in the Ayub government was Bhutto who was too engrossed in pushing his own career to worry about the plight of the people.

Khuhro was deeply concerned about these conditions. He had negotiated the terms for Sind's entry into the West Pakistan Province and although the situation had altered fundamentally with the imposition of military dictatorship, Khuhro felt that he must play his part to see that Ayub Khan's government be induced to honour the commitments that had been made to the Sindhi people. Thus the older leadership of Sind tried its best to remedy the situation. Khuhro was specially concerned that an adequate protest was registered against every action which was against the interests of the people. He kept a watchful eye on issues which affected the welfare of Sind particularly. As Syed Ghulam Mustafa Shah then Director of Education in West Pakistan says in his inimitable style:

"Ayub was a coward... He was in jitters because Khuhro issued a number of statements on Ayub Khan's educational policy and Tikka Khan's misbehaviour with the Vice Chancellor of Sindh University, I. I. Kazi, and Tikka Khan's effrontry to the Sindhi language. Khuhro had given creeps, phantoms and sleepless nights to Ayub on this issue. Already anti-One Unit agitation was burgeoning and crystallising and these statements of Khuhro, Hyder Baksh Jatoi, G. M. Syed and Shaikh Abdul Majeed Sindhi were rather politically and morally disturbing for Ayub and his coadjutors."[4]

When EBDO restrictions were lifted in December 1966 and he could do more than make statements, Khuhro headed the anti-One Unit Front to amend the constitution and restore the provinces to their former status.

But there seemed to be no stopping the inexorable momentum of the military dictatorship. The leadership felt so emboldened that in 1968 Ayub Khan decided to celebrate his 'decade of reforms'. There was an official blitz of sycophantic propaganda but in fact this had the opposite effect. The public fed up with the prolonged military dictatorship was ready to sieze on any opportunity to show its displeasure:

"No one quite understood how the country was suddenly engulfed by an agitation which spread like wild fire across the land in January 1969."

says Altaf Gauhar one of the inner circle of the Ayub regime:

"Was Ayub abandoned by his lukewarm allies as they saw his system come under mounting public pressure? Was it the natural culmination of years of political suffocation? Was it the result of a conspiracy hatched by the armed forces in collusion with some politicians? Or, was the Central Intelligence Agency of the United States(CIA) responsible for Ayub's downfall? Like the scholars who would later study the period, Ayub too was haunted by these questions."[5]

But within months Ayub fell ill as had his regime. So sick was the regime that it collapsed almost completely. In February 1969 Yahya Khan another military general had taken over from Ayub as Chief Martial Law Administrator. Yahya Khan announced that there was need for a new constitution and that elections would be held. In his second major address to the nation on 28 July Yahya Khan said that his mind was open on constitutional issues although he was still considering the restoration of the 1965 constitution:

"On the constitutional issue some feel that the 1956 is the only answer. While others feel equally strongly against this constitution.

Others says that elections should be held on the basis of population. Others contend that the principle of parity should be maintained.

On the issue of One Unit opinions are divided. There is a view that apart from a few administrative requirements there is no need to change the One Unit status of West Pakistan. There is a very strong feeling however in certain sections that One Unit is not acceptable to them and West Pakistan should revert to the pre-One Unit position.[author's italics]

Then there is the question of autonomy raised by our brethren of East Wing."[6]

It seemed that at last the military bureaucratic regime had recognised the absurdity of their ways.

Khuhro reacted characteristically. He was in no doubt that the previous decade of military rule had been a terrible anamoly in Pakistan's history and that democratic procedures would put things back on course. He was convinced that the decade of military rule had been an aberration that could be quickly eliminated much as British rule had been rightly removed. This was an undoubted personal strength but proved to be a severe underestimate of the desperate situation at that time. He never, even at the end would realise the dark opportunistic forces which were at work. His was always the long view – the inevitablility that the people of Sind would prevail as they had from time immemorial and moreover their leaders were duty bound not to betray them when their interests and welfare were at risk. Now the people were struggling to get out of the 'years of political suffocation'. Khuhro was not at all surprised. He had closely followed the effects on the people of the inept and arrogant decisions of a ruling class completely neglectful of ordinary people. He judged that the ten years of military dictatorship had left Pakistan with problems which were difficult but not impossible to solve. He knew that the most important of these was the feeling of neglect and isolation of the provinces like Sind, Baluchistan and East Pakistan which had little or no representation in the armed forces and very little in the bureaucracy. Khuhro had seen that military rule had deprived the people of these provinces from a sense of participation in the affairs of the country and had deprived them of their freedom which an independent state of Pakistan, which he had fought for had promised. The sense of deprivation and economic neglect had been especially well articulated and politicized in East Pakistan. Khuhro had known this first hand and he was ready to fight for what he knew was right.

Khuhro realised that there was an urgent need to re-organise and re-invigorate the political parties which had been practically moribund since Miss Jinnah's election. His first priority was to put this right and get political activity going. He recognised that the split in the Muslim League Party needed to be mended and that the existing three groups be merged to form one strong countrywide party. He decided to call a meeting to consider the problem:

On 13 July 1969 Khuhro called a widely representative gathering of Sind leaders particularly those associated with Muslim League, at his house in Karachi, to consider the new situation arising from the imposition of the second Martial Law regime. The meeting put forward 13 resolutions including the demand for the dismemberment of One Unit. The resolution urged that the new provinces should be streamlined and the states, frontier regions etc be amalgamated with the four provinces. The provinces so formed should be former Sind (with Khairpur state), Baluchistan, Punjab with Bahawalpur and Frontier province with adjoining states and tribal areas. The meeting also demanded an Upper House with equal representation for all the future provinces, control of WAPDA (West Pakistan Water and Power Authority) and Communications in West Pakistan by the Central Government to maintain the solidarity of Pakistan as one unified country.

Khuhro was very much aware that political forces needed to work together and not remain fragmented if they were to succeed in restoring democracy:

"The Sind leaders' meeting... was of the view that the three Leagues be brought on a common platform. If this effort failed, Khuhro added, the politicians from Sind will join a Muslim League party that had a programme which incorporated all the conditions for the purpose of future elections and the future form of government.

If this too was not possible then we from the Sind zone will try and form a common party with Baluchistan and NWFP in West Pakistan and make an alliance with major parties in East Pakistan on an agreed programme."

This was Khuhro at his best. Undimmed by ten years of marginalised political activity, he was as decisive and forthright now at 69 years of age as he had been when he had worked relentlessly to remove Sind from the Bombay Presidency more than thirty years previously and when he had dealt so effectively with the extraordinary problems which independence had thrown up in 1945. He was back at doing what he was best at: giving principled leadership about the real issues which concerned the people of Sind and Pakistan: their yearning for freedom and their right to a prosperous future. He was supremely sensitive to the public will and his actions reflected the peoples' anguish and their desperate misgivings of a decade of military rule. And in the first instance he was spectacularly successful. Within four months of his July meeting, on 14 December 1969 Yahya Khan announced that the One Unit would be broken up and the smaller provinces would be restored before the elections.

Khuhro realised immediately that this announcement meant that a crucial issue had been taken away from the Sind United Front election programme. Again he reacted quickly and called a meeting on 20 December at his Karachi residence to consider the situation arising out of the President's announcement. His letter of invitation pointed out that the fast changing situation required that a joint decision by like minded Sind politicians as to which political party they should join. After a couple of meetings they were able to issue a joint statement on 10 January 1970 announcing their decision to join Council Muslim League.* Khuhro ruled

---

* Many of the Sind politicians who joined Council Muslim League were also members of the Sind United Front and at the suggestion of Khuhro, Daultana drafted a press note to set out their position clearly *vis a vis* the S.U.F:

"1. That the Sind United Front is not a political party but a front consisting of members of various different political parties formed for the purpose of working for the interest of all the people of the people of Sind of promoting their welfare in a separate province while fully maintaining the stability and solidarity of Pakistan, and of bringing about the fullest co-operation and comradeship between all sections of the people of Sind.
2. Prominent leaders of the Pakistan Muslim League have been the members of the Sind United Front from the very beginning i.e. Justice Z. H. Lari, Nawabzada Zahid Ali Khan, Haji Najamuddin Sireval Laghari and others.
3. Many other important Sindhi leaders who were also members of the Sind United Front, have since joined the Pakistan Muslim League.
4. The intention of the statement which was issued recently under the joint signatures of leaders of the Pakistan Muslim League and the Sind United Front was a re-iteration of the already existing co-operation and co-ordination of efforts for this common objectives. It did not constitute a new development or an alliance between two different political parties.
5. All the activities and political efforts of the Pakistan Muslim League are subject to its following objectives:-
(a) Dedication to the Islamic way of life.
(b) Efforts to bring about an Egalitarian, Economic and Social system accordingly to the principles of Islam.
(c) Maintenance of the solidarity and stability of Pakistan.
(d) To see that the fullest regard is paid to the wishes and interest of the people of all the Units and Regions and Provinces of Pakistan. In the establishment of a Federal Parliamentary Government.
(e) Establishment of complete co-operation mutual regard and comradeship between all sections and elements of the people of Sind.
(f) Establishment of a full democratic system of Government in Pakistan.

out any collaboration with Bhutto's Peoples Party "because of the unclear and vague attitude of the undoing of One Unit and an undefined socialist programme."⁷

While these discussions were going on Khuhro, mindful that not a moment was to be lost and that the interests of Sind needed to be safeguarded in the aftermath of the break up of One Unit, called a meeting of the Larkana District Council of the Sind United Front. The meeting passed a number of resolutions on matters which Khuhro felt needed to be urgently addressed in view of the break up of One Unit. The resolutions expressed satisfaction over the decision to introduce adult franchise and went on to speak of the actions that needed to be taken on the break up of the West Pakistan province:

"This Council ... urges upon the President Aghá Mohammed Yahya Khan to take early steps to appoint a committee to determine assets and liabilities of the provinces that will be formed, as a result of the undoing of one unit.

People of Sind have grave apprehensions that unless Sind and other small provinces are effectively represented on this committee justice may not be done to those provinces. Consequently it is urged that experienced non-officials should also be associated with this very important Committee, as also with the Committee that will deal with future setting of the administration of these newly formed provinces."⁸

Khuhro also realised that the question of Karachi's future would come up now that it was no longer the federal capital and had been merged with West Pakistan. He hoped that Karachi would become part of Sind once again but at the same time he knew that such a decision would have to come from the citizens of Karachi itself. Resolution number 3 referred to this problem:

"This Council urges upon the President of Pakistan that while defining the boundaries of the new provinces, wishes of the people of Karachi be ascertained whether they would like to join Sind province or they would prefer to remain a separate province? This Council however is in favour of Karachi being joined with Sind, as historically Karachi always was part of Sind uptil June 1948. That Karachi was separated from Sind only because it was made capital of Central Government. But now that the capital is shifted to Islamabad, there is no justification in not joining Karachi with Sind again. This in view of the Larkana District Council will be beneficial to both Karachi and Sind."⁹

When Karachi was in fact returned to Sind, Khuhro felt deep satisfaction that in just over two decades that which he had considered a wrong against democracy and justice had been rectified and Karachi had become part of Sind again. The city had grown, its demographic map had changed somewhat but it was still the capital of which Sind was proud and which the people felt an inalienable part of their historic province. It was also deeply satisfactory for Sindhis that the newer citizens of Karachi opted to join with them in restoring historic Sind.

With the President's announcement that,"West Pakistan will revert as closely as possible to the pre One Unit position."¹⁰ It was now urgent for Sindhis to concentrate their minds and work methodically. Writing to Syed in February 1970 Khuhro pointed out that order and respect for rules was necessary to run the Sind United Front of which Syed was president, successfully. Khuhro had been surprised at the undisciplined method in which Syed had conducted the SUF meetings and the way in which any passerby could sit in on the Working Committee meetings, resolutions were brought in without any prior notice and even a regular agenda was lacking to conduct the business of meetings. He suggested to Syed that this state of affairs be remedied.

"Time has come that you should put SUF organisation in proper shape. You know that you created this organisation only by inviting a few of your friends from all over Sind...and you named it a Working Committee.

For every political organisation there has to be membership in villages and then district and Provincial organisation. Working Committee is to be selected from among the members of the Provincial Council. In the case of SUF none of these lower tiers exist. All that one has of SUF is a congress of a few people gathered from here and there on consideration of personal attachments. Such a thing can by no stretch of imagination be termed as a regular full-fledged political party. However you cannot be blamed for it because you started SUF only in July last when some ray of hope appeared on the horizon that democracy may be restored. And within about four months from that date President General Yahya Khan announced his decision of breaking up One Unit in West Pakistan. So naturally you had no time to organise a political party. Now after this announcement much of the purpose of this organisation has been achieved and therefore its scope will now be considerably restricted.

My object in writing this letter is that till you are able to popularize this organisation all over Sind and put it on sound footing you must at least have the constitution and rules properly framed. The Working Committee of this type of hotch-potch be re-organised and representation be given to all districts and large cities of Sind. I would suggest that there should be two members from each district. There should be two seats for the city of Hyderabad and one each for Mirpurkhas, Nawabshah, Sukkur and Larkana. This makes a total of 26 and 4 may be given to recognised student leaders or some writers and poets of renown. This brings the total to 30, plus President and Secretary."[11]

"The list [of Working Committee] members may be prepared in consultation with reliable friends and then published for the knowledge and information of every one. At present whatever meetings I have attended so far I have found at each meeting some new faces who have never been in politics of Sind and not even of any known identity. It is only fair that we should know in advance who the members of SUF Committee are with whom we have to deal in the meetings.

I have of late notices that you bring highly controversial matters in the form of resolutions without previously circulating these among your SUF members. This causes considerable confusion and frustration to many of those present in the meeting. There are some who, perhaps intend to create disruption in the organisation and have no genuine and honest intention, to promote the cause for which SUF was set up..."[12]

It was unlikely that Syed would change his ways but Khuhro was anxious that SUF should set out its aims clearly and organise to fight the elections on a well-thought out and relevant manifesto. He got a resolution to this effect passed in the Working Committee and a committee was formed under his chairmanship to draft the manifesto. He wrote to Syed confirming the membership of the committee:

> "In this morning's papers I don't find any mention of the Resolution passed yesterday appointing a committee of seven members to prepare the constitution of SUF and its manifesto etc. As far as I remember the names were, myself, Shaikh Abdul Majid, Pir Ali Mohammed Rashdi, Ghulam Hyder Shah, Pirzada Abdul Sattar and Agha Ghulam Nabi. Please release this to the press and send me a copy. I propose to convene a meeting on 10th and 11th of this month, so that this work be completed early and we should be able to put it before the next meeting of the Working Committee for approval."[13]

A relevant and popular manifesto was an urgent necessity in view of the fact that the popular slogan of breaking One Unit was now redundant. Khuhro wanted the Sind United Front to address itself to the problems which would arise from the breaking of One Unit and to safeguard Sind's interest in the aftermath:

> "...to deal with matters arising out of un-doing of One Unit, as for example boundaries of Sind Province, question of Karachi's re-unification with Sind, assets and liabilities of the the Province; administration of railways, WAPDA [Water and Power Development Authority] of West Pakistan, WIPDC [West Pakistan Industrial Development Corporation] and Agricultural Development Corporation etc."

Khuhro wanted the Sind United Front should therefore henceforth function only as a Sind party

> "Serious effort must be made by Mr. G. M. Syed and everyone else to bring all Sind politicians, to whatever political party they may owe their allegiance now, to join together to safeguard interests of Sind. In all Pakistan matters they could function in their respective parties."[14]

Syed however was not interested in these details of assets and liability and the economy of the province and went off to Dacca to talk to Shaikh Mujib-ur-Rahman, President of Awami League and to try and forge a grand alliance. Khuhro knew that given the peculiar phobias of the Punjab and of the army leaders who were still in control, this action of Syed smacked of foolhardiness. In the interests of ensuring that the transfer of power to an elected parliament took place smoothly it was necessary not to put such a cat among the pigeons of the Pakistan Government. Khuhro cautioned Syed not to support the Six Point Programme which could put the whole process of democratisation in jeopardy.

He knew that it was necessary to tread delicately on the ground. He reminded Syed of the agreed programme of SUF:

> "...the resolution passed at his [Syed's] residence on 10 August 1969...makes no mention of Six Points at all. It evisages a federal form of government at the Centre with a bicameral legislature, representation on population basis in the Lower House and equal representation to all federating units in the Upper House. This resolution does not support separate currency, or power of all taxation to provinces or separate foreign trade."[15]

Khuhro knew and felt instinctively that it was necessary to tread carefully. The military regime appeared exhausted and seemed to be making gestures towards restoring normal political conditions in the country. But appearances were deceptive. The military had held power for ten years and were not going to give up easily. In addition, a new and potentially explosive political trajectory was moving alarmingly over the country's firmament and would break apart its fragile post independence polity.

Z. A. Bhutto had been abruptly removed from his cosy perch in the military regime in 1965 in the aftermath of the disastrous war with India. At first Bhutto was confused and tearful, asking whoever he met what would happen to him. But Ayub Khan had treated him well and given him a fully paid holiday in Europe as a gentle let down.[16] While there he met the retired diplomat and scholar J. A. Rahim. Together they hatched a reckless and ambitious plan. The sixties in America and Europe was an exciting and optimistic place to be. Anything was possible: the poor would be rich; the planet saved; everything could be managed etc. Bhutto and Rahim (as were many third world persons at the time) were easily seduced by this rhetoric. As Khuhro had noticed Bhutto had no roots and little idea what real life in Pakistan was about.

J. A. Rahim, steeped in the then current European intellectual jargon wrote the 'foundation papers' and a manifesto for a political party which Bhutto launched in December 1967 as Pakistan People's Party (PPP). When increasing unrest emerged in the autumn of 1968 Bhutto, quick on the uptake realised fully the potential of the situation and assumed his people's leader role. He "effortlessly embraced the tenets of extreme populism. It was a flawless impersonation."[17] Soon Bhutto was touring the country with an uncanny display of political showmanship. "Pakistan Peoples Party was unique and unstable blend of the Right and Left wings of West Pakistan's leadership spectrum."[18] The sloganising, the rallies and propaganda was something which had not been seen in Pakistan before. Even in the heyday of the Pakistan national movement when huge crowds of people used to gather to listen to their leaders, speeches and behaviour was restrained. Bhutto used a language which was deliberately coarse and designed to appeal to the 'man in the street'. He modelled himself on socialist leaders so popular at the time. Basically his approach was 'Peronist' with its accompanying showmanship and its solidarity with the 'shirtless' masses.

Khuhro tried his best to warn his countrymen of the dangers of this flood of rhetoric and play acting that seemed to be taking in the people particularly those of the Punjab. Watching the histrionics in the pre election period, with disbelief, the Parliamentary Board of the Sind Provincial Muslim League issued a caution:

"The Sind Provincial Muslim League (Council) Parliamentary Board views with grave concern the deteriorating law and order situation in the Province due to the abusive and highly irresponsible statements, speeches and other provocative activities of workers of the Peoples Party who have openly defied Martial Law Regulations 6, 16-A and 60 and other relevant rules and regulations for the conduct of peaceful elections; with a view to undermine the prestige of the present regime. Consequently this Board urges upon the Government to take firm and determined steps to curb such nefarious activities on their part and direct local officials to maintain law and order with a firm hand."[19]

In fact Bhutto had turned a complete somersault on all his attitudes and pronouncements while he was Minister during his eight year tutelage under Ayub

Khan's authoritarian regime. He was now bitterly critical of 'Basic Democracies' as undemocratic and a fraud. He constantly promised to reveal 'secrets' of the Tashkent Declaration which he ofcourse never did. He had a different approach to India from the one he had during his days of power which was to 'fight India for a thousand years'.[20] He arranged to meet the Indian embassy officials 'like a thief from the back door.'* When he could not justify his present stand he would ask the crowd wherever he happened to be for 'forgiveness'. It was play acting of a high order.

Apart from Ayub Khan, Bhutto was the best known face at least in the western part of the country and he traded on that as well as showmanship and his abilities to abuse all his rivals be they religious or political leaders. He reserved his special invective for Khuhro whom he considered his most dangerous rival in Sind and ofcourse in Larkana. Conveniently disregarding his 8 year long intimate association with the military dictatorship of Ayub Khan he accused Khuhro of 'throttling democracy' when he was Premier of Sind.

Khuhro knew that what made Bhutto tick was the acquisition of power pure and simple. He had seen him embrace the short cuts to power offered by the military regime. He had seen him serve the dictatorial regime in whatever capacity they wanted to the utmost of his ability. He had been chosen by Iskander Mirza, been a long serving civilian in the military regime of Ayub Khan. Here he had been regarded as the most favourite minister and his most faithful agent. He had masterminded the Ayub Khan campaign against Fatima Jinnah in Sind using every means fair or foul. He had advocated the One Party State where every civil servant would be a party member. Khuhro had seen Bhutto operate in the B.D. elections where he had gone back on every promise he had made without the slightest scruple. Khuhro was amazed at the new pose of Bhutto as the champion of the people. Here was the faithful lackey of dictatorship now reborn as a David of socialism. Khuhro found Bhutto's programme a hoax which was being touted as a solution for the ills of the people by a fraudulent politician. Khuhro was revolted by the spectacle of Bhutto crying hypocritical tears, making long and noisy speeches which made little sense, tearing his shirts open, wearing a Mao cap as if that transformed him into a revolutionary. Khuhro could see that all loafers in Larkana had gathered round him as they had from all over the country.

But there was no stopping Bhutto. On the campaign trail, there were no limits to his rhetoric, he lashed out at everyone he could think of, Maulana Maudoodi, the chief of Jamaati Islami came in for his share of vitriol as did other clerics. Bhutto also attacked the two senior politicians of Sind, Khuhro and G. M. Syed, using

---

* General Musa the Governor of West Pakistan at this time was forced to make a public statement to correct some of the more extravagant claims of Bhutto:
"He wants an aggressive confrontation with India and yet he associates himself with and has even offered to defend those who are accused of hatching a plot for the secession of East Pakistan ...
He has said that he contacted the Indian High Commissioner in Karachi. The latter wanted to see him in order to discuss with him his views on India, because India was shivering due to his ideas about that country. If this statement is correct why did he enter the Indian High Commissioner's house like a thief from the back door... It shows that his conscience was guilty and that he wanted to hide from the people of Pakistan the fact that he was in touch with India's representative in this country." General Musa, *The Pakistan Times*, 12 Oct. 1968.

vulgar and derogatory language. Khuhro again felt that he had to cut the flood of vicious invective short. He issued a statement to the press drawing attention to Bhutto's disregard of the norms of normal election campaign behaviour:

"It appears as if M. L. R. No. 60 recently promulgated by the President is a dead letter and no notice is to be taken of it."

Khuhro reminded the public of his record in the service of the country as that of G. M. Syed who had also been attacked by Bhutto:

"Everyone in Sind and in the country at large knows me and my record in getting Sind separated from Bombay and made a separate Muslim majority province and my constant and untiring efforts to build up All India Muslim League in Sind from 1937 to 1947, which resulted in the achievement of Pakistan under the able guidance and leadership of Quaid-e-Azam Muhammed Ali Jinnah. Mr. G. M. Syed was with us in that struggle during that crucial period from 1937 to 1945. He got the resolution for Pakistan passed by overwhelming majority in the Sind Legislature."

As opposed to the experienced and seasoned politicians who had earned their status in the white heat of the struggle for freedom was this spurious leader with suspect antecedents:

"My young friend Bhutto has no political background. In October 1958, when he was hardly thirty years of age he was made a Minister by the late Iskander Mirza overnight when the latter, in conspiracy with the then C-in-C General Ayub Khan, brought in Martial Law to escape the general elections scheduled by our Cabinet for February 1959. Bhutto stayed on as Minister in collaboration with the dictatorial regime. The role that he played from October 1958 to June 1966, nearly eight long years, is known to every one in Pakistan. He accuses me of throttling democracy during the time I was Chief Minister of Sind. What brilliant record of democratic system and practice has he established during his eight years of power and influence with dictatorial regime of Ayub Khan? Is he not the same Bhutto who got all the senior politicians 'EBDOed' to make the field clear for himself and his colleagues? Was he not the prime author of B.D. system which denied the people the right of adult franchise and made it easy for him and his friends in power to rig the elections in 1962 and 1965? Is he today proud of the role he played in getting the late Mohtrama Fatima Jinnah defeated by his then Godfather Ayub Khan – now the target of his mean attacks? Was he not the one to advise his boss to be the permanent President of the country like Dr. Soekarno and Nkrumah? And who suggested to Ayub Khan to have a `one party' state with all the officials high and low to be its members to loot the country with impunity. Surprisingly today he has emerged as a great champion of democracy and socialism in the country."[21]

But Bhutto was riding high. His immoderate and threatening speeches and the breaches of peace by his followers went unchecked much to the surprise of other parties. Few knew at the time how close were the links that Bhutto had with the regime. Bhutto's biographer shows Bhutto as Yahya's drinking and shooting companion and that he was deeply involved in the inner councils of the regime. He also reveals the close consultation that existed between Bhutto and Lieutenant General S. G. M. M. Peerzada who was the head of C.M.L.A. Headquarters and Principal Staff Officer to Yahya Khan. Access to Yahya Khan was exclusively through Peerzada during those critical months leading up to the elections.[22] Almost every important document was shown to Bhutto by Peerzada and he was consulted on most political issues.[23] These facts would come to Khuhro's knowledge after the elections which took place in December 1970.

Bhutto deliberately targeted Khuhro as the most important political leader of Sind with popular support. He was insecure about fighting the elections in Larkana and therefore had decided to file from a number of other constituencies. But he knew that he would need the credibility of winning a seat from his own home district. It was therefore important for him that Khuhro be painted in the blackest colours possible as 'traitor' to Sind. With his close links with the Yahya regime through the Generals, particularly General Peerzada, in the immediate circle of the new Martial Law Administrator[24] and the new methods of propaganda available to him, Bhutto set out to destroy Khuhro as a political force. Already Khuhro was no match for him financially. Bhutto appeared to have vast reserves of wealth with which he covered the highways of Pakistan with his party's flags draped on what seemed every thorn bush in the desert to the smallest tea shop.

Khuhro contested from his seat in Larkana against Bhutto. He was depending on his lifetime of service to the district and to the province, his wide and intimate knowledge of the people and on their loyalty. He was now 69 years of age and had not represented Larkana for the twelve years during the period when a sea change had taken place in the political culture of the country but Khuhro felt that he had a duty to contest. Bhutto had sent him messages that he would give him two seats in the provincial assembly if he stood down from the National Assembly seat. He realised that Bhutto had enormous funds and certainly the regime appeared to favour him but he felt that the people could not possibly vote for a man who was so obviously a charlatan and who had been associated so intimately with the hated dictatorship of Ayub Khan. Khuhro was contesting on behalf of 'Council' Muslim League, but the party was divided and fragmented with the Qayyum Khan faction being supported by the regime. A recent historian of the period refers to
> "the special relationship which Qayyum had from the beginning developed with the regime. He had the blessings of the National Security Division and the intelligence agencies..."[25]

The Yahya regime had appropriated the funds of Muslim League and also took money from industrialists and gave it to certain favourites. This meant that Muslim League was weakened financially and politically and could not put up a solid front. Its chances of success therefore were not too good.

The elections took place in December 1970. During the elections the support of the state machinery for Bhutto became obvious. The military personnel on duty actively intervened and stopped Khuhro's voters from going into the polling stations. Bhutto went round the polling booths accompanied by district officials. He blustered and bullied but remained insecure till the last moment. When a woman election agent of Khuhro's made a remark in English to the polling officer at a women's polling booth in a secure Bhutto area, his father in law's home town of Naudero, his first wife Shereen who was acting as his agent immediately sent a message to Bhutto that Khuhro's agent was conspiring with the Polling officer. Bhutto came rushing to the polling booth to check on the 'conspiracy'.[26]

As well as his loudly proclaimed appeal to the common man Bhutto had tried every means to win over the major landowners and the influential men of the district. He had Khuhro's supporter in Dokri district Wadero Ghulam Umar Unnar arrested under the Goonda Act. Khuhro met the Martial Law authorities to protest against the arrest but could not get him released. Bhutto negotiated with him through intermediaries and got the promise of his support in return for his release. Similarly with the regime's support Bhutto used threats and promises to win over the other zamindars who were till then supporting Khuhro. When the zamindars saw that the Military regime was definitely with Bhutto they decided that it would serve their interests best if they sided with the man who had that support.

One of the major supporters of Khuhro in the election was Pir Pagaro who had opposed any compromise with Bhutto and had promised Khuhro his full support. On the eve of the elections Khuhro organised a big public meeting in the Larkana stadium where Pagaro was to be the leading speaker to publicly demonstrate his support for Khuhro. But at the last minute Pagaro failed to turn up so that the meeting had to go ahead without him. It was a major blow to Khuhro's campaign that the Pir failed to show up at this crucial public meeting. Pagaro had in fact left his house in Karachi and gone to Thatta ostensibly to support candidates there, an area where his support was minimal. It was generally believed that Pagaro had been sent messages from the Martial Law Headquarters that he was not to attend the meeting for Khuhro – a message which obviously he felt he could not ignore.*

The voters of Khuhro's home taluka and the Larkana town stayed with Khuhro in spite of all the blandishments and gave him a majority in these areas. In the town he was fully and loyally supported by the Urdu speaking migrants whom he had help settle there. Ratodero (which included the Bhutto stronghold of Naudero) was expected to go with Bhutto but the decisive vote was lost in Dokri taluqa which Bhutto won with his pressure tactics. Bhutto took 70,763 votes to Khuhro's 31,009, with just over 3,000 votes going to religious and other parties.

Khuhro took his defeat as stoically as he did all the adverse strokes of fortune in his life. When his workers and family came in from the tough day's work, downcast at the results, they found him calmly studying the results and analyzing the votes from the different polling stations, quite calm and collected. With the way the circumstances had shaped up he had come to the conclusion that the election was in fact lost sometime before the results were known. Khuhro knew that he had given a good fight, the best that he could under the circumstances against a candidate who had not only much greater funds but also government support.

---

* The election campaign would not have suffered if Pagaro had not been expected at all. It was the build up of expectations of the public, many of whom were Pagaro followers, and the let down which created an atmosphere of despondency. Pagaro missed the meeting and turned up shamefaced in Larkana at 5 the next morning when it was no use to anybody. Pagaro was clearly under pressure by the Martial Law authorities and unable or unwilling to disregard their instructions.
Pagaro also played a treacherous role in the elections of Khuhro's close friend Wadero Ghulam Mohammed Wassan of Tharparkar. This extremely upstanding politician had never been defeated even in the Martial Law regime of Ayub Khan now lost the elections in 1970 because Pagaro went back on his word to give his support to him.

Khuhro had succeeded in pinning Bhutto down to Larkana during much of the course of the election even though he was fighting in several other constituencies including some in the Punjab which were crucial to his ambition to rule the country.

The results of the elections were contrary to the designs of the Martial Law regime who were expecting East Pakistan to have a much less decisive result and take advantage of a divided mandate to continue their rule. As it was the Awami League got a definite majority in parliament with 162 seats out of just under 300 and Bhutto's Peoples Party got 81 seats from the Punjab and Sind, 1 from N.W.F.P. and none from Baluchistan. It had only 42% of the vote in Punjab and Sind and no representative status for two out of four provinces of Western Pakistan. As the clear majority leader, Shaikh Mujib-ur-Rahman, the leader of Awami League had every expectation that he would be Prime Minister and President Yahya Khan on his visit to Dacca in the second week of January 1971 actually referred to him as the future Prime Minister of Pakistan.

Almost immediately on his return from Dacca, Yahya Khan went to Larkana as Bhutto's guest for a shoot. He took with him a number of his key advisers including Generals Peerzada and Hameed. He told Bhutto of his discussions with Mujib. Bhutto, very skilfully, put doubts in his mind and succeeded in sabotaging the straightforward programme of transfer of authority to an elected parliament. Bhutto now introduced a number of red herrings about how East Pakistan would secede from Pakistan although he did not explain why the majority province should secede from a number of minority provinces. He also put himself forward as the sole spokesman for the western wing of the country and suggested a grand coalition of the two wings. He convinced Yahya Khan that no transfer of power could take place without his agreement. The 'Larkana conspiracy' as it came to be known, changed the direction of events. The generals now filled with distrust, were in no mood to accommodate the majority party and Bhutto became their collaborater.

Bhutto went to Dacca at the end of January to 'talk' to Mujib but these talks were clearly to demonstrate to the public and the generals that there was no meeting point between East and West Pakistan and that the Assembly session should be postponed. Naturally Mujib could not agree to a postponement which could only give more time to Bhutto to conspire against the majority party.

Bhutto met Yahya after his return from Dacca and reported that Mujib would economically weaken the West Pakistan provinces and that he would impose his own constitution. He asked Yahya to postpone the Assembly till the end of March so that he had a chance to have public meetings throughout West Pakistan. Bhutto was determined not to let his party members or even other members from western Pakistan attend the Assembly session which was scheduled for early March. He was not sure that he could retain his West Pakistan members in an open session and it was clearly not in his interest to meet in a House where he would be seen to be a minority. He threatened to 'break the legs' of any member who dared to go to Dacca and talked of the division of the country between himself and Awami League-'idhar hum, udhar tum' (We on this side, you on the other). He threatened other West Pakistan leaders with reprisals if they went to Dacca-"..what Bhutto was asking for was outside the system and could only be resolved by extra constitutional means."[27]

On 19 February Bhutto met Yahya Khan for five and half hours and Yahya agreed to change the Legal Framework Order to allow Bhutto to remove members of his party who defied him and went to Dacca for the session. Following this meeting it appeared that the understanding between the Martial Law authorities was further deepened and cemented. Just three days later Yahya Khan called a meeting of the provincial Governors and Martial Law Administrators and made known his intentions of postponing the Assembly session indefinitely. He was now convinced that 'a whiff of the grapeshot' would restore the situation to that of 1969. On the afternoon of 1 March the further postponement of the Assembly was announced by Radio Pakistan leading to an immediate storm of protest. Admiral Ahsan was removed as Governor of East Pakistan on account of his advocacy of reconciliation and compromise and General Yakub was appointed Governor instead. But Yakub could not last as he was not hardline enough and was replaced by Tikka Khan possibly on Bhutto's advice.[28]

The decision to take army action in East Pakistan had presumably been taken sometime in February as the air lifting of troops into East Pakistan had been taking place for sometime. With army in 'advanced state of preparation to regain control of East Pakistan,' Yahya Khan went to Dacca on 14 March meeting Bhutto on the way in Karachi. Immediately after that Bhutto addressed a public meeting in Karachi and proposed transfer of power to the majority parties in their respective Wings.!

The meaning of the events became clear as the news of the tragic events following the army action in East Pakistan at the end of March filtered through to the western wing. On the night of the 25th and 26th March the army action started in Dacca with an attack on the University hostels.The events would unfold with inevitably tragic consequences for Pakistan and for the Muslims of the sub-continent. Bhutto who flew back on the day after the actions announced on landing in Karachi: "Thank God Pakistan is saved."

Khuhro made a comprehensive statement making the situation clear for the public:

"Mr. Bhutto cannot be absolved of the role he played in bringing about the crisis. His talks with Shaikh Mujib did not succeed in early February in Dacca, where he had gone mainly to press his claim to share power with him in the event of Awami League forming the Government after framing the Constitution.

Mr. Bhutto and his party's right place was Opposition. In any democratic form of Government majority party forms the Government and minority party which P.P.P. was, had to sit in Opposition. The situation put him completely out of his wits and his public speech in Lahore on 28th February was most unfortunate. He publicly advocated boycott of the Assembly session summoned by the President on 3rd March at Dacca and threatened all MNAs of West Pakistan that if they did go to attend the session at Dacca they will not be allowed to return alive to their homes and thus brought about the crisis."

Khuhro pointed out that Bhutto did not confine himself to the destruction of democratic norms at home but was equally bent upon harming Pakistan's position abroad:

"He talks of negotiating settlement with Shaikh Mujibur Rahman and of making peace with India on Bangla Desh and other issues while giving interview to the foreign press in Iran and when he returns to Pakistan he talks of going to war with India. Does Mr. Bhutto realize that war at this time may turn our country as well as India into another Vietnam where particularly after Defence alliance between Russia and India world powers are bound to come in and it will prove ruinous for both countries.

Mr. Bhutto was mainly responsible for the war with India in 1965 which proved to be very costly both for India and Pakistan.

He was not only one of the signatories to Tashkent agreement but also played his role in drafting it and publicly praised it in the press as also on the floor of the National Assembly. And yet after his removal by the then President Ayub Khan from his Cabinet, he denounced it in his public meetings and went on playing with the sentiments of our gullible public for quite a long time that he would expose some secrets about the Tashkent declaration. There were no secrets about it and none were exposed but only the public was being misled to get votes for his party men in his election campaign."

Turning to the situation of Larkana, Khuhro drew attention to the victimisation of Bhutto's opponents:

"God save our country from such turn coat politicians whose main aim in life is to get power anyhow and use it to victimize their political opponents. What his men are doing in Larkana in particular when he is not yet in power has repeatedly appeared in details in local newspapers. Such politicians want to copy Hitlerian tactics, in reality, believe in dictatorial rule and are not fit to run a government working under a Constitution based on Islamic ideology."[29]

There was a defeaning silence among the politicians of West Pakistan immediately after the army action. With the exception of a few Baluch leaders who registered their unhappiness at the East Pakistan situation there was no voice of dissension or protest. The excuse that there was censorship was hardly tenable as until the 25 of March events were being reported and the foreign press and radio carried the news about the events in East Pakistan.

Khuhro's daughter who was a Fellow at St. Antony's College, Oxford at the time saddened and outraged at the tragic events that were taking place in Pakistan, wrote to *The Times* of London expressing her view of the situation. In this letter she fully implicated Bhutto in the tragedy:

"Today, I, a Sindhi, would be ashamed to be called a West Pakistani if it were West Pakistan that was "restoring discipline" in East Pakistan. But the people of Sind, Baluchistan, the North West Frontier and, I am sure, the people of the Punjab, abhor and disavow the coercion of Bangladesh. This action is an absolute denial of the spirit in which Muslims of the Indian sub-continent fought for a separate homeland – a fight in which Bengali Muslims were, if anything, ahead of those who live in the provinces of West Pakistan. Muslim League was born in Dacca at the time of the first partition of Bengal into Muslim and Hindu majority provinces and Bengal's Muslims have pride of place in the Pakistan movement.

But the present situation is not, as I have said, a struggle for political or economic power between the people of East and West Pakistan. It is another struggle and one which has raged for the past 20 years, that is, of the Army and the Civil Service, overwhelmingly Punjabi in composition, to retain its predominance, both in the West over smaller provinces and in the East over the majority province of Bengal, by crushing political activity and politicians. For the first ten years after 1947 the anti politicians of the Punjab manoeuvred behind the scenes and manipulated politicians for their own ends; for the next ten years from 1958 to 1968 they ruled openly through ex President Ayub Khan; now we see another attempt to re-establish their authority by crushing the one threat to their power, Bengali political representatives supported by the representatives of the smaller provinces and to their credit, the old politicians of the Punjab.

In this present phase of the struggle, Mr. Bhutto of Pakistan Peoples Party, has indeed played the role of a "political bastard". A Sindhi by birth, he presides over a party which has adopted a spurious socialist stance. He won votes, particularly in the Punjab, by his election slogan of economic reform: "Bread, cloth and house" for everyone. He was given no other mandate. Since the election he has not spoken in any serious manner about economic reforms but has concentrated on histrionics and meaningless and inconsistent poses. His party is increasingly revealed as Fascist in behaviour with a para-military `volunteer' organization, threats against other political groups and leaders and against the press and a naked pursuit of power by any means. At present he is providing a convenient front as elected leader of West Pakistan to the forces that would like to crush legitimate political activity.

One cannot absolve Awami League leaders and the leaders of West Pakistan of shortsightedness in the events leading up to the present crisis. They have played right into the hands of the antidemocratic forces. But however tragic the present events and whatever their immediate outcome–we, the people of Sind, appeal to our Bengali brothers to remember that the idea of Pakistan is greater than those who now manipulate the country for their own ends an appeal to them not abandon us in West Pakistan to our fate."[30]

The letter was published in *The Times* of 1 April and got an immediate response from people from across the world. It was picked up by the B.B.C. which, unable to get any public and political reaction from West Pakistan, used the letter fully. The Urdu service which was heard by practically every Pakistani also fully used the letter to portray public reaction in Pakistan. Hamida Khuhro got a large number of letters from England, North America and the sub-continent with varied reactions: appreciative letters from Bengalis and abusive ones from the Punjab.

Bhutto fully alive to the importance of the media and very sensitive about his image was very annoyed at the letter and gave his reaction in a statement against Khuhro who was at that time engaged in bringing about a merger of the three factions of Pakistan Muslim League:

"Commenting on the proposed merger of the three factions of the Muslim League, Mr. Bhutto wondered how would the same Muslim League leaders who always jeopardised the interests of Pakistan for the fulfilment of other vested interests work for the preservation of national ideology...

He said these so-called politicians are meeting at the residence of Ayub Khuhro to discuss the ideology and integrity of Pakistan. Bhutto said that Dr. Hamida, Khuhro's daugh-

ter recently made statements in England which appeared in London Times.

She had stated that she was ashamed to be called a Pakistani, Mr. Bhutto said and added that she is a strong supporter of so-called Bangladesh. So how could Khan Abdul Qayyum Khan and Mian Mumtaz Daultana discuss these issues at Khuhro's residence when his daughter supports "Bangladesh", he asked."[31]

Khuhro never one to watch helplessly while the country was being torn apart by the demogogues in both eastern and western wings of the country felt that the most effective way to prevent certain disaster was to unite potentially the most mature political party with the most experienced leadership – the Muslim League. He had been working on the idea of unification even when Ayub Khan had been alive and had prepared points to be discussed by Muslim League leaders. These had included the proposal for a merger of Muslim League factions and the basis for a future constitution of Pakistan.[32] It was difficult for the merger to take place while Ayub Khan was at the height of his powers and one of the Muslim Leagues was his instrument but with his decline the merger became a possibility.

On the morning of 13 August 1971 an informal meeting of some members of Council Muslim League was held at the house of G. A. Madni M.P. A. There Khuhro brought up the question of the merger and the members present appeared to be keen on the idea. Khuhro undertook to talk with the different factions. He started the negotiations with the groups the same day. He first talked to Khan Abdul Qayum Khan and his party men and also Daultana. The next two days saw prolonged discussions for the next three days. By the morning of Sunday 15 August Qayum Khan had agreed to the merger. Daultana also agreed to Khuhro's formula. Malik Mohammed Qasim and Fazlul Qadir Chaudhry of the Convention League also approved and Khuhro was able to release the agreement to the press on the evening of the 15th:

> "I have been having talks with the representatives of the Pakistan Muslim League (Qayyum group), Council Muslim League and Convention Muslim League for the last three days at my residence. It has now been unanimously agreed that all the three factions of Muslim League will summon their Councils shortly and it is expected that resolutions will be prepared by the respective Councils giving full powers to their Working Committees or to Special Committees of selected members with respect to the merger of the three Leagues, and selections of all office bearers of one Combined Organisation, and in such case it will not be necessary to refer back the matter thus decided to the respective Committee for approval."[33]

A joint press statement was issued by the leaders of the three factions emphasising the urgent need of achieving the unity within the ranks of the Muslim League and of transforming the organisation into one powerful mass organisation 'to maintain the integrity and solidarity of Pakistan and to defend the ideological and geographical frontiers of Pakistan'. Khuhro had also issued a press statement in answer to Bhutto's insinuations against the meeting at Khuhro's house:

> "One can easily understand Mr. Z. A. Bhutto getting exasperated at the news that the leaders of the three Muslim League parties might meet at my residence for talks of merger. Power hungry that he is, he naturally feels very upset about

it as in that event his party will lose all its bargaining power. Even now it is a minority party confined only to Sind and Punjab but after the merger of Muslim League it will be in a worse position. Mr. Bhutto naturally therefore cannot relish the idea of Muslim League leaders meeting together."[34]

But by August 1971 it was already too late for Muslim League. If the factions had got together in 1968, they might have had a chance of winning the elections which were held in the winter of 1970-71, as one party. But conflicts between the leaders together with the interference of the Martial Law regime prevented their unification. Qayyum Khan League had been chosen as the special protege of the regime and was given material support to fight the elections. Now with the regime deeply involved with Bhutto, and with the censorship and the restrictions on political activity in the critical months of 1971, there was little room for a third force to emerge or to introduce sanity and Pakistan continue unchecked on its way to disaster.

23

A REVEALING EXCHANGE OF LETTERS

In the months after March 1971 when any hope that an elected government would take power faded, Pakistan went blindly and inexorably to disaster. That disaster was not to end with the humiliation of surrender of Dacca in December 1971. It was to continue when total power came into the hands of a man completely without principle or conviction– "A man born to be hanged."*

Bad as had been the Martial Law periods from 1958, the period of 'civilian Martial Law' and subsequent 'democratic rule' would not only be a nightmare for the country but an incredibly difficult period for Khuhro. Bhutto's attitude to Khuhro and his family had been clear to him much earlier even during Ayub's rule when Bhutto had constantly tried to undermine Khuhro's political reputation and position by every means available legitimate or otherwise. During the 1970 elections and afterwards his enmity had become more open. After winning the elections of 1970-71, Bhutto and his party men, confident that the regime favoured them began to behave as if they ruled the country and set about it by browbeating officers and victimizing their opponents. By May of that year Khuhro made a public statement deploring this behaviour. The statement set out in Khuhro's usual forceful and unambiguous manner the situation that Bhutto was fermenting in the country. It is interesting that even after ten years of dictatorship the judiciary had obviously maintained certain standards as Khuhro asked for an enquiry to be made into various scandals which had occurred. The press statement was carried prominently in the main newspapers and read as follows:

"Mr. Z. A. Bhutto, Chairman PPP has been claiming the right, as the leader of

---

* Sir Morrice James (Lord Saint Brides), British High Commissioner in Pakistan in the '60s, in his book *Pakistan Chronicle* (OUP 1993), pp. 74-75, writes one of the most penetrating observations on Bhutto ever made: "Bhutto certainly had the right qualities for reaching the heights – drive, charm, imagination, a quick penetrating mind, zest for life, eloquence, energy, a strong constitution, a sense of humour and thick skin...

But there was – how shall I put it?–the rank odour of hellfire about him. It was a case of *corruptio optimi pessima*. He was a Lucifer, a flawed angel. I believe that at heart he lacked a sense of the dignity and value of other people; his own self was what counted. I sensed in him a ruthlessness and a capacity for ill-doing which went far beyond what is natural... Lacking humility he thus came to believe himself infallible, even when yawning gaps in his own experience (e.g. of military matters) laid him–as over the 1965 War–wide open to disastrous error.

Despite his gifts I judged that one day Bhutto would destroy himself... In 1965. so I reported in one of my last despatches from Pakistan as British High Commissioner. I wrote by way of clinching the point that Bhutto was born to be hanged."

majority party in two provinces (Punjab and Sind) to interfere, right from now, in the day to day administration, to expect officials to kowtow to him and receive orders from him and his partymen, to demand transfers of officials and to direct officials whom he thus gets posted, whom to favour and whom to harass. In order to create a climate of awe and to demoralize the executive, he claims sometimes to be in status next only to the President of Pakistan, and sometimes, in the same position as President-elect of the United States. As a consequence of this situation, what has been happening, for example in Larkana has been making front page stories in the national press, though, I am afraid, the exposure of these scandals has not yet been seriously taken notice of by the Authorities that be. Such serious complaints made by applications to the higher authorities and openly through newspapers, should be enquired into through an independent judicial officer of the rank of not less than a District Judge."[1]

Khuhro pointed out that the administration was still the exclusive responsibility of the Martial Law regime of Yahya Khan and that Bhutto had no *locus standi*–

"Mr. Bhutto's claim that he has a right to interfere in the day to day administration... is untenable both constitutionally and from the stand point of good and impartial administration."

Khuhro accused Bhutto and his party of using the Martial Law administration to 'do things which are intended only to promote their own political and party interests.' He warned that any discredit from such compulsions and actions would be laid at the door of the Martial Law administration. Khuhro advised the administration that politicians should be allowed to take the responsibility for their own actions which would be the case when power was transferred–

"when power is transferred to political parties it will be be directly their responsibility to run the administration of the country. And in that event, victims of their vendetta and political persecution will have various means of seeking relief."

Khuhro was ofcourse speaking from his own experience of democracy where flawed as it was, he had been able in the end to get just decisions from courts. Relief had been available to the public in the courts and in the working of the parliamentary system itself. In a remarkable paragraph he set out very clearly what democratic accountability by politicians entails:

"Ministries functioning under Democracy are subject to the vigilance and control of legislatures. There, in order to bring an erring Ministry to book, vote of censure could be brought, debates could be raised, and cut motions and adjournment motions could be moved. In addition, there will be courts of law where their actions could be challenged with a regular constitution defining and sustaining the fundamental rights of the citizens...Press will be available for the exposing the misdeeds of the party in power. These are the checks and balances that could be availed of when there is full democracy functioning. I dare say that even these very politicians who today try to exploit the present position and try to wield power indirectly, will think twice before they commit any acts of indiscretion on their own responsibility."[2]

Khuhro uneasily aware that a PPP government under Bhutto would be the fate of Sind, even if the majority Awami League formed a coalition with Muslim League at the Centre, was informing people of the safeguards the citizen had under a democracy. He suspected at this stage that Bhutto would try to circumvent these rights and safeguards but he could not have imagined that the situation would change so drastically and that within months Bhutto would emerge as the Chief Martial Law Administrator and that he would eventually suspend these precious funadamental rights indefinitely!

With mayhem raging in East Pakistan in 1971 Bhutto was rushing around the western part of country threatening violent action and worse, if he was left out of power. He was having frequent meetings with Yahya Khan and being consulted at each stage of the fiasco being staged in East Pakistan. It was a masterly mixture of collusion and blackmail. Such were the twists and turns of Bhutto's performance that the politicians could only guess at the secret negotiations taking place, and the public were completely in the dark. Khuhro who found subterfuge impossible could hardly bring himself to believe in the drama that was being staged. He grew more alarmed everyday at the emotional pitch to which the public rose as Bhutto reached greater and greater heights of acting at the successive public meetings. On 8 September in Hyderabad he boasted:"...I have the strength and courage to organise a movement." What kind of movement was he planning? Again on the death anniversary of the Quaid-e-Azam on 11 September he addressed a rally at the *Mazar* and made what amounted to a seditious speech:

"What happened in East Pakistan, can happen in West Pakistan as well... We will not permit another Jallianwala Bagh."[3]

Khuhro was alarmed and outraged and decided that he could not remain silent while the people were being so wickedly misled and possibly dragged into violence and disorder. He wrote on 14 September to the CMLA pointing out the dangerous nature of Bhutto's speeches and behaviour:

"Mr. Z. A. Bhutto Chairman PPP harangued a huge crowd that came to pay homage to Quaid-e-Azam at his *Mazar*, on Saturday morning. If your Intelligence organisation serves you well, they must have reported to you full contents of this bitter and highly provocative speech. He openly incited the listeners to violence, particularly students, labour, peasants and semi-educated unemployed... This was an unauthorised and unexpected meeting which comes within the mischief of Martial Law Regulations. He talked of civil war resulting in blood bath as in East Pakistan. If your Government is not prepared to take action even in such a dangerous situation, then why at all are there Martial Law Regulations in force, which are used against smaller fry and far less dangerous elements. Surely we the peace loving citizens in West Pakistan do not want to go through once again the terrible holocaust similar to that ...in East Pakistan. I am convinced that if this kind of mischief, namely, preparing ground for civil commotion on a large scale which may engulf the whole of West Pakistan, is not fully controlled at once, after sometime the situation will become uncontrollable. It is believed by everyone here that laws of the country apply to everyone equally, irrespective of the consideration whether the offender is a big and influential man or is an ordinary man in the street.

I have done by duty as a citizen of this country and it is for you to act in the interest of maintenance of Law and Order in the country."[4]

This letter was shown to Bhutto by General Peerzada as was most other correspondence which came to CMLA Headquarters. Bhutto who, while unmoved by appeals to democratic values which Khuhro made in his public statements, was very aware that the generals would be sensitive to the charge of not taking action to maintain Law and Order and to the idea that the ungovernable situation of East Pakistan could be repeated in West Pakistan.

Bhutto's haranguing and intemperate language at public meetings hid a desperately insecure personality that showed itself in an extra-ordinary series of letters which he exchanged with Khuhro at that time. After Khuhro's daughter's letter appeared in *The Times*, Bhutto had written to complain and urged Khuhro to reprimand her. Khuhro had written back to say that since his daughter was adult, married, independent and working at Oxford University, he was hardly in a position to control her writing or her assessment of events. If she had written something to hurt him personally however he was sorry and would write and let her know that Bhutto had minded her remarks.

Insecure and furious at receiving this letter Bhutto wrote a long six page typed letter to Khuhro flinging past and present grievances at him and writing 'creatively' about events in his father's and his own life, detailing largely imagined injuries:

"On the 17th of September 1971 you wrote me a letter apologising for the unsavoury behaviour of your daughter, Dr. Hameeda Khuhro, who seems to have lost all sense of propriety by employing words unbecoming of a respectable person. However, characteristic of your attitude towards me and my family for last sixty years or more, about two days earlier, as a 'citizen', you wrote a letter to President Yahya Khan, demanding my arrest for the speech I delivered at the Quaid-e-Azam's Mazar on the 11th of September for the restoration of the rights of the people. I hope you will pardon me if I tell you that this is really the epitome of hypocrisy and cowardice. But I was not surprised. We know you too well, too well I am afraid. We know exactly how you have behaved throughout your chequered career as a person and a politician.

I do not intend here to catalogue one by one your conduct towards us despite our generous attitude towards you. Whenever God Almighty has given us the opportunity to serve the people, we have always taken a magnanimous view towards you. How long do you think this one-sided traffic should continue?

Allow me to remind you that my father, Sir Shah Nawaz Khan Bhutto for whom you have expressed respect in your letter under reference but whom you have viciously attacked on numerous other occasions was always good to you. My father met you for the first time when as a young man, you visited our village to beg him to use his influence on Mr. Bolus to spare Shah Mohammad Khuhro who was a small but hardworking Khatedar of the district. Both of you expressed your gratitude to my father for his assistance and pledged to remain loyal to him for ever.

On the introduction of Minto Morley Reforms in 1919[5] my father went to the Imperial Council but returned to provincial politics in 1923. In all the elections since 1923 you intrigued against my father but he secured the highest number of votes in all of them until the fatal elections of 1937. Despite your hostile attitude my father continued to be good to you and made you Vice President of the Sind Mohammedan Association of which he was President. During the 1928 riots you would have been put into serious trouble had not my father once again intervened on your behalf. My uncle, Sardar Wahid Baksh Khan Bhutto was implicated in the well-known Khanzadi murder case, you moved heaven and earth to see him convicted, a conviction which might have led to his death.

This is the way you repaid him for his kindness towards you obtaining your own acquittal in 1928.

You made every conceivable effort but in vain to prevent my father from representing Sind and the Muslims of Bombay Presidency in the first and second Round Table Conferences held in London. In contrast, my father allowed you to give evidence in London in support of the findings of the Sub-Committee on the Separation of Sind. Incidentally, although you went to London only to give evidence in support of the findings of a certain Sub-Committee like many others who went for the same purpose, you have falsely claimed that you were a delegate to the Round Table Conference.

As a socialist I am opposed to feudalism. It nevertheless amuses me when I see you lay absurd claims to a great feudal past. What a monstrous lie? I do not want to open up the past as that might embarras you. I would not like to injure your feelings despite your daughter's unnecessarily provocative attitude.

Before the elections were held in 1937 my father and you agreed not to oppose each other. But you blatantly violated this understanding. Despite this breach of faith on your part, my father stuck to his word and did not put up a candidate against you. Less due to your intrigues and more on account of the stupidity of our close relatives, my father who was then the Chief Adviser to the Governor of Sind, was 'defeated' in the 1937 elections. At that time he was only 49 years old and he held sway over the politics of Sind for more than a decade. He was not only the acknowledged leader of the Mussalmans of Sind but that of Bombay Presidency as a whole. This notwithstanding, at that relatively young age he honourably decided to withdraw from the political scene.

Even after my father withdrew from politics he continued to assist you. When you were involved in the Allah Baksh murder case he helped you. He saved you from the gallows because he was a gentleman. Begum Khuhro met him in the Circuit House at Sukkur and begged him to be merciful.* He did this because he knew you as a boy and had helped you to come into prominence. Mark you, he did this although Allah Baksh was very close to him. After his evidence in your favour Allah Baksh's brother Moula Baksh hysterically told my father that he did not expect that a man who had been like a father to Allah Baksh would "save a murderer" to quote Moula Baksh. You acknowledged your gratitude in a telegram addressed to my father in Bombay immediately on your release. Since the time you went to my father in distress for help against the wrath of an imperial Deputy Commissioner to the time of his death he maintained the most cordial relations with you. Before his death in 1957, in the last elections held in his lifetime in 1954, he helped you in instructing his cousin and uncle and father-in-law, Khan Bahadur Ahmed Khan Bhutto, to support you. As a result, Khan Bahadur Ahmed Khan Bhutto lost his own seat but you and your brother were returned from Sanghar and Larkana.

In the earlier part of your association with my family I was not born. Later on, I was too young to be aware of your impeccable (sic) enmity towards us. For instance, in 1931 I was only three years of age when my father participated in the Round Table Conference in London, you tried to take advantage of his ab-

---

* Khuhro's wife who was in strict *purdah* at the time did not leave Karachi the entire time that Khuhro was in jail in Sukkur. Her father had come to Karachi to look after her.

sence from Larkana by trying to replace him as President of the Larkana District Local Board. Despite your best efforts you could not dislodge him from that office which he held continuously for over fifteen years. Since those days to the present I have either heard of your hostility or seen it in action.

When Martial Law was declared in 1958 and you were arrested for black-marketing, I took the step of visiting your house in Karachi to express my sympathy. I told your brother, the one who resides in Hyderabad, that I was prepared to represent you as a lawyer in the Martial Law proceedings. I took this initiative although the gesture might have cost me my ministership.

Your brother was so touched by my gesture that tears trickled down his eyes. Soon after that when I became a Minister, you were convicted to suffer rigorous imprisonment as a third-class convict. I was sitting with President Ayub Khan when the then Deputy Commissioner of Karachi, Mr. Muzaffar Hussain, now Chief Secretary of East Pakistan, came and reported to Ayub Khan your pathetic condition in jail. After he left I told President Ayub Khan to be generous in victory and allow you the facilities of an important political prisoner.* President Ayub Khan expressed surprise because he was under the impression that an ancient feudal rivalry existed between your family and my family. I informed him that since our association began from the time when your father was a small zamindar struggling very hard to improve his status, the question of an ancient feud could not arise. At the time when my great ancestors were owning vast tracts of land in Larkana and Jacobabad, and were held in high esteem, you were nowhere in the picture.

After you were released on bail in November 1958** you came to my residence in Karachi along with your son Shah Mohammed. You told me that you were a shattered person and that as an old man with failing health you could not endure the rigours of extended imprisonment. I assured you of my support. Partly if not chiefly on this account, your bail plea was confirmed. When the martial law authorities sent a high powered team of officials, both civil and military, to investigate your dubious claim to land holdings in the riverian tracts in Larkana taluka, President Ayub Khan asked me to assist them with information and evidence. Although I could have given the Government convincing evidence to adversely affect your contested possessions, I refrained from doing so. I told President Ayub Khan that I was his Minister of Commerce and not his chief of Police. Indeed, not on a single occasion throughout my long tenure as a Minister in the Martial Law Government and subsequently in the Cabinet under the Constitution of 1962, did I ever seek to harm your interests. If I had chosen to do so, I could literally have crushed you by using the efficacious martial law machinery and thereafter by employing the administration against you. But you will

---

* Mr. Muzaffar Hussain, C.S.P. was Collector of Karachi and I. G. Prisons Sind at the time of Khuhro's trial. He denies any such incident ever having taken place where he saw Ayub Khan in connection with Khuhro's privileges in jail or even meeting Bhutto in this regard. Muzaffar Hussain was himself the authority for granting privileges and he granted these in spite of strong opposition from the Commissioner Karachi, N. M. Khan who was a co-conspirator with Mirza in bringing the prosecution against Khuhro. Interview with Muzaffar Hussain C.S.P. by Shah Zaman Khuhro, 30 Jan. 1996.

**Khuhro was released on bail by the Supreme Court in March 1960 and acquitted just a few weeks later when his case was heard by the full bench of the Supreme Court in April 1960. There could be no reason to ask Bhutto for any favours after coming out on bail and with Suhrawardy arguing the case for Khuhro.

admit that instead of falling into this temptation, nay, of doing my duty, I chose to maintain cordial relations with you. The Home Minister Mr. Zakir Hussain and his Home Secretary, Mr. N. M. Khan tried to send you to jail in 1960. You came flying to Rawalpindi and begged me to save you. Please remember that I immediately went to Zakir Hussain and to President Ayub Khan to quash the investigations. You expressed abiding gratitude when I informed you that I had managed to stop further investigations.

On a number of occasions as a Minister I came to your house on your invitations. I flew specially from Dacca to Karachi to attend your daughter's wedding. On one occasion to show my goodwill I came with my wife to your house for lunch, the same person whom your goondas and gangsters tried to attack violently on the 4th of December 1970 when they thought that she was in my car along with other ladies. After that unpardonable incident you did not have the elementary decency to apologise to us.

Despite your own suspicious activities I gave you indirect support in the 1962 elections by not coming out openly against your brother Ali Gohar. On this account he was returned to the Provincial Assembly of West Pakistan in a Basic Democracies election. This would simply not have happened if I had openly and effectively opposed him.

You were delighted when I left office after Tashkent. You could not conceal your joy and jubiliation. You could not contain yourself. You thought the time had come for you to destroy me. You offered your services to Ayub Khan for this purpose. You had it conveyed to him that you were a strong man, the master in the art of employing brute force and that you alone could destroy me. Along with the other despicable politicians of your type you sought to form a front against me. But God in his infinite mercy saved me because I championed the people's cause. All your conspiracies failed. You threatened to take vengeance against me in a speech you delivered in Ratodero in January 1967. You spared no efforts to bring this about but in spite of your intrigues and the power of the former dictator, I launched a great movement of the people against Ayub Khan and destroyed his regime. When I was in jail you and another notorious politician of Sind suggested to Ayub Khan that I should be involved in a false murder case to implicate me with Hashim Khan who had tried to assassinate Ayub Khan in Peshawar on the 10th November 1968. Even when the regime of Ayub Khan was tottering you gave statements in Larkana in support of him. Taking undue advantage of the changed times, in January 1968, a day after Ayub Khan had dined with you at Larkana, you took the law in your hands and demolished my cousin's orchards and hand-pump to illegally extend your boundary wall on his property. It is alleged that you have usurped about 19,000 sq. ft. of municipal property ...[and the land of my cousin and Nawab Lahori to build a house in Larkana.]

During the period of the present martial law regime, on a number of occasions you have tried to intrigue and prejudice the Government against me. You threatened to bring about my Waterloo in the elections of last year. You spent plenty of money, you bought Mashori's support,* you got Pagaro's help, you misused

---

* Mashori was a *pir* in the Dokri taluka of Larkana District who was in fact paid by Bhutto to support him and did so. In this case as was usual with him, he accused his opponent of what in fact he had done himself.

the holy name of Islam, nevertheless I gave you a crushing defeat and secured more votes than you even in your own village. But alas! because of your inveterate hatred for me and my family you refused to see the writing on the wall even after such a humiliating defeat. During those elections, I cannot forget, how low you stooped by having my friends attacked by your gangsters. I repeat you had my wife's automobile attacked in the belief that she was seated in it. You crudely and falsely boasted that you had made my father flee from Sind in 1937 by defeating him in that election.

Now also when I am engaged in the struggle for the restoration of democracy you are intriguing against me day in and day out, as per your letter to President Yahya Khan a couple of days after my speech of September 11th at the Quaid's Mazar. A few days later you send me a written apology for the atrocious language employed by your daughter in her letter to the *Times* of London of April 1st, 1971. In that letter your daughter has not only chosen to attack me in indecent language but she has not spared the Armed Forces and the majority of the people of this part of Pakistan. She has maliciously called me "an agent of the Punjab" little forgetting (sic) that her own father is considered to be the greatest of all agents, the man who imposed One Unit on Sind. I have never been anybody's agent, I am a socialist and I believe in the rights of all the peoples. Your daughter has gone on to say that she is ashamed of calling herself a Pakistani. I presume she is not a jouvenile (sic) delinquent. She claims to be a Doctor doing research in one of the finest universities of the world. Surely she should be little more refined but it seems that blood is thicker than college books.

How can you expect me to attach any credibility to your apology when, in 1932 you apologised to my father's servant Husain for having him attacked by your goondas? You have repeatedly repented whenever we have been in power but you have always sought to strike us whenever even a remote opportunity has arisen in your favour.

I am far too engaged in the battle for Pakistan's survival to attend to your pranks. I am so completely engrossed in higher responsibilities that I cannot find the time to consider whether this is yet another well timed but insincere gesture of yours. Please reflect a little, please think back over the years, draw a balance sheet and arrive at objective conclusions. Do not indulge in halucinations built on falsification of events and resting on equally tenuous foundations."

Khuhro got the letter when he returned to Karachi from Larkana on 26 September. Bhutto's diatribe was absolutely shocking in its no holds barred abuse based as it was on "hallucinations built on falsification of events and resting of equally tenuous foundations." which he was accusing Khuhro of. Khuhro's letter to the President pointing out the inflammatory nature of Bhutto's speeches and behaviour had been confidential and Khuhro had never expected that confidentiality would be betrayed at such a high level. He had always known government circles which were highly principled and discreet. This was his introduction to the new style of government in Pakistan. But his letter had obviously found its mark with Bhutto and his daughter's analysis of events made as early as 1 April was still rankling with a man who was "so completely engrossed in higher responsibilities" that he found time now to write a six page closely typed letter and would within a few weeks write another 15-page invective again raking over the past and myriad imagined grievances. Khuhro could not ignore a letter so full of distortion of past events which included his own political career, personal life and his relationships with his contemporaries. No doubt Bhutto was listening to garbled stories from servants and sycophants and giving them his own interpretation filtered through a mind riddled with complexes. Khuhro decided to write back as factually as possible and try to correct the erroneous views that Bhutto had taken on certain events. He knew by now that Bhutto's principal motivation was his self-aggrandisement. It would be difficult to get through to him that there were people who acted from a sense of public responsibility. Khuhro could but try and on 4 October he sent his reply spread over 10 pages somewhat less closely typed than those of Bhutto:

"I got your letter dated 21 September, 1971, full of abuse and reproach quite uncalled for and based on wrong and misleading information.

The real reason why you have got so infuriated that you have thrown to winds all decency and decorum and have often used provocative language is, that the President General Yahya Khan has deemed it fit to show you my confidential letter.

I have said nothing new in my letter to the President. Your speeches, one at Hyderabad on 7th and another at Quaid-e-Azam's Mazar on 11th September were very provocative, inciting industrial labour in urban areas, peasantry in rural areas, students and semi-educated unemployed youth of the country to violence. This has been publicly resented not only by me, but by various other experienced political leaders in West Pakistan in the press and in their restricted workers meetings. Newspapers too, have been publishing and criticising your violent trend of speaking from time to time. It may be due perhaps to frustration. No other party or public man except you could be blamed for creating this impasse. They have repeatedly sounded a note of warning to the present regime about yours and some of your party men's activities of this kind. We the peaceloving and law abiding citizens of the country cannot afford to see West Pakistan also passing through the same ordeal as East Pakistan. So I have done my duty in drawing attention of the President to this situation. You seem to draw your own conclusions when you say that in my letter I have asked for your arrest. But you will agree that law of the land is the same for everyone, high or low.

You have traced the history of more than the last fifty years, even much before you were born, about occasional political differences between late Sir Shahnawaz and myself. It seems some people are determined to give you wrong information and have placed before you some kind of record wholly or substantially fabricated. Let me briefly answer your allegations against me.

I have never been to your village to see your father the late Sir Shahnawaz Bhutto, not even once in my life. My first meeting with him was when I was a student in Larkana Madressah and your father was on its governing body. I was in 5th English in 1917 when he came there for the oral examination of my class and he, I learnt later, gave me more marks than I should have got. It was a bit of partiality. He talked to me sweetly and enquired about my father's health. Mr. E. J. Bolus whom I knew as President of our Madressah Board, was a very polite and good natured gentleman and, therefore, any quarrel or misunderstanding between him and my father is unthinkable and therefore the question of your father's magnanimity does not come in. My father Shah Mohammed Khan was not a small *khatedar* though he must have been hard working in his young days which every zamindar should be. People of the whole District and Sind know that he was one of the top zamindars of the District. Only two years after his death I contested Bombay Legislative Council elections, that is in November 1923. District Larkana then also included the present Dadu District and the District had three plural seats and, therefore all the candidates had to canvass the entire area of the District although the number of votes was small as voting qualification was on property basis. Your father first contested Bombay Legislative Assembly seat from Larkana in November 1920 and not in 1923 as you have wrongly stated. K. B. Dhanibaksh Jatoi of Mehar and K. B. Ghulam Mohammed Isran were elected then along with him. In November 1923 I came in the field to fight elections and K. B. Ghulam Mohammed Isran withdrew from the contest and transferred all his support to your father and that is why he secured the first position. I got elected as well as K. B. Karimbaksh Jatoi the brother of K. B. Dhanibaksh Jatoi. Nawab Amir Ali Lahori and Pir Hamid Shah were defeated. If I were a son of a small *khatedar*, however hardworking, I would not have dared to contest the elections of such a vast area running from Ratodero to Sehwan which required considerable expense and influence. Sir Shahnawaz got so exhausted in this election, although he was only about 40 years old, that he fell very ill and was removed to Karachi for treatment and therefore could not attend the Budget session at Bombay in February-March 1924, the first session after the elections.

Unlike you he was not vindictive nor petty-minded. K. B. Isran had filed objection against my nomination papers before the Larkana Collector who was also the Returning Officer and who rejected the objection and upheld my nomination. After the result of my elections K. B. Isran wanted to file an election petition against me, that as I was 22 years of age I was not qualified to contest. When your father heard of this he came to my house and took me along with himself to K. B. Isran's house and persuaded him not to file the election petition.

On my return from Bombay to Karachi by sea in early April, 1924 I stayed in Karachi for sometime and during that period I often used to go and visit him at the old bungalow of Haji Dossul at Clifton where he was convalescing. He came in contact with your mother there. I was then staying at Carlton Hotel near Cantonement Station, which was then considered to be the best hotel in Karachi. In early May your father came and occupied the room next to mine in the hotel. He took your mother to Quetta and I saw them off. After the Nikah ceremony there at the residence of the late Nawab Bahadur Aazam Jan, father of the present Khan of Kalat a fortnight later, they returned to Larkana and stayed at my house in Larkana. This will show you what intimate connections I had with your parents. From 1924 to 1929 Sir Shahnawaz was the leader of Muslim group in Bombay Council and I was the Deputy Leader and in Sind he was President of Sind Mohammaden Association of which I was Vice-President and K. B. Vali Mohammed Hassanali was the General Secretary.

Towards the end of 1928 Sir Samuel Hoare the then Secretary of State for India sent a Commission headed by Sir John Simon to make recommendations about further instalment of reforms to Indians. The Commission comprised only of Englishmen and therefore the Indian National Congress boycotted it. The Provincial Governments had then appointed local Committees to collaborate with the Simon Commission within their respective provinces. From Sind Sir

Shahnawaz Bhutto and the late Syed Miran Mohammed Shah were appointed on the collaborating Committee. In January 1929 I led a deputation before the Simon Commission and presented a Memorandum for the separation of Sind from the Bombay Presidency and its constitution as a separate province. Many senior gentlemen from Sind like the late Mir Ayub Khan, K. B. Hassanali, Ghulam Ali Chagla, K. B. Allah Baksh Soomro and various others were in the delegation. When the Simon Commission in its Report opposed the proposal of separating Sind from Bombay, Syed Miran Mohammed Shah wrote a comprehensive minute of dissent strongly advocating the cause of the separation of Sind. Sir Shahnawaz refused to subscribe to it and he affixed his signature to the Simon Report endorsing the view that Sind may continue to be part of Bombay. This happened sometime in early 1930. In January 1931 the first Round Table Conference of Indian leaders was called by the British Government in London. Mr. M. A. Jinnah was in Karachi in December 1930 to argue the appeal in the then Judicial Commissioner's court, Karachi, on behalf of the late Pir Pagaro (father of the present Pir) against his conviction in the lower Court. I invited him to dinner at the Carlton where Messrs. G. M. Syed, Hatim Alvi, Syed Miran Mohammad Shah, Pir Ali Mohammed Rashdi and various other politicians of Sind were present. After dinner I presented an address to him urging him to press the case in the Round Table Conference for separating Sind from Bombay and making it an autonomous province. This view was fully endorsed by him in his reply. On the other hand the Government of Bombay got Sir Shahnawaz nominated on the RTC to oppose separation of Sind. Both of them, that is, Mr. M. A. Jinnah and Sir Shahnawaz left by the same steamer from Karachi in the third week of December for London. When all the delegates met in London in January 1931 Muslim delegates from India selected the late His Highness Sir Agha Khan as their leader and the late Dr. Sir Shafaat Ahmad as Secretary. Mr. M. A. Jinnah went from here bag and baggage to settle down in London and practice there. As the Muslim opinion was very strong for separation of Sind Sir Shahnawaz could not oppose it. In the meantime Lord Willingdon who was at one time Governor of Bombay, took over as Viceroy of India. He was very anti Congress and also Mr. Jinnah.

Lord Willingdon put Mr. M. K. Gandhi and some other prominent Congress leaders in jail and he also got the name of Mr.Jinnah struck off from the subsequent RTC meetings. Sir Shahnawaz's name was also dropped because Government of Bombay was by then convinced that the British Government may take a favourable view towards the persistent demand of the Muslim delegates of RTC of making Sind a separate province. The rift between Sir Shahnawaz and myself in fact came on this issue of Sind separation.

After the third RTC I was invited to appear before the Joint Parliamentary Committee on Indian Reforms in June-July 1933 to present the case for the separation of Sind as I was playing a leading role among the politicians of Sind for getting the province separated from Bombay. On behalf of Hindus who were opposing the separation of Sind, Professor Chhablani was invited. I went all alone but the Hindus sent a strong delegation to assist Mr.Chhablani. Thus you will see that I had no hand at all in your father's selection on the first RTC or his removal from the 2nd and 3rd RTC.

I have given this long description just to keep the record straight and that the history of this period is not falsified in the manner you have attempted to do. You have made a mention of the Hindu–Muslim riot in Larkana in May 1928. I played the leading role to defend Muslims who were victims of false and malicious propaganda by the vocal class of Hindus in Larkana. Muslims were very backward and were very frightened and, therefore, I had to take this bold step to defend their just cause. I therefore organized a defence committee and engaged the best available lawyers for their defence in Courts. A large number of people were put on trial, but with the Grace of God, I got them all acquitted. Your father was then playing a diplomatic role of pleasing both sides. It is absolutely untrue that he saved me from going to jail on charges of instigating riots. In fact I came to Larkana a little after the riot was over and I could not have been implicated for taking any part in the riots. My only role was to defend innocent Muslims who were brought into trouble.

You have claimed in your letter that you are a Socialist and are opposed to Feudalism. This claim indeed amuses me. You are a product of feudalism and in some of your speeches during the elections you claimed that your are a much bigger zamindar and much richer person than myself. This does not embarrass me as this is quite true. During 1959 when Ayub Khan introduced the so-called Land Reforms you were his Minister and right hand man. You saved all your landed property from the effects of Martial Law Regulation No. 64, but everyone of us suffered. Your palatial buildings in Karachi, Larkana and home town Naudero and other urban and rural properties bear ample evidence to your being a wealthy man. If you were really Socialist you would have long ago distributed much of your properties among the poor citizens in urban areas and the peasantry in villages of Larkana district. Socialism was only your election slogan. In fact you are a fascist. The way you have victimised the poor people in Larkana district getting their small bits of land and residential houses occupied by your goondas on mere suspicion that they voted for me, is a clear proof that you believe in Hitlerian tactics. No Socialist will dare do that. Shall I say in the words of your own party Information Secretary, Maulana Qausar Niazi that "you are Jagirdar (capitalist) but yet a Socialist."

As written above political rift came between your father and myself in the end of 1930 on Sind separation issue, and this continued upto 1937 when your father was defeated in the elections of separated Sind province, although I personally played no role of opposition against him. Against me the late Sher Mohammad Khan Abro was put up; but he could not do much and lost his deposit. In fact I should not be blamed for your father's defeat in 1937. He was then heading the newly formed United Party in Sind and I was with Sir Ghulam Hussein in the Democratic Party. All his close relatives except K. B. Ahmad Khan did not support him and most of them actually worked against him. Your father knew full well that I was not instrumental to his defeat, and therefore, he maintained good relations with me even after he left Sind and went on the Bombay–Sind Public Service Commission as Sind's representative. We used to meet whenever he came to Karachi on his annual trip. In 1943 when I went to Bombay to attend Quaid-e-Azam M. A. Jinnah's Working Committee in the month of April-May, the late Sir Shahnawaz came to the Taj Hotel where I was staying and insisted that I should go and stay with him in his flat on Cumballa Hill and he took me in his car. I spent at least a week or ten days with him. When he came finally to Sind after the occupation of Junagarh by the Indian Government, where he was Divan for a year or more, he stayed on McNiel Road, and we often met. I was sometimes a Minister and sometimes in the Opposition. You would recall that in 1954 when you returned after completing your studies abroad he sent you to invite me to a private dinner at McNiel Road house, where I came. You will also recall that you came to see me in Larkana in December 1954 to present me a small book you had written in support of One Unit in West Pakistan. You will also recall that in the indirect elections to the West Pakistan Assembly at Lahore, held in January 1956, your father deputed you to help me in the elections and you went to Sardar Sultan Ahmad Chandio in Karachi to secure his help for me and also you went to K. B. Ahmad Khan Bhutto your father-in-law to help me and my group as against that of Kazi Fazlullah.

The other day while searching my old papers I came across a letter written by your father, the late Sir Shahnawaz from Hyde Park Hotel, London, dated 26th August 1955. I enclose a photostat copy of it and you will see how intimate he was with us. He had been to London for medical treatment. Your dear mother was also very friendly with us both and she often came to our house on friendly visits.*

Sardar Wahid Bux Bhutto

You have stated in your letter that I moved heaven and earth to get the late Sardar Wahid Bux Khan convicted in the Khanzadi (w/o Chatto Buriro) murder case. I am not only surprised but am pained to hear this from you. Sardar Wahid Bux and myself and his brother Nabibux Khan were studying in Larkana Madressah at the same time. Nabibux was my contemporary, but Wahid Bux was two or three years senior. We were all good friends and later used to invite each other for *shikar* parties.

In fact he was one of those friends who persuaded me, to contest elections in October-November 1923. And he promised his full support to me. He did work for me in the beginning but suddenly about two weeks before the date of the elections, at very great family pressure, when Sir Shahnawaz (then K. B. Bhutto) went and stayed for a week or more at his house in Mirpur village he changed over to your father's side. But yet our good relations continued. I had no hand at all, I can say on oath, in this unfortunate Khanzadi episode. Public generally had sympathy with that poor peasant Chatto Buriro whose wife was kidnapped and later murdered and buried in Thatta district as far as I remember. But I had nothing to do with that area to which he belonged i.e. Village Buriro in Ratodero taluka, near Naudero. I had no witnesses in the case nor was I even remotely concerned. Fact of the matter is that I could neither have harmed nor helped Wahidbux Khan. The Collector at that time A. D. Gorwalla ICS and SP Mr. Rusby happened to be friendly with me. But even if I had approached them for or against Wahidbux they could not have done anything in a kidnapping or murder case. They both were honest and independent officers, quite unapproachable. Later when Sir Ernest Hotson, Home Minister in the Bombay Governor's

---

* Lady Bhutto counted the Khuhros among her closest friends. She complained to them bitterly about Zulfiqar's choice of an Iranian wife and afterwards brought Nusrat Bhutto with herself on visits to the Khuhros in Larkana and Karachi. Later she also complained to them about Zulfiqar's behaviour to her after Sir Shahnawaz's death and even suggested that if he threw her out of the house she would come and live with them. Apparently he was forcing her to give all the family jewellery to him so that she would not give it to her daughters. Conversations and visits in author's presence.

Cabinet ordered the withdrawal of the case against Wahidbux at the persuasion of Sir Shahnawaz, I did not oppose it, although Hotson was equally friendly with me. Late Wahidbux Khan and myself were on visiting terms even after this criminal case, till his death, which I went to condole with his brother and family.

Late Allah Bux Murder Case Episode:[6]

Allah Bux was killed by Hurs of Pir Pagaro in May 1943. The Hurs had a strong grievance against him. Pir Sahib and Allah Bux had made a political alliance and therefore during the Budget session in February March 1941, Pir Sahib came and stayed in Karachi in the house of late Sir Ghulam Hussain who had earlier been Home Minister in Allah Bux's cabinet. Pir Sahib told his followers who were members of the Sind Legislature to cross over to Allah Bux's side under threats of violence and thus got our Ministry headed by Mir Bundehali Khan in which I was number 2 Minister, defeated.[7] Soon thereafter Pir Sahib's Hurs started acts of lawlessness in Sind on a large scale. Trains were derailed and in one of those derailments Sir Ghulam Hussain's son was also killed, many people were butchered on highways and motor buses and cars looted. Sir Hugh Dow was then Governor of Sind. He forced his Ministry to restore law and order and Pir Sahib was arrested and lodged in Jubbulpore (C.P.) jail. He then was brought back to Hyderabad in early 1942 and tried under Martial Law and was given capital punishment. This was sufficient ground for Hurs to retaliate.[8]

I was the victim of political intrigue... As leader of Opposition by virtue of being the leader of the Muslim League block in Sind Assembly, I was approached by Sir Ghulam Hussain through Mr. Yusuf Haroon, as he was called upon by the Governor in early October 1942 to form the Ministry on dismissal of Allah Bux, that our party should join his and form a combined Ministry. Sir Ghulam Hussain was anti-Muslim League at the time. G. M. Syed was President of the Provincial Muslim League. We both negotiated terms which were that Sir Ghulam Hussain with all his followers will join Muslim League and out of four Muslim Ministers he will have two including himself and we will have two. This was agreed to and finally approved by Quaid-e-Azam. I nominated Mr. M. H. Gazdar as second Minister from Muslim League in addition to myself. This strengthened the position of the Hidayetullah Ministry which became Muslim League Ministry for the first time in Sind and continued in office right up to the time of Partition. Mr. Allah Bux had been dismissed under instructions from the Viceroy in early October 1942 as he renounced his title of Khan Bahadur... at the pressure of Congress block in Sind Assembly who were his supporters. My political opponents conspired against me and brought up a case of conspiracy against me for Allahbux's murder and the police was heavily bribed. Governor Hugh Dow also acquiesced in this.

This British Governor had an old rancour against me. In 1933 when I came back from U.K. after giving evidence before the Joint Parliamentary Committee on the Sind Separation issue, Viceroy Lord Willingdon appointed an Administrative Committee in October of the same year because he got instructions from the Secretary of State that Sind was becoming a separate autonomous province. This Committee was headed by the same Sir Hugh Dow who was then a Secretary in the Government of India. Myself and late Sir Abdullah Haroon were the two Muslim representatives on the Committee and D. B. Hiranand Khemsingh was the Hindu representative and there were two Government representatives Mr. Mclaughlin, Chief Engineer and Mr. Kaula the Auditor General of India. The function of this Committee was to suggest a machinery for the administrative set up in the new province of Sind. I raised the issue that as Sind was becoming a separate province it must have a separate university. Sir Hugh Dow did not like the idea but as the proposal was carried he wrote a chapter on this subject for the Committee, which was very nasty, criticising Muslim zamindars and jagirdars in Sind in particular and the backward Muslim community in general in highly provocative language and suggested that as Sind was an extremely backward and illiterate province two renowned British Professors be deputed to survey the area and suggest what type of university, if at all, be given to Sind. This clearly implied that the University should be almost wholly manned by Britishers. I could not tolerate this and strongly protested in the meeting and told him that he should withdraw this language and re-write the chapter recommending the constitution of the University of Sind immediately on creation of the Province, and this be largely manned by Indian Muslims from whatever part of the country they came as the proper course to help educationally backward province was to set up a University as quickly as possible and not put it into cold storage as he meant to do. There were some hot words exchanged and ultimately he gave in, but he never forgave me for that and also for my anti-Government speeches in the Bombay Council where he was a Government whip for some years.

Sir Shahnawaz at that relevant period of time, i.e., 1942 to 1945 was member on Bombay–Sind Public Service Commission and lived in Bombay and had no evidence to give in this false murder case. He was unnecessarily troubled to come to Sukkur in June-July 1945 to appear as prosecution witness in the case. He was perhaps called to prove my opposition with the late Allah Bux politically. It was not necessary to call him because there was enough material on record to show that I was the top leader of Muslim League in Sind and Allah Bux was enjoying the support of the Hindu Congress. I must say to the credit of your father that he did not add anything and did not give false evidence as he might have been expected by the prosecution. He must have thought of his own reputation also in addition to whatever sympathy he may have for me or for the Muslim League organisation. Quaid-e-Azam was very perturbed at this false prosecution of me and sent Mr. Somjee, Bar-at-Law a famous Criminal lawyer in Bombay to appear for me and he was very happy on my acquittal. He sent a telegram of felicitations to my wife. Soon thereafter Quaid-e-Azam came to Karachi. I received him at the airport and he came to our residence and had a private dinner with us next day.

I am sorry to hear that some micreants attacked your car in which Begum Nusrat Bhutto was travelling during elections in last December. I hear this from you for the first time after nearly ten months. Nusrat Bhutto has been quite friendly particularly to my daughter Hameeda and my wife. Please convey my apologies to her for this unfortunate incident.

It is a big lie to say that I offered my services to Ayub Khan after your removal from the cabinet. All politicians of any consequence in Pakistan were EBDOed by Ayub Khan mainly on your advice. In fact you played a very dirty role during your association with him for eight long years 1958–66. It was you who suggested that politicians should all be banished under EBDO; it was you who suggested that there should 'one party Government like Communist or semi-Communist countries with officials controlling at Tahsil, District and Province levels; it was you who got Convention League started in the end of 1962 and thus brought about rift in the organisation.

After your dismissal from Ayub Khan's cabinet and after completion of the course of EBDO in December, 1966, I called a meeting at my residence in Karachi, of prominent Sindhi politicians and the issue was discussed whether we should form the opposition or support Ayub's regime and it was decided by an overwhelming majority that we must oppose the regime, although Qazi Fazlullah and some others did not agree. Agha Ghulam Nabi who is now close to you, was present and will bear me out. I made it very clear to Qazi Fazlullah that I do not want to come in the Ministry in the Centre or the Province but if he wanted he could do so. Six months later Qazi Fazlullah was actually taken in the provincial cabinet. You will notice my speeches during 1967 and 1968 criticised the Government every time for the wrong actions and corruption all round at a large scale, so much so that for my speeches at times Qazi Fazlullah was taken to task by Governor Musa and F. M. Ayub Khan because of his association with me. I was one of the few public men in West Pakistan who every time that met him [Ayub Khan] told him plainly all the defects and shortcomings of his administration.

You have made a mention in your letter of certain acts done by you in my favour during Ayub's regime when you were his Minister for Industries and later Foreign Affairs. I gather this from your letter for the first time as you never said so in the past whenever we met here and there. The case of the sale of the car started against me by N. M. Khan under the inspiration from Iskander Mirza and perhaps Ayub Khan who arranged the coup when I was Defence Minister, was a false and fabricated case as the unanimous judgement of the Supreme Court clearly shows. Because I was Defence Minister at the time of the coup in a democratic government, such kind of trouble was expected from the succeeding (undemocratic) regime. I may tell you, however, that it is absolutely untrue and your memory has failed you when you say that you helped in getting my bail confirmed. The bail was refused by the High Court and granted by the Supreme Court and it was final so there was no question of confirmation. Mr. A. K. Brohi was my Advocate at that time. Later on, however, Mr. Brohi went to India as High Commissioner and actually the case itself was argued on my behalf by the late Mr. H. S. Suhrawardy before the Supreme Court in Lahore.

There remains yet one point to explain, however minor or petty it may be you have referred to the incident of your father's favourite servant, who as far as I recollect, was named Hussain and belonged to Bombay side. This was somewhere in 1929-30. Sir Shahnawaz and myself had jointly bought a property near Seo Bazar in Larkana, and I had to arrange collection of rent and looking after of the property. Tenants there usually fell in arrears. One day this servant appeared in the afternoon at my house and demanded the share of the rent of his master for three months or so, which had fallen in arrears and my man had not been able to collect it. So he was told that it would be sent as soon as the rent was received. He was not satisfied and said that his master needed the money.

I therefore told him that I will arrange to give him the required amount on the following day. This did not satisfy him, it appears. So, when he left my room, outside in the courtyard he used some abusive language about me which my servants overheard. Next day while in Seo Bazar he and some of my servants crossed each other by accident and finding a good opportunity my servants gave him a sound thrashing. He was a bad tempered fellow and when dissatisfied with his master did not even spare him and in his absence would use foul language about him. In this case however Sir Shahnawaz thought it to be his own insult and got a complaint lodged at the Larkana Police Station, and saw the Collector and D. M., Mr. H. M. Patel ICS personally about it. But as it was not a cognisable offence and outside influence did not work in those days of British rule, the complaint was dismissed by the police. Then a face saving device was to be arranged. Mr. Patel the D. M. who was friendly with both of us. He called us to tea and as Sir Shahnawaz was senior to me by about twenty years and also in politics, I told him I was sorry for what had happened and hoped that good relations between us would not be affected by such trivial incidents.

Finally I must answer the false and frivolous charges that

1. I have usurped some 2,500 sq.ft. of Sardar Pirbux Khan's land while erecting the compound wall on the south of our new house under construction.

2. that I have encroached upon Municipal land, some 9,000 sq.ft. in the north east corner of our house.

As far as Pirbux Khan, this area was measured in his presence by the City Surveyor, in February 1968. He was not satisfied, so he complained to the then Deputy Collector Larkana who is also City Survey Officer (Mr. Illias Baloch). Mr. Baloch therefore got a Survey Party from Hyderabad. They measured the area and determined the boundary between his and our land. And thereafter we started raising the wall, with his full knowledge and approval. If he had not been satisfied he would have filed a civil suit and not kept quiet for the last nearly four years.

Regarding the Municipal dispute, the facts are that this piece of land in dispute is 2,750 sq.ft. only and not 9,000 sq.ft. as you say in your letter. This is our land according to Revenue Record. Municipal Committee however laid false claim to it in 1968. Ahmed Hussain Lahori and his brothers claimed, on the other hand, that this piece belonged to them. So they went to Civil Court and filed a suit against us and made the Municipal Committee also a party in the suit. In that suit Municipality took the stand that they have no interest in the land as it was not their property. We have also filed a suit in the Civil Court for declaration and injunction, as it is clearly our property. So the matter is subjudice.

I have taken pains to aswer your tirade as best as I could and you must be knowing in your own mind that much of what you have said against me is false and fabricated, due to political animosity.

Let me in the end tell you that in politics there are no permanent friends and no permanent enemies. These changes take place as situations and circumstances change. I have very long experience of political life and I have seen many ups and downs in the past nearly fifty years.

In elections parties win and parties lose. No party in a democracy can claim to remain in power for all time."[9]

Bhutto was not happy with this comprehensive answer to his letter which did not give him the last word and rebutted his charges convincingly. He did not let the matter rest and penned another long list of grievances and sent them off to Khuhro. This time the letter covered 16 pages of closely typed material. Understandably Khuhro was amazed that Bhutto could find time to rake up the past for his mixture of trivial and absurd charges. He had not suspected the extent of Bhutto's complexes and the depth of his bitterness. Khuhro was hard put to it to account for these feelings. There were no blood feuds with the Bhuttos. He had reasonably cordial relations with his parents. He had known the young man only slightly before he was picked up by the Martial Law regime as Minister in 1958. Bhutto had been in power for most of the time of their acquaintance therefore definitely had the upper hand. Now he was the leader of the majority party in West Pakistan, he had defeated Khuhro in the elections and had himself written that he was busy with 'higher matters' so how was he able to find time to think about and write down the list of complaints from the past? Where had all this bitterness come from? Khuhro's weariness with the tirades from Bhutto was obvious from his reply to the second letter:

"Thanks for your letter dated 16th November delivered to me at Larkana, covering as many as sixteen typed pages.

1. I don't propose to reply to all the points, as I wish to avoid writing a lengthy letter, so that your valuable time is not wasted in going through it.

It is immaterial whether my father was a big zamindar or a small one. If he was a self made man, all the more creditable for him to have left enough property that I could contest elections to the Bombay Legislature two years after his death, against well established zamindars of the district like your father late Sir Shahnawaz Khan. Nawab Haji Amir Ali Lahori, K. B. Ghulam Mohammed Isran and K. B. Karimbaksh Khan Jatoi, at 22 or 23 years of age.

2. I am surprised to find that you have taken the trouble of getting the order of precedence for Commissioner Sind's Darbar of January 1932. Sir Shahnawaz then was not only a member of Bombay Legislative Council, but also the President of District Local Board, and a Ist Class Magistrate. So naturally he will get a higher position in a formal Darbar. He was, as I have already said, much senior to me in age and politics.

You have said in para. eight of your letter that I contested for Presidentship of D. L. Board against your father. This is absolutely untrue. Sir Shahnawaz was the first non-official President of District Local Board, at first nominated by the Collector and later from 1921 to 1934 by election. During this period I was never a candidate. On the contrary I always supported him in District Local Board."[10]

Khuhro picked out some of the points which he felt could not go unrefuted and answered them. He again contradicted the charge that he had opposed Bhutto senior personally:

"I have never claimed at any time that I got your father defeated in elections in 1937. Late Nawab Lahori, K. B. Isran and I made an agreement between ourselves to help each other. I offered myself from Larkana town and taluka, Lahori from Dokri–Warrah and Isran from Mehar-Kambar. All three of us got elected. I am not much interested whether you are a socialist or a fascist. Time will show what you will really be when you get or sieze power and control of country's affairs."[11]

Bhutto had once again brought up the Allah Baksh Soomro murder case and Khuhro replied once again:

"Para 21 of your letter regarding the K. B. Allah Baksh Soomro murder: Everyone is convinced including the Soomro family that I was quite innocent and a false case was made out against me through a deep rooted conspiracy, as I have stated in my earlier letter to you. I have nothing more to add in that respect."

Another point Khuhro felt he had to answer was the accusation that Khuhro had got close to Ayub Khan after Bhutto's removal and that he had supported Ayub Khan in the elections against Miss Jinnah, a wild accusation indeed:

"Para 23 of your letter, page 11: It is absolutely untrue that I went to see President Ayub Khan on late Haji Khan Kalhoro's fields where he went on *shikar*. I have never seen Haji Khan's lands up to this day. So the question of my offering him services does not arise.

You have mistaken me for Qazi Fazlullah who went there to see him and as he later told me, had dinner with Ayub Khan. This was in February 1967. In fact I had made it plain to Kazi Fazlullah that I do not want to join Ayub's Cabinet, much less go under Moosa Khan in the Provincial Cabinet. I never sang any praises of Ayub Khan. Will you please quote any public utterances on this subject. But I can quote your Assembly speeches and public statements, etc. wherein you praised him to the skies. You compared him to Sultan Salahuddin Ayubi, to Abraham Lincoln, to Lenin and to other great heroes that the world has produced. Your bitterness against him started much after your removal from his cabinet and after he started investigations against you in the Tractor fraud case. I saw Ayub Khan for the first time after extinction of EBDO restrictions, in July 1967 at Murree, where he invited me to lunch. This was after Fazlullah was taken up as a Provincial Minister."

Para 24 of your letter:

I was in Europe from August to mid October 1964. When I arrived here by about the 20th October, Miss Jinnah had already announced her candidature. So the first thing I did was to go and call on her and assure her of my support. Mumtaz Daultana was in Karachi then and I informed him of it and also many other friends like Justice Z. H. Lari, Hassan A. Shaikh, Mohammed S. Mitha and others.

... you saw that I worked for Miss Jinnah in the whole of Sind. I spent my own funds, as she had no funds at all. I also contributed to her central election fund. As far as your part in this affair, I am sure you can't be proud of it. I don't want to say more, as I don't want any more bitterness to be created in your mind."

Bhutto had claimed that in the elections of 1970 he had got more votes than Khuhro even in his own village of Akil and that Khuhro was victimizing the Bhuttos in that village. Khuhro made a reply gently reasoning as if with a angry child throwing ill considered accusations:

"Para 30, page 15 of your letter:

At my village polling I got nearly 1,500 votes. You got only 92. There were over a hundred bad votes and a few that Moulana of Jamiat ulemai Islam got. Please check up your record of polling results. I got almost the same number of votes (93) at your village Naudero polling station as you got at Akil village. So, on a tribal basis Khuhros voted for me and Bhuttos of Akil for you. I have no grouse against them. I challenge anyone who says that I have ever attempted to victimize them. They are all there in the village as happy in their homes as ever. Not an acre of land is taken away from them nor any shop or house. Some of them are in my private service as they were before. I have dismissed none."

Bhutto went somewhat overboard in his insults to Khuhro writing that he was financed by Nawab Chandio for his travel to Bombay to which Khuhro replied:

"It is not only surprising but also amusing to hear from you that late Nawab Ghaibi Khan financed my trips to Bombay for attending the Legislative Council sessions and committees, etc. The fact is that Nawab Ghaibi Khan did not support me in the elections of 1923 and 1926. In 1930 we three candidates came unopposed i.e. Sir Shahnawaz, K. B. Isran and myself. When the first elections of Sind Legislative Assembly were held on 1st February 1937 after the separation of Sind from Bombay, I had opposed Nawab Ghaibi Khan's son Mir Mohammed Khan from Kambar taluka and had put up Pir Turab Ali Shah of Kambar against him. Actually Nawab Sahib became friendly with me only from 1940 onwards when I became Minister in the Sind Cabinet. So the question of Ghaibi Khan giving me any financial help simply does not arise."

Finally Bhutto flung another insult at Khuhro telling him that his house in Larkana opposite the Bhuttos' house was very large and ugly. Khuhro wrote back patiently in the face of this amazing behaviour:

"My house opposite yours may be ugly architecturally as you say. I would not like to contradict you on this personal point of view. But it is a large house, my family being large."

Oddly Bhutto had sent his 'creative work' in the words of his biographer, *The Great Tragedy*, to Khuhro along with his incredible letter. Khuhro thanked him with complete self possession:

"Your book *The Great Tragedy* I have already read in the English version, as the book was presented to me by a friend as soon as it was put on sale. Thanks for sending me its Sindhi edition. Time will show whether you were right or wrong in acting politically as you have done in the present situation that we are faced with after the general elections of last December.

All best wishes and prayers that God Almighty guides you on the right path."[12]

This exchange of letters reveal with startling clarity the differences in character between the two men. Bhutto obssesive, bombastic and deeply consumed with a fixated idea of his own importance. He had sucked deep from the waters of the Western obsession with self and had virtually ignored the deep traditions of life in rural Sind. Khuhro, on the other hand shows a mind and a personality sure in its purpose and place in the scheme of things. He saw and related details with a context of the whole; he was objective and clear in his reporting of matters and had a scepticism about worldly events which made him see people for what they were.

Khuhro had uncannily predicted in the letter that Bhutto would take over power,

"Time will show what you will really be when you get or sieze power and control of the country's affairs",

a possibility not clear at that stage in November 1971 before the Indian invasion of East Pakistan. But just over a month later, on 20 December 1971 this eventuality came about when Bhutto became Chief Martial Law Administrator of the country. Khuhro and Pakistan were about to find out how he would really be in that situation.

24

A TEST OF ENDURANCE

The worst possible catastrophe had occurred. Pakistan went through self inflicted agony and a blood bath, was militarily defeated, dismembered, internationally humiliated and execrated. In December 1971 after the surrender of Dacca the capital of East Pakistan to the Indian army, power passed into the hands of the adventurer who was in large measure responsible for bringing about the catastrophe. Bhutto and his co-conspirators had taken the country into the depths of humiliation and disaster. Not able to face the consequences of their criminal actions the military junta now handed the country to the civilian who was their accessory. The 'joker'* was put in charge. Bhutto had trampled over the ruins of the country and thousands of corpses to achieve his dearest wish, supreme power in Pakistan.

Ironically the bewildered public of Pakistan fed on lies about the political and military situation welcomed Bhutto as saviour. In the ensuing five years the 'joker' would win many tricks but even in the midst of the most serious matters facing the country and the sleight of hand required to keep the country surviving, Bhutto did not forget Larkana or Khuhro.

The next few years were to be extremely trying for Khuhro, his family and his supporters. Bhutto was a curious character. Behind the bluster was a complex ridden, thin skinned man who took revenge for his imagined grievances by bullying and humiliating people–whether friends or foes. He would see how far he could go with people and then withdraw suddenly. He would use threats which ofcourse were sometimes carried out.

With Khuhro he now tried his favourite cat and mouse games. Even before coming into power Bhutto had used official machinery as well as unofficial means to harass those who had supported Khuhro in the elections. He continued the harassment with a will. Respectable zamindars, heads of tribes who had supported Khuhro were humiliated and insulted. Sardar Ali Hasan Depar was one such who was jailed. When he was released Bhutto sent for him and said, "Well, has the fat melted from your heart?" (presumably meaning that was he now brought down a peg or two and ready to support Bhutto). Depar, not a man to be bullied, replied, 'It has not'. The fate of Fakir Mohammed Kalhoro, a zamindar of Warah taluka near Nasirabad, who had been vociferously anti Bhutto in the elections, was more

---

* At the time a remark was widely attributed to one of the two generals, General Gul Hassan and Air Marshal Rahim Khan who were supposed to have brought Bhutto into power and one of whom apparently said: " Let the Joker look after it now"

serious. He was murdered in the *Mukhtiarkari* (the local administrative headquarters) in front of eyewitnesses and it was strongly rumoured that the murderers were rewarded by the government. Similarly vengeance was visited upon greater and lesser inhabitants of the district who had been known to vote against Bhutto. Occupation of land, criminal charges, jail became routine for these unfortunate people.

One of Khuhro's staunchest supporters in the election was a first cousin of Bhutto who had worked for Khuhro openly defying a dangerous man like Zulfiqar Bhutto. Now he paid for that defiance. He was put in jail and his house in the village Garhi Khuda Baksh in Taluka Ratodero, which was also the ancestral village of Zulfiqar, was requisitioned.

On landing at Moenjodaro airport on his first visit to Larkana soon after assuming power, Bhutto turned to the local officials and said: "What have you done about Habibullah Narejo?" Narejo was a young student worker of Khuhro whom Bhutto had noticed because of his energy and fearless confrontations with him during the elections. This young man was to be in jail for prolonged periods during the Bhutto years.

Sometimes the harassment took a farcical turn. A teacher at a Government school who was at school with Khuhro's daughter in Karachi, and who had exchanged a remark with Khuhro's polling agent on election day, was ordered to be suspended. Those who gave the orders of suspension only knew the first name of the teacher which was Zuleikha. The Education Ministry armed with just the first name and unable immediately to identify her, suspended all the Zuleikhas working for the Department. Thus three or four Zuleikhas suddenly found themselves out of favour quite unable to account for their misfortune.[1]

It was said that some people such as Alam Khan Gopang, Qaisar Khan Jatoi and others had taken money from Bhutto to vote for him. After coming into power he had them arrested and brought before him. The three begged for mercy. Bhutto then took out diary and checked through it and told each of them the amount he had paid them and that the money must be returned by that evening. The money was returned.

A lot of people who had opposed Bhutto, seeing the state of affairs escaped from Sind and went to live in Quetta under the protection of Sardar Ataullah Khan Mengal's Government. Even after the ANP government was removed, Quetta continued to be a safe haven compared to Sind and the refugees stayed there for the duration of Bhutto's rule.

Bhutto organised the administration of Larkana to suit his style. Khalid Kharal, highly recommended, was brought in from the Punjab as Deputy Commissioner, Larkana. For the crucial post of Superintendent Police he eventually found the perfect man, S. P. Pinial. Pinial had come to Bhutto's notice when he was Sub-Inspector and had won his confidence when he had been D.S.P. in Naudero in the election. He was promoted to S.P.Larkana and eventually to D.I.G. when Larkana was made a Division and spent his entire career without moving out of Larkana. Pinial was close enough to Bhutto be in charge of *faislas* (deciding disputes etc.) on his behalf in Naudero. He could also on occasion exercise enough influence on Bhutto to moderate some of his more excessive decisions. He certainly had more influence with the Prime Minister than successive Chief Ministers of Sind.

After Bhutto metamorphosed from President to Prime Minister he liked to play the role of the mediaeval ruler receiving the local notables. On Eid days he would hold court in the house of his late father-in-law, K. B. Ahmed Khan Bhutto. Bhutto would sit in the verandah, with the D. C. Kharal and S. P. Pinial standing behind him. The notables would line up and would be brought up to be presented one by one. Pinial would have a list of people to check to see who had come and who had not. Those who had missed out would be asked as to why they had not attended. If they had a plausible excuse they could be left in peace but if the S.P. was not convinced they would be arrested and jailed.

Some of Khuhro's close supporters asked him what to do and realising that dealing with Bhutto was like trying to please *Kali Devi*, he advised them to attend the 'durbars', as it appeared to him not worthwhile for them to antagonise this tyrannical and petty minded man. He even sent his sons along on Eid. Bhutto recognized the gesture by having them seated near himself. On one occasion after the public reception Bhutto took Khuhro's son Shah Mohammed into the drawing room and started reminiscing about the past. Invariably on such occasions he would bring up the matter of his father's defeat in the 1937 elections. He turned to Shah Mohammed and said:

"You know why my father lost the elections? It was because he was very pleasure loving and he was having an affair with Mrs. Parpia at the time which is why he delayed coming to Sind to organise his elections."[2]

Bhutto would also always try to find out from Khuhro and others who were likely to know, how far his cousins and relations were responsible for the defeat of his father. He seemed well aware of the role his family had played but wanted corroboration if he could get it.

Bhutto also started holding 'kutcheries' on the pattern of colonial 'durbars' except that he included the *'Awam'* or the common people who were to bring their grievances to him so that the Prime Minister could personally deal with them. He would arrive in Larkana and hold a 'kutchery' which was well advertised in advance. This would be either in his house or in the Circuit House. He would be flanked by whatever members of his government were present including the Chief Minister. All the important people of the district would be present and selected *'Awam'* would come with their petitions to be presented to the Prime Minister. These would be taken by the D.C. who would tell the P.M. what was required and the great man would put his note or signature. Jobs would be also given with these 'chits' or signatures. The Prime Minister would also distribute largesse in the shape of bicycles, hand pumps and sewing machines. On Eid days a henchman would keep a pile of hundred rupee notes which were handed out by Bhutto to the poor who came to pay their respects. In this way Bhutto by-passed the due process of government and introduced the system by which all decisions were taken by the Prime Minister himself without going through the required formalities. He not only effectively centralised the business of government but he turned it into a personal fiefdom in which all power was concentrated in the person of the Prime Minister. By handing out free gifts on behalf of the Government of goods ranging from bicycles to plots and quarters, albeit built with funds from the rulers of Abu Dhabi or wherever; by forcing people to ask for personal favours rather than getting their work done by due process, he introduced the culture of beggary in Sind and no doubt elsewhere in Pakistan.

Larkana was also elevated into the ancestral family seat of the Bhuttos. Here he invited potentates and Presidents to shoot duck, partridge and wild boar on the lakes of neighbouring zamindars and on the banks of the Indus. The national airline set up the P.I.A. dancing troupe to entertain his guests. Dancers from the night clubs of Karachi were brought to entertain distinguished visitors including the Shah of Iran. From their house across the road Khuhros could see the helicopters carrying the guests to and from the airport. They could hear the strains of music floating across from the Prime Minister's house. On one occasion when the Shah of Iran was Bhutto's guest at Larkana the Khuhros were invited to dinner and accepted the invitation. For after dinner entertainment folk singers performed and much to Khuhros' astonishment were followed by Bhutto's cabinet ministers and the Sind cabinet ministers dancing on the stage. Sometime on, the same man would introduce prohibition, losing the country a huge amount of revenue* and declare Friday a holiday instead of Sunday. No one could claim that these actions had been taken from conviction.

Bhutto was bent upon making life as difficult as possible for the Khuhros. If any well-known or influential person was seen visiting the Khuhro house he would be questioned by Bhutto himself as to why he had gone there. Word got about that it was dangerous to visit the Khuhros and it soon became an act of bravery or foolhardiness to be seen in the neighbourhood of Khuhro's house. Rumours were put out that Khuhro's house would be requisitioned and made a government guest house or some other institution. Khuhro's old house had already been acquired by the government on nominal rent for the purpose of a 'technical college'. Major and minor harassments were the order of the day.

Khuhro was spending a considerable amount of time in Larkana to deal the problems that were being faced by his supporters. But in spite of the way things were he was not expecting the next blow that fell. Khuhro had been in Larkana from 7 May 1972 when early on the morning of the 13th a friend came to see him on an urgent errand. The friend informed him that the next morning Bhutto's cousin Pirbux, whose house was next to Khuhro's, was planning to demolish the southern boundary wall of Khuhro's house with police help. Khuhro telephoned the Deputy Commissioner who completely denied any such plan. He then telephoned Pirbux who refused to discuss the matter thus confirming that something was afoot. Khuhro immediately asked his lawyer to apply for an injunction restraining the District Magistrate from taking any such step. Notice of two days was issued by the Court which was served on the District Magistrate who was also the Deputy Commissioner, at 1 o'clock that afternoon. But in spite of this court order at about 4 o'clock the same afternoon a large police force came along with about a hundred men and bulldozers from the Agricultural Department started demolishing the boundary wall of Khuhro's house. The demolition went on well after dark with flood lights provided for the work. As the evening went on the Khuhro family hardly knew what to expect. They could not be sure if it was the boundary wall or the house itself which was to be destroyed. President Bhutto was expected in Larkana the same evening and duly arrived to stay in his house opposite.

Among other complaints Bhutto had, in his letter to Khuhro some months earlier mentioned that his cousin Pirbux Bhutto had a grievance regarding the bound-

---

* When Khuhro had been Premier of Sind he had gone to the Quaid-e-Azam to get his views on the introduction of Prohibition in the country but the Quaid had warned him against taking any such step. He had pointed out that only would precious revenue be lost but that instead of decreasing the use of alcohol, Prohibition would make it much more widespread and would also increase smuggling and crime. This had been the experience of Prohibition in the U.S.A. Khuhro, *Notes*, KP.

ary wall between his and Khuhro's house. No complaint had however been made by Pirbux Bhutto to Khuhro after the survey had been made by the Municipal authorities and boundaries fixed four years earlier. Nor had Pirbux Bhutto gone to the Urban Area Civil Court but as Khuhro said,

"Suddenly in 1972 after the present regime came into power I heard he made a complaint that we encroached upon his piece of land of about 2,200 sq.ft. No explanation however was called for from us even by the Revenue Department regarding this petition of his."[3]

Now without warning the bulldozers had been sent and the walls demolished with the help of the local administration. Even if there were a rumbling dispute about the boundary of Khuhro's house nothing could have prepared Khuhro for these extraordinary events. Not only was the wall dividing Khuhro's house from that of Pirbux Bhutto knocked down but at the same time the wall of Khuhro's house which was bordering the road on the north of the house was demolished by the administration. The excuse given for this was that this was Municipal property. Khuhro issued a press statement showing that the sudden claim of the Municipality that there were 'streets' or pathways on the edges of his property was false and that this had been decided by the Courts years earlier but now in April 1972 the claims had been revived. Khuhro added with irony:

"This somersault on the part of the Municipal Administrator is understandable."[4]

The whole matter had been settled during the Ayub regime when Khuhro was in no position to use any influence. Zulfiqar Bhutto would explain afterwards to Khuhro that he had been pushed into this action by his cousins Pirbux and Mumtaz and had allowed them to go ahead in order to keep peace in the family! It was obvious to anyone who cared to look that this was a heavy gesture of intimidation to show the public that henceforth Khuhros were the underdogs in Larkana and in Sind.

In the process of destroying all sources of Khuhro's influence in the district, Bhutto manoeuvred to remove him from the Presidentship of the Larkana Zamindari Co-operative Bank. Khuhro had been President of this Bank since he had started it in the early days of the co-operative movement in Sind in the 'twenties and had run it extremely efficiently ever since. Bhutto had bogus elections in the Bank in which he got his own nominees as directors and proceeded to get his own man elected President.[5] The Bank soon went into liquidation leaving a vacuum in the financing of the agriculture of the district. The local knowledge that the Bank had accumulated over 40 years of operation and the convenience that it offered for the local agriculturists was thus lost forever. Nor was this the limit of the intimidation that the Khuhro family would suffer in the the years that Bhutto was in power. Cases were instituted against Khuhro's eldest son Shah Mohammed, varying from cutting the wood from the riverain jungles, for which he was arrested and kept in jail until released by the court, to going on *shikar* (hunting) in the desert for gazelle in the month of May. In this latter case, fortunately, the bureaucracy had not thought out the case properly.

Along with Khuhro's son, others who had helped in the elections were also accused of going on this shoot. These were Sikander, the son of Moosa Khan Bughio of Dokri taluka, Pir Jial Shah of Gambat and Bahawal Unar of the Unar tribe of Dokri. Attempts were also made to involve Shah Mohammed in murder cases which luckily for him were so flimsy that the administration did not have the courage to pursue them. On one occasion Shah Mohammed was arrested and taken to the police station lock-up. The judges at that time had not been completely demoralised and Shah Mohammed was given bail the next morning. Bhutto who had been out of the country the previous day in Dubai, telephoned Khuhro and said, "I am very sorry. It was Mumtaz's mischief and not my doing." In fact on a number of occasions Bhutto would telephone to say that such or such problem inflicted on Khuhro was not of his doing. Khuhro knew well the tactics were deliberate and sometimes would say so to Bhutto when he telephoned. Shaikh Rashid, the Minister specially chosen by Bhutto to be in charge of disposing land reform case and deal as brutally as possible with Bhutto's opponents, threatened Khuhro's younger son Mahmood with seven years jail for 'not declaring' two acres of land which he did not even own.

The local police officers were ordered from time to time to raid the Khuhro house and arrest Khuhro's son but everytime the officials, with a greater sense of decency than the ruler, gave a timely warning to the Khuhros. D. C. Kharal was apparently ordered to insult the zamindars who had opposed Bhutto and not allow them a seat when they came to see him. Kharal had the grace to let Khuhro know that he had these instructions and not to let any of sons to go to Collectorate.

One of the first things that the Bhutto government did was to get Khuhro's daughter Hamida removed from her job as lecturer at Karachi University. Hamida who had a lien on her job while she was a Fellow at St. Antony's College, Oxford, was told that she had no job to go to when she went back. When Dr. Mahmud Husain, the Vice Chancellor of Karachi University was asked why had he thrown out Hamida, he said he was helpless as the Government had insisted. The Government's spies never let up on Khuhro's daughter. In April 1975 the Home Secretary of the Government of Sind wrote to Khuhro complaining that she had been seen having tea in a public restaurant in the company of Air Marshal Asghar Khan and Nawab Akbar Khan Bugti and that she had visited the Embassy of the U.S.S.R. Khuhro wrote back that while it was true that she had had tea with the two distinguished Pakistani leaders she had not gone to the Soviet Embassy and in fact had been unable to attend an official reception there because she had been busy with her teaching duties at the University of Sind.[6]

When Bhutto announced his 'Land Reforms' in 1972 all the matters relating to the Khuhro lands which had been finally settled, or so Khuhro thought, were revived and were to drag on throughout the next five years. All this time hearings were kept in different places at different times and most of the time Khuhro had to appear personally to oversee the work of the lawyers. Crops from Khuhro's land were forcibly cut and taken away under police supervision leaving the cultivators penniless and starving. After Bhutto's removal Khuhro's land reform file was found in Prime Minister's House, Rawalpindi. Khuhro sent his son Barrister Mahmood Khuhro to get it finally disposed off by the Federal Land Commission in Rawalpindi.

The telephones of all politicians were tapped. It was believed that Bhutto, who apparently needed very little sleep, spent most of his nights listening to tapes of telephone conversations and other bugged talk. The Khuhros had personal experience of this when Khuhro's daughter returning to Karachi from London by road at the end of 1973 came through Baluchistan where Nawab Akbar Khan Bugti was Governor. A good friend of Hamida and her husband, he gave them a very warm welcome, an escort from the Afghan border and they were his guests in Quetta. Hamida talked to her parents in Karachi from Quetta describing their visit to Baluchistan. After their arrival in Karachi they were both invited to dinner by Nusrat Bhutto who innocently repeated verbatim Hamida's conversation with her parents. At the wedding reception of Khuhro's son, Bhutto's sister Manna conveyed a message to Hamida that Bhutto was very displeased that she had gone to G. M. Syed's birthday celebrations!

Socially Bhutto observed the norms with the Khuhros throughout the 'sixties and the 'seventies, although in his own fashion. In January 1973 Khuhro's second son Shah Zaman was to get married. The Bhuttos were ofcourse invited and accepted. On the day of the wedding at 7 o'clock in the evening the telephone rang in the Sind Governor's house. Mir Rasul Baksh Talpur, the Governor, was getting dressed to come to the wedding. On the telephone was Prime Minister Bhutto. "What are you doing Rasul Baksh?" he asked. Talpur replied that he was getting dressed to go to the Khuhro wedding reception. "But we are not attending", said Bhutto. "Ofcourse Sir" said Talpur and phone was put down. Talpur immediately sent for his son and told him to go to the Khuhros, attend the wedding on his behalf and apologise for his absence due to ill health. The next day Talpur was chagrined to read in the papers that Begum Nusrat Bhutto accompanied by her sister-in-law, Bhutto's sister, had attended the wedding.[7] Bhutto would maintain social civilities himself but he was not about to allow that privilege to his cohorts. The PPP colleagues and government officials were so terrified of Bhutto that they dared not greet or meet any one who was seen not to be "in favour". The only exception in Bhutto's close circle was his wife Nusrat who continued her friendship with the Khuhro family the entire time that he was in power.

Bhutto was a curious mixture of pique and pettiness. In 1973 Khuhro decided to go to England for a holiday. He required a health check and needed to take a break from the tensions in Pakistan but he found that he was on the Exit Control List. Khuhro sent his son to the Home Secretary to find out the reason for this restriction. The Home Secretary who seemed to be beseiged by people asking for permission to go abroad, took Khuhro's son aside and showed him the file where there was a note in Bhutto's own hand saying that on no account was Khuhro to be allowed to travel abroad. At a later meeting Bhutto explained to Khuhro that he had prevented his visit to London because London was very hot that year!

Occasionally Bhutto bowed in the direction of history and overcame his antipathy and would invite Khuhro on some 'historic' occasion. One such was the Islamic Summit at Lahore in February 1974. Khuhro was happy to be present on an occasion, the first in Pakistan, where the most important leaders of the Muslim world were gathered. Another occasion was the 100th anniversary of Quaid-e-Azam's birthday in December 1976. Khuhro had written his memoirs of the Quaid which were to be published by the official committee but not before objections had been made to various passages which Khuhro refused to change and gave the paper to *Dawn* instead.[8]

Bhutto invited some of Quaid's colleagues to a small dinner party. The guests were the Daultanas, Ispahanis and the Khuhros. At the dinner Bhutto was very affable and asked Khuhro what was the secret of his success as administrator. Khuhro replied shortly that it was natural talent. He then asked Khuhro, 'How many times were you Chief Minister?", "Three times", replied Khuhro. Bhutto asked, "Why did you resign?" Khuhro replied that he resigned in a variety of circumstances but usually when he lost the majority in the House and came back as Chief Minister when he regained the majority. Bhutto remarked,"I think a person who resigns from power is a fool. I shall never resign. I will hold one election and I shall never hold another election after that." The final comment of Bhutto throws into transparent relief his obvious contempt for democratic procedures and his urge to retain power at all costs.

Ironically all his assertions came true. At this dinner Bhutto hinted that he would be holding elections shortly. Seeing Bhutto at the dinner and noting his assurance and barely concealed arrogance, his slighting references to the Shah of Iran, the thought that crossed Khuhro's mind was that this was hubris indeed and he wondered how long it would last.

For Khuhro these years were very difficult indeed. Used as he was to being at odds with the Governments of the day and suffering as a result, the experience of Bhutto in power was a new low. He could not know where the next attack was coming from-if a son was to be arrested, if his supporters were being charged with murder or being murdered. If his house was being requisitioned or knocked down; if his crops were being taken or his lands sequestered or whether he was being prosecuted on any kind or number of charges. If it were just himself at the receiving end as had been the case until 1958, the troubles were bearable. It had meant losing power or being unable to take part in politics. After the imposition of Martial Law a new dimension of the unknown was added. Martial Law had meant the dehumanising of civilian life and defrauding people of their freedom. Martial Law had been defined as 'no law' by the leading jurist of Pakistan, A. K. Brohi. It was far worse than the colonial regime of the British. Under that at least the law of the rulers was sacrosanct and on the whole the people knew the rules by which they were living. There was no redress or fairness under Martial Law.

Bhutto's regime whether as CMLA or as Prime Minister after the imposition of the 1972 constitution can only be described as Fascist. The constitution for which the vote had been taken from politicians of all shades of opinion on the grounds that fundamental rights would be guaranteed was amended immediately to suspend those very same fundamental rights. Amendments were introduced further curtailing democratic practice. The entire leadership of the Opposition was put in jail to be tried for anti-state activities. Army action against the Baluch was pursued ruthlessly and relentlessly. Bhutto was bent upon teaching a lesson to these Sardars they would not forget. He could not forgive their stiff necks. On one occasion he was going on and on about the Baluch Sardars in the presence of Khuhro who warned him that he should moderate his behaviour and realise that he would have to live in the same country as these Baluch Sardars and so would his children, unless he migrated and that he should not rely on being in power for ever.

One instance of the way Bhutto's love of inflicting humiliation on people occurred when he was visiting Baluchistan while the Khan of Kalat was Governor. Bhutto was in his Falcon about to land in Quetta. On the ground the Governor, the Ministers and other notables were lined up to receive him. At the last minute he said to his companions,"I will made the bastards wait" and ordered the pilot to fly around for the time being. The pilot was to tell Quetta airport constantly he was about to land so that the reception line on the tarmac was kept at the ready but the plane continued to fly. It was fully one hour before Bhutto decided to land and the pious old man, the Khan, was kept standing, waiting for him.[9]

Bhutto was not only pursuing this military action in Baluchistan against a civilian population, he was also ruling through spreading terror in Sind. His opponents were mercilessly victimised and even killed. Six of Pir Pagaro's khalifas were murdered in cold blood. In 1972 the ineptness of the Government led to the disorder in Karachi known as 'the language riots' which pitched the Urdu speaking people against the Government. These riots were in reality confined to the urban centres of Karachi and Hyderabad and did not involve the Sindhi population as such. In Larkana however the regime decided to turn it into an opportunity to drive out the Urdu speaking community which had been living there since 1947 merely because they had voted for Khuhro and Muslim League.

A conspiracy was hatched in the house of a Sind Minister from Larkana and riots instigated against the Urdu speaking community which at that time owned most of the shops in the bazar. In this the Shaikhs of Larkana were co-opted by the Minister by being told that they could take over the shops and the business. In a shameful act quite unprecedented in the annals of the history of Sind, attacks were encouraged against the shop keepers in which some deaths also occurred. Early on the morning on which the riots were planned a police contingent surrounded Khuhro's house. For two days the siege continued and was only withdrawn in the evening of the next day. Immediately after the siege was lifted Khuhro went out in his red coloured jeep with a couple of servants armed with a shotgun, and toured the affected areas of the city. He saw for himself the bazaar and the areas where the riots had taken place and sympathised with the people. There was little else he could do. As a result of these riots most of the community which had fully assimilated and become Sindhi speaking was frightened into leaving Larkana.

It was only Khuhro's stoicism and his enduring religious faith that carried him through the Bhutto period. Here was a man who was a powerful ruler, cruel and capricious like the some mediaeval king but at the same time he had a deeply complexed and insecure post Freudian personality. It was safest to be at a distance from him. Unfortunately for the Khuhros they found themselves in close proximity with him in Larkana. Khuhro had to exercise great patience and tact to get some breathing space for the people who were dependent on him. Much as he would have liked to, he could not cut himself off during this trying period. People had to be rescued from false cases, have their livelihoods restored, their cultivation kept safe, their security safeguarded from a tyrannous government and its pitiless police.

Bhutto deliberately undermined the traditional systems of justice and local government, denigrated and vilified the traditional leaders of society and gave the villages over to his corrupt administration and police. A people used to cheap and quick justice, to a society where the criminal had no place to hide were now at the mercy of the police which jailed the poor who could not afford to pay and let off those who could pay, without regard for the criminal or the innocent. The respectable were insulted and abused and the dregs of society were elevated.

Khuhro faced all these changes which had set society as he knew it on its head, with extreme fortitude. He discharged his responsibilities faithfully in the face of the gravest provocations. In the end his patience and forbearance called up some reserves of decency in the officials whom Bhutto had specially chosen to do his bidding in Larkana and in Sind. Deputy Commissioner Kharal and S. P. Pinial themselves moderated the excessive commands of their master and when necessary warned Khuhro of what was to happen.

In January 1977 it was announced that elections would be held in March. Bhutto had carefully laid his plans and expected to win them without much trouble. In this the man proposed but God disposed somewhat differently. The Opposition parties combined into a formidable force and set up a strong challenge to the PPP in Larkana. But Bhutto had no intention of a fair election. The Jamaat-i-Islami put up a token candidate Jan Mohammed Abbassi who could not find the D.C. in his office to receive the papers. The D.C. along with the elite and the public were already at the Prime Minister's residence, Al-Murtaza, with garlands to congratulate the candidate who was assumed to have come in unopposed. Abbasi was kidnapped for his temerity and Bhutto was declared elected unopposed.

When the results came in of PPP's victory the country was outraged. The result was countrywide agitation which obviously surprised Bhutto. He began to look increasingly beleaguered, searching for ways to counter the Opposition. In March after the elections had taken place and while Khuhro was in Larkana, Bhutto suddenly made an unannounced visit to Khuhro's house in Karachi. Khuhro's son Shah Zaman and some family members were at lunch when the servant came in and announced that Bhutto Sahib had arrived. Shah Zaman, thinking it was some other Bhutto of their acquaintance, asked the servant to show him to the sitting room while they finished lunch. The servant insisted that it the Prime Minister. Thinking it was some sort of elaborate joke, Shah Zaman went out of the dining room and was confronted by Zulfiqar Bhutto, accompanied by his entourage of an A. D. C. and Secretaries, smoking a cigar and looking nonchalant, except for his eyes which looked haunted. He shook hands with Khuhro's son who apologised for his father's absence and asked him if he would have lunch.

"No, no," said Bhutto, "I only came to call as I was passing by. Please give your father my regards and say that I came to call."

It was a curious incident. Had he come to mend fences, look for support and perhaps a bridge with the Opposition? The question was never cleared up because he did not follow up the visit.

The agitation throughout the country gathered enough momentum from March onwards and eventually forced Bhutto into negotiations with the Pakistan National Alliance (PNA) which dragged on till July. On 4 July 1977 the army staged a coup and General Zia-ul-Haque took over as CMLA inaugurating the fourth Martial Law rule in Pakistan.

Even though Khuhro was a die hard believer in the democratic process he could not help taking a breath of relief at Bhutto's removal. But was the nightmare really over? The next two years saw Bhutto out of detention, bullying and blustering as ever, preparing for elections and taking swipes at Khuhro whenever he got the chance. But he was back in prison soon facing the charge of conspiracy of murder for the killing of Nawab Ahmed Khan Kasuri. The case was long drawn out but by March 1978 it was clear that Bhutto's fate was hanging in balance. He had lost the case in Lahore High Court and the Appeal in the Supreme Court. Now it was up to the CMLA to make the final decision. There was much tension and speculation in the country. Presumably Zia-ul-Haque was sounding out his associates for the crucial decision. He had been rumoured to say that even Bhutto's best friends did not want him freed. Khuhro reflected on the situation and decided that it was his duty to put the situation in perspective for President Zia-ul-Haque so that the best decision for the future of the country could be taken. On 21 March 1979 Khuhro wrote to the President:

"Dear General Mohammed Zia-ul-Haque,
I have been thinking for sometime about writing to you about a matter of national importance as I feel that it is my duty to put before you the situation in the country as I see it in relation to Mr. Z. A. Bhutto.

As you are well aware I hold no brief for Mr. Z. A. Bhutto. Although my own family has good social relations with the Bhutto family and I had particularly friendly relations with his father the late Sir Shahnawaz Bhutto, the vengeful, mean and intolerant behaviour of Mr. Z. A. Bhutto had strained our relations to the limit. I do not need to remind you that my family suffered greatly at his hands. Even today, we are not clear of the many and complicated problems he created for us. You may remember that he went so far as to order the bull-dozing of the compound wall of my residence at Larkana soon after he came to power. In fact it would not be too much to say that he was bent upon the destruction of my family.

However inspite of all this, in the larger interests of the nation, as one of those who took a leading role in the struggle for independence and was with the Grace of God one of the co-founders of the Islamic Republic of Pakistan, I feel it incumbent upon me to put before you my views on a matter which seems to me crucial to the survival of Pakistan as a cohesive nation.

You may recall that at the time Mr. Z. A. Bhutto was ousted from power his government was very largely unpopular in the country. The corruption, the large scale rigging of elections, maladministration, political victimization of opponents etc. (the list of the regime's misdeeds is indeed long) had sunk it low in the estimation of the public. The time that has elapsed since his ouster has by now dimmed the memory of these misdeeds in the public mind and moreover the long drawn out trial has created sympathy among the masses for his present pathetic state. This is specially the case in Sind. The common people of Sind in keeping with people everywhere have a somewhat simplistic view of things and in the case of Mr. Bhutto they tend to see a Sindhi leader who has been removed, put to trial and will possibly be executed by non Sindhi forces. This feeling is very strong in the towns and villages of this Province. In this connection it is important to remember that Mr. Bhutto's image has been before the people of this country and especially the Province of Sind, for twenty years, i.e. since the imposition of the first Martial Law in 1958.

In a period where politicians as a whole have been abused and derided and accused of all kinds of crimes, a period in which the bureaucracy was supreme and politician was a dirty word, Mr. Bhutto then great favourite of President Ayub Khan, was given tremendous publicity by the Government controlled press which continued even after his dismissal. This helped him win elections of 1970-71 in the Punjab and Sind, and in the crisis of 1971 the people turned to him as the only leader they knew. You are well aware how the media was subsequently used by him to project himself as a progressive leader. It would only be fair to say that Mr. Bhutto's administration tried to introduce certain reforms, to remove certain injustices and anamolies in the society, however inadequately, which have stayed in the public mind and will undoubtedly earn him a place in the national pantheon.

I have tried briefly to identify the reasons for Mr. Bhutto's dominance of the political scene for two decades and also the reasons for his popularity among the masses. The two years that have elapsed since his removal from power have succeeded in dimming the memory of the wrongs of his regime and only the positive aspects of his policy are remembered. If Mr. Z. A. Bhutto pays the extreme penalty of death, the public will bestow on him the crown of martyrdom. All his sins would be wiped away when he pays for them with his life. History has shown that martyrdoms rent the society apart, create revolutions and bring chaos. I do not wish to sermonize on the historical aspects of the Bhutto case, but to point out only the possible adverse effects it may have on our country. His death will surely cause deep bitterness in the minds of the masses of Sind and maybe in the Punjab and elsewhere. It would prepare the ground for possible class conflict. We know already that the proponents of class conflict (i.e.Communists) are exploiting Bhutto's name.

In the present delicate international situation in this region this could prove the match to light the conflagration. The very existence of Pakistan could be endangered. At the very least Mr. Bhutto's death would create hatred against the majority Province with consequences which may not be apparent immediately but would make themselves felt sooner or later. I would also like to point out that the politics of our country, including the successive coups d'etat have been free from the taint of blood and violence which characterize so many other countries. Although Mr. Bhutto would be punished under ordinary criminal law of the country, it would be treated by the people and the world at large as a political decision. This is already apparent from the number of appeals your Government has received from Abroad. As a sincere worker and well-wisher of the country and one who has enjoyed the confidence of the people of Sind, and of Pakistan over a long period, I would like to advise moderation and mercy. May Allah Almighty grant you the wisdom to take the correct steps for the welfare of this country and its people. With kind regards,

Yours sincerely
M. A. Khuhro"[10]

This was a remarkable letter and reflects very clearly the untrammelled and unprejudiced way Khuhro approached even the most emotionally fraught and complicated situations.

Khuhro did not get a direct response from the President but he was asked to a meeting with General Abbasi, the Governor of Sind, who hinted that the decision had been taken to hang Bhutto but that he had been asked to take advice as to what to do with Bhutto's remains. The option of burying the body in an unknown place or at sea, was being considered. Khuhro was quite clear in his answer. He said that the body must be returned to the relatives. He gave the example of the late Sibghatullah Shah, Pir Pagaro, whose body had not been returned by the British and for a long time he was believed to be alive by his followers. In death he had assumed mythical proportions. Bhutto was hanged on 4 April 1979 and his body was returned to his relatives. With Bhutto's sons out of the country, Khuhro went to condole with Pirbux Bhutto who was the head of the family.

The Government had taken precautions in case any trouble occurred at the death of Bhutto but in fact there was no sign of any disturbance. There was a kind of stunned stillness in the country. As it happened the assessment of Khuhro of the situation that would obtain in the country if Bhutto was hanged, came true almost as he had analysed.

25

A QUIET EXIT

"In the name of Allah, Most Gracious, Most Merciful.

1. Have We not
   Expanded thee thy breast?

2. And removed from thee
   Thy burden

3. That which did gall
   Thy back?-

4. And raised high the esteem
   (in which) thou (art held)?

5. So verily,
   With every difficulty,
   There is relief;

6. Verily, with every difficulty
   There is relief.

7. Therefore, when thou art
   Free (from thine immediate task)
   Still labour hard,

8. And to thy Lord
   Turn (all) thy attention."

The Holy Quran
Sura XCIV

Khuhro's life assumed a quiet tranquillity in the last three years of his life. As usual he divided his time between Larkana, the lands and Karachi. His routine continued as it had even in the darkest days. His daily life was as strictly regulated as it had ever been. He continued to do his public work, meeting people and taking notice of any government action or ordinance that might seriously affect the country. He issued statements on crucial public issues or wrote to the President on such matters.

President Zia-ul-Haque was always polite and deferential. He wrote and asked Khuhro for advice on some matters as for instance on the matter of appointing an Ombudsman. Khuhro wrote back to say that if elections were held and a democratic process effected there would be no need for an Ombudsman as elected members would act to prevent injustices. Although a strict observing Muslim, Khuhro did not like the overt Islamisation process and the encouragement given to Mullas under Zia's regime. He wrote to Zia opposing the imposition of Ushr, giving historical reasons. He wanted the tax system to remain strictly secular.

Khuhro enjoyed the role of elder statesman during this time. He took an extremely objective view of his own career and gave impressively balanced interviews to journalists and archivists. He continued to advise those who asked him for help whoever came for help with officials or for jobs until the end. He kept his faith in the struggle for freedom and for Pakistan although his children took pleasure in pointing out the many things that had gone wrong with the country.

Occasionally old friends came to call. On a rare visit to Karachi with special permission from detention at his village of Sann, G. M. Syed came to see him. Khuhro invited Rashdi to join them. It was a memorable morning with Syed and Rashdi, talking about old times, about Jinnah and the Working Committee meetings in Bombay, even about Rashdi's extraordinary influence over the two most senior and formidable Sind politicians.

Khuhro who had been to Haj twice thought about going again. He dictated notes on his life to his daughter to be part of his biography and was anxious that it should be completed in his lifetime. He passed away peacefully surrounded by his family, on the evening of Eid-ul-Azha, 20 October 1980.

As the ambulance carried his body to Larkana, villagers hearing its wailing sirens came out of their homes to see Khuhro as he wound his way northwards through the towns and villages of the Sind that he loved so much and for which he had dedicated his life. He was buried in his ancestral graveyard in village Aqil.

Khuhro and wife welcome the Prime Minister and Begum Liaquat Ali Khan.

Taking Sardar Abdur Rab Nishtar, President, Pakistan Muslim League for a tour of Sind.

The Constituent Assembly of Pakistan, 1952.

Greeting the Shah of Iran.

A chat with Queen Soraya of Iran.

Begum Khuhro with Celal Bayar, President of Turkey.

Khuhro with the President of Turkey.

Habib Ibrahim Rahimtoola, Madame Sun Yat Sen, Khuhro.

Greeting King Zahir Shah of Afghanistan.

Meeting the young Aga Khan.

Khuhro and wife with Pandit Jawaharlal Nehru.

With Syed Abdul Qadir Al Gaylani.

Begum Daultana, Khuhro, Yusuf Khattak, at the back Saifullah Marwat and Mumtaz Daultana.

Khuhro and Khan of Kalat.

Khuhro and Z. A. Bhutto.

Khuhro with H. S. Suhrawardy.

Khuhro, Sind Premier for the third time with Governor Sind Nawab Mamdot and Cabinet colleagues, 1954.

Showing King Hussein of Jordan the model of Lower Sind Barrage.

West Pakistan Administrative Council. Khuhro with his back to the camera next to Firoze Khan Noon–Gurmani and others facing camera.

Talking to Prime Minister Chaudhry Mohammed Ali, Yusuf Haroon. Dr. Khan Sahib (on the right).

Speaking in Constituent Assembly of Pakistan, 1955.

Official tour of Sukkur Central Jail.

Moscow, in conference with Nikita Khruschev and Bulganin.

Friday prayers in Tashkent.

Baghdad Pact Conference, London, July 1958.

Khuhro and Ayub Khan.

Arriving in Larkana by train.

Dastarbandi of Pir Pagaro.

Sind United Front meeting with G. M. Syed presiding.

Khuhro's dinner party for Miss Jinnah just after the presidential election, 1964.

Khuhro on a boat on the Indus with younger sons Shah Zaman, Masood and Khalid Mahmood.

Boundary wall of Khuhro's house in Larkana being demolished under Bhutto's government.

G. M. Syed visits Khuhro, 1978. *Left to Right*: Hamida, G. M. Syed, Khuhro, Ali Qutb Shah, Pir Ali Mohammed Rashdi.

Khuhro with grandchildren.

Khuhro, Begum Khuhro, daughter Hamida and granddaughter Nuha Elisabeth Marui.

END NOTES

CHAPTER 1

1. The Viceroy and the Governor of Bombay and other Governors of Presidencies were known as *Lat Sahib* which roughly translated means Lordship.
2. Bombay was part of the dowry of the Portugese princess Catherine of Braganza who married Charles II on 20 May 1662, and therefore a British possession nearly two hundred years before the conquest of Sind.
3. For a detailed account of the position of jagirdars, zamindars and the land revenue arrangements in Sind see H. Khuhro, *The Making of Modern Sind*, Karachi, 1972, Chapters 2 and 3.
4. During the time the Panhwar chieftains ruled the Dadu area, Khudabad was known as Shikarpur (the Dadu Shikarpur was distinct from the famous Shikarpur located near Sukkur in Upper Sind) and was renamed Khudabad by Yar Mohammed Kalhoro (early 18th century) who defeated the Panhwars, to commemorate his title of Khudayar Khan bestowed on him by the Mughal Emperor.
5. *Chachnama* is the earliest historical text of the sub-continent and relates the story of the conquest of Sind by the Ommayed general Mohammed bin Qasim in 711 A.D. The original Arabic version was written by a contemporary historian but the version available to scholars at present is a Persian translation made sometime later.
6. Ellenborough to Napier, 12 Apr. 1843, see H. Khuhro, *op.cit.*, pp. 12-13.
7. See *John Jacob of Jacobabad*, H. T. Lambrick, London, 1960, for the career of John Jacob in Sind.
8. See H. Khuhro, *op. cit.*, Chapter 6.

CHAPTER 2

1. There is also an occasional legend that Khuhros are the descendants of the surviving Kurus who fled the battlefield of Kurukeshetra after their defeat by the Pandus and took refuge in Sindhu Sauvira, the kingdom of their ally King Jaydratha, who himself had been killed in a battle by Arjuna.
2. The Arab descent of the Khuhros is chronicled in *Twarikh Ganjina Jahan Numa* of Raees-ul-Ulema Hazrat Makhdum Mian Pir Moḥammed also known as Mohammed Aqil, the *sajjada nashin* of Dargah Khuhra Sharif in Gambat in Khairpur State, who wrote the book in 1288 A. H. circa the earlier part of the 18 century A. D. The account is based on earlier histories and relates the origins of different towns of Sind as well as its saints. The hand written Mss. in Persian is preserved in the library of the Makhdums of Khuhra.
3. Hostages were taken from as far as Dadu district where a Abdur Rahman Panhwar of the Khuhai Panhwars came back home after many years from Calcutta where he was taken along with the ruling Talpur family. Eyewitness account of residents of the village *Abdur Rahim jo Khooh*.
4. Parliamentary Papers (House of Commons), 1854, vol. XLIX, part XXXII
5. Khuhro, *Notes*, KP.
6. Dr. U. M. Daudpota, *Muhn ji Mukhtasir Atam Kahani*,(Sindhi), edit. Begum Khadija Daudpota, Karachi, 1959, pp. 26-27.
7. *Ibid*, p. 32.
8. Khuhro, *Notes*, KP.
9. The foundation stone of the building of Sind Madressah in the Qafila Serai area was laid in 1887 by Lord Dufferin, the Viceroy of India, and the building was completed by 1890.
10. Khuhro, *op.cit.*

CHAPTER 3

1. Edwin Montagu, Secretary of State for India in the House of Commons, 20 Aug.1917, quoted in P. Moon, *The British Conquest and Dominion of India*, London, 1989, p. 977.
2. Interview with Pir Ali Mohammed Rashdi, Karachi, March 1981.
3. Rashdi, *Uhe deehan uhe sheenhan*, vol. I, pp. 194-5, has a pithy account of the plight of the *muhajireen* in Afghanistan.
4. On going home later when his father lay seriously ill, Khuhro found out that the Commissioner-in-Sind, Sir Louis Rieu, had especially asked *Wadero* Shah Mohammed to advise his son against joining the agitators. The old man was in any case averse to such activities and alarmed that his son might be involved but he need not have worried as Khuhro was not in the least inclined to what he considered essentially quixotic activities.
5. Reply to Questionnaire, Government of Bombay, 1924, KP. The replies contributed to the Report that was compiled by Taunton I.C.S., a good friend of Khuhro who was posted to Khairpur during these years. It was published in 1926.
6. Ibid.
7. Ibid.
8. Ibid.
9. Ibid.
10. The story of Khuhro's dinner for Mir Ali Nawaz is recounted in A. M. Rashdi's book *Uhe Deenhan Uhe Sheenhan*, Vol. 3, Chapter on Khuhro. The Mir's courtship of Bali was pursued for many years at great cost to the Khairpur treasury. Numerous stories of the courtship are still recounted by the people of Khairpur.
11. Khuhro, Notes, KP.
12. Khuhro, Notes, KP.

CHAPTER 4

1. Bombay Legislative Council Debates, Spring Session, 1924.
2. Ibid.
3. Ibid.
4. Ibid.
5. Khuhro, Notes, KP.
6. Bombay Legislative Council Debates, Autumn Session, 1924.
7. Khuhro, *Note on Muslims in Government Service for the Government of Bombay*, KP.
8. Khuhro, Notes, *op. cit.*
9. Ibid.
10. *vide infra* Chapter 10.
11. Secretary Home Dept., Govt. of Bombay to Khuhro, 1 Jul. 1924, KP
12. Rieu to Khuhro, 28 Jul. 1924, KP.
13. KP. Imdad Ali Kazi popularly known as Allama I. I. Kazi was a member of the distinguished Ansari family of Paat in Dadu district which traced its origins to the Ansars of Medina. Allama Kazi went to England at the age of 21 in 1907 where he was called to the Bar and was also a student at the London School of Economics and the School of Oriental and African Studies. He was a notable Islamic scholar and an educator. He was Vice Chancellor of the University of Sind in the late '50s.
14. Governor of Bombay to Khuhro, 23 Aug. 1924, KP.
15. Secretary, General Department, Govt. of Bombay, 9 Sep. 1924, KP.
16. Daudpoto served as Director, Public Instruction, in Sind and ended his career as Member, Public Service Commission of Pakistan. In 1940 in recognition of his scholarly work Dr. Daudpoto was conferred the title of *Shamsul Ulema*, one of the four such conferred in Sind in the British period. His scholarly work was mostly in the field of Arabic and Persian literature which had also been the subject of his Cambridge thesis: "The influence of Arabic poetry on Persian poetry." Dr. Daudpoto was also a scholar of the Sindhi language and in his retirement worked on the Risalo of Shah Abdul Latif.
17. Khuhro to Governor of Bombay, 17 Sep. 1924, KP.
18. KP.

19. KP.
20. *Ibid.*
21. Khuhro to Governor of Bombay, 11 Oct. 1925, KP.
22. Governor of Bombay to Khuhro, 16 Oct. 1925, KP.
23. Governor of Bombay to Khuhro, 30 Nov. 1925, KP.
24. Register of members and subscriptions, KP.
25. Lists of candidates, KP.
26. Khuhro to Governor of Bombay, 30 Jul. 1928, KP.
27. Governor of Bombay to Khuhro, 1 Aug. 1928, *ibid.*
28. Governor of Bombay to Khuhro, 20 Aug. 1928, KP
29. Khuhro to Governor of Bombay, 12 Sep. 1928, KP.
30. Khuhro to Minister of Education, Govt. of Bombay, 7 Mar. 1926. KP.

CHAPTER 5

1. Khuhro, Notes, KP.
2. Khuhro to G. A. Thomas, 28 Aug. 1930, KP.
3. *Ibid.*
4. *Ibid.*
5. Thomas to Khuhro, 29 Aug. 1930, KP.
6. Khuhro, Notes, KP.
7. Khuhro to Thomas, 7 Sep. 1930, KP.
8. A. A. Agha, *The Daily Gazette*, Karachi, 27 Aug. 1930.
9. Draft in KP.
10. *Ibid.*

CHAPTER 6

1. *Vide infra* Chapter 10.
2. *Farman* of Pir Pagaro, dated 3 Aug. 1930, issued from Karachi Jail. KP.
3. Khuhro, Notes, KP.
4. The issue of the separation of Sind was one of the 'Fourteen Points' which Jinnah formulated as the minimum Muslim demands after the failure to reach an agreement at the All Parties Conference at Calcutta.
5. See H. Khuhro, *Documents on the Separation of Sind*, vol. 1., 'Proceedings of the 17th Session of All India Congress.', Karachi 1913, Doc. 1.
6. Edwin Montagu, *An Indian Diary*, London 1930, p. 151.
7. See Hamida Khuhro, *ibid,* for a detailed discussion of the history as well of the Separation and the major documents dealing with it.
8. *The Nehru Report,* 1975 edition, quoted H. Khuhro, *op.cit.*, vol. 1. p. 186.
9. Report of the Brayne Conference, 1932.
10. *Ibid.*
11. *Ibid.*
12. *Ibid.*
13. Khuhro to Allama Iqbal, 21 Nov. 1932. KP.
14. Syed Miran Mohammed Shah to Khuhro, 10 Jun. 1933, KP.
15. Khuhro sent his account of the journey to *New Era*, a Karachi newspaper immediately after his arrival in London. There were briefer accounts in other newpapers. The Dutts' account was published in a newspaper in Jubbulpore.
16. Khuhro, *New Era,* Karachi, 1 Aug. 1933.
17. *Ibid.*
18. Sir Shafaat Ahmed Khan had supported the case for separation strongly. He remained in close touch with Khuhro all the while and had presented the case for financial subvention for Sind from the Government of India with great skill and success.(H.Khuhro, *op. cit.*). After the separation Khuhro wrote to Sir Shafaat very warmly thanking him for his help.

19 The Aga Khan to Sir Ghulam Hussain Hidayetullah, 3 Aug. 1933 KP.
20 Private Secretary to the Viceroy to Khuhro, 9 Sep. 1933, KP.
21 A. M. Rashdi, *Uhe Deehan Uhe Sheenhan*, (Sindhi), vol. 1, pp. 294-317.
22 Willingdon to Brabourne,19 Mar. 1934, IOL, Mss. Eur. F. 97/5A
23 Brabourne 'Diaries', IOL. Mss. F. 97/51. Brabourne notes in his Diary: "Khuhro, K. B. (M. L. C. Larkana), 17-3-34. Pro Ghulam Hussain. 26-6-34 – to make peace after one stormy interview in early March when he 'threatened' me. 25-8-35 – Re Sind Zemindar's woes. 13-3-36 – to day Goodbye otherwise as b-y as usual." Brabourne was to bear Khuhro a grudge after the episode of the interview of March 1934.
24 Willingdon to Brabourne, 9 Apr. 1934, IOL Mss. Eur. F. 97.
25 Brabourne to Willingdon, 12 Apr. 1934, *ibid*.
26 Willingdon to Brabourne, 14 Apr. 1934, *ibid*.
27 Eric Mieville to Brabourne, 29 Apr. 1934, *ibid*.
28 Brabourne to Willingdon, 3 Jul. 1935, Mss. Eur. F. 97/9.
29 Brabourne to Willingdon, 5 Dec. 1934, *ibid*.

CHAPTER 7

1 Khuhro to the Aga Khan, 3 Apr. 1934, KP.
2 Khuhro, Draft Statement for the Sind Azad Conference, KP.
3 *Ibid*.
4 *Ibid*.
5 *Shah Jo Risalo*, edited by Dr. Gurbaxani was the first standard compilation of the poetry of Shah Abdul Latif, the 18th century poet who is regarded as the greatest poet of the Sindhi language. Dr. Gurbaxani was the Professor of Persian at D. J. College and a scholar of Persian and Sindhi as well as an elegant writer of Sindhi.
6 Dr. Gurbaxani, Reply to Questionnaire, *Proceedings of the Sind Administrative Committee*, 1934, KP.
7 *Ibid*.
8 *Ibid*.
9 *Progs. of the Sind Administrative Committee*, and Khuhro, *Notes*, KP.
10 Khuhro to Allama Iqbal, 8 Jan. 1934, KP.
11 Allama Yusuf Ali to Allama Iqbal, enclosure to letter from Allama Iqbal to Khuhro, KP.

CHAPTER 8

1 Willingdon to Zetland, 10 Nov. 1935, IOL Mss. Eur. D. 609.
2 Linlithgow to Zetland, *ibid*.
3 Graham to Brabourne, 27 Dec. 1936, IOL Mss. Eur. F 97/16.
4 Graham to Brabourne, 29 Jan. 1937, IOL Mss. Eur. F 97/16.
5 A. K. Jones, *Muslim Politics and the Growth of the Muslim League in Sind, 1935-1941*. Ph.D. dissertation, Duke University.
6 The *Daily Gazette*, Karachi, 20 Aug. 1935, p. 14.
7 Brabourne to Graham, 16 Mar. 1937, IOL Mss.Eur.F. 97/16.
8 Handwritten marginal note by Khuhro in his copy of G. M. Syed's book *Struggle for New Sind*, p. 6. 'includ. also Isran, Lahori, Jatoi and Mir group'. Also Khuhro, *Notes*, KP.
9 Khuhro to Syed, 17 Nov. 1937, Syed Papers, Khuhro file.
10 *Ibid*.
11 *Ibid*.
12 G. M. Syed, *Struggle for New Sind, Karachi*, 1949, p. 7.
13 Khuhro to Syed, 22 Jan. 1938, Syed Papers, Khuhro file.
14 Graham to Brabourne, 3 Sep. 1937, IOL L/P&J/5/251.
15 Jones, *op. cit.*, pp. 140-141.
16 Syed, *op. cit.*, p. 8.
17 Syed, *op. cit.*, p. 10.
18 Syed and Rashdi related this episode in a number of interviews with the author.

CHAPTER 9

1. *Fortnightly Report*, second half of March 1938, IOL, L/P&J/5/252.
2. Jones. *op. cit.*
3. Syed, *op. cit.*, p. 13.
4. Rashdi, Interview with author, June 1981.
5. Syed, *op. cit.*, p. 15.
6. Zetland–Linlithgow correspondence, June 1937, IOL Mss.Eur.D.609, Vol. 10.
7. Zetland to Brabourne, 21 Jun. 1938, *ibid.*
8. Syed, *ibid*, pp. 16-17.
9. Syed, *op. cit.*, p. 19.
10. Jones, *op. cit.*, pp. 154-5.
11. Khuhro to Kader Mian, 3 Aug. 1938, QAP F 1095/321.
12. Haroon to Jinnah, 2 Aug. 1938, QAP, F 109/57.
13. Graham to Linlithgow, 17 Jun. 1938, IOL, Mss.Eur.F.125/93.
14. Brabourne to Zetland, 19 Aug. 1938, IOL, Mss.Eur.D.609, vol 10.
15. Graham to Brabourne, 29 Jul. 1938, IOL, Mss.Eur.F.97.
16. *Ibid.*
17. Acting Governor to Viceroy, 14 Sep. 1938, IOL,L/P&J/5/253.
18. Graham to Brabourne, 7 Jul. 1938, IOL, Mss.Eur.F.97.63.
19. Brabourne to Zetland, 5 Aug. 1938, IOL, Mss.Eur.D.609.
20. Silawats were originally immigrants from Rajasthan and were skilled stone workers who had traditionally done the stone construction and carvings in Sind.
21. Rashdi quoted by Jones, *op. cit.*
22. Chief Secretary, Government of Sind, *Fortnightly Report*, first half Oct. 1938, IOL, L/P&J/5/253.
23. Interview with A. M. Rashdi, March 1981.
24. Jinnah, *Handwritten notes*, QAP, F. 134.
25. *Ibid.*
26. Syed, *op. cit.*, p. 24.
27. Acting Governor, Sind to Brabourne, 12 Oct. 1938, IOL,Mss.Eur.F.97.63.
28. Garret to Brabourne, 17 Oct. 1938, IOL Mss.Eur.F.97.63
29. Chief Secretary to Govt. of Sind, *Fortnightly Report*, second half December 1938, *op. cit.*
30. Garret to Linlithgow, 21 Nov. 1938, *op. cit.*
31. *Ibid.*
32. Graham to Linlithgow, 9 Dec. 1938, *op. cit.*
33. Graham to Linlithgow, Jan. 1939, IOL, Mss.Eur.F 125/95.
34. *Ibid.*
35. *Ibid.*

CHAPTER 10

1. The Report of the Court of Inquiry appointed under Section 3 of the Sind Public Inquiries Act of Investigate the nature of the Manzilgah buildings at Sukkur. The Report published at Karachi in 1941 detailed the history of the buildings and came to the conclusion that Masjid Manzilgah was in fact built as a mosque.
2. *Ibid.*
3. *Vide ante* Chapter 6.
4. *Vide* Chapter 4.
5. *Vide* Chapter 2 and later in this chapter.
6. Khuhro to Syed, *9 Mar. 1939, Syed Papers*, Khuhro file.
7. *Al Wahid*, Karachi, 16 Apr. 1939.
8. *Causes of the Sukkur Disturbances*, Important findings of the Court of Inquiry into Sukkur riots of November, 1939 presided over by Mr. Justice Weston. October 1940, hereafter referred to as Weston Report, p. 10
9. *Ibid*, p. 12.
10. *Ibid*, p. 21.

11 *Causes of the Sukkur Disturbances*, Important findings of the Court of Inquiry into Sukkur riots of November, 1939 presided over by Mr. Justice Weston. October 1940, hereafter referred to as Weston Report, p. 22.
12 *Ibid*, p. 26.
13 *Ibid*, p. 43.
14 *Al Wahid*, Karachi, 25 Jul. 1939.
15 *Ibid*.
16 Chief Secretary, Government of Sind, to Secretary Home, Government of India, IOL,L/P&J/5/251.
17 *Al Wahid*, Karachi Aug.–Oct. *passim*.
18 Linlithgow to Graham, 29 Oct. 1940, IOL., Mss. Eur. F.125.
19 Linlithgow to Zetland, 19 Oct. 1939, IOL., Miss. Eur.D.609/17.
20 Zetland to Linlithgow, 5 Sep. 1939, IOL.L/P&J/5/254.
21 *Ibid*.
22 *Ibid*.
23 Maulana Chishti, *Al Wahid*, Aug. 1939.
24 Khuhro to Syed, (undated) Sep. 1939, Syed Papers, Khuhro file.
25 Government Press Note, *ibid*.
26 *Al Wahid*, 28-29 Sep. 1939.
27 Interview with Aligohar, a 'Manzilgah volunteer', 23 Apri. 1991.
28 *Al Wahid*, Karachi 3 Oct. 1939
29 *Ibid*.
30 *Ibid*.
31 Syed, *Struggle for New Sind*, pp. 34–38.
32 *Ibid*.
33 Khuhro to Syed, 10 Oct. 1939, Syed Papers, Khuhro file.
34 Syed, *op. cit.*, pp. 34–38.
35 Syed *op. cit.*, pp. 29–31.
36 Haroon to Jinnah, 2 Oct. 1939, QAP F.274., p. 3.
37 QAP, F/274, p. 48.
38 Khuhro to Syed, 26 Oct. 1939, Syed Papers, Khuhro file.
39 Khuhro *Notes*, KP.
40 Weston, *Report*, p. 6.
41 The Governor refers to this in his report to the Viceroy: "The Muslim League continues to scream for the blood of my Cabinet, though Sir Abdullah Haroon has thought fit to remove himself with his minion, Ali Mohammad Rashdi to Lahore. From there he is puring out propaganda and I am waiting my chance to pick him up for a substantial offence under the Penal Code." Governor's Situation Report, 16 Dec.1939, L/P&J/5/254.
42 Zetland to Linlithgow, 22 Nov. 1939, IOL, Mss. Eur.F.125.
43 Linlithgow to Graham, 21 Oct. 1940, IOL, Mss. Eur.F.125.
44 The term 'dictator' was very fashionable from the late 'twenties' to the late 'thirties. With Mussolini and Hitler as super efficient organisers who were called 'dictator' the term was used by those aspiring to organising any quasi military operation or to organising any efficient operation. Thus the head of Khaksars called himself 'dictator' and in this case the organiser of volunteers and *jathas* for the *Satyagraha*.
45 Weston, *Report*, p. 6.
46 *Ibid*.
47 *Ibid*.
48 *Ibid*.
49 The stretch of the river bank under the control of Khuhro family. The *keti* land was on long term lease from the government and in this case from the state of Khairpur. The control of the land went along with the responsibility for law and order and the general administration of the area.
50 Khuhro to Syed, *12 Dec. 1939, Syed Papers*, Khuhro file.
51 Khuhro to Syed, *24 Dec. 1939, ibid*.
52 Governor's Situation Report for December, 1939, *op. cit.*
53 Khuhro to Syed, 12 Jan. 1940, *op. cit.*
54 Khuhro to Jinnah, 8 Jan. QAP F/518, p. 27.
55 Linlithgow to Zetland, IOL Mss. Eur.D.609.18.
56 Khuhro, Sind Legislative Assembly Proceedings, 26 Feb. 1940, p. 51.

57. Khuhro, *Notes*, KP.
58. Syed, *op. cit.*, p. 47.
59. Zetland adds superciliously: "Our Indian friends being as sensitive as they are, anything short of fulsome and unqualified praise is almost bound to be violently resented."
60. Governor's Situation Report, 16 Jan. 1940, *op. cit.*
61. Linlithgow to Zetland, 27 Feb.1940, IOL, Mss.Eur. D.609.18, p. 27.
62. QAP F/518, p. 21.
63. The Agreement between the Hindu Independents and Muslim League members was as follows: *Demands for the safety of minority community and the measures to be adopted regarding Sukkur tragedy agreed upon by the Muslim League party and the Hindu Independent party which parties are now dissolved and have formed themselves into a Nationalist Party and which Party have approved and ratified the said demands.*
    (1) Immediate appointment of impartial and independent tribunal to determine whether any of the domed buildings in the Sukkur Manzilgah was originally a mosque or not. In case Tribunal holds that to be a mosque, then along that to be given with safeguards which will not lead to breach of peace.
    (2) Sufficient number of additional police to be employed for *mofussil*. As minority communities in police are few, recruitment should be made as to make up minority representation to 40 of the total strength in all cadres.
    (3) Compensation proceedings to be expedited and compensation to be ascertained as early as possible. Twenty per cent of the compensation to be paid by the Government as advance which sum can be recouped from recoveries made towards compensation.
    (4) Orders regarding entertainment of punitive police in villages where dacoities, arson and murder have taken place during November disturbance to be passed immediately and sanction asked for in the current Assembly.
    (5) Court of Inquiry already decided to be appointed by Government should start their work immediately (looking) into all causes of riots, etc., including misbehaviour of officers.
    (6) A Consultative Committee dealing with the situations like the one arising out of the Sukkur riots and dealing with questions relating to law and order should be formed with Premier as Chairman, one Hindu minister as a member and also Congress Party Leader as member.
    (7) Immediate firm action should be taken against those responsible directly or indirectly for the murder of Bhagat Kanwar Ram.
    (8) Action should be taken against all those who were concerned in the Sukkur riots or who incited or abetted the same.
    (9) No cases in connection with Sukkur riots to be withdrawn except those considered by the District Magistrate and Commissioner to be proper ones for reference to the *jirga*. Sind Frontier Regulations should be extended to Sukkur district for disposal of such cases arising out of recent riots which are referred to *jirgas*.
    (10) Villages should be got rehabilitated and intensive propaganda to be carried on for communal harmony.
    (11) Strong immediate action to be taken against all Police Officers and public servants who failed to discharge their duties properly during riots.
    (12) Postings of officers in each district should be so made as to have proportionate assortment from all communities. The necessary changes to be effected at once.
    (13) Officers of the minority communities already serving in Judicial, Police and Revenue should be posted in larger numbers in charge of executive posts in the *mofussil*, so as 40 of executive posts be held by them. Necessary changes should be effected at once.
    (14) Riverine police which formerly existed should be re-employed as otherwise cattle lifters take shelter on the river and (in) forests.
    (15) Government plots should be given either free or at nominal *malkano* to the villagers who want to shift to bigger towns,
    (16) Gun licences should be given to the following persons:–
        (1) Zamindars paying assessment Rs. 250.
        (2) Lessees who pay Rs. 1,000 assessment.
        (3) Income tax payers.
        (4) Panchayats.
        (5) All who need protection including working partners of big zamindars.
        (6) Applications for gun licences should be disposed of within a month.

(17) Parliamentary Secretary should not be allowed to represent accused in Crown cases.
(18) All legitimate interests of minority communities should be safeguarded Minority communities should get 40% ratio in public services.
(19) Strict orders should be issued to all public servants not to indulge in any communalism and that any such tendency on their pat shall be taken serious notice of.
(20) No Bill should be brought by Government before the Assembly except with the previous consultation of the parties supporting the Government.
(21) Introduction of Joint Electorates. Signed by:
  (1) Nichaldas Vazirani
  (2) K. B. M. A. Khuhro
  (3) G. M. Syed
  (4) Shaikh Abdul Majid.

64 Khuhro, *Notes*, KP.

CHAPTER 11

1 Linlithgow to Zetland, 31 Aug. 1939, IOL, Mss.Eur.D.609.
2 Linlithgow to Zetland, 21 Dec. 1939, *ibid.*
3 Zetland to Linlithgow, 12/13 Sep. 1939, *op. cit.*
4 Pirzada, S. S., *Foundations of Pakistan*, vol II, p. 340.
5 Ibid, pp. 340–342.
6 See Ayesha Jalal, *The Sole Spokesman*, Cambridge University Press, 1985, p. 55 and passim for a detailed analysis of the problem.
7 Ibid, p. 57, Wolpert in his book *Jinnah of Pakistan*, misses the point by asserting that Jinnah was absolutely serious about Pakistan from this moment on. Not only does the evidence of his subsequent conduct belie that assumption but the top Muslim League leadership continued to believe till the collapse of the Cabinet Mission Plan at least that the Pakistan demand was a 'bargaining counter' and were completely taken by surprise at the bargain they eventually got.
8 Ibid.
9 Graham to Linlithgow, IOL, H/P&J/5/420.
   The Hindus had put the condition that on no account was Khuhro, the leader of the Muslim League Parliamentary Party and the Leader of the Opposition in the Assembly, to be made Premier and the compromise candidate agreed on was Mir Bandeh Ali who had the support of the Talpur group.
10 Ibid.
11 Ibid.
12 Graham to Linlithgow, 29 Jul. 1940, *op. cit.*
13 Ibid.

CHAPTER 12

1 Moon, P, *The British Conquest and Dominion of India*, London 1989, pp. 1104–1109.
2 Ibid, p. 1110.
3 Khuhro to Syed, 13 Mar. 1969, Syed Papers, Khuhro file.
4 Syed's interview with author, January 1990.
5 *The Daily Gazette*, Karachi, 1 Aug. 1942.
6 Dow had a great shock when Allah Baksh whom he considered a most 'loyal' Premier announced his decision to renounce his title of Khan Bahadur and O.B.E. in keeping with Congress policy. Dow pleaded with him not to go ahead with this decision and writes in bewilderment to the Viceroy:"He did not give any indication of this last evening when he had a discussion with me on the general political situation. He was very bitter about the uncompromising attitude of the British Government and also Jinnah, but his own idea of compromise did not go beyond accepting the Congress demands in full... I suppose he cannot really make up his mind which way to act in order to secure his political future. Things are getting a little too big for him... He does not think renunciation of titles would mean leaving the Government." Dow to Linlithgow, 18 Sep. 1942, IOL R/3/1/71.

7 Syed, *op. cit.*, p. 89.
8 Dow to Linlithgow, 22 Oct. 1942, IOL, R/3/1/71
9 Shaikh Abdul Majid to Jinnah, 24 Oct. 1942, QAP F/576, p. 7.
10 *Ibid.*
11 Telegram, Jinnah to Yusuf Haroon, 13 Oct. 1942, QAP F/274, p. 273.
12 Yusuf Haroon to Jinnah, Oct. 1942, QAP F/274, p. 268.
13 Khuhro, *Notes*, KP.
14 Dow to Linlithgow, 25 Jan. 1943, Mss.Eur.F.125/99.
15 Dow to Linlithgow, 22 Feb. 1943, *ibid.*
16 *Ibid.*
17 Linlithgow to Dow, 15 Aug. 1943, IOL.Mss.Eur.E.327 Box 2.
18 Dow to Linlithgow, 23 Mar. 1943, IOL R/3/1/72.
19 Dow to Linlithgow, 20 Apr. 1943, *ibid.*
20 Dow to Wavell, 22 Nov. 1943, IOL. Mss.Eur.F.125/99.
21 *Ibid.*
22 Dow to Linlithgow, 23 Mar.1943, *ibid.*
23 Dow to Linlithgow, 18 Jun. 1943, *ibid.*
24 Linlithgow to Dow, 15 Aug. 1943, IOL,Mss.Eur.E.372.
25 Dow to Linlithgow, 5 Aug. 1943, IOL, L/P&J/5.
26 *Ibid.*
27 *Ibid.*
28 In September 1944 Khuhro resigned as Minister as he had to face charges in the Allah Baksh murder case and was arrested shortly afterwards. This allowed Dow an excuse to postpone giving his assent.
29 Dow to Linlithgow, 26 Oct. 1944, IOL, L/P&J/5 Box 61.
30 *Ibid.*
31 Khuhro to Syed, 17 Jan. 1943, Syed Papers, Khuhro file.
32 Khuhro to Jinnah, 17 Jan. 1943, KP.
33 *Ibid.*
34 *Ibid.*
35 *Ibid.*
36 Dow to Wavell, 20 Dec. 1943, IOL L/P&J/5/259.
37 Stanley Wolpert, *Jinnah of Pakistan*, Oxford University Press, New York, 1984, p. 226.
38 Syed, *op. cit.*, p. 95.
39 *Ibid.*
40 *Ibid.*
41 *Ibid.*
42 *Ibid*, p. 111.
43 Shamsul Hasan, K., *Sindh's Flight for Pakistan*, p. 6.
44 Intelligence reports on Gazdar during the Hur troubles gave a resume of his career: "Mohamed Hashim Gazdar is a Civil Engineer and possesses the degree of B.A., M.I.E. He served the Government in the Bombay Provincial Engineering Service in the Bombay Back Bay Reclamation Scheme. It is said that he resigned under compulsion after enquiries were made regarding charges of corruption against him which, apparently, were not substantiated." Gazdar would prove a courageous politician in his later career championing the Muslim cause before Partition and the Sindhi cause after 1947.

CHAPTER 13

1 Dayaram Gidumal, Memorandum, *The Hur Sect*, 1896, IOL, Mss.Eur.F.208
2 *Ibid.*
3 Gidumal, *ibid.*
4 Sardar M. Yakub, Acting Deputy Commissioner, Tharparkar District to Commissioner-in-Sind, 30 Sep. 1898, *ibid.*
5 *Ibid.*
6 Evan James, Commissioner-in-Sind to Sandhurst, *ibid.*
7 *Ibid*, For details of Lucas' Operations against the Hurs see Lucas to Commissioner-in-Sind, 25

May 1896, Appendix H & I, with above letter.
8. *Ibid.*
9. *Ibid.*
10. *Ibid.*
11. Government of India's 'Adviser' to the Mir of Khairpur was known as 'Vizier'.
12. The *kot* or the citadel of Pir jo Goth had protective mud walls so thick that 'a bullock cart could drive along the top.' Khuhro, *Notes*, KP.
13. The police officers involved in the investigation of the Pir case were the same ones involved in concocting the Allah Baksh murder case against Khuhro in 1944, They were G. G. Ray at this time S.P., Sukkur and Ghulam Akbar, S.H.O., Pir jo Goth.
14. G. A. Thomas known as 'god almighty' Thomas, Commissioner-in-Sind, later Executive Councillor, Bombay, was an arrogant and autocratic official who had a confrontation with Khuhro over the incident of Sukkur riots in 1929, *vide* Chapter 5.
15. Mohabat Fakir figures prominently in H. T. Lambrick's *The Terrorist*, a brilliant 'docu-novel' of the Hur insurgency of the 'forties'.
16. Khuhro, *Notes*, KP.
17. Fortnightly Report for the first half February, 1939. IOL L/P&J/5/254.
18. IOL, Mss. Eur. F. 208/17.
19. IOL, Mss. Eur. F. 208/69, pp. 137-8.
20. Khuhro, *ibid.*
21. Wells, A. G., *op. cit.*
22. Khuhro, *Notes*, KP.
    Intelligence reports of the time suggest close links between Pagaro and both Hidayetullah and Soomro. Hidayetullah's links with Pagaro were well-known and informants of the government repeatedly asserted these links: "It is reliably reported that Mr. N. C. Vazirani the ex Minister to Government of Sind, before proceeding to Hyderabad to give defence evidence in the case against Pir Pagaro fixed for Sunday (14 February 1945) told his thick [sic] friend that he would not give evidence in favour of the Pir and added that not his but Sir Ghulam's palm was in the past was being greased by Pir Pagaro.
    After Mr. Nihchaldas' departure for Hyderabad, Allahbux ex-Premier of Sind went to his residence and enquired from his people if he had left any instructions for him (Allahbaksh) in connection with the case against the Pir in order to enable other people to decide whether or not they should depose in the Pir's favour." IOL Mss. Eur. F. 208/17.
23. Khuhro, *Notes*, KP.
24. All were leading members of the Congress Party in Sind.
25. Mohammed Hussain, Deputy Superintendent Hur Bureau, Hyderabad, to Lambrick, 12 Feb. 1946, IOL, Mss. Eur. F. 280/16.
26. Lambrick, 26 Jan. 1946, Mss. Eur. F. 208/16.
27. *Ibid.*
28. *Ibid.*
29. Executive Engineer Mithrao to Superintendent Engineer. IOL, Mss.Eur.F/208/24.
30. Evidence of Mohammed Khan, son of Fateh Khan Pathan, armed police constable, Nawabshah. *ibid* 208/19.
31. Harris, J. R., Memorandum, 10 Jun. 1942, *ibid* 208/25.
32. Extract from the Minutes of the meeting of the Working Committee Sind Provincial Muslim League, Karachi 14-9-1942. IOL, Mss. Eur. F. 208/60.
    The confidential proceedings of the Sind Muslim League Working Committee were provided to the British authorities by Rashdi who was himself a member of the Working Committee but at the same time a trusted adviser of the Martial Law authorities in the matter of Hur activities and the case against Pagaro. His speech in the Working Committee with its open advocacy of Martial Law authorities is obviously made with an eye to these very same authorities as he well knew that the report would be seen by them.
33. *Ibid.*
34. *Ibid.*
35. Lambrick, *Notes*, IOL Mss. Eur. F. 208/18.
36. Khuhro, *Notes*, KP.
37. IOL, Mss. Eur. F. 125/99.
38. *Ibid.*

END NOTES

39 Lambrick, *Memo*, No. 41/18-H(S), *ibid.*
40 Khuhro, *Notes*, KP.
41 Dialmal Lalwani to Lambrick, 26 Jan. 1943, IOL, Mss. Eur. F. 208.
42 *Ibid.*
43 Dow to Wavell, 9 Sep. 1944, L/P&J/5/260.
44 Barty to Lambrick, 15 Feb. 1943, This and subsequent correspondence in IOL, Mss. Eur. F. 208/20.
45 Lambrick, *Note*, 17 Feb. 1943, *ibid.*
46 IOL, Mss. Eur. F. 208/21.
47 Rashdi, Representation to Secretary, Government of Sind, 18 Sep. 1943, IOL, Mss. Eur. F. 208/75.
48 Rashdi to Lambrick, 16 Sep. 1943, *ibid.*
49 Lambrick, *Memo*, No. 41/18-H(S) *ibid.*

CHAPTER 14

1 Shamsul Hasan Collection, Papers on Sind, *passim*.
2 *Vide supra*, Chapter 7.
3 *Vide supra* Chapter 13.
4 Dow to Wavell, 4 Mar. 1944, IOL, Mss. Eur. E. 372/7.
5 Sessions Court Sukkur, Case No. 28 of 1945. *Judgement*, p. 27.
6 Interview with Kasim Mangrejo's nephew, Larkana, January 1980.
7 *Ibid.*
8 Governor to Viceroy, 20 Sep. 1944, L/P&J/5/260.
9 Khuhro to Jinnah, *Memorandum*, Sep. 1945.
10 *Ibid.*
11 *Ibid.*
12 Governor to the Viceroy, 6 Oct. 1944, L/P&J/5/260 .
13 Dow to Wavell, 4 Nov. 1944, *ibid*. Partabrai Punwani was the former Advocate General who had prosecuted some well-known cases and was a very experienced lawyer. He was specially brought back by Dow for this case.
14 *Ibid.*
15 *Ibid.*
16 *The All India Reporter*, Sind Chief Court, A. I. R.(33) 1946, Sind 1. Mohammed Ayoob Khuro - Applicant v. The Emperor.
17 *Ibid.*
18 *Al Wahid*, Sep. 1944 – Aug. 1945, *passim*.
19 Yusuf Haroon to Jinnah, 4 Oct. 1944, Shamsul Hasan papers.
20 Khuhro, *Notes*, KP.
21 Evidence of G. M. Syed in Sub-Divisional Magistrate's Court, 15 Jan. 1945.
22 Paymaster, *Judgement*.
23 M. H. Sufi, Sub-Divisional Magistrate, Shikarpur, Committal Enquiry Proceedings, 7 Feb. 1945.
24 *Judgement*, p. 37.
25 *Ibid*, pp. 36–39.
26 *Ibid*, p. 40.
27 *Ibid*, p. 41.
28 *Ibid*, p. 42.
29 *Ibid*, p. 46.
30 *Ibid*, pp. 80-81.
31 *Ibid*, p. 83.
32 *Ibid*, p. 83.
33 *Ibid*, pp. 110-111.
34 *Ibid*, p. 116.
35 *Ibid.*
36 *Ibid*, p. 120.
37 *Vide* Chapter 13 for Hur reasons for the derailment of Lahore Mail being the murder of Allah Baksh.
38 *Judgement*, p. 121.
39 *Ibid*, p. 121.
40 *Al Wahid*, 4 Aug. 1945.

41 *Al Wahid*, Editorial, 4 Aug. 1945.
42 *Ibid.*
43 Khuhro to Jinnah, *Memo*, Sep. 1945.
44 Dow to Wavell, 20 Sep. 1945, IOL, Mss. Eur. E. 372/7.
45. Governor to Viceroy, 21 Feb. 1946, IOL, L/P&J/5/262.

CHAPTER 15

1   Linlithgow to Zetland, 21 Dec.1939, IOL, Mss.Eur.D.609.18.
2   Sharma, *op. cit.*, p. 88.
3   Shamsul Hasan, *op. cit.*, p. 27.
4   *Ibid.*
5   *Ibid*, p. 29.
6   *Ibid*, p. 29.
7   Syed, *op. cit.*, p. 121
8   Syed, *op. cit.*, pp. 125-126. The full text of the telegram and the explanation of Syed's position and the opportunism of Hidayetullah is recounted by Syed. For details of the crisis see K. S. Hasan, *Sindh's Fight For Pakistan*, Chapters 1–3.
9   Syed, *ibid.*
10 Syed, *ibid.*
11 Syed, *op. cit.*, p. 128.
12 The resolutions of the Council relating to the autonomy of the provincial organisation are interesting for the fact that almost similar battles would be fought by Khuhro against the Central *dictat* after independence. An indication of the mind set of Syed at this time is obvious from a resolution laying down that every member of Muslim League should sign a pledge to say his prayers at least once a day in congregation.
13 S. Pirzada, *op. cit.*, pp. 9-10. Both Jinnah and Miss Fatima Jinnah had sent congratulatory telegrams to Khuhro on his release. K. S. Hassan, *op. cit.*, pp. 109-110.
14 Syed, *op. cit.*, p. 140-141.
15 K. S. Hassan, *op. cit.*, pp. 126-127.
16 *Ibid.* p. 127.
17 *Ibid.*
18 Jinnah to Khuhro, 13 Oct. 1945, KP.
19 Dow to Wavell, 21 Dec. 1945, IOL, Mss.Eur.E.327/7.
20 *Ibid.*
21 Liaquat Ali Khan, *Report*, 20 Oct. 1945.
22 Minutes of the Central Parliamentary Board, A.I.M.L., KP.
23 Khuhro, *Notes*, KP.
24 Series of interviews by author with Rashdi, Karachi, Winter of 1981-2.
25 Syed, *op. cit.* p. 143.
26 *Ibid.*
27 Rashdi, Interviews with author, Winter 1981-82. Also Mir Ali Ahmed Talpur, Interviews, Summer 1972, London.
28 Isa M. Buxani, Secretary, Sind Muslim League, Tharushah, District Nawabshah, to Jinnah, 21 Nov. 1945. K. S. Hassan, *op. cit.*, pp. 136-137.
29 Khuhro to Syed, 16 Nov. 1945, K. S. Hassan, *op. cit*, pp. 136-137.
30 *Ibid*, p. 146.
31 Syed, *op. cit.*, pp. 156-158.
32 K. S. Hassan, *op. cit.*, p. 151.
33 Durga Das, *Sardar Patel's Correspondence*, vol. 3., p. 93.
34 Mudie to Wavell, 26 Apr. and 24 May 1946, IOL, L/P&J/5/262.
35 QAP F/1133, p. 18, Syed, *op. cit.*, p. 170.
36 Khuhro, *Notes*, KP.
37 *Ibid.*
38 Mudie to Wavell, 27 Apr. 1946, IOL L/P&J/5/262.
39 Mudie to Wavell, 24 May 1946, *ibid.*
40 Mudie to Wavell, 11 Jun. 1946, *ibid.*

END NOTES

41 *Ibid.*
42 *Ibid.*
43 Khuhro, *Notes*, KP.
44 Durga Das, *op. cit.*, p. 105.
45 Speaker, Legislative Assembly of Sind to M. A. Khuhro, 11 July 1946, KP.
46 The contacts suspected at the time were later confirmed, Sudhir Ghosh, *Gandhi's Emissary*, London, 1967 and Moon, *Wavell, The Viceroy's Journal*, London, 1973.
47 Nehru, 14 Jul. 1946, quoted in Moon, *op. cit.*, p. 1153.
48 Moon, *op. cit.*, p. 1155.
49 Vallabhai Patel to Sidhwa, Congress MLA from Sind, Durgadas, *op. cit.*, p. 145.
50 Khuhro to Jinnah, May 1946, KP.
51 Khuhro to Jinnah, 26 Aug. 1946, KP.
52 Khuhro, *Notes*, KP.
53 Moon, *Wavell, The Viceroy's Journal*, p. 413.
54 Mir Bandehally Talpur was given unspecified promises to defect from Muslim League but settled for Ministership in the Muslim League Ministry. Patel writes rebuking the Sind Congress for its stupidity in making underhand deals: "Up to now the Coalition Party was able to hold its head high as it stood on clean record and on principles. By making a settlement with Mir Bundeh Ali, the Coalition Party compromised its position and damaged its reputation, as it had to offer a very high price for inducing him to come out of his party and join the Coalition. On top of this, the failure of Mir Bundeh Ali to stand by his promise made the position of the Coalition more vulnerable and ridiculous." Patel to Mehrotra, 27 Mar. 1946, Durga Das, *op. cit.* p. 121.
55 Durga Das, *op. cit*, pp. 127–131.
56 Vazirani to Patel, 13 Dec. 1946, *ibid*, p. 136.
57 Khuhro to Syed, 13/17 Mar. 1969, Khuhro file, Syed papers.
58 Syed, *op. cit.*, p. 181.
59 Mudie to Wavell, 8 Jan. 1947, IOL L/P&J/5/262.
60 *Ibid.*
61 Mudie to Wavell, 22 Jan. 1947, *ibid.*
62 Mudie to Mountbatten, 10 May 1947, IOL L/P&J/5/63.
63 Mudie to Wavell, 8 Jan. 1947, *ibid.*
64 Mudie to Mountbatten, 26 Mar. 1947, *ibid.*
65 Mudie to Mountbatten, 7 Apr. 1947, IOL L/P&J/5/263.
66 Mudie to Mountbatten, 25 Apr. 1947, *ibid.*
67 Abdul Rasul Memon, Chief Engineer, Irrigation and Power Dept., Government of Sind, letter to author, 17 Aug. 1992 and also see *Agreement between the Punjab and Sind regarding the Sharing of the Waters of the Indus and Five Punjab Rivers. 1945.*
68 Government of Sind, *Post-War Development, 1945*, Government of Sind Press, 1945.
69 *Ibid*, p. 6.
70 Moon, *Wavell*, p. 424.
71 Mudie to Wavell, 24 Feb. 1947, IOL/L/P&J/5/263.
72 Khwaja Nazimuddin quoted in Jalal, *op. cit.*, p. 238.
73 Sharma, M. S. M., *op. cit.* p. 113.
74 Mudie to Wavell, 22 Jan. 1947, *op. cit.*
75 Jalal, *op. cit.*, p. 262.
76 Alan Campbell-Johnson, *Mission With Mountbatten*, London 1951, p. 103. This story has been repeated by other writers and has not been denied.
77 Mudie to Mountbatten, 26 Jun. 1947, *op. cit.*

CHAPTER 16

1 The sixty nine seats included members from the fully-fledged provinces of British India and included Muslim members from the minority provinces. Several areas of Pakistan such as the states of Bahawalpur, Khairpur, the Frontier states, Baluchistan states and the tribal areas would be representation quite a while later.
2 *The Daily Gazette*, Karachi, 12 Aug. 1947.
3 Chaudhri Muhammad Ali, *The Emergence of Pakistan*, p. 198.

4   Khuhro was occupying the house on Victoria Road opposite the Sind Club which is the State Guest House at present and which was renamed '10, Victoria Road' by Begum Liaquat Ali Khan. Echoes of 10 Downing Street perhaps!
5   Chaudhry Muhammad Ali, *op. cit.*, p. 199.
6   In view of the majority opinion in favour of Khuhro all other aspirants for the post namely Mir Bandeh Ali Talpur, Mir Ghulam Ali Talpur, Pirzada Abdul Sattar, and Pir Illahi Baksh had issued a joint statement as early as 4th August that "...the Honourable M.A.Khuhro, our Deputy Leader now should unanimously be elected as the leader of the Sind Muslim League Assembly Party and assume charge of Premiership of Sind." *The Daily Gazette*, Karachi, 5 Aug. 1947.
7   *The Daily Gazette*, Karachi, 11 Jul. 1947.
8   *Dawn*, Karachi, 4 Nov. 1947.
9   Khuhro, *Notes*, KP.
10   *The Daily Gazette*, Karachi, 15 Jul. 1947.
11   *The Daily Gazette*, Karachi, 3 Sep. 1947.
12   Jalal, A. *The State of Martial Rule*, p. 31.
13   Author interview with Salar, Muslim League National Guard, Nawabshah, 30 Sep. 1994. When the killings were reported the Government of Sind took serious notice of the incidents but Masood covered his tracks by holding meetings of the minority community leaders to clear him of any blame. In one such meeting in the Durbar Hall of DC house in Nawabshah the much respected Hindu community leader Rai Bahadur Hotchand gave Collector Masood 'a clean chit'.
14   *The Daily Gazette*, Karachi, 22 Sep. 1947.
15   *The Daily Gazette*, Karachi, 16 Sep. 1947.
16   *Dawn*, Karachi, 21 Oct. 1947.
17   *Ibid* Khuhro came in for a good deal of criticism from the press for what was supposed to be the Sind Government policy and gallantly though perhaps foolishly tried to justify the ordinance: "His attention being drawn to to the stoppage of various articles of luggage which were being carried by the refugees, the Premier stated that the Customs examination was a necessity because it was not Government's intention to allow prohibited goods from going out-i.e...arms, ammunition, bombs, explosive materials, unsewn cloth..." *Daily Gazette*, 14 Sep. 1947.
18   *Dawn*, Karachi, 24 Oct.1947.
19   *Ibid.*
20   *Ibid.*
21   Sri Prakasa, *Pakistan; Birth and Early Days*, Meerut, 1965, pp. 54, 71 and *passim*.
22   Khuhro not only sent what he could spare from Sind but also made efforts to obtain arms from abroad for the fight in Kashmir as well as to set up an arms industry in Pakistan, sending at least one well-known business man to make the arrangements. His unexpected removal from office within a few months however put a stop to that venture. Rahim Bux Khan, *My Beloved Pakistan*, pp. 29–44.
23   Liaquat Ali Khan to Jinnah, 4 Feb. 1948, QAP F/25.
24   Khuhro, 'My personal contacts and impression about Quaid-e-Azam Mohammed Ali Jinnah', *Papers Presented at the International Congress on Quaid-e-Azam, 19–25 December 1976*, vol V, Quaid-e-Azam University, Islamabad.
It was obvious that not every provincial government was able to meet the level of efficiency set by Khuhro who writes, "According to Liaquat Ali Khan's own version, he told me that he had to stay in Lahore because (Provincial) Ministry was not able to face the refugee problem and were too afraid to deal with them." *ibid*, p. 84.
25   Sharma, *op. cit.*, p. 168.
26   Khuhro, *Notes*, KP.
27   *Ibid.*
28   Eye witness account of I. K. Gujral, later to be Indian Ambassador to the U.S.S.R. External Affairs Minister, Government of India, and Prime Minister of India, was living in Karachi as his father was member of the Constituent Assembly of Pakistan, saw the attack and Khuhro's action from Lakshmi Building on Bunder Road (now M. A. Jinnah Road). Interview with author at Karachi.
Rashdi, interviews cited above.
29   Khuhro, *Notes.*
30   Khuhro, *Notes*, KP.

31 Khuhro, *Notes*, KP. *Ibid* Khuhro recounts: "I personally saved some of the Hindus removing them with their families from the dangerous areas, Dingomal Thadani, the Sind Government Law Secretary, Hardasmal and M. P. Mithrani, the Additional Chief Engineer, among others."
32 *Ibid.*
33 I. K. Gujral said that Khuhro was one of the best administrators the subcontinent had produced. (interview cited above) Admiral Ahsan, Pakistan Navy. Admiral Ahsan gave his opinion that it was a cause for regret that a man like Khuhro whom Pakistan could have used and indeed needed badly in its formative years had been renedered ineffective by political intrigue and manipulation. Interview with author, October 1980, Karachi.
34 Khuhro, *Notes*, KP.
35 Sharma, *op. cit.*, pp. 172-173.
36 Khuhro, *Notes*, KP.
37 Khuhro, *Notes*, KP.
38 Khuhro to Jinnah, 4 Jan. 1948, *Sind Special Court of Enquiry Papers* 1949.
39 Chief Secretary, Sind to Governor, Sind, 24 Feb. 1948, QAP, (G.G.file).
40 *Dawn*, Karachi, 21 Jan. 1948.
41 Resolution of the Council of Sind Muslim League, 2 Feb. 1948, KP.
42 *Ibid.*
43 Khuhro to Chundrigar, 8 Feb. 1948, QAP (G.G.file).
44 Chundrigar to Khuhro, 12 Feb.1948, *ibid.*
45 Khuhro to Chundrigar, 14 Feb.1948, *ibid.*
46 Chundrigar to Khuhro, 17 Feb.1948 *ibid.*
47 Khuhro to Chundrigar, 19 Feb.1948, *ibid.*
48 Khuhro to Chundrigar, 24 Feb.1948, *ibid.*
49 Khuhro to Jinnah, 22 Apr. 1948, *Special Court of Enquiry Papers, 1948.*
50 Khuhro to Jinnah, 23 Apr. 1948, *ibid.*
51 The contents of the interview of the two Ministers and the Governor with Jinnah was widely discussed by their friends and colleagues at the time.
52 Khuhro, *Notes*, KP. The letter of dismissal from the Governor said that it was issued on the instructions of the Governor General. The citing of this authority, it was reported, annoyed Jinnah who did not want to be openly associated with this blatantly unconstitutional action.
53 Rashdi, Interview with author. Rashdi was one of the guests at lunch on 26 April.
54 *Al Wahid*, Karachi, 28 Apr. 1948,(translated from Sindhi). *Al Wahid* carried the full text of Khuhro's press statement which was not fully reported by *Dawn*.
55 *Ibid.*

CHAPTER 17

1 Some months later in 1949 the question came up before the Sind Assembly of paying the cost of the Sind Special Court of Inquiry. The members objected strongly to the demand on the grounds that the expenditure had not been sanctioned by the Assembly nor had it been consulted in the matter. Yusuf Haroon, the Premier at the time, agreed that the whole thing had been irregular but that someone had to foot the bill!
2 *Sind Special Court of Inquiry*, Karachi, Government Press, 1948. (Government Blue Book)
3 *Ibid.*
4 Written Statement of M. A. Khuhro before the Sind Special Court of Inquiry, Thursday, 30 Sep. 1948, para. 2.
5 *Ibid*, para 3.
6 *Ibid.*
7 *Ibid.*
8 *Ibid.*
9 *Ibid.*
10 *Ibid*, paras. 71–82.
11 *Ibid*, para. 63.
12 *Vide supra* Chapter 16.
13 *Ibid.*
14 *Ibid.*

15 *Ibid.*
16 *Vide supra* Chapter 16.
17 *Ibid*, para. 44.
18 *Ibid.*
19 *Ibid.*
20 *Ibid*, para 42.
21 *Ibid.*
22 *Ibid*, para. 84.
23 *Ibid*, paras. 86, 87.
24 *Ibid*, paras. 88, 89.
25 *Ibid*, paras. 90, 91, 92.
26 *Ibid*, para. 92.
27 IOL L/P&J/5/330, p. 30.
28 *Ibid.*
29 *Ibid.*
30 *Ibid.*
31 *Ibid*, p. 30.
32 The way the Inquiry had gone had led to rumours that there was a behind the scenes agreement between Khuhro and the Central Government but this was not based on fact and was eventually belied by the actions of the Central Government enacting PRODA and disqualifying Khuhro from politics.
33 IOL L/P&J/5/330, P. 217.
34 Hamid Yusuf, *Pakistan In Search Of Democracy, 1947–77*, Lahore, 1980.
35 In the Chief Court of Sind at Karachi. Original Civil Jurisdiction. Suit No. 480 of 1949.
36 Khuhro *Notes*, KP.

CHAPTER 18

1 IOL, L\P&J\5\33, p. 170.
2 *Dawn*, 24 Mar. 1951.
3 *Ibid.*
4 Constituent Assembly of Pakistan, Debates, 22 May 1948.
5 *Ibid.*
6 *Ibid.*
7 Mohammed Sharif Ansari to Quaid-e-Azam at Ziarat, 22 Jun. 1948, QAP (G. G. file).
8 Resolution of the Sind Muslim League Assembly Party, 12 Jun. 1948.
9 Telegram to Quaid-e-Azam from Hashim Gazdar, Secretary, Sind Muslim League Assembly Party, 14 Jun. 1948. QAP (G. G. file).
10 *Dawn*, 23 Jun. 1948.
11 *Ibid.*
12 Press Note from G. G.'s Camp at Quetta, dated Ziarat, 21 Jun. 1948, QAP (G. G. file).
13 Few historians have dared to criticise the sacred cows of Pakistan so that objective assessments of events are virtually non existent. One article on the subject which is reasonably balanced is that of Malik Mohammed Jafar in *Viewpoint* 30 Aug. 1990, which I quote here.
14 *Ibid.*
15 *Ibid.*
16 G. Swayne Thomas to G. G.'s Secretariat, 16 Mar. 1948, QAP (G. G. file).
17 M. W. Abbasi, Joint Secretary, Ministry of Interior to Personal Secretary to Quaid-e-Azam, 19 Jun. 1948, *ibid*.
18 Malik Mohammed Jafar *op. cit.* and other writers have discussed the possible motives of Liaquat Ali Khan and his insecurity which led to the hasty and politically ill considered actions taken by the Central Government with regard to Karachi.
19 *Ibid.*
20 Press Note, G. G. Secretariat, Ziarat, 21 Jun. 1948, reported in *Dawn*, 22 Jun. 1948.
21 Constituent Assembly, Debates, reported in *Dawn*, 24 Mar. 1951.
22 *Ibid.*
23 *Pakistan Times*, Lahore, 1 Apr. 1950.
24 S. M. Akhter, *Distribution of Revenue Resources between the Centre and the Provinces*, p. 12.

CHAPTER 19

1. British High Commissioner to Pakistan to Secretary Commonwealth Affairs, (HCR), 5-11 Nov. 1948, IOL, L/P&J/5/331.
2. *Ibid.*
3. *Ibid*, HCR, 6–12 Jan, 1949,
4. *Ibid.*
5. *Ibid*, p. 317.
6. *Mr.Khuhro's Note on the Recommendations of the Retrenchment and Reorganisation Committee*, Government of Sind Printing Press, Karachi, 1950.
7. *Ibid.*
8. *Ibid*, 20–26 Jan. 1950.
9. *Ibid*, 6–12 Apr. 1950.
10. See Khuhro, H. *The Making of Modern Sind. British Policy and Social Change in Sind in the 19th Century*, Karachi, 1972.
11. *vide* Chapter 1 *et seq.*
12. IOL, Mss.Eur.F.235/260.
13. *Ibid.*
14. IOL, Mss.Eur.F. 235/264.
15. *Ibid.*
16. M. Masud, *The Hari Report, Note of Dissent*, p. iv and *passim*. There are numerous errors and exaggerations in the Minute as well as in the Introduction by a S. A. Imtiaz who claims that Khuhro was heading the Sind Government in February 1948 when in fact Khuhro did not become Premier for the second time till March 1951. Although the Report (minus the Note) was published in December 1948, the Introduction quotes newspaper editorials written five months earlier in July 1948 demanding the publication of the Note of Dissent!
17. Sir Roger Thomas to Sir Francis Mudie, Governor of West Punjab, 28 Sep. 1948, IOL, Mss.Eur.F.235/260.
18. *Dawn*, Karachi, 28 Mar. 1951.
19. *Evening Times*, Karachi, 9 De. 1950.
20. *The Sind Observer,* Karachi, 1 Apr. 1951.
21. *Ibid.*
22. *Ibid.*
23. HCR 23–29 Mar. 1949 L/P&J/5/331.
24. HCR *ibid.*
25. *Ibid.*
26. *Ibid.*
27. HCR, 19-26 APR. 1949, *op. cit.*
28. *Daily Al Wahid*, Karachi, 1949 *passim.*
29. HCR 19-26 Apr. 1949, *op. cit.*
30. *Dawn*, Karachi, 28 Jan.1951.
31. In 1951 £1 sterling was equivalent to Rs.6 approximately and today £1 is equal roughly to Rs. 56 which makes Rs. 7000 equal to Rs. 65,333 approximately in terms of present day.
32. In 1942 when Khuhro had become President of Sind Provincial Muslim League he had to resign in a few months when he became Minister, because of this decision of the Quaid-e-Azam.
33. *Dawn*, Karachi, 27 Mar. 1951.
34. *Ibid.*
35. *Ibid.*
36. *Ibid.*
37. *Dawn*, Karachi, 21 Apr. 1951.
38. *Ibid.*
39. Constituent Assembly Debates, 11 Apr. 1951.
40. *Report of the Court of Inquiry on the Rioting and Firing at Hyderabad (Sind) on 23rd October 1950*, Government of Sind Press, Karachi, p. 29.
41. *Ibid.*
42. *Dawn*, Karachi, 10 Apr. 1951.
43. Syed Nur Ahmed, *From Martial Law to Martial Law*, (edit. Craig Baxter) Lahore, 1985, p. 317.
44. Khuhro, *Statement to the Press*, 2 Feb. 1953.

END NOTES

45 Khuhro, *Statement to the Press*, 2 Feb. 1953.
46 *Dawn*, Karachi, 3 Feb. 1953.
47 Nur Ahmed, *op. cit.*, pp. 319-20.
48 Bogra told Khuhro later that he had hinted to Nazimuddin "that perhaps the Governor General is thinking of making me Prime Minister" but Nazimuddin had not understood what he was driving at. Khuhro, *Notes*, KP.
49 The controlling power behind the formation of the Sind Cabinet was the all powerful Governor General, Ghulam Mohammed.
50 Rafique Afzal, *Political Parties in Pakistan*, Islamabad 1986, vol I, p. 146.
51 CAP Debates, 20 Sep. 1954.
52 Keith Callard, *Pakistan, A Political Study*, p. 104.
53 Nur Ahmed, *op. cit.*, p. 343.
54 Proceedings of the Constituent Assembly of Pakistan, September 1954.
55 *Dawn*, Karachi, 6 Oct. 1954.
56 *Gazette of Pakistan Extraordinary*, 20 Oct. 1954.
57 Khuhro asked Suhrawardy about his support of Ghulam Mohammed and the One Unit scheme at a dinner party given by Khuhro's neighbour, K. R. S. Captain, sometime afterwards. Suhrawardy who could be very candid when he chose, said that he had been made certain promises in return for his support such as maximum autonomy for East Bengal and Prime Ministership.
58 Rashdi who was close to the Central clique at this time related this to Khuhro. *Notes*, KP.
59 Ayub Khan, *op. cit.*, pp. 52-53.

CHAPTER 20

1 Altaf Gauhar, *Ayub Khan*, Lahore, 1993, p. 44.
2 Mohammed Ayub Khan, *Friends Not Masters*, Karachi, 1967, p. 54.
3 Iskander Mirza actually came from a Nawab family of Bengal which claimed descent from Mir Jaffer through whose treachery the Battle of Plassey was lost by Nawab Siraj-ud-Daulah in 1757.
4 'Red Shirts' was the popular name for members of the Khudai Khidmatgar Party led by Khan Abdul Ghaffar Khan, the brother of Dr. Khan Sahib.
5 The *Dawn* of 26th and 27th October 1954 carried the statements of Mir Ghulam Ali Talpur and Sind Chief Minister Pirzada supporting the action of the Governor General.
6 Khuhro, *Notes*, KP.
7 Apparently Sardar Rashid had been promised that the capital of West Pakistan would be Abbottabad in N.W.F.P. and that he would be made the first Chief Minister of the Province, a promise which was also made by Iskander Mirza to Dr. Khan Sahib in order to bring him into the Central Cabinet.
8 Khuhro, *Notes*, KP.
9 K. P. The details are also given in Rashdi, 'The History of One Unit', *Jang*, Karachi, 6 Jul. 1970 (7 instalments).
10 The Karachi newspaper *Dawn* under the editorship of Altaf Hussain had continually advocated the unitary form of government for Pakistan, including both the wings divided by a thousand miles of Indian territory! The sponsorship of this idea by *Dawn* had led people to assume that this was an idea of Liaquat Ali Khan and subsequently of the powerful Central clique.
11 Rafique Afzal, *op. cit.*, vol. 1, p. 155.
12 Rashdi, 'The History of One Unit', article in *Jang*, Karachi, 6 Jul. 1970.
13 *Ibid*.
14 CAP Debates, 16 Sep. 1955.
15 Khuhro had been present at the meeting and Sardar Rashid had been among the most enthusiastic about the scheme.
16 Rashdi, Interview with author, Karachi, 1982.
17 CAP Debates, 10 Sep. 1955.
18 *Ibid*.
19 CAP Debates, 14 Sept. 1955.
20 Sind had built the magnificent Dow Medical College which had been completed just before Partition.
21 CAP Debates, 14 Sep. 1955

22 By 'Oriental' Khuhro meant literature of the province written in languages other than Sindhi as for instance in Persian, etc.
23 CAP Debates, *ibid*.
24 *Ibid*.
25 *Ibid*.
26 *Ibid*.
27 *Ibid*.
28 Khuhro, *Notes*, KP.
29 *Dawn*, Karachi, 9 Apr. 1956.
30 Rashdi. 'The History of One Unit', *Jang*, Karachi, 6 Jul. 1970 and seven subsequent weekend supplements.
31 Khuhro, Text of Speech, Moscow, KP.
32 M. H. Zuberi, *Voyage Through History*, Karachi, 1987, vol II, p. 315, says that with the creation of the Republican Party and the prospect of his defeat, Nishtar advised Chaudhry Mohammad Ali to have elections as provided in the constitution but he chose to take the advice of President Mirza who advised him to resign, drop the Muslim Leaguers and he would be asked to form a new government with Republican support. According to Zuberi he accepted this advice and resigned from the Prime Ministership as well as Muslim League. The call from the President to form a new government never came.
33 The Khuhro Papers include a document which appears to be the original draft of the agreement between N.A.P. (G. M. Syed's party) and Muslim League. It is signed by Sardar Bahadur Khan, Mian Mumtaz Daultana, M. A. Khuhro, Qayyum Khan, G. M. Syed, Pir Illahibaksh and Ghulam Mustafa Bhurgri. The text is the same as that produced in G. M. Syed's *The Case of Sindh*, but the date given on the document on three separate pages is 17 March 1958. The date of the agreement between Muslim League and NAP is 17 March 1957. Could this be a mere case of mistake in writing?
34 *Dawn*, Karachi, 27 Mar. 1957.
35 *Ibid*.
36 Reported by Agha Ghulam Nabi Pathan, Minister, West Pakistan Government at this time.
37 The Constitution of 1956 gave the President viceregal powers regarding the appointment of the Prime Minister who had to be chosen at his discretion. (Article 37(3)).
38 Khuhro, *Notes*, KP.
39 Hamidul Huq Chowdhury, *Memoirs*, Dacca, 1989.
40 Khuhro, *Notes*, KP.
41 *Ibid*.
42 The violation of the commitments given to Sind before One Unit is detailed in G. M. Syed's *The Case of Sindh. G. M. Syed's Deposition for the Court*, Karachi 1995, pp. 140–144. Syed also quotes Professor Azizuddin's *Kya Hum Ikatthey Reh Saktey Hein, Barrage Zaminen Aur Ghair Sindhi Abadkari* (Urdu), pp. 347–350) giving an account of the infraction of the agreement with the Sind Government.
43 Daultana had told Khuhro several times that the Punjab was also unhappy with the One Unit as it had to sacrifice a great deal in terms of representation and also the demands of the smaller provinces were being found difficult to meet. Whatever the worth of these complaints Khuhro felt that as far as dismantling of One Unit was concerned the Punjab leadership should back his stand.
44 *Dawn*, Karachi, 24 Jan. 1958.
45 *Dawn*, Karachi, 1 Apr. 1958.
46 *Ibid*.
47 *Dawn*, Karachi, 13 Apr. 1958.
48 *Ibid*.
49 *Dawn*, Karachi, 5 May 1958.
50 *Ibid*.
51 Altaf Gauhar, *op. cit.*, pp. 131-132.
52 Nawabzada General Sher Ali Khan Pataudi of the Pakistan Army relates an incident when he called on Khuhro one morning at his residence in Karachi and Khuhro showed him a letter he was sending to Ayub Khan regarding some request the latter had made. General Sher Ali said that though the letter was absolutely correct it was rather curt. This could certainly have ruffled the feathers of Ayub Khan but Khuhro was not being gratuitously rude only blunt in his usual style.
53 In March that year the Khuhros had invited Mirza and his wife and the Daultanas to dinner. Mirza had specially requested that no one else be invited. Mirza had taken Khuhro and Daultana

outside on the lawn and discussed the possibility of toppling the Noon Ministry. Daultana told him that it was not possible for Muslim League to form a government with Awami League support and Suhrawardy had only a few days earlier issued a categorical statement supporting the Noon government unconditionally. In fact Mirza wanted a situation in which it looked as if it was not possible to carry on a civilian government and had been working towards this end for sometime.

54 Khuhro, *Notes*, KP.
55 *Dawn*, Karachi, 8 Jul. 1958.
56 Khuhro, *Notes*, KP.
57 The central leaders of Muslim League did not attend the conference.
58 Quoted in Jalal, *The State of Martial Rule*, p. 266.
59 Khuhro, *Notes*, KP.
60 *Ibid*.
61 Altaf Gauhar, *op.cit.*, p. 145.
62 Hamidul Huq Chowdhury, *op.cit.*
63 Khuhro, *Notes*, KP.

CHAPTER 21

1 Related by G. M. Syed to the author, November 1980. Shah Abdul Latif is the 18th century Sindhi mystic poet regarded as the greatest poet of the Sindhi language.
2 On a visit to London in the early sixties, Khuhro met Mirza who was living there in exile with his wife Naheed. Mirza denied having had anything to do with the prosecution of Khuhro and insisted that it was at the behest of Ayub Khan.
3 *Dawn*, 12 Dec. 1958.
4 *Dawn*, Karachi, 1 Feb. 1959, Khuhro's evidence and *Dawn*, 4 Feb. 1959, evidence produced in Court.
5 *Dawn*, Karachi, 30 May 1959.
6 P.L.D. 1960, Cases decided by the Supreme Court of Pakistan, pp.237–253.
7 Khuhro to Ayub Khan, Aug. 1966, KP.
8 Khuhro to President of Pakistan, 12 Jan. 1972, KP.
9 *Ibid*.
10 *Dawn*, Karachi, 14 Jul. 1960.
11 For a pithy account of the system see Altaf Gauhar, *op. cit*, passim.
12 See Altaf Gauhar, *op. cit.*
13 *Ibid*, pp. 158–193. Gauhar relates how the civilians around Ayub Khan, particularly Manzur Qadir and Z. A. Bhutto, played up to his ideas and advocated a highly centralized form of government with Ayub as the supreme arbiter or even 'monarch'.
14 Samuel P. Huntington, *Political Order in Changing Societies*, Yale University Press, 1968, pp. 250-251
15 Telegram to the Election Commission by the Larkana Opposition candidates, November 1964. KP.
16 Quoted in M.Rafique Afzal, *op. cit.*, vol II, p. 150.
17 Khuhro, *Notes*, KP.
18 Bhutto told Khuhro that he had personally paid Rs. 50,000 to Bhashani and that the Governor of East Pakistan had paid him Rs. 300,000 for the 'institutions he was running'.

CHAPTER 22

1 In his book *Political Parties in Pakistan*, M. Rafique Afzal mentions Khuhro and Suhrawardy as well a some other politicians as having filed petitions for the waiving of EBDO. Khuhro and Suhrawardy did not file any such petition. The Government did float such rumours at the time to malign the politicians.
2 Mahmudul Aziz, 'Late Ayub Khuhro' *Pictorial News Review*, Jan. 1981, p. 26.
3 Khuhro Papers contain a number of files with details of the companies Khuhro set up and the loans that were sanctioned by the private banks as well as the correspondence with the officials

of the concerned Ministries. The efforts proved fruitless even after the loans had been sanctioned but permission was not forthcoming from the Government.
4. Sayid Ghulam Mustafa Shah, *Bhutto The Man and The Martyr*, Karachi, 1993, pp. 26-27.
5. Altaf Gauhar, *op. cit.*, p. 434.
6. 'President's Broadcast to the Nation'. *Dawn*, Karachi, 29 July 1969.
7. *Dawn*, 13 Jul. 1969. While making extensive tours to set up his party and popularize it, Bhutto had on various occasions publicly refused to endorse the breaking up of One Unit. On one occasion when addressing the students of Sind University at Hyderabad he was asked if he would demand the dismantling of One Unit, he said. 'I will never betray the Punjab.' – a remark typified Bhutto for the Sindhi students who on the whole remained aloof from him.
8. Resolutions Nos.1 and 2, Larkana District Council of Sind United Front, 1st week December 1969. KP.
9. *Ibid.*
10. President's 'Address to the Nation', *Dawn*, Karachi, 29 Mar. 1970.
11. Khuhro to Syed, 3 Feb. 1970, KP.
12. *Ibid.*
13. Khuhro to Syed, 2 Feb. 1970, KP.
14. *Jang*, Karachi, 29 Feb. 1970.
15. *Ibid.*
16. Wolpert, *op. cit.*, pp. 108-109.
17. Ian McIntyre, *The Times*, London, 6 Jan. 1994.
18. Wolpert, *op. cit.*, p. 111.
19. Resolution of SPML (Council), KP.
20. *The Pakistan Times*, Lahore, 20 Oct. 1968.
21. Khuhro, Press statement, Oct. 1970, KP.
22. Richard Sisson and Lo E. Rose, *War and secession in Pakistan, India and the creation of Bangladesh*, 2nd edition, 1992, p. 25.
23. S. Wolpert, *Zulfi Bhutto of Pakistan*, Oxford University Press, Chapter 8, *passim*.
24. Wolpert, *op. cit.*, pp. 115, 131 and *passim*.
25. Hasan Zaheer, *op. cit.*, p. 124.
26. Interview with Khuhro's election agent Mrs Kulsum Adil, March 1972
27. Hasan Zaheer, *The Separation of East Pakistan*, p. 140.
28. *Ibid*, p. 148.
29. Khuhro, Press statement, 13 Aug. 1971, KP.
30. *The Times*, London, 1 Apr. 1971.
31. The Associated Press of Pakistan (APP) and Pakistan Press International (PPI) report carried by all Pakistani newspapers including *Dawn*,12 Aug. 1971.
32. Khuhro, *Note*, Aug. 1968, KP.
33. Khuhro, Press statement, *Daily Sun*, 13 Aug. 1971.
34. Khuhro, Press statement, 13 Aug. 1971, *Daily Sun*, Karachi.

CHAPTER 23

1. Khuhro, Press Statement, May 1971, KP.
2. *Ibid.*
3. Wolpert, *op. cit.*, pp. 160-161. For Bhutto's collusion with the Martial Law regime see *ibid* Chapter 8.
4. Khuhro to General Yahya Khan, 14 Sep. 1971, KP.
5. In 1919 Montague Chelmsford Reforms were promulgated and not Minto Morley Reforms which had already been enacted in 1909.
6. *Vide supra* Chapter 14.
7. *Vide supra* Chapters 11 and 12.
8. *Vide supra*, Chapter 13.
9. Khuhro to Z. A. Bhutto, 4 Oct. 1971, KP.
10. Khuhro to Z. A. Bhutto, 27 Nov. 1971.
11. *Ibid.*
12. *Ibid.*

CHAPTER 24

1. Incident related by the Secretary of Education, Government of Sind, 1972.
2. Interview with Shah Mohammed Khuhro, 31 March 1996, Karachi. Mrs. Parpia was the glamorous wife of an I.C.S officer in Bombay who was later posted to Sind.
3. Khuhro, Press Statement, *The Daily Sun*, Karachi, 22 May 1972
4. Khuhro, Press Statement, *The Daily Sun*, Karachi, 22 May 1972.
5. Notice to the Registrar, Co-operative Societies, Province of Sind, Hyderabad, from Advocates for M. A. Khuhro, ex-Chairman of the Board of Directors, Larkana Zamindari Co-Operative Bank Ltd., AK/138/1972, (June 1972). KP.
6. Khuhro to Home Secretary, Government of Sind, 7 Apr. 1975. KP.
7. Mir Rasul Baksh Talpur related this incident to Khuhro on a visit a year or so after the incident.
8. Khuhro's article was eventually reproduced in the proceedings of the conference.
9. Related by Ahmad Khan Khuhawar of Shahdadkot in Larkana district, a close friend and drinking companion of Bhutto who was accompanying him on this trip.
10. Khuhro to President Zia-ul-Haque, 21 Mar. 1979, KP.

BIBLIOGRAPHY

Over the several years that I have spent researching and writing this book I have read and referred to innumerable books and documents and have interviewed a large number of people. It would be difficult to include all the books and the people I have seen and interviewed. I append below a comparatively brief bibliography which includes printed books, pamphlets, newspapers and collections of private papers both here and abroad and some of the people I have interviewed. A very important source has been information which I got from my family and friends who lived through many of the events I have written about and much is the result of long and indepth discussions with people who experienced this recent history:

PRINTED BOOKS

Abbassi, Muhammad Yusuf, *The Political Biography of Syed Ameer Ali*, Lahore, 1989.
Afzal, M. R., *Political Parties in Pakistan, 1947–69, 2 vols*, Islamabad, 1986.
Aitken, E. H., *Gazetteer of the Province of Sind*, Karachi, 1907.
Aiyar, Mani Shankar, *Pakistan Papers*, New Delhi, 1994.
Allana, G., *Quaid-e-Azam Jinnah, The Story of a Nation*, Lahore, 1967.
Altaf Gauhar, *Ayub Khan, Pakistan's First Military Ruler*, Lahore, 1994.
Amjad Ali, S., *Glimpses*, Lahore, 1992.
Andrew, W. P., *The Indus and its Provinces, Their Political and Commercial Importance*, Lahore, 1976.
Ansari, Sarah, F. D., *Sufi Saints and State Power, The Pirs of Sindh, 1943–47*, London, 1992.
Aziz, K. K., *The Indian Khilafat Movement, 1915–1933*, Karachi, 1972.
Azizuddin Ahmed, *Kya Ham Ikhathey Rah Saktey Hai* (Urdu), Lahore, 1988.
Baloch, N. A. (Edit.), *Chachnama*, Hyderabad, 1954.
Baloch, Sher Mohd, *Pani Majh Pasah* (Sindhi) (Place and date of publication not given).
Baluchistan, The Govt. of, *Baluchistan Gazetteer*, 1908.
Batalvi, A. H. (Edit.), *The Forgotten Years, Memoirs of Sir Mohammed Zafrullah Khan*, Lahore, 1991.
Bernard Lewis, *The Assassins*, London, 1967.
Binder, Leonard, *Religion and Politics in Pakistan*, Los Angeles, 1963.
Brohi, A. K., *Sahar Ja Seenghar (Sindhi)*, Letters to G. M. Syed from Allama I. I. Qazi, Hyderabad, 1969.
Burki, Shahid Javed, *Pakistan Under Bhutto, 1971–77*, Hong Kong, 1988.
Butler, Iris, *The Viceroy's Wife, Letters of Alice, Countess of Reading From India, 1921–1925*, London, 1969.
Callard, K., *Pakistan, A Political Study*, London, 1957.
Campbell Johnson, Alan, *Mission with Mountabatten*, England, 1953.
Chaudhri Muhammad Ali, *The Emergence of Pakistan*, Lahore, 1967.
_____ *The Task Before Us*, Lahore, 1974.
Choudhry Khaliquzzaman, *Pathway to Pakistan*, Lahore, 1961.
Daudpoto, Dr. O. (Edit. Khadija Daudpoto), *Munhji Mukhtasar Atam Kahani*, Karachi, 1959.

Durga Das, *Sardar Patel's Correspondence 1945–50, 10 Vols.*, Ahmedabad, 1972.
Erikson, E. H., *Gandhi's Truth, On the Origins of Militant Nonviolence,* London, 1970.
Farhat Mahmud, *A History of U.S.–Pakistan Relations,* Lahore, 1991.
Ghulam Mustafa Shah, Syed, *Bhutto–The Man And The Martyr,* Karachi, 1993.
Glendevon, John, *The Viceroy at Bay, Lord Linlithgow in India, 1936–1943,* London 1971.
Government of Pakistan, *White Paper on the Crisis in East Pakistan,* Islamabad, 1971.
Gul Hassan Khan, Lt. Gen., *Memoirs,* Karachi, 1993.
Gujra, B. T., *Sind's Role in the Freedom Struggle,* Bombay, 1986.
Haider, S. M., Dr. (Edit.), *Kashmir and South Asian Security,* Rawalpindi, 1992.
Hamidul Haq, Chowdhury, *Memoirs,* Dhaka, 1989.
Hardy, P., *The Muslims of British India,* New York, 1972.
Hughes, A. W., *Gazetteer of Sind,* London, 1876.
Hughes Thomas, R., *Memoir on Sind, 1855,* Selections from the Records of the Bombay Government, No. XVII, New Series.
Jalal, Ayesha, *The State of Martial Law, The Origins of Pakistan's Political Economy of Defence,* England, 1990.
_____ *The Sole Spokesman, Jinnah, The Muslim League and The Demand for Pakistan,* Hyderabad (India), 1985.
James, Sir Morrice, *Pakistan Chronicle,* Karachi, 1993.
Jones, A. K., *Muslims Politics and the Growth of the Muslim League in Sindh, 1935-1941,* Ph.D. Thesis, Duke University, 1977.
K. S. Hassan, *Sindh's Flight for Pakistan,* Karachi, 1992.
Kameruddin bin Abbas, *The Constitution of Pakistan,* Lahore, 1958.
K. S. Hassan, *The Transfer of Power,* Karachi, 1966.
Kamal Hossain, Dr., Talukdar M. H. R. (Edit.), *Memoirs of Huseyn Shaheed Suhrawardy,* Dhaka, 1987.
Khairi Saad, R.,*Jinnah, Reinterpreted,* Karachi, 1995.
Khan, Muhammad Zafarullah, *The Agony of Pakistan,* London, 1974.
Khan Muhammad Ayub Khan, *Friends Not Masters, A Political Autobiography,* Karachi, 1967.
Khuhro, Hamida (Edit.), *Documents on Separation of Sindh from the Bombay Presidency, Vol. I,* Islamabad, 1982.
_____ *The Making of Modern Sind,* Karachi, 1978.
_____ (Edit.), *Sindh through The Centuries,* Karachi, 1981.
Khuhro, M. A., *Reminiscences of the Day of Deliverance,* Karachi, 1976.
_____, *Sufferings of Sind,* Karachi, 1930.
Lambrick, H. T., *Sir Charles Napier and Sindh,* London, 1952.
_____ *John Jacob of Jacobabad,* London, 1960.
_____ *The Terrorist,* London, 1972.
Lifschultz, L., *Bangladesh: The Unfinished Revolution,* London, 1977.
Malik Iftikhar Haider, *Sikandar Hayat Khan, A Political Biography,* Islamabad, 1985.
Mansergh, N, Lumby, E. W. R. (Edit.), *Transfer of Power Documents,* 12 vols. H. M. S. O., London, 1970–83.
Maugham, W. S., *The Memoirs of Aga Khan,* London, 1954.
Maulana Abul Kalam Azad, *India Wins Freedom,* Madras, 1959.
Mayne, Peter, *The Saints of Sind,*
McGrath, Allen, *The Destruction of Pakistan's Democracy,* Karachi, 1996.
Montagu Edwin, *An Indian Diary,* London, 1930.
Montagu P. de Webb, *The Karachi Handbook,*
Moon, Penderel, *The British Conquest and Dominion of India,* London, 1989.
_____ *Divide and Quit,* London, 1962.
_____ (Edit.), *Wavell, The Viceroy's Journal,* London, 1973.
Munir, Justice Muhammad, *From Jinnah to Zia,* Lahore, 1979.

Mushtaqur Rahman, *Land and Life in Sindh, Pakistan*, Lahore, 1993.
Nanda, B. R., *Gandhi, Pan Islamism, Imperialism and Nationalism*, Bombay, 1989.
Nazir H. Ch., *C. J. Muhammad Munir, His Life, Writings and Judgments*, Lahore, 1973.
Nehru, Jawaharlal, *Autobiography, Centenary Edition, 1985*.
_____ *The Discovery of India, Centenary Edition, 1985*.
Niazi, Kausar, *Last Days of Premier Bhutto*, Lahore, 1991.
Niazi, Zamir, *The Press in Chains*, Karachi, 1986.
Noon, Firoz Khan, *From Memory*, Islamabad, 1993.
Nur Ahmed, S. (Edit. Baxter Craig), *From Martial Law to Martial Law, Politics in the Punjab 1919–1959*, Lahore, 1985.
Page, David, *Prelude to Partition*, Delhi, 1982.
Pakistan Historical Society, *A History of the Freedom Movement*, 4 vols., Karachi, 1970.
Pakistan, *The Interim Constitution of the Islamic Republic of*, Islamabad, 1972.
Peerbhoy, A. A., *Jinnah Faces An Assassin*, Bombay, 1943.
Pherwani, Prof. Shewaram Nirsinghdas, *Diwan Dayaram Gudumal (Sindhi)*, Hyderabad, 1938.
Pirzada, D. A., *Growth of Muslim Nationalism in Sindh*, Karachi, 1995.
Pirzada, Haji Shahnawaz, *Ade Ayub Ji Azmaish* (Sindhi), Karachi, 1945.
Pirzada Syed Sharifuddin, *Foundations of Pakistan, All-India Muslim League Documents 1906–1947*, 3 vols., Karachi, 1969.
Ponomarev, Y., *The Muslim League of Pakistan, 1947–1977*, Lahore, 1986.
Ramwani, Motiram, S., *Sindh and Asanjo Warso (Sindhi)*, Bombay, 1987.
Rashdi, Pir A. M., *Rand Aieen Pandh (Sindhi)*, Karachi, 1988.
_____*Rooedad-e-Chaman*, Karachi, 1986.
_____*Uhe Deehan, Uhe Sheenhan*, 3 Vols., Hyderabad, 1966–81.
_____ *Faryad e Sind* (undated, 1947?).
Safdar Mahmood, *Pakistan Divided*, Lahore, 1984.
_____ *Pakistan: Muslim League Ka Dour Hukumat* (Urdu), Lahore, 1973.
Sen, Dr. (Edit.) *Dictionary of National Biography*, Calcutta, 1973.
Shabbir Hussain, S., *The Death Dance, Suicidal Politics of Pakistani Trio!*, Islamabad, 1979.
Shahnawaz Jahan Ara, *Father and Daughter, A Political Autobiography*, Lahore, 1971.
Sharma M. S. M., *Peeps Into Pakistan*, Patna (India), 1954.
Sisson, Richard and Rose, Leo E., *War and Secession Pakistan, India, And The Creation of Bangladesh*, Karachi, 1990.
Sri Prakasa, *Pakistan; Birth and Early Days*, Meerat (India), 1965.
Sayeed, K. B., *Politics in Pakistan, The Nature and Direction of Change*, New York, 1980.
Soomro, M. Q. *Muslim Politics in Sindh, 1938–47*, Hyderabad, 1989.
Sorley, H. T., *The Gazetter of Sind* (The former province of Sind) Karachi, 1968.
—— *Shah Abdul Latif of Bhit*, London, 1940.
Suhrawardy, Begum, S. I., *Huseyn Shaheed Suhrawardy, A Biography*, Karachi, 1991.
Syed, G. M., *Struggle for New Sind*, Karachi, 1949.
_____*Jadeed Syasat Ja Nav Ratan (Sindhi)*, Hyderabad, 1967.
_____*Janam Guzarium Jin Seen (Sindhi)*, 2 vols, Hyderabad, 1967.
_____*Kujh Khat (Sindhi)*, Hyderabad, 1985.
_____ *Religion and Reality*, Karachi, 1986.
Taylor, P. M., *Confessions of A Thug*, London, 1986.
Talbot, Ian, *Provincial Politics and The Pakistan Movement, The Growth of the M. L. In North, West and North East India*, Karachi, 1988.
Wilcox, Wayne Ayres, *Pakistan, The Consolidation of Nation*, New York, 1963.
Wolpert, Stanley, *Jinnah of Pakistan*, Karachi, 1989.
_____ *Zulfi Bhutto of Pakistan, His Life and Times*, New York, 1993.
Zaheer, Hasan, *The Separation of East Pakistan, The Rise and realisation of Bengali Muslim Nationalism*, Karachi, 1994.

Zardari, Mohammed Laiq Dr., *Tehrik Pakistan Mey Sindh Jo Hiso (Sindhi)*, Moro, 1984.
Ziauddin Ahmed Prof., *Shaheed-e-Millat Liaquat Ali Khan, Builder of Pakistan*, Karachi, 1990.
Ziring Lawrence, *Pakistan, The Enigma of Political Development*, England, 1980.
Zuberi, Musarrat Hussain, *Voyage Through History*, 2 vols, Karachi, 1987.

OFFICIAL PUBLICATIONS

The Bombay Legislative Council Debates, 1924–1936.
Constituent Assembly of Pakistan Debates.
Sind Legislative Assembly Debates, 1937–1958.
The Govt. of India Act, 1935 (As adopted by the Pakistan "Provisional Constitution" Order, 1947). Government Press, Karachi, 1948.
District Gazetteers of Sind, 1926.

REPORTS AND PAMPHLETS (SELECTED)

Report on the Subject of Legislation to restrict the alienation of land in Sind by members of the agricultural classes. S. H. Covernton, Karachi, 1927.
Sind Financial Enquiry Report, 1931.
The Sind Conference Report (The Brayne Report), 1932.
A Memorandum on the Question of Sind's Separation from Bombay submitted by M. A. Khuhro to the Joint Parliamentary Select Committee on Indian Reforms on Behalf of the Sind Separation Conference, June-July 1933.
A Rejoinder to the Criticism of Anti-Sind Separation Committee by M. A. Khuhro, September, 1932.
Report of the Inquiry appointed under Section 3 of the Sind Public Inquiries Act to enquire into the riots which occurred at Sukkur in 1939, Karachi, 1939.
Report of Inquiry appointed under Section 3 of the Sind Public Inquiries Act to enquire into the nature of the Manzilgah Buildings at Sukkur, Karachi, 1941.
Causes of the Sukkur Disturbances, published by The Sind Provincial Moslem League, Karachi, 1940.
Report of the Sind University Committee, Karachi, 1942.
Basic Principles Committee, Interim Report, Karachi, 1950.
Report of the Basic Principles Committee, Karachi, 1952.
Address of H. H. Prince Sir Aga Khan at the Session of *Motamer e Alam-e-Islami* on 9th February 1951 at Karachi.
Report of the Court of Inquiry on the Rioting and Firing at Hyderabad (Sind) on 23rd October 1950, Karachi 1950.
Report of the Government Hari Enquiry Committee, 1947-48, Karachi, 1948.
Hari Report, Note of Dissent, M. Masud, 1948.
Sind Tenancy Act 1950, Rochiram, Sind Hari Publications, 1950.
The Province of West Pakistan (Dissolution) Order, 1970.

NEWSPAPERS AND PERIODICALS

Al-Wahid, Karachi
The Daily Gazette, Karachi
Dawn, Karachi
Hindustan Times, Bombay
Jang, Karachi
The New Era, Karachi
The Pakistan Times, Lahore
The Sind Zamindar, Sukkur
The Sind Observer, Karachi

The Sun, Karachi
The Statesman, New Delhi
The Times of India, Bombay
The Times (London)
Pictorial News Review, Karachi, January 1981
Punch, vol 6, 1844, London

COLLECTIONS/MSS.

G. M. Syed Papers
Quaid-e-Azam Papers
Muslim League Papers
The Shamsul Hasan Collection

AT THE BRITISH LIBRARY (India Office Library)

The Athol Papers
The Brabourne Papers
The Brayne Collection
The Curry Papers
The Cross Papers
The Dow Papers
The Fazle Hussain Collection
Sir Eric Franklin Papers
The Green Collection
The Halifax Papers
The Harris Papers
The Lambrick Papers
The Linlithgow Papers
The Lewis Pelly Papers
The Sykes Papers
The Roger Thomas Papers
The Symington Papers
The Willingdon Papers
The Zetland Papers
The Private Office Papers (L/PO/-)
Governor of Sind Correspondence with the Viceroy
Fortnightly Reports from the Government of Sind to the Government of India

ABBREVIATIONS

AIML	All India Muslim League
AINC	All India National Congress
BD	Basic Democracy
CAP	Constituent Assembly Proceedings
CP	Central Provinces
CSP	Civil Service of Pakistan
DC	District Collector (now Deputy Commissioner)
DSP	Deputy Superintendent of Police
EBDO	Elective Bodies Disqualification Order
GOC	General Officer Commanding
HCR	High Commissioner's Report
ICS	Indian Civil Service
IGP	Inspector General Police
IOL	India Office Library
IPC	Indian Penal Code
KB	Khan Bahadur
KP	Khuhro Papers
KS	Khan Sahib
KSP	Krishak Sramik Party
ML	Martial Law
MLA	Member Legislative Assembly
MLC	Member Legislative Council
NAP	National Awami Party
PIDC	Pakistan Industrial Development Corporation
PLD	Pakistan Law Digest
PML	Pakistan Muslim League
PP	Public Prosecutor
PPP	Pakistan Peoples Party
PRODA	Public Representatives Officers Disqualification Act
PWD	Public Works Department
QAP	Quaid-e-Azam Papers
RB	Rai Bahadur
RTC	Round Table Conference
SHO	Station House Officer
SP	Superintendent Police
SUF	Sind United Front
UP	United Provinces

GLOSSARY

Allah lok	God's people
Amanat	In Trust
Amir	Ruler
Angrez sarkar	The English or British Government
Ashram	Religious sanctuary
Autaq	Part of the house reserved for meeting visitors.
Badmash	Bad character
Badshah	King
Bafta	Unrefined cotton cloth
Bania	Hindu belonging to Vanya or trader caste
Barani	Rain fed land
Be Murshid	Without guide
Bhaiband	Hindu trading caste in Sind
Bund	Flood protective wall
Charkha	Spinning wheel
Chhakro (Raath)	Bullock cart
Chhoot	Untouchability
Dargah	Shrine
Darvish	Holy man
Darul Islam	Abode of Peace
Darul Harb	Abode of War
Dastarkhwan	Cloth spread to place food on.
Diwan	Finance Minister
Durbar	Holding Court
Faisla	Adjudicate
Fakir	Mendicant
Farman	Edict
Fatwa	Religious ruling
Firqa	School of thought or sect
Gadi	Seat
Gadi Nashin	Head/Occupier of seat
Ghazi	Soldier for right cause
Ghitti	Lane
Goonda	Bad character
Graeen	Fellow villager
Hari	Cultivator
Hijrat	Migration
Inam	Present/Award/Prize
Jagirdar	Feudatory
Jatha	Batch
Jirga	Council for Tribal leaders

Jumptee	River house boat
Kafila Serai	Caravan inn
Kamdar	Land steward
Kameez	Shirt
Katcha	Unsurveyed land on bank of the river
Karez	Water channel
Keti	Riverain area leased to and under a landowner's control
Khaddar	Handloom material
Khalifa	Caliph
Khatedar	Owner of Land
Koh Kaf	Caucasian mountain, legendary home of enchantresses and demons.
Kot	Protective wall or fort
Kutcherry	Gathering of Court
Landhi	Shelter or an extension of house
Lat Sahib	Lordship
Lorha	Fence
Lungi	An ornately woven piece of material bestowed as mark of honour
Maafa	A covered palanquin
Madressah	School
Mai Baap	Father and mother, i.e. protector
Majzoub	Handicapped
Maktab	School
Manat	Offering
Mashirnama	Situation Report
Maurusi	Hereditary
Mehri	Special riding camel
Mir Munshi	Senior official in office of Commissioner in Sind
Mofussil	Rural Area
Muhajir	Emigrant
Mukh	Head/Leader
Mukhi	Head of Village Town Councillor
Mukhtiarkar	Revenue Official
Mulla (or *Maulvi*)	Religious scholar
Munshi	Account Keeper/Official under Talpurs
Murid	Disciples
Murshid	Spiritual guide
Mushaira	Poetry Recital
Nafl	Prayer
Naib Vazir	Deputy Minister
Namaz Janaza	Funeral prayer
Nikah	Marriage contract
Pagdar	Wearer of Turban
Panchayat	Council
Pandal	Tent enclosure
Pargana	Equivalent of district
Parwana	Official letter
Patharidar	Patron of anti-social elements
Pir	Spiritual guide/saint
Piri Muridi	Guide/disciple relationship
Pucca	Surveyed land
Rais al Muhajireen	Leader of Emigrants
Raiyat/raiya/ryot	Subject (Anglo-Indian application) tenant of the soil.

Raj	Rule
Ryotwari	Type of land settlement
Ram Raj	Righteous Rule
Rasai	Corrupt practices
Razo	Builder
Saag	Green leaf vegetable
Salaam	Greetings
Sardar	Chief
Sarkar	Government/Ruler
Satyagraha	Sit in, protest
Shalwar	Trousers
Shamiana	Canopy
Shikar	Shoot or hunt
Sheedi	Sindhis of African descent
Shehnai	Musical instrument
Shia	Muslim sect
Shuddhi	Purification
Taccavi	Loan to farmer
Tapedar	Revenue official
Tazia	Float during Shia (Moharram) mourning
Tehsil	Sub division of district
Ulema	Islamic learned men
Vilayet	Abroad
Wadero	Elder of the tribe and village
Zaat	Caste
Zakat	Religious tax
Zamindar	Land owner/owner of rural land
Ziarat	Pilgrimage
Zoolum	Injustice/cruelty

INDEX

A

Abbasi, General, S. M., 512
Abbassi, Maulvi Jan Mohammad, 510
Abbot, Collector, 31
Abbottabad, 408
Abdel Aziz Ibn Saud, King of Saudi Arabia, 372
Abdul Hamid Khan, (of Old Sukkur), 87
Abdul Qadir Mohammed Hussain, 38, 67
Abdul Qaiyum, Sir, 94,
Abdul Rehman Barrister, 74, 87
Abdullah Khan, 450
Abdur Rashid Sir, Justice, 349
Abid Hussain, Colonel Syed, 424
Abid Shah, 292
Abro, Sher Mohammad Khan, 492
Abu Dhabi, 503
Abu Jalal (Amr, Abu-l-Hakam), 27,
Abyssinia, 238
Accott, A.S.V., 74,
Achakzai, Abdus Samad, (Baluchistan Gandhi), 279
Advani, Durgadas, 52
Afghanistan, 18, 24, 38, 40
Agha Khan III, H. H., Sir, 94, 99, 100, 104, 105, 111, 112, 112, 113, 118, 197, 491
Agha Mohammad Yahya Khan, General, 443, 464, 467, 468, 472, 473, 475, 476, 482, 483, 484, 489
Agha Nizamuddin, K.B., 276
Agha Shahi, 327, 328
Agha Shamsuddin, 145
Ahmedabad, 51
Ahsan Ali, 246
Ahsan, Admiral, 476
Air Orient Service, 102
Aitichison College Lahore, 450
Aizaz Rasul, Begum, 299
Ajmer, 38, 331, 332, 358
Akbar Khan, General, 327
Akbar the Great, 19, 71, 169
Akhund Abdullah, 57
Akhund Rasul Baksh, 227
Al Aqsa, Mosque of, 462
Al Gaylani, Al Sayed Abdul Qadir, *(Piran Pir)*, 462,
Al Gaylani, Al Sayed Abdul Qadir,(Iraqi ambassador) 463
Alamut, 223
Alavi, Hatim, 137, 280, 292292, 491
Alexander the Great, 24
Alexander, A. V., 285
Al-Gaylani, Al Sayed Yusuf, 462,
Ali brothers, 38, 253
Ali, Maulana Shaukat, 159
Alipur, 429
All India Muslim League Working Committee, 274, 277, 285, 287, 302
All India Muslim League, 40, 88, 119, 139, 147, 158, 172, 173, 174, 199, 202, 210, 211, 216, 223, 227, 231, 233, 235, 269,291, 292,300,302, 335, 336, 373, 454, 475
All India Muslim League, Lahore Session 1940, 193-199
All India National Congress Working Committee, 204, 205, 288, 301
All India National Congress Party, 40, 52, 88, 91, 151, 155, 284,287
All Parties Conference, (Calcutta), 88, 90
All Sind Hindu Association, 92
Allana, G., 321
Al-Radi Selma, 462
Al-Radi, Mohammad Salim, 462
Al-Radi, Suad, 462
Altaf Gauhar, 464
Altaf Hussain, (Editor of *Dawn*), 330, 364, 388, 418
Al-Wahid, (newspaper), 84, 91, 145, 267
Alwar, 331, 334
Amin-el-Hussaini, Al Haj, The Grand Mufti of Jerusalem, 397
Amir Taimur, tomb of, 428
Amiruddin Ahmed, Justice, 449
Amman, 462
Anderson, 107
Ankara, 442, 443
Ansari, Mohammed Shafi, 380
Anti One Unit front, 437
Aqil village, (Akil), 27, 29, 31, 35, 36, 258, 259, 499, 514
Arya Samaj, 73
Asghar Khan, Air Marshal Mohammad, 440, 506
Assam, 98, 218, 285
Ataturk, Mustafa Kemal Pasha, 20,39
Ataur Rehman, 420, 432
Athens, 104
Attlee, Clement, 269
Aurangzeb Road, No. 10, New Delhi, 80
Aurangzeb, (Mughal Emperor), 72,
Australia, 39, 369, 391, 454
Awami League, 416, 429, 431, 432, 434, 445, 469, 475, 476, 478, 482

Ayub Khan, General Mohammad, 409, 410, 411, 412, 415, 432, 439, 440, 441, 442, 443, 452, 453, 455, 456, 458, 459, 461, 463, 464, 470, 471, 472, 473, 481, 485, 487, 492, 495, 496, 499
Azad Kashmir, 426, 441
Azad, Maulana Abul Kalam, 38, 154, 165, 166, 168, 280, 287,
Azim Khan, 101, 145, 146

B

Babur, (Mughal Emperor), 72
Babylon, 462
Bachu 'Badshah', 226
Badr, Battle of, 194
Badshahi Mosque, Lahore, 194, 195
Baghdad Pact Conference, 442, 443
Baghdad Pact, 443
Baghdad, 27, 103, 442, 443, 462, 463
Bahawalpur House, 328
Bahawalpur State, 415
Bakapur, 48
Bali (courtesan), 45
Baluch, Haji Mir Mohammed, 101
Baluchistan States Union, 436
Baluchistan, 19, 21, 25, 41, 50, 118, 436, 444, 465, 466, 475, 477, 506, 508
Bande Mataram (anthem), 40, 157
Bangladesh, 477, 479
Barakzai, Agha Shamsuddin, 146
Barelvi, Sayed Ahmed, 224
Basic Principles Committee, 376, 377, 412
Batheja Professor, 98, 99
Beach Luxury Hotel, 446
Behan, Fakir Mohabat, 87, 228, 259, 268
Behan, Majnu, 259
Bengal, 69, 98, 119, 155, 159, 193, 206, 211, 216, 230, 231, 243, 288, 295, 297, 299, 301, 302, 303, 316, 320, 334, 412
Bethlehem, 462
Bevan-Petman, (Barrister), 75

Beyrout, (Beirut), 103, 104
Bhagat Kunwar Ram, 246
Bhaiband Community, 23, 187, 190
Bhakti Tradition, 72
Bharatpur, 331
Bharchundi, Pir of, 209, 231, 246
Bhashani, Maulana, 407, 458
Bhateja, Professor, 95, 98, 99
Bhavdakar, 254
Bhayo, Abdul Haq, 260
Bhayo, Osman, 260
Bhayyo, Abdul Haq Karim Bux, 251
Bhil (tribe), 21
Bhiri village, 259
Bhogi village, 259
Bhumbatpur, (dacoity at), 258
Bhurgri, Jan Mohammad, 52,
Bhurgri, Rais Ghulam Mohammed, 45, 46, 48, 52, 88, 89, 90, 106, 131, 154, 415
Bhurgri, Rais Ghulam Mustafa, 415
Bhutto, Khan Bahadur Ahmed Khan 485, 503
Bhutto, Lady Khurshid, (also known as Lakhi Bai), 50
Bhutto, Nabi Baksh, 493,
Bhutto, Nusrat, 493, 495, 506, 507
Bhutto, Pirbux Sardar, 497, 504, 505, 512
Bhutto, Sardar Wahid bux 32, 253, 484, 493, 494
Bhutto, Sir Shahnawaz, 32, 33, 38, 40, 41, 47, 48, 49, 50, 52, 64, 74, 80, 81, 82, 92, 93, 94, 101, 102, 107, 108, 133, 134, 135, 137, 139, 140, 141, 142, 248, 257, 263, 459, 484, 489, 490, 491, 493, 494, 495, 496, 497, 498, 500, 511, 514
Bhutto, Zulfiqar Ali, 50, 452, 455, 457, 458, 459, 460, 461, 462, 470, 471, 472, 473, 474, 475, 476, 477, 478, 479, 480, 481, 482, 483, 488, 489, 498, 500, 501, 502, 503, 504, 505, 507, 508, 510, 511, 512
Bihar, 139, 204, 234, 288, 290, 331
Bijarani, Khan Saheb Sher Mohammed Khan, 52
Bikaner, 331
Black and Tans, 237

Boar's Hill, Oxford, 55, 104
Bodleian Library, Oxford, 116
Bodley, Sir Thomas, 116
Bogra, Mohammed Ali, 404, 405, 406, 408, 409, 411, 413, 414, 417, 420
Bokhara, 428
Bolan, 17
Bolari Camp, 243, 332, 432,
Bolus, E. J., 484, 489
Bombay Baroda Central India Railway (BBCI), 51,
Bombay Legislative Council of, 43, 45, 46, 47, 48, 50, 57-86 *passim*, 92, 109, 113, 132, 138, 140, 150, 211, 250, 498
Bombay Mail, 237
Bombay Sindh Public Service Commission, 141, 142, 492, 495
Bombay University, 115
Bombay, 88, 107, 110, 114, 115, 116, 131, 168, 166, 241, 243, 323, 324, 351, 359, 372, 423, 452, 455, 461, 473, 485
Bombay, Governor of, 25, 45, 51, 58, 81, 83, 89, 106, 107, 228, 492
Bombay, Presidency of, 17, 24, 87, 88, 110, 119, 170, 214, 331, 337, 372
Bose, Sarat, 303
Bose, Subhas Chandar, 165
Boucher, General, 300
Boundary Commission, 303
Bozdar, Sardar Kaisar Khan, 231, 232
Brabourne, Lord, 106, 107, 108, 109, 111, 131, 135, 141, 157, 163
Brahmo Samaj, 72
Brauhui, 21
Brayne A. F. L., 95, 97, 100
Brayne Report, 99
British Broadcasting Corporation (B.B.C),478
British East India Company, 17, 24
British Empire, 17, 18, 37, 64, 88, 385
Brohi, A. K., 441, 448, 496 497, 508,
Brussels, 443, 444
Bughio, Moosa Khan, 505

INDEX

Bughio, Sikandar, 505
Bugti, Nawab Mohammad Akbar Khan, 506
Bugti, Nawab Shahbaz Khan, 226
Bugtis, 25
Bukkur, 23
Buledi, Sardar Jaffar Khan, 248
Bulganin, 427
Burdi Sardar Jafar Khan, 265
Buriro village, 493
Buriro, Chatto 493
Burton, Richard, 24
Bushire, 103

C

Cabinet Mission Plan, 284-291, 299, 302
Cadell, Sir Patrick, 65, 81
Café Grand, 123
Calcutta, 24, 51, 63, 72, 88, 90, 197, 205, 288, 290, 333, 334, 407, 429
Cambridge University of, 32, 34
Cambridge, 34, 59, 450, 462
Cambridge, Emmanual College, 59
Cambridge, Girton College, 462
Canada, 39, 454
Cargill, P., 231, 244, 245, 246
Carlton Hotel, Karachi, 50, 81, 132, 490
Caroe, Mrs., 50,
Carr, Sir Hubert, 94
Central Asia, 23, 24, 72, 428
Central Indian Railway, 233
Central Intelligence Agency of the United States (CIA), 464
Central National Mohammedan Association, 63
Chablani, Professor, H. L., 92, 95, 98, 491
Chachnama, 23
Chagla, Ghulam, Ali, 491
Chandio, Illahi, 260
Chandio, Mir Mohammad Khan, 500
Chandio, Nawab Ghaibi Khan, 48, 500
Chandio, Sardar Sultan Ahmad, 493
Chandio, Tajoo, 260
Chandiram, 86

Chandookah (or Chandukah), Pergunnah of, 19, 28
Chang Mewo, 259
Channa, A., 65
Charbar, (Chah Bahar), 102, 103
Chattari, Begum, 462
Chattari, Nawab Rahat Saeed, 462
Chaudhri Abdul Ghani, 32
Chaudhri Mohammed Ali, 316, 318, 401, 405, 409, 411, 412, 413, 419, 420, 421, 424, 425, 429, 441
Chaudhry Ghulam Abbas, 441
Chaudhry Zafrulla, 316
Chaudhry, Fazlul Qadir, 479
Chhajro, Mehardil 260
Chhor, 237
Chimandas, 320
China, 23, 203
Chintamini, C. Y., 94
Chowdhry Hamidul Haq, 406, 408, 429, 434
Chundrigar, I. I., 289, 318, 320, 334, 335, 337, 338, 433, 434, 435
Church of Christ, Jerusalem, 462
Churchill, Sir Winston, 203, 269, 284
Ciminal Tribes Act XXVII of 1871, 43
Clee, Sir Charlès, 233
Coltman, 254, 297
Commonwealth Parliamentary Conference, 434
Communist Party, 426
Constantine Justice, 369
Constituent Assembly Parliamentary Committee for Fundamental Rights, 315
Convention Muslim League, 457, 458, 479
Copts, (Christian minority of Egypt), 88
Corfu, 104
Corin John, 232
Cornelius, A. R. Justice, 449
Council Muslim League, 457, 466, 479, 480
Cox and King's Ltd., 104
Craik, Sir Henry, 237
Cripps Offer, 204
Cripps, Sir Stafford, 203 (and Cabinet Mission Plan), 284-291

Currimbhoy, Sir Ebrahim, Fazalbhoy, 45, 59, 159, 185
Curzon, Lord George Nathaniel, (Viceroy of India), 51, 88, 429

D

D. J. (Dayaram Jethmal), Sind College, 34, 35, 39, 115
Dacca, 316, 429, 435, 436, 437, 438, 457, 469, 475, 476, 477, 481, 487, 501
Dadu District, 18, 23, 46, 47, 52, 131, 200, 444, 449, 490
Daharki, 229
Dahiri, Issan, 259
Daily Gazette, (newspaper), 84, 99, 325, 326
Dajla (Tigris), 463
Damascus, 103
Darbelo, 270
Daresh (Khuhro), 'approver' witness in Allahbaksh Soomro murder case, 251-268
Dasti, Abdul Hamid, 424
Daudpoto, Dr. Omar bin Mohammed, 32, 59, 114
Daultana, Mian Mumtaz Mohammed Khan, 346, 373, 388, 401, 403, 404, 407, 419, 424, 425, 426, 429, 434, 457, 479, 499, 507
Davis Sir Godfrey, 192, 229, 255
Dawn (newspaper), 323, 330, 364
'Day of Deliverance', 185, 186
Dayo, Wadero Ghulam Qadir, 48
Dehlavi, Sir Ali Mohammed, 25,
Dehli Sultanate of, 18
Delhi Club, 318
Delhi Muslim Conference, 197
Delhi, 24, 51, 170, 171, 179, 188, 189, 202, 203, 206, 218, 220, 221, 229, 248, 249, 250, 294, 297, 298, 303, 304, 317, 322, 324, 326, 327, 434, 435
Democration Coalition Party, 145
Depar, Sardar Ali Hasan, 501
Dera Ghazi Khan, 444
Desai, Bhulabhai, 148
Dhoro Naro, 237
Din Mohammed, Justice, Governor of Sind, 364, 387, 401, 402, 402

District Local Board, Larkana, 40
Diwan Gidumal, 22, 90
Djask, 102, 103
Dodo, village of, 31
Dokri, (Larkana District), 73, 474, 498, 505
Dossul, Haji, (family), 49, 490
Dow, Sir, Hugh, 57, 95, 113, 114, 117, 201, 202, 206, 207, 208, 211, 212, 213, 214, 215, 216, 218, 233, 245, 246, 252, 253, 268, 275, 282, 295, 494, 495
Drabhi Jungle, 260
Drabhi Village, 260
Drew, 135
Dubbo, (battle of), 18
Dulles, John Foster, Secretary of State, U.S.A., 443
Dumlotee, 329
Durrani, Agha Badruddin, 265
Dutt, Mr., 102, 103
Dyarchy, 39, 46
Dyer, General, 38

E

East Pakistan Legislature, 431
East Pakistan, 379, 433, 434, 435, 443, 445, 458, 465, 466, 475, 476, 477, 483, 484, 486, 489, 500, 501
Eastwick, E. B., 169
EBDO Tribunal, 374, 375, 454, 456, 459, 461, 464, 472, 495, 496, 499
Effendi, Khan Bahadur Hassanally Bey, 34, 63
Egypt, 17, 18, 19, 24, 88, 106, 169, 190, 372, 453
Ejaz Ali, Syed, Vizier of Khairpur, 233
Elburz, Mountains, 223
Ellenborough, Lord, 18, 24
Empire Road, Larkana, 38, 50, 74, 132
Encumbered Estates Act, 54
England, 38, 55, 59, 71, 93, 101, 102, 103, 104, 105, 107, 111, 117, 247, 248, 269, 298, 429, 478, 479, 507
European Chamber of Commerce, Karachi, 46

F

Faisal ibn Abdel Aziz, King of Saudi Arabia, 462
Fakir Shahabuddin, 31
Faruqui, N. A., 281
Fazal Mohammed, K. B. Haji, 350
Fazl u Rehman, 407
Fazle Hussain, Sir, 119
Fazlul Haq, Maulvi, 159, 160, 161, 163, 385, 406, 407, 412, 420
Federal Court of Pakistan, 416
Federal Finance Committee, 98, 99, 100
Federal Land Commission, Rawalpindi, 506
Federation of Sind Panchayats, (Bhaiband Panchayats), 187, 188, 191
Fernandez, 102
Ferozepur, 324
Financial Enquiry (Miles Irving) Committee, 94, 95, 97, 153
Foot, Isaac, 94
France, 17
Frere, H.B.E. (Sir Bartle), 24, 25, 51, 202

G

Gaad, 21
Gabole, Sardar Allah Baksh, 142,
Gambat, 23, 27, 505
Gandhi, Mohandas Karamchand, 37, 39, 40, 73, 166, 174, 204, 205, 230, 240, 242, 302, 322, 491
Garang Bungalow, 233, 264
Garhi Khuda Baksh Bhutto, 260, 264, 502
Garret, 157, 163, 166
Gazdar, M. H., 143, 151, 159, 161, 164, 216, 222, 245, 250, 252, 256, 257, 266, 268, 270, 274, 280, 292, 319, 380, 381, 390, 407, 408, 494
Georgia, 428
Germany West, 20, 454
Ghana, 459
Ghanshyamdas Jethanand, Professor, 320, 321

Ghar Channel, 28
Ghazanfar Ali Khan, Raja, 290, 334
Ghotki, 52, 237
Ghulam Akbar, 228, 254, 257, 267, 268
Ghulam Faruque, 447
Ghulam Hussain, Inspector Police, 254, 268
Ghulam Mohammad (Shop), 447
Ghulam Mohammed, (Governor General of Pakistan), 316, 317, 328, 329, 331, 334, 377, 401, 403, 404, 405, 406, 407, 408, 409, 410, 411, 412, 414, 419, 447
Ghuznavi, 107
Gibson, Commissioner-in-Sindh, 134
Girohri, Abul Rahim, 229
Gokaldas, Rai Sahib, 200, 215
Gokhale, G. K., 37, 110
Gokhale, Professor, 95
Gopang, Alam Khan, 502
Gorwalla Report, 153
Gorwalla, A.D., I.C.S., 493
Government of India Act of 1919 (Montagu Chelmsford Reforms or Montford Reforms) 53, 39, 46, 86, 91
Government of India, Act of 1909 (Morley Minto Reforms), 89, 106
Government of India, Act of 1935, 91, 105, 112, 119, 139, 353, 367, 368
Graham, Sir Lancelot, 57, 134, 142, 147, 153, 157, 158, 166, 231, 232, 245
Green Report, 183
Gul Hassan, General, 501
Gurbaxani, Dr. Hotchand, 34, 35, 114, 115, 116
Gurmani, Nawab Mushtaq Ahmed, 401, 403, 405, 408, 410, 413, 414, 416, 419, 420, 424, 425, 426, 430, 432, 435
Guru Mandir, 326
Guru Nanak, 22, 72

H

Hafiz, (Persian Poet), 428

Hagar, (Bibi Hajera), 371, 462
Hakim Ahson, 461
Hakro, Khan Bahadur Ali Hassan, 73
Hala, 224, 275
Halaku Khan, 223
Hameed General, 475
Hamid Ali, 73, 74
Hamidul Haq Group, 433
Hanuman Mandir, 180
Hari Committee, 221
Hari Enquiry Committee, 'The Hari Report', 22, 392
Haripur, 425
Haroon Yusuf, 208, 209, 216, 218, 220, 221, 256, 257, 265, 267, 273, 276, 277, 278, 280, 292, 321, 366, 369, 388, 389, 390, 391, 418, 434, 494
Haroon, Abdullah Sir, 8, 52, 79, 84, 85, 87, 91, 95, 101, 106, 113, 137, 138, 142, 154, 155, 156, 160, 161-192, 195, 220, 239, 240, 249, 388, 494
Haroon, Lady Nusrat, 133, 266
Haroon, Saeed, 266
Harrison, Sir Charlton, 52
Hasan bin Sabah, 223
Hasham bin Abdul Malik, 462
Hashim Khan, 487
Hasnie, S. A., 322
Haymarket, London, 104
Hayward, Sir Maurice, 52, 57, 58
Hazara, 425
Hebron, 462
Hendraningrat, Brigadier General Roekmito 460, 461
Hidayetullah, Sir Ghulam Hussain, 49, 52, 94, 105, 106, 107, 108, 109, 135, 137, 138, 139, 143, 144, 145, 148, 149, 151, 153, 155, 156, 161, 162, 164, 167, 168, 170, 172, 175, 180, 207, 208, 209, 210, 212, 218, 230, 231, 232, 233, 236, 243, 245, 249, 255, 257, 266, 269, 270, 271, 273, 279, 280, 281, 282, 283, 292, 293, 294, 295, 304, 318, 339, 340, 341, 350-364, 492, 494,
Hindu Independent Party, 168, 271
Hindu Mahasabha Party, 73, 74, 99, 151, 155, 181

Hindu Sabha Conference, 182
Hingorani, Dr., 86, 95
Hingoro, Rahim, 247
Hiranand Khemsingh D. B., 494
Hiroshima, 269
Hitler, 180
Hizbullah Shah, 224, 225
Hoare, Sir Samuel, Secretary for State for India, 490
Holt, Mr., 241
Holy Quran, 101, 118, 267, 376, 393, 513
Hotson, Sir Ernest, 493, 494
House of Commons, (British parliament) 37, 354
Hudson, W., 32
Humayun, (Mughal Emperor), 72
Hur Act (Act I of 1942), 237
Hur movement, Chapter 12, *passim*, 234, 244
Hussain Imam, 274
Hutheesingh, Krishna, Mrs., 205
Hyde Park Hotel, London, 493
Hyderabad (Deccan), 205, 219
Hyderabad (Sind), 18, 21, 22, 23, 24, 28, 29, 33, 45, 46, 50, 51, 52, 57, 58, 70, 71, 93, 99, 101, 106, 115, 118, 137, 138, 146, 185, 187, 216, 217, 224, 236, 247, 255, 264, 275, 304, 320, 321, 322, 326, 331, 333, 363, 365, 378, 388, 399, 400, 405, 415, 417, 432, 483, 486, 489, 494, 509
Hyderabad Circuit House, 417
Hyderabad Jail, 182, 185, 236, 243, 244, 246, 402I
Hyderabad, District Local Board of, 106

I

Ibrahim Kori, 227,228
Ibrahim, (Prophet Abraham), 462
Icchra, Lahore, 160
Ikramullah, Begum Shaista, 299
Imam Hussain, 27, 224, 462
Imam Mahdi, 462
Imam Moosa Kazim, 462
Imam Muhammad Taqi, 462
Imambux Khatti, 260
Imperial Airways, 102

Imtiaz, S. P.,
India, Constitution of, 112
India, Interim Government of, 286, 289-291
India, Viceroy of, 89, 269, 315, 491
Indian Chamber of Commerce, 46
Indian Independence Act 1947, 368
Indian Round Table Conference (First), 94
Indian Round Table Conference (Third), 84, 99, 100, 105
Indian Round Table Conference, (Sub Committee IX, on Sind), 94, 96, 131
Indus (Sindhu), 17, 18, 20, 23, 24, 27, 41, 44, 504
Indus Delta, 24,
Iqbal, Sir Mohammed, 99, 100, 113, 117, 118, 119, 197
Iran, 477
Iraq, 443, 447, 453, 461, 462
Irwin, J. B., 48
Isa, Mrs. Pyari, 299
Isani, G. M., 65, 66, 67
Islamabad, 384, 467
Islamic Summit Conference, 507,
Ispahani, M. A. H., 205, 412, 507
Isran, Ghulam Mohammed, 38, 47, 49, 490, 498, 500
Israr Mohammed Khan, 446
Issarsing, 232
Istanbul, 20, 39, 462
Ivan the Terrible, 427

J

Jacob, General John (of Jacobabad), 24, 25
Jacobabad, 25, 46
Jadhav, B. V., 94,
Jadoon, Khushal Khan, 194
Jafri, Nawaz Ali, 32
Jagan Village, 260,264
Jaipur, 331
Jairamdas Daulatram, 234, 235
Jalal, Ayesha ,199, 302
Jallianwalla Bagh, 38, 195
Jam, Nawab Jan Mohammed, 236
Jam, Nawab Kambho Khan, 245
Jamaat-i-Islami, 510
Jamaat-i-Ulemai Hind, 159, 279

INDEX

Jamaat-I-Ulemai Sind, 171
Jamali, Sardar Jafar Khan, 164, 265, 350, 444
James, H. E. M. (Sir Evan), Commissioner-in-Sind, 226, 227
James, Lieutenant Hugh, 19, 28
James, Sir Morrice, (Lord Saint Brides), 481
Jamiat Ulemai Islam, 499
Jamrao Canal, 226,237
Janvri, Karim Baksh alias Redho, 259
Japan, 269
Jatoi, Abdul Hamid Khan, 415
Jatoi, Dhani Baksh, K.B., 47, 490
Jatoi, Ghulam Rasool, 275
Jatoi, Hyder Baksh 464
Jatoi, K. B. Karimbaksh, 47, 49, 52, 490, 498
Jatoi, Khan Saheb Serai Imambaksh Khan, 52
Jatoi, Qaisar Khan, 502
Jayakar M. R., 52, 84, 94
Jeddah, 371, 462
Jehangir Kothari Parade, 49
Jehangir, Sir Cowasji, 52
Jericho, 462
Jerusalem, Al Quds, 462
Jethanand, Mukhi, 52
Jethmall Parsram, 114
Jhandeware jo Goth, 224
Jinnah, Miss Fatima, 205, 293, 315, 327, 328, 452, 456, 458, 471, 472, 499
Jinnah, Mohammed Ali, (Quaid-e-Azam), 34, 87, 88, 91, 93, 94, 113, 137, 139, 154, 155, 156, 157, 158, 159, 160, 162, 163, 164, 180, 181, 185, 187, 190, 193, 195, (Fourteen Points of, 197), 203, 204, 205, 206, 208, 209, 216, 217, 218, 219, 228, 229, 239, 242, 243, 249, 250, 253, 256, 270, 271, 272, 273, 274, 276, 277, 280, 281, 285, 287, 288, 289, 291, 293, 294, 295, 299, 301, 302, 303, 304, 315, 316, 318, 319, 324, 327, 328, 329, 333, 335, 336, 337, 339, 340, 341, 345, 346, 347, 351, 352, 356, 357, 364, 374, 378, 380, 381, 382, 384, 385, 397, 437, 491, 492, 504, 513

Jodhpur State, Political Agent of, 237
Jodhpur, 51, 323, 331
Joint Parliamentary Committee on Indian Reforms, 101, 491
Joint Refugee Council, 325
Jordan, 461
Jubbulpore (C.P.) Jail, 494
Jubbulpore, (C.P.), 103
Jugtu front, (UnitedFront), 378, 385
Junagarh State, 142, 493
June 3rd Plan, 303
Junejo, Jan Mohammed, 38
Junejo, Khan Bahadur Mohammed Hayat, 245
Junejo, Khan Sahib Din Mohammed, 245
Junejo, Wadero Sahib Khan, 48

K

Ka'aba, 371, 372, 462,
Kabul, 18,
Kadir, Shaikh Mohammed, 44, 45, 47, 155, 156
Kakul Academy, 441,442
Kalabagh, Nawab Amir Mohammed, 457, 461
Kalat, 444, 445, 446
Kalat, Khan of, 25, 50, 279, 444, 445, 446, 490, 508, 509
Kalhoras, 18, 22, 23, 28
Kalhoro Haji Khan, 499
Kalhoro, Fakir Mohammed, 501
Kalhoro, Ghulam Shah, 22
Kambar, Larkana District, 47, 498, 500
Kapadia, 259
Karachi Cantonement Station, 266
Karachi Central Jail, 415, 447
Karachi Club, 107, 400
Karachi Daily (newspaper), 222
Karachi Garden Police Station, 327
Karachi Municipal Corporation, 159, 323, 415
Karachi University, 506
Karachi, 18, 23, 29, 34, 35, 37, 44, 46, 49, 50, 97, 115, 179, 181, 185, (Karachi take over by Centre, 335), 404, 406, 407, 408, 413, 415, 419, 420, 422, 424, 429, 432, 434, 436, 439, 442, 443, 444, 445, 446, 447, 457, 458, 459, 460, 461, 463, 465, 466, 467, 469, 474, 476, 486, 487, 488, 490, 491, 492, 493, 494, 495, 496, 499, 502, 506, 509, 510, 514
Karam Fakir, 31
Karbala, 224, 462
Kasai, Allahrakhio, 260
Kasai, Ibrahim Motayo, 251
Kasai, Ibrahim, 260
Kasai, Kabir 260
Kasai, Kambar Bahadur, 251
Kashmir, 324, 364, 365, 378, 418, 427, 442
Kashmir, Maharaja of, 324
Kasuri, Nawab Ahmed Khan, 510
Kathiawar, 331, 332, 358, 362
Kaula, G, C.I.E., 494
Kayani, M. R., Chief Justice, 449
Kazi Fazlullah, 158, 182, 318, 341, 381, 389, 390, 401, 402, 405, 406, 418, 425, 426, 435, 440, 461, 493, 496, 499
Kazi Jan Mohammed, 32
Kazi Mohammed Akbar, 292, 381, 405, 410
Kazi, Imdad Ali, (I. I. Kazi), 58, 114, 464
Kedleston House, Derbyshire, England, 429
Kehar, Khan Sahib, 32
Kennedy, 58
Kenya, 238
Keti Khuhro, 259, 262
Khadda, Madressah Mazhar ul Uloom, 271, 279
Khahi, 260, 264
Khairpur State of, 21, 27, 41, 44, 45, 47, 131, 171, 185, 223, 231, 238, 241, 259, 415, 465
Khairpur Zamindari Association, 184
Khairpur, (town of) 21, 27, 28, 31, 44, 45
Khairpur, Mir of, (Ruler of), 45, 87
Khaksars, 194, 195, 279
Khalifa Hazrat Ali, 27
Khaliqdina Hall, Karachi, 328
Khalique-u-Zaman, Chaudhry, 209, 271, 300, 366

Khamiso, Haji Gul Mohammed, 52
Khan Abdul Ghaffar Khan, 119, 409, 418, 435
Khan Sahib, (Dr.), 373, 409, 412, 418, 419, 424, 425, 426, 430, 431, 432, 434
Khan, Abdul Qayyum Khan, 404, 436, 437, 438, 439, 443, 457, 473, 479
Khan, F. M., 441
Khan, N. M., 487, 496
Khan, Qurban Ali Khan, 401, 419, 424
Khanzadi (w/o Chatto Buriro), Murder case, 484, 493
Kharal, Khalid, 502, 503, 506, 509
Kharal, Wali Mohammed (Walu) Hur activities of, 252-268
Kharas, J. G., 362,
Khaskheli, Waryam, 238
Khattak, Yusuf, 457
Khemchand, 264
Khilafat Committee, 159
Khilafat Conference of 1920, 38
Khilafat Movement, 37, 38, 39, 40, 71, 76, 106, 139, 159, 170
Khipro, 227, 238
Khirthar wah, 260
Khokhrapar, 324, 325, 400
Khoso, Ali Baksh, 260
Khoso, Sardar Azizullah, 402
Khoso, Sardar Khan, 402
Khruschev, Nikita, General Secretary Communist Party of USSR, 426, 427
Khudabad (Dadu District), 23
Khudai Khidmatgar Party, 119, 409
Khuhra (town of), 25, 27
Khuhro Road, (later named Club Road), 450
Khuhro, Aligohar, 339, 487
Khuhro, Begum Fatima, 131, 205, 485
Khuhro, Emnah, 29, 30
Khuhro, Hamida, 429, 462, 506, 477, 478, 484, 488, 495, 507
Khuhro, Jan Mohammad, 28, 30, 31, 33, 34, 35, 36, 40, 46
Khuhro, Khalid Mahmood, 506
Khuhro, Mohammad Nawaz, 36, 252, 452

Khuhro, Mohammed Ayub, Birth, family background and early education 27–36, college, attitude to Khilafat movement, entry into politics 37–41, understanding of Sind conditions 41–43, elected to Bombay Council 46-50, public issues taken up in Bombay Council 53–72, Larkana riots 73–75, Sukkur riots 76, confrontation with Commissioner-in-Sind, 76-86, first meeting with and lunch for M. A. Jinnah 87, role in separation of Sind 87-110, plane crash in Iran 102-103, in England 104-105, role in setting up Sind administration 111–120, domestic life 131–134, Sind politics 134–154, 1938 ML session 155–168, Masjid Manzilgah 169–192, at the 1940 Lahore AIML session 193–199, Minister in Coalition Government 199–202, President Sind ML, member AIML Working Committee 202–206, Muslim League government in Sind 206–210, Muslim League programme and problems with Governor 210–216, AIML 1943 session 217–219, Khuhro and Pir Pagaro 228–233, Hur Movement 239–248, Allabaksh Soomro murder case 249–268, strengthening ML working for Pakistan 269–304, first Premier of Sind after independence 315, dealing with problems of Partition 316–328, differences with Centre over Karachi 328–346, removal from office 346–348, Court of Enquiry 349–366, PRODA 366-370, first Haj 371-372, expectations from independence belied 372, lifestyle of Pakistani elite 375, delay in constitution making 375-377, central monopoly of resources 377-378, Karachi taken over by Centre 379-385, Sind's financial deprivation 389–391, stand on Liaquat Ali's 'agrarian reform' plans 391-396, Chief Minister second time 397, refugee rehabilitation 399-400, PRODA again 401–409, Central crisis 404-405, Sind ministerial crisis 405-406, third time Chief Minister 410, formation of One Unit 411–424, Suhrawardy's speech on 'Khuhroism' 420-421, historic One Unit speech 421–424, West Pakistan ministerial crisis 424–426, leads Parliamentary delegation to U.S.S.R. 426-429, visits Calcutta 429, views on Governor's rule in West Pakistan 430–432, differences with ML leadership 433–439, Minister of Defence 439, Mirza's intrigues and imposition of Martial Law 441–446, imprisonment and prosecution under Martial Law 447–450, out of politics 450-452, Ayub's land reforms 452–454, EBDO 454, Convention Muslim League, Council Muslim League and Presidential elections 456-458, second Haj and Middle East tour 461-463, effots to unite Sind political forces 464–469, views on Bhutto's behaviour 471–473, 1970 elections 473-474, efforts to unite Muslim League 479-480, criticism of PPP and Bhutto 489–497, reply to Bhutto's letter 487–489, reply to second letter 489–500, boundary walls of K's house in Larkana demolished 504, Khuhro family persecuted 505–507, letter to General Zia-ul-Haque 511-512, death 514.
Khuhro, Rashida, 429
Khuhro, Shah Mohammad, 27, 134, 450, 458, 485, 503, 505, 506

Khuhro, Shah Zaman, 485, 507, 510
Khuhro, *Wadero* Dost Mohammad, 28,
Khuhro, *Wadero* Mohammed Ayub,27, 29, 30, 31, 33, 34, 46, 137 (17, 26, 29, 85)
Khuhro, *Wadero* Shah Mohammed, 27, 484, 489
Khwaja Nazimuddin, 209, 290, 300, 364, 378, 437, 384, 401, 402, 403, 404, 405, 437, 457
Khwaja Seth Mohammed Din, 73
Khwaja Shahabuddin, 370, 379, 396, 401
Khyber, 17
Kirov Theatre, Leningrad, 428
Kolhis, 21
Kot Lashari, 260, 264
Kotri (taluka, District Dadu), 47
Kremlin, 427
Kripalani, (Chief Secretary, Government of Sindh), 134, 135,148
Kripalani, Acharya, 165, 320
Krishak Sramik Party, 416, 433, 434
Krishna, Lord alias Shama, 27
Krishnan Nair, 107
Kufa, 462
Kundandas R. B., 257
Kwame Nkrumah, 459, 472

L

Labour Party, 269
Lahore 'Pakistan' Resolution, 160, 198, 199, 284, 300, 315,335, 336,379, 381, 451
Lahore Mail, 234, 236, 237, 264, 266
Lahore, 32, 45, 75, 160, 178, 186, 193, 194, 195, 196, 233, 286, 324, 325, 342, 346, 403, 404, 425, 440, 441, 462, 476, 493, 496, 507
Lahore, Hira Mandi, 45
Lahori Nawab Amir Ali, 38, 41, 47, 48, 73, 74, 248, 487, 490, 498
Lahori, Ahmed Hussain, 497
Lahori, Sarai Shah Mohammed, 32

Lahri Bandar, 24
Lakhi Tar, 259
Lala Menghraj, 234
Lalchand Navalrai, 86
Lalwani, Dialmal, 243, 245, 256, 264
Lalwani, Dr., 222
Lambrick, Hugh Trevor, 113, 134, 225, 235, 237, 240, 240, 243, 244, 245, 246, 248
Land Alienation Bill (and Debt Reconciliation Bill) 33, 54, 143, 148, 211, 215, 216, 221, 296, 282, 296, 378
Lari, Justice, Z. H., 466, 499
Larik, 27
Larkana District Local Board, 486
Larkana District Mohammedan Association of, 47
Larkana Madressah of, 31, 32, 33, 38, 47, 489, 493
Larkana Municipal Committee, 41, 47, 48
Larkana Zamindari Co-operative Bank, (District Co-operative Credit Bank), 47, 505
Larkana, 19, 23, 27, 28, 29, 30, 31, 32, 33, 35, 36, 38, 45, 46, 47, 48, 49, 50, 58, 68, 73, 74, 87, 99, 111, 132, 133, 135, 140 , 141, 158, 164, 176, 181, 182, 184, 185, 186, 216, 222, 228, 239, 258, 259, 261, 265, 273, 274, 275, 318, 444, 454, 457, 458, 460, 461, 468, 471, 473, 475, 477, 482, 485, 486, 487, 488, 490, 492, 493, 498, 502, 503, 504, 505, 509, 510, 514
Larkana, Collector of, 32
Lawrence, Sir Henry, (of the Punjab), 55
Lawrence Madressah, 69
Lawrence, John (later Lord),
Lawrence, Lady Rosamund, 104
Lawrence, Sir Henry, (Commissioner-in-Sind), 52, 55, 65, 104, 114, 202
Legal Framework Order, (L.F.O.), 476
Leghari, Haji Fazal Mohammed, 52
Leghari, Haji Najamddin Sireval, 466

Leghari, Nawab Wali Mohammed, 19, 21, 22, 28
Lenin, 427, 499
Leningrad, 427
Leslie Wilson Hostel, (Jinnah Courts), 44, 339
Liaquat Ali Khan, Beguam Ra'ana, 375, 400
Liaquat Ali Khan, Nawabzada, 159, 209, 219, 271, 274, 276, 281, 289, 299, 315, 316, 318, 324, 327, 329, 330, 366, 367, 369, 370, 373, 377, 382, 383, 385, 388, 391, 396, 397, 398, 411, 426
Lincoln, Abraham, President of USA, 499
Lingah (Bandare Lengeh), 103
Linlithgow, Lord (Viceroy of India), 153, 157, 175, 182, 187, 189, 190, 196, 204, 245, 269
Lintotts, (restaurant), 418
Lloyd (Sukkur) Barrage, 19, 24, 34,52, 96, 97,114, 152, 250, 297, 421
Local Self Government, 30, 200, 282, 323, 337
London, 84, 94, 99, 104, 112, 429, 485, 491, 506, 507
Lower Sind Barrage (Kotri Barrage), 282, 297, 384,395, 398, 414, 421,435
Luari Haj, 173
Lucknow Pact, 1916, 40
Lucas, W. H., 225, 226
Lulla, Sri Krishna, 257
Lund, Khan Sahib Sardar Dadan Khan, 245
Lutyens, Sir A. (architect of New Delhi), 51, 318
Lycurgus, 456

M

MacArthur, General Douglas, 269,
Macdonald, Ramsay, 95
Maclachlan, R.B. I.S.E. Chief Engineer Sindh, 495
Macmillan, Sir Harold, 443
Madinat ul Nabi, 27, 371
Madni, G. A., 479
Madras, 98, 107, 114, 454
Magsi, (tribe), 21

INDEX

Mahmud Hussain, Dr., 506
Mahmud Shevket Pasha, 462
Mahmudabad Raja Sahib, 159, 205
Mahmudul Aziz, 461
Majlis-i-Ahrar-i-Islam, (Ahrar), 194
Makhdum Hassan Mahmud, 426
Makhdum Mohammad Aqil, 27
Makhdums of Khuhra, 27
Makhi Dandh, 225-248
Makkah Mukarammah, 371, 372
Makrani, 102
Malik Barkat Ali, 194, 195
Malik Mohammed Qasim, 479
Malik, Dr. A. M., 412
Malir Cantonment, 304, 317, 328
Mamdot, Nawab Iftikhar Hussain, 373, 384, 410
Mamdot, Nawab Sir Shahnawaz, 185
Mandal, Jogendra Nath, 290
Mangrejo, Kamal, 250–268
Mangrejo, Kasim, 250–268
Manila, 444
Manzilgah Mosque Restoration Committee, 174, 176, 179, 181, 182, 186
Mari, Haji Ali Mohammed, 381
Mari, Hashim, 402
Marina Hotel, Delhi, 180
Marseilles, 104
Marwan, 27
Marwar, 50
Marxism, 420
Mashori, Maulana, (Pir of Mashori), 487
Mashriqi, Allama, 194, 279
Masjid Manzilgah, 168–192
Masood, Ross Sir, 45
Masud, M. I.C.S. 292, 320, 321, 346, Hari Report 'Minute of Dissent', 393
Masur-ji-wai, 259, 264
Maulana Abdul Hamid Badauni, 159
Maulana Maudoodi, 471
Maulana Zafar Ali Khan, 178
Maulvi Tamizuddin, 407, 416
Mauripur Airport, 299, 330
Maurya, 18
Maxwell, Sir Reginald, 237, 238, 239
Mazari, (tribe), 25

Mediterranean Sea, 104
Mehar, Dadu District, 47, 52
Mehrabpur Railway Station, 259
Mehrali, Yousif, 165
Mehta, Jamshed Nusserwanji, 85, 240
Mehta, Pheroze Shaw, 37, 110
Mehta, Rt. Hon. M.C.V., 52, 55, 60
Memon, Justice Azizullah, 449
Memon, Zuleikha, 502
Mengal, Sardar Ataullah Khan, 502
Mesopotamia, 462
Metharam Hostel, 34
Mian Aminuddin, 402
Mian Iftikharuddin, 380
Miandad, 259, 260
Miani,(battle of), 18
Midnapore Central Jail, 229, 235
Mir Ayub Khan, 491
Mir Ghulamullah, 253
Mir Mohammed Khan, 500
Miro Khan (Larkana District), 58
Mirpur Sakro, 446
Mirpur village, 493
Mirpurkhas, 21, 46, 137, 138, 216, 236, 250, 264, 417, 468
Mirza Ismail, 22
Mirza Kalichbeg, 114
Mirza, Iskander, 401, 404, 407, 409, 412, 415, 416, 418, 419, 420, 421, 424, 425, 426, 429, 430, 432, 434, 435, 440, 441, 442, 443, 444, 445, 452, 459, 471, 472, 496
Mirza, Kambar Ali , Special Judge, 448
Mitha, Seth Mohammad Suleman Kassim, 499
Mithi, 417, 418
Mithrao Canal, 238
Mody, H. P., 94
Moenjodaro, 502
Mohammed Ali Group, 433
Mohammed bin Qasim, 23, 24, 27, 223
Mohammed Khan, 251, 252, 257, 258, 259, 260, 261, 262, 264
Mohammed Sadiq, Maulvi, 171, 172, 193, 198, 279
Mohammed Taqi, 462

Mohan Mia (Yusuf Ali Chowdhury), 435
Montagu, Sir Edwin, Secretary of State for India, 37, 89, 93
Moonje, B. S. Sir, 94
Moonje, Dr. 94, 181
Morley Minto Reforms, (see Government of India Act, 1919)
Moses (Hazrat Moosa), Prophet, 462
Moslem Voice, (newspaper), 143, 244
Mount of Olives, Jerusalem, 462
Mountbatten, Lady Edwina, 298, 299
Mountbatten, Lord Louis, Viceroy of India, 299, 302, 303, 315, 316
Mudie, Sir Francis, 114, 117, 294, 295, 296, 297, 300, 304, 324, 339
Mughal Empire, 17, 71
Mujumdar, G. N., 52
Mukhi Gobindram, 143, 145
Multan, 24, 167, 325, 439
Munir Abbas, 462
Munir, Justice, M. (Chief Justice of Pakistan), 409, 444, 449
Munshi, K. M., 155
Munshi, Khan Bahadur Pir Baksh, , 87
Murree Club, 418
Murree, 418, 419, 442, 499
Musa, General, 471, 496, 499
Muslim Educational Conference, 45,
Muslim League Central Parliamentary Board, 274, 276, 277, 278, 279, 280, 292, 404
Muslim League, (see All India Muslim League),
Mustansir Street, Baghdad, 463
Muta'sim Billah, Abbassid Khalifa, 27
Muzaffar Hussain, C.S.P., 447, 486

N

N.E.D. Engineering College, 34
Nabi Baksh Mohammed Hussain, K. B., 38, 57, 275
Nadir Shah, ruler of Iran,132
Nagpur, 233

N

Naidu Padmaja, (Governor of West Bengal), 429
Naidu, Sarojini, 165, 279, 429
Naik Mohammed, 32
Najaf, 462
Nanak Panthis, 22
Nanak Shahis, 22
Naoroji, Dadabhoy, 110
Napier Barracks, 317
Napier, Sir Charles, 18, 24, 25, 29, 88, 93, 104, 109
Naples, 104
Napoleon, Emperor, 17
Nara, 28
Narejo, Habibullah 502
Narejo, Wadero Mohammed Waris, 227
Nariman, K. F., 52
Naseerabad, 23
Nasik District, 53
Nasser, Gamal Abdel, President of Egypt, 453
Nathiagali, 441, 442
National Awami Party, 432, 433, 438
National Democratic Front, 457
National Library, Belvedere, Calcutta, 429
National Party, 191, 301
Naudero, 473, 474, 492, 493, 499, 502
Naushahro Feroze, 259
Nawab Bahadur Aazam Jan, 490
Nawab Bahadur Yar Jung, 205, 219
Nawab Ismail Khan, 205, 209, 271, 274, 290
Nawabshah, 46, 52, 468
Nazi, 428
Nazir Ahmed, 322
Nehru Report, 88, 90
Nehru, Jawaharlal, 279, 285, 287, 288, 289, 299, 302, 303
New Delhi see Delhi,
Niazi, Maulana Kausar, 492
Nile, 17
Nishtar, Sardar Abdur Rab, 289, 315, 396, 404, 408, 425, 426, 433, 436
Nizam ul Mulk, 223
Nizame Islam, 433
Noakhali, 290
Non-Cooperation Movement, 38, 39, 40, 71, 76, 170
Noon, Lady Vicarunissa (Vicky), 299, 445
Noon, Sir Feroze Khan, 204, 299, 413, 417, 434, 435, 437, 440, 445, 446, 451
Noonari, Abdullah Rasulbux, 251
North West Frontier Province (NWFP), 89, 94, 119, 198, 284, 285, 290, 293, 319, 324, 373, 393, 395, 404, 411, 415, 436, 437, 439, 466, 475
Nur Nabi, K. B., 101

O

O'Sullivan. Justice J., 254, 255
Oad, 21
Om Mandli, 173, 180,
Omar Khyyam, 223,
Ommayed, 27, 223, 224, 462
One Unit Bill, 412, 419, 421, Scheme 384
Ottoman, 371, 462
Oxford University, 484
Oxford, 34, 55, 104, 116, 290, 459, 477, 484, 506

P

P&O Ships, 105
P.I.A.(Pakistan International Airlines), 463, 504
P.N.A. (Pakistan National Alliance), 510
Pahlajani, Bhojsingh, 52, 95, 143, 145,
Pakistan Indonesian Cultural Association, 460
Pakistan Muslim League (Qayyum group), 479,480
Pakistan Muslim League Council, 438
Pakistan Muslim League, 435, 438,439
Pakistan People's Party (PPP), 467, 470, 507
Pakistan Refugee Fund, 397
Pakistan Times (newspaper), 471
Pakistan, 204, 279, 303, 304, 315, 348, 352. 358, 373, 383, 385, 386, 394, 395, 397, 398, 400, 401, 403, 404, 406, 409, 410, 411, 412, 415, 416, 418, 419, 420, 421, 426, 427, 428, 429, 433, 439, 440, 441, 443, 451, 452, 454, 456, 458, 460, 465, 466, 470, 472, 475, 476, 477, 478, 480, 481, 495, 500, 501, 503, 512, 514
Pakistan, Constituent Assembly of, 315, 336, 369, 380
Pakistan, Government of, 317, 320, 324, 335, 336, 337, 338, 375, 379, 461
Palestine Fund, 397
Palestine, 104, 397
Pandava, 18
Panhwar, Khan Sahib Mohammed Parial, 131
Panjudero, 260
Parmanand Kundanmal, 339, 350
Parpia, 254
Parpia, Mrs., 503
Parsi Colony, 133
Parsi, 51, 52, 67, 85, 95, 133, 286, 317
Pasha Zaghlul, 88, 190
Patel Park, (Nishtar Park), 35, 133, 134, 171, 189, 266, 276
Patel, H. M., I.C.S., 497
Patel, Sardar Vallabhai, 154, 155, 165, 166, 280, 284, 286, 287, 288, 302, 303
Pathan, Agha Ghulam Nabi, 182, 265, 270, 273, 275, 277, 280, 381, 389, 426, 469
Pathan, Agha Nazar Ali, 73, 174, 182
Pathan, K. B. Jan Mohammed, 52
Patiala, 331
Paymaster, Justice, (trying Session Judge in Allahbaksh murder trial), 254-268
Peace Board (for Sind), 321, 326
Pearl Harbour, 203
Peerzada, Lieutenant General M. M., 472, 473, 475, 483
Pehlavi Mohammed Reza, Shah of Iran, 455
Persia, 18, 102, 103, 223
Perumal, Seth Sitaldas M.L.A., 236, 264
Peshawar, 419, 445, 487
Pethick Lawrence, Lord, 285
Philby, St. John, 372
Phillipines, 444
Phull family, 33
Phulloo, (village) 73

Piccadilly, London, 104
Pinial, S. P., 502, 503, 509
Pir Aligohar Shah, (Pir Pagaro), 224, 225, 227
Pir Fatehali Shah, 234
Pir Hamid Shah, 47, 490
Pir Illahi Baksh, 151, 152, 157, 160, 161, 162, 270, 273, 282, 318, 340, 342, 344, 345, 356, 361, 365, 387, 388, 415
Pir Jial Shah, 505
Pir jo Goth (village), 223, 225
Pir Pagaro (the seventh), Shah Mardan Shah, 227, 248, 474, 487, 509
Pir Pagaro (the sixth), Syed Sibghatullah Shah, and the Hur movement 223-248, 87, 256, 259, 264, 491, 494, 509, 512 494, 512,
Pir Qurban Ali, 275, 417
Pir Rasulbaksh Shah, 52
Pir Turab Ali Shah, 500
Pirpur Report, 185
Piru, 226
Pirzada Abdus Sattar, 276, 281, 282, 318, 319, 333, 405, 406, 407, 409, 410, 415, 425, 426, 469
Pirzada, Haji Shahnawaz, 257
Poona, 52, 62, 63, 83, 116, 204, 205
Pradhan, R. G., 53
Primary Education Bill, 453
Prince of Wales, (Edward VIII), 429
Pringle Keith, (Commissioner-in-Sind), 25
PRODA, 349, (Legislation of, 366), 367, 368, 369, 372, 384, 397, 401, 402, 403, 407, 408,
Progressive Party, 416
Pryde, I.C.S., 363
Pucca Qilla, 22
Punjab Alienation of Land Act, 282
Punjab House, Karachi, 420, 432
Punjab Murderous Outrages Act No. XXIII of 1867, 227
Punjab, 17, 22, 24, 25, 118, 119, 155, 272, 277, 284, 285, 286, 289, 290, 293, 296, 297, 299, 301, 302, 303, 304, 320, 321, 325, 329, 332, 360, 366, 373, 378, 383, 384, 389, 392, 393, 395, 404, 411, 412, 413, 414, 415, 418, 423, 424, 425, 430, 435, 437, 444, 445, 450, 454, 457, 465, 469, 470, 475, 477, 478, 482, 488, 511, 512
Punjab, Government of, 91, 325 334
Punjabi, K. M., 66, 135, 226, 292, 397, 405, 409, 478
Punwani, Partabrai, 254

Q

Qadiris, 132
Qadri, Ghulam Sarwar, 32
Qalandar Lal Shahbaz, 31
Qazi Isa, 209, 271, 425, 426
Qizilbash, Nawab Muzaffar Hussain, 297, 433, 437, 445, 446
Quetta Mail, 50
Quetta Municipality of, 415
Quetta, 50, 219, 220, 271, 273, 320, 358, 445, 446, 490, 502, 506, 508
'Quit India' Movement, 204, 206, 234, 443
Quraishi, Makhdum Ghulam Hyder, 275
Quraishi, Makhdum Nawab Murid Hussain, 167
Quraishi, Naimutullah, 181, 182
Qurbani, newspaper, 359
Qutb Minar, 290

R

Rabb, Air Commodore, 440
Radio Pakistan, 476
Raffles Hotel, Singapore, 52
Rafiuddin Ahmed, Maulvi, 52
Rahim Khan, Air Vice Marshall, 510
Rahim, J. A., 470
Rahimtoola, Habib Ibrahim, 412
Rahimtoola, Sir Ibrahim, 45, 52, 93, 412
Rahman, Justice, S. A., 449
Raja Narendar Nath, 94
Rajasthan, (Rajputana), 50, 51,223, 237, 239,321, 358
Rajpar Ali Mohammed, 250, 251, 252, 259
Rajputs, Induvarsi, 27
Ramchandani, Dingomal, 255, 367
Ramzo, 260
Rao Commission, 297
Rashdi, Pir Ali Mohammed, 75, 87, 91, 101, 102, 106, 107, 141, 147, 149, 152, 154, 160, 195, 220, 244, 246, 248, 272, 274, 275, 276, 277, 278, 405, 410, 417, 418, 444, 469, 491, 513
Ratodero, (taluka District Larkana), 47, 48, 239, 325, 474, 487, 490, 493, 502
Rawalpindi, 324, 439, 440, 441, 487
Ray, (S. P.), 228, 251, 254, 258, 261, 267
Raza, Kazim, (DIG Police), 326
Reading, Marquess of, 94
Red Sea, 106
Red Shirts, (also see under Khudai Khidmatgar), 412
Red Square, Moscow, 427
Refugee Settlement Officer, 322
Rehman, Justice, S. A.,
Republican Party, 426, 429, 432, 433, 434, 437, 438
Revolt of 1857, (War of Independence), 25, 72
Richardson, General, 234
Ridley, Sir Sidney, 233
Rieu, Sir Jean Louis, (Commissioner-in-Sind), 58, 65,
Ripon Lord, 30, 455
Ritz Hotel, London, 104
Rohillas, 41
Rohri, 23,223
Roshan Ara Club, New Delhi, 299
Rotary Club, 393, 446
Royal Commission on Agriculture in India,392
Royal Statutory Commission on Indian Reforms (Simon Commission), 64, 91, 92, 93, 94, 101, 138, 141, 169, 170, 490, 491
Ruk Station, 265
Ruki Bai, 50
Rupchand, 73, 74
Rusby, S. P., 493
Russell, Earl, 94
Russia, 18, 23, 477
Russian Empire, 24
Ryotwari System, 110, 454

S

Saddar, Karachi, 134, 266
Sadh Belo, 169, 170
Sadhayo, Khan Bahadur 270
Saiyid Ghulam Nabi Shah, 52
Saiyid Mohammed Kamil Shah, 52
Sakrand College, 422
Salahuddin Ayubi, Sultan, (Saladin), 223, 499
Samarkand, 428, Afrasiyab, 428,—Registan Square, 428, —Ulugbek Observatory, 428, —Shah i Zinda, 428
Samarra, 462
Samma, 24, 27
Sammat, 27
Samon, 27
Sams (restaurant), 418
Sanaullah, (shop), 447
Sanghar, 225, 227, 233, 236, 238, 245, 257, 322, 485
Sanjrani, Imam Bux, 237
Sanjrani, Sono 259, 260
Sann (village), 514
Sansar Samachar (Sindhi newspaper), 145
Sarabhai, Mridula, 205
Sardar Aurangzeb, 218
Sardar Bahadur Khan, 413, 424, 425, 426, 430, 457
Sardar M. Yaqub, 225
Sardar Mohammed Baksh, 321
Sardar Sampuran Singh, 94
Sardar, Abdur Rashid, 413, 415, 419, 432
Sarfraz, Ms. Zari, 299
Sarhindi, Pir Ghulam Mujaddid, 181, 182
Sarhindi, Pir Sahibzada Abdul Sattar Jan, 143,
Sarkar, Abu Hussain, 420
Satyagraha, 37, 172, 173, 174, 175, 176, 177, 178, 179, 190
Sayed Ahmed Khan, Sir, 45
Sayed Ali Akbar Shah, 364, 381
Sayed Khairshah, 168, 273, 275
Sayed Noor Mohammad Shah (Bakapur), 48
Sayed Nur Mohammad Shah, 138, 164, 292, 389, 411
Scott, Major W. 24, 25
Scott, Sir Walter, 24
Secheyelles, 238
Sehwan, (Siwistan), 23, 31, 47, 223, 490
Sehwani, Hakim Fateh Mohammed, 172
Seo Bazar, Larkana 496, 497
Seoni Jail, 233
Sethna, Pheroze Sir, 94
Shafaat Ahmed Khan, Sir, (Dr.), 94, 99, 104, 491
Shafi, Sir Mohammad, 94, 113, 197
Shafiabad, 320
Shah Abdul Latif, 448, *Risalo* of, 35
Shah Bunder, 24
Shah Subhan Ali, 32
Shah, Abdul Rahim, 101
Shah, Baqadar, 275
Shah, Ghulam Rasul 237, 246
Shah, Qabul Mohammed, 275
Shah, Sayed Hassan Baksh, 275
Shah, Sayed Hyderali, 257
Shah, Syed Ghulam Mustafa, 464
Shah, Syed Karam Ali, 87
Shah, Syed Masoom, 87, 169
Shah, Syed Mohammad Ali, 270, 271, 275, 292
Shahabuddin, Fakir, 31
Shahabuddin, M. Justice, 350, 409, 449
Shahani, Dayaram Gidumal, 114, 225,
Shahani, S. C., 34, 85, 86,
Shahdadpur, 238
Shahi Bazar, Hyderabad 22,
Shahi Jirga of Baluchistan, 415
Shahid Hamid, General, 441
Shahid Hamid, Mrs., 441
Shaikh Abdul Majid, 74, 85, 90, 91, 101, 136, 139, 141, 142,43, 145, 151, 154, 156, 160, 161, 162, 164, 165, 168, 181, 186, 188, 189, 198, 199, 200, 272, 321, 464, 469
Shaikh Ghulam Mohammed, 47
Shaikh Hassan A., 499
Shaikh Khurshid, 415
Shaikh Mujibur Rahman, 420, 421, 432, 475, 476
Shaikh Rashid, 506
Shaikh Wajid Ali, 177, 181, 182, 183, 265
Shaikh Zafar Ali, 417
Shaikh, General, K. M., 327, 445
Sharif Khan (S.P. Police), 326
Sharif, Justice M. 409
Sharma, M. S. M, (Editor *The Daily Gazette*), 325
Shepheards Hotel (Cairo), 52
Sher Bahadur, General, 446
Shikarpur, 18,19, 23, 29, 32, 70, 86, 177, 260, 265, 268, 270, 271, 275
Shuddhi Movement, 72, 73, 75, 76, 230
Sibi, 25
Sidhwa, Rustom, 95, 234, 245
Sidiki, 66
Sikandar Hayat, Sir, 157, 159, 160, 161, 162, 163, 167, 191, 186, 191, Lahore Session of AIMS and Sir Sikander 193-199, 204, 218
Sikhs, 119, 194, 224, 289, 301, 303, 321, 326
Silawat community, 143
Simla Conference, 266, 272
Simla, 106, 156, 176, 231, 285, 289, 297, 298, 299, 333, 334
Simon Commission, (see Royal Statutory Commission on Indian Reforms)
Simon, Sir John, 90, 91, 490
Sind (Brayne) Conference, 95, 100, 153
Sind Act, 88,
Sind Administrative Committee, 113, 153, 250, 295
Sind Azad Conference, 99, 101, 118, 136, 137
Sind Azad Party, 139, 141
Sind Governor's House, 315, 507
Sind Hindu Sabha, 139, 183
Sind Industrial Trading Estate (SITE), 298
Sind Land Mortgage Restoration Bill, 387
Sind Legislative Assembly, 139, 148, 155, 165, 170, 188, 217, 315, 337, 347, 360, 361,398
Sind Madressah, 34, 70, 131
Sind Mohammedan Association, 63, 64, 83, 89, 90, 92, 108, 484
Sind Muslim Democratic Party, 139, 141, 142,

INDEX

Sind Muslim League Assembly Party, 163, 164, 167, 171, 203, 206, 207, 319, 341, 342, 352, 380, 419, 430
Sind Muslim League Conference, 159-160
Sind Muslim Students Federation, 266,355
Sind Observer, (newspaper), 84, 145, 186, 254, 349, 366, 394
Sind Primary Education Bill, 296
Sind Provincial Conference, 89,
Sind Provincial Muslim League Council, 165,335
Sind Provincial Muslim League Working Committee, 171, 176,240,389
Sind Provincial Muslim League, 170, 179, 203, 217, 221, 240,249, 277, 278, 279, 280, 335, 364, 365, 380, 381, 388, 391, 396, 397, 403, 404, 436, 437,438, 439, 470
Sind Punjab Water Dispute, 289, 297
Sind Rural and Land Transfer Bill, 296
Sind Separation Day, 101
Sind Tenancy Act, 392, 395
Sind United Front, 466, 467, 468, 469
Sind United Party of, 138, 141, 142, 143, 149, 152, 154, 158
Sind University Bill 295-296, 495
Sind University, 114,115, 296, 422,495,506,
Sind *Varkies*, 23
Sind Zamindar, (newspaper), 44, 46, 47, 60, 73, 75, 84, 87, 145, 170, 174, 186, 395
Sind, Chief Court of , 229, 255, 367, 369, 372, 397, 404
Sindh Landholders Mortgage Bill, 296
Sindhi Language, 25, 32, 44, 145, 414, 463, 464
Sindhi, Maulana Ubaidullah, 171
Sindhu - (see Indus)
Singapore, 52, 203
Sinjhoro, 233, 238, 259
Sipahimalani, Kumari Jethi, 291, 321

Sochi, 428
Soekarno, President, 460, 461, 472
Solon, 456
Somjee, Bar-at-Law, 256, 495
Soomro, K. B. Allah Baksh, 86, 91, 137, 142, 143, 146, 147, 149, 151, 152, 154, 156, 157, 162, 163, 164, 165, 166, 167, (Role in Manzilgah Movement 168-192), 206, 207, 208, 210, 230, 232, 233, 236, (murder case of 248–268), 485, 491, 494, 495, 499
Soomro, Maulabaksh, 257, 263, 270, 271, 272, 275, 350, 402, 410, 485
Soomro, Mohammed Usman, 248, 257
South Africa, 39
Special Court of Inquiry, 349-370, 374, 398
Sri Prakasa, High Commissioner of India, 324
St. Antony's College, Oxford, 477, 506
St. George Hotel, Beirut, 104
Stafford Cripps, Sir, 203, 284
Stalin, Joseph, 426, 427, 428
Stalingrad, 428
Suez Canal, 51, 106, 429
Suez invasion, 429
Sufferings of Sind, 93, 94
Sufi, M. H. I.C.S., 258, 363, 455
Suhrawardy H. S., 288, 303, 321, 404, 406, 409, 412, 416, 419, 420, 421, 423, 429, 431, 433, 441, 445, 449, 457, 485, 496
Sukhia, Khan Sahib, S.K. 80, 83
Sukkur Barrage, (see Lloyd "Sukkur" Barrage,)
Sukkur District Jail, 87, 256
Sukkur, 23, 32, 44, 46, 48, 73-94, 297, 301, 321, 392, 421, 437, 439, 451, 454, 468, 495
Sukkur, Manzilgah Movement in, 168–192
Sultan Abdul Hamid II, 371,
Sultan Abdul Majid, 371
Sultankot, 270
Sumar, 259
Surahio, Seth Khudadad, 73
Surat, (Gujerat), 44
Swaraj Party, 52

Syed Ali Makki,223
Syed Amir Ali, 63
Syed Amjad Ali, 104, 409, 434
Syed Miran Mohammad Shah, 90, 92, 93, 95, 100, 101, 114, 137, 138, 145, 268, 280, 282, 292, 294, 324, 491
Syed Wajid Ali, 415
Syed, G. M. 91, 94, 101, 133, 136, 137, 138, 143, 144, 145, 147, 148, 149, 152, 153, 154, 157, 161, 162, 165, (Manzilgah Movement 168-192), 196, 198, 200, 207, 205, 207, 209, 219, 220, 221, 222, 240, 242, 249, 250, 256, 257, 266, 267, (G.M.Syed's quarrel over distribution of 'tickets' 269-281), 291, 292, 293, 300, 359, 415, 430, 435, 448, 464, 468, 469, 471, 472, 491, 494, 507, 514
Syed, Ghulam Hyder Shah, 221, 276,469
Sykes, Sir Frederick, Governor of Bombay, 57, 201
Syria, 27, 104

T

Tahilramani, M.P., 321, 326
Taj Hotel, (Bombay), 51, 52, 492
Tajar Bagh, (Jinnah Bagh), Larkana, 28, 159
Talpur, Mir Ali Murad, 224
Talpur, Mir Ali Nawaz, 45, 400, 425, 426
Talpur, Mir Bandeh Ali, 143, 145, 161, 162, 164, 167, 189, 191, 192, 193, 199, 200, 282, 293, 294, 493, 494
Talpur, Mir Ghulam Ali , 161, 164, 266, 270, 273, 276, 280, 294, 317, 318, 340, 342, 344, 345, 361, 362, 363, 388, 389, 401, 409, 412, 414, 415, 417, 418, 433, 445, 446
Talpur, Mir Ghulam Mahommed, 69
Talpur, Mir Hussain Baksh, 275
Talpur, Mir Rasul Baksh 507
Tando Adam, 236
Tando Agha, 22
Tando Mir Mahmood, 22

Tando Mohammed Khan, 270, 275, 417
Tando Thorho, 22
Tando Wali Mohammed, 22
Tashkent, 428, 487
Tata, 51, 52
Tayyabji, Abbas 73
Tayyabji, Begum, 133
Tbilisi, Georgia, 428
Tehrik Reshmi Roomal, 171
Thadani, Rewachand, 95
Thakur, B.T., 429
Thakurdas, Sir Purshotamdas, 91
Thar, (Great Thar Desert), 17, 18, 19, 322
Tharparkar, 138, 223, 236, 238, 245, 257, 273, 362, 417
Thatta, 24, 46, 292, 369, 446, 454, 474
The Times, London,(newspaper), 477, 478, 484, 488
Thomas, George A., (Commissioner-in-Sind), 77–83, 228, 229
Thomas, Sir Roger, 392
Thorne, Sir John, 237, 238, 239
Tikka Khan, General 463, 464
Times of India, (newspaper), 99, 137
Tiwana, Khizr Hayat Khan, Sir, 218
Todar Mal, 72
Tughlaq House, 317
Turkey, 442

U

U.P, (United Provinces of Agra and Oudh), 204, 234
U.S.A.(United States of America), 369, 404, 408, 426, 454, 460
U.S.S.R.(Soviet Union), Embassy of , 506
U.S.S.R., visit of parliamentary delegation, 426-429
Ubauro, 229, 363
Udaipur, 331
Uderolal, 236
Udharam, Mr., 228
Union Powers Committee of the Constituent Assembly, 302
Unionist Government of Punjab, 91, 119,193, 194, 272

Unionist Party of Punjab, 136, 137, 139
United Nations, 327
United Pressive Party (of East Bengal), 433
Unnar, Wadero Ghulam Umar, 474
Upper Sind Frontier District (later Jacobabad), 52
Ustad Manzoor Ali Khan, 400
Uzbekistan, 428

V

Vakil, Noor Mohammed, 52, 91
Vazirani, Nihchaldas, 145, 146, 147, 149, 151, 157, 163, 167, 189200, 236, 275, 276, 286
Victoria Queen Empress, 20
Vietnam, 477
Vishindas Harchandrai, 89, 90
Voroshilov, Soviet President, 426

W

Wadhio, 262
Wadhwani, Hemandas, 66, 145, 189
Wadia, Navrojee Jehangir, 52
Wah Ordinance Factory, 440
Wahiduddin Ahmed, Justice, 449
Wali Mohammad Hussanally, K. B., 92, 490, 491
Walid bin Abul Malik, Ommayed Khalifa, 27
Warah taluka, Larkana, 501
Washington, 420
Wasim (Advocate General), 340
Wassan, Khan Bahadur Ghulam Mohammed, 257, 265, 276, 474
Wassan, Nuro, 237
Wassand, Kazak, 227
Waterloo, 487
Wavell, Lord, (Viceroy of India), 268, 272, 284, 287, 289, 295, 298, 300, 301
Wells, A.G., 192, 231, 232, 233
West Pakistan Assembly, 424, 429, 430, 432, 435, 493
West Pakistan Cabinet, 414, 424, 426

West Pakistan, 316, 396, 404, 409, 410, 412, 413, 414, 416, 418, 421, 422, 423, 425, 429, 430, 432, 433, 435, 436, 438, 458, 460, 464, 467, 470, 475, 477, 478, 483, 484, 489, 496, 498
Weston Court of Inquiry, 171
Weston Report, 232
Weston, Mr. Justice, 171, 175, 183, 254
Willingdon (Lord), Viceroy of India, 106, 107, 108, 109, 491, 494
Wilson, Sir Leslie, Governor of Bombay, 45, 57, 58, 59, 60, 61, 62, 63, 64, 65, 66, 67, 68, 114, 201
Wilson, Woodrow, President of U.S.A., 197
Wolpert, Stanley, 219
World War I, 36, 37, 55, 64, 104, 462
World War II, 117, 119, 197, 231, 428
WPIDC (West Pakistan Industrial Development Corporation), 469

Y

Yacoob (Jacob), Prophet, 462
Yadav Rajput tribe, 27
Yamin, Dr. Mohammed, 173, 182
Yar Mohammed, 58
Yezid, 224
Yousuf Ali, Allama Abdullah, 101, 118, 119

Z

Zafrulla Khan, Sir, 193, 327, 328
Zaghlul Pasha, 88, 190
Zahid Ali Khan, Nawabzada, 466
Zahiruddin, 421
Zainal Reza, Ahmed Yusuf, 462
Zakir Hussain, 487
Zetland, Marquess of, 94, 157, 134, 182, 187, 189, 193, 196
Ziarat, 219,
Zia-ul-Haque, General, President of Pakistan, 510, 511, 514
Zurich, 409